✓10/15 PA Lib Sale 1.00
Lib 10/21

A HISTORY OF THE
UNITED STATES OF AMERICA

Volume Three

A HISTORY OF THE
UNITED STATES OF AMERICA

VOLUME ONE
The Search for Liberty
From Origins to Independence

VOLUME TWO
An Empire for Liberty
From Washington to Lincoln

VOLUME THREE
The American Dream
From Reconstruction to Reagan

The American Dream

From Reconstruction to Reagan

ESMOND WRIGHT

First published 1996

Blackwell Publishers Inc.
238 Main Street
Cambridge, Massachusetts 02142
USA

Blackwell Publishers Ltd
108 Cowley Road
Oxford OX4 1JF
UK

Library of Congress Cataloging-in-Publication Data

Wright, Esmond.
The American dream : from Reconstruction to Reagan / Esmond Wright.
p. cm. – (A History of the United States of America; v. 3)
Includes bibliographical references and index.
ISBN 1–55786–589–2
1. United States – History – 1865. I. Title. II. Series:
Wright, Esmond. History of the United States of America; v. 3.
E661.W75 1995
973–dc20 94–48715
CIP

British Library Cataloguing in Publication Data

A CIP catalogue record for this book is available from the British Library.

Typeset in 11 on 13 pt Sabon Symposia by Apex Products, Singapore
Printed in Great Britain by T. J. Press Ltd, Padstow, Cornwall

This book is printed on acid-free paper

Contents

Maps

Plates

Chronologies

Foreword

When I began the writing of what is now volume III of this trio of books, I did not envisage that they would in the end grow into three distinct volumes. The zealous reader will note how my indebtedness has grown to many distinct sources: the causes of and the prelude to the War of Independence are very different themes from the topics of volume II or III; if Columbus was a hard man to know, so were John C. Calhoun, Andrew Carnegie – and Martin Luther King.

My indebtedness to a host of sources will be obvious. I recognize, too, and I would like to salute my indebtedness to my collaborators: to Enid MacDonald, who has made sense of an unreadable script and typed every page sometimes more than once but always without complaint; Sue Martin, my zealous and skilful copy-editor; Ginny Strand-Lewis, for her inspired choice of illustrations; and John Davey of Blackwell's, not least for his patience.

General Chronology

1867	First Reconstruction Act; purchase of Alaska from Russia.
1869	Completion of first transcontinental railroad.
1875–6	Second Sioux War; defeat of General Custer's cavalry in Battle of the Little Big Horn.
1876	Invention of the telephone by Alexander Graham Bell.
1877	Withdrawal of federal troops from the South marked end of Reconstruction.
1880	US population c. 50 million.
1881	John D. Rockefeller's Standard Oil Trust established; Henry James, *Portrait of a Lady*.
1885	Mark Twain, *The Adventures of Huckleberry Finn.*
1887	Dawes Severalty Act provided for the settlement of Indians on homesteads.
1890	Sherman Antitrust Act; Eleventh US Census declares frontier closed.
1891	Formation of the People's (Populist) party.
1893	Chicago World's Columbian Exposition.
1895	J. P. Morgan & Co, established; Stephen Crane, *The Red Badge of Courage*.
1896	*Plessy* vs. *Ferguson* case: Supreme Court upheld legality of " separate but equal" facilities for blacks.
1898	Spanish-American War; annexation of Hawaii and Philippines.

1900	Twelfth US Census showed population of 76 million.
1901	US Steel Corporation established.
1903	Henry James, *The Ambassadors*; Jack London, *Call of the Wild*; W. E. B. DuBois, *The Souls of Black Folk.*
1906	Upton Sinclair, *The Jungle.*
1907	Peak immigration year: 1,285,000 immigrants enter US.
1909	First Model T Ford.
1913	Armory Show exhibition of modern European art.
1914	Eight-hour day with $5 minimum wage introduced in all Ford plants; President Wilson proclaimed US neutrality on outbreak of World War I.
1915	British liner *Lusitania* torpedoed with loss of over 100 American lives; Germany restricted submarine warfare; D. W. Griffiths, *Birth of a Nation.*
1917	German resumption of unrestricted submarine warfare; US enters World War I.
1918	President Wilson outlined his 14 Points to Congress; Armistice ended war in Europe.
1919	Prohibition Amendment ratified; Senate voted down US membership of League of Nations.
1920	"Red Scare" leads to mass arrests of labor agitators; Fourteenth US Census showed urban population exceeded rural.
1921–4	Quota laws restricted immigration.
1922	T. S. Eliot, *The Waste Land.*
1923	Henry R. Luce launched *Time* magazine.
1925	F. Scott Fitzgerald, *The Great Gatsby;* Gertrude Stein, *The Making of Americans*; Scopes (evolution) trial in Dayton, Tennessee; Harold Ross launched the *New Yorker.*
1927	Execution of Italian-born anarchists and Vanzetti; Charles Lindbergh flies the Atlantic.
1928	First full-length sound film; 26 million cars and 13 million radios in use in US.
1929	Stock market crash.
1932	William Faulkner, *Light in August.*
1933	Inauguration of Franklin D. Roosevelt as President; beginning of New Deal; end of Prohibition.

1935–7	Neutrality legislation passsed in order to prevent US being drawn into future foreign wars.
1936	John Dos Passos, USA.
1939	John Steinbeck, *The Grapes of Wrath*; Britain and France declared war on Germany.
1940	Richard Wright, *Native Son*.
1941	Land-Lease Act; Orson Welles's film *Citizen Kane*; Japanese attack on Pearl Harbor led to American entry into World War II.
1942	American troops in Pacific and North Africa; UN Declaration signed in Washington.
1943	Rodgers and Hammerstein, *Oklahoma*.
1944	Allied invasion of Normandy; advance of Russian forces into Czechoslovakia, Hungary and Poland.
1945	German capitulation; surrender of Japan following dropping of atomic bombs on Hiroshima and Nagasaki; UN Conference in San Francisco.
1947	Truman Doctrine and Marshall Plan designed to counteract Soviet expansionism and provide for European reconstruction; Taft-Hartley Act restricted trade union power; Tennessee Williams, *A Streetcar Named Desire*.
1948–9	Berlin blockade and airlift.
1949	NATO established; Arthur Miller, *Death of a Salesman*.
1950–3	Korean War.
1950	Alger Hiss convicted of perjury; Senator Joseph McCarthy launched antiCommunist crusade; Seventeenth US Census shows population of 151 million.
1950–60	Advent of mass television.
1951	J. D. Salinger, *The Catcher in the Rye*.
1953	James Baldwin, *Go Tell it on the Mountain*; execution of Julius and Ethel Rosenberg for atomic espionage.
1954	J. Robert Oppenheimer denied security clearance; Senate censured McCarthy; Supreme Court ruled against school segregation.
1956	Suez crisis; Soviet invasion of Hungary; Eugene O'Neill, *Long Day's Journey into Night*.
1957	Jack Keronac, *On the Road*; federal troops enforced school desegregation in Little Rock, Arkansas.

1961	Inauguration of President John F. Kennedy, who called for a "New Frontier"; Bay of Pigs (Cuban invasion) fiasco.
1961–8	Birth control pill came into general use.
1962	Cuban missile crisis; international live telecasts by satellite.
1963	Martin Luther King gave his 'I Have a Dream' speech at the Lincoln Memorial; assassination of President Kennedy.
1964	President Johnson called for a Great Society; Gulf of Tonkin Resolution led to build-up of US ground forces in South Vietnam.
1965	Civil Rights Act; Race riots in Los Angeles, Cleveland, Chicago, Newark, Detroit and other major cities continued through 1966 and 1967.
1968–72	Student protest on US campuses.
1968	Assassinations of Robert Kennedy and Martin Luther King.
1969	US astronauts landed on moon.
1970	US forces invaded Cambodia; National Guard fired on students at Kent State University, Ohio.
1971	Severing of historic link between the dollar and gold marked the end of the postwar international monetary system.
1972	President Nixon visited China; SALT agreement with Soviet Union.
1973	US ground troops withdrew from Vietnam; Allende government overthrown in Chile; October War between Egypt and Israel; OPEC quadrupled price of oil.
1974	Watergate scandal led to resignation of President Nixon.
1975	South Vietnam and Cambodia surrendered to Communist forces.
1978	Egypt and Israel signed peace agreement at Camp David; President Carter launched national campaign to conserve energy.
1979	Revolution in Iran; Soviet invasion of Afghanistan.
1980	Japan overtakes US in steel and automobile production.
1983	President Reagan introduced "Star Wars" – the Strategic Defence initiative.

1985–8 Reagan held four summit meetings with Russian premier Mikhail Gorbachev.

1986–7 "Irangate" scandal over illegal arms deals.

1988 President Reagan left office, succeeded by his former Vice-President, George Bush.

I say to you today, my friends, that in spite of the difficulties and frustrations of the moment, I still have a dream. It is a dream deeply rooted in the American dream. I have a dream that one day this nation will rise up and live out the true meaning of its creed: "We hold these truths to be self-evident: that all men are created equal."

Martin Luther King
Address at the March on Washington
August 28, 1963

Introduction: From Appomattox to Reagan

The century from Appomattox to the presidency of Ronald Reagan wrought a vast transformation in American society, in road, rail and air, in cinema, radio and television. From what had been two societies and many regions, a single nation emerged, and almost all its legion of inventions enhanced its unity, if not its nationalism. Moreover, once the war was won, the single united nation was invaded by immigrants, overwhelmingly non-British, some of them refugees from persecution. In transport and communications, in its taste for food and drink, and in a growing host of fast-food chains, the nation might come to be unified, but in population and in religion it was a land of many diverse groups and cults – even if the objective was *e pluribus unum*. It has long been a point of contention whether the best comparison is a melting pot or a salad bowl.

Vast, polyglot and proud; the nation could be swept by hurricanes, storms and crises – and passions: climatic, economic, religious, patriotic, emotional and – especially after the coming of television – psychological and synthetic. Democrats easily became demagogues, witness William Jennings Bryan, Joe McCarthy, Martin Luther King, Billy Graham, and a host of others. Thanks more to Supreme Court judgements than to street violence, the mid-twentieth century brought legal equality to people of all colors of skin, and women achieved more freedom and more earning power than ever before. Indeed, there was more affluence for more people than ever before. But William Howard Taft's judgment was apt – and he was Supreme Court chief justice as well as President: "We became the worst governed people because we were the most governed people."

Nor was the reach of government limited to the Atlantic or Pacific. In the twentieth century one plank in the platform has finally gone: the Monroe Doctrine. In 1823 the US pledged itself, and the Americas, to a foreign policy of isolation. That held for two generations, until the purchase of Alaska in 1867 and the invasion of Cuba in 1898 (though in the latter at least the cause was "Cuba Libra," the objective to give Cuba freedom from Spain). Since then, the US has been the arsenal of democracy in two world wars until intervening itself (in 1917 and 1942); its economic and military commitments reach from the Philippines to the Panama Canal, from the eastern Mediterranean to Somalia. Contrast the agonies suffered by Thomas Jefferson when he argued with himself over his powers to acquire Louisiana or his capacity and justification to strike down the Barbary corsairs. Now American preoccupations are worldwide and imperial, though, with memories of 1776, it must not call itself an empire.

The US today is polyglot and variegated, white and black, red and yellow, and usually a bit of each. It includes the great and the not-so-great, Marxists and Ku Klux Klan, Black Muslims and members of the John Birch Society, the Wobblies, the Dixiecrats and the various cults of the West. There are many of all of them, and some of their habits are peculiar.

In the US, the twentieth century began in a wave of war-inspired patriotic high Republicanism. With Reagan towards the end of that century, it was Republican again, high this time with the rhetoric of freedom, capitalism, and a curb on the power of the state. But two world wars had bred state power, and one President, Franklin D. Roosevelt, had learnt to use the state to check the abuses and excesses of economic freedom.

Can any theses be held to be constant through these years of turmoil? It is always the unexpected that happens. Political labels and reputations often mean little in office, especially for presidents. Franklin Roosevelt campaigned to cut spending and balance the budget until he chose a new slogan, "Win the War." What began as the Welfare State became the Warfare State – and in both cases the spendthrift state. Harry S. Truman of Missouri was not expected to take much interest in foreign affairs, but he dropped the atom bomb on Japan, presided at the Potsdam peace conferences, and inaugurated the Marshall Plan and the Doctrine named after him that gave aid to Greece and Turkey. Dwight D. Eisenhower, a military man and an adopted Republican, kept the defense budget steady and raised domestic spending more on the Interstate project than on troops. Lyndon Johnson, a Southern Democrat suspected by liberals, pushed through the Civil Rights Act. Richard Nixon, the free enterprise conservative and "who lost China?" cold warrior, imposed wage and price controls and went to Beijing. Jimmy Carter, a conservative Southern populist campaigning under Democratic colors, who promised lower defense spending and national health insurance, raised the first and never got around to the second. What is striking in this list is that until Carter, every President governed less conservatively than he campaigned. Each President, regardless of party, very broadly accepted what could be called the Democratic Idea of strong, activist government, both at home and in foreign affairs. Lyndon Johnson's hero was not John Kennedy, but FDR, under whom he had his first experience of politics: the Great Society was LBJ's version of the New Deal. It is the Democratic Idea that provides a thread through the labyrinth for the better part of 40 years. Under other names, the Democratic Idea is also Welfare Capitalism or the Liberal Consensus.

But the twentieth century has also been the century when the US became the world's greatest superpower, an empire of a republic. The 48 states became 50 with the transition of territories to states: Alaska, rich in oil, became a state, as did Hawaii in the Pacific. Puerto Rico became American territory, and its people made New York City a goal. The US has participated in wars in Europe and Asia, in the Persian Gulf and in Somalia, in a fashion that neither Washington nor Jefferson, Jackson nor Lincoln, could have foreseen or welcomed. For all of them, the ideal of the republic was to be distinct, serene, and free from Old World tensions. Today's America is, in involvement – and perhaps in understanding – closer to the Europe and Asia from which their ancestors and Founding Fathers and Mothers came.

A third feature is the phenomenal growth of bureaucracy, particularly of the federal branch of government. And the power of that Man in the White House is much greater – and more intrusive. Thanks to the media, he – and his wife – are more familiar persons than were their predecessors; so, as he is more powerful, he is more vulnerable, not only physically, but by day-to-day cross examination and near-crucifixion in the press – even to the point that, for once in a 200-year history, in 1974 a President actually chose to resign. It is an office with an intense, complex and human history. No one now can doubt that America's is also a story that is unique.

1
The American Dream

1 THE LAND

You are the buffalo-ghost, the broncho-ghost
With dollar-silver in your saddle-horn,
The cowboys riding in from Painted Post,
The Indian arrow in the Indian corn...[1]

The history of the United States is strikingly different from the history of Britain or of Europe. It cannot be assessed by European standards or be read in European terms. Five of America's characteristics stand out clearly and give its history distinction: the land itself; the origins and polyglot composition of the people; their social mores; their political ideas; and, not least, their sense of national identity – their image of themselves to themselves, and the role in the world that they see themselves as playing.

The United States will soon have a population of 270 million people, forming, after China, Russia, and India, the world's fourth largest single nation. That nation inhabits a land area of 3 million square miles, the third largest politically unified land mass in the world, and certainly the most thoroughly tamed of all the continents. The land itself is rich, providing supplies and resources sufficient to feed and sustain all its people (except for tin, rubber, coffee, and uranium, which have to be imported), and allowing them to enjoy the highest standard of living ever reached in world history. Though

[1] Stephen Vincent Benet, "Invocation," *John Brown's Body* (London, Oxford University Press, 1945).

they form only 7 percent of the world's population, they regularly, and indeed wastefully, consume some 40 percent of its resources. And their technical skills can triumph even over their few natural disabilities – synthetic rubber is now not only an alternative to natural rubber, and available in quantity, it is for many purposes superior.

Yet, unlike the story of China, Russia, or India, American history is brief; it is now not much more than 200 years since independence was won, only some four centuries, since the first European settlements were made. Two centuries span only some four or five generations. American history is intense, ruthless, colorful, and dramatic. The history is short and memory long; of this, myths are natural progeny.

The first theme, then, is that of the speedy mastery of a vast and unknown continent. This land was rich and attractive. "The air at twelve leagues' distance smelt as sweet as a new-blown garden," wrote John Smith in praise of Virginia, the colony he helped to found: "Heaven and earth never agreed better to frame a place for man's habitation." Of his colony, William Penn, the founder of Pennsylvania, said: "The air is sweet and clear, the heavens serene." As inviting as the climate were the native foods. The sea abounded in oysters and crabs, cod and lobster; and in the woods there were turkeys "fat and incredible of weight," and quail, squirrels, pheasants, elk, geese, and so many deer that in places "venison is accounted a tiresome meat."

From the beginning the land, in all its size, mystery, and grandeur, was seen as at once opportunity and enemy. "The great fact was the land itself ... the land wanted to be let alone, to preserve its own fierce strength; its peculiar savage kind of beauty, its uninterrupted mournfulness." The words are Willa Cather's. And the probing and conquest of it has been a recurrent topic, a series of sagas: the first journeys of the French into the Great Lakes country and down the St Lawrence to the Gulf of Mexico; the adventures of the *coureurs de bois* and of the missionaries, serving God and Gold; the journey, part expedition, part frolic, of the Knights of the Golden Horseshoe into the Blue Ridge of Virginia; the repeated thrusts south of the German and "Scotch-Irish" frontiersmen down the Valley of Virginia and into the Carolinas; the individual epics of men like Daniel Boone, or George Croghan, or John Sevier – there were many like them – in the 1750s, and of Jedediah Smith, Kit Carson, Jim Bridges, or other Indian scouts and mountain men in the 1820s: 70 years apart in time and 2,000 miles apart in space, but in dress and characteristics, in function and vocabulary, very alike, and forming

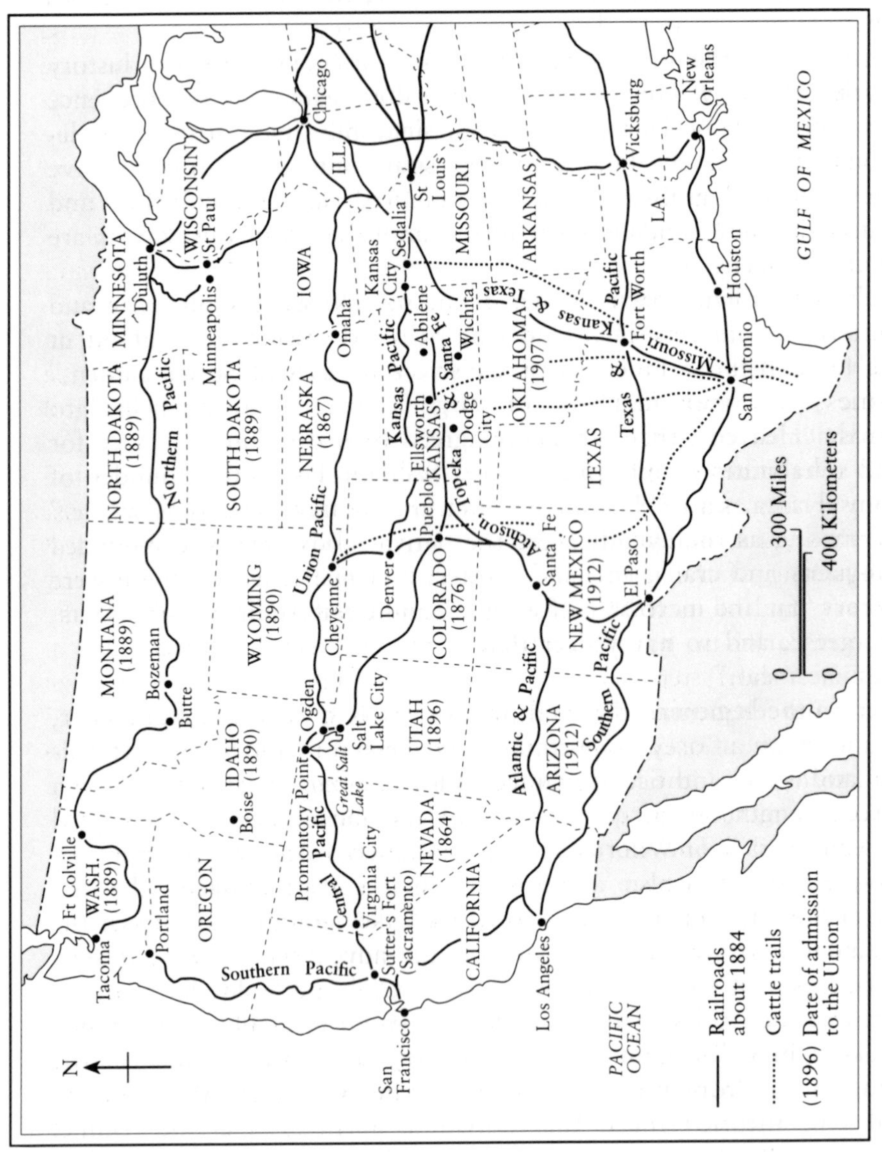

Map 1 The western states.

the coonskin-capped and buckskin-jacketed stereotype of the pioneer exploited by a host of writers and film cameramen ever since. There were the expeditions of Lewis and Clark in 1804–6; the exploration of the "Great American Desert;" the trek of the Mormons led by Brigham Young in 1847, or of the tragic Donner and similar parties crossing the High Sierras in the 1850s; the cutting of canals, not least the Erie in 1825 and the Panama in 1906–14; the meeting of the Union Pacific and Central Pacific railroads on the Utah salt-flats in May 1869, where a golden spike was driven into the ground to mark the linking of East and West coasts by rail. There were the land grabs – Texas in the 1820s and formally in 1836, Kansas in 1856, Oklahoma in 1889, even the dreams of the Knights of the Golden Circle of an empire on the Caribbean; the struggles with the Indians on many a dark and bloody ground from the Eastern coastal clashes of 1608 or 1620 to Custer's Last Stand on the Little Bighorn in 1876, or the last sad years of Sitting Bull; the stories, now inextricably mixed with legend, of cowpunchers and herdsmen driving their Texas longhorns over dry and dusty paths – and over other people's farms – to the Kansas cow towns, of the Pony Trails and of Wells Fargo, and of the law west of the Pecos. All these, and many other episodes in the discovery, mapping, and conquering of the land itself, are part of the texture of American history, and of its folklore, as the greatest American historians, like Francis Parkman, have captured in prose.

It is a short step from Parkman's thoroughly researched history and from elemental but real-life heroes like Davey Crockett and Daniel Boone, Casey Jones and John Henry, Billy the Kid and Buffalo Bill, to legend and fiction, to the Leatherstocking tales and Fenimore Cooper's pictures of the forests, to the landscapes and skyscapes of Edna Ferber or Willa Cather, or to the icy wastes of Jack London. It is a short step also to miracle men like Paul Bunyan, who dug Puget Sound, and ring-tailed roarers like Mike Fink, the Mississippi keelboatman, who could "out-run, out-jump, out-shoot, out-brag, out-drink, an' out-fight, rough-an'-tumble, no holts barred, any man on both sides of the river from Pittsburgh to New Orleans an' back ag'in to St Louiee." It was only one generation and a rich imagination from the real frontier to the world of Mark Twain. Even the historic George Washington, who stood, his contemporaries noted, "six feet two and straight as an Indian," could throw a rock clean across the Rappahannock, chop down trees with ease, even as a boy, and found it difficult, we are assured, to tell a lie.

In 1893 the frontier was closed, even if its legends were slow to fade. In that year a young Wisconsin historian, F. J. Turner, wrote a paper on *The Significance of the Frontier in American History*, and first gave expression to the view that it was the moving belt of human population pushing ever-westwards that was the unique feature in the story; and that to this were due many of the characteristics of American society. A safety valve for urban tensions and discontents, it created a resourceful, independent and egalitarian society, with freedom of opportunity and free land available to every man who had the energy, courage and will to work it; it called for initiative, ingenuity and self-reliance; it was hostile to remote authority because it was remote and because it was authority; it was activist, un-intellectual, and strongly optimistic.

> They went with axe and rifle, when the trail was still to blaze,
> They went with wife and children, in the prairie-schooner days,
> With banjo and with frying pan – Susanna, don't you cry!
> For I'm off to California to get rich out there or die.[2]

Its possibilities had indeed no obvious limits: "Why, sir, on the north we are bounded by the Aurora Borealis, on the east ... by the rising sun, on the south ... by the procession of the Equinoxes, and on the west by the Day of Judgment." It was the uniqueness of this environment in agriculture and topography which explained, Turner believed, the differences between the Old World and the New.

In recent years, his view has been contested. The Tennessee and Kentucky frontier was marked less by dignity and democracy than by cheap politics, crude individualism, and bigoted sectarianism. Born of two parents, protestant fundamentalism and radical democracy, its egalitarianism easily lapsed into anti-intellectualism. The romantic exaltation of "the common man," of the "voices of the people" and the "truths of the heart," the celebration of "common sense" and "plain talk," the insistence that government is an activity which requires no special training or abilities, the distrust of "high-falutin' speculation," the suspicion of intellectual authority, the scornful equation of art with artifice – all this is in the mainstream of American democratic thought, which flows with little interruption (though many detours) from Tom Paine through Andrew Jackson to Joe McCarthy. The frontiersmen of fact, as distinct from the frontiersmen who were the product of Eastern imagination, emptied the forest with their rifles as later they destroyed the buffalo of the plains (and with it the Indian culture which was based on the

[2] Stephen Vincent Benet, "Western Wagons," *The Stephen Vincent Benet Pocket Book* (New York, Pocket Books, 1946).

buffalo); they overgrazed the land with sheep and cattle, overworked the cotton and tobacco land, and then moved on; they overploughed the prairie so that wind could erode it into dustbowls, over-cut the timber on the hills, overmined everywhere, and repaired nothing – for they did not linger long enough to see the result. When they moved West they burned their houses – timber was abundant – and raked the ashes for nails, which were precious. Only a vast and rich land could have survived such despoliation. But in the process it was certainly conquered and subdued.[3]

The land is fertile and in climate frightful – tundra-cold in winter, jungle-hot in summer, humid whenever it is not freezing, swept by northern blizzards in the Mid-West, by hurricanes from the Atlantic in the summer and the fall. John Smith found it so as a discoverer in the seventeenth century, and in that it has changed little:

> The summer is hot as in Spain; the winter cold as in France or England. The heat of summer is in June, July, August, but commonly the cool breezes assuage the vehemency of the heat. The chief of winter is half December, January, February and half March. The cold is extreme sharp, but here the proverb is true, that no extreme long continueth.

Yet it can be swept by blizzards, and by emotions. It has bred strange and native religions, in all its faith in rationalism. Indeed, the US has been irregularly swept by religion. In its pre-Enlightenment colonial origins, the religion was Puritan; in the nineteenth century, Roman Catholics and Jews began to arrive; then, divinely inspired, the US began to invent new religions: Mormon, Christian Scientist, Scientologist. Today the US is a teeming bazaar of fundamentalist-style religion. As the various religions are largely exempt from taxation, religion is the US's greatest growth industry.

2 A MOBILE AND IMMIGRANT PEOPLE

If the size and scale and variety of the land itself and the sense of physical space and freedom form the first theme in the story, the

[3] There are a number of original and reflective studies of the frontier: Henry Nash Smith, *Virgin Land: The American West as myth and symbol* (Cambridge, MA, Harvard University Press, 1950); Edwin Fussell, *Frontier: American literature and the American West* (Princeton, NJ, Princeton University Press, 1965); R. W. B. Lewis, *The American Adam: Innocence, tragedy and tradition in the nineteenth century* (Chicago, Chicago University Press, 1955); and Leo Marx, *The Machine in the Garden: Technology and the pastoral ideal in America* (New York, Oxford University Press, 1964).

Plate 1 Immigrants entering the US at Ellis Island wait in line for railroad tickets to continue their journey.
(Library of Congress.)

second is the matching diversity of its people. They came from many different countries and from many different social groups to form a new nation: *e pluribus unum*. From the first beginnings, 40 million people have migrated to America – and many more planned and failed to do so or died in the attempt. Thirty-five million immigrants arrived between 1800 and 1924: Scots, Irish and Scotch-Irish, Germans, Italians, Scandinavians, often in organized groups, Eastern and

Middle Europeans. It was the greatest migration of people in recorded history. Every American is in some sense an immigrant – even the Indians who came millennia before Columbus, and by another ocean. Will Rogers, who was part Cherokee Indian, used to boast that his ancestors did not come on the *Mayflower*, they were at the dock to meet it; but they too were migrants, at long remove. When President Franklin D. Roosevelt greeted a convention of the now highly conservative assembly, the Daughters of the American Revolution, he could correctly, if mischievously, begin by addressing them as a "Fellow Revolutionaries and Fellow Immigrants." His cousin, Teddy, boasted of being descended from English, Dutch, French, Scotch, and Irish forebears. Nothing like this had occurred before. It was a movement of individuals, even if, as in Norway or Scotland, an organized movement; and if in scale it was a folk-wandering, it was the product of individual choice, of human fears and hopes and dreams – and sometimes of travel prospectuses that were calculated to attract and to deceive.

In 1890, when the frontier was closed, millions of immigrants had come to America, but most had settled on farmlands. Already there had been massive movements to American cities, but many of those migrants were colonial-stock Americans moving off their farms. But beginning in the 1890s, the numbers of immigrants increased, the sources of immigrants became increasingly Eastern and Southern Europe, and their destinations became almost exclusively the great cities of the North, where they accounted for the lion's share of the nation's exceedingly rapid metropolitan growth. Greater New York City in 1890, with four out of five residents of foreign birth or parentage, was the greatest immigrant center in the world. In Boston and Philadelphia, one-fourth to one-third of the population was foreign-born in 1860. The combined population of Chicago, Cleveland, Minneapolis, and Detroit in 1890 was two-fifths foreign-born. In the 18 largest cities in 1890, a large percentage of all males were of foreign birth or parentage.

Throughout the decades from 1890 to 1930, about one out of three Americans was of foreign stock – born abroad or having at least one parent born abroad. In 1930, 15 percent of Americans were foreign-born and a total of 36 percent were of foreign stock, the highest such figures in American history. Add to their number those with ancestors who had been of foreign stock in 1890 and nearly half the population and more than half the whites were of immigrant stock. What might be called, with just a little poetic license, the Ellis Island immigration – New York being by far the largest entry point – in effect superimposed another America on top of the country

Table 1 Immigration (in millions) 1840–1925

Years	*Britain*	*Ireland*	*Germany*	*Scandinavia*	*Italy*	*Eastern and Central Europe*	*Russia*	*Total*
1840–1860	0.7	1.7	1.4	–	–	–	–	4.2
1860–1880	1.1	0.9	1.5	0.3	–	–	–	4.8
1880–1900	1.1	1.1	2.0	1.1	0.9	1.0	0.6	8.9
1900–1925	1.1	0.6	0.7	0.8	3.6	3.9	2.7	17.3

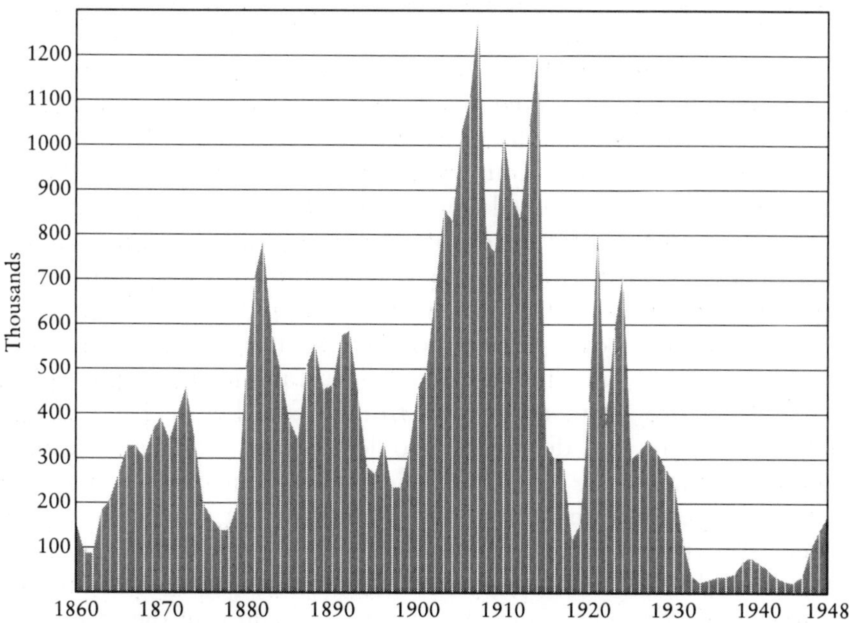

Map 2 Immigration 1860–1948.

already in place. These immigrants inevitably formed new, distinct groups, with cultural attitudes and political behavior different from those of other Americans.

In 1882 formal immigration restrictions were introduced, and later, as a result of World War I emotions, extended. And in 1921 and in 1924 came a radical departure. Until then there had been no curbs on numbers or source, but in 1924 Congress passed the National Origins Quota Act, a law providing that, after a preparatory period, the number of European immigrants annually admitted to the United States should be restricted to 150 thousand, and that these should be so apportioned among the various countries as not to alter the existing composition of the American people. Both provisions of the statute involved a radical break with historic practice. The flood became a trickle. The "quota" – a fixed number admitted each year for different races – became standard: based on the population of the United States in 1890, it greatly favored the then dominant strains, British or North European. It made entry for all the rest, Asiatics, Indians, or Slavs, very difficult. For a number of years after 1930, more people left the country than entered (although of course the population continued to grow). By 1960 only 5 percent of the population was foreign-born.

The shifting flow of immigration is apparent from Map 1 and from table 1, which shows the number and sources of immigrants arriving from 1840 to 1925 (the last period shown spans 25 years, since immigration was halted briefly by World War I and then continued at high rates until the passing of the Act of 1924).

More than any other country in the world, the United States accepted and even welcomed immigrants from diverse sources. But sudden surges of certain kinds of immigrants often alarmed many Americans. The arrival of millions of Catholic Irish after the potato famine of the 1840s and of Germans in the mid-1850s stirred nativist feeling in the years before the Civil War. Even more striking, there was virtually no immigration from Scandinavia before 1880, from Italy before 1890, or of Jews from Russia before 1900. These immigrants were not desperate people without skill, no huddled masses yearning to be free: the lands from which they came had made some political and economic advance in the years before they moved. And they had enough skill to get through Ellis Island and to find a job: in New York's Lower East Side tenements, in the coal mines of Pennsylvania or the factories of Ohio, in the farmlands of Wisconsin and Illinois or beyond, or, if they were Irish, overwhelmingly to the Boston which before 1850 had been above all an English city.

In 1790, the year of the first census, no American city had a population of 50,000 persons and only five had more than 10,000. In the middle decades of the nineteenth century changes in communication and transportation, especially the railroad, enhanced trade and urbanization, while the development of the steam engine enabled urban manufacturing to increase, drawing native migrants and foreign immigrants to the city. By 1870, 168 places had populations over 10,000, and 15 cities had populations over 100,000.

For the urban dweller in 1850 the city was a multiplicity of environments, many of them unknown and even frightening. The slum, where the "other half" lived, became a part of the urban imagination. In retrospect, however, the midcentury city was more ordered than many contemporaries recognized. Distinct commercial areas, often extensions of the waterfront in coastal or river cities, had emerged. Nearby were small manufacturing enterprises, especially those associated with the port or likely to be organized by merchant capital. Farther out, toward the fringes but near a working-class neighborhood, were a few heavy industrial enterprises. Within the commercial district lay a cluster of major financial institutions, some retail blocks (forerunners of department stores), and entertainment establishments. Not far from the center would be at least one fashionable neighborhood (Beacon Hill in Boston was typical) and a slum, such as Five Points in New York.

After 1870, technology, facilitating both vertical and horizontal movement, provided the basis for a dramatic reorganization of urban form in America. The first elevator in an office building was installed in New York's Equitable Life Assurance building. Elevators equalized the rental value of all floors, which raised land values in city centers. Between 1870 and 1930 the tall central-city office building and business block gave both a new appearance and a new function to the central business district, as it came to be called. By the 1890s it was apparent, first in New York and later in other large cities, that dense clusters of tall buildings had created a new kind of urban skyline. The New York City skyline was indeed unique. The US, it has been said, was born in the country and moved to the city.

Urbanization is by definition a process whereby the number of urban dwellers increases in relation to rural dwellers. By the 1990s this process had been largely completed in the United States. Although in recent decades cities have continued to receive migrants, the pattern of migration has been within an urban system – from city to city, from city to suburb, from suburb to city, as well as from foreign to American city.

So much of the nineteenth-century history of the United States is associated with western movement that one naturally wonders about the relation of urbanization to continental expansion. The two movements reinforced each other. Cities were "the spearhead of the frontier." Urban markets and marketing mechanisms gave value to agricultural land in the United States. The combination of local trade and an agricultural base enabled many cities, especially inland ones, to develop small-scale manufacturing.

Much nineteenth-century American development was fueled by urban rivalry. Boosters sought to make their cities regional centers by promoting transportation improvements and often encouraging investments in cultural institutions: a museum, a theater or opera house, a college, a scientific society, a large park.

Except in the case of the South under slavery, in the United States economic development and urban growth were intertwined. The result was an exceptionally dynamic economy and a dense network of cities. Unlike many developing countries in the post-World War II era, where a single overgrown metropolis dominates, in America large cities are to be found in every region, each in turn surrounded by networks of medium-sized cities.

Urbanization encompasses changes in form and social character that illuminate larger changes in American social and economic history. At the time of the American Revolution all the major cities were seaports. The port provided the basis of the urban economy, and it supplied a principle of order for the social and physical organization of the city. Nearly all eighteenth-century views of New York, Boston, and Philadelphia place the harbor with its ships and wharves in the foreground. This idea of the city as a port dominated urban perception until Independence.

The most striking symbol of America's new urbanism – in myth and poetry as well as in fact – was the Brooklyn Bridge, which helped to "create" New York City. It took 14 years to build (1869–83), and was the product of the genius and energy of the Roeblings, father and son. John A. Roebling was an immigrant civil engineer from Germany, who died from tetanus poisoning shortly after the bridge was begun. The work was completed by his son, Washington Roebling, who had built bridges for the Union Army in the Civil War; he himself suffered from "the caisson disease" ("bends") from working under water at too intense a pressure, but for many years he directed the work from his sickroom overlooking the bridge; he was greatly aided by his wife Emily, part messenger, part co-director. The great steel cables were built by J. Lloyd Haigh of Brooklyn.

The completion of the bridge in 1883 stimulated mass migration from New York (then consisting only of Manhattan) to more open Brooklyn, and the outflow accelerated after the two cities, together with Queens, the Bronx, and Staten Island, were united as Greater New York in 1898. The first subway line was completed in 1904, and in the quarter-century that followed tens of thousands of immigrants moved out from the crowded tenements of Manhattan to the freshly minted and spacious apartment buildings of Brooklyn and the Bronx and even Queens. Manhattan's population fell from 2.3 million in 1910 to 1.9 million in 1930, while that of the Bronx rose from 430,000 to 1.3 million and that of Brooklyn from 1.6 million to 2.6 million in the same 20 years. The city's population nearly doubled in the first three decades of the century, to 6.9 million in 1930, and it spread out.

One aspect of life that may have contributed to the possible equality of Americans is not just their immigration but their mobility. Since the end of slavery Americans have had few restrictions to prevent them from moving. In comparison to persons in many other countries Americans are more prone to move. Everett S. Lee wrote of the significance of mobility on the American character:

> The point is that migration has been a force of greatest moment in America civilization, and that from the magnitude and character of migration within

> this country certain consequences logically follow ... It is therefore not maintained, paraphrasing [Frederick Jackson] Turner, that migration explains American civilization. It certainly does not, but that it was and is a major force in the development of American civilization and in the shaping of American character hardly anyone will deny. ...
>
> ... Migration has been phenomenally successful for Americans. The immigrant from abroad did find superior economic opportunities and if they were fleeing oppression they found freedom. Within our country the major flows of migration have been from areas of lower to higher economic returns. ... The natural interpretation by the migrant is that migration has been a good thing; having done it once he is willing to do it again if another area looks more attractive. This attitude he imparts to his children and to nonmigrants with whom he comes in contact. ...[4]

This mobility was further encouraged by the widespread car ownership that came to the US between 1912 and 1923. In the earlier year registrations equaled only 4.2 percent of US households; by 1923 they had reached 50 percent of all households. As President Harding put it: "the motorcar has become an indispensable instrument in our political, social and industrial life."[5]

Thus the diverse land was matched by a diverse and mobile labor force, geographically and psychologically restless. It formed an open, not a static, society which was always in flux, a society which gave, it seemed, opportunity to all. Even before the Revolution, Crevecoeur enthused:

> It is not composed, as in Europe, of great lords who possess everything, and of a herd of people who have nothing. Here are no aristocratic families, no courts, no kings, no bishops, no ecclesiastical dominion, no invisible power giving to a few a very visible one, no great manufacturers employing thousands, no great refinements of luxury. The rich and the poor are not so far removed from each other as they are in Europe. Some few towns excepted, we are all tillers of the earth, from Nova Scotia to West Florida. We are a people of cultivators, scattered over an immense territory, communicating with each other by means of good roads and navigable rivers, united by the silken bands of mild government, all respecting the laws, without dreading their power, because they are equitable. We are all animated with the spirit of an industry which is unfettered and unrestrained, because each person works for himself.[6]

[4] Everett S. Lee, "The Turner Thesis reexamined," *American Quarterly*, 13 (1961), pp. 78–9, 83.

[5] Peter J. Ling, *America and the Automobile: Technology, reform and social change, 1893–1923*, Manchester, Manchester University Press, (1992), p. 127.

[6] J. Hector St John de Crevecoeur, "Letters from an American Farmer," (1782; repr. Garden City, NY; Doubleday, n.d.), p. 50.

It was not all blessings. In the New World as in the Old, equality meant equality of chance, not equality of reward; diversity of racial and economic origins could produce unrest and violence, as in the lynching of Negroes or in the War Between the States; nor has equality of opportunity been matched by easy acceptance of differences of color or of religion or of taste; the price of diversity of origins has been to stress conformity rather than individualism, the normal rather than the eccentric. Despite the size and diversity of the land, the people of the continent have been disciplined into a compelling uniformity by a network of daily life that is strikingly similar – the product of fast communications and of standardized press, radio, and television advertising. Main Street can be anywhere and everywhere. In consequence the United States is more a free than a tolerant society. And not all who moved to it have stayed there permanently. Of the 16 million immigrants who moved to the United States from Europe in the three decades after 1900, nearly 4 million returned; it was often a poignant return indeed, for they were driven back to Scotland or Sicily, Greece or Norway by the Depression, by failure, by a sense of not belonging, or by simple homesickness. But where differences could be reconciled, the life of the nation has been deepened and enriched and made distinct from any other by the infinite variety of its component stocks. Archibald MacLeish describes it vividly:

> It's how we marry says Maine. We ain't choosers.
> We scrabble them up and we mingle them in. We marry the
> Irish girls with the shoes with the quick come-after.
> We marry the Spaniards with the evening eyes.
> We marry the English with the tiptoe faces.
> We marry the golden Swedes: the black Italians:
> The German girls with the thick knees: the Mexicans
> Lean and light in the sun with the jingling and jangling:
> The Chilenas for luck: the Jews for remembrance: the Scots girls
> Tall as a tall man – silver as salmon;
> The French with the skillful fingers: the long loves.
> I gather we marry too many says Maine: too various.
> I gather we're bad blood: we're mixed people.
> That's what they say, says Texas.[7]

The story can be told less lyrically but quite as movingly for almost every national group. In the 100 years between 1820 and

[7] Archibald MacLeish, Colloquy for the States," in *Land of the Free* (New York, Harcourt Brace, 1938), pp. 83–4.

1920, and especially after the great famine of 1846–7 in Ireland, some four and a half million Irish crossed the Atlantic. They helped to build the early railroads and canals, they worked in mills and mines. Staying largely in the Northeast and becoming urbanized – and very slowly "suburbanized" – they took to politics and administration, and to the police and fire departments of local governments. The roll call of Eastern city mayors and bosses is strongly Irish – witness President Kennedy's Boston grandfathers, Patrick Kennedy and John Fitzgerald ("Honey Fitz").

The Italian contribution is equally strong. They moved in great numbers only after 1880. Like the Irish, many remained urbanized, to move into the clothing trades and become masons and stonecutters. But they moved West and South also, as truck gardeners around the great cities, into the vineyards of Northern California and the cotton and rice fields in the Deep South, into baseball like Joe Di Maggio, music like Gian-Carlo Menotti and politics like Fiorello Enrico La Guardia – Indeed, La Guardia, mayor of New York from 1934 to 1945, is in many respects the prototype immigrant figure; he was the son of an Italian father and a Portuguese-Jewish mother, and one of his grandmothers was Greek. And, when Democratic party leaders go on political trips abroad, they are still likely to ensure that their itineraries include Israel, Italy, and Ireland (North and South).

The German groups had moved more steadily to the New World, and they went farther West; by the Hudson to the Mohawk, or down the Susquehanna to the Pennsylvania frontier. Among the first German settlements were the Pennsylvania "Dutch" (or Deutsch), who developed the area around Philadelphia and "Germantown;" in the 1740s the youthful Benjamin Franklin was afraid that German would become the language of the state. Voices were raised at the First Continental Congress of 1774 querying whether English was the appropriate language for the new nation: should not Huron or one of the Iroquois tongues be adopted as the national speech? (Roger Sherman had, as was his way, a brusquer proposal: let the new nation keep the English language and let the British learn Greek.) The first campaign for a free press and free speech was Peter Zenger's in 1735. Many Germans moved south down the valley of Virginia into the pine-barrens country of the Carolinas and Georgia. When George III recruited "Hessians" to fight as mercenaries in the British armies during the Revolution, he forgot that on meeting German-speaking Pennsylvanians they would be sorely tempted to change sides; and many did. Later waves of German migration – the "48ers" – came into exile after the failure of the European revolutions, many with the thought of returning to Europe as liberators. Instead, hundreds of them served as liberators in Union armies in the Civil War, and one, Carl Schurz, became a brigadier, a close friend of Lincoln, and an advocate of the establishment of a civil service. He was excited by what he saw, and his observations have obvious echoes of de Tocqueville. Wendell Willkie of Indiana, Republican opponent of F. D. Roosevelt in the 1940 elections, was a descendant of 48er Germans. By 1910 there were 8 million Americans who were either themselves German-born or whose parents had been born there. Their roots, however, became Mid-Western and agrarian; they were industrious, conscientious, strong in family and civic loyalties. Charles F. Adams's impression of them is that of a Yankee but its imagery is apt:

I like to see a hand dot's brown,
  Und not avraid off vork;
Dot gifes to dose vot air in need,
  Und nefer tries to schirk:
A man dot meets you mit a schmile,
  Und dakes you py der hand,
Shust like dey do vhere I vas born,
  In mine own vaterland, –

Vhere bier-saloons don'd keep a schlate;
  Vhere tailors get deir pay,
Und vashervimmin get der schtamps
  For vork dey dake avay;
Vhere *frauleins* schtick righdt to der vork
  So schteady as a glock,
Und not go schtrutting droo der schtreets
  Shust like a durkey-cock;
Vhere blenty und brosperity
  Schmile ubon efery hand:
Dot ist der Deutscher's paradise;
  Das ist das Vasterland.[8]

By the end of the nineteenth century the major source of settlers was Southern and Eastern Europe: Italians and Russians, Poles and Slavs – new groups, more difficult languages, sharper social tensions. The transcontinental railroads were largely the work of Chinese coolie labor, and now Chinese-Americans make San Francisco their

[8] Charles F. Adams (1835–1915) in his *Autobiography* (Boston, Little, Brown, 1916), p. 122.

own western American capital. Many Mid-Western farmers are of Swedish, or Norwegian, or Czech descent. Slovaks are prominent in the heavy industries of the Eastern and North Central states, not least in the steel mills of Pittsburgh. Mexicans have built most of the irrigation canals in the Imperial valley of California, and work the beet fields of Colorado and Michigan. And the black contribution is evident: singers Paul Robeson, Marion Anderson and Lena Horne; educators like Robert R. Moton, Booker T. Washington and John Hope Franklin; poets like Langston Hughes and Claude McKay; athletes like Jesse Owens; jazz musicians like "Duke" Ellington; and countless others.

For this last-mentioned group, the blacks, now numbering 30 millions and sometimes preferring to be described as African-Americans, the story has been, of course, sharply different: their ancestors did not cross the Atlantic by choice.

3 AFRICAN-AMERICANS

Negro slave trade with the Americas was a vast commercial operation that lasted for 300 years, on which great fortunes – British, Dutch, Portuguese, French, and American – were founded and which was basic to the prosperity of Glasgow and Liverpool, Newport and Providence, and the West Indies. Some 15 million black cargoes were shipped, packed like cattle into holds where they were often forced to sit upright throughout the voyage – there was, indeed, an argument in the trade between the "tight-packers" and the "loose-packers." They died by the thousand: of disease and filth, foul air, poor food, and broken hearts. Those suspected of contagion were thrown overboard to protect the rest of the investment. After the prohibition of the slave trade in the early nineteenth century, ships were ready to jettison live cargoes to escape being caught with slaves aboard. Those that survived were, on arrival, sold on the block, to be the absolute property of their owners. Until 1865 they had no protection in law or in any moral code. For the last century of nominal and legal freedom blacks have been struggling to find a real economic and political base for their formal freedom. The sense of guilt and the fight for civil rights are major themes in recent American literature and in contemporary politics.

After Reconstruction, whites regained control of Southern legislatures and passed "Jim Crow" laws to enforce racial segregation and discrimination. The most important test of Jim Crow laws was the case of *Plessy vs. Ferguson* in 1896 in which the Supreme Court upheld a Louisiana law segregating rail passengers by race. Eight of the nine justices reasoned that, so long as the facilities provided for the races were equal, there was nothing wrong with racial segregation. If colored persons chose to believe that "enforced separation of the two races stamps the colored race with a badge of inferiority," said the majority, "it is not by reason of anything found in the Act, but solely because the colored race chooses to put that construction upon it." This decision endorsed "separate but equal" facilities. However, since most Southern blacks were disenfranchised and politically powerless, separate facilities were not, and could not be, equal.

The only Supreme Court justice to dissent from the Plessy decision was John Marshall Harlan (1833–1911). Harlan achieved a reputation as a forceful dissenter, particularly on matters involving the protection of black rights, and his famous dissent in *Plessy vs. Ferguson* was quoted in the early 1950s by lawyers for the National Association for the Advancement of Colored People in their successful legal attack on racial segregation.

Not that the blacks were a united people: the approaches of black leaders differed widely. Booker T. Washington (1856–1915) was for compromise and accommodation. Born a slave, in 1872 he enrolled at Hampton Normal and Agricultural Institute and paid his way by working in the school as a janitor. After teaching and further studies, he was chosen to lead Tuskegee Normal and Industrial Institute. Over the next 34 years, Washington built Tuskegee from an impoverished school into a major institution with 1,500 students. He believed that the path to advancement for blacks was through industrial education, small-scale entrepreneurship, and hard work. Invited to address a white audience at the Atlanta Exposition on September 18, 1895, in his speech he counseled fellow blacks to cultivate "the common occupations of life," to develop friendly relations with their white neighbors, and to begin "at the bottom," not the top.

Other black leaders such as W. E. B. Du Bois rejected Booker T.'s counsel of patience and moderation, and called his speech the "Atlanta Compromise;" they also denounced Washington's emphasis on industrial education at the expense of academic education. At the time, black rights in the South were imperiled by the passage of the Jim Crow laws. Black farmers were mainly tenant farmers, exploited by a system of sharecropping, and black workers in the cities were excluded from labor unions. Whites, however, cheered Washington's speech, and he was feted by white Southerners and Northerners. In 1901, he was invited to the White House by President Theodore

Roosevelt. From 1895 until his death, he was considered the most powerful black American of the day. He wrote a dozen books, including his autobiography, *Up from Slavery*. In his address at the Atlanta Exposition, he said:

One-third of the population of the South is of the Negro race. No enterprise seeking the material, civil, or moral welfare of this section can disregard this element of our population and reach the highest success. I but convey to you, Mr President and Directors, the sentiment of the masses of my race when I say that in no way have the value and manhood of the American Negro been more fittingly and generously recognized than by the managers of this magnificent Exposition at every stage of its progress. It is a recognition that will do more to cement the friendship of the two races than any occurrence since the dawn of our freedom.

Not only this, but the opportunity here afforded will awaken among us a new era of industrial progress. Ignorant and inexperienced, it is not strange that in the first years of our new life we began at the top instead of at the bottom; that a seat in Congress or the State Legislature was more sought than real estate or industrial skill; that the political convention or stump speaking had more attractions than starting a dairy farm or truck garden.

A ship lost at sea for many days suddenly sighted a friendly vessel. From the mast of the unfortunate vessel was seen a signal: "Water, water, we die of thirst." The answer from the friendly vessel at once came back, "Cast down your bucket where you are." A second time the signal, "Water, water, send us water," ran up from the distressed vessel and was answered, "Cast down your bucket where you are," And a third and fourth signal for water was answered "Cast down your bucket where you are." The captain of the distressed vessel, at last heeding the injunction, cast down his bucket and it came up full of fresh, sparkling water from the mouth of the Amazon River.

To those of my race who depend on bettering their condition in a foreign land, or who underestimate the importance of cultivating friendly relations with the Southern white man who is their next-door neighbor, I would say: Cast down your bucket where you are; cast it down in making friends, in every manly way, of the people of all races by whom we are surrounded. Cast it down in agriculture, mechanics, in commerce, in domestic service, and in the professions. And in this connection it is well to bear in mind that whatever other sins the South may be called upon to bear, when it comes to business pure and simple, it is in the South that the Negro is given a man's chance in the commercial world.

What has been seen as his philosophy, he summed up as:

In all things that are purely social we can be separate as the fingers, yet one as the hand in all things essential to mutual progress.[9]

[9] Booker T. Washington, *Up from Slavery* (New York, Bantam Books, 1963), p. 88.

John Hope (1868–1936) was born in Augusta, Georgia, and graduated from Worcester Academy in Massachusetts and then Brown University in 1894. He went on to become a professor of classics and sciences at Roger Williams University in Nashville, Tennessee. Hope was one of the founders of the Niagara Movement, which preceded the National Association for the Advancement of Colored People. In 1906, he became the first black president of Atlanta Baptist College (Morehouse College), and in 1929, the president of Atlanta University. A strong advocate of liberal education for blacks, Hope opposed Booker T. Washington's advocacy of technical training. He heard Washington's famous Atlanta Exposition speech and disagreed strongly. On February 22, 1896, he delivered a speech in rebuttal to Washington to a black debating society.

W. E. B. Du Bois was the moving force in the creation of the Niagara Movement, an organization of prominent black leaders that first convened in the summer of 1905 at Niagara Falls. The purpose of the organization was to establish an assertive alternative to the accommodationist politics of Booker T. Washington. The group, however, was unable to develop enough funding to establish a permanent staff or headquarters and appeared to be heading for the same fate as previous efforts to establish a black protest organization. However, in 1908 the race riots in Springfield, Illinois, the hometown of Abraham Lincoln, prompted a group of whites to plan an organization that would revive the abolitionist spirit on behalf of black rights. Mary White Ovington, a social worker, William English Walling, a journalist, and Oswald Garrison Villard, publisher of the *New York Post*, convened a national conference to renew "the struggle for political and civil liberty." The white leaders joined forces with the black leaders of the Niagara Movement to create the National Association for the Advancement of Colored People. The principles of the Niagara Movement became the principles of the new NAACP. For Du Bois, his viewpoint was that "Any discrimination based simply on race or color is barbarous, we care not how hallowed it be by custom, expediency or prejudice."

There is another aspect to the story: in music, song and dance. The songs of the slaves, working in the fields and on the plantation, form a distinct element in American literature. Negro spirituals were composed, as the black poet James Weldon Johnson put it, by "black and unknown bards." These beautiful and poignant songs spread far beyond the physical confines where they were created and entered the American consciousness as a fundamental part of the national culture. James Weldon Johnson held in 1925 that the spirituals were "America's only folk music and, up to this time, the finest distinctive artistic contribution she has to offer the world." With more than a touch of irony, he observed, "It is strange!" The spirituals fused characteristics of African music with elements of the Old Testament to become dignified and rhythmic expressions of faith. Most were written for group or choral singing. Immediately after emancipation, educated blacks discouraged the singing of spirituals as a reminder of slavery; but the old songs nonetheless remained popular in black churches and in time received wide public recognition. The spirituals were introduced to a large popular audience by the Fisk University Jubilee Singers, who toured the country in 1871. In time, songs like "Swing Low, Sweet Chariot," "Gimme Dat Ol'-Time Religion," and "Nobody Knows de Trouble I Seen" became popular American standards.

Even after the Civil War, the rural character of the black population remained virtually intact, although there was some movement into new agricultural areas in Louisiana and Texas. The first exodus from the South occurred in the period 1879–81, when freedom in law allowed mobility. Some 60,000 blacks moved into Kansas. This spontaneous movement was made under the most difficult of circumstances by riverboat, railroad, decrepit wagons, and on foot. The in-migration to Kansas created situations that strained the state, and several cities became refugee camps. The drive behind this initial thrust to new lands was the need for social and economic freedom and the avoidance of political abuse after "Reconstruction".

By 1910, the first signs of the urbanization of America's black population began to appear. By this date, some 27 percent of them were in the cities. While in the South the black population was virtually all rural, in the North and West almost 80 percent of blacks lived in cities.

The first large northward migration of Negroes occurred between 1910 and 1920, resulting in a drop in the Southern Negro population from 89 percent to 85 percent. The most dramatic change in the black population between 1940 and 1970 has not been in terms of numbers or percentage of the total US population, but rather in location – away from the South and into the urban areas of the North and West. In 1940 over 77 percent of the black population was in the South. By 1970 this figure had dropped just below the 52 percent level. During the 1950s blacks were leaving the South at a rate of some 146,000 people a year, and although the pace slackened during the 1960s the annual out-migration rate was roughly 88,000 people per year.

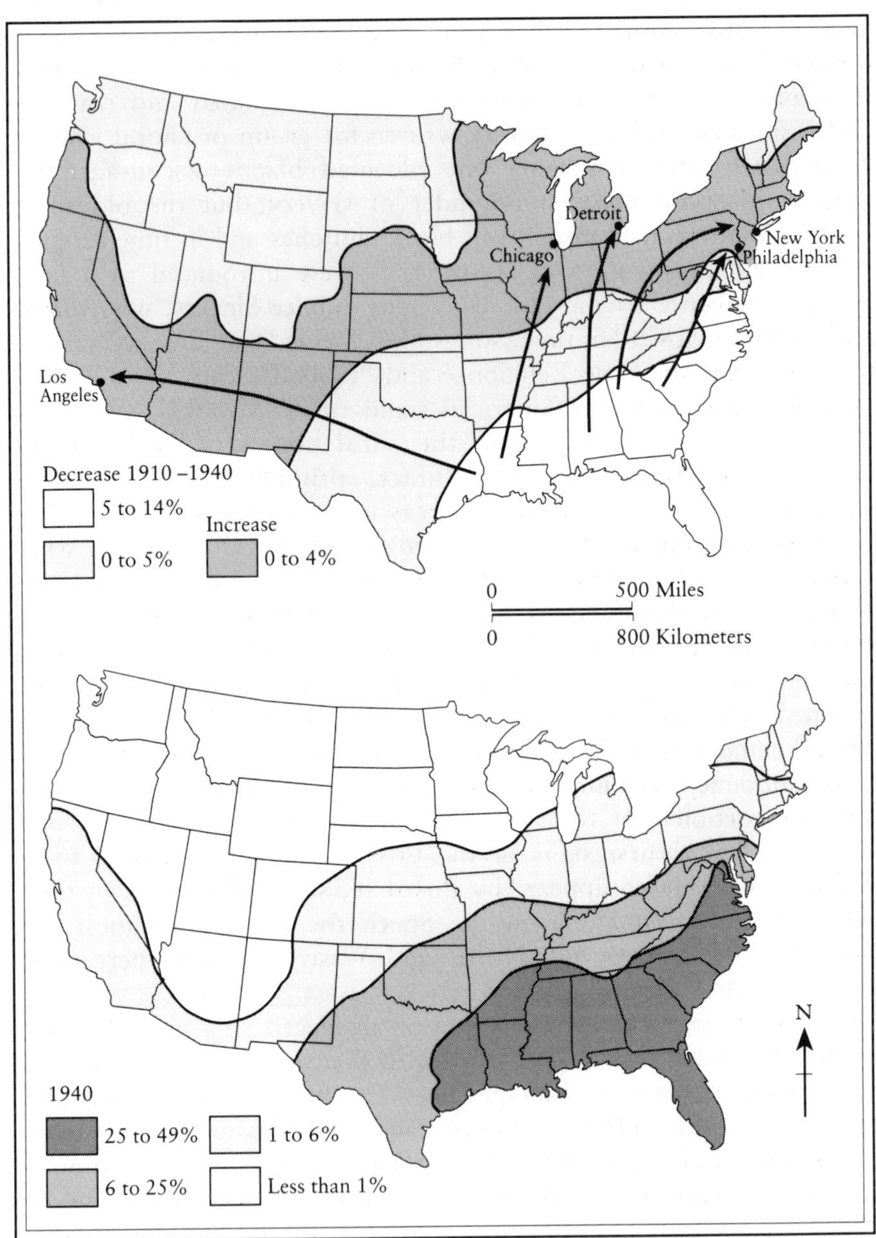

Map 3 Distribution of black population, 1940. The movement north of blacks during the years between 1910 and 1940 resulted in a higher proportion of blacks in the Northern industrial areas, but still by far the highest numbers were in the Deep South.

As of 1970 most of the nation's blacks who still lived on farms or in rural areas were to be found in the South. Nevertheless, even in the South, almost three out of five lived in urban centers. In the nation as a whole, 75 percent of the black population now reside in urban areas: the heaviest urban concentrations are in the North and West, where approximately 97 percent of the black population of the area reside in urban centers. Since the beginning of the 20th century, the percentage of blacks in the total population has remained relatively stable, at around 11 percent.

It took two generations after the end of the Civil War and participation in two World Wars, before segregation would cease; and that as much the result of the protest of the streets, of riots and civil disturbance, as from the decrees of the Supreme Court. Race has been one of the central themes of the history of the US in the so-called "American century;" for African-Americans, the dream of equality has been as intense as ever it was to Thomas Jefferson.

The last two generations, in which the word black has been given a new deference, has seen many developments: the civil rights court battles, the landmark march on Washington in 1961, the long hot summers for which Watts, in August 1965, acted as a flashpoint, when in all over 100 cities burned. In the same vein came the rise of the Black Panthers and the "Nation of Islam." If Martin Luther King's oratory was Christian, that of Malcolm X and of Stokeley Carmichael and of Eldridge Cleaver broke with gradualism, and its imagery was that of the clenched fist. On the West Coast, Hoyt Fuller retitled the *Negro Digest, Black World* as steps to a Black Cultural Nationalism, a movement in which Ross Karenga would share. Yet the same decade witnessed the award of the Nobel Prize for Literature to a black woman, a teacher at Princeton, Toni Morrison, and Black Studies were established everywhere. Violence and equality marched almost step by step.

Desegregation, and the decrees of the Court, were one dimension. There were others – as Richard Wright, in his semi-autobiographical novel *Native Son*, (1940) had testified. Alongside grew the cultural phenomenon of Black Power itself. Black Power was essentially a cultural phenomenon which offered African-Americans psychological emancipation from the constraints of white racism and a new sense of collective worth. Regardless of political orientation, Black Power ideologues shared a passionate belief in their distinctive African-American culture. They accordingly sought to bolster racial pride in "soul" music, in clothing, cooking, and tonsorial styles, in "Black Studies," "Black English," and African language and customs. Rather than reflecting the despair and disillusionment of separatist black militants following the fragmentation of the integrationist civil rights movement, Black Power updated the concerns of the "Freedom Schools" of the mid-1960s to "spread a positive, empowering sense of pride throughout black America." Thus Ron Karenga led the West Coast "back to black" movement, advocated the teaching of Swahili as a language of "self-determination," and inaugurated the celebration of such holidays as Uhuru Day (commemorating the 1965 Watts riot), Kuzawila (celebrating the birth of Malcolm X), and Kwanzaa (the black alternative to a white Christmas). The new black consciousness was particularly evident on college campuses, with demands for "revolutionary" Black Studies programs and black instructors. The new aesthetic was also apparent in the Black Power protests (and salutes) of black athletes and servicemen, the vogue for "natural" hairstyles (or wigs), the chart hits of James Brown ("Say It Loud: I'm Black and I'm Proud"), the writings and artistic/musical enterprises of Amiri Baraka, and the "soul theology" of the Reverend Albert B. Cleage.[10]

4 *PLURES*, NOT *UNUM*

With all its tensions, immigration is a central theme in the story; the United States is a society of immigrants. The Revolutionary leaders alongside Washington included Frenchmen like Rochambeau and Lafayette and Girard, Poles like Kosciuszko and Pulaski, Germans like Steuben. The intermixture has continued ever since. If many Americans, even in the seventh generation, are in name and in emotion hyphenated with Europe, the fact of immigration is also a fact of national distinction. And the story still continues. In the mid-term elections of November 1966, California elected to the governorship a film star, Ronald Reagan, and New York a millionaire, Nelson Rockefeller; but the governor of Maryland was the son of Greek immigrants, the governor of Massachusetts was an Italian Catholic, and the governor of Nevada was the son of a Basque shepherd. Even more strange, they were all members of the same Republican party, the party of conservatism and wealth.

The crossings the immigrants made were full of hazards – leaky ships, the risk of scurvy, disease and shipwreck, and of capture by

[10] William L. Van Deburg, *New Day in Babylon: The Black Power movement and American culture, 1965–1975* (Chicago and London, University of Chicago Press, 1992).

pirates or in war by the enemy, or the still bigger risk of mutiny or exploitation *en route* by their own crews. Exile was never easy and often never thought of as permanent. Throughout the history of emigration, the dream of a prosperous return was never far away. In the first colonies, to desert was to run the risk of execution after recapture – until in Virginia subtler devices were introduced: the promise of 50 acres of land on arrival, or the introduction of shiploads of maidens, "whereby the Planters minds may be the faster tyed to Virginia by the bonds of Wyves and children."

Even if all Americans were immigrants, not all the immigrants were well received by earlier arrivals. "Foreigners" were unwelcome even in the first English settlements, and this term included Scots, Irish, and Welsh. Huguenots, although both Protestants and good cultivators, were far from welcome – only in South Carolina did they find acceptance; elsewhere they were treated with suspicion and sometimes with violence. If the newcomers were peasants, they were apt not to fit into town life; differences of language, religion, dress, and social orientation made for perennial difficulty; however liberal in politics they might be, they learned only slowly the curious processes of democratic government. Even Jefferson thought the immigrants of the 1780s likely to be either vicious or despotic. In the 1790s immigrants tended to be either French royalist emigrés – politically unwelcome; Jacobins – even less welcome; or Irish and British radicals, least welcome of all. Qualifications for citizenship were raised in 1795 from two to five years. In the 1840s a familiar sign was "No Irish need apply," and a political party, the Know-Nothings, was established to exploit anti-foreign and nativist sentiments. On the immigrants it was possible to blame slums and city crime, sweat shops and disease, bossism and intemperance. If their numbers stimulated the movement West, their restlessness and rootlessness made for a wasteful agriculture; the land was mined, not farmed, the soil impoverished. Every fresh group has met distrust, contempt, suspicion, and open violence. If this was true of the "Old" migration, it was much truer of the "New." When the Founding Fathers thought of America as a land of refuge, they thought of the refugees as basically coming from Western and Northern Europe, escaping from the oppressions of royal or religious tyranny. By the 1890s, they were coming from East, South or Central Europe. When the first Italians began to come in, a New York paper had this to say:

> The floodgates are open. The bars are down. The sally-ports are unguarded. The dam is washed away. The sewer is choked ... the scum of immigration is viscerating upon our shores. The horde of $9.60 steerage slime is being siphoned upon us from Continental mud tanks ...

But in the 1920s, in the aftermath of World War I, the floodgates were closed. When he served as junior Senator from Massachusetts, John F. Kennedy campaigned to alter the quota system that had been introduced in 1924, and had regulated immigration ever since. He wrote:

> The famous words of Emma Lazarus on the pedestal of the Statue of Liberty read: "Give me your tired your poor, your huddled masses yearning to breathe free." Under present law it is suggested that there should be added: "as long as they come from Northern Europe, are not too tired or too poor or slightly ill, never stole a loaf of bread, never joined any questionable organization and can document their activities for the past two years."

"We must avoid", he said, "what the Massachusetts poet John Boyle O'Reilly once called:

> Organized charity, scrimped and iced,
> In the name of a cautious, statistical Christ."

As President, Kennedy called on Congress to change the 1924 law and to allow in each year, without regard to race or national origins, 165 thousand people. In 1965, two years after his assassination, Congress so ordered.

To seek to identify and describe the social characteristics of the inhabitants of the US as they have emerged over 350 years is to explore dangerous and twisting ground; the landscape is vast and varied, and different vantage points give very different views. The strands that form the American character are not in themselves difficult to disentangle; less tractable are the issues of emphasis and interpretation and the many paradoxes.

One such strand obviously is the pioneer tradition, the effect of the frontier itself, the challenge posed to Americans not only by the foreign enemy, when they faced the nations of Europe, but the personal challenge to survival in the wilderness, the call to adventure and to hardihood. As a result, even today and even in its urban settings, life is still lived close to nature. The qualities needed became the qualities admired: the manual skill to produce food, to build a house and its contents so that, in Dixon Wecter's phrase, the American equivalent of the Greek motto "Know thyself" is "Know thy stuff." Respect is for ingenuity and for the "doer" – "Skill to do comes of doing," said Emerson. Hard work was basic to survival, class origins and titles irrelevant, so that Americans today remain loose and casual about honors and dignities, strong in self-assurance, short of deference. The respect each won was due to personal, not inherited, merit, and to the pride and equality conferred by ownership of land. And, as always, paradoxes were obvious: if life was rough, the shortage of women led to a certain veneration for them; if it was hard, it was rich in hospitality to strangers; and, as in religious practices, rich in emotion. But despite the myth, the frontier was less productive of independence than of gregariousness, as witness the communal house-building or the quilting bees of colonial times, the town-meetings and the active community spirit of today. Conformism and ready hospitality, and not solitude and privacy, were its characteristics.

Again, the impact of Puritanism is as striking as the frontier spirit. One reason for the colonial migration was the quest for freedom of religious worship; and despite periods of aberration in seventeenth-century New England, and waves of anti-Catholic hysteria in the mid-nineteenth century, the record of the United States is admirable here. To many of the Founding Fathers, the freedom sought was freedom of the mind and of the conscience. Jefferson assessed his own career in the epitaph he wrote himself: author of the Declaration of American Independence, the Statute of Virginia for Religious Freedom and Father of the University of Virginia, "by these as testimonials that I have lived I wish most to be remembered." The Revolution saw the rise of, and was in part consequence of, the more liberal and democratic churches, especially the Baptist and the Methodist. Not only did these groups emphasize individual interpretation of the Bible, but their services were expressive, emotional and non-doctrinal; their most striking preachers were possessed by the Word and could raise visions of hellfire and damnation; they stressed personal salvation and had great effect on the frontier.

Puritanism has taken other forms than freedom of worship. As Max Weber and R. H. Tawney have shown, Calvinism and the business ethic are closely linked. Benjamin Franklin derived a career of conspicuous secular success largely from the adages of Cotton Mather. The Yankee emphasis on sobriety and earnestness – even if in twentieth-century New England both gaiety and Catholicism have indeed broken in; the search for wealth as a symbol of success and the promptness to see God and Mammon as twin deities; the mysticism indeed of success itself as at once reward and justification; these also became American characteristics. It is more blessed to give than to receive, because prosperity and affluence are more blessed than poverty. The United States is indeed a strongly religious society, church-going, publicly pious, and addicted to ceremony, however loosely shaped and at times absurd may seem its ceremonial forms. But the religious creeds have become oddly approximate to each other so that a Baptist sermon can sound very like an Anglican; they are strongly civic and socially motivated; they are bathed less in a sense of personal awareness of sin and humility than in a mood of guileless and well-meant optimism. Religiosity is more striking than faith; the emphasis is less on theological content than on a subjective experience.

Worldly achievement and business success, physical energy and activity, and with it youth and virility, are the real objects of adulation; and Rotary, Elks and Kiwanis are in a sense churches too. Popular religion has become, in some measure, a religion of accommodation to the secular humanism of the surrounding society; throughout the nineteenth century its message was strongly a social gospel, preoccupied with human needs, either of the self (witness the peace-of-mind cults of the West Coast) or of society. In recent years there has been a distinct theological revival. But, however transmuted into a code of civic good and assessed by the Community Chest budgets, Puritanism is deeply entrenched in American history from Cotton Mather, through unlikely Benjamin Franklin, by way of Andrew Carnegie and Frederick W. Taylor's faith in scientific management of machines and men, to Herbert C. Hoover and Calvin Coolidge. At intervals it erupted into waves of reform whose intensity often took strange direction: the witch-trials of Salem; the Great Awakening on the frontier; the religious sects of the West Coast; the fundamentalism of the Bible Belt and the campaign in Tennessee against the teaching of evolution; the Temperence Movement in the nineteenth century and Prohibition in the 1920s. And there has been an easy overflow from religion into politics that is also characteristic; Know Nothingism in the 1840s, the Ku Klux Klan in the 1860s and intermittently since 1919; the call to turn away from false gods that marked the crude campaign of Senator McCarthy. It is easy to write cynically of some aspects of American religious and political/religious experience; Americans have sought God in some very strange places and sometimes recognized Him in some very unlikely forms. But it is idle to minimize the place of the Calvinist ethic in the story; and the most native of the American faiths – Mormonism and Christian Science – have been strongly marked by respect for personal and for business success.

American society is a society of laws. It is governed by a written Constitution, and one major branch of government is the Supreme Court. Yet, equally, American society – because of its democratic qualities, its wealth of physical and human resources, and perhaps because of its polyglot character – is also a society of such zest and vigor that it is marked as much by lawlessness as by respect for Law. Much of the writing of Cooper, and Melville, and Jack London, is preoccupied with the tension between a tiny man and his vast environment, whether of land or sea, just as the writing of Charles Brockden Brown, Poe, Faulkner, and Hemingway is concerned with the clash between society and the primitive forces of the soul, the "Gothic," the eruptive, the violent. If the "Western" is one of the classic expressions of this conflict in American film art, so are the bar-room fight and the ritualized duel. Law, after all, was slow to reach the frontier, whether it was in the Tidewater in the seventeenth century or on the Rockies in the nineteen. The Pilgrim Fathers marched to church with scouts and riflemen to protect them. The colonial preachers in the valley kept their muskets beside them in the pulpit below the Holy Book, and the first sheriffs and marshals had short and hectic lives. Effective justice depended for three centuries on being alive to tell the tale. Teddy Roosevelt spoke for his world, and his country's history, when he said in 1900: "Speak softly, and carry a Big Stick; you will go far."

But the tradition is more than this. Even in the settled East, the law and its guardians play little more than a surface role: bosses like George Washington Plunkett, Mayor Tweed of Tammany Hall, Governor Huey Long and James Hoffa of the Teamsters' Union, skate over and round it merrily; robustly to defy it wins a certain reluctant public approval. Nor does it curb the racial infighting of Al Capone, the lynchings of the Deep South, the clashes over civil rights in Mississippi and Chicago. The gusto and energy that give American life its dynamic quality, the restlessness and drive that give it progress, are impatient forces. The law respected might be that of the classic portico of the Supreme Court Building or the calm of the Court House Square, but the law invoked is apt to be lynch law and vigilante justice.

Again, if the pressure to conformity is striking, so is the tradition of dissent: Roger Williams and Anne Hutchinson, Sam Adams and Paul Revere, Tom Paine and George Logan, William Lloyd Garrison, Thoreau, and E. V. Debs; Big Bill Haywood, Joe Hill, and Lincoln Steffens; Horace Greeley, Ignatius Donnelly, and Altgeld of Illinois; Mary Ellen Lease of Kansas, Dorothea Dix, and Elizabeth Cady Stanton; and not least in such a gallery, Justices Holmes and Brandeis. They were attacked and vilified and were called everything from "dreamers of the dream" to "the lunatic fringe," "crusaders," and "mavericks." But they serve as reminders of the chameleon-like quality of freedom. To each of them liberty meant something different: to Garrison, Negro emancipation; to Thoreau, freedom from coercion; to Debs, economic equality. They are conspicuous because they crusaded against the dominant conformity and babbittry of American life.

And yet again, alongside the tradition of democracy, of egalitarianism and civic good causes, is another tradition, now lost except to history and myth: the tradition of aristocracy as expressed in the Old South. The plantation system bred other things than staple crops for export, and slaves to work the fields. It bred America's only native feudal system, the big house at the center of vast estates on the James River (or the Santee or the Hudson), and the patroonage of New York, the Carolinas and Chesapeake Bay. Newport had its wealth, drawn largely from shipping, the sea and the slave trade. But there emerged farther south the lords of great acres, who, in families like the Byrds and the Carters, the Randolphs and the Lees, produced an elite that stands comparison with the aristocracy of Old England – on which indeed it modeled itself. The master was perforce law and laird, estate manager, doctor, guardian, guide, and glad host to an extensive family, in which the blood-tie now and then took strange forms. He was usually educated in England, and from it he imported his cambrics and linens, his glass; and tableware, his dress and his coaches, books for his library and busts for his drawing room. Occasionally he read widely, like Peter Harrison, or Thomas Jefferson, or William Byrd II of Westover. At its best, this was the world of Mount Vernon or Monticello, of Tuckahoe or Stratford Hall, of Newport or of the James River homes. Its worst manifestations have left a more bitter legacy in backwardness that still characterizes parts of the South, the tensions of race and the passion of the civil rights cause.

This society was destroyed by the Civil War, the ugliest scar in the history of the United States. It has been abundantly chronicled by historians, and the memory of it is deeply enshrined in the writing of Stephen Crane and Stephen Vincent Benet, of William Faulkner, and of the Fugitive School of writers. But perhaps the significance of it has never been better described than by C. Vann Woodward in his essay "The burden of Southern history."[11] The fact of defeat, of devastation, of the occupation of the land by a "foreign" army, the circumstances of the fight back and all the devices, including the Ku Klux Klan, that were used to win it, the economic and racial

[11] C. Vann Woodward, *The Burden of Southern History*, (New York, Vintage Books, 1960).

consequences for the New South that slowly emerged: this is a rare and moving chapter in the American story. It is sharply at odds with the straightforward and unstructured world of contemporary America, itself now invading even Dixie. As Nathaniel Hawthorne saw it, this bourgeois society of the North had "no shadow, no antiquity, no mystery ... nor anything but a commonplace prosperity, in broad and simple daylight." For a short time there was a prospect of another America, but it was to be a destiny unmanifest.

Central to all American characteristics is a faith in political freedom. Men should not exercise power over one another; power therefore should be as limited and as diffused as possible. "That Government is best," said Jefferson, "which governs least." The government set up in 1787 – and that, though designed for a farmer's world of three and a half million souls, has shown itself surprisingly well suited to the industrial world of 250 million – was carefully balanced: Executive *versus* Legislature *versus* Judiciary. If there is respect for and primitive satisfaction in size – of industrial organization and architecture as well as of mountain and cascade – and if today there is a deep respect for presidential authority, there is the equally durable tradition of ingrained suspicion of all those who wield power, whether political, economic or social. Americans have repeatedly acted either to prevent power from growing too menacing or to destroy it after it has emerged. Nor does apprehension stop at the boundaries of political power. Elections have been decided on the basis of promises to control economic power. Jacksonian Democrats promised to deprive Eastern bankers, above all Nicholas Biddle and the Bank of the United States, of their supposed capacity to limit Western economic growth. William Jennings Bryan's three unsuccessful campaigns for the presidency were founded on a similar fear of J. P. Morgan and other Eastern financiers. The small banker as well as the small farmer of the West knew in his bones that his troubles stemmed from the malevolent domination of his affairs by a few giants of finance located in Wall Street or Threadneedle Street. Franklin D. Roosevelt promised to drive the money-changers from the temples of power.

These curbs on and suspicions of authority, the faith in balanced government, the belief in visibly subjecting the Executive to a searching cross-examination of policy and motive – a far more searching, more public and more vitriolic cross-examination than takes place in the House of Commons – these are not merely matters of constitutional practice or of political doctrine, whether derived from the Mayflower Compact or from 1688, from Tom Paine, or from

Locke, from Calvin, or from the Levelers. They became entrenched because of the possibility of the enjoyment of freedom due to the availability of cheap, or even free, land. "Those who labor in the earth are the chosen people of God, if ever he had a chosen people," said farmer Jefferson. It was no mere form of words for him to write as his first draft for the Declaration of Independence:

> We hold these truths to be self-evident, that all men are created equal, that they are endowed by their Creator with certain unalienable rights, that among these are life, liberty and property.

If the final form became "life, liberty, and the pursuit of happiness," "property" has been seen, from the beginnings, as giving man a real sense of independence, a capacity to stand on his own feet and to be himself. The colonial headright system, whereby a man, or whoever financed his journey, got the promise of 50 acres of land, the Homestead Act whereby in 1862 he got 160 acres on condition that he settled and worked it himself – these are at the root of American's proper pride in the notion of equality. As Louis Hartz has brilliantly shown, the uniqueness of the American experience is that it never had to pass through a feudal period; the American people inherited liberty without having to struggle for it.[12] And even semi-feudal Virginia was, it now seems, more middle-class (and even "democratic"?) than we used to think, with land ownership widely enjoyed and political practices boisterously public.

The faith in land ownership has met its challenges, especially in the Dustbowl in the drought of the 1930s, when the land became a subsoil that was useless for cultivation. The farmers of the Western plains, and of Oklahoma, became rootless wanderers, dependent on seasonal jobs, picking peas and fruit in California, gathering melons in Colorado, working in the beet fields of Montana. And there have been many millions in the United States who have been unable to share the gospel of a property-owning democracy.

To the Homestead Act of 1862, two other measures should be added: Jefferson's Ordinances of 1785 and 1787. These opened the land lying west of the Allegheny and the Appalachian Mountains to indefinite increase in population, and promised admission of newly formed states to the Union on a basis of absolute equality with the original states in the East. This was a complete departure from the European doctrine that colonies should occupy a position inferior

[12] Louis Hartz, *The Liberal Tradition in America* (Cambridge, Mass., Harvard University Press, 1955).

to that of the mother country, and should be developed for its benefit. It made possible a totally new society in which variety and distance were themselves enlisted to build a new federal system; the United States was the product not only of the Constitution of 1787 but of the imaginative liberalism of the writers of the North-West Ordinances. Without them, Vermont could have been driven into Canada, or left isolated; without them, the men of the Western Waters might well have sold themselves to Spain; without them, the threats of secession of 1812 and 1830 would have been dangerous indeed. The new state – aided by Europe's quarrels, be it said – was held together by its very looseness. As once used to be said of the British Commonweath – though it is hardly possible to say it still – it was the product of its own capacity for freedom.

Even more daring in 1787 was the notion of republicanism itself. No priests, no king: it had taken many centuries to achieve the dream of a society truly free and independent in mind. Free from European entanglements, it should be possible to develop a centralized and federal republic and a weak central government. The clearest expression of the American political ideals, as the Founding Fathers saw them, was expressed by Jefferson in his first inaugural address:

> Kindly separated by nature and a wide ocean from the exterminating havoc of one-quarter of the globe; possessing a chosen country, with room enough for our descendants to the thousandth and ten thousandth generation; entertaining a due sense of our equal right to the use of our own faculties, to the acquisitions of our own industry, to honor and confidence from our fellow-citizens, resulting not from birth, but from our actions and their sense of them; enlightened by a benign religion, professed indeed and practiced in various forms, yet all of them inculcating honesty, truth, temperance, gratitude, and the love of man; acknowledging and adoring an overruling Providence, which, by all its dispensations, proves that it delights in the happiness of man here, and his greater happiness hereafter; with all these blessings, what more is necessary to make us a happy and a prosperous people? Still one thing more, fellow-citizens, a wise and frugal government which shall restrain men from injuring one another, shall leave them otherwise free to regulate their own pursuits of industry and improvement, and shall not take from the mouth of labor the bread it has earned. This is the sum of good government; and this is necessary to close the circle of our felicities.

Yet, despite all these political factors, despite a highly mobile and mixed population, in the twentieth century freedom has been menaced. The threat has not been from external enemies, not from the growth of authority of the Executive, nor from the arrogance of self-appointed inquisitors like Senator McCarthy, but from human nature itself. By the steady erosion of differences inside the United States, by the destruction of status, by the emphasis that one individual is as good as the next, an emphasis on freedom can lead to a loss of identity; people in our time have sought to escape from freedom in the idea of service to a cause outside themselves. True freedom, in a society in which the compulsions exercised are not politically coercive but socially conformist, can be hard to sustain.

Finally, what of the image of the US's own role in the world? The state was born in a Revolution, a Revolution seen as harbinger of many more. But the attitude of Americans to the fact of revolution today is distinctly ambivalent.

> We feel a certain obligation to like revolution on principle, having been born in one ourselves. On the other hand, we are also afraid and suspicious of revolutions. This, no doubt, can be traced back to a suppressed guilt feeling about the treachery to a parent culture which any revolution implies. Our attitude toward revolution, therefore, is a compound feeling of both love and hate, affectionate regard for the infants toddling in our early footsteps and unresolved guilt about our own breakaway.[13]

Clearly in today's world, revolution is a familiar phenomenon. It is even more necessary to national pride than its consequence, independence. To assert the rights of man is now to stake a claim to the right to affluence. Every African and almost every Asian country has passed or is passing through social or political changes, many of them violent, that can be traced back in lineal descent to the events of 1776. Thirty new nations have been born in Africa in the last 20 years. And the role of world leader enjoyed by, or thrust upon, the United States gives its own revolution a peculiar importance outside and inside the country. It was the first true revolution in modern history. Its relative smoothness makes it in some measure an event worthy of emulation.

Yet here again the facts deny the legend. Whatever might have been the revolutionary forces at work, they were soon tamed. There can be little debate among historians on one point, that by 1787 perhaps, and by 1793 certainly, the Revolution was – whether concluded or not at home – no longer (perhaps never?) meant for

[13] K. E. Boulding, "The US and Revolution," in *The US and Revolution* (Washington, DC, US State Department, 1976), p. 4.

export abroad. Whatever the storms in Europe or Latin America after 1789, the United States would have no part of them. If its own revolution was herald of a new order of things across the world, its leaders were unwilling to assume the role of world crusaders. Not only was this a revolution that acquired an ideology belatedly, but it was a revolution that curbed itself at its own frontiers. Abstention from, not involvement in, Europe was the dominant notion of the Founding Fathers. Washington proved very deaf to Miranda's call to be not once but twice *El Libertador*. It is natural in today's world to seek to trace the ideas of American leadership back, like everything else, to the Founding Fathers. But they were not crusaders. The new order of the ages that they were building was to be a model, but for emulation and example only.

It is not merely that the world has changed, but that the revolutions are very different. When Locke, and Jefferson, and Paine proclaimed the ultimate right to revolt, their enemies were the traditional divine-right or hereditary monarchies; they sought to replace them by tightly limited republican institutions which would be in the hands of a new elite, not of the people. "Your people, Sir, is a great beast." The words were Alexander Hamilton's, but if the people had been an urban proletariat they could have been Jefferson's too. They could even have been Tom Paine's. His hopes in France were for limited liberal republican constitutionalism, and when the French abandoned these goals, Paine's criticisms put him in prison and almost led him to the guillotine. The Revolution of 1776 was a Whig revolution; it was not intended to make the world safe for Jacksonian Democrats.

And yet, if the events of 1776 and 1787 were not in this sense a totally new order of the ages, in spirit and in consequence they proved to be so. For they created a new nation and a new ideology. American nationality was not inherited but achieved, and the achievement gave those who won it, and those who followed after, a new security, a new prosperity, and a new pride. Other revolutions, though like everything else they have their own momentum, have this dream too. For Americans the consequences – the enjoyment of the wealth and exploitation of a continent without being the victim of foreign interference – were attributed to the cause. Less fortunate continents will have a less fortunate history, and other consequences will follow their revolutions. But the nineteenth century in the USA was unlike anything in previous history. Nor could the forces it generated be confined to the United States alone, despite the Monroe Doctrine. When in 1898 the United States followed an imperial course in the War with Spain, its course was distinct from all preceding imperialisms. It was not merely that "it did not last," but that its motivation was distinct. And by the same forces the Revolution of 1776, though it might be the source and origin of many of the modern forces in the world, is no longer the stereotype of revolution.

The solution, however, is not for America to abandon her traditional devotion to revolution as such. The solution is for her to come to appreciate that if the American Revolution were to take place in the twentieth century it would look more like the revolutions that have occurred in Israel, in Puerto Rico, and in India than like the American Revolution of 1776. Indeed, the America of General Motors and TVA, the America of Levittown and Los Angeles, the America of Columbia University and Cal. Tech., is no longer the America of the American Revolution. The America of Walter Lippmann is not the America of Thomas Paine. And yet it is the America of Walter Lippmann at which the entire world – including Russia most especially – aims. But the world knows something that we have hidden from ourselves. And that is that you don't produce TVA, Cal. Tech., and General Motors in twentieth-century India or Africa by starting with prototypes drawn from the American eighteenth century.[14]

And it is these, TVA and Cal. Tech. and General Motors, products at once of the individualist dynamic and of the social conscience of the nineteenth and twentieth centuries, that have come to be the objects of admiration and regard. These constitute the ideas and ideals of the American free society. The Revolution of 1776 set Americans free. American progress since 1776 has been the consequence of that freedom: of free men and women, free movement of goods and ideas in a vast, abundant, and open society.

[14] Harvey Wheeler, "The US and revolution," in *The US and Revolution* (Washington, DC, US State Department, 1976), pp. 20–1.

2

Reconstruction

1 THE WAR BETWEEN THE STATES

The Civil War is the great traumatic experience of the American people. For once the Federalist dream was broken, sectionalism proved stronger than the nation, and no compromise could be found.

The imbalance of numbers and resources was obvious. The North had nearly 23 million people, the South less than 9 million, of whom 3½ million were slaves. The North had immense advantages in the extent of its railroads, the number of its factories and of what could become the infrastructure of total war. In skill and courage, however, the sides were well matched. The South had experience in the field, and in the handling and organization of men; its cotton exports, it thought, would be so cardinal to European industry that Britain and France would sooner or later support it; for command there was an array of talent experienced in the Mexican War, names that are a rollcall of cavalry leaders. And General Robert E. Lee showed himself an able tactical commander. The center of the war was the 100 square miles of country between the rival capitals, Richmond and Washington. Yet Northern Virginia, which still bears the scars of that long grim struggle, was not the decisive theater of war. Brilliant and devoted as was Lee, the war was won outside Virginia.

It was won for five main reasons. First, because Lincoln's leading officer, General Ulysses Grant from the North, drove south through Kentucky and Tennessee to take Chattanooga in 1863, and Admiral David Farragut forced the surrender of New Orleans; Texas, Arkansas and Louisiana were cut off from the rest of the Confederacy, which by 1863 was essentially the southeastern seaboard ringed round by mountains which were largely in Union hands. Second, because the sea blockade cut off Southern exports (of cotton and of ambassadors) and imports; clothing, shoes, and medicines became desperately short. Against this, Northern resources began to tell – of men, money, railcars, and ammunition, of flour and meat, boots and shoes. Northern exports boomed, and for the next generation corn, not cotton, was king, with decisive effects on the world economy, on the new interest in Indian and Egyptian cotton supplies, and on the food policies of Europe. Third, because as deprivation, hardship, and shortage hit the South, the North enjoyed a war boom. The making of the Great American Fortune was begun in the years of war and (as usual) by men not in uniform: J. D. Rockefeller in oil and railroads, C. H. McCormick in reaping machines, Andrew Carnegie in steel. Fourth, because Europe stayed aloof: the working men of Lancashire, hard-hit though they were by the cotton famine, stayed loyal to the cause of liberty. If they had had any doubts – and originally, certainly, both their political leaders Palmerston and Gladstone had – their doubts were stilled by Lincoln's Emancipation Proclamation of January 1863; given also Alexander II's liberation of the Russian serfs in 1861, the South was branded as barbarous, alien, and uncivilized. And fifth, behind all the heroism of the struggle, the South itself was not a united nation; at intervals its member states talked of seceding from the Confederacy.

When Lee surrendered to Grant at Appomattox Court House in April 1865 the South was in ruins. As a (no doubt apocryphal) Johnny Reb said to a (no doubt apocryphal) Billy Yank, "You-all never licked us. We-all got plumb tired out lickin' you-all."

On the occasion of his Second Inauguration in 1864 Lincoln had used words that have become immortal:

> With malice toward none; with charity for all, with firmness in the right, as God gives us to see the right, let us strive on to finish the work we are in; to bind up the nation's wounds; to care for him who shall have borne the battle, and for his widow, and his orphan ... to do all which may achieve and cherish a just and lasting peace among ourselves and with all nations.

It was both ironical and tragic that five days after Lee's surrender, Lincoln was assassinated in Ford's Theater in Washington. His achievement was remarkable: ill-educated and very poor, he had held the highest office in the land through its worst ordeal. The Union was preserved and the question of secession permanently outlawed.

Indeed, government now was no longer federal but national. Hereafter any President could be, if he wished, and if the crisis warranted, a dictator by consent. Lincoln himself had grown into greatness: an awkward, patient, humble man, in whom the penchant for a tall tale never quite died, he had revealed great political dexterity, remarkable timing, and a deep and real compassion. He became the incarnation of the Union. To the black population, he was more than life-size, his humility touched with the spirit of Christ. The great brooding figure that today looks out on the Reflecting Pool in Washington from his memorial has become the center of a pilgrimage.

Appomattox was the prelude to one of the least heroic periods in American history. The South was all but destroyed in war. The savings and investments of two centuries were wiped out, its farms gutted, its railroads destroyed, one in five of its men of military age wounded, its government in chaos. As a legacy of the war, the South's transportation systems were paralyzed, manufacturing had almost ceased, few banks or insurance companies were solvent, Confederate securities were worthless, labor was demoralized, plantations in chaos, and in some sections starvation was imminent. Few civilian administrations functioned, churches had been destroyed, and schools were closed. On the South for a decade the North wreaked a morbid vengeance.[1]

2 PRESIDENTIAL RECONSTRUCTION

The word "reconstruction," used to indicate Lincoln's (and his successor, President Andrew Johnson's) plan for the gradual restoration of political rights to the South and the gradual enfranchisement of the blacks, became at the hands of the Radicals a word synonymous with revenge. Civil War leaders in the South were, inevitably perhaps, proscribed; but the result was that Southern politics and business were left at the mercy of "scalawags" (white Southern Republican sympathizers) and "carpetbaggers" (Northern migrants into the South, usually "on the make"), and of newly enfranchised blacks, who were extravagant, incompetent, and easy

[1] "The South had undergone an experience that it could share with no other part of America – though it is shared by nearly all the people of Europe and Asia ... military defeat, occupation and reconstruction": C. Vann Woodward, *The Irony of Southern History*, p. 3 (Southern Historical Association Presidential Address, Nov. 7, 1952).

prey to corruption. The Radicals' intention to guarantee political and economic liberty to the blacks became fundamental law in the Fourteenth and Fifteenth Amendments to the Constitution (1868; 1870), but the idealism of the cause of emancipation and protection of blacks was swamped by the welter of greed for jobs, profits, and power.

The situation thus required that the President, as intermediary between the victor and the vanquished, give a clear indication of the rituals appropriate to peacemaking. The issues involved, however, were beyond the ability of President Johnson to handle, despite his good intentions. Politically, they had been raised two years before Johnson came to office. In his proclamation of December 1863, Lincoln had outlined a reconstruction plan whereby any Southern state government would receive executive recognition as soon as one-tenth of the voters in the state took an oath to support the Constitution, and affirm their loyalty to the cause of emancipation.

But the deadlock between the President and the Radical Republicans in Congress was clearly manifest in the Wade-Davis Bill of 1864, a punitive measure demanding far more submission by the states before their governments would be recognized, including a ban against Confederate office-holders and soldiers; it was designed to show that Reconstruction was the prerogative of Congress rather than the President. Lincoln's pocket veto of the bill presaged a contest which Lincoln, a political insider, probably would have won. However, the issue was inherited by Johnson, a political outsider as a War Democrat from Tennessee elected Vice-President on the Union (Republican) ticket with Lincoln in 1864. As a former Jacksonian Democrat, Johnson was a firm believer in states' rights, and held that blacks were innately inferior. He stubbornly refused to permit Congress to modify his lenient policy of dealing with the South. Johnson offered a pardon to all Southern whites except Confederate leaders and wealthy planters (although most of these subsequently received individual pardons), appointed provisional governors, and outlined steps whereby new state governments would be created. Apart from the requirements that they abolish slavery, repudiate secession, and abrogate the Confederate debt – all inescapable corollaries of Southern defeat – these governments were granted a free hand in managing their affairs. Johnson offered blacks no role whatever in the politics of Reconstruction. Having long identified himself as a tribune of the South's (white) common people, with whom he identified (he had had no schooling, and had been chosen as his Vice-President by Lincoln to balance his ticket and to appeal to those non-slaveholders in the South), Johnson assumed that ordinary yeomen would replace in office the planters who had led the South into secession. But when Southern elections restored members of the old elite to power, he did not modify his Reconstruction program. Jefferson Davis understood him: "Mr Johnson was a Democrat of pride, conviction, and self-assertion – a man of the people, who not only desired no higher grade of classification, but could not be forced into its acceptance." But so did others. Thaddeus Stevens was, as was his manner, vituperative: "In Egypt, the Lord sent frogs, locusts, murrain, lice, and finally demanded the blood of the first-born of all the oppressors. ... We have been oppressed by taxes and debts, and He has sent us worse than lice, and has afflicted us with Andrew Johnson." William Tecumseh Sherman was shrewd: "Johnson never heeds any advice. He attempts to govern after he has lost the means to govern. He is like a General fighting without an army – he is like Lear roaring at the wild storm, bareheaded and helpless."

As the South cast its votes in 1865, as directed by Johnson, the old-time Whigs swept to a large triumph. They had joined the Confederacy reluctantly, but once committed they gave it yeoman service. But as the war drew to its grim conclusion, many of them hastened to point out how catastrophic a decision secession had proven to be. They gained 8 governorships, 11 Senate seats, and no less than 36 seats in the House of Representatives. The Democrats were swamped by a three-to-one margin. Again, in the constitutional conventions called to revise the state constitutions, the Whigs commanded substantial majorities.

The Whigs accused the Democrats of fostering the secession that had brought the state to the verge of ruin, to which the Democrats counter-charged that disaster had resulted from Whig supineness and coldness on behalf of the war. Numerous Whigs agreed to join the Republican party as the best guarantee to revive the old Whiggery. To achieve their objective, many agreed with Mississippi's first Republican governor, James L. Alcorn, a wealthy Whig planter, that a political alliance with the freedmen made sense. But the Republican Congressional leadership refused to seat the Southerners who arrived to claim their seats. Too often, these Southerners had been in the field fighting the Union only months earlier, and Northerners were not prepared to forgive and forget.

When Congress finally convened in December of 1865, the Radicals meant to be heard. Their immediate targets were the newly elected Southern Senators and Representatives. Convinced that their erstwhile enemies were morally corrupt, the Republicans were animated with a good measure of high idealism. This was particularly true of the Radicals, who in the words of one of their leading spokesmen, Ben Wade, were "men of principle."

If Johnson were to prove unyielding, they were uncompromising. Harshest in its formulation was the "conquered provinces" theory of Thaddeus Stevens. It had its origins in the debates early in the war over the punitive action to be taken against the South. Stevens – a lame and bitter diehard – thought that the Southern states had lost their rights as states. When the war ended, he argued that the defeated states had been reduced to mere pawns in the hands of their conquerors. In Stevens's mind, Congress possessed the power to restructure the Southern social system, give the freedmen land through wholesale confiscations, and to do as they willed with the lives and property of the conquered.

Midway in this spectrum of Congressional theories was that of Charles Sumner of Massachusetts. Under the circumstances, Sumner concluded, "The whole broad Rebel region is ... 'a clean slate,' where Congress ... may write the laws." This position was further modified in 1866 by Rep. Samuel Shellabarger of Ohio, who argued that the seceded states had forfeited their rights. Since Congress alone possessed the power to guarantee the individual states "a republican government," it followed that Congress alone had the power to determine whether the seceded states had secured such a government.

The course adopted by the new Southern governments turned much of the North against Presidential Reconstruction. Alarmed by the apparent ascendancy of "rebels," Northern Republicans were further outraged by the Black Codes enacted by Southern legislatures in 1865–6. These laws required blacks to sign yearly labor contracts, declared unemployed blacks vagrants who could be hired out to white landowners, provided for the apprenticing of black children to white employers without the consent of their former owners, and in other ways sought to limit the freedmen's economic options and re-establish plantation discipline. Blacks strongly resisted the implementation of these measures, and the evident inability of the white South's leaders to accept emancipation fatally undermined Northern support for Johnson's policies. By driving the dominant party in Congress into the hands of the Radicals, Johnson lost what influence he had for moderation. In his effort to assert executive authority, Johnson misinterpreted the North's mood to the South, and by playing up the intent of vindictive Radicals to subjugate "the proud traitors," he encouraged the South to assume a rigid posture of defiance that in turn persuaded the North that it had been cheated of its dearly won victory.

The South turned in upon itself. It made a legend out of the Lost Cause; alongside the Black Codes it also developed its own ugly and extra-legal methods of browbeating the Negro, in the White Camellia, the Black Horse Cavalry, and the Ku Klux Klan, murdering, lynching, raping, beating. It became not only a solid South but also a solidly Democratic South, since Republicanism was associated with Northern domination. Gradually there grew up the "Jim Crow" system of segregation of the races, in schools and hotels and public life, that was a feature of the South until it was declared illegal by the Supreme Court in 1954.[2]

When Congress assembled in December 1865, Radical Republicans like Thaddeus Stevens and Charles Sumner called for the abrogation of the Johnson governments in the South and the establishment of new ones based on equality before the law and manhood suffrage, though the more numerous moderate Republicans hoped to work with Johnson while modifying his program. Congress refused to seat the Congressmen and Senators elected from the Southern states under the "provisional" governments set up under the Johnson plan, and in early 1866 passed and sent to Johnson the Freedmen's Bureau and Civil Rights bill. The first extended the life of an agency that Congress had created in 1865 to oversee the transition of the black population from slavery to freedom. The second defined all persons born in the United States as national citizens and spelled out rights they were to enjoy equally without regard to race – making contracts, bringing lawsuits, and enjoying "full and equal benefit of all laws and proceedings for the security of person and property." The Radicals constituted an ugly blend of moral purpose and self-interest.

A combination of personal stubbornness, fervent belief in states' rights, and deeply held racist convictions led Johnson to reject the radical bills. His vetoes caused a permanent rupture between the President and Congress. The Civil Rights Act was the first major piece of legislation in American history to become law over a President's veto. In 1868, Congress would approve the Fourteenth Amendment, which forbade states from depriving any citizen of the "equal protection of the laws," barred many Confederates from holding state or national office, and threatened to reduce the South's representation in Congress if black men continued to be kept from voting.

[2] Woodward, *The Irony of Southern History*; idem, *The Burden of Southern History* (New York, Vintage Books, 1960), and *The Strange Career of Jim Crow* (New York, Oxford University Press, 1957); Howard N. Rabinowitz, *Race Relations in the Urban South 1865–1890* (Champaign, Ill., University of Illinois Press 1978).

Not until 1867, however, was Congress prepared to endorse black suffrage directly. This happened after three developments further strengthened the Radical Republicans. In July 1866 there was an ugly race riot in New Orleans when whites attacked blacks who were demanding racial equality: 37 were killed and 119 wounded. Another riot in Memphis convinced Republicans of the need for strict Reconstruction. Second, Northern voters overwhelmingly repudiated Johnson's policies in the fall 1866 Congressional elections. Third, the Southern states, with the exception of Tennessee, rejected the Fourteenth Amendment. Congress now decided to begin Reconstruction anew. In the Congressional elections of November 1866 the Republicans, now dominated by Radicals, won a two-thirds majority in both Houses. In March 1867 Congress prescribed that all military orders from the President should emanate from the General of the US Army in Washington, who could not be removed without approval of the Senate. On March 2, 1867, the Tenure of Office Act was passed over Johnson's veto, prohibiting the President from removing any civil officer without the consent of the Senate. On March 2, 1867, the First Reconstruction Act was passed, also over Johnson's veto, dividing the South into five military districts under martial law. In order to return to the Union a state had to call a constitutional convention (elected by universal manhood suffrage) and set up a government that would grant the Negro suffrage and ratify the Fourteenth Amendment. When the South took no action to call conventions, Congress passed supplementary Acts (March 23 and July 19, 1867, and March 11, 1868) allowing the military commanders to launch all statehood proceedings.

In August 1867 President Johnson suspended the secretary of war, Edwin M. Stanton, who was loyal to the Radicals, and made General Grant secretary of war *ad interim*. On January 13, 1868, the Senate refused to accept the suspension of Stanton, and, despite an understanding with Johnson, Grant turned the office back to Stanton. On February 21, 1868, President Johnson finally dismissed Secretary Stanton. The House impeached President Johnson on February 24 for violating the Tenure of Office Act and for behaving in an undignified way. After a lengthy partisan trial (March 5-May 16), the Senate voted 35–19 in favor of conviction, falling by a single vote short of the necessary two-thirds. Seven Republicans voted for Johnson, including Edmund G. Ros (Kansas), William P. Fessenden (Maine), and Lyman Trunbull (Illinois). Thus began the period of Radical or Congressional Reconstruction, which lasted until the fall of the last Southern Republican governments in 1877.

By 1877, all the former Confederate states had been readmitted to the Union, and nearly all were controlled by the Republican party. These groups made up Southern Republicanism. Carpetbaggers, or recent arrivals from the North – former Union soldiers, teachers, Freedmen's Bureau agents, and businessmen, most of whom had come South before 1867, when the possibility of obtaining office was remote – leapt at the opportunity to help mold the "backward" South in the image of the North.

The central figure and the most difficult problem in Reconstruction was the black, a freedman after the passage of the Thirteenth Amendment in 1865. The sudden release from bondage of some 4 million persons, most of whom lacked even elementary training for the responsibilities of a free society, was without parallel in history, and the complexity of the problem was compounded in those regions where the ratio of blacks to whites was narrow. To assure his rights, such Northern organizations as the Union League moved into the South, and Congress created the Freedmen's Bureau. By the time that it ceased to function, it had become avowedly a device for Republicans to organize the black vote.

3 "BLACK RECONSTRUCTION"

It was in an attempt to meet this problem, which was especially acute in the Deep South, where whites were outnumbered by blacks and large numbers of blacks chose no form of employment, that the Southern states enacted the series of laws known as the Black Codes in 1865–6. In the Deep South the codes were severe, in North Carolina and Virginia they were mild, in Tennessee no codes were adopted. All of the codes gave certain limited civil rights, but not the right to vote. To such radical organs as the Chicago *Tribune*, the codes virtually established a system seen as peonage for blacks. As we have seen, the effect in the North was to increase support for the Radicals' position.

To the Southern whites the codes were constructive measures enacted as stopgap legislation to prevent chaos at a moment when the whole economic system erected on slavery had been destroyed and when no machinery existed for educating blacks to civic responsibility. Many Northerners viewed them differently. Those Radical Republicans who intended to make political capital of the defeated South wanted the black vote, and idealists saw the codes as a covert attempt to revive slavery. The Reconstruction Acts of 1866–8 were therefore pushed through Congress to give the Radicals complete military control of the South. Southern whites responded by organizing vigilante patrols, such as the Ku Klux Klan, to intimidate the blacks and frighten them from exercising their votes. Enactment of the Fourteenth Amendment (1868), conferring citizenship on blacks was followed by the Fifteenth in 1870, granting suffrage, and by passage of a series of Enforcement Acts (1870–5) designed to compel recognition of these statutes. This period of "Black Reconstruction", from 1868–1877, when Southern state legislatures were controlled by the Radicals and blacks participated in politics under Republican protection, was sometimes characterized by corruption, extravagance, and vulgarity (as in the North during the same period), but these so-called "carpetbag legislatures" nevertheless introduced public schools for both races, welfare institutions, and essential postwar recovery measures, which were necessarily costly.

Blacks were segregated in all social and cultural spheres. They lived in sections of towns and cities set apart for them. They went to a separate school, if they went to school at all. Both sets of schools were supported by taxpayers, white and black alike, but the whites had by far the greatest burden because they owned most of the property. The financial burden was overwhelming, particularly for a section of the country that had been plunged into poverty by the war.

In many ways, Reconstruction at the state level profoundly altered traditions of Southern government. Serving an expanded citizenry and embracing a new definition of public responsibility, Reconstruction governments established the South's first state-funded public school systems, adopted measures designed to strengthen the bargaining power of plantation laborers, made taxation more equitable, and outlawed racial discrimination in public transportation and accommodations. They also embarked on ambitious programs of economic development, offering lavish aid to railroads and other enterprises in the hope of creating a New South whose economic expansion would benefit black and white alike. But the program of railroad aid did much to undermine support for Reconstruction, spawning corruption and rising taxes, and it alienated increasing numbers of white voters. Black Reconstruction disfranchised 150,000 whites and registered 700,000 black voters; however, it was only in South Carolina, Mississippi, Louisiana, Alabama, and Florida that black voters constituted a majority. Only in South Carolina did they dominate the legislature. They held few offices. There was no black governor during Reconstruction; only 2 blacks served in the Senate and 20 in the House of Representatives. Reconstruction governments were corrupt, but not more so than some governments in the North, and corruption was biracial and bipartisan.

If blacks in the state legislatures never played a dominant role as a group, many of them were prominent and influential as individuals. In South Carolina, Jonathan J. Wright served for nearly six years as associate justice of the State Supreme Court. In Louisiana, William G. Brown discharged the duties of superintendent of education with marked ability. Jonathan C. Gibbs was Florida's secretary of state for four years and its superintendent of instruction for two years. A score of additional blacks held high posts, including such offices as prosecuting attorney, superintendent of the poor, sheriff, and mayor. However, the vast majority of black officeholders were local officials, such as justices of the peace.

By far the most notable group of blacks to hold office were those who went to Congress. From eight Southern states came 22 black Congressmen. Two of these sat in the Senate: Hiram R. Revels and Blanche K. Bruce, both from Mississippi. Of the 20 blacks who sat in the House of Representatives, South Carolina accounted for 8, North Carolina for 4, Alabama for 3, and Florida, Georgia, Louisiana, Mississippi, and Virginia for 1 apiece. Thirteen of them had been born in slavery; 10 had college training, including 5 with college degrees. The best educated was Robert B. Elliott, who had graduated from Eton in 1859 and who read French, German, Spanish, and Latin. Perhaps the most respected of the black Congressmen was John R. Lynch, who at the age of 24 had become speaker of the Mississippi House and who in Washington made many influential friendships, including that of President Grant.

The black Congressmen were not destined to leave any mark on national legislation. Their numbers were small, and their tenure in office was short, the two Senators serving a total of seven years and the 20 House members serving a total of 64 years. But as legislators they won praise, including that of their fellow Congressman James G. Blaine, who characterized them as studious and earnest.

Far more lasting than the work of the black Congressmen was that of the Republican-Negro regimes in the Southern states after their readmission to the Union. To begin with, the new constitutions adopted by these states as a condition of their readmission were a distinct improvement over the documents they supplanted. They provided for expanded suffrage by removing all property qualifications for voting and holding office (North Carolina's abandoning the religious test for those seeking election to public position). Equally important, every one of the new constitutions provided for a statewide system of free public education. Without redistributing the land, the new constitutions exempted small property-holders from taxation. Imprisonment for debt was abolished in many states, and such punishments as branding, whipping, and the stocks were declared illegal. In the South Carolina constitution the number of capital crimes was reduced from 20 to 2.

The constructive work of the Republican-Negro regimes was marred by evidences of fraud and corruption in such states as South Carolina, Florida, Alabama, and Louisiana. In the first-named, the legislature reimbursed a Speaker of the House the sum of $1,000, which he had lost on a horse race, and such items as wines, cigars, and groceries were listed under legislative expenses. It should be carefully noted, however, that fraud and corruption in public life were new neither in the South nor in the nation.

The essential reason for the growing opposition to Reconstruction, however, was the fact that Southern whites could not accept the idea of former slaves voting and holding office or the egalitarian policies adopted by the new governments. Increasingly, the opportunity of Reconstruction turned to violence. The Ku Klux Klan launched a campaign of terror that targeted for beatings or assassination local Republican leaders as well as blacks who asserted their rights in dealings with white employers. The Klan decimated the Republican organization in many localities. Increasingly, the new Southern governments looked to Washington for survival.

By 1869, the Republican party was firmly in control of all three branches of the federal government. After his impeachment trial, even though the Senate failed to convict him, Johnson's power to obstruct the course of Reconstruction was gone; and Republican Ulysses S. Grant was elected President in the fall of 1868. Soon afterward, Congress approved the Fifteenth Amendment, prohibiting states from restricting the franchise because of race, followed by the Enforcement Acts authorizing national action to suppress political violence. In 1871, the administration launched a legal and military offensive that destroyed the Ku Klux Klan. Grant was re-elected in 1872 in the most peaceful election of the period.

Nonetheless, Reconstruction soon began to wane. Democrats had never accepted its legitimacy, and during the 1870s, many Republicans retreated from both the racial egalitarianism and the broad definition of federal power spawned by the Civil War. Southern corruption and instability, Reconstruction's critics argued, stemmed from the exclusion of the region's "best men" – the old planters – from power. Conservatives began to capture control of state governments – beginning in 1870 with Virginia and North Carolina. The blacks lost their two greatest champions in Congress – Thaddeus Stevens died in 1868 and Charles Sumner six years later. As the Northern Republican party became more conservative, Reconstruction came to symbolize both misgovernment and a misguided attempt to use state power to uplift the lower classes of society. The depression that began in 1873 pushed economic questions to the forefront of politics, eclipsing Reconstruction. And when Democrats, for the first time since the Civil War, won control of the House of Representatives in 1874, it was clear that Southern Republicans could expect little further help from Washington. When violence again erupted in the South in the mid-1870s, Grant failed to intervene.

By 1876, only South Carolina, Florida, and Louisiana remained under Republican control; the remaining Southern states had been "redeemed" by white Democrats. The outcome of the presidential election of 1876 between Republican Rutherford B. Hayes and Democrat Samuel J. Tilden hinged on the disputed returns from these states. Three Southern states sent in two sets of election returns, one Republican, one Democratic. A specially created Electoral Commission decided in favor of Hayes. After negotiations between Southern political leaders and representatives of Hayes, a compromise was reached: Hayes would recognize Democratic control of the remaining Southern states, and Democrats would not block the certification of his election by Congress. Hayes was inaugurated, federal troops returned to their barracks, and Reconstruction came to an end. The South was returned to the South.

Self-rule gradually returned to the states, and when President Hayes withdrew the last Federal troops in 1877, state jurisdiction was completely restored and the crucial race problem was left to the Southern whites. Conservatives revised the state constitutions, deleting from them all guarantees of equal rights. Although animosities between the sections were all but forgotten by 1890, the moral and racial scars of Reconstruction were visible well into the twentieth century, to be seen until late in the 1920s in a persisting pattern of the solid South.[3]

Although in the plantation belt the planter still stood atop the social pyramid, in a few areas, such as the sugar region, large numbers of planters saw their lands pass into the hands of Northern investors. Generally, however, the majority of planter families

[3] General studies include J. G. Randall and David Donald, *The Civil War and Reconstruction* (Lexington, Ky, D.C. Heath, 1961); John Hope Franklin, *Reconstruction After the Civil War* (Chicago, University of Chicago Press, 1961); Kenneth E. Stampp, *The Era of Reconstruction, 1865–1877* (New York, Knopf, 1965); Eric Foner, *Reconstruction: America's unfinished revolution* (New York, Harper Collins, 1988); (abridged edn), *A Short History of Reconstruction*, (New York, Harper Collins, 1990).

managed to retain control of their land. Yet Reconstruction altered their world. Stripped of political influence at Washington and often at the state level, and lacking the ability to control their volatile labor force, many planters found themselves reduced to poverty.

The South's economic problems were exacerbated by the depression that began in 1873. Within four years, the price of cotton fell by nearly 50 percent, plunging farmers into poverty and drying up the region's already inadequate sources of credit. The depression shattered what hopes remained for the early emergence of a modernizing New South, and forced long-established businesses into bankruptcy. It facilitated the penetration of Northern capital, as outside corporations bought up bankrupt Southern railroads and other enterprises. Hard times accelerated the spread of tenancy among white farmers, ruined many planters, and reversed much of the very modest economic progress blacks had made in the post-emancipation years. Long into the twentieth century, the South would remain the nation's foremost economic problem – a legacy not only of slavery but of the social and economic changes that began during Reconstruction, and of Reconstruction's political failure.

4 CARPETBAGGERS AND SCALAWAGS

The ugliest aspect of the Reconstruction of the South was less the maneuvers of Radicals in Congress than of the adventurers, Southerners as well as Northerners, who sought to exploit the situation to their own advantage. Carpetbaggers – Northerners who went south after the Civil War, presumably to exploit unsettled conditions – were contemptuously so named because they allegedly could transport their entire assets in a satchel. They swarmed through the South in the decade following the Reconstruction Acts of 1867, which brought the states of the former Confederacy under Radical control. In alliance with Southern white "Scalawags," they often sought financial and political profit. Some were sent as agents of the Freedmen's Bureau, and others were impelled by missionary zeal. Many of these were exemplary individuals, genuinely interested in the black, who identified themselves with their adopted Southern communities, and several were elected to Congress by the newly reconstructed states. But often they were venal.

Of the seven governors in states restored to the Union in 1868, four were carpetbaggers, and the resulting administrations, executive, legislative, and judiciary, were sometimes extravagant and sordidly corrupt. Their misrule (as well as legitimate postwar costs) trebled and even quadrupled the debts of Southern states. Governor Warmoth of Louisiana, typical of the mischievous spoilsmen, though more successful than most, in four years built a personal fortune of half a million dollars by looting the state treasury. After the rule of the Radical Republicans had ended, and Hayes had succeeded to the presidency in 1877, white home rule in the South was restored, and the carpetbaggers as a class disappeared.

The carpetbaggers were a mixed lot. Many of them were veterans, who saw in the South unique investment opportunities. Many brought much-needed capital into the impoverished South. The lure of profits persuaded such well-known Northerners as Whitelaw Reid to invest in Louisiana and John Hay to lose a sum in Florida orange groves. Elsewhere, numerous Northern retailers established businesses in Southern towns. It was precisely this class of people who reinforced Southern convictions that they were the victims of rampaging Yankee exploitation. They were seen as the ones who before the war had siphoned off Southern wealth through the tariff and after the war came with carpetbags protected by Federal bayonets. Equally unacceptable to Southerners were the Northerners attracted by purely philanthropic motives. These included teachers and churchmen, and a goodly number of the Freedmen's Bureau were generally honest men. Their corruption (in the mind of the Southern white) resulted from their representing an alien authority.

Simultaneously, the restoration of Federal control opened up to Northerners a chance to fill the numerous patronage offices. Since many Southerners were not eligible to hold such posts, and since freedmen often lacked the background to obtain such appointments, they fell by default to Northerners. These included not only Freedmen's Bureau agents but also treasury agents, tax collectors, and customs officers, among others. Although surprisingly few entered Southern politics, the occasional exceptions, such as Governor Robert Scott of South Carolina, only served to prove the rule.

Corruption was widespread. Not all of it was the work of carpetbaggers. State indebtedness rose sharply in the South after the war, much of it as a result of the costs of restoring war-damaged facilities, and even more frequently as a result of the various states underwriting new railroad construction. The immediate beneficiaries of this activity were railroad promoters, construction agents, bond speculators, and the lobbyists whose corrupting activities knew no sectional boundaries. Not infrequently, Southern whites of unimpeachable credentials allied themselves with carpetbaggers to share the loot.

The corruption was indefensible, but it reflected a national malaise rather than a sectional plight. What made the Southerner suffer more was that his region could ill afford to have any of its funds taken as graft. Not only the South, but such cities as New York and Washington endured wholesale corruption. It is estimated that the Tweed Ring alone robbed New York City of more than $100 million in the closing years of the 1860s.

Many of the difficulties grew out of the inadequacy of the federal system's administrative plant. Developed in the Antebellum period when limited government was the rule, the American political system could not expand rapidly enough to meet its new obligations. In using the term "carpetbagger," Southern whites indulged in a form of double-think; they judged behavior not on the basis of the action itself but on the origin of the actor. It followed that if a Northerner entered politics as a Republican, he was automatically deemed a carpetbagger, no matter what his honesty, while if a Southerner entered politics as a Democrat, he was automatically an honest man, no matter how dubious his use of office was to advance his own well being.

Alongside the carpetbaggers from the North were the scalawags. The word "scalawag" entered common American parlance to describe inferior cattle, and subsequently to characterize men of dubious character. During the Civil War, it became the accepted Southern description of white "Union men," and after the war it came to mean any white Southern Republican. Obviously it required a tough skin for a Southern white openly to embrace the Republican party.

The story of one well-known carpetbagger, General Milton S. Littlefield, symbolizes the greed that reigned after Gettysburg. Littlefield, who drifted into Illinois from New York via Michigan, was one of the Republican Wide-Awakes who delivered Menard County to Lincoln. He was at Shiloh, at Memphis with Grant and the cotton speculators, with Sherman in various pursuits, and lord over Charleston when the unhappy climax arrived. He was on the spot when the opportunity was hot, whether as one of Lincoln's "military protégés" or through sheer Yankee luck.

The open facts of Littlefield's career from 1865 to 1869 fall into three phases. In the first he was an advocate of the bustling, perhaps all black metropolis (such as Hilton Head then promised to become) that might very well dominate the new South. A respite afterward in Philadelphia, where his timber and oil ventures aroused unkind suspicions, gave Littlefield the time and experience to think out another approach to the New South. This time he returned, affable and persuasive, to demonstrate on a grand scale the larcenous art of bond speculation. Railroads (or rather, plans for railroads) were Littlefield's principal stock in trade, but this imaginative fellow also managed to own a newspaper, hold the contract as state printer for North Carolina, and have a finger in many dubious real-estate operations, Funds – other people's not Littlefield's – were juggled across state borders, and his enemies in North Carolina charged that Littlefield had "the legislature in his pocket," along with control over state bonds worth $7,000,000.

Whiskey and graft were powerful weapons, and Littlefield and his crowd knew how to employ both.

Littlefield brazened out the disaster of 1869 longer than most, and, even as a bare-faced swindler in the cause of freedom and Grant, deserved better than the unmarked grave in upstate New York where he has so long rested.[4]

5 AN AGRICULTURAL ECONOMY

In the South, as in the rest of the nation, the period between 1865 and 1930 saw remarkable changes in agriculture take place. With the end of the war the planters had expected that the freedmen would remain on the plantations, working for wages. This hope was quickly dashed. Many blacks happy to be free, wandered about the South. Some of those who stayed on or near the plantation worked only long enough to get enough cash; to many, freedom meant an opportunity to do no work.

A partial solution to the labor problem was found in the breakup of the plantations. Portions were sold to the more prosperous independent farmers. To some extent the poorer whites living on the least fertile land acquired portions of the former plantations. As a consequence, the number of farms more than doubled between 1860 and 1880, while the size of the average farm decreased. By 1930 not one in 100 farms was as large as 500 acres. Indeed, by 1930, 79.9 percent of all the farms in the United States smaller than 100 acres were in the South. The black, who had emerged from slavery without schooling, without land, almost without clothes to wear upon his back, also benefited from the breakup of the large plantations. By 1875 nearly 5 percent of the freedmen had acquired

[4] Jonathan Daniels, *Prince of Carpetbaggers* (Philadelphia, Lippincott, 1958). For a more recent treatment of the carpetbaggers, cf. Richard N. Current, *Those Terrible Carpetbaggers: A reinterpretation* (New York, Oxford University Press, 1988).

small farms, and as the years passed more and more became landowners. By 1890 the number had increased to 121,000, and by 1920 to 219,000.

The growing number of smaller landowners gave a new direction to Southern politics. In the 1880s and 1890s more and more small farmers began to challenge the political monopoly that the older, more conservative, aristocratic planters had enjoyed since the restoration of white rule. These smaller farmers, together with others beneath them on the agricultural ladder, joined with discontented Western farmers in various political revolts designed to improve the lot of agricultural workers.

While some poor whites and an even smaller number of blacks became owners of small farms, many others entered into a tenant relationship with the large landowners. The planter parceled out his land to tenants who paid either cash or a specified number of bales of cotton as rent. In some instances these tenants – who supplied their own seed, mules, and provisions – paid for the use of the owner's land by giving him one-third to one-quarter of the crop. The owner managed the scattered tenant holdings much as if these made up the oldtime plantation, in this way retaining some of the advantages of large-scale production. Frequently the landlord owned the country store where the sharecropper bought his provisions. Since he was always in debt, the sharecropper paid higher prices than other men who had cash in their pockets and could buy where they wished.

Moreover, their monotonous diet, deficient in vitamin C, produced pellagra, a disease that exhausts the victim's strength and leads to insanity and death. Hookworm, which thrives in filth and which the poor people picked up in their bare feet, also saps the energy of those infected with it. During the twentieth century medical science began to make considerable progress in the South as elsewhere. Slowly dietary habits began to change and sanitation improved, with a resulting improvement in the health of Southerners. Yet as late as 1930 the death rate was much higher among Southern whites than among Northerners, and especially high among blacks. Malaria, typhoid fever, pellagra, anemia, and childbirth continued to cut short the lives of far too many Southerners.

Despite the formidable problems confronting the Southern farmers during the years between 1865 and 1930, considerable progress was made. Southerners, like farmers in other parts of the United States, benefited from the new developments in science and technology. In 1872 Alabama and Virginia established agricultural colleges. Cotton continued to be the most important single crop. Indeed, by 1879 the South was producing more cotton than it had in 1860. The older states increased their yield per acre by liberal use of commercial fertilizers and improved farming methods. Much of the total increase, however, came from the opening of new cotton lands in the western part of the South, and by 1900 Texas's production alone was one-third of the nation's total. Between 1900 and 1930 the amount of land planted in cotton increased from 25 million acres to 40 million acres.

During this same period tobacco also remained one of the major agricultural products of the South, which by 1930 produced about 85 percent of the nation's total crop. After World War I the production of the older tobacco states of Virginia, Maryland, North Carolina, and Kentucky was supplemented by new fields in eastern South Carolina, southern Georgia, and northern Florida.

Rice production shifted from the coast of South Carolina to Louisiana, Arkansas, and Texas, where improved seeds and the use of machinery rapidly increased the yield per acre. Improved methods made it possible for an American worker to produce 60 to 70 times as much as an Oriental farmer. Sugar planters likewise benefited from the development of scientific agriculture, and sugar remained an important part of the economy of Louisiana and Texas.

The most important change in the agricultural life of the South was the development of truck farming. As a consequence of the expansion of railroads and the invention of the refrigerator car, it became possible to ship fresh vegetables to the urban centers in the North. Longer growing seasons and an abundance of cheap labor also stimulated truck farming. As early as 1900 more than 60,000 refrigerator cars were rolling northward day and night, hauling to market the welcome supplies of green vegetables, watermelons, strawberries, oranges, apples, and peaches.

Southern industry, notably textile milling, did boom after the end of Reconstruction. But the region remained disproportionately poor, and was characterized by staple-crop monoculture, low-wage industry, and external ownership of much of its resources.

6 THE NEW SOUTH

The Civil War and Reconstruction had given a few Southerners dreams of a business-oriented, manufacturing South. The vision of a New South described by Edwin De Leon in magazine articles in the early 1870s was taken up by skillful propagandists like Henry Grady of the *Atlanta Constitution*, Henry Watterson of the

Louisville Courier-Journal, and Richard Edmonds of the *Manufacturers' Record*, and became a favored prescription for a rejuvenated Dixie. Instead of cultivating a few staple crops, the South, with the aid of Northern investment, could become a land of industry, entrepreneurship, and scientific farming. In addition, although insisting upon white supremacy, the New South should devote itself to sectional reconciliation.

The influence of science and technology was not confined to agriculture. Even more remarkable was the industrial development of the South after the War between the States. In this respect the South was responding to the same forces that were transforming the economic life of most of the nations of the Western world.

The industrial development of the South began before the outbreak of the War between the States. By 1860 about 10 percent of the manufactured wealth of the United States came from Southern textile mills, iron works, lumber projects, and sugar refineries. But the economic disorganization that came with the war ruined many Southern industries, and for more than 20 years the industrialization of the South was halted. By the 1880s small amounts of capital became available as the incomes from the staple cash crops of cotton and tobacco increased. Some of this capital was invested in new industries. A group of Southerners, typical of whom was Henry Grady, began to talk about "the New South." Grady and his fellow Southerners pleaded with the South to abandon the one-crop system and to develop all the resources of a rich land – the minerals and the forests, as well as the soil that yielded cotton, tobacco, sugar, rice, corn, wheat, and other crops. Above all, the South was urged to convert these raw materials into manufactured goods in Southern factories and mills.

The enthusiasts for industrial development called attention to the advantages that the South offered to industry. They pointed to the numerous swift-flowing rivers from which to generate abundant electricity to turn the wheels of industry. They called attention to the human resources available in the South – especially the tenant farmers, many of whom were eager to quit their poverty-stricken farms for wages and town life.

The War between the States left the railroads in a terrible condition; but the old railroads were quickly rebuilt and new lines were constructed. By 1880 the South possessed a modern rail system twice as large as that of 1860, and by 1930 the South, with approximately one-third of the area of the United States, possessed one-third of the railroad mileage, or 82,000 miles of track.

Cotton furnished an important source of raw material for the industrial development of the South. During the 1880s the number of cotton spindles and looms in the South doubled, and by 1930 two-thirds of all the nation's spindles were in Southern mills. Most of this development took place in the upland (piedmont) sections of North and South Carolina and Georgia. The advantages enjoyed by Southern textile manufacturers – nearness to the cotton fields, cheap labor, cheap power, and low taxes – struck a severe blow at New England's textile interests, and many of the older Northern mills moved to the South. Southerners also found a use for the cotton seeds, and factories sprang up to convert these seeds into many products. The seed itself was processed into food for cattle and into fertilizer. The oil from the seed proved useful as a substitute for olive oil and lard and as an ingredient for oleo-margarine. The cottonseed oil mills spread over the South; Texas, the largest producer of raw cotton, became the major source of cottonseed oil products. The result was that in some of the new industrial centers, as in the older agricultural regions of the South, economic and political power continued in the hands of a relatively few individuals.

Tobacco also proved to be another source of raw material for the growing industries of the South. Great tobacco factories sprang up in Durham and Winston-Salem, both in North Carolina. Huge new fortunes, such as those of the Dukes and the Reynolds, were rapidly accumulated. By 1930 the South was manufacturing 60 percent of the nation's tobacco products and 84 percent of its cigarettes.

The vast Southern forests likewise provided material for the growing industrial economy. Much of the lumber used to build homes for the rapidly increasing population of the United States during the opening decades of the twentieth century came from the South. Indeed, by 1930 almost half of all the lumber produced in the United States came from Southern forests. Hardwood from these same forests helped to furnish America's new homes. By 1930 Southern factories were manufacturing one-third of the nation's household furnishings.

The industrial demand for minerals led to a number of significant developments in the South, as well as in other parts of the country. One measure of this development is revealed by the fact that in 1930 the South was producing 35 percent of the entire mineral and quarry output of the United States. The South had salt from Louisiana, phosphates from Florida and Tennessee, sulphur from Texas, marble from Tennessee and Georgia, and bauxite (used to make aluminum) from Arkansas. The most valuable mineral resources, however, were iron, coal, and oil. Starting in the 1880s, a feeble coal and iron industry soon began to expand so greatly that within a few years Birmingham, Alabama, became known as the little Pittsburgh of the South.

The oil industry, which had begun in 1859 in Titusville, Pennsylvania, shifted steadily southwestward as new fields were discovered and opened. By 1931 more than two-thirds of the nation's total supply of oil (and 40 percent of the world's total production) was gushing from wells in Texas, Oklahoma, and Louisiana. In addition, one-half of the nation's natural gas, a by-product of oil, was also produced in the western part of the South, with pipelines carrying the surplus gas to markets as far away as Chicago. Other pipelines carried petroleum from the oil fields to refineries located on the Gulf of Mexico and in the Northeast.

While these developments were taking place, Southerners were converting their coal and their rapidly flowing rivers into electric power. By the early 1930s one-third of the nation's electricity was produced in the South. Electric power, cheap labor, and raw materials – coal, tar, petroleum, cotton, pulpwood, sulphur, phosphate rock, and natural gas – enabled the South to develop an important chemical industry. By 1927, 20 major chemical plants in the South were producing one-quarter of the entire chemical output of the United States. Much of the research for this industry was done by chemists from other parts of the country. Indeed, a large part of the American chemical industry was originally constructed on basic processes developed in Germany and taken over by the United States during and immediately after World War I. However, there were notable Southern contributions, among them those of a former slave, George Washington Carver of Tuskegee Institute, who discovered ways to transform the peanut and the sweet potato into scores of useful industrial products.

In no other section of the country did cities grow more rapidly than in the South. Between 1870 and 1890 Durham, North Carolina, developed from a small village to a flourishing tobacco center. Richmond, Virginia, and Chattanooga, Tennessee, as well as older towns, took their places as leading urban centers in the New South. Atlanta's population increased from 37,000 to 65,000 between 1880 and 1890. Birmingham, Alabama, changed from a crossroads village to a bustling industrial city within a few years. In the oil regions cities mushroomed. In 1926 in the Texas Panhandle one ranch was converted into a city of 25,000 inhabitants within a few weeks.

The industrial development itself should not be overemphasized. In 1929 only 9 percent of the nation's total industrial output came from the Southeastern states, compared with 42 percent for the Northeast and 36 percent for the Middle states. Southern wages were also low, an average of $844 per person in the Southeastern states as compared with $1,364 for the Northeastern states and $1,447 for the Middle states. Nevertheless, the evidence of progress was real and unmistakable. By 1930 the South possessed in its newer industries the most modern and efficient machinery in the United States. By 1930 older established industries were moving into the South and newer industries were being developed. And this was only the beginning. World War II and the postwar years were to bring even greater changes to the new South.

Basic to the changes and the progress in the South was black advance through educational opportunity. Part of the stimulus came from the North. Some of these Northerners, like John Slater (a new England industrialist) and Julius Rosenwald (of Sears, Roebuck and Company), were devoted exclusively or primarily to black education. Others, like George Foster Peabody (a banker) John D. Rockefeller, and Edward S. Harkness (both of whom made millions from oil), were interested in the education of both races. Gifts from their funds helped to provide elementary schools, teacher-training institutions, and scholarships for able blacks. Because the money was not used to break the color line, Southern leaders cooperated in these efforts to improve the education and welfare of black people. Gradually the states did more to support black public schools, though in nearly every community in the South black schools received less money than the white schools.

Prominent among institutions was Tuskegee in northern Alabama. Its principal, Booker T. Washington, as we have already seen, was a former slave who had got his own schooling the hard way, at Hampton Institute in Virginia. There in the deep South he trained carpenters, masons, mechanics, cooks, nurses, and teachers, who learned some history and other academic subjects in addition to acquiring vocational skills. At Tuskegee, under Washington's heroic leadership, the black students designed and constructed the buildings, made their own clothing, and raised their own food on their own farm. By the time a student graduated from Tuskegee, he was prepared to take his place in society, fully equipped to earn a living and to get along with his fellow men. Washington believed that practical knowledge and skills were worth far more to black people than book learning or political and social equality. Obsequiousness, he hinted, would pay in the long run.

The number of blacks engaged in professional work increased from 68,350 in 1910 to 136,925 in 1930 – most of these in teaching.

By 1930 black colleges had 1,500 competent professors, among them a number of outstanding scientists and scholars, such as George Washington Carver, to mention probably the best-known example. By 1930 there were 4,000 black physicians, 1,500 dentists, and 1,100 lawyers.

Between 1890 and 1920 some two million blacks migrated from the South to the Northern cities, to Chicago in particular. Migration to the North secured the political recognition that many of them were seeking. They went to the polling places and voted like other Americans. And in some states, notably New York, they in time came to exercise an influence far larger than their numbers indicated.

Southern blacks sought to make the best of the situation. Long before Booker T. Washington proclaimed in his 1895 "Atlanta Compromise" speech that blacks and whites should be like the separate fingers of the same hand, a new middle class of black ministers, teachers, and business people had emerged with a vested interest in segregation. Until the middle of the twentieth century, despite sporadic opposition to segregation, most black leaders preferred to attack instances of exclusion or unequal separate treatment. But increased migration of blacks northward after the turn of the century, and post-World War I competition with immigrants and white veterans for jobs and housing – sometimes marked by violence – led to the creation of large-scale black urban ghettos with their own schools, community institutions, and businesses. These ghettos had become a fixture of Northern urban life by the 1920s, as conditions for blacks in the North and South came to resemble each other more closely, especially in their dire environments: bad plumbing, poor hygiene, spasmodic refuse collection and malnourishment, bad schooling, working mothers, and one-parent families, brought high crime rates and generational conflict. The ghetto was a magnet for exploiters, racketeers, and criminals of varied hues.

Prior to the 1950s, Northern blacks were more likely than their Southern counterparts to challenge segregation *per se*. But during the so-called Second Reconstruction of the mid-twentieth century the federal government intervened, partly in response to demands for change from blacks and white liberals and partly out of concern for world opinion. The North's *de facto* segregation, visible in its poverty and crime potential, however, proved more entrenched, more difficult to overcome than the South's primarily *de jure*-based system. Today, *de jure* segregation is a thing of the past, but in many areas, especially housing and public education, *de facto* segregation persists in the nation's cities.

7 THE LEGACY: JIM CROW

After 1865, the Southern states drew a sharp color line that divided back from white in all things; and these were enshrined in the new constitutions of the Southern states in the post-Reconstruction period.

Tennessee led the way with the first "Jim Crow" law in 1875, and was quickly followed by the other states of the former Confederacy. Among the early targets for the separate but equal treatment were the railroads, which had to put on special coaches for blacks only when they reached the Jim Crow states. To many people this seemed a violation of the Fourteenth Amendment. The Supreme Court settled the matter in the Civil Rights Case of 1883, which declared that the Fourteenth Amendment did not dictate to the states what they must or must not do.[5] Following the passage of Louisiana's railroad law in 1890, a citizens' group challenged it. A test case was made of Homer Plessy, who in 1892 brought a suit after being arrested for riding on a white-only coach. The railroads secretly supported the challenger because of the enormous expense they incurred in providing separate coaches. Plessy lost in the state courts and the appeal went up to the US Supreme Court. In 1896 the highest court in the land ruled by a majority of eight to one that the Fourteenth Amendment, which granted citizenship rights to blacks, did not debar separate but equal accommodations: this made the Jim Crow laws constitutional.

The South was ingenious in devising methods to disfranchise the blacks. The standard devices for accomplishing disfranchisement on a racial basis and evading the restrictions of the Constitution were invented by Mississippi, a pioneer of the movement and the only state that resorted to it before the populist revolt took the form of political rebellion. Other states elaborated the original scheme and added devices of their own contriving, though there was a great deal of borrowing and interchange of ideas throughout the South. The plan set up certain barriers such as property or literacy qualifications for voting, and then cut certain loopholes in the barrier through which only white men could squeeze. The loopholes to appease

[5] The origin of the term "Jim Crow" applied to blacks is lost in obscurity. Thomas D. Rice wrote a song and dance called "Jim Crow" in 1832, and the term had become an adjective by 1838. The first example of "Jim Crow law" listed by the *Dictionary of American English* is dated 1904. See Woodward, *The Strange Career of Jim Crow*, p. 7.

(though not invariably accommodate) the underprivileged whites were known as the "understanding clause", the "grandfather clause," or the "good character clause." Some variation of the scheme was incorporated into the constitutions of South Carolina in 1895, Louisiana in 1898, North Carolina in 1900, Alabama in 1901, Virginia in 1902, Georgia in 1908, and Oklahoma in 1910. The restrictions imposed by these devices were enormously effective in decimating the black vote, but in addition all these states, as well as the remaining members of the old Confederacy – Florida, Tennessee, Arkansas, and Texas – adopted the poll tax. With its cumulative features and procedures artfully devised to discourage payment, the poll tax was esteemed at first by some of its proponents as the most reliable means of curtailing the franchise – not only among blacks but among objectionable whites as well. And if the black did learn to read, or acquire sufficient property, and remember to pay the poll tax and to keep the receipt on file, he could even then be tripped by the final hurdle devised for him – the whites-only primary election. The statewide Democratic primary was adopted in South Carolina in 1896, Arkansas in 1897, Georgia in 1898, Florida and Tennessee in 1901, Alabama and Mississippi in 1902, Kentucky and Texas in 1903, Louisiana in 1906, Oklahoma in 1907, Virginia in 1913, and North Carolina in 1915.

In spite of the ultimate success of disfranchisement, the movement met with stout resistance and succeeded in some states by narrow margins or the use of fraud. In order to overcome the opposition and divert the suspicions of the poor and illiterate whites that they as well as the blacks were in danger of losing the franchise – a suspicion that often proved justified – the leaders of the movement resorted to an intensive propaganda of white supremacy, Negrophobia, and race chauvinism. The South was kept a White Man's Land; it was solidly one-party; the Democratic nominating primary – limited to white delegates – was more important than actual elections.

The effectiveness of disfranchisement is suggested by a comparison of the number of registered black voters in Lousiana in 1896, when there were 130,334, and in 1904, when there were 1,342. Between these two dates the literacy, property, and poll tax qualifications were adopted. In 1896 black registrants were in a majority in 26 parishes; by 1900 in none.[6]

[6] Woodward, *The Strange Career of Jim Crow*, pp. 66–8.

8 THE NEWEST SOUTH

A feature of the years since 1890 has been the gradual industrialization of the South, since labor was cheaper there than in the North. Cotton mills were built, and later artificial fibres were produced. Tobacco processing – particularly cigarette making – steadily increased. Birmingham's steel industry has made it the Pittsburgh of the South; the mineral riches of the Gulf Coast are transforming Louisiana; and Texas is probably the wealthiest and most diverse state of all, from cattle to cotton, from oil to tin and zinc. As well as the efforts of private enterprise, there has been the aid of the federal government. In 1933 President F. D. Roosevelt declared that the South was still the nation's "economic problem number one," and that one-third of its people were ill-fed, ill-housed and ill-clothed; he set up the Tennessee Valley Authority to develop the Tennessee River basin. The Authority's dams and power plants, its flood control system, soil conservation, and housing schemes made an immense improvement in the area. Land, sucked dry and eroded by cotton and tobacco, and then devastated by war and its aftermath, was saved by afforestation schemes. All this provided much employment, and also brought a great lift to the morale of the South.

The South, like the Far West, also benefited paradoxically from the two world wars. Shipbuilding became a Southern development; so did aircraft manufacture at Dallas and Fort Worth in Texas. Northern industries opened branches and assembly plants in the South. The improvement in Southern incomes brought an increased demand for manufactured goods as the standard of living rose. But in the South more than a century after the Civil War, "The War" is still not Hitler's War or the Kaiser's War, but "The War Between the States."

3

The Growth of Urban Society

1 THE INDUSTRIAL PIONEERS

The North won the war: it had more men, and more and better equipment: iron and steel, railroads, coal – and by 1861 oil. It attracted entrepreneurs and rewarded them generously. It was a place for hard work and thrift – for Calvinist qualities. It was a climate that encouraged invention. It was a place for Scottish virtues: two of the most conspicuous men of enterprise were from the Auld Country. The results were astonishing – the output of goods and services (Gross National Product) increased by 44 percent between 1874 and 1883, and continued to develop *pro rata*; the value of manufactured products rose from $1.8 billion in 1859 to $3.3 billion in 1869, to $5.3 billion in 1879, to $9.3 billion in 1889, and to over $13 billion in 1899.

The careers of Carnegie and Rockefeller, of Henry Ford, Edison, and the Wright brothers, and of a legion of inventors and entrepreneurs, were made possible by the philosophy summarized in Emma Lazarus's words inscribed beneath the Statue of Liberty: "Give me your tired, your poor, your huddled masses yearning to breathe free." The US was the greatest – and the most generous – of all immigrant nations, and stayed so until Congress passed the successive laws in 1921 and 1924 that effectively ended immigration; cheap labor was no longer so badly needed. But mass immigration and the all-but-endless demand for workers on farm and in factory was the secret of the astonishing economic growth of the United States in its golden age of industry, the half-century between the Civil War and World War I.

Andrew Carnegie

The career of Andrew Carnegie (1835–1919) was, of course, unique. A poor ill-educated boy, born in Dunfermline in 1835, who emigrated with his parents at the age of fourteen when his handloom-weaver father was broken by the slump of the 1840s, he got a job in Pittsburgh as a telegraph boy and railroads clerk. By the age of thirty however, he had made shrewd and farsighted investments, which by 1865 were concentrated in iron, and had an annual income of $50,000. He never in fact received another salary cheque. By the time he was forty-five he was the foremost ironmaster in America. Within a few years he had organized or had stock in companies making iron bridges, rails, and locomotives. Ten years later, the steel mill he built on the Monongahela River in Pennsylvania was the greatest in the country. Year by year Carnegie's business grew. He acquired commanding control not only over new mills, but also over coke and coal properties, iron ore from Lake Superior, a fleet of steamers on the Great Lakes, a port town on Lake Erie, and a connecting railroad. His business was allied with a dozen others; it could command favorable terms from railroads and shipping lines; it had capital enough for expansion and a plentiful supply of labor. Nothing comparable in the way of industrial expansion had ever been seen before in America. The Carnegie Steel Company was formed in 1899, with profits of 40 million dollars. His income grew by what it fed on: by a series of mergers, and shrewd investments, he became one of the richest men of his own, or all, time. At his death in 1919 he had given away 350 million dollars. So Carnegie became and for many remains a key figure in the American experience – the Americanized immigrant, the self-made man, the dedicated philanthropist, and in Professor Wall's words, "the democrat who could not only walk with, but argue with Kings."[1]

As with other success stories – and there are obvious parallels with Benjamin Franklin and Cecil Rhodes – much of it was due to chance, in Carnegie's case his meeting with Thomas A. Scott of the Pennsylvania railroads, who made him his assistant and who became his friend and mentor. It was Scott who put investments in his way; the young boy who received his first dividend payment from 10 shares in Adams Express and shouted "Eureka, here's

[1] Joseph Frazier Wall, *Andrew Carnegie* (New York, Oxford University Press, 1970); see also Andrew Carnegie, *The Autobiography of Andrew Carnegie* (New York, Houghton Mifflin, 1920).

the goose that lays the golden eggs," from the first put his faith in the capitalist system. He was industrious, enquiring, intelligent and, in his youth, likable. It was, in other words, very largely the story of the industrious apprentice. He retired, aged 66, as a multi-millionaire. Like Franklin and Rhodes, he came up the hard way; like Franklin, but unlike Rhodes, he did not believe in fighting an enemy if you could destroy him as easily by negotiation. And, like Franklin, he was addicted to epigrams, most of which his own career flatly contradicted.

It is not of course a career that will commend itself to all tastes. When on Carnegie's death an old blacksmith was asked what he thought of him, he gave the reply: "maybe you have heard the saying that every honest man has hair growing in the palms of his hands."

What Frazier Wall establishes is that Carnegie was the product of Radical and Chartist Dunfermline, and he never forgot all three. His speeches and adages were more evocative of Chartism than of the Gilded Age; he learned to like and cultivate men of power, from Theodore Roosevelt to Kaiser Bill, but in all the roles he played – Laird of Pittsburgh, Laird of Skibo in Sutherland (the ruined castle that he restored and saw as home, on the shores of the Dornoch Firth in northern Scotland), and ultimately Laird of Pittencrieff in Dunfermline (his boyhood ambition) – he never quite outlived the anti-monarchism and the secularism imbibed from his Chartist youth. He continued to see America, the very America he had helped to create, as simply the realization of the hopes of Chartist Scotland. And he saw in the Republican party of Lincoln a merger of the Radical idealism of Dunfermline with the business opportunism of America. There was no dissembling here, since it had been true for him. But he continued to see in the Republican party of Blaine, Teddy Roosevelt and Taft, evidence of the same idealism, evidence few others were able to detect. In other words, Carnegie, who all through his life could give Radical speeches in Britain, miraculously transformed himself into a Conservative Republican when he crossed the ocean. The advocate of an American protective tariff was in Britain a believer in free trade; he was as ready to give financial help to John Burns in Britain as he was to Roosevelt or Taft in the United States. The Radical and Pacifist of Dunfermline, with noble thoughts about the dignity of labor and *The Gospel of Wealth* (the title of the book he wrote), was the same man who called in the Pinkertons to break the Homestead Strike in 1892. One maxim that he did not inscribe over his mantelpiece – there were already so many that there was hardly room for more – was that of Rochefoucauld:

"old men are fond of giving good advice because they are no longer in a position to set bad examples."

This is of course in part the contrast between youth and age, between three generations and two worlds. But in other ways also it becomes clear that Carnegie was no true model of the industrious apprentice. He was no lover of hard work or of dirt for their own sakes. He was proud to be an American citizen and a Lincoln Republican, but he was not willing to fight in the American Civil War for the cause of free men and free land; he bought a replacement, an Irishman, and thought him cheap at 850 dollars. He was no inventor, unlike the man who developed the railroad sleeping car and died in poverty. And he was ruthless with his own mentor, Tom Scott, when he ran into difficult times. One moral that can be drawn from the Carnegie story is: don't invent, just exploit the inventions of others.

Yet this egocentric extrovert was one of the real founders of modern America. It was more than the accidental coincidence of a man whose temperament suited the times. The industries in which he worked and invested – railroads, iron, steel, oil – united a diverse continent, and produced both an economic common market and an opportunity state. And the skill of the money-making was in the end so gigantic that he was able to move from it to good works on a hitherto unknown dimension, and in the end to make philanthropy itself big business. He gave away vast amounts that his investments brought him, and he strove hard to avert the outbreak of World War I, and to halt it when it came. He established Hero Funds, the Hague Peace Temple, and the Pan-American Union. It is this aspect that contributes at once the almost paradoxical feature of his career and its most significant. How is it possible to assess the value of his investments in knowledge and research? There is no evidence whatever, either in 1835 when he was born, in 1919 when he died, or now over 70 years later, that, had he not made the fortune he did, or if he had not, assuming that his workers would have made, retained and invested an equivalent amount of money, the world would have somehow produced the observatories, the libraries, the medical research programs or the universities that Carnegie (and Rockefeller and Ford and Harkness) supported and endowed, in the US, in Britain, in Canada, and beyond. There is no evidence whatever that without the Robber Barons any of these things would have been done at all. Massive philanthropy was not in the Six Points of Chartism, nor is it a necessary part of the capitalist creed. It proved, however, to be Carnegie's great invention, and there can be no question that the extent of it must go a long way to justify the methods by which the fortune was made – if indeed, in today's world, justification is any longer needed. That is the real divide between the Chartist world and our own. It is what gives Frazier Wall's study of him a moral dimension. It is a good story, and it leaves the reader both enlightened and disturbed.

Stung by competition, Carnegie at first threatened to acquire new mines, and build an ever more powerful business; but, as an old and tired man, he was finally willing to listen to the suggestion that he merge his holdings with the new organization which would embrace most of the important iron and steel properties in the nation. The story of Carnegie's United States Steel Corporation can be only matched by Rockefeller's Standard Oil Company, by Vanderbilt or Hill in railroad consolidation, or by the enterprises of Ford or Mellon or Frick.

John D. Rockefeller

John D. Rockefeller (1839–1937) was a pioneer too: of big business, nationally organized, and of big philanthropy: a combination that was not unique, except perhaps in its scale. In 1853 he moved with his family from Tioga County, New York, to a village near Cleveland, Ohio, where during his twenties he formed a partnership to establish an oil refinery, which in 1870 became the Standard Oil Company. He owned 26.7 percent of the stock. He combined meticulousness of detail in guiding the rapid expansion of a new industry with a broad vision regarding the problems of top-level management. Whereas in the 1860s, the oil business was chaotic, haphazard, and vigorously competitive, with barrel prices rising as high as $13.75 and falling as low as 10 cents, Standard Oil was consistently profitable and growing. Rockefeller used then-legal tactics like railroad rebates and predatory pricing. He created one of the first and largest of the "trusts:" his objective was order, rather than total monopoly. He selected his associates astutely. Rockefeller was convinced that the company's success depended upon eliminating competition, and before 1890 he had created a petroleum empire, close to a monopoly, which dominated the oil market on a global scale: almost from the start 75 percent of its markets were in Europe. But the trusts and interlocking directorates that he created led to antitrust suits and in 1911 to Supreme Court action, which dissolved them.

Although Rockefeller did not formally retire until 1911, after 1890 he devoted most of his time to planning how to distribute his vast fortune and he organized large charities as meticulously as he had organized his industries. They included establishment of the

University of Chicago (1892), to which he gave $600,000 in 1889 as an establishment fund, and to which the family would ultimately give more than 80 million dollars, the Rockefeller Institute for Medical Research (1901), the General Education Board (1903), and the Rockefeller Foundation (1913) for programs in the fields of medicine, public health, science, and the humanities.

But the story of Rockefeller will always be the story of the rise of Standard Oil, and so it is in Allan Nevins's biography.[2] It begins with Rockefeller's first investment in a Cleveland refinery partnership in 1863 (four years after Drake's well was brought in at Titusville) and ends, with the Supreme Court decree ordering the dissolution of the Standard Oil Co. of New Jersey in 1911, some ten years after Rockefeller's retirement. (There were no years of financial struggle, incidentally; Rockefeller seems to have made money on oil in every single year from the first to the last.) The story – the wild competitive disorder of the Oil Reign, the alliances and mesalliances of the oil companies and the railroads, the rebates and drawbacks, the abortive South Improvement Co., the vision of the trust, the acquisition – or, as some would have it, the destruction – of the independents, the struggle for pipelines and the fabulous untaxed millions which poured in on Rockefeller and his colleagues – is superbly told.

Furthermore, Nevins points out that the rebates received by Standard, and even the notorious drawbacks on competitors' shipments, were not in fact significantly out of line with the business ethics of the day, and that those who regretted them most regretted mostly that it was Rockefeller, not they, who were the beneficiaries. He also shows – a rather more dubious defense – that after making a competitor desirous of selling out by price cutting or the denial of transportation outlets the trust usually paid good prices for the property. Finally – and also rather dubiously – Nevins argues that Rockefeller was repeatedly blamed for the acts of his subordinates. But Rockefeller profited from the extraordinary capacity of his captains and lieutenants, and his ability to recruit men was a prime source of his success. He can hardly escape responsibility for their lapses.

The railroad barons

It was a similar story at almost every turn: the US Patent Office registered 1,000 inventions a year in the 1850s, over 12,000 in the

[2] Allan Nevins, Study in Power: *John D. Rockefeller, industrialist and philanthropist*, 2 vols (New York, Scribner's, 1953).

1870s, and in 1890 alone issued 25,322 patents. So too with railroad tracks: in 1865 less than 35,000 miles of track existed; by 1875 it was over 74,000, and by 1890 it was 166,000. There were entrepreneurs here too. One was Commodore Cornelius Vanderbilt, who had made a fortune in shipping before turning to railroads. By the time of his death in 1877 his New York Central operated a network of over 4,500 miles of track between New York City and most of the principal cities of the Middle West. Carnegie's first employer Tom Scott, was busy making the Pennsylvania Company into a second major trunk line, fusing roads to Cincinnati, Indianapolis, St Louis, and Chicago to his Pennsylvania Railroad, which linked Pittsburgh and Philadelphia. By the mid-1870s, the Baltimore & Ohio also reached Chicago; so did the Erie, which boasted 1,400 miles under one management and 860 miles without a change of cars; it was the product of three railroad freebooters: Daniel Drew, Jay Gould, and Jim Fisk.

It was that same Jay Gould, soft-spoken and insignificant-looking but ruthless and cynical, who invaded the West in the 1870s, buying 370,000 shares of Union Pacific stock. He also took over the Kansas Pacific, running from Denver to Kansas City, which he consolidated with the Union Pacific; the Missouri Pacific and the Texas and Pacific also became part of his empire. Henry Villard and James J. Hill also owned Western networks.

The effect of railroads on the economy was all but limitless: they demanded iron and railroad trackmen, and they gave stimulus to every locality. They had their own inventors too: George Pullman's sleeping car in 1864, George Westinghouse's air brake, which enabled an engineer to apply the brakes simultaneously to all his cars. They bought and sold land. They offered cheap rates to travellers interested in buying farms, even through "bureaux of immigration" – so that the pleasures of the American West were advertised across Europe. Occasionally whole colonies of new settlers migrated to America under railroad auspices, such as the 1900 Mennonites who moved from Russia to Kansas in 1874 to settle on the land of the Atchison, Topeka, and Santa Fe.

Moreover, one industry fostered another. Railroads usually allowed Western Union to string wires along their right of way. By 1883 Western Union was transmitting 40 million messages a year over 400,000 miles of wire. The two industries, in Jay Gould's words, went "hand in hand," "integral parts" of American civilization.

Bell and Edison

There were other entrepreneurs. Alexander Graham Bell (1847–1922) was Edinburgh-born; he came to Boston in 1871. As a professor of vocal physiology at Boston University he applied the method of his father, Alexander Melville Bell, a distinguished phoneticist, to the education of the deaf. By means of "visible speech," or graphic diagrams of letters as uttered in talking, he taught the deaf to speak. His transmission of sound by electric waves led to the invention (1876) of the first telephone. His later inventions helped Edison to perfect the phonograph, and aided S. P. Langley in problems involving balance in aeronautics. He talked in his mature and elder years of little but aviation – his preoccupation was with the mastery of space and communication.

When Western Union realized the importance of the telephone, it sought to compete with Bell. It commissioned Thomas A. Edison, who in 1869 was granted his first patent for an electrical vote recorder; in the course of experiments with "the mysteries of electrical force," he devised a multiplex telegraph capable of sending four messages over a single wire at the same time. More than this, he set up in 1876 at Menlo Park, New Jersey, a research laboratory for the concerted attack on specific problems by teams of researchers. Its first major product was the phonograph. Even more significantly, the Wizard of Menlo Park perfected his incandescent lamp or electric light bulb. Late in 1879 he produced a carbonized filament that would glow brightly in a vacuum tube for as long as 170 hours without crumbling. In 1884 he had 500 consumers using over 10,000 lamps in New York City – where the first two customers were the *New York Times* and the banking house of J. P. Morgan. By the end of the decade Edison was producing a million lamps a year. In his life he was granted well over 1,000 patents. To many he came to symbolize the archetypal inventor, proof of America's genius at technology and invention.

Henry Ford

The discoveries and inventions of Rockefeller and Carnegie made Henry Ford's invention possible. If Henry Ford (1863–1947) did not invent the automobile, he certainly developed design concepts and production techniques that allowed its manufacture in such volume and at such cost as to bring it within reach of the average wage earner. It can be said that he, more perhaps than any other individual, invented the twentieth century – or at least made its significant emblem possible.

Henry Ford was born on a farm near Dearborn, Michigan. From his earliest days he displayed a marked mechanical aptitude, and all his life he delighted in working with machinery. In 1879 he became an apprentice in a machine shop in Detroit, repairing watches at night to make ends meet. In the early 1890s he began experimenting with the new internal combustion engine and in 1896 produced his first car, built in the garage of his home. In 1903 he established the Ford Motor Company with $28 thousand in capital provided by others. Profitable from the first, it became much more so when he introduced the Model T in 1908.

As Ford developed his production ideas, fully introducing the assembly-line principle in 1913, the price of the Model T dropped steadily. In 1908 the company made 10,607 cars and sold them for $850 apiece; in 1916 it manufactured 730,041 priced at only $360. Originally Ford held a quarter of the firm's stock, but by 1920 he had become the sole owner of one of the largest industrial enterprises on earth. In 1927, when the last of more than 15 million Model T's was produced, the company boasted undistributed earnings of nearly $700 million along with billions more in plant and equipment.

In 1914, when industrial workers were averaging about $11 a week, Ford announced that his employees would be paid $5 for an eight-hour day. His purpose was not only to motivate his workers to endure the drudgery of the assembly line but to bring his automobiles within their economic reach. The policy made Ford famous around the world, and it seemed for a time that he might have a political career.

Once an industrial revolutionary, in his later years Ford became set in his ways. He refused to make changes in his production system, his automobiles, or his labor policies, even when the need and the market signals were clear. Finally, a plummeting market share left him no choice but to shut down production of the Model T and retool to produce the Model A. Other automobile companies, especially General Motors, took advantage of the hiatus, and the Ford Motor Company never regained its once overwhelming dominance.

Ford, a mechanical genius, was otherwise ignorant, narrow, and naive. He published many scurrilous antisemitic articles and fought unionization with every weapon at his disposal, including a private police force. Nor would he allow modern management techniques to interfere with his autocratic ways. By the mid-1930s the company was riven by factions. A decade later the Ford Motor Company, once the most prodigious engine of wealth creation in the American economy, was on the brink of ruin, losing a million dollars a day.[3]

The Wright Brothers

Although two of the five sons of a highly respected bishop in the Church of the United Brethren in Christ, neither of the Wright brothers, Wilbur (1867–1912) and Orville (1871–1948), had a college education. In commenting on the importance of his family background in later years, Orville Wright remarked: "We were lucky enough to grow up in a home environment where there was always much encouragement to children to pursue intellectual interests, to investigate whatever aroused curiosity. In a different kind of environment, our curiosity might have been nipped long before it could have borne fruit."

The brothers launched their first joint venture, a print shop in their home town of Dayton, Ohio, in 1889. While continuing to operate the print shop, the brothers entered the bicycle trade in 1892. By 1896 they were manufacturing bicycles for sale on a small scale. Never more than moderately successful as small businessmen, the Wrights nevertheless enjoyed a modest prosperity during the years 1890 to 1905. They financed their flying machine experiments solely from the profits of their business enterprises.

The brothers became interested in flight as a result of newspaper articles reporting the death of the German aeronautical experimenter Otto Lilienthal in a glider crash in 1896. Between 1899 and 1905, Wilbur and Orville constructed seven aircraft: one kite (1899), three gliders (1900, 1901, 1902), and three powered airplanes (1903, 1904, 1905). The disappointing performance of the first two gliders led them to undertake a series of key experiments with a wind tunnel of their own design during the fall of 1901. The wind tunnel tests, coupled with two years of gliding experience, opened the road to success. The Wrights made the world's first powered, sustained, and controlled flights with a heavier-than-air flying machine at Kitty Hawk, North Carolina (now Kill Devil Hills), on December 17, 1903. They returned to Dayton and continued their experiments in

[3] Peter Collier and David Horowitz, *The Fords: An American epic* (New York, Summit Books, 1987); Allan Nevins and Frank Ernest Hill, *Ford*, 3 vols, (New York, Scribner's, 1954–63); Peter J. Ling, *America and the Automobile: Technology, reform and social change 1893–1923* (Manchester, Manchester University Press, 1990).

the relative secrecy of a local cow pasture for two more years. By the close of the 1905 flying season, they had transformed the marginally successful machine of 1903 into the world's first practical airplane. They won world fame with their first public demonstration flights in Europe and America in the summer and fall of 1908.

The brothers founded the Wright Company to build and sell aircraft in the United States and licensed various manufacturers to produce their machines in Europe. With their business in the hands of professional managers, the Wrights devoted most of their time and energy to pursuing patent infringers in courts on both sides of the Atlantic.

Wilbur Wright died suddenly of typhoid fever in 1912, and Orville sold the Wright Company to a group of investors in 1915.[4]

One other name should be mentioned here – a name that in the end absorbed many others: Morgan. The Morgan perspective so illuminates the rise of the modern American economy, its maturation, and its extraordinary overseas expansion that the reader will frequently have the sense of a large field opening up before him. The firm's early history can be briefly summarized. It was formed in England by George Peabody in 1838. Peabody was a Baltimore entrepreneur who slowly built his London establishment into the principal conduit for British investment in America. He eventually took into partnership a Boston financier, Junius Morgan. When Peabody died Junius stayed in London, appointing his son Pierpoint (1837–1913) as New York agent. The business was therefore international from the outset, with a large Paris branch also soon attached. A domestic axis was formed with the Philadelphia-based Drexel interests in 1871. The result was a superbly strong, elastic financial combination that, by the time Pierpoint's son Jack took control in 1913, could look back on several decades at the top of American finance and industry.

The Morgans and their partners paid a price for their power, however, especially in the stormy years 1880–1920. Cartoonists delighted to draw Pierpoint, with his bulbous nose, his fierce glare, and his pneumatic bulk weighed down with bulging money bags. Behind the ridicule lay a deep brew of genuine hatred, envy, and fear. Populists, progressives, socialists and millions of ordinary Americans viewed them as cynical bloodsuckers. Their bankers' hard

[4] Tom D. Crouch, *The Bishop's Boys: A life of Wilbur and Orville Wright* (New York, Norton, 1990); Marvin W. McFarland (ed.), *The Papers of Wilbur and Orville Wright* (Salem, Ayer Co., 1971; repr. of 1953 edn).

money policy, traitorously serving British financial interests, worked to ruin the farmer, rob the laborer, and stifle enterprise. Carnegie and Rockefeller at least produced something and gave employment. The House of Morgan seemed, by comparison, unredeemably parasitic.

Today, it all looks a little different. The modern reader, steeped in relativism, may feel a certain sympathy for the Morgans. Many historians now portray them, especially Pierpoint, as economic statesmen. Their London financial channel, on this view, furthered American growth. They had to maintain the gold standard to keep British investors happy. They brought order to a chaotic industrial economy, and especially to the railroad business which was its bedrock. They rescued New York City three times. And they successfully led the country through the great financial crises of 1893 and 1907. In the post-1920 period, the House of Morgan, its radical tormentors at last in retreat, was slowly woven into a more co-ordinated system of national power increasingly dominated by Washington. It remained enormously influential internationally. Its interwar record was patchy. It cooperated in European reconstruction in the 1920s but blotted its copybook in the 1930s by dubious associations with Mussolini, the Nazi regime, and the Japanese militarists. Yet the House of Morgan persisted, under the resourceful leadership of Thomas Lamont and other partners, and emerged after 1945 still the leading American merchant bank and a substantial international force. It remains today, in much modified form, a powerful, successful presence.[5]

2 PIONEERS OF INDUSTRY: AN ASSESSMENT

These were only a few of the many pioneers of the new industrial society. Like other pioneers – cattlemen, prospectors, frontier farmers – they helped to develop the resources of a new land. They were endowed with great energy and rare ability. They were gamblers, willing to take chances for the hope of gain. They were highly competitive men in a highly competitive society, where few laws had been enacted to bring order into the mad rush of business enterprise in the early days of industrialism. The tycoons were strikingly of one mould; usually Scottish, Scotch-Irish or English;

[5] Ron Chernow, *The House of Morgan: An American banking dynasty and the rise of modern finance* (New York, Touchstone Books, 1991); F. L. Allen, *The Great Pierpoint Morgan* (London, Gollancz, 1949).

usually non-aristocratic in origin and indeed ill-educated (though venerating and endowing education in their later years, when it became a habit to act as if *richesse oblige*); and usually – though here Carnegie was an exception – pious and religious. ("God gave me my money," said J. D. Rockefeller.) They were absorbed in the wild excitement of building a new industrial world, of creating huge fortunes, of securing power. Their methods were often selfish and ruthless. They have frequently been condemned for their ruthlessness and for the power that they came to hold; but at the same time their critics have admitted that they built new industries, introduced efficient organization, and provided opportunities for many people to invest their savings profitably in the new industries that were springing up all over the nation.

Leaders of this type were the products of their time. They will probably never appear in American life again, but while they were on the stage, they played an important part in an important period of the nation's development, and they helped to give new direction to American life.

During the second half of the nineteenth century industry in the United States grew by leaps and bounds. By 1900 the United States had become the leading industrial nation in the world. Smoking factory chimneys, the rumble of steam-driven and electric machinery, and long trains of freight cars pulling into congested urban centers were symbols of the industrial revolution that was taking place. Particularly in the northeastern and north central states, but to a lesser extent throughout the nation, industrialism was transforming the lives of the people. Raw materials from America's vast reservoir of natural resources poured into the mills and factories. Finished products in evergrowing quantities became available at lower prices to more and more people.

Mass production led to specialization. Financiers raised the capital to build the railroads and the factories. Manufacturers developed more efficient methods of producing goods. Merchants developed new methods of advertising and selling. Wage-earners – clerks, stenographers, managers, miners, factory workers, and others – manned the new industrial plants. New methods of business organization were developed, and great corporations (and even combinations of corporations) increasingly replaced the earlier family-owned factory, mill, or store.

Throughout America a new spirit of fierce competition drove men at a faster and faster pace. It was an exciting and a productive period in the nation's history. But some of the changes created problems for many people. Much of the nation's history since the

War Between the States centers in the efforts of Americans to adjust their ways of life to the new industrial society.

The objective of the new approach was to dominate the industry; to control the source, the production, and the market. Business consolidation followed, in steel, or railroads, or oil. By 1904, 5,000 hitherto independent concerns had been consolidated into 300 trusts. The corporations and trusts were powerful not only at home but abroad, and, despite wars, they remain so. In the late nineteenth century they certainly influenced and they sometimes bought politicians; the presidency of General Ulyssess S. Grant (1868–76) was an age of corruption, marked by the attempts to defraud the Federal Government in the Crédit Mobilier scandal, and attempts to defraud the city of New York in the activities of Boss Tweed. It was an Era of Good Stealing, of Honest (and sometimes of Dishonest) Graft. And in the years between the presidency of Grant and Theodore Roosevelt, the Presidents were less important and less influential figures than the tycoons.

Certainly the age of unlimited and unchecked enterprise brought immense wealth to a few; *per capita* income mounted steadily, and the land was disciplined. But to many of its people it was an age of hardship. Despite the high agricultural productivity – or perhaps because of it – the farmer did not benefit. He saw himself as the victim of the exorbitant rates charged by the railroad companies; he was at the mercy of high tariffs, scarce credit and falling prices, of erratic rainfall, freezing winters, and grasshopper plagues. Only the Eastern banker benefited. Only cheap money would help the farmer, and he came to see in the unlimited coinage of silver – vast supplies of which were available in the mountain states – a way to salvation. To increase the volume of money available would send farm prices up, and allow farmers to pay off their debts more readily. Slowly the farmer began to organize, in the Grange Lodges, in the Farmers' Alliance, and ultimately in the Populist party. Populist proposals seemed absurd and alarming to those sleeping safely in the East; so did Populist leaders, who advised the farmers to raise less corn and to raise more hell – which was crude but, in fact, wise advice, both economically and politically. The Omaha platform of the People's party – as it was first called – in 1892 included the free coinage of silver, the government ownership of railroads, the abolition of national banks, the direct election of Senators, an eight-hour day and a graduated income tax. Its eloquence was the handiwork of Ignatius Donnelly (1831–1901), leader of liberal crusades in Minnesota politics and editor of the *Anti-Monopolist*. The Party polled over a million votes. When in 1896 the Democrats nominated William Jennings Bryan for the presidency, they channeled Populist feeling to their cause, and Bryan, a pious and Fundamentalist, but rabble-rousing, figure, the "silver-tongued orator of the Platte," was the first major challenge to the big-business Republican party, and to the American Establishment. But Bryan was defeated, and the trend to insurgency diminished – in part because the reform planks of this third party were gradually taken over and incorporated into the platforms of one or other of the two major parties.

With the exception of Grover Cleveland (President 1884–8, 1892–6), Republicans monopolized the White House from Lincoln's day until Woodrow Wilson; and both Cleveland and Wilson won because of Republican splits. Republicans capitalized on the Civil War spirit – waving "the bloody shirt;" until 1904 every successful Republican presidential candidate was a Civil War veteran, most of them members of an Ohio dynasty that seemed self-perpetuating. To this school, the total abstainer Bryan, shirt-sleeved and passionate, was alien, and and anathema. He carried his crusade to the people and stormed over 18,000 miles, the young man eloquent: "You shall not crucify mankind on a cross of gold."

Nevertheless, his Republican opponent in 1896, William McKinley of Ohio, running on a platform of high-tariff protection and the maintenance of the gold standard, but sitting firmly on his own front porch in Canton, Ohio, had an easy victory. He won 7,100,000 popular votes to Bryan's 6,500,000. The electoral college votes were 271 to 176. Bryan did not carry any Northern industrial states, and the agricultural states of Iowa, Minnesota, and North Dakota also went Republican. The discovery of rich gold deposits in Alaska removed one of the major Populist objections to it, its scarcity. And the demands for agricultural and factory products that was the result of the Spanish-American War eased the tensions of the 1890s.

3 AMERICAN SOCIETY

The US in 1900 was mainly British in its roots. By 1700, twice as many Britons as Spaniards had emigrated to the New World, even though Spain had the larger empire. In the 1780s, France still had a bigger navy and four times the population, but could not establish a comparable foothold. And in the century following 1832, half of all European emigrants from Europe came from Britain. The British emigrants tended to be low-church Protestants – class-climbing Nonconformists – who went abroad "putting profits over grandeur," ignoring the French and Spanish *mission civilitrice*. This is, of course, no more or less than the "Protestant ethic" described by Weber and Tawney, which exalted thrift, deferral of gratification, and devotion to work, and viewed prosperity as an outward sign of God's grace. Britain not only provided the tools for the global economy (from accounting principles to the opening of trade routes) but also set the standards. Today, when we talk about "success," we mean success in a Calvinist world.

After the 1880s, two changes occurred in the character of immigration into the US: first the annual volume of immigration greatly increased, and second a greater proportion of the new immigrants were peasants from Southern and Eastern Europe. Thus the new immigrants were culturally, linguistically and occupationally differentiated from the earlier immigrants. Moreover, the new immigrants settled predominantly in industrial cities, and found employment in mass-production industries, in which they comprised the bulk of the unskilled and semiskilled workforce. A parallel pair of stratifications thus existed among US workers, who were divided socially as well as vocationally. One group, the "native" Americans, had immigrated to the US in earlier times, were skilled and organized; the other group, the new immigrants, were unskilled and unorganized. The craft unions, composed of skilled men, tightened their organizations in competition against the newcomers.

Other causes for the domination of the American labor movement by craft unions have roots still further back in American history. From the early years of American history there has been a lack of class-consciousness among the American laboring population. As opposed to European laborers, who have been decidedly class-conscious, American laborers have been job-conscious. Out of a number of conditions which might be cited to explain the lack of class consciousness among American workers, two appear to be the most important: American society has never been a stratified society; there has been nothing comparable in the US to the European idea, developed out of the background of feudal society, that a person was born to a particular class, whose barriers he could not cross. Although the lack of this tradition in the US is an intangible matter, its importance in explaining the absence of class-consciousness among American workers can hardly be exaggerated. The American worker obtained the right to vote with great ease, in sharp contrast with developments in Europe. There the franchise was obtained only as the result of trade union agitation. The trade union was the mechanism by which the civil rights of the European worker were extended. Thus the European worker was a trade unionist first and a citizen second. The US worker got all his civil rights without organizing; therefore he was a citizen first and a trade unionist second.

Political passiveness and the absence of socialist agitation: two further characteristics of the American labor movement before World War I should be noted at this point. In both of these aspects, the American labor movement was sharply different from the European. American trade unions as such evinced virtually no interest in political objectives. The only political formula of these unions was an attempt to reward their friends and punish their enemies. They did not try to influence, in any important way, either of the two major parties; nor did they try to form a powerful third party. Nor were the American labor unions influenced, except to a minor degree, by the general philosophy of socialism. There is a tendency among historians to stress certain dramatic incidents in the American labor movement in which various socialist organizations were engaged; but in so emphasizing these incidents, they exaggerate the influence of the socialist organizations. The Industrial Workers of the World, or "Wobblies," provide an illustration of this tendency. Although this group made the headlines, it was not influential in the day-to-day developments in American labor. The IWW was a union revolutionary in its aim, and as such it was not supported by any substantial portion of American labor. Although it was particularly active among certain groups, particularly lumber men and migratory workers, its representation in the broad sweep of American labor was negligible. The average American worker was neither informed about nor interested in socialism.

Some historians put an emphasis on socialism, because some labor leaders, even in the American Federation of Labor, had an orientation that originally was socialistic. The point is, however, that these leaders did not attempt to instill their ideology into the unions they led. They discarded their ideas, for one reason or another, in favor of "bread and butter" unionism. The AFL, regardless of the background of some of its leaders, never adopted a socialist program.

4 THE GROWTH OF THE CITIES

Urbanism and industrialism bring problems as well as benefits. One of the most striking changes in American life during the nineteenth century was the rapid growth of cities. Beginning about 1820 and during the remainder of the nineteenth century, the rate

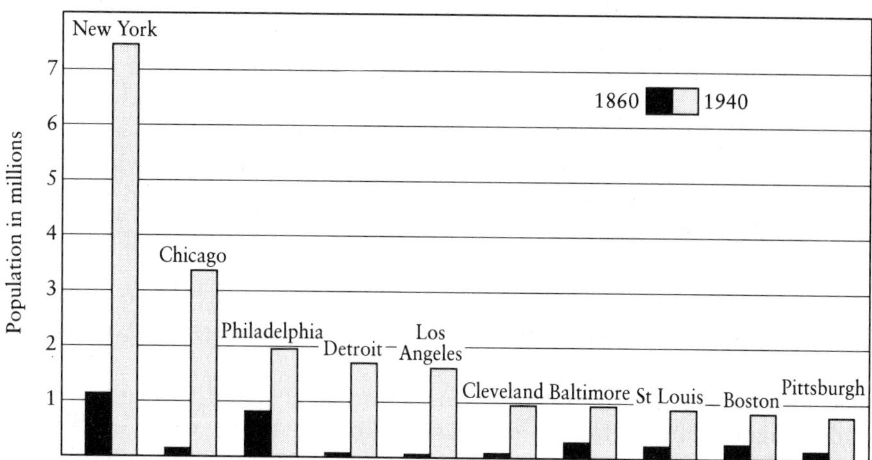

Map 4 Industry and the growth of cities. Between 1860 and 1940, industrialization changed the pattern of growth of cities. New York, the gateway for immigration, shot ahead of all the rest.

of American urbanization accelerated. The nation had only 61 cities in 1820, but forty years later that number had increased to 392, and by 1900 the United States contained 1,737 cities. At the outbreak of the War Between the States only one-sixth of the population of the United States lived in cities of more than 8,000 people. By 1900 one-third of all Americans lived in cities.

Simply put, the reason for this dynamic change in America was industrialization, according to Charles N. Glaab and A. Theodore Brown:

From 1820 on, technological and economic transformations had contributed to a high rate of urbanization in the United States. The continuance of this urban trend in the years after 1860 led to an ever increasing concentration of Americans in cities of all sizes and engendered the view on the part of many social critics that the "rise of the city" was a fundamental problem facing American society. ... Urbanization did not proceed at an even pace during the fifty years. Movement to the city naturally accelerated in times of prosperity and fell off in times of depression when economic opportunities in the city diminished. ... But throughout the period the urban trend was unmistakable; the United States was clearly becoming a nation of cities and city dwellers.

As cities grew, their natures and functions in many cases changed. At the beginning of the nineteenth century, the sizable cities of the United States were strung out along the coast; they were ports and ... faced the sea and the maritime trade which had nurtured them. By the time of the Civil War, however, this could no longer be said. Maritime trade, indeed, was still directly or indirectly an important element of the life of the cities, but new cities had appeared deep in the continental interior and the older ones, the great seaports, had engaged in great metropolitan rivalries with one another to secure as much as possible of the commerce which came from the interior. Manufacturing had begun to influence the shape of many of the cities. ...[6]

Why did urbanization accelerate during the late nineteenth century? Blake McKelvey offered another explanation for urban expansion:

The historic process of America's urbanization acquired new momentum and a significantly different emphasis following the Civil War. As the improved transport facilities reached farther inland rival trading centers sprang up to serve each frontier. The discovery and exploitation of rich mineral deposits and other natural resources, increasing the national output manyfold, added tremendously to the flow of commerce in which many cities shared and over which the national metropolis on the Hudson continued to exercise a loose domination. But New York's former pre-eminence, based on the strategic location of its great port, was lessened as the rise of new factory towns transformed America, during the second half of the century, into an industrial nation. This process, which relegated exports and imports to a secondary position, created new demands for technological improvements and for organizational services. As competing cities and metropolitan centers endeavored to perform these functions, new trade patterns developed, and new civic and cultural patterns as well.[7]

The growing cities created numerous problems. In the country, the poor somehow manage to survive, even if they had to resort to the country poorhouse. But in the city neither private nor government charity was adequate to meet the needs of the jobless in periods of hard times. In the rural areas very poor people often lived in miserable shacks, but they were far enough from each other to prevent dangerous overcrowding. Such was not the case in the city tenements. The ill-lighted, dingy, filthy slums bred new social problems. Many children of the slums toiled in gloomy and wretched sweatshops or roamed the streets like wild animals. Juvenile crime became a problem. Contagious diseases flourished. And those who lived in the slums, mostly newly arrived immigrants, paid rents far

[6] Charles N. Glaab and A. Theodore Brown, *A History of Urban America* (New York, Macmillan, 1967), pp. 107–8, 27.

[7] Blake McKelvey, *The Urbanization of America, 1860–1915* (New Brunswick, NJ, Rutgers University Press, 1963), p. 17.

too high for such firetraps and disease-breeding hovels. As Blake McKelvey put it:

> The cities had also paid sacrifice for their surging growth. Expanding commercial districts engulfed many old residential wards, while factories and freight lines segmented established communities and invaded suburban retreats. The inrush of newcomers from abroad had transformed many once-friendly neighborhoods into heterogeneous slums whose densely packed inhabitants often dwelt as indifferent or hostile strangers under the same roof. It was, many felt, a transition period, and the great majority, imbued with a boundless optimism, looked hopefully to the future. Yet the number who rebelled or inadvertently fell out of step was increasing, as the mounting crime ratios disclosed; and recurrent dislocations of the economy left vast hordes destitute.[8]

Writers such as Herman Melville, Nathaniel Hawthorne, Henry Thoreau, Henry James and Stephen Crane, described cities as evil and corrupting. Agricultural periodicals told how the city caused the depravity of young farm boys and girls. And, by the late decades of the century, notable Protestant writers, like the Reverend Josiah Strong, warned of impending urban disaster due to the unchecked growth of Roman Catholicism, socialism and political corruption.

The rapid growth of cities put a great strain on the traditional institutions of local government, and the resultant problems were difficult to rectify because of city corruption. Constance McLaughlin Green elaborated on urban corruption:

> Corruption in municipal government had sprung up like a toadstool wherever community leadership faltered. ... Incompetents and scalawags moved into public office. If accumulating civic needs brought about appeals to state legislatures for special commissions to handle such problems as building and managing city waterworks or taking charge of police departments, the usual result was a division of authority, the resignation of honest officials, and a breakdown in civic morale that strengthened boss rule. Once bosses were in the saddle they cracked the whip over underlings. ...
>
> 'Bosses' financial support came chiefly from ... traction and gas companies for franchises and from the underworld of gamblers, prostitutes, and operators of the unlicensed liquor establishments known as "blind pigs." Political support, on the other hand, rested quite as much upon the gratitude slum dwellers and voters a few economic notches above them felt toward the men who gave their wants some consideration. ... The rank and file of citizens were slow to see that boss rule with its perversion

[8] Ibid., pp. 231–2.

of power hurt the entire community, that it made a mockery of the fundamental concept of a "government of laws, not men."[9]

As the cities grew in size and population it became increasingly difficult, if not impossible, for the average citizen to know what was going on. To most people, the candidates for public office were merely names on a piece of paper. And yet these officials held enormous power. They gave contracts for an almost endless number of services – sewers, water mains, electric lighting systems, trolley lines, and other public utilities. A few businessmen willingly paid the city officials fat bribes to get these contracts. These businessmen added the cost to the expense of operating the utilities or performing the contract, and the taxpayers in the end footed the bill. In cities of any size, liquor dealers, gamblers, and others needing favors often paid "protection" money to the police and city officials. Thus every large city came, in the years after the War Between the States, to be ruled by so-called "rings." Some of these rings were Republican; some were Democratic. Such rings made fabulous fortunes for the politicians, while the public paid the bill.

It was the age of the political boss. Of these William Marcy Tweed (1823–1878) was probably the first. He was Grand Sachem of Tammany Hall and boss of the New York State Democratic party in the late 1860s and early 1870s. Tweed was master of the "Tweed Ring" and of numerous techniques for extracting personal profit from city construction projects. He was exposed by *Harper's Weekly* and the *New York Times*, caricatured brutally by the cartoonist Thomas Nast, and convicted of graft. He died in jail.

Richard Croker (1841–1922) rose from being a prizefighter and fireman to become Grand Sachem of Tammany Hall in 1886. After that, "for sixteen years his word was law in the Democratic organization of New York City." By obtaining the stock of construction companies dependent on city contracts, he amassed enough wealth to buy a large farm and a stable of racehorses. After his candidate for mayor was defeated by a reform slate in 1901, Croker spent most of his time in Great Britain. One of his horses won the 1907 English Derby.

Thomas Collier Platt (1833–1910), Republican Congressman and Senator, was known as the "easy boss" because of the seemingly effortless way he controlled the New York Republican party in the late nineteenth century. Platt handpicked most party candidates and

[9] Constance McLaughlin Green, *The Rise of Urban America* (New York, Harper and Row, 1965), pp. 111–12.

dispensed patronage with cold-blooded efficiency. His one monumental mistake came when he promoted the nomination of then-Governor Theodore Roosevelt as the party Vice-Presidential candidate in 1900. He did so in order to get the popular Roosevelt, who threatened his control of the New York party, out of the state and into a traditionally powerless office. Alas for Boss Platt, the assassination of William McKinley made Roosevelt President and marked the beginning of the end of Platt's influence in the state.

The "uncrowned king" of the Lower East Side of New York City around the turn of the century was Timothy D. "Big Tim" Sullivan (1862–1913). "Big Tim," also known as "the Big Feller," was both an extremely efficient collector of graft and a lavish distributor of political largess. He supplied thousands of poor people with turkey dinners and gifts each Christmas, distributed shoes to schoolchildren on his birthday, and sponsored picnics and other public festivals – entertainments for constituents, rich and poor alike. He was mentally unbalanced in his later years and died under mysterious circumstances. His funeral was attended by 215,000 people.

Charles Francis Murphy (1858–1924), a saloon keeper, was Grand Sachem of Tammany Hall from 1902 until his death. Although superficially unprepossessing, he had a brilliant political mind, so brilliant that he was able to control the organization without resorting to corrupt practices. Before World War I, Murphy advanced the careers of Alfred E. Smith and Robert F. Wagner, but he clashed with young Franklin D. Roosevelt, then a member of the state Senate. An intuitive, unflamboyant type, unusual among politicos, Murphy raised Tammany, a biographer has written, to "the highest point of its prestige and power."

Tammany Hall was a political force in New York City from its 1789 inception as a benevolent association to mayoral campaigns in the 1950s. Frequently its leadership was identical with that of the executive committee of the local Democratic party, and it was a major or controlling faction in the party in the years 1821–72 and 1905–32. Key Tammany bosses through the years included Tweed, Croker, and Murphy. Although its name was synonymous with corruption to many, Tammany Hall's popularity and endurance resulted from its willingness to help the city's poor and immigrant populations. Irish emigrés forced Tammany Hall to admit them as members in 1817, and the Irish thereafter never lost their tie with it. Because in the 1820s Tammany successfully fought to extend the franchise to all propertyless white males, it was popular with the working class. A close association with the Democratic party was also forged in the Jacksonian era. Tammany's decentralized organization enabled ward leaders to act as advocates for individuals when they had difficulties with the law: a criminal judge, for example, appointed or kept in office by Tammany Hall would have to listen carefully to a local ward leader asking for a suspended sentence in a particular case. Later, the hundreds receiving Tammany Hall assistance with problems or baskets of food on holidays would show their gratitude at the polls. "Reform" administrations periodically took power away from the Hall, but for many years it always made a comeback.

New York, while outstanding in the field, has never had a monopoly of the state and local political boss market. Abraham Ruef (1864–1936), a lawyer, dominated San Francisco politics in the first decade of this century through his control of the Union Labor party. He extracted huge fees from various corporations in return for franchises and other favors. In 1909 he was convicted of bribing municipal officials and served five years in San Quentin prison. Edward H. Crump (1874–1954) was a successful insurance salesman and businessman who dominated the politics of Memphis, and to a lesser extent Tennessee, from 1909 until his death. During his long reign, he was elected mayor several times and served two terms in Congress. Crump gave Memphis an efficient government, but he used corrupt means to control elections.

What did urban citizens finally do about their problems? Ultimately, in desperation, some banded together to try to solve their problems. Blake McKelvey commented on their efforts:

> Alarmed by these miseries, some humanitarian citizens had begun to transform urban charities into welfare agencies; others, blazing with varied degrees of indignation, were demanding political and economic reforms. The sudden upsurge of the progressive movement around 1910 gave cumulative expression in state and national politics to a multitude of grievances dating back several decades in many communities. And since the state legislatures failed to master numerous issues of control, the urban interests, both public and private, turned increasingly to Washington for administrative supervision. Many of the leaders in this movement had served an apprenticeship in local reform campaigns, and their triumphs in the larger arena further revealed the extent to which urban problems had become national issues.[10]

How did the South fit into the urban pattern? Because the South lagged behind the rest of the nation in industrialization, it made a

[10] McKelvey, *Urbanization of America*, p. 232.

meager contribution to American urbanization. T. Lynn Smith noted the slow industrial development in the South:

> The Census of 1790 showed that Charlestown ... was the fourth city in the nation. ... By 1810 the Louisiana Purchase land added New Orleans to southern cities, giving the region another large center. ... Thirty years later, important urban centers were still conspicuously absent in the South. New Orleans ... in 1840 stood in a class by itself and ranked fourth in the nation. ... On the eve of the Civil War (1860), New Orleans with 168,675 inhabitants was still the only metropolis in the South, although Louisville had begun to come to the fore. No other southern city had passed the 25,000 mark. ...
>
> It is doubtful that the twenty years of war and reconstruction greatly retarded the development of urban centers in the South. ... [Nevertheless] as the twentieth century opened, the South contained only six of the nation's 50 large cities, ... [and by] 1920 was held to seven only.[11]

It is clear that Southerners did not create and move into cities as readily as did Northerners and Westerners. But why did not the immense foreign immigration of the nineteenth century swell Southern urban populations? Maldwyn Allen Jones offered an answer to this question.

> That the southern states attracted such a small proportion of immigrants was not due, as contemporaries sometimes thought, to the European's moral aversion to slavery. ... [The South] could offer neither the employment opportunities nor the facilities for obtaining land that were available in the free states [before the Civil War].
>
> Most of the southern states ... joined in the [post-Civil War] ... scramble for immigrants. The South had practically no unsold land to dispose of, but it wanted cheap foreign labor to replace its allegedly inefficient Negroes. ... The truth was that the absence of free land and – until the twentieth century – of large-scale industry deflected the current of immigration elsewhere.[12]

The growth of cities thus presented at least two major problems to these who were honestly concerned with the public welfare. In the first place, it was necessary to curb the dishonesty in city governments so that the people's money would not be stolen from

[11] Rupert B. Vance and Nicolas J. Rath (eds), *The Urban South* (Chapel Hill, NC, University of North Carolina Press, 1954), pp. 25–6.
[12] Maldwyn Allen Jones, *American Immigration* (Chicago, University of Chicago Press, 1960), pp. 120–21, 188.

them by the dishonest politicians. In the second place, the urgent need for protecting the large urban populations from fire, disease, and crime required increased governmental regulation of private enterprise.

America had always prided itself on the large amount of equality of opportunity which prevailed in the land. But during the years after the War Between the States, wealth was increasingly concentrated in the hands of a small fraction of the population. As we have seen, the resources of the nation were being brought under the control of immense corporations and combinations of corporations.

Because statistics of wealth and its distribution were inadequately kept, it is impossible to state precisely what the situation was at the end of the nineteenth century. George K. Holmes, an official of the United States Census Office, estimated in 1893 that 20 percent of the wealth of the country was owned by 0.03 percent of the population, and that 29 percent of the wealth was all that fell to 91 percent of the population. These figures were, to be sure, criticized as an overstatement of the case. But according to a leading economist, Professor Richard Ely of the University of Wisconsin, there was a greater concentration of wealth in the United States than in any other modern country. That, despite the wealth of the country, there was widespread poverty could not be denied. In 1904 one student of the problem, Robert Hunter, estimated that 10 million Americans were living in poverty. His estimate was also challenged. Much depended, of course, upon the definition given to "poverty." But official figures and estimates in 1914 indicated that a majority of American wage-earners did not earn enough to ensure their families a standard of living considered adequate by students of such matters.

A growing number of people were concerned over these revelations. They blamed the great monopolies, which they believed were the cause of many of their troubles. All this quite naturally led to demands that the government control the trusts and bring about a more equal distribution of wealth and power.

5 LABOR AND STRIKES

In the cities the workers too began to organize. The Knights of Labor were formed in 1869, the American Federation of Labor in 1881. The Knights of Labor began as a secret society of tailors in Philadelphia in 1869. The organization grew slowly during the hard years of the 1870s, but worker militancy rose toward the end of the decade, especially after the great railroad strike of 1877, and the Knights' membership rose with it. Grand Master Workman Terence V. Powderly took office in 1879, and under his leadership the Knights flourished; by 1885 the group had 110,000 members. Powderly dispensed with the earlier rules of secrecy and committed the organization to seeking the eight-hour day, abolition of child labor, equal pay for equal work, and political reforms including the graduated income tax.

Unlike most trade unions of the day, the Knights' unions were vertically organized – each included all workers in a given industry, regardless of trade. The Knights were also unusual in accepting workers of all skill levels and both sexes; blacks were included after 1883 (though in segregated locals) On the other hand, the Knights strongly supported the Chinese Exclusion Act of 1882 and the Contract Labor Law of 1885; like many labor leaders at the time, Powderly believed these laws were needed to protect the American work force against competition from underpaid laborers imported by unscrupulous employers.

Powderly believed in boycotts and arbitration, but he opposed strikes. He had only marginal control over the union membership, however, and a successful strike by the Knights of Labor weakened his grip.

The AFL was established at about the same time that the Knights of Labor was becoming less important. The new organization, a federation of craft unions, began to assume importance in the 1880s and by the 1890s it was the dominant American labor organization. By this time, the philosophy of the craft unions had become increasingly crystallized into "business unionism" – that is, the craft union no longer pushed long-term programs, but concentrated instead on making narrow economic gains through individual craft union action. The principal function of the AFL in this new situation was that of acting to minimize jurisdictional disputes among the craft unions.

On the eve of World War I, the American labor movement consisted almost entirely of craft unions, and this situation continued until 1935. Only 8 percent of the total number of American workers were organized at this time – particularly small in comparison to that obtaining in Europe. In the earlier history of American labor, the wage-earner characteristically believed that he would eventually become a proprietor, and this goal was indeed frequently achieved by the wage earners. But with the growth of big business, it became less and less possible for large numbers of workers to alter their status in a significantly upward direction. As wage-earners grew to realize that the chances of their becoming proprietors were seriously reduced, a change in the climate of their ideas took place. It began to seem logical to them to support only those unions which acted in such a way as to provide their members with job security. Whereas formerly, wage-earners had derived a sense of security from the hopeful anticipation of eventually becoming proprietors, and so had joined in mass movements for the advancement of industrial democracy, by 1890, they found it increasingly necessary to belong to craft unions, which could obtain for them a security that would otherwise be denied them.

Throughout the latter part of the nineteenth century, strikes were launched against railroad companies and coal owners, with bitter strike-breaking, the use of private detectives (the Pinkertons) and with, at times, in Pennsylvania, West Virginià or Chicago, troops being used. Violence was common; some of it was a deliberate political tactic, as by the Industrial Workers of the World (IWW, the "Wobblies") in the rough mining camps of the West; to them capitalism could only be overthrown by violence and sabotage.

The Railroad Strike of 1877 broke out when firemen and other workers of the Baltimore & Ohio Railroad walked out in protest against a wage out. The strike spread throughout the East and Mid-West until roughly two-thirds of the nation's tracks were inactive. Rioting, arson, and looting convulsed Pittsburgh, Baltimore, and other cities. Federal troops were called in, and a number of people were killed before order was restored. This was the first industrial strike to approach national proportions. The Missouri Pacific Railroad Strike of 1885 began after two wage cuts had been imposed. In March, when the entire southwestern rail network controlled by Jay Gould had been paralyzed, the management agreed to restore the cuts. A few months later, the Knights of Labor struck the Wabash Railroad, another Gould line, and again won a victory. But in March 1886 a general strike against the Gould system – involving 60 thousand workers – was broken – a heavy blow to the Knights of Labor.

The McCormick Harvester Machine Company Strike in Chicago in 1886 was part of a campaign for the eight-hour day that involved about 80 thousand workers. The strike's chief historical importance rises from the fact that local anarchists staged a protest meeting in Chicago's Haymarket Square after a striker was killed by the police. When 180 policemen arrived to break up this meeting, someone threw a bomb. Seven policemen were killed, some apparently as a result of bullets fired into the crowd by their fellows. Eight anarchists were convicted of the crime on very flimsy evidence and four of them were hanged. Although the strikers were not involved in the bombing, the incident caused a reaction against them and against organized labor in general, and the eight-hour movement suffered a serious setback.

The Homestead Strike of 1892 involved the Carnegie Steel Company's plant in Homestead, Pennsylvania, a town on the Monongahela River near Pittsburgh. When the Amalgamated Association of Iron and Steel Workers struck Homestead, Henry Clay Frick, Andrew Carnegie's man in charge, determined – with Carnegie's full approval – to prove that "we had a right to employ whom we pleased and discharge whom we pleased." He engaged 300 Pinkerton guards to "protect" the plant. But when the guards arrived by barge from Pittsburgh on July 4, they were met by a hail of bullets from picketers. After a day-long battle, in which seven Pinkertons and two strikers were killed, the Pinkertons surrendered and were allowed to march off. Troops were then brought in, and by late July the plant was again operating, using non-union workers. The attempt of anarchist Alexander Berkman to assassinate Frick in his Pittsburgh office was a further blow to the union, though Berkman had no connection with it. In any case, the strike was crushed, and Homestead remained non-union for nearly half a century. A number of strikers were tried for murder, but acquitted.

The Pullman Strike of 1894 began as a walkout in the Pullman Palace car factory outside Chicago. Since some Pullman workers belonged to the newly formed American Railway Union, the union refused to move trains with Pullman cars, and this closed down most of the railroads leading in and out of Chicago. Trains were stopped and a certain amount of railroad property was damaged in resulting clashes. The fact that the mails were held up by the strike led to the issuance of a federal court injunction against the union on the ground that it was a combination in restraint of trade. (The union was willing to move mail trains if no Pullmans were attached, but the railroad operators would not agree to this.) When the union ignored the injunction, President Cleveland sent troops to Chicago to preserve order and move the mails. The strike then collapsed. Eugene V. Debs, president of the union, was sentenced to six months in jail for ignoring the court order.

The Anthracite Coal Strike of 1902 was called by John Mitchell, head of the United Mine Workers, in an effort to obtain recognition of the union by the mine companies, most of which were owned by railroads. A strike two years earlier had resulted in a 10 percent wage increase, but not in recognition of the union. This walkout began in June and dragged on throughout the summer and early fall. The strikers won much public support by avoiding violence and by offering to submit the dispute to arbitration, a proposal the operators rejected. With coal in short supply and winter approaching, President Theodore Roosevelt summoned both sides to Washington and sought to force a settlement. When the operators refused even to discuss the issue with the union, Roosevelt announced that he would send in troops to mine the coal. The operators then agreed to abide by the determination of a Presidential Commission, and the strike ended. The Commission granted the miners a wage increase, but did not compel the operators to recognize the United Mine Workers.

The union movement, and labor in general, made important gains during World War I, and when the war ended there were many strikes as workers sought to preserve these gains during a period of inflation. In the steel industry, largely unorganized since the time of the Homestead Strike, the AFL created a special committee in an effort to unionize the workforce. When the steel companies, led by Elbert H. Gary of US Steel, refused to recognize the union, engage in collective bargaining, and put an end to the twelve-hour day, the committee called a strike. About 350,000 workers walked out. The strike was a failure, however. State and federal troops were called in and the companies hired strikebreakers. Hysteria over Communist revolutions was at its height, and public opinion was much influenced by the fact that the most important strike leader, William Z. Foster, was an avowed revolutionary, head of the Syndicalist League of North America. Early in January 1920, the committee called off the strike without obtaining any concessions from management.

Another of the many strikes of the postwar period was the Boston Police Strike of 1919. When the Boston police commissioner, Edwin Curtis, discharged 19 officers who were active in the local policemen's union, more than two-thirds of the 1,500-man force walked out. The result was widespread looting and other unlawful activity in the city. Curtis refused to arbitrate the dispute, fired the strikers, and began recruiting a new force. Though he had done nothing to prevent the strike or to negotiate a settlement, Governor Calvin Coolidge then called out the state militia and announced: "There is no right to strike against the public safety by anybody, anywhere, any time." The largely undeserved praise that Coolidge received for having broken the strike led to his choice as Harding's running mate at the 1920 Republican National Convention.

The West was equally prone to violence: considering the atrocious living and working conditions that the lumber men were subjected to, one may wonder why the discontent had not broken out earlier. But the migratory character of the industry meant that lumber companies had always been able to leave their problems behind and move to another area; the lumber man too, when he objected to the working conditions, would take his bedding and his gear and move on. Such a highly migratory labor force could not form a conventional union. However, the Far West was the end of the road for both the industry and the lumber men, and the discontent finally found its organizational outlet in the Industrial Workers of the World, founded in 1905.

One can, perhaps, describe the members of this union – "Wobblies", as they came to be called – as a group of young radicals. The intellectuals in Chicago and New York who had founded the organization looked upon it as comprising a heterogeneous group of intellectual radicals, held together by their common disenchantment with the American Federation of Labor. If we look at it from the West and follow its development on this coast, then the organization seems to be, in essence, a fraternity of lumberjacks: a group of lumberjacks who had come together not to discuss the finer points of some sophisticated socialist idea, but to demand a better life for workers. Considering the character of the lumber men – their recklessness, for example – it is not surprising that the IWW was an activist union. It was this reckless activism that set the IWW apart from all other unions in the US.

The influence of the Eastern theorists and intellectuals declined, and the IWW became essentially a nonpolitical organization. It lost some of the insights of European socialism, and espoused an oversimplified, apolitical program which called for a society that would fulfill basic human needs. Slogans like "One Big Union" kept the Wobblies spiritually united, and they hoped that through the general strike they would achieve their goals. But the slogans remained only slogans, because they knew only how to fight well, and were never much interested in the intricacies of maintaining a union, nor did they ever develop an effective program.

The Wobblies were straightforward activists who disliked and shunned theory. Often their public pronouncements would be in sharp contrast to their actions. Whereas in the lumber camps they advocated sabotage, publicly they would admit only of supporting "soldiering on the job," i.e. passive resistance. Soldiering, of course, existed: men tried their best to accomplish as little as possible in the greatest amount of time; they would suddenly become too stupid to understand the simplest order. The actions advocated in the IWW's pamphlets were nothing more than pranks to play on the boss.

The IWW was not a highly structured political organization. It was held together not by a program but by a mystique. It is best expressed, perhaps, in its songs. The IWW was known as a singing organization, and the *IWW Song Book* went into its twenty-eighth edition in 1945. "The Preacher and the Slave," by Joe Hill, was one of the favorites:

Long have preachers come out every night,
Try to tell you what's wrong and what's right.
But when you ask how about something to eat,
They will answer with voices too sweet:
"You'll eat bye and bye in that glorious land above the sky.
Work and pray, live on hay, you'll get pie in the sky when you die."

Such bitter humor occurs often in their songs; they were cynical about American ideals. Many of the verses were sung to the melodies of Christian hymns. They expressed their antimilitarism and cynical view of US society in: "Onward Christian soldiers, at them tear and smite,/That the gentle Jesus bless your dynamite."

The Wobblies were different from other unionists. Their bitter humor, cynicism, and recklessness, and the great spirit they showed in their singing all tended to set them apart. Their IWW halls were also different from any ordinary union hall. At one time these could be found in every major city in the West. These halls were, for the Wobblies, a substitute home, a post office, a social club, and a lounge. They were usually located near the main railyards exchange (which was usually in the cheapest part of town), since most of the Wobblies were continually on the move. Inside, one might have been surprised to find a piano and a small library. They were not intellectuals, but reading took up much of their time. Many Wobblies would decide which hall to spend the winter in on the basis of the quality of the library.

Even though the IWW was not a sophisticated political organization, it had great cohesiveness, because (in addition to fulfilling an economic function) it met emotional and psychological needs. The emotional function explains the undying loyalty that the union commanded from so many of its members. Although this cohesiveness gave the union its appeal and strength, it proved, in the end, to be also its undoing. As modern technology was introduced into the lumber industry, it became possible for ordinary laborers to do the work of skilled lumberjacks. The lumber industry became more stable, and lumber camps became communities with family dwellings. Both developments brought more and more ordinary laborers and family men into the industry – men whom the Wobblies had always looked upon with disdain. They refused to associate with them, and hence the IWW, instead of becoming the envisioned "One Big Union," became a very small union.

The ordinary union emphasized practical and tangible benefits. It did not stress the finer points of idealism or men's emotions, but rather the importance of the few pennies more or the longer vacation it was able to obtain through bargaining. If some Wobblies tried to change the IWW into a union with more practical goals, they would be accused of selling out the birth right of the IWW for some mere economic betterment. The Wobblies, in the face of the growing necessity to change their union, became even more determined to maintain the kind of organization they had envisioned – to remain the ideal union, regardless of how impractical it was. This insistence only increased the IWW's isolation and exclusiveness, as more and more men joined ordinary unions. That the Wobblies did not see that a solution could be found through an analysis of their situation, but sought it in still more uncompromising legendary exploits should not, then, be considered as a sign of their strength, but of their weakness.

Under their system, any Wobbly could be a full-time organiser and yet remain on the job as a lumberjack. He would supply himself with membership cards and spread the IWW gospel as he moved from job to job. He would recruit new members, collect dues, keep records, and establish an IWW headquarters at each new job site. This system made it possible for the IWW to spread its message into even the most remote camps, and it did make it influential. The system, however, also brought the IWW into conflict with, and alienated it from, other unions, because the job delegate would often show up and begin activities in an area where a union had already been established.

The strikes that the IWW conducted were usually unsuccessful, and, with two or three major exceptions, were small and brief. The IWW founded its reputation less on ordinary union activities – on the bargaining process – than on its guerrilla tactics: on the often-reported gun battles with vigilantes, on court trials, on street oratory, and on fracases with the police.

One tactic that was very successful in its early stages was the free-speech fight. The Wobblies would converge on a town that prohibited street meetings and begin to give speeches, allowing themselves to be arrested and going to jail willingly. The jails, however, would soon be overflowing, and there would still be Wobblies giving speeches. The authorities discovered not only that they did not have enough space for the other Wobblies, but also that they could not, for any length of time, afford to provide room and board to the many Wobblies they had imprisoned. By this tactic the Wobblies hoped to impress the citizens with their solidarity and willingness to fight for constitutional ideals. They had their first spectacular success with this tactic in Spokane in 1909. Other towns, however, soon learned their lesson, and would meet the invading Wobblies with a small army of vigilantes or deputies. It is not surprising that, as battles ensued, most Americans began to see the IWW as an internal enemy, doing its best to undermine the foundations of American society.

In 1917 the IWW suddenly found itself leading a major strike, which had broken out not so much because of agitation by the IWW as because of the atrocious working conditions in the lumber industry. Although to many Wobblies the strike came as a pleasant surprise, it turned out to be a disaster for the IWW.

There were several elements in the situation that prevented a successful strike. The employers in the lumber industry were adamantly opposed to any form of unionism. Many of them had started from the bottom of the industry; they had worked on the logging crews and had endured the same working conditions. So the strike did not break out because the employers did not speak the same language as the workers and did not understand what it meant to work under such conditions; it broke out precisely because they did. The employers considered their own experience and endurance to be an example of how to achieve success; they would, therefore, almost sanctify the miserable working conditions. As one employer said: "I have lived in the woods, slept on the ground ... blistered my hands, worked the 16 hours a day and have worked my way out of it into something better. Why should a husky man make such a holler about the working conditions?"

Also, the strike coincided with US entry into World War I. Lumber, especially spruce, was needed for the war. Consequently, the demand for an eight hour day and the strike which brought the production of spruce to a standstill became national concerns. State governments, as well as the federal government, intervened and the IWW had little chance to capitalize on its leadership of the strike. The Wobblies found no other alternative but to return to the job and end the formal strike.

The Wobblies went back to work, but they explained that they had not given up – that they were "taking the strike to the job." They continued soldiering on the job and acted as if the demands of the strike had been met; they would cease work after eight hours and return to camp. Many Wobblies were fired, but they would simply take their gear and move on to the next camp, which was in need of workers, since it too had fired several. These methods were effective until the War Department sent army officers into the Pacific Northwest. They soon organized a soldierlike union called the Loyal Legion of Loggers and Lumbermen (the Four L, as the Wobblies called it), which managed to get the industry going again.

The IWW was the only labor union in the US that formally opposed the war, but in its actions it tended simply to ignore it. The Wobblies did not consider it to be their concern, and, in any case, they disliked organized antiwar activities because these involved politics, which to them was distasteful. This attitude naturally fostered the impression that the IWW was an internal enemy, and it was considered especially dangerous during the war. Rumors soon spread that the Wobblies were allies of the Kaiser, and that they received financial aid from the Imperial German government. Americans have always been suspicious of socialism; it is not surprising that Samuel Gompers, leader of the American Federation of Labor, charged that Bismarck had fostered the international socialist movement to prepare the world for German conquest.

A "Red scare" set in after the Russian Revolution of 1917, and since the Wobblies always stood up and fought for their socialist ideas, they bore the brunt of the US reaction. Under the espionage and sedition laws of 1917 and 1918, the Wobblies were arrested *en masse* and thrown into jail. Many states adopted criminal syndicalism laws that made the IWW illegal and drove it underground, and scores of Wobblies became victims of vigilante mobs. The Centralia Armistice Day riot, in Centralia, Washington, in 1919, is perhaps the best example of the degree to which national fury descended upon them.

With the Russian Revolution, the Communists proved that the "great revolution," about which the Wobblies had at times spoken, had been possible to accomplish. The radical movement in the rest of the world gained a new focus. The glamor of the Communist achievement made the few successes that the Wobblies had been able to achieve seem insignificant. Many Wobblies joined the Communists. When, in the late 1920s, the IWW made its final decision not to join the Communist party, many Wobblies who had been able to be Communists as well were faced with a difficult choice, and many chose Communism. The Wobblies became bitter enemies of the Communist party, and much of their energy was devoted to quarrels with the Communists.

Because the IWW disdained the whole philosophy of job unionism and abhorred the concept of the business union, it did not profit from the policies of the New Deal – from the collective bargaining laws that were enacted. The IWW shrank to insignificance. During World War II, there were reports of renewed activity in the mining regions of the West and on the waterfronts of New Orleans, San Francisco, and New York, but this revival was more imaginary than real, and today the IWW is only a living legend.

The legend is, however, instructive. It is the story of downtrodden laborers; it makes us realize that there was a time in our history when men had to use force in an attempt to gain that measure of dignity that we now think the right of all men.

6 MUCKRAKERS AND ANARCHISTS

It was the concentration in the cities of industrial workers, often recent immigrants unfamiliar with American life, that made reform both urgent and possible. The slums bred crime and disease, which was no respecter of persons or of sensitiveness. They were marked by fire-trap tenements and poor sanitation, by gambling, alcoholism, and prostitution (10,000 professional prostitutes in Chicago in 1908). In almost all the cities there was corruption and bossism, not least in Chicago, St Louis, and Pittsburg; the scale and sources of it were brilliantly etched by Lincoln Steffens in his *The Shame of the Cities* (1904). But the cities also made possible mass organization and a public education system, labor unions and social service settlements like Hull House, Chicago, Henry Street, New York, or Andover House in Boston; they bred – even if they were rare animals – reform mayors like "Golden Rule" Jones in Toledo and Tom Johnson in Cleveland.

The era of big business was quickly followed by the era of the Muckraker. The Muckraking movement received its name from Roosevelt in 1906, in his attack upon allegedly biased and sweeping charges of corruption in politics and business. (The term originally alluded to a character in *Pilgrim's Progress*, who was so intent upon raking up muck that he could not see a celestial crown held over him.) The Muckraking movement in the US began in 1902 and in four years had spread throughout the nation. It reached another climax in 1911, but ended as a movement with America's entry into World War I. *The Arena* a dignified journal of protest, was the precursor of many popular magazines that became the medium for the exposure of unscrupulous methods and motives in private business and in city, state, and national government. *Everybody's*, *McClure's*, *The Independent*, *Collier's*, and the *Cosmopolitan* were the leading periodicals devoted to the movement. The magazines campaigned against the trusts. Steffens examined civic misgovernment, Ida Tarbell exposed the ethics of the oil industry, and Upton Sinclair's *The Jungle* (1906), an indictment of the meat packing industry, led to the passage of the Pure Food and Drugs Act of 1906. Theodore Dreiser, in *The Financier* (1912) and *The Titan* (1914), attacked the role of finance capital in big business. In an age of a new and strident popular press, the American people were weaned for a decade on a rich diet of scandal, exposure, and corruption. From it came the Progressive Movement, and a great crusader for reform in Robert La Follette, governor of Wisconsin (1900–6) and from 1906 to 1924 Senator for Wisconsin, which he made the prototype state for the democratic idea. And by 1901, with Theodore Roosevelt as President, there was in the White House at long last a crusader on the people's side.

A considerable literature of social protest had been growing for many years, however. In 1879 Henry George published *Progress and Poverty*. A San Francisco newspaperman, he was increasingly disturbed by the enormous profits that reached land speculators simply by their holding property as the population remorselessly rose – and the consequent ever-widening gap between rich and poor. His demand was for a property tax, a tax on "unearned income" that came from the ownership of land. It would make all other forms of taxation unnecessary and provide enough money to build new and better schools, museums, and other valuable public institutions. *Progress and Poverty* attracted wide attention and "single tax" clubs sprang up all over the nation, though of course such a tax was never enacted.

Thorstein Veblen's *The Theory of the Leisure Class* (1899) was an even more savage assault on the acquisitive character of American society than Henry George's. Veblen, the son of Norwegian immigrants, argued that Americans tended slavishly to ape the standards and values of the wealthy. He coined the term "conspicuous consumption" and heaped scorn on those who practiced it. He taught at Stanford and at the New School for Social Research in New York. *Wealth Against Commonwealth* (1894) by Henry Demarest Lloyd, a powerful, if somewhat exaggerated, attack on the Standard Oil monopoly, attracted wide attention even earlier than Ida Tarbell's indictment of its ethics. Besides denouncing Standard's business practices – Lloyd quipped that the trust did everything to the Pennsylvania legislature except refine it – he denounced *laissez-faire* economics and the application of Darwinian ideas about the survival of the fittest to social affairs. As an activist he opposed Tammany, and as a lawyer he defended the men convicted in the Haymarket Riot and the socialist Eugene Debs in the Pullman strike.

In the field of education, the philosopher John Dewey in *The School and Society* (1899) developed the basic ideas of what was later to be known as "progressive" education. Schools should build character and train children to be good citizens, not merely provide them with new knowledge. They should make use of the child's curiosity, imagination, and past experience, not rely on discipline and rote memory to teach.

Edward Bellamy's *Looking Backward 2000–1887* (1888) met with immense popularity, which led to the founding of Bellamy clubs and a Nationalist party. *Equality* (1897), a sequel, is more a tract than a novel. Conceived as a "fairy tale of social felicity," the book describes a future social and economic order through the narrative of Julian West, a young Bostonian, who enters a hypnotic sleep in 1887, and is revived 113 years later in the changed city. He falls in love with Edith Leete, a descendant of his former fiancée, and through her father, a physician, learns of the scientific and social developments that have taken place. In contrast with the squalor of the slums and the injustices and inequalities of the earlier time, he finds an America in which the business monopolies have evolved to become "The Great Trust," economic chaos having been replaced by a democratic form of state capitalism. Private enterprise has disappeared, each citizen is both an employee and a member of the state, and the collective organization of wealth and industry has eradicated crime, poverty, advertising, warfare, and many diseases. The cultural level of the people has consequently risen, and Dr Leete ascribes these changes to the spread of social intelligence and social ethics among a good people formerly victimized by an evil system.

None of these quite matched in contemporary effect Lincoln Steffens's writings in *McClure's* and other magazines, which made him a leading Muckraker. His analysis of political corruption and of the alliance between business and politics was published in book form in *The Shame of the Cities* in 1904, and in *The Struggle for Self-Government* in 1906. He tells the story in crisp and vivid detail in his *Autobiography* (1931).

H. L. Mencken was equally critical. While he viewed with alarm the provincial hatred of the city, his own comment on the metropolis was scarcely favourable. "During many a single week, I daresay, more money is spent in New York upon useless and evil things than would suffice to run the kingdom of Denmark for a year":

All the colossal accumulated wealth of the United States, the greatest robber nation in history, tends to force itself at least once a year through the narrow neck of the Manhattan funnel. To that harsh island come all the thieves of the Republic with their loot – bankers from the fat lands of the Middle West, lumbermen from the Northwestern coasts, mine owners from the mountains, oil speculators from Texas and Oklahoma, cotton-mill sweaters from the South, steel magnates and manufacturers from the Black Country, blacklegs and exploiters without end – all laden with cash, all eager to spend it, all easy marks for the town rogues and panders ... What town in Christendom has ever supported so many houses of entertainment, so many mimes and mountebanks, so many sharpers and coney-catchers ... so many miscellaneous servants to idleness and debauchery?[13]

Perhaps the most influential of all was *The Jungle* (1906) by Upton Sinclair. Few novels have had an impact on public policy even approaching that of this book. Sinclair's story of the life of a Chicago stockyard worker described both the filthy conditions under which cattle were slaughtered and the ways in which the meat packers exploited their workers. A strike of the workers had been crushed in 1904 and Sinclair had gone to Chicago to study their surroundings, living in their houses, hearing their stories, taking notes about their work and the dumps of city garbage that lay festering around them. In the stockyards the races had displaced one another, first the Germans, then the Irish, the Bohemians, the Poles, the Lithuanians, the Slovaks, largely misled by agents of the packers, who had found them in their villages and promised them unheard-of wages to lure them over. Ignorant, and stunted by European tyranny, only to be utterly destroyed by American indifference, they were swindled by house agents, political bosses who played havoc with their womenfolk, and judges who refused to recognize their rights. No one either knew or cared when their babies were drowned in the stinking green water that lay in puddles about their wretched shacks, when their daughters were forced into prostitution, when their sons fell into boiling vats because the employers had provided no safety devices. The government inspectors were commonly bribed to look the other way when rotten meat was doctored and sold with the rest.

The novel was a bestseller. President Theodore Roosevelt reacted to it by setting in motion a government investigation that led to federal meat inspection and the passage of the Pure Food and Drugs Act of 1906. Later, as a Democrat in name but a socialist by

[13] H. L. Menaken, *The American Dictionary* (1936 edn).

conviction, Sinclair ran for the governorship of California, leading the organization he labelled EPIC (End Poverty in California). He wrote over 100 books, some of which won Pulitzer prizes. Jack London described *The Jungle* as the *Uncle Tom's Cabin* of wage-slavery. Van Wyck Brooks describes Sinclair in lyrical terms:

> This was the chief concern, for instance, of the young Baltimorean Upton Sinclair, the child of a run-down Southern family who had been struck, like Dreiser, by the contrast of wealth and poverty in the American scene. He was one of those hypercompassionate men who cannot sleep at night when they think of ten-year-old children working in mills and who, convinced that society is ruled by organized greed, feel that the burden of changing it rests upon them. There were many who had felt this in Brook Farm days and who never lost hope of abolishing the evils of the world – who had even succeeded in abolishing a few of them, at least – and Sinclair, albeit a Southerner, was a reincarnation of these Yankees of old, tirelessly sanguine as they were and eager to be useful. A Puritan in grain, he hated self-indulgence and shared the contempt of Savonarola for the "little shining stones" with which rich women "deck their bodies," while, speaking of wine as a kind of "red chemical," he could not see a man playing golf – "hitting little balls around a field" – without thinking of peasants starving in a famine on the Volga. He was a born promoter of isms, a teetotaller whose father had drunk too much and who ate raw food himself or none at all, a pacifist, a non-smoker, a physical-culture enthusiast, and a "conscientious objector to capitalism". By preference he lived in Single-tax colonies in Alabama or Delaware, except when he lived alone in a hut in the woods, and he always felt that by starting a magazine, writing a novel, or winning a strike he might change the world into what it ought to be.[14]

There was also – part cause, part legacy of the Haymarket Riot of 1886 and of the assassination of President McKinley in 1901 by an anarchist – a distinct anarchist thread weaving through these stormy times for all who worked in cities and in industry. By law, anarchists were not permitted as immigrants, but that did not stop the doctrine spreading.

Russian-born Emma Goldman (1869–1940) came to the US in 1886. Her inflammatory speeches led to riots and to her imprisonment in 1893. She edited the anarchist journal *Mother Earth* in collaboration with Alexander Berkman (1870–1936), the anarchist who attempted to assassinate the industrialist Henry C. Frick. Imprisoned in 1916 for publicly advocating birth control, and again

[14] Van Wyck Brooks, *The Confident Years 1885–1918* (London, Dent, 1937), p. 220.

for obstructing the draft (1917), she was deported to Russia in 1919 but left there two years later because she objected to Bolshevism. A woman without a country during the 1920s, she was permitted to return to the US in 1934 on a 90-day visa. In 1936 she published her autobiography. Unable to resist the ferment of revolution, she went to Spain during its years of civil war (1936–9). She died in Toronto, Canada.

Alexander Berkman was the perpetrator of the first *attentat*, or terrorist act, in America, committed in open defiance of all laws and restrictions. "A revolutionist," as he said, "first" and only "a man afterwards," he made an attempt on the life of the Pittsburgh magnate who had crushed the steel workers' union shortly before, fully persuaded that his victim was as much an enemy of the people as any of the classic tyrannicides of antique times. Theodore Dreiser had seen Pittsburgh as the dividing point between the humane old America and the industrialized nation, but there was only one America for immigrants like Berkman, for whom Pittsburgh struck the "key-note of the great republic." Cold and hard as the steel it produced, it dominated all chords, he felt, "sacrificing harmony to noise, beauty to bulk," and, convinced by his philosophy that the law was a "a conspiracy of rulers and priests against the workers, to continue their subjugation," he followed the logic of his own revolutionary ethics.

The anarchist movement was a cult that had long flourished in tsarist Russia, where remedial democratic measures could never have been hoped for, and the immigrant anarchists were still fighting the tyranny of Russia, unchanged themselves, on a totally different soil. They opposed the state on principle at a moment when the state was becoming a powerful instrument of the exploited masses, and they insisted that all laws were unjust when there was nothing but the law with which to oppose the oppression of the weak by the strong. But in certain ways Berkman was admirable for all his delusions. Only a high-minded man could have written his *Prison Memoirs of an Anarchist*, a man without guile who was shocked in prison by every encounter with criminal types and could scarcely believe at first in the existence of baseness. It was this in part that distinguished the book, with the writer's perception of human worth under the destructive conditions of existence in the cell-house that tended to drive them all into perversion or madness. There was much graphic skill as well in Berkman's scenes of prison life; the basket-cell, the solitary, the shops, the dungeon, the misery and dread in which the days went by, the shadow-like giant figures in the corridors at night.

7 TEXAS: THE RELUCTANT EMPIRE

Capital was the most needed commodity on the American frontier in the late nineteenth century, to buy land, to expand cities, to open new agriculture, to build homes, to start or develop businesses, to stock ranches, to buy farm equipment. And capital was in short supply. Of the money westerners were able to secure, substantial sums came from the wallets of Scots investors.

In *Scottish Capital on the American Credit Frontier*, W. G. Kerr gives the reader a brief look at the background for British and Scottish investment in the American West. Then he studies the financiers, mostly Scots, who recognized and took advantage of the frontier's urgent need for money; he analyzes the character and the policies of the men who guided the early mortgage companies. Finally, using Texas as a representative location, he examines three companies whose impact on that state's development was almost unmeasurable: the Scottish-controlled Texas Land and Mortgage Company (the Texas specialist among mortgage companies); the Scottish American Mortgage Company and the Alliance Trust Company, both giant firms whose activities spread across almost the whole Western frontier and the redeveloping South, and whose investments in Texas were massive and vital. An early Texan comment about the Texas Land and Mortgage Company could be echoed regarding almost any county or city in Texas:

> to it [the mortgage company] is due the credit, in a large part, for the present agricultural development of Dallas County lands. During the first twenty years of its existence the Company loaned thousands of dollars to citizens of Dallas for building purposes and in this way greatly aided the development of this city.

Without the money which such firms provided, Texan economic history would have been a drastically different story. Furthermore, not only were these Scottish mortgage companies invaluable to the pioneer Texans who borrowed their money, but they proved highly profitable investments for the pioneering Scots who provided that cash.[15]

By the mid-1880s, British ranching interests spread from the Montana and Wyoming ranches south to the breeding lands of Texas.

[15] W. G. Kerr, *Scottish Capital on the American Credit Frontier* (Texas State Historical Association, Austin, 1976).

Scottish and English companies poured millions of pounds into cattle ranches and land, contributing heavily to the development not only of Texas but of the West in general. In most cases these investments failed because of distance, weather conditions, and falling markets, and, most important, because the British investor knew nothing about ranching on the Western plains. Such was not the case with Scottish mortgage companies organized to do business in Texas, the South, the Mid-West, the Pacific Northwest, and the plains states. The directors of these companies knew their business and their investments prospered.

Texas, "The Reluctant Empire," all 267,339 square miles of it, did not emerge shyly; it splashed into the international scene. Unlike many areas in the United States which sent people scurrying for their atlases in order to identify them, Texas from the beginning was known. The struggle for independence from Mexico, followed by the Anglo-French rivalry for diplomatic supremacy in Texas during the days of the Republic, gave Texas an advance billing, if not financially, certainly romantically, in the imagination not just of the eastern United States, but of Britain too. From the very beginning everything was big about Texas – and it was not a native Texan or American who helped create this image. It was Scotland, and its investors.[16]

Nobody put it better than W. A. Baillie-Grohman, a British-traveller, who commented:

> Cowboys can be divided into two classes: those hailing from the Lone Star State, Texas, the others recruited either from Eastern States ... or from the Pacific slopes. ... the Texans are, as far as true cowboyship goes, unrivalled: the best riders, hardy and born to the business; the only drawback being their wild reputation. The others are less able but more orderly men. The bad name of Texans arises mostly from their excitable

[16] W. Turrentine Jackson, "British interests in the range cattle industry," in M. Frink, W. T. Jackson, and A. W. Spring, *When Grass Was King* (Boulder, Colo. 1956), pp. 135–322 (Jackson's monograph, as well as the rest of the book, is most useful); Morton Rothstein, "A British firm on the American West Coast, 1869–1914," *Business History Review*, 37 (1963), pp. 392–415; Richard Graham, "The investment boom in British-Texan cattle companies, 1880–1885," ibid., 34 (1960), pp. 421–45; W. G. Kerr, "Scotland and the Texas mortgage business," *Economic History Review*, 38 (1965), pp. 53–71; Gene M. Gressley, "Broker to the British: Francis Smith and Company," *Southwestern Historical Quarterly*, 71 (1967), pp. 7–25; Gene M. Gressley, *Bankers and Cattlemen* (New York, Knopf, 1966), pp. 134, 261, and *passim*; W. Turrentine Jackson, *The Enterprising Scot: Investors in the American West after 1873* (Edinburgh, Edinburgh University Press, 1968).

tempers, and the fact that they are mostly "on the shoot" (that is, very free in the use of their revolvers.)[17]

[17] W. A. Baillie-Grohman, *Camps in the Rockies* (London, 1882), pp. 344–5; idem, "Cattle ranches in the Far West," *Fortnightly Review*, 34 (1880), p. 447.

4

The Presidency in the Gilded Age

1 INTRODUCTION

The years after the Civil War witnessed an absence of leadership from the White House. No one man held the office long enough to make much impact. Major questions – tariffs, gold versus silver as currency, the plight of distant regions like the South and the West – were debated but without consensus emerging; and no permanent solution was found for them. And when markets were found abroad and imperialism was born as a result, it too fostered contentions before it bred leadership and a philosophy of its own.

Only one Democrat occupied the White House in the 47 years from Appomattox to Woodrow Wilson – Grover Cleveland – against nine Republicans. More than this, there was a high casualty rate; indeed, it is surprising that there were so many volunteers for the office. But then most of the candidates were veterans: soldiers were ready for the fray, now that many of them saw politics as but a continuation and consequence of the War Between the States. The bulk of the people – farmers, laboring men, shopkeepers, white-collar workers – distributed their ballots fairly evenly between the two parties in most elections; the balance of political power after 1876 was almost perfect. Between 1856 and 1912 the Democrats elected a President only twice (1884 and 1892), but most of the contests were extremely close. Majorities in both the Senate and the House fluctuated back and forth continually. Between 1876 and 1896, the "dominant" Republican party controlled both houses of Congress and the Presidency at the same time for only one two-year period.

The presidency in these years was, as it still is, a high-risk vocation. Three men have been assassinated; attempts were made to kill both FDR and Ronald Reagan; Gerald Ford was attacked twice. Moreover, if there is a "curse" on the Kennedys, it is comparable to that on Lincoln. Abraham Lincoln's oldest son Robert was in Washington the night his father was shot, and was summoned to the house opposite Ford's Theater, where the President lay dying. In 1881, as Secretary of war in President Garfield's cabinet, he went to the station to meet the President, moments after his assassination. In September 1901 he was invited to the Pan-American Exposition in Buffalo to meet President McKinley; he arrived just after McKinley's murder by Leon Czolgosz.

The Presidents were not great men in the period between Lincoln's assassination in 1865, the murder of President Garfield in July 1881, and that of President McKinley in 1901. It was the age of the flaunting of the "bloody shirt," when Northerners had the whip hand, and Radical Reconstructionists were in political control of Congress and the country, North and occupied South. Presidential elections were won almost uniformly by Republicans: General Ulysses Grant in 1868 and 1872, Rutherford Hayes in 1876, James A. Garfield in 1880. Although Grover Cleveland, a Democrat, won the presidency in 1884, he lost in the Electoral College (168 to 233) in 1888 to Benjamin Harrison, the Republican. Although in 1892 Cleveland won the majority of popular votes (5,556,918 to 5,176,108), and more decisively in the Electoral College, to return to the White House, it was his second but final term. The Republican William McKinley triumphed both in 1896 and in 1900.

One topic obsessed the politicians in these years. That was the "bloody shirt," which Paul H. Buck has called "possibly the greatest weapon any American party ever possessed." The term, which became part of the language after a Massachusetts Congressman had dramatically displayed to his colleagues in the House the blood-stained shirt of an Ohio carpetbagger who had been flogged by terrorists in Mississippi, referred to the tactic of reminding the electorate of the Northern states that the men who had taken the South out of the Union and precipitated the Civil War had been Democrats, and that they and their descendants were still Democrats. Should their party regain power, former rebels would run the government and undo all the work accomplished at such sacrifice during the war. "Every man that endeavored to tear down the old flag," a Republican orator proclaimed in 1876, "was a Democrat. Every man that tried to destroy this nation was a Democrat. ... The man that assassinated Abraham Lincoln was a Democrat. ... Soldiers, every scar you have on your heroic bodies was given you by a Democrat." Naturally every scoundrel or incompetent who sought office under the Republican banner waved the bloody shirt in order to divert the attention of Northern voters from his own shortcomings, but the technique worked so well that many decent candidates could not resist the temptation to employ it in close races. Nothing, of course, so effectively obscured the real issues of the day.

2 ULYSSES S. GRANT

The victorious Northern commander Ulysses S. Grant (1822–1885) won a decisive victory in the presidential contest in 1868. He was a Republican, but the convention that nominated him was Radical in character; it championed a vigorous Reconstruction policy in the prostrate South, and was a defender of Northern banking, manufacturing, and railroad interests against the agricultural leaders of the West and South. In the electoral college Grant defeated the Democratic candidate Horatio Seymour by 214 to 80 votes, but his 300,000 popular majority was made possible only by the 650,000 black votes cast for him in a South under military control. In fact the white voters in the reunited nation had not endorsed the Radical Republican program.

Grant's two administrations (1869–77) were marred by indecisive leadership, by an inconsistent policy on Southern Reconstruction, and by massive corruption. Coupled with a severe economic depression that began in 1873, administration scandals cost Grant much of his popularity. Nonetheless, his presidency did have some solid accomplishments. The Treaty of Washington in 1872 resolved a major dispute with Great Britain over damages inflicted on American shipping by Confederate raiders built in British shipyards during the Civil War. The Enforcement Acts of 1870–1 broke the power of the Ku Klux Klan in the Reconstruction South, and the Civil Rights Act of 1875 marked an unprecedented attempt to extend federal protection of black civil rights to areas of public accommodations.

After returning to the United States from a world tour in the late 1870s, Grant went bankrupt as a result of foolish investments in the fraudulent banking firm of Grant & Ward. Though once again a failure in civilian life, Grant did much to redeem his place in history by writing his *Personal Memoirs*. Finished just before his death from throat cancer in 1885, his memoirs stand as one of the clearest and most powerful military narratives ever written.

3 RUTHERFORD B. HAYES

Rutherford B. Hayes (1822–1893), President from 1877 to 1881, came to office with a distinguished record. Born in Delaware, Ohio, in 1822, he attended Kenyon College and the Harvard Law School before settling down to practice in Cincinnati. Although he had a wife and family to support, he volunteered for service within weeks after the first shell fell on Fort Sumter. "This is a just and necessary war," he wrote in his diary, "I would prefer to go into it if I knew I was to die ... than to live through and after it without taking any part."

Hayes fought bravely, even recklessly, through nearly four years of war. He was wounded at South Mountain, on the eve of Antietam, and later served under Sheridan in the Shenandoah Valley campaign of 1864. Entering the army as a major, he emerged a major-general. In 1864 he was elected to Congress; four years later he became governor of Ohio, serving three terms altogether. The Republicans nominated him for President in 1876 because of his reputation for honesty and moderation and his war record; his election, made possible by the Compromise of 1877, seemed at last to presage an era of sectional harmony and political probity.

Hayes was a long-faced man with deep-set blue eyes and a full beard. Outwardly he had a sunny disposition, inwardly, in his own words, he was sometimes "nervous to the point of disaster." Despite his geniality, he was utterly without political glamour. Always abstemious, as President he became a total abstainer and refused even to serve wine at state dinners. Politically temperate and cautious, he had never been a vigorous waver of the bloody shirt, although in the heat of a hard campaign he was not above urging others to stress the dangers of "rebel rule" should the Democrats win. He tended to play down the tariff issue whenever possible, favoring protection in principle but refusing to become a mere spokesman for local business interests. On the money question he was conservative. He cheerfully approved the resumption of gold payments in 1879 and vetoed bills to expand the currency by coining silver. He accounted himself a civil service reformer, appointing Carl Schurz, a leader of the movement and a "48er German" to his Cabinet. He opposed the collection of political contributions from federal officeholders and issued an order forbidding them "to take part in the management of political organizations, caucuses, conventions, or election campaigns."

As President he saw himself more as a caretaker than a leader, and felt that Congress should assume the main responsibility for settling national problems. He hated having constantly to make decisions on controversial questions. As we have seen, he complained about the South's failure to treat its black population decently after the withdrawal of federal troops, but he took no action.

In the eyes of his contemporaries his administration was a failure. Neither he nor they seriously considered him for a second term. "I am not liked as President," he confessed to his diary, and the Republican minority leader of the House admitted that the President was "almost without a friend" in Congress.

4 JAMES A. GARFIELD

Hayes's successor, James A. Garfield (1831–1881), was cut down by an assassin's bullet only four months after his inauguration. Even in that short time, however, his ineffectiveness had been clearly demonstrated. Garfield grew up in poverty on an Ohio farm. He was only 29 when the Civil War broke out, but he helped organize a volunteer regiment and soon proved himself both a fine disciplinarian and an excellent battlefield commander despite his inexperience. He fought at Shiloh and later at Chickamauga, where he was General Rosecrans's chief of staff. He rose in two years from lieutenant-colonel to major-general. Then, in 1863, he won a seat in Congress, where his oratorical and managerial skills soon brought him to prominence in the affairs of the Republican party.

Garfield was a big broad-shouldered man, balding, with sharp eyes, an aquiline nose, and a thick, full beard. Studious, industrious, with a wide-ranging, well-stocked mind, he was called by one friend "the ideal self-made man." His one great weakness was indecisiveness – what another of his admirers described as a "want of certainty" and a "deference for other men's opinions." As President Hayes put it, Garfield "could not face a frowning world. ... His course at various times when trouble came betrayed weakness." "The scholarship of modern times," he said in 1870, "is ... leading in the direction of what is called free trade." Nevertheless, he would not sacrifice the interests of Ohio manufacturers for a mere principle. "I shall not admit to a considerable reduction of a few leading articles in which my constituents are deeply interested when many others of a similar character are left untouched," he declared. Similarly, though eager to improve the efficiency of the government and resentful of the "intellectual dissipation" resulting from time wasted listening to the countless appeals of office seekers, he quickly wilted under pressure from the spoilsmen. "I believe in party government and that the spirit and doctrines of the Republican party should prevail in the Executive departments," he assured a close associate at the time of his nomination. Only on fiscal policy did he take a firm stand: he opposed categorically all inflationary schemes.

The assassination of Garfield elevated Chester A. Arthur to the presidency. Arthur was born in Mexico, but was brought to the United States as an infant in 1830. After graduating from Union College he studied law and settled in New York City. An abolitionist, he became an early convert to the Republican party and rose rapidly in its local councils. In 1871 Grant gave him the juiciest political plum in the country, the collectorship of the Port of New York, which he held until removed by Hayes in 1878 for refusing to keep his hands out of party politics. The only elective position he ever held was the Vice-Presidency. Before Garfield's death he had paid little attention to questions like the tariff and monetary policy, being content to collect annual fees ranging upwards of $50,000 and oversee the operations of the New York customs office, with its hordes of clerks and laborers. (During Arthur's tenure, the novelist Herman Melville was employed as an "outdoor inspector" by the Custom House). Of course Arthur was an unblushing defender of the spoils system, although it must be said in fairness that he was personally honest and an excellent administrator.

In 1883 Congress passed the Pendleton Act, "classifying" about 10 percent of all government jobs and creating a bipartisan Civil Service Commission to prepare and administer competitive examinations for these positions. The law also made it illegal to force officeholders to make political contributions and empowered the President to expand the list of classified positions at his discretion. Better-educated civil servants were recruited; and bribery, if still a fact of politics, was curbed.

Arthur also took an intelligent and moderate position on the tariff. He urged the appointment of a nonpartisan commission to study existing rates and suggest rational reductions, and after such a commission was created, he urged Congress to adopt its recommendations. He came out for federal regulation of railroads several years before the passage of the Interstate Commerce Act. "Congress should protect the people ... against acts of injustice which the State governments are powerless to prevent," he said. He vetoed "pork-barrel" legislation and pushed for much-needed construction of a modern navy. As an administrator he was systematic, thoughtful, businesslike, and at the same time cheerful and considerate. Yet, he, too, was a political failure. Although he naturally sought election in his own right in 1884, he was callously shunted aside by the politicos at the Republican convention.

5 GROVER CLEVELAND

The record of Stephan Grover Cleveland (1837–1908) is distinguished. He apprenticed himself to a law office in Buffalo, New York, was admitted to the bar, and made a name for himself as the "veto mayor" of Buffalo (1881), because of his efforts to thwart a council that sought to raid the city's treasury. Elected Democratic governor of New York in 1882, Cleveland vigorously opposed the corrupt machine politics of Tammany, and as a "clean government" candidate for President won the 1884 election, against the Republican James G. Blaine, in a campaign notable for its close contest. Nevertheless, his election was a surprise. It was a bitter campaign: Blaine was charged ("the Mulligan letters") with the corrupt granting of federal favors to the Little Rock and Fort Smith Railroad; Cleveland, a bachelor, was charged with being the father of an illegitimate child. So Republicans rejoiced in the chanting of the ditty: "Ma! Ma! Where's my Pa?" In the so-called Gilded Age, when corruption and lavish spending was usual, he was frugal with public money, brutally honest, undramatic, ungracious and obstinate. He was the first and the only victorious presidential candidate lacking a military career, and he was a bachelor. He possessed a contrariness that appealed to reformers. In 1884 he carried New York by 1,100 votes, and, ditty or no ditty, just managed to win the election.

As President, Cleveland emphasized civil service reform, vetoed the disgraceful Civil War pension bills, and opposed the spoilsmen of his own party who tried to push through "pork barrel" legislation. He incurred the wrath of veterans and politicians alike. "I feel myself strongly attracted to Mr Cleveland as the best representative of the higher type of Americanism that we have seen since Lincoln was snatched from us," said James Russell Lowell in 1887. Benjamin Tillman was frank in 1894: "When Judas betrayed Christ, his heart was not blacker than this scoundrel, Cleveland, in deceiving the Democracy. ... He is an old bag of beef and I am going to Washington with a pitchfork and prod him in his old fat ribs." Cleveland signed the Indian Emancipation (Dawes) Act of 1887, and the Interstate Commerce Act (1887), but he initiated no major legislation. His most popular act was personal: he married his 22-year-old ward, Frances Folsom, in the White House. As his party's standard-bearer in 1888, he supported lower tariffs. The government was embarrassed by a large surplus revenue, which Cleveland hoped to reduce by cutting the duties on necessities and on the raw materials of manufacturing. He devoted his entire annual message of December 1887 to the tariff, thus focusing public attention on the subject. When worried Democrats reminded him that an election was coming up and that the tariff might cause a rift in the organization, he replied simply: "What is the use of being elected or re-elected, unless you stand for something?" Although he won popular support at the polls on the issue, he lost the electoral college vote to Benjamin Harrison.

6 BENJAMIN HARRISON

The next president, the 23rd President of the US, Benjamin Harrison (1833–1901), was – as they almost all were – a lawyer; he was the grandson of a President, and he had emerged from the Civil War as a brigadier-general. But he was a strange general: his personality has been described as iceberg-like. "Outside the White House and at dinner [Harrison] could be a courtly gentleman. Inside the Executive Mansion, in his reception of those who solicited official appointments for themselves or their friends, he was as glacial as a Siberian stripped of his furs" (Thomas Collier Platt, 1910). "We have one of the smallest Presidents the U.S. has ever known. [Harrison] is narrow, unresponsive and, oh, so cold. ... As one Senator says: 'It's like talking to a hitching post'" (Walter Wellman, 1889). But Harrison came from a crucial state, Ohio, where he was the leading Republican. After graduating from Miami University (Ohio) in 1852 at the age of 18, he studied law. He settled in Indiana, where for a number of years he was Indiana Supreme Court reporter, editing five columns of *Reports* with considerable skill. He fought under Sherman at Atlanta and won a reputation as a stern but effective disciplinarian. In 1876 he ran unsuccessfully for governor of Indiana, but in 1881 he was elected to the Senate.

Harrison believed ardently in the principle of protection. Though Cleveland in 1888 received more popular votes, Harrison was elected by a majority in the electoral college. Dignified, honest, and conscientious, but unskillful in arousing public opinion, Harrison lacked the ability to check the spoilsmen of a party controlled largely by his very astute secretary of state, James G. Blaine. With "Czar" Reed as Speaker of the House, however, and with a majority of both Houses obligated to the machine that had placed them in office, the connection between government and business during the Harrison administration was frankly avowed. His approach to fiscal policy was conservative, although he was extremely freehanded in the matter of veterans' pensions. He would not use "an apothecary's scale," he said, "to weigh the rewards of men who saved the country." No more flamboyant waver of the bloody shirt existed. "I would a thousand times rather march under the bloody shirt, stained with the life-blood of a Union soldier," he said in 1883, "than to march under the black flag of treason or the white flag of cowardly compromise." During his term the high McKinley Tariff Act (made palatable by his reciprocity provision) and the Sherman Silver Purchase Act (which he hoped would help the silver industry by the Government's agreement to buy 4.5. million ounces of silver each month) were passed, Civil War pensions were augmented, and imperialist policies were pressed in the Pacific. With Blaine as secretary of state, a vigorous imperialist policy was followed: bases in the Caribbean and the Pacific, a naval build-up and the beginning of the isthmian canal. He failed, however, to persuade the Senate to annex Hawaii. Congress also passed the Sherman Anti-Trust Act, one of major significance. Defeated for re-election in 1892 by Cleveland, however, by over 350,000 votes, Harrison returned to his law practice.

7 CLEVELAND'S SECOND TERM

In 1892 Cleveland's re-election was due chiefly to the support of those who were irritated by the high McKinley Tariff Act of 1890. The panic of 1893, the passage of the Wilson-Gorman Tariff Act of 1894 without Cleveland's signature, and Cleveland's effort to preserve the gold standard against insurgent party opposition, created a gulf between the President and the radical Democrats which was never bridged. The rift was widened when Cleveland used federal troops on the side of the railroads in the Pullman strike of 1894, thereby alienating labor. By staying on the gold standard, and persuading a reluctant Congress to repeal the Sherman Silver Purchase Act, he was blamed for the depression of 1894. In foreign affairs the Cleveland administration was anti-imperialist: he enlarged the scope of the Monroe Doctrine by its stand in the Venezuela Boundary Dispute, forcing Britain to arbitrate a boundary dispute. He refused to annex Hawaii. By 1896, however, the "silver Democrats," under the control of William Jennings Bryan, dominated the party, and they were decisively defeated at the polls.

Cleveland's stature derives chiefly from his stubborn championship of tariff reform and of honesty and efficiency in the civil service. His two terms marked a cooling of the post-Civil War mood. His strength of character made him the most distinguished President between Lincoln and Theodore Roosevelt, and his counsel continued to be in demand after his retirement. He was a man of great physical courage. During his second term he was afflicted with cancer of the mouth, the growth necessitating the removal of his upper left jaw. The operation was carried out without any publicity on July 1, 1893, aboard Commodore E. C. Benedict's yacht *Oneida* on Long Island Sound. In a second secret operation, July 17, other parts of the growth were removed; the President was fitted with an artificial jaw of vulcanized rubber. By August 7 he had recovered sufficiently to be able to address Congress.

8 WILLIAM MCKINLEY

William McKinley (1843–1901), also Ohio-born, 25th President of the US (1897–1901) served in the Union army during the Civil War, from which he emerged a major in Rutherford B. Hayes's regiment; he returned to his state and practiced law at Canton. Entering politics, he was elected as a Republican to Congress in 1876, where, except for one term, he served until 1891. It was to Hayes that he owed his political rise. Although he voted for the Bland-Allison Silver Act (1878) and advocated the original Free Silver bill of 1890, both favoring subsidies to silver producers, he pleased Ohio industrialists by his ardent support of protection in the McKinley Tariff Act (1890). He was the strongest protectionist in Congress. He thus gained the attention of the powerful capitalist-politician Mark Hanna, who steered McKinley into the Ohio governorship (1892–6) and secured the presidential nomination for him on the first ballot in 1896. By making an endorsement of the gold standard his chief campaign issue, McKinley fought Bryan on free silver. The Democrats, and Bryan as their leader, were discredited, demoralized, and divided by the depression that followed the panic of 1893. Whereas Bryan wished to inflate the currency by the unlimited coinage of silver, McKinley's platform was protection and prosperity, and the defense of the gold standard. The popular vote was close, but by Hanna's masterful adroitness (he persuaded McKinley not to vie with Bryan's oratorical platform appearances, but to receive delegations at his own front porch), McKinley was carried into office by an electoral vote of 271 to 176. With the Republicans in control of Congress, and a thorough going Republican tariff in effect, McKinley could turn his attention to foreign affairs. Theodore Roosevelt, however, had no illusions about him: "McKinley has

Plate 2 The McKinley Flying Machine: pen and ink cartoon by G. Y. Coffin. (Library of Congress.)

about as much backbone as a chocolate eclair." Joe Cannon improved on the verdict: "McKinley keeps his ear to the ground so close that he gets it full of grasshoppers much of the time."

Questions of war and empire rather than domestic issues dominated McKinley's presidency. A rebellion in Cuba against Spain stirred American opinion, which steadily became hysterical. The threat of American intervention in Cuba secured some concessions from Spain, but it refused to surrender Cuba. Yielding to this popular hysteria, McKinley directed Congress in entering the brief and needless Spanish-American War (1898), asked the peace commissioners to demand the Philippines for the US, and imposed a tight control on Cuba. He signed the bill annexing Hawaii, supported the Open Door policy promulgated by his secretary of state, John

Hay, to deal with China, pushed on with plans for an isthmian canal and thus was carried along by the imperialist trend of the times. Defeating Bryan again in 1900 (by 292 to 155 electoral votes), he had time only to organize his new administration. While attending the Pan-American Exposition at Buffalo, McKinley was shot on September 1901 by the anarchist Leon Czolgosz. He died nine days later. A gentle man, simple and friendly, McKinley himself had no distinctive policy, but he left the US with a colonial empire in the Caribbean and the Pacific.

The striking feature of the post-Civil War years was less the insignificance of the men in the White House than the absence of men of stature in Congress itself. In these years there were no men who bore comparison with Clay, Webster, or Calhoun. The only one of stature was himself corrupt: James G. Blaine of Maine (1830–1893), who served from 1863 to 1881, first in the House and then in the Senate. Blaine had many of the qualities that mark a great leader personal dynamism, imagination, political intuition, oratorical ability, and a broad view of the national interest. He was a follower of Henry Clay and shared his "nationalism." President Lincoln spotted him when he was a freshman Congressman, calling him "one of the brightest men in the House" and "one of the coming men of the country." Blaine was essentially a reasonable man, favoring sound money without opposing inflexibly every suggestion for increasing the volume of the currency, supporting the protective system but advocating reciprocity agreements to increase trade, adopting a moderate and tolerant attitude toward the South. Almost alone among the men of his generation, he was deeply interested in foreign affairs. His personal warmth captivated thousands. He never forgot a name. This was perhaps calculated, yet he was capable of impulsive acts of generosity and kindness too.

That Blaine, although perennially an aspirant, never became President was partly a reflection of his very abilities and his active participation in so many controversial affairs over the years. He was alleged as Speaker to have helped finance an Arkansas railroad. He aroused jealousies and made many enemies, not least Roscoe Conkling of New York. But some inexplicable flaw marred his character. He had a streak of recklessness entirely out of keeping with his reasonable position on most issues. He waved the bloody shirt with cynical vigor, heedless of the effect on the nation as a whole. He showered contempt on civil service reformers, characterizing them as "noisy but not numerous ... ambitious but not wise, pretentious but not powerful." There is also reason to doubt his general honesty, for he became wealthy without visible means of support. His services in foreign affairs, however, are important: he was secretary of state for Garfield, then for Benjamin Harrison; he helped organize the Pan-American Conference of 1889 advocated reciprocal trade agreements, and the annexation of Hawaii. He was a key figure in the Republican party between 1870 and 1890.

William Jennings Bryan (1860–1925), born in Illinois, inherited from his parents an intense commitment to the Democratic party and a fervent Protestant faith. After graduating from Illinois College and Union Law School, he married, and, seeing no political future in Illinois, moved to Nebraska in 1887. In 1890, when the new Populist party disrupted Nebraska politics, Bryan won election to Congress; he was re-elected in 1892. In Congress, he earned respect for his oratory and became a leader among free-silver Democrats. In 1894 he led Nebraska's Democrats to support the state Populist party.

Bryan electrified the 1896 Democratic convention with his stirring Cross of Gold speech favoring free silver and thereby captured the presidential nomination. Also nominated by the Populists, Bryan agreed with their view that government should protect individuals and the democratic process against monopolistic corporations. "The Boy Orator of the Platte" travelled 18 thousand miles, made 600 speeches, was heard – so it was reckoned – by some 5 million people, and spoke to thousands of voters, but lost: William McKinley's victory initiated a generation of Republican dominance in national politics. Bryan's 1896 campaign, however, marked a long-term shift within the Democratic party from a Jacksonian commitment to minimal government toward a positive view of government. The Democratic party was re-committed to its original principles, to the cause (or is it causes?) of Jefferson, of Populism, of the poor, the weak, and – in the end – the black. Bryan was to commit his party to lose votes in the East, and in the near future. But he committed it to the future, to the Gospel of the West. Vachel Lindsay recalled the echoes: "Bryan, Bryan, Bryan, Bryan":

> ... It was eighteen ninety-six, and I was just sixteen
> And Altgeld ruled in Springfield, Illinois,
> When there came from the sunset Nebraska's shout of joy:
> In a coat like a deacon, in a black Stetson hat
> He scourged the elephant plutocrats
> With barbed wire from the Platte.
> The scales dipped from their mighty eyes.
> They saw that summer's noon

A tribe of wonders coming
To a marching tune.
Oh, the longhorns from Texas,
The jay hawks from Kansas,
The plop-eyed bugaroo and giant giassicus,
The varmint, chipmunk, bugaboo,
The horned-toad, prairie-dog and ballyhoo,
From all the newborn states a row,
Bidding the eagles of the west fly on,
Bidding the eagles of the west fly on ...[1]

During the Spanish-American War, Bryan served as a colonel in a Nebraska regiment, but after the war, he condemned McKinley's Philippine policy as imperialism. Nominated again by the Democrats in 1900, Bryan hoped this time to make the election a referendum on imperialism, but other issues intervened, including his own insistence on free silver and attacks on monopolies. McKinley won again.

After his defeat, Bryan launched a newspaper, the *Commoner* (based on his nickname "the Great Commoner") and made frequent speaking tours. Although he was a superb orator, he was neither a deep nor an original thinker. He used the *Commoner* and the lecture circuit to affirm equality, to advocate greater popular participation in governmental decision making, to oppose monopolies, and to proclaim the importance of faith in God. "Shall the People Rule?" became the watchword of his third campaign for president, in 1908, when he lost to William Howard Taft.

In 1912, Bryan worked to secure the Democratic presidential nomination for Woodrow Wilson, and when Wilson won, he felt obliged to name Bryan secretary of state. As secretary, Bryan promoted conciliation, or cooling-off, treaties, in which the parties agreed that, if they could not resolve a dispute, they would wait a year before going to war and would seek outside fact-finding. Thirty such treaties were drafted. When the European war broke out in 1914, Bryan, like Wilson, was committed to neutrality. But he went beyond Wilson in advocating restrictions on American citizens and companies to prevent them from drawing the nation into war. When Wilson strongly protested Germany's sinking of the *Lusitania*, Bryan resigned rather than approve a message he feared would lead to war.

[1] J. Hollingsworth, *The Whirligig of Politics* (Chicago, University of Chicago Press, 1967).

Thereafter in the years of anti-climax, Bryan worked for peace, prohibition, and women's suffrage, and he increasingly criticized the teaching of evolution. In 1925, he joined the prosecution in the trial of John Scopes, a Tennessee schoolteacher charged with violating state law by teaching evolution. In a famous exchange, Clarence Darrow, defending Scopes, put Bryan on the witness stand and revealed his shallowness and his ignorance of science and archaeology.[2]

[2] Paolo E. Coletta, *William Jennings Bryan*, 3 vols (Lincoln, University of Nebraska Press, 1964–9); Robert W. Cherny, *A Righteous Cause: The Life of William Jennings Bryan* (Boston, Little, Brown, 1985).

5

Empire

1 WHY IMPERIALISM?

Imperialism is an alien term for Americans, and has been so since 1776. Since then, and notably as expressed in the Monroe Doctrine in 1823, they had banned the invasion of their own and of neighboring territory by European empires, and committed themselves for their own part to isolation. Yet in the years after 1865 – forty years or so after Monroe's declaration – the term imperialism, and what it implied, came into use, both in Britain and in the US. Lord Carnarvon could say in 1787: "I have heard of imperial policy and imperial interests, but imperialism, as such, is new to me." By the 1890s the term had been adopted both by those who approved and by those who rejected the doctrine; by the Westminster Gazette, which explained how the "vivid realization of the British Empire as "a world-wide Venice with the sea for streets,' gave a decisive impetus to what may be called, in the slang of the day, 'the new Imperialism'" (1895); and by the *Daily News*, which spoke of "that odious system of bluster and swagger and might against right on which Lord Beaconsfield and his colleagues bestowed the tawdry nickname of Imperialism" (1898).

If Burke could state his theory of empire adequately without using the term "imperialism," why did Lord Rosebery feel the need for it? The answer seems to lie in the special characteristics of this late nineteenth–early twentieth-century phase of colonial expansion. First, its scale and tempo: between 1880 and 1920 the greater part of the African continent, of the Arab world, of China and Southeast Asia, with such oceanic islands as had hitherto been left unmolested, was brought directly or indirectly under the control of the chief colonial powers: Britain, France, Belgium, Germany, the Netherlands, Portugal, Italy, and the USA.

Second, the competing claims of these powers for colonies, protectorates, spheres of influence and – later – mandates, brought into being new zones of inter-European tension in the world outside Europe: Egypt, Morocco, the Nile valley, the Congo basin, Persia, Manchuria. Europeans were compelled to think of their future as in some way linked with the outcome of crises in remote places with unfamiliar names – Agadir, Fashoda, Kiao-Chow.

Third, since the states involved in this struggle for empire were for the most part parliamentary democracies, operating systems of universal or manhood suffrage, their governments were faced with the problem – new, apart from Athenian experience – of conducting imperialist policies with the consent of the governed; and of presenting these policies – involving expenditure of blood and treasure, and a reversal of earlier liberal attitudes – in terms which would secure the approval of "all or most men."

Hence the need for an imperial ideology, which could be stated in suitable ethical language, and commend itself alike to British Nonconformists, German Lutherans, Belgian Catholics, and French *libres penseurs*. It was partly for this reason that the imperial idea affected all aspects of national life and thought – above all in Britain; and found expression in imperial history, imperial sociology, imperial philosophy, imperial theories of government, imperial poetry, imperial romance, and an imperial popular press.

One further characteristic of this phase of colonial expansion was the fact of controversy: imperialist orthodoxy was quickly challenged by an anti-imperialist heresy – or heresies. And, though Britain has been rightly regarded as the best laboratory specimen of the new imperialism, the debate itself was international: Joseph Chamberlain, Jules Ferry, Karl Peters, King Leopold II, Theodore Roosevelt, on the one side; J. A. Hobson, Jean Jaurès, Rosa Luxemburg, Lenin, Emma Goldman, on the other.

The imperialist thesis – though, of course, it was stated in cruder and subtler forms – consisted in the main of an amalgam of doctrines, drawn from different sources: a pseudo-Calvinist belief in one's own nation as a nation "elect" – specially ordained by God (or 'Providence' or 'History') to increase the welfare and improve the manners of less-favored peoples; a neo-Hegelian view of the nation-state as the embodiment of an ethical idea; a neo-mercantilist theory of the necessity for colonies as a market for manufactures, and an insurance against poverty, unemployment and class war;

and a neo-Malthusian theory of their usefulness as a dumping-ground for surplus population.

The classic statement of the anti-imperialist heresy is to be found in J. A. Hobson's *Imperialism* (1902). His argument can be reduced to three main propositions. First, the "tap-root" of modern imperialism is economic. The drive for empire arises out of the chronic "under-consumptionist" tendencies of advanced capitalist economies. Thus the main purpose of expansion (however justified in colonial apologetics) is to maintain a falling rate of profit. At this stage of history the governments of imperialist countries become little more than executive committees of merchants and investors, interested in the goldfields of the Rand, a Berlin-Baghdad railroad, or Congo rubber.

Second, the effect of imperialism is not merely to disrupt the traditional social systems and values of the colonial peoples; but also to corrupt the colonizing nation: to stimulate a spirit of jingoism, racial arrogance, moral humbug, delight in violence; to strengthen the pressures for intellectual conformity (particularly in Oxford and Cambridge); to weaken the institutions of liberalism by re-exporting into the Home Counties retired proconsuls and nabobs, who introduce into British public life the authoritarian habits of mind which they have acquired in their dealings with Asians and Africans; and, above all, to increase the tensions leading to international war.

Third, the solution to the problems raised by imperialism is to be found in social reform, and a progressive raising of domestic standards of consumption – which will render unnecessary the drive for colonial markets and investment outlets.

Lenin, who in the preface to his *Imperialism* (1917) warmly acknowledged his debt to Hobson, accepted, in essentials, Hobson's first two propositions, and rejected his third. Drawing on a work of Rudolf Hilferding's, *Das Finanzkapital* (1910), Lenin placed greater emphasis upon the role of the banks, of monopolies, and of the export of capital, in the genesis of imperialism. He was more interested, too, in the effect of imperialism upon the Labor movement – particularly in the development of the attitude which he described as "opportunism" among the Labor and trade union leadership of the wealthier imperial countries, bought, as Lenin saw it, with the proceeds of colonial loot; and he quoted with approval Engels' remark that "even Tom Mann ... is fond of mentioning that he will be lunching with the Lord Mayor."

For Hobson's reformism Lenin, of course, had no use. Imperialism, in his view, could be abolished only by the combined attack of the revolutionary proletariat in the imperial countries and revolutionary nationalists in the colonies. One consequence of this critique of empire was that "imperialism" acquired a rhetorical – in addition to its original descriptive – meaning: it became a rude word. We are none of us imperialists now. Indeed, there are hardly any empires: only a Commonwealth of Nations, a French Union, an integral Belgian-Congolese State, no longer even a Union of Soviet Socialist Republics.

2 AMERICAN IMPERIALISM

In the US, imperialism had never consistently commanded support. Yet it was itself an imperial product. Its own history began with the settlements in North America created by European nations in their attempts to find areas for capital investments, to exploit raw material, and to build up markets for home exports. These empires were erected according to theories of mercantilism, the pursuit of economic power through national self-sufficiency. If it can be argued that its own extensions of territory were done from motives of purchase and security rather than greed – the Louisiana Purchase in 1803, the acquisition of Alaska on the Pacific in 1867 by the Civil War secretary of state, William H. Seward – yet there can be no denying that the motives that led to the occupation of Texas and the War with Mexico in 1846 spelt imperialism, though it was disguised by the journalist John L. O'Sullivan, who enriched the political vocabulary by calling it Manifest Destiny. O'Sullivan died in 1895, when there was need for his services again, for by that time there was much to describe.[1] In 1898 McKinley could refer to the years preceding his administration as "the period of exclusiveness." With the possible exceptions of Seward and Hamilton Fish, all thirteen secretaries of state between 1865 and 1898 were politicians much more concerned with the political scene at home than with diplomatic developments abroad. Yet, however unpopular they each might be, they were all involved in controversy.

Central to the explanation of the origins of American imperialism was America's own prosperity. By 1900 its markets, and the profits they brought, were found abroad as well as at home; so were many of its needs. The economies of New York and Chicago were

[1] Julius W. Pratt, *The Expansionists of 1898* (Albert Shaw Lecture; Baltimore, Johns Hopkins University Press, 1936), and idem, "John L. O'Sullivan and Manifest Destiny," *New York History*, 14 (1938), pp. 213–34.

now keyed to consumers who lived in Europe, Asia, and Latin America as well as in the US, even though Americans might express nominal indifference to the affairs of Europe or Asia. Their sugar came from the Caribbean and the Pacific, their coffee from Brazil. Within a generation, they would construct and own their own factories abroad, employ foreign as well as American workers, and own foreign resources and divert their profits homeward. It is a matter of debate whether Europe, Asia, Africa, Mexico, or Latin America, all by comparison low-wage economies, benefited or lost from this exchange. It was certainly no longer possible to speak of "isolation."

By the end of the nineteenth century, the United States had emerged as a world power, rich in people and resources and strong in moral convictions of its righteousness. No country in the world produced so much grain and fruit, so much iron, coal, and steel as did the United States. This nation's banking wealth rivaled Britain's, its navy equaled Germany's and its population surpassed that of all European nations save Russia. Although the Western advance on the American continent ended with the closing of the frontier in the 1890s, habits of expansion and pioneering were then transferred overseas. The settlement of the West also led to a greater economic and military interest in the Pacific region.

Expansion into Europe and into the Pacific was spurred by the growing industrialization of the United States. Every decade after 1870 revealed the increase in its exports and, what was more important, the steady rise in the proportion of manufactured goods in the totals of its foreign trade. As the industrial system took shape, the need for markets gave added impetus to the demand that American political control over areas in the Pacific be strengthened.

Ernest R. May assessed the dramatic emergence of America as a world power:

> Up to the 1890s ... European diplomats and political analysts coupled it [the US] with such states as Sweden, the Netherlands, Belgium, and Spain. By the early twentieth century, on the other hand, some of the very same people had begun to say in all seriousness that Europe was in danger from America. The distinguished French historian, Henri Hauser, for example, asserted in a little volume on American imperialism in 1905 that the principal topic of conversation in France was the so-called "American peril". In little more than a decade the United States had moved from among the second-rate powers to a front rank among first-rate powers.[2]

[2] Ernest R. May, *The Reconstruction of American History*, ed. John Higham (New York, Harper and Row, 1962), pp. 181–2.

The motives for expansion were not only commercial and economic. The US had been compelled to enforce the Monroe Doctrine ("Hands off the Americas!") in Mexico. Near the close of the Civil War, Napoleon III, in flagrant violation of the Monroe Doctrine, had placed Archduke Maximilian of Austria upon an unstable Mexican throne. Secretary of State Seward had vainly protested; but with the conclusion of hostilities the United States government ordered General Sheridan's troops to take up positions along the Rio Grande. Though war seemed imminent, Seward scored a diplomatic victory when Napoleon's troubles in Europe caused him to withdraw French troops (1867). Without French support, Maximilian lost his throne and was executed by his former subjects. Thus the attempt of a European power to intervene in the affairs of an independent American nation was thwarted.

Moreover, the US was beginning to become a Pacific power. Secretary Seward deserves credit for stating clearly the traditional basis of the US's commercial interests in the Pacific. In 1867 he found Russia eager to get rid of its outpost on the North American continent, and he persuaded Congress to purchase Alaska for $7,200,000. This rich base, Seward hoped, would start the United States on an expansionist policy. He also arranged for the United States to annex the Midway islands (1868), and to acquire rights to a canal route across Nicaragua. At the same time he urged eventual acquisition of the Hawaiian islands.

The usual reason given for imperialism was the necessity to make the nation secure: compare the usual arguments in Britain for a strong navy. Naval expansionist Captain Alfred T. Mahan expressed this reasoning at the time. Despite his arguments, however, neither he nor any noted spokesmen of naval power before 1898 demanded indiscriminate territorial annexation.

To provide this [national defense], three things are needful: First, protection of he chief harbors by fortifications and coast-defense ships, which gives defensive strength, provides security to the community within, and supplies the bases necessary to all military operations. Secondly, naval force, the arm of offensive power, which alone enables a country to extend its influence outward. Thirdly, it should be an inviolable resolution of our national policy that no European state should henceforth acquire a coaling position within three thousand miles of San Francisco – a distance which includes the Sandwich [Hawaiian] and Galapagos islands and the coast of Central America. For fuel is the life of modern naval war; it is the food of the ship; without it the modern monsters of the deep die.[3]

[3] Alfred T. Mahan, "The United States looking outward," *Atlantic Monthly*, 66 (Dec. 1890), p. 823.

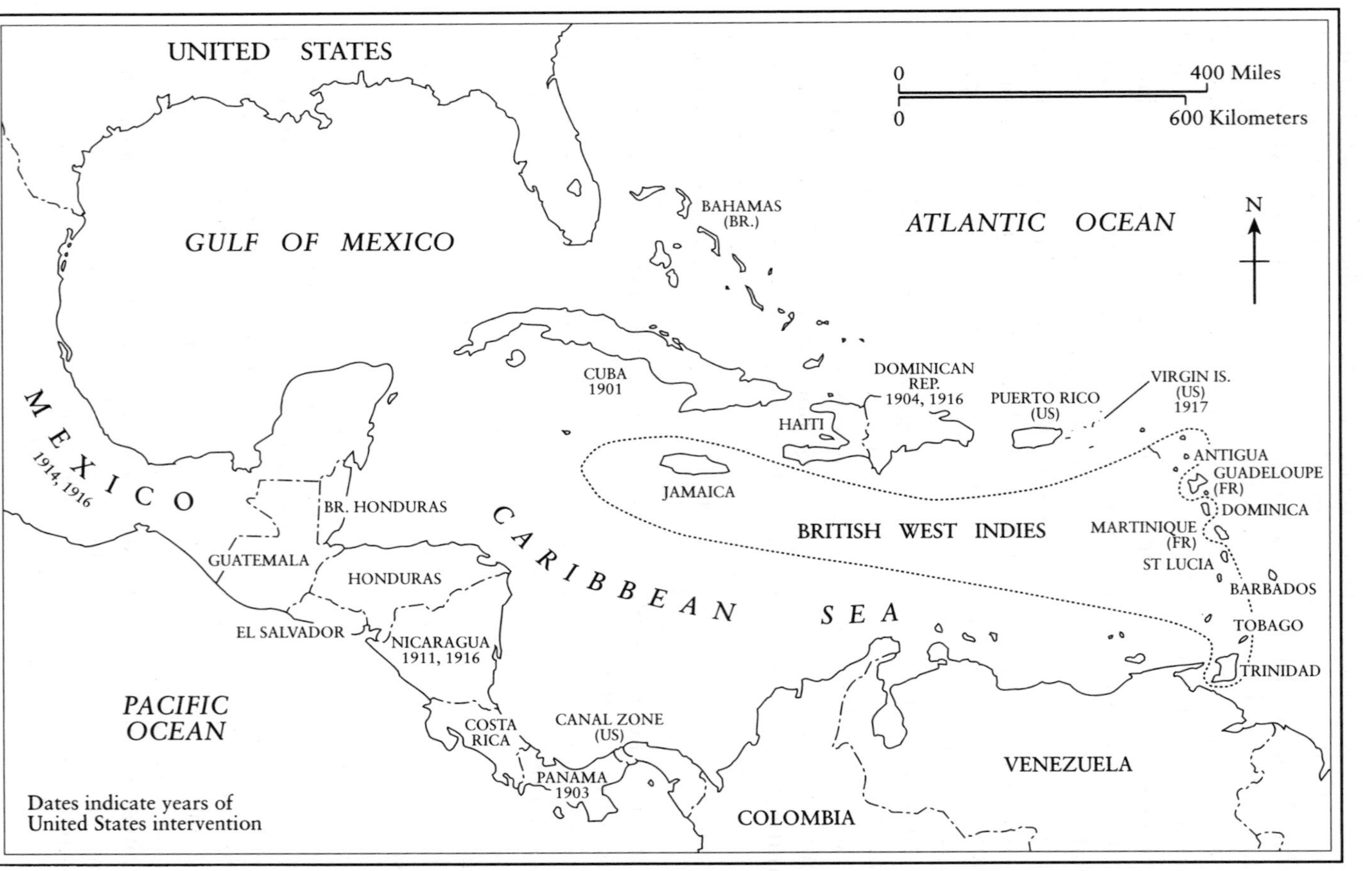

Map 5 The US in the Caribbean.

3 THE LURE OF THE PACIFIC

The American case for a strong navy was by the 1890s largely put with the Pacific in mind. There the arguments for American presence came not only from chambers of commerce and investors in the sugar of the Philippines and Hawaii, but from missionaries – mariners and missionaries, indeed, were American pioneers in Samoa, Hawaii, and other Pacific islands. Though the United States had never maintained a large standing army, the people had long cherished the high tradition of the American navy. But naval strength had been allowed to decline after the Civil War and a new steel navy was not constructed until the late 1880s. The Naval Act of 1890 marked the acceptance by the government of the concept of a navy capable of meeting any potential foe on the Atlantic or the Pacific. The new policy was being put into effect in the very years that Americans in large numbers were reading Mahan's books and articles on the importance of sea power and its relation to commercial expansion.

The Samoan islands

An early example of the changed attitude of many Americans toward overseas imperialism was the peaceful penetration of the Samoan islands. Contacts with the islanders, first stimulated by the China trade, passed through several stages. First came trading concessions. Casual relations established by seamen and traders led in 1872 to the negotiation of a treaty granting the United States a naval station which the Senate failed to ratify. Six years later, however, a Samoan proposal that the United States establish a protectorate over the islands resulted in an agreement (1878) that gave American ships most-favored-nation rights in the harbor of Pago Pago and the opportunity to establish a naval base.

At the same time, however, Germany and Great Britain received commercial privileges in Samoa, and the three nations entered into a competition for favored treatment by Samoans, which was not always friendly. This rivalry aroused a nationalistic spirit in the United States which was only partially satisfied in 1889, when the three nations established a condominium over Samoan affairs. Ten years later, after the Spanish-American War had been won, the United States permitted Germany to take over many of the islands, but retained the most important, Tutuila, with the fine harbor of Pago Pago (1899), as an American possession.

Hawaii

Acquisition of the Hawaiian islands (1898) was the result of forces similar to those which brought to the United States colonial responsibilities in Samoa. As early as 1820 New England missionaries had established themselves on several of Hawaii's islands, where their descendants were joined by Yankee ship captains, traders with the Orient, and sailors on the whaling ships, who steadily augmented the American population in the islands. Within a generation, sugar became the chief interest of Americans in Hawaii. The sugar planters, a majority of whom were Americans, worked indefatigably for closer relations with the United States. In 1875 they secured a treaty of reciprocity between the United States and the islands which greatly stimulated their sugar trade. However, the McKinley Tariff of 1890 removed the duty on imported sugar and provided for a bounty of two cents a pound on domestic sugar. Thus the Hawaiian planters lost their favored position and looked to annexation as their best prospect.

The American faction in the Hawaiian islands, led by the great planters and financed by American capital, staged a successful revolt against Queen Liliuokalani in 1893. Her government was determined in its opposition to foreigners, and the American minority became alarmed when she boasted that Hawaii was for the Hawaiians. The revolution of the foreign elements was quickly accomplished after the American minister, John L. Stevens, gave his support to the temporary government of the revolutionists and had American marines landed to preserve order.

President Harrison, who favored annexation, left office before a treaty could be acted upon. The incoming President, Grover Cleveland, withdrew the annexation treaty from the Senate and appointed anti-imperialist James H. Blount as special commissioner to investigate the situation. After receiving Blount's report, Cleveland attempted to restore the government of Queen Liliuokalani on the condition that she pardon the revolutionists. The queen refused to do this, and the revolutionary government continued in power. On July 4, 1894, this government proclaimed the Republic of Hawaii, and the following month it was recognized by the United States.

When McKinley became President in 1897, sentiment in favor of annexation was running strong. Acquisition of the Hawaiian Republic, said the expansionists, was imperative because (1) it might otherwise fall under the control of a foreign power; (2) it would provide badly needed naval bases in the Pacific; and (3) it offered opportunities for commercial expansion and for investment of American capital. These arguments were reinforced in the minds of many citizens by the belief that it was the manifest destiny of the United States to control the Pacific and that the nation had a duty to bring the Christian gospel and American democratic institutions to the native populations in that area. A Japanese protest against annexation also spurred on the move, and the war with Spain gave it added impetus. These considerations brought annexation of Hawaii by a joint resolution of Congress, which President McKinley signed on July 7, 1898.

4 CUBA

Strategy and security were also factors in American imperialism. During the second half of the nineteenth century the United States frequently showed its concern over the fate of Cuba, its close neighbor, which was Spain's chief possession in the Caribbean – and only 90 miles from the Florida keys.

Early in the century the American government had expressed fear lest the sovereignty of Spain in the island should be replaced by that of a more formidable European power. For a decade after 1850 there was much discussion of the acquisition of Cuba either by purchase or seizure. The prolonged revolt of the Cubans against Spanish authority in the Ten Years' War of 1868–78 not only brought devastation to large areas of the island, but also pushed the United States to the verge of war with Spain, because of Spanish charges that Americans were aiding the rebels in violation of international law. Despite Spanish mistreatment of American citizens in Cuba and the execution of Americans taken from a filibustering ship (the *Virginius*), the United States at this time had no desire for war. The close of the war in 1878 left the Cuban leaders resentful over unfulfilled promises made by the Spanish government, and sent many of them to the United States, where they carried on propaganda for Cuban independence.

Continuing discontent in Cuba flared into revolt again when declining prices of sugar and tobacco, partly induced by American customs duties under the Wilson-German tariff, brought widespread economic depression to the island. Nevertheless, the wealthier classes in Cuba and most Americans with investments in the island were opposed to the rebels' demand for independence.

Unable to cope with the guerilla tactics of the revolutionary forces, which were terrorizing the countryside, Governor-General

Weyler tried to confine military operations within a limited area and to concentrate the civilian population in camps closely supervised by Spanish troops. Though Weyler's policy was misrepresented in sensational newspapers in this country, he probably deserved the sobriquet of "butcher" for the brutal effects of his concentration camps on noncombatants. Equally brutal, however, were the tactics of the insurgents as they tried to "fight fire with fire" and embarked on a campaign of destruction.

During the closing months of his administration, President Cleveland strove to maintain genuine neutrality and to persuade the Spanish government that the grant of Cuban autonomy was the surest means of establishing peace and political stability. He feared, however, that the demand for intervention would compel his successor, McKinley, to act.

American intervention in the Cuban situation was not desired by those who had the largest financial interests in the island, since they believed that Spain could eventually restore peace and order. The groups most enthusiastic for a war to secure Cuban independence included humanitarians who believed that Spanish policy, as exemplified by Weyler, had been not only dictatorial but also "brutal and inhuman"; certain "jingoes" who felt that war was the high road to commercial and industrial prosperity; partisan politicians who hoped that a successful struggle with Spain would quicken patriotic support of the McKinley administration; a few public officials, like Roosevelt and Lodge, nationalistic in spirit, who were eager to have the United States assume its place as a world power; and a powerful portion of the sensational press, which was fattening its circulation by publishing exaggerated stories of Spanish "atrocities" and erroneous accounts of events in Cuba.

On February 15, 1898, the battleship *Maine*, which had been sent to Havana to be ready in case Americans there needed protection, was sunk at her moorings with the loss of 260 officers and men. Though it was impossible to determine whether the sinking had been the work of Spanish loyalists or Cuban insurgents, or was entirely accidental, the war faction immediately made "Remember the *Maine*" a slogan. Although he was truly desirous of averting war, President McKinley realized that a "peace at any price" policy might split his party and wreck his administration. Therefore, on April 11 he sent a message to Congress charging that the Spanish government was unable to suppress the Cuban rebellion and yet was unwilling to grant an armistice. Spain had actually yielded to McKinley's demands between the time that he wrote his message and the date that he sent it to Congress; nevertheless, the pressure for war was so great, not only in Congress but throughout the nation, that he could no longer resist it. The war resolution of April 20, 1898, contained the so-called Teller amendment, which pledged the United States to withdraw from Cuba as soon as its independence and political stability had been established.

In spite of serious blunders by military and civilian authorities, the United States won the Spanish War with relative ease. During the 30 years following the Civil War the United States government had been negligent of its military establishment, since no powerful foe seemed to threaten the nation. The American people paid the price of this lack of preparedness in the Spanish War. But fortunately, the brunt of the conflict fell upon the navy, which was better prepared than any other part of the military establishment. It was the first test of the new steel ships, construction of which had been going forward since 1883. In addition to the Atlantic Fleet under Admiral Sampson, the Flying Squadron under Commodore Schley and the Asiatic Squadron under Commodore Dewey, the Navy Department had put into service more than 100 auxiliary ships acquired during the spring of 1898. Thirty million dollars had been spent, the personnel of officers and men had been doubled, and contracts had been placed for munitions and supplies.

In contrast, the army was ill-prepared for the conflict. For a generation Congress had been miserly in its appropriations for the War Department. Furthermore, too many high officials in the Department had been political appointees rather than men trained in the technical and administrative skills which the military service required. As a result, when war broke out the normal processes of the War Department broke down. It could not double the size of the regular army and train 200,000 volunteers with the speed and efficiency that war demanded. The record made distressing reading for Americans, who slowly learned that spoiled food, inferior guns and ammunition, lack of proper clothing, and insufficient medical service both in camp and in the field accounted for a heavier loss of life than did the actual fighting on the battlefield.

With the outbreak of war Spain became vulnerable not only in her Caribbean colonies, but also in her Pacific possessions. The first blow for Cuban independence was struck not in Atlantic waters but in the far-distant Philippines. Commodore George Dewey's squadron (which was in Asiatic waters as a result of Assistant Navy Secretary Theodore Roosevelt's orders) steamed from Hong Kong to Manila and destroyed the Spanish fleet in Manila Bay – and was then compelled to wait from May 1 until August 13 for reinforcements which finally enabled American troops to capture the city of Manila.

Meanwhile, Admiral Sampson and Commodore Schley had established an effective blockade of all Cuban ports. They were not able, however, to prevent Admiral Cervera, with the most important Spanish fleet, from taking a position under the batteries of Santiago harbor. Lieutenant Hobson's attempt to sink the collier *Merrimac* across the mouth of the harbor failed, and the fleet waited for the arrival of American troops before beginning the Cuban campaign in earnest.

The campaign against Santiago was brief and decisive. Its two phases were: (1) the operations of the American expeditionary forces to the north and east of the city; and (2) the destruction of Cervera's fleet. On June 14, 1898, 17,000 troops under the command of General W. R. Shafter embarked at Tampa, Florida. Within three weeks General J. F. Kent's division had taken San Juan Hill; General H. W. Lawton's division had reached El Caney; and General Wheeler's dismounted cavalry, with the Rough Riders, a volunteer cavalry group, organized and led by Theodore Roosevelt, who had resigned from the Navy Department to become an army colonel, had stormed Kettle Hill. Admiral Cervera, learning that the Americans controlled the heights above Santiago, made a desperate effort to escape. His entire fleet was destroyed, while the American casualties were 1 killed and 16 wounded. On July 17, Santiago surrendered.

After the termination of the Santiago campaign, General N. A. Miles undertook to conquer Puerto Rico. So feeble was the military resistance in the island that "Mr Dooley," the creation of American humorist Finley Peter Dunne, described the "campaign" as "Gin'ral Miles' Gran' Picnic an' Moonlight Excursion." It was cut short in August 1898 by the peace protocol (the Peace of Paris).

The terms of the treaty with Spain revealed to the American people how far and how fast they had traveled along the road of empire-building. McKinley had decided that the country favored the retention of the Philippines and that humanitarian, as well as economic, considerations justified it. The chief clauses of the treaty which was finally signed on December 10 were: (1) the grant of Cuban independence and assumption of the Cuban debt by Spain; (2) the cession to the United States of Puerto Rico, Guam, and the Philippines; (3) the payment by the United States of $20 million for the Philippines. This overseas expansion was the result of many motives: the desire to increase the national prestige, to promote new business enterprises, to tap the expanding trade with the Orient, to frustrate the designs of Germany in the Pacific, and to "uplift and civilize" the population of the islands.

However, President McKinley encountered great difficulty in persuading the Senate to ratify the treaty. A few Republicans, led by Senator Hoar of Massachusetts, denounced any attempt to subjugate and rule distant Oriental possessions. The Democrats sought to make political capital out of the debate over ratification. Though he was opposed to overseas expansion, William Jennings Bryan persuaded some Democratic Senators to vote for ratification, because he believed that this would make the new imperialism a clear-cut issue in the presidential campaign of 1900. Thus the administration got the treaty ratified with the aid of Democratic votes.

5 GEORGE ARMSTRONG CUSTER, AND THE INDIANS

General George Armstrong Custer, the most flamboyant of Northern cavalry generals in the Civil War, added to his reputation after the war ended by leading the Seventh Cavalry in skirmishes against Indians in Kansas and Nebraska. He wrote up and justified his escapades during these years in *My Life on The Plains*, telling in particular of his raid into the Indians' sacred Black Hills, where gold was discovered; the gold rush that followed led the US Government thereafter to confine all northern Plains tribes to reservations. In June 1876, the year when Philadephia was about to celebrate the US's first century of independence, Custer led the Seventh Cavalry in a dangerous three-pronged campaign against Sitting Bull's alliance of Sioux and Cheyenne camps in the valley of the Little Bighorn River in Montana. Custer and some 250 of his men were surrounded and annihilated by greatly superior Indian numbers. Custer's legend as a *beau sabreur* owes much to the writing and lectures of his widow Elizabeth Bacon Custer during the next half-century. She wrote of their life together in *Boots and Saddles* (1885). Sitting Bull fled to Canada but, when he returned in 1881, he was confined to a reservation where he continued his campaign for the Sioux retention of their lands; he travelled for a season with Buffalo Bill's Wild West Show. The popularity among Dakota Sioux of the Ghost Dance, a tribal religion that proclaimed that all whites would disappear and dead Indians and buffalo would return, brought him into disfavor with government officials. Sitting Bull was killed in a mêlée while trying to escape arrest. Some 250 Indians were killed in the battle – or near-massacre – at Wounded Knee in 1890: to many whites it was a revenge for the Little Bighorn disaster.

In 1890 the Bureau of the Census formally announced the closing of the frontier. The General Allotment (the Dawes) Act 1887 converted all Indian tribal lands to a system of individual land ownership to facilitate the assimilation of Indians with white culture. After individual allocations had been made, much land was thrown open for sale to non-Indians. There was in 1889 a white land rush into the Indian Territory, which became Oklahoma as a result. In 1934 the Indian Reorganization Act (largely the work of Indian commissioner John Collier) reversed the policy, and attempted, with federal assistance, to strengthen tribal life. Surplus land was returned to tribal ownership. American Indians, now a rapidly growing minority group, possess a unique legal status, and are better educated, in better health, and are more prosperous than ever before in their history.

6 THE LEGACY

Even before the Treaty of Paris was signed, an Anti-Imperialist League had been organized in Boston (November 1898). Its members, led by Charles Francis Adams, William Graham Sumner, and Carl Schurz, denounced the acquisition of colonial possessions as a policy which would conflict with democratic principles, impose heavy burdens upon the national treasury, and compel Americans to conquer millions of people hostile to their rule. The literature of protest sent out by the Anti-Imperialists was generally inspired by Eastern "intellectuals."

Imperialism became the paramount issue in the political battle for the presidency in 1900. The Republicans renominated McKinley with great enthusiasm; drafted Theodore Roosevelt (against his wishes) for the vice-presidency; and praised the administration for its successful conduct of a "righteous war" and for its courageous assumption of a "moral duty" in the Philippines. For the Democrats, Bryan, nominated by acclamation, endeavored to spread the gospel of anti-imperialism. Denunciation of the trusts, condemnation of high protection, and support of free silver received less attention from the Democratic candidate than his demand that the country repudiate the course of empire upon which the Republicans had entered.

Bryan's cause was hopeless. The country was enjoying heightened prestige abroad and widespread prosperity at home. The electorate was ready to assume the burdens imposed by the new possessions and to reward the party which had brought a revival of commercial and industrial activity. Bryan carried only four states outside the Solid South and received 155 electoral votes to 292 for McKinley.

There has been much controversy over the priority of economic and business interests before strategic or security arguments. For decades, historians have argued over whether American businessmen demanded the annexation of colonies to increase their trade. Julius W. Pratt contended that they did not:

> It seems safe to conclude, from the evidence available, that the only important business interests (other than the business of sensational journalism) which clamored for intervention in Cuba were certain of those directly or indirectly concerned in the Cuban sugar industry; that opposed to intervention were the influence of other parties (including at least one prominent sugar planter) whose business would suffer direct injury from war and also the overwhelming preponderance of general business opinion. ...
>
> However when Dewey's dramatic victory on the first of May offered a far eastern base from which the threatened markets in China might be defended, ... business had gladly accepted the result, and long before the close of the wonderful year 1898 it was building high hopes upon the supposed opportunities for trade and exploitation in a string of dependencies stretching from the Philippines to Porto Rico. ... In no section of American opinion had the year wrought a greater transformation than in that of the business men.[4]

Walter LaFeber argued that businessmen had convinced President McKinley to declare war:

> The President did not want war; he had been sincere and tireless in his efforts to maintain the peace. By mid-March, however, he was beginning to discover that, although he did not want war, he did want what only a war could provide: the disappearance of the terrible uncertainty in American political and social life, and a solid basis from which to resume the building of the new American commercial empire. ...
>
> Influences other than the yellow press [sensationalism] or congressional belligerence were most important in shaping McKinley's position of April 11. Perhaps most important was the transformation of the opinion of many spokesmen for the business community who had formerly opposed war. ... This transformation brought important financial spokesmen, especially from the Northeast, into much the same position that had long been occupied by pro-interventionist business groups and journals in the trans-Appalachian area. McKinley's decision to intervene placated many of the same business spokesmen whom he had satisfied ... by his refusal to declare war.[5]

4 Julius W. Pratt, "American business and the Spanish-American War," *Hispanic American Historical Review*, 14 (1934), pp. 178, 200–1.

5 Walter LaFeber, *The New American Empire; An interpretation of American expansion, 1860–1898* (Ithaca, NY, Cornell University Press, 1963), pp. 400, 403.

In addition to strategic and economic reasons for imperialism was the Neo-Manifest Destiny. This new version of Manifest Destiny was both a revival and a revision of that which was prominent in the middle of the century. Religious and racial superiority were evident in both. Indiana Republican Albert J. Beveridge reflected this feeling of superiority in his speech "The March of the Flag" in late 1898:

> It is a noble land that God has given us; a land that can feed and clothe the world. ... It is a mighty people that He has planted on this soil; a people sprung from the most masterful blood of history. ... It is a glorious history our God has bestowed upon His chosen people; a history heroic with faith in our mission and our future. ...
>
> Have we no mission to perform, no duty to discharge to our fellow-men? ...[6]

A decade earlier the influential religious leader Josiah Strong wrote in a similar vein:

> It seems to me that God, with infinite wisdom and skill, is training the Anglo-Saxon race for an hour sure to come in the world's future. ... Then this race of unequaled energy, with all the majesty of numbers and the might of wealth behind it – the representative, let us hope, of the largest liberty, the purest Christianity, the highest civilization – having developed peculiarly aggressive traits calculated to impress its institutions upon mankind, will spread itself over the earth. ...[7]

Richard W. Leopold provided an amplification of the above statement:

> Only after the War with Spain had begun did American religious bodies and periodicals launch a systematic campaign for overseas territory. For some years before, however, they had helped develop a climate of opinion which made that campaign successful. By asserting that injustice and suffering everywhere is the concern of all and by stressing the responsibility of the powerful to lift up the weak, they contributed toward destroying the provincialism of American citizens and toward reminding them of their obligations before God and man ...[8]

[6] Albert J. Beveridge, "The March of the Flag," speech quoted in *Modern Eloquence*, vol. IX, ed. Ashey H. Thorndike (New York: Lincoln Scholarship Fund, 1928), pp. 372–3.

[7] Josiah Strong, *Our Country* (New York, The Baker and Tayloe Co., 1885), pp. 174–5.

[8] Richard W. Leopold, *The Growth of American Foreign Policy: A History* (New York, Knopf, 1962), pp. 125–6.

However, unlike the earlier version of Manifest Destiny, the imperialist binge of the late nineteenth century had Social Darwinism to support the religious and philosophical assertions. Richard Leopold elaborated on the rationale for Neo-Manifest Destiny:

By the middle of the 1880s racists and political scientists were also drawing upon the Darwinian hypothesis when they described international relations as a jungle in which the weak were crushed and the virile spread themselves over the globe. It was impossible, they declared, for any nation to remain aloof. To stand still was to fall behind in the march of civilization. ... Annexing distant possessions, then, promoted the national interest and insured the nation's survival. But it did more. It benefited backward peoples by raising their standard of living and by teaching them the art of self-government. Here was an ennobling purpose, a civilizing mission that it was the duty – indeed, the destiny – of certain races to undertake.[9]

By the Treaty of Paris, signed in late 1898, Spain yielded to the United States its colonies in Latin America and Asia. To test public reaction to the acquisition of overseas colonies, politicians debated the issue openly. Bernard A. Weisberger suggested that President McKinley's victory over William Jennings Bryan and the anti-imperialists should not have surprised anyone in the election of 1900:

The anti-imperialist debate provides a final footnote on the story of the years from 1877 to 1900. Many of the most outspoken opponents of annexation come from the ranks of intellectuals and reformers who were past fifty, and had been birthright Republicans. They believed that the republic they had known – of equality under law, self-restraint in appetite, and probity in government, would not survive the creation of an empire, complete with military adventurers and swindling proconsuls. But the republic of which they were dreaming had been disappearing for years; 1896 was its funeral rite.

On the other side were the imperialists, many of them vigorous young men, soon to become Progressives. They had reached maturity when the transcontinental railroad, the trust, the city, and the battleship were already realities instead of threatening novelties. They welcomed the power and challenges of the new society. They believed that an empire abroad could coexist with progress at home, and that strong, efficient, modern government could carry on the paternalistic and moralistic goals of the old Protestant tradition. The kind of nation that they dreamed of had been gestating for a long time and, in a sense, the year 1896 was its birth-year.[10]

[9] *Ibid.*, p. 88.

[10] Bernard A. Weisberger, *The New Industrial State* (New York, John Wiley, 1960), pp. 136–7.

The rewards of the war were immense and novel. Cuba was, in form, free, but in fact became, by the Platt Amendment of 1901, an economic colony of the United States. The United States acquired outright Puerto Rico, Guam, and the Philippines – the beginning of major commitments in the Pacific and the occasion of the great debate on imperialism. Was it consistent with the American tradition to subjugate alien and distant people? By 1939 the case for retaining an imperial control had become military and naval, not economic – imperialism has a momentum of its own. Certainly it was as a consequence of its acquisition of Pacific bases, and from the great debate on imperialism that they occasioned, that the decision was taken to build and fortify a canal at Panama and to stage a revolution in Colombia to ensure that that canal when built would be under the sole control of the United States. In the next decade American marines would land at intervals in Haiti, Nicaragua, the Dominican Republic, and Mexico. There arose also an interest in the China trade and in an Open Door for it that began to involve the United States permanently in Asia, as in the suppression of the Boxer Rising in 1900. There arose also a sentimental and missionary-minded concern for China, and a deep suspicion of Japan, that were both to be rich in stormy dividends.

From the end of the Spanish-American War in 1898 to the American entrance into World War I in 1917, the United States government engaged in an aggressive policy of expansion in Latin America. By means of purchase, coercion and military intervention, the United States made the Caribbean virtually into an "American lake." A critic of American imperialism, Samuel Guy Inman, described the expanse of this empire a quarter-century after America fought Spain:

> Run your eyes rapidly down the map and note the countries where the United States is now in practical control. And remember that this control always brings resentment and enmity among the people, though their officials may approve it. Here is the list:
>
> Cuba, where the United States has a navy base, with marines often found in the interior of the country, with the threat of intervention always held over the Cuban Government. ...
>
> Haiti, where two thousand United States marines direct and protect the Haitian Government, elected under their supervision; where an American financial adviser exercises absolute control over finances. ...
>
> Santo Domingo, where for the first time in the history of republics, one republic, without declaring war on another, landed an army, dismissed the president and congress, and for seven years ruled entirely, without even a semblance of national government. ...

> Panama, where, as President Roosevelt said, "I took Panama," since which time it has been under control of the United States. ...
>
> Nicaragua, where we have maintained one hundred marines since 1912, keeping in control a government which – according to the United States Admiral in charge – is opposed by eighty percent of the Nicaraguans, but which is favorable to American bankers. ...
>
> Honduras, where the American minister and two American corporations have long been the controlling powers, and where recently marines have been landed for "protection of American life and property." ...[11]

Next, Inman listed five Central and South American nations where United States financial interests directed the fiscal policy of each nation. These included Salvador (New York bankers collected customs receipts to insure payment of their loans); Colombia (diplomatic pressure protected US petroleum concessions); Peru and Ecuador (American advisers influenced national decisions); and Bolivia (a commission of American bankers controlled national finances).

Finally, Inman assessed American capitalist influence in three other Latin American nations:

> We must now retrace our steps on the map and look at the third class of countries. These are the ones dominated by North American capitalists, though not having Americans officially appointed to direct their fiscal programme. They number three as follows:
>
> Guatemala, where American bankers control the business, American money is the medium of circulation, and the United Fruit Company and other American financial interests have secured control of the railroads, which now become a part of the International Railways of Central America – the largest American-owned railway enterprise outside of the United States.
>
> Costa Rica, where after thirty years' peace, American oil and banana interests recently fomented a revolution against a reform government and at present largely control the economic life of the country and often act as brokers for the government.
>
> Mexico, where Americans own one third of the $2,500,000,000 of the nation's wealth, with seventy-three percent of the oil lands and much the largest part of the 54,874,557 acres of land owned by foreigners (an area equal to France, Spain, Portugal, and Switzerland), and where American financial representatives are the most important plenipotentiaries received by the Mexican Government.[12]

[11] Samuel Juy Inman, "Imperialistic America," *Atlantic Monthly*, 134 (July 1924), pp. 107–8.
[12] *Ibid.*, p. 109.

Eventually, in the 1930s, the United States terminated its occupation in Latin America. However, it never kept its eye off the Caribbean. At present, the United States still retains two colonies, Puerto Rico (conquered in 1898) and the Virgin Islands (purchased in 1916). And it maintains a naval base at Guantanamo, Cuba, and military fortifications in the Canal Zone. It also holds 99-year leases in the Corn Islands of Nicaragua, Guayana, Trinidad, Antigua, and Santa Lucia.

Behind the war with Spain, the jingoism of Roosevelt, and the emotions they aroused, were deeper forces – the new, highly industrial America of iron and steel and finance capital, in search of foreign markets. In the decade after 1897 American investment abroad quadrupled. The United States, though protected by both oceans, now sought the security of a two-ocean navy, and a quick link at Panama between the two; in mood it was no longer isolationist. It was an age of heavy involvement in ducal England, of the marriages of wealthy American girls in quest of coronets to poor but prestigious nobility. Speedy communication by ship and telegraph now made the Atlantic more a bridge than a barrier. Investment overseas, a quest for markets, for goods, and for brides were all part of the legacy of empire.

6

The Learned Presidency

1 THE NEW NATIONALISM

After Thomas Jefferson, Theodore Roosevelt (1858–1919) was the most versatile of Presidents. "The Roosevelt family fortune, derived from trade and banking, rested squarely on the twin pillars of law and property," writes David Burton, "and rejoiced in heaven's approval."[1] Born in New York City to a wealthy family, he was educated at Harvard, from which he graduated in 1880; after a spell at Columbia Law School he emerged as the leader of reform Republicans in the New York State Assembly in the early 1880s. Thereafter he pushed practical reforms as head of the US Civil Service Commission (1889–95). He was a rancher in the Dakota Territories, police commissioner and governor of New York (1899–1900), assistant secretary of the navy (1897–8), Colonel of a troop of volunteers known as the Rough Riders in Cuba, historian, and activist. As governor of New York he alienated the boss of the Republican machine, who decided to get rid of him by making him the vice-presidential nominee on William McKinley's ticket in 1900. The relentless overachiever was supposed to fade into quiet oblivion, but when McKinley was assassinated by the factory worker and anarchist Leon Czolgosz in September 1901, Roosevelt became president – the 26th, and at 42 the youngest, President of the US.

Like Andrew Jackson, "Teddy" saw himself as the tribune of the people, and, like Jackson too, he had skill at self-projection and

[1] David H. Burton, *The Learned Presidency* (New Jersey, Fairleigh Dickinson University Press, 1988), p. 41.

self-dramatization. The coming of a popular press helped his cause: his teeth, his eye-glasses, his immense vitality and advocacy of "the strenous life," his gift for phrases – "Speak softly, and carry a big stick," "the malefactors of great wealth," "I am feeling like a bull moose" – provided rich material for cartoonists and journalists. "Roosevelt is still mentally in the Stürm and Drang period of early adolescence, ... gushes over war as the ideal condition of human society, ..."[2] As David Burton makes plain, two ideas especially were the legacy of his years in the West: rugged individualism, with its Darwinist overtones (Darwin's *Origin of Species* appeared in the year after Roosevelt's birth), and the welfare of mankind, redolent of religious conviction.[3] After Roosevelt, the presidency ceased to be an office for shy men. When by accident they attained it, like Calvin Coolidge in 1923, they were strangely out of place. The most dynamic of American presidents, Roosevelt was at once a realist and a romanticist in foreign affairs and a progressive in domestic policy. He was also a fervent nationalist and a consummate moralist. He was the first American recipient of a Nobel Peace Prize, in 1906, for his services in concluding the treaty of peace between Russia and Japan at the end of the Russo-Japanese War. He was also the first President to ride in an automobile, and to be a passenger in an airplane. "Roosevelt was very likeable, a big figure, a rather ordinary intellect, with extraordinary gifts, a shrewd and I think pretty unscrupulous politician. He played all his cards – if not more," said Oliver Wendell Holmes, Jr, in 1921.

Roosevelt delivered one of his most popular speeches on April 10, 1899, in Chicago, a few months after he was inaugurated as governor of New York. Only six weeks previously, William Jennings Bryan had spoken in Chicago, denouncing imperialism. Roosevelt responded to Bryan on Appomattox Day in a speech that merged his personal view of life as a physical challenge with his conception of America's role in the world:

> In speaking to you, men of the greatest city of the West, men of the state which gave to the country Lincoln and Grant, men who preeminently and distinctly embody all that is most American in the American character, I wish to preach not the doctrine of the strenuous life; the life of toil and effort; of labor and strife; to preach that highest form of success which comes not to the man who desires mere easy peace but to the man who does not shrink from danger, from hardship, or from bitter toil, and who out of these wins the splendid ultimate triumph. ...

[2] Ibid., p. 42.
[3] Ibid., p. 42.

As it is with the individual so it is with the nation. It is a base untruth to say that happy is the nation that has no history. Thrice happy is the nation that has a glorious history. Far better it is to dare mighty things, to win glorious triumphs, even though checkered by failure, than to take rank with those poor spirits who neither enjoy much nor suffer much because they live in the gray twilight that knows neither victory nor defeat. If in 1861 the men who loved the Union had believed that peace was the end of all things and war and strife a worst of all things, and had acted up to their belief, we would have saved hundreds of thousands of lives, we would have saved hundreds of millions of dollars. Moreover, besides saving all the blood and treasure we then lavished, we would have prevented the heartbreak of many women, the dissolution of many homes; and we would have spared the country those months of gloom and shame when it seemed as if our armies marched only to defeat. We would have avoided all this suffering simply by shrinking from strife. And if we had thus avoided it we would have shown that we were weaklings and that we were unfit to stand among the great nations of the earth. Thank God for the iron in the blood of our fathers, the men who upheld the wisdom of Lincoln and bore sword or rifle in the armies of Grant: Let us, the children of the men who proved themselves equal to the mighty days – let us, the children of the men who carried the great Civil War to a triumphant conclusion, praise the God of our fathers that the ignoble counsels of peace were rejected, that the suffering and loss, the blackness of sorrow and despair, were unflinchingly faced and the years of strife endured; for in the end the slave was freed, the Union restored, and the mighty American Republic placed once more as a helmeted queen among nations.[4]

Despite the phrases, Roosevelt's achievement was less dramatic than his personality. The new President's first message to Congress, calculated to quiet the fears of his party associates, was nevertheless a blueprint of far-reaching reforms. He called for greater control of corporations by the federal government; more authority for the Interstate Commerce Commission; conservation of natural resources; extension of the merit system in the civil service; construction of an isthmian canal; and a vigorous foreign policy. Implicit in all of his recommendations was his theory that the President should be the leader in the formulation of governmental policies. But he extended the civil service rules over numerous classes of federal employees. The Sherman Antitrust Act of 1890, till then powerless, was used to regulate the railroads: their rates had to be published and standardized. The Department of Commerce

[4] Quoted in H. K. Beale, *Theodore Roosevelt and the Rise of America to World Power* (Baltimore, Johns Hopkins University Press, 1984).

and Labour was set up. The operations of the great business trusts came under scrutiny, especially their secret arrangements over rebates with the railroad companies. Whereas the first three Presidents had initiated only 18 suits, Theodore Roosevelt's administration in nearly eight years sued 44 trusts, to win him the title of "Trustbuster" – a term he disliked.

During Roosevelt's administrations the Department of Justice obtained 25 indictments and brought 18 bills in equity against the trusts. The most important of the judicial decisions were the injunction forbidding the members of the Beef Trust to engage in certain practices designed to restrain competition (1905); the suit that resulted in the dissolution of the Standard Oil Company of New Jersey, a holding company which had a monopoly of oil refining (1906–11); and the order dissolving the American Tobacco Company as an illegal combination (1907–11). In the course of its decisions under the Sherman Antitrust Act, the Supreme Court formulated the "rule of reason:" that only "unreasonable" combinations in restraint of trade were prohibited. William Howard Taft in the next four years initiated 90 suits; Woodrow Wilson before 1921 challenged another 80 trusts.

The first gun in the fight against illegal combinations was fired when Attorney General P. C. Knox filed suit against the Northern Securities Company, a holding company which controlled the Northern Pacific, the Great Northern, and the Chicago, Burlington & Quincy railroads. This meant, in effect, curbing the Big Three in railroads: J. P. Morgan, E. H. Harriman and James J. Hill. And Morgan had his own way to defy trust busters. When Knox instituted legal proceedings, he went to the White House and told Roosevelt "If we have done anything wrong, send your man to my man, and they can fix it up." The President, who had announced that the largest corporation, like the humblest citizen, would be compelled to obey the law, was pleased that the government won its case in the lower federal courts and that the Supreme Court upheld the decision (1904).

The Hepburn Act of 1906 gave the Interstate Commerce Commission, which had been set up 20 years earlier by Grover Cleveland, real authority in rate regulation and forced the railroads to surrender their interlocking interests in steamship lines and coal companies. By the end of the Roosevelt administration, rebates had practically disappeared, and the public regulation of railroads was an accepted principle.

In defining the government's relation to business enterprise, Roosevelt manifested a lively concern that there should be a "square deal" for all – capital, labor, and the public. This concern prompted his actions in the anthracite coal strike of 1902. For many years the miners in the anthracite districts of eastern Pennsylvania, unable to effect a satisfactory organization to protect their interests, felt that they had been exploited by the mine operators. Their grievances included long hours and low wages; the policy of compelling them to live in company houses and to trade at company stores; the compulsion to produce 3,000 pounds to a "ton;" and the refusal of the operators to recognize the union and collective bargaining. When the mine-owners refused to arbitrate, 140,000 miners went on strike (May 15, 1902), and the strike dragged on until the fall of that year.

Waiving the question of his constitutional prerogative, President Roosevelt invited John Mitchell, president of the United Mine Workers, and the mine-owners led by George F. Baer, president of the Philadelphia & Reading Coal & Iron Company, to confer with him. But the President's attempt to mediate failed completely, as the mine-owners still refused to make any concessions; and Baer he found to be arrogant, whereas Mitchell he thought a "gentleman." However, Roosevelt quietly exerted pressure in financial circles, and he also threatened to use federal troops to run the mines. He persuaded the operators to agree to his plan for an arbitral board to review the questions in dispute. The decision of this arbitral board granted a 10 percent wage increase and a nine-hour day, but did not recognize the union. It became the basis of industrial peace in the anthracite districts for 15 years.

Having served three and one-half years of McKinley's term, Roosevelt was eager for an election in his own right. For a time he feared that the reactionary Republicans would refuse him the nomination and would name Mark Hanna. But Hanna's death in the spring of 1904 removed all possibility of opposition, and Roosevelt was nominated by acclamation at the Republican convention. The Democrats, turning aside from the "radicalism" of Bryan and ignoring the claims of William Randolph Hearst, selected a conservative New York jurist, Alton R. Parker, as their standard-bearer. The issue of the campaign was really the policies of Theodore Roosevelt. The President was re-elected by an electoral vote of 336 to 140 for Parker. He carried every state outside the Solid South. Thereafter he became increasingly progressive, and by 1909 had endorsed proposals for graduated income and inheritance taxes and other concepts then deemed radical – "The New Nationalism".

One issue very dear to Theodore Roosevelt was conservation, the preservation of the natural resources of the country. He called for programs of irrigation, reclamation, and preservation for forest reserves, and for national parks – by no means the least of all his legacies. In 1907 he appointed an Inland Waterways Commission to canvas the whole question of the relation of rivers and soil and forest, of water power development, and of water transportation, and in 1909 a National Conservation Association was formed to engage in wide public education on the subject. For seven and a half years, Roosevelt strove to balance the interests of farmers, workers, and business people. Despite his image as a trustbuster, he preferred continuous regulation of giant corporations to dissolution under the antitrust laws, and to that end he drove through Congress legislation creating the Bureau of Corporations and strengthening the regulation of railroads. He also supported regulation of the food and drug industries. But his most significant accomplishment was probably the transfer of 125 million acres of public land into the forest reserves, the doubling of national parks, the creation of 16 national monuments such as California's Muir Woods, the establishment of 51 wildlife refuges, and the construction by 1907 of 28 irrigation projects in 14 states. The result of a White House Conference in 1908 was the appointment of a National Conservation Commission, with Gifford Pinchot as chairman, and the creation of 36 state boards to cooperate with the national body.

In foreign affairs, Roosevelt willingly shouldered the responsibilities of world power. As he put it after his retirement, while touring Africa in 1910, "I am, as I expected I would be, a pretty good imperialist." As Vice-President, he had strongly supported the use of force to suppress the nationalists in the Philippines, seeing Aguinaldo as similar to Sitting Bull. He broke precedents, acted independently of Congress, and held himself ready to invoke force in defense of the national interest if necessary.

Roosevelt's conspicuous and aggressive activity in the conduct of foreign relations increased the influence and prestige of the United States as a world power. The growing interests of the United States in the Caribbean, tremendously stimulated by the acquisition of the Panama Canal Zone – "I took Panama," he boasted, with some pride – caused the Roosevelt administration to develop a theory of responsibility for the preservation of order in that area. Under Roosevelt's direction, the Monroe Doctrine was reinterpreted to justify United States intervention in Latin-American affairs.

In 1902, Great Britain and Germany, endeavoring to collect debts owed to their citizens by the government of Venezuela, established a blockade of Venezuelan ports. Roosevelt feared that the debt question might be made the pretext for a violation of the Monroe

Doctrine. His diplomatic pressure behind the scenes, particularly against Germany, probably helped both nations to decide to grant Venezuela's plea for arbitration. Mixed commissions reviewed the claims against the South American republic, and Venezuela agreed in 1903 to devote 30 percent of its customs receipts to pay the valid claims. However, the Venezuelan incident caused Luis Drago, the Argentine minister for foreign affairs, to announce the doctrine that no state had a right to make the financial claims of its citizens against another state the pretext for military intervention: the Drago Doctrine. The American State Department gave its support to the principles of the Drago Doctrine, and at the Second Hague Conference in 1907, the United States delegation secured the adoption of a resolution that no nation should resort to armed force to recover the debts due its citizens "unless the debtor nation refused arbitration, or, having accepted arbitration, failed to submit to the award."

When in 1904 France, Italy, and Belgium threatened to use force in collecting debts owed their citizens by the Dominican Republic, Roosevelt announced in his annual message to Congress in December 1904 that chronic wrong doing, or an impotence which results in a general loosening of the ties of civilized society, may in America, as elsewhere, ultimately require intervention by some civilized nation, and in the Western Hemisphere the adherence of the United States to the Monroe Doctrine may force the United States, however reluctantly, in flagrant cases of such wrongdoing or impotence, to "the exercise of an international police power." Under this so-called Roosevelt Corollary of the Monroe Doctrine the administration negotiated a treaty with the Dominican Republic providing for control of the collection of the Dominican customs by the United States. When the Senate refused to ratify the treaty, Roosevelt put the receivership into effect by executive order. This manifestation of "police power" was widely criticized in the United States and aroused grave apprehension throughout Latin America. Roosevelt and later Presidents cited the Corollary to justify intervention in the Dominican Republic, Cuba, Nicaragua, Mexico, and Haiti. In 1934, however, Franklin D. Roosevelt renounced interventionism and established his Good Neighbor policy, prompting one commentator to say, "A Roosevelt gave and a Roosevelt hath taken away."

The results of the Spanish-American War dramatically emphasized the desirability of a canal between the Atlantic and the Pacific under the control of the United States. By the Clayton-Bulwer Treaty of 1850 the United States had agreed that any isthmian canal should be under the joint guarantee of Great Britain and the United States. The abrogation of this agreement was secured by Secretary of State Hay in the Hay-Pauncefote Treaty of 1901, which provided that America might build the canal and have full control and policing of it if its use was accorded to all nations on equal terms. Meanwhile, Congress had decided to build the canal across Panama, then a province of Colombia, rather than across Nicaragua as originally proposed, and had offered the New Panama Canal Company $40 million for the rights of the old French company which had tried to construct a canal during the 1880s. The Hay-Herran Treaty with Colombia was signed, whereby Colombia granted the United States a 99-year lease over a zone ten miles wide in Panama in return for $10 million in cash and an annual rental of $250,000 beginning nine years after the agreement was ratified. However, the Colombian Senate, much to the disgust of President Roosevelt, refused to ratify the treaty, probably hoping to get better terms.

Colombia's rejection of the Hay-Herran Treaty not only irritated the United States government, but it alarmed those who were interested in the New Panama Canal Company and it aroused patriotic Panamanians who feared the canal would be built in Nicaragua. In the summer of 1903, therefore, it was no surprise to the American government when revolution was fomented in Panama. The revolutionists were successful because the United States, basing its action on a treaty of 1846 with Colombia, maintained "free and uninterrupted transit" across the isthmus. Actually, this action prevented the Colombian government from moving the necessary troops to quell the revolt. Two weeks after the revolution the United States concluded a treaty with the Republic of Panama, which Roosevelt had already recognized. The Hay-Bunau-Vanilla Treaty of 1903 granted to the United States in perpetuity the use of a canal zone ten miles wide; transferred to its government the properties of the New Panama Canal Company and the Panama Railroad Company; awarded Panama $10 million and an annuity of $250,000 for its concessions. In 1921 the United States quieted Colombian complaints by a treaty in which it agreed to pay the South American republic $25 million.

Both the Roosevelt and Taft administrations gave constant support to those building the Panama Canal. Construction, after several false starts, went forward rapidly under Colonel G. W. Goethals, while Colonel W. C. Gorgas conquered sanitation difficulties in the Canal Zone. The first steamer passed through the Canal in August 1914.

In the Far East, Roosevelt, and Taft after him, supported and extended John Hay's vigorous assertion of American interests. At the outbreak of the Russo-Japanese War in 1904, Roosevelt persuaded both powers to recognize the neutrality of Chinese territory outside of Manchuria, and he warned France and Germany that if either power aided the Russians the United States would side with Japan. Having succeeded in limiting the extent of the war, President Roosevelt intervened to bring it to an end. At his suggestion, representatives of Japan and Russia met at Portsmouth, New Hampshire, and finally signed a treaty terminating hostilities. Roosevelt managed to guide the deliberations of the wrangling delegates and was awarded the Nobel Peace Prize for his efforts.

Japan's easy victory convinced many Americans that the Japanese were a threat to the interests of the United States in the whole Pacific area. In 1905, by a secret understanding (the Taft-Katsura Memorandum), Japan recognized the sovereignty of the United States in the Philippines, while the United States recognized Japan's control of Korea. The two nations pledged themselves to maintain peaceful conditions in the Far East. But within a year Japanese resentment flared over California's demand that all Japanese immigration be forbidden by Congress, and the action of the San Francisco Board of Education in segregating all Oriental students in special schools. Elihu Root, who had succeeded John Hay as Roosevelt's secretary of state, found a formula of "Gentlemen's Agreement," in which Japan promised to restrict the emigration of laborers to the United States and the California school officials modified their rulings concerning Japanese pupils. By the Root-Takahira Agreement (1908), both countries agreed to uphold existing territorial arrangements, to respect the political integrity of China, and to maintain the Open Door principle.[5]

2 THEODORE ROOSEVELT: CRUSADER ON THE PEOPLE'S SIDE

TR was an Easterner by birth and breeding, Westerner in style and bravado, an Anglo-American imperialist by instinct and by taste. But he was also a crusader for social justice. "Muckraker" was his own term for some journalists of that same stripe. The Muckrakers whom Roosevelt so named because of their preoccupation with scandalous conditions in business and politics, exerted a powerful

[5] Lewis L. Gould, *The Presidency of Theodore Roosevelt* (1990); William H. Harbaugh, *Power and Responsibility: The life and times of Theodore Roosevelt* (Oxford, Oxford University Press, 1975); Burton, *The Learned Presidency*; Henry F. Pringle, *Theodore Roosevelt, a Biography* (New York, Harcourt Brace, 1931); Edmund Morris, *The Rise of Theodore Roosevelt* (New York, Coward, McCann and Geoghagen, 1979).

influence in stirring public opinion to the point of action. The President's crusade for social justice was aided by their work, even if he did not always recognize his indebtedness. As we have seen, one can trace to their efforts such federal legislation as the Meat Inspection Act and the Pure Food and Drug Act (1906). They were also largely responsible for the government's suit against the Beef Trust and the proceedings against the subsidiaries of the American Sugar Refining Company for defrauding the government of customs duties.

Reformers of the Roosevelt era also endeavored to make government organization and processes more democratic and to enact legislation that would directly benefit the people. The accusation that American legislative bodies were unrepresentative and dominated by privileged interests led to a demand that the popular will be translated more directly into governmental action. Various devices were put in place to further this end.

The initiative and referendum, first adopted by South Dakota in 1898, permit a certain percentage of the electorate to initiate by petition measures which the state legislature or the people may vote upon. Likewise, a certain percentage of the electorate may have a law, which has passed the legislature, referred to the voters for acceptance or rejection. Twenty-two states have at various times tested the initiative and referendum. Another plan, the recall, intended to make public officials more responsive to public opinion, was first used in Los Angeles in 1903; it permits the voters to remove an official from office before the expiration of the regular term for which he has been elected or appointed. Its use in connection with the recall of judges, as provided in Arizona's constitution, aroused bitter controversy, but there have been few examples of summary removal.

The system of direct primaries, introduced in Wisconsin by Robert M. La Follette in 1903, represented an attempt to give the voters a chance to name candidates, as well as to choose between candidates, for public office. By 1933 some form of the direct primary was used in all but six of the states. However, the promises of the reformers that the power of the political boss would be broken and that the character of candidates for public office would be improved were over-optimistic.

The champions of direct government were particularly insistent in their demand for popular election of United States Senators. Claiming that election by the state legislatures resulted in a Senate controlled by an alliance between predatory wealth and unscrupulous politicians, they persuaded state after state to permit the voters to express a senatorial preference at the polls which the legislature was bound to accept. At the same time the reformers worked hard to secure a constitutional amendment. Not until 1911 did the Senate finally capitulate and join the House in passing a resolution (which was ratified by three-fourths of the states in 1913 and became the Seventeenth Amendment) providing for direct popular election of the upper house of Congress.

Probably no part of the program of the political progressives was more valuable than their attack upon the structure and administration of city government. The notorious failure of municipal government in the United States was attributed in part to the anachronistic mayor-and-council system. In 1900 Galveston, Texas, experimented with a new form of government – the commission plan. All municipal functions were vested in a small commission – usually of five – with each commissioner being responsible for the management of a department. By 1914 more than 400 of the smaller cities of the country had tried the plan, but some with such indifferent results that they abandoned it. In 1914 Dayton, Ohio, introduced the "city manager" type of municipal organization, in which the politically responsible commission appoints a business manager to run the city as if it were a going business concern. As in the case of the commission plan, the results have not been uniformly satisfactory. Both new types, however, have done much to arouse the electorate to an appreciation of the problems of municipal government.

The Progressive era was marked by a notable extension of the suffrage, as state followed state in granting the ballot to women. The pioneer advocates of women's rights in the 1840s had started a suffrage movement which began to bear fruit after the Civil War. The discussion of the civil and political status of blacks; the equalitarian philosophy of the Far Western frontier; the entrance of women into factories, trades, and professions; and the opening of the doors of institutions of higher learning to women; all gave impetus to the campaign for sex equality and for female suffrage. Wyoming, the first female suffrage state, was admitted to the Union in 1890; by 1912 Colorado, Utah, Idaho, Washington, Kansas, Arizona, California, and Oregon had granted the ballot to women.

Many of the feminists believed that an amendment to the Constitution was the royal road to equal political privileges with men. Susan B. Anthony proposed such an amendment as early as 1869; nine years later it was introduced in Congress. There it languished for forty-one years, until 1919, when Congress passed it as the Nineteenth Amendment and referred it to the states. Ratification came in August, 1920, in time to permit the women of the nation to vote in the presidential election of that year. This result was a testimonial to the effective work of such leaders as Susan B. Anthony, Elizabeth Cady Stanton, Ann Howard Shaw, and Carrie Chapman Catt.

The Progressives were also responsible for a good deal of state welfare legislation passed during this period. A number of states enacted laws regulating wages, hours, and working conditions; restricting the labor of women and children; providing for workers' compensation; granting public aid to mothers with dependent children and the needy aged; and setting safety and health standards for industry. Progressive reforms in the cities included the establishment of settlement houses, slum clearance, and recreation facilities.

The publicity that plays about the White House began in the years before 1900: not with TR, but with McKinley. Before the 1890s the press did not cover the White House on a regular basis: Capitol Hill was a far richer source of news. But the McKinley administration, and the Spanish-American War in particular, reversed this situation. McKinley himself recognized the growing press interest in the chief executive and set aside an outer reception room for the use of the growing number of White House correspondents, with permanent accommodation in the heart of the executive mansion.

It is possible that George Juergens passes too quickly over McKinley's role in the birth of the White House press corps. Ida Tarbell, in an article published in 1898, laid a good deal of emphasis on McKinley's cordial relationships with newsmen. But whereas for McKinley good relations with reporters were an added bonus, for his successor they were a vital necessity. Theodore Roosevelt lacked a secure political base: to become a strong leader, he decided to appeal directly to public sentiment. Whether Roosevelt was engaging in dramatic acts (the Northern Securities Company prosecution) or using well-timed leaks to assist the progress of legislation in which he was interested (as in the successful attempt to secure a Bureau of Corporations and the long-running battle over the Hepburn Bill), he saw the press as an essential tool to be used in furtherance of his own purposes. When it seemed to be going too far, as it did in 1906, he made his famous "Man with the Muckrake" speech reining it in. Roosevelt had no notion of an independent press. Indeed, his manipulation of reporters, his reserving of the juiciest pieces of news to a group of "fair-haired boys" who would publish it when and how he wished, showed a determination to reduce press comment on his administration to the level of propaganda. Roosevelt upgraded the press corps at the price of corrupting it. But his methods were only successful because he was dealing with a press not yet assertive about its rights.

Roosevelt's successors, Taft and Wilson, had to cope with expectations aroused by TR, that the President would be a media figure, and with a new militancy on the part of reporters more conscious now of their role and status. Taft, easy-going, indolent and oddly sensitive to criticism, totally failed to grasp the importance of using the press to build support for his programs. His presidency was a disaster in the field of public relations. Wilson, an even more reserved and remote man, believed as Roosevelt had done that the President should control the news and the way it was written, but lacked TR's finesse in achieving his aims. It is more than a little ironic, as Juergens points out, that the one genuine newsgathering innovation of the Wilson years, the presidential press conference, should have owed its origin to a president who distrusted newsmen profoundly and sought to limit his contact with them to a formal, almost ceremonial level. Once America entered World War I, George Creel's Committee on Public Information assumed responsibility for publicizing Wilson's words and deeds, making it unnecessary for him to see reporters any more on a regular basis. Juergens is critical, and rightly so, of Wilson's failure to restrain those members of his own administration who saw in the war an opportunity to stifle dissent. He makes it clear that a large part of the blame for the Senate's rejection of the League of Nations lay in Wilson's refusal until it was too late to use the press to mobilize public support behind his peace proposals.[6]

3 WILLIAM H. TAFT

At the end of his second term Roosevelt could have been nominated again had he permitted his friends to carry out their plans. Instead, he directed all his political power toward the selection of William Howard Taft, secretary of war, as his successor. The convention of 1908 was a Roosevelt convention. The delegates were wildly enthusiastic over the President, and at his behest nominated Taft and adopted a platform which had been written at the White House. Bryan, once more dominant in Democratic circles, was unable to make any headway in the campaign against Roosevelt's

[6] George Juergens, *News From the White House: The presidential-press Relationship in the Progressive era* (Chicago, University of Chicago Press, 1981), pp. x, 338.

trusted lieutenant. Indeed, there was much in the Republican platform which met with the approval of the Democratic leader. Bryan's electoral vote of 162 to 321 for Taft indicated, however, that the Nebraskan had regained some of the ground lost by Parker four years earlier.

The reform movement continued under President Taft, who sought to carry on and to strengthen the reforms of his predecessor. But Taft, however genial in manner, was heavy and lethargic; he lacked the ability, the temperament and volubility of Teddy Roosevelt. "Taft is evidently a man who takes color from his surroundings. He was an excellent man under me, and close to me. ... He has not the slightest idea of what is necessary if this country is to make social and industrial progress" (Theodore Roosevelt, 1910, 1911). He accepted in 1909 proposals for an inordinately high protective tariff, and seemed to be the prisoner of conservative Republicanism. But then he was an Ohio man.

Like many of his predecessors, Taft was a lawyer. A native of Cincinnati and a graduate of Yale, Taft was an able administrator and an intelligent, if unimaginative, lawyer and jurist. "Taft is a large body, entirely surrounded by men who know exactly what they want" said Jonathan P. Dollier in 1909. He was fully aware of W. G. Sumner's views of the rights of capital in a *laissez-faire* economy, but he was no believer in *laissez-faire*. Indeed, he was a believer in government, and had spent his whole life administering it. Taft had served as US solicitor general from 1890 to 1892 and as a federal circuit court judge from 1892 to 1900. He became head of the Second Philippine Commission in 1901 and the first governor-general of the Philippines the following year. In both posts he did much to advance civil government and to reconcile the Filipinos to American rule. Appointed secretary of war in 1904, he faithfully executed President Theodore Roosevelt's policies. He was a competent executive officer. But he had long believed that life was in fact a long series of compromises. As a judge he did set limits to the power of government, limits that permitted governments to do many things that he considered unwise. There was a place, that is, for the judgment of the politician, for patronage, back-scratching, and boodle; but for Taft, government came first.

Conservative in temperament though Progressive in convictions, Taft deemed it his mission as president to consolidate rather than expand the Roosevelt reforms – to give them "the sanction of law," as he privately phrased it. He was, in David Burton's words, "a partially wrought social Darwinist." Moreover, he surrounded himself with conventionally-minded lawyers, and allowed Old Guard

Republican leaders to control his lines to Congress. Partly in consequence, he compromised on the tariff, the Payne-Aldrich Bill, after a courageous initial call for reform. He also suffered the resignation of Roosevelt's intimate, Chief Forester Gifford Pinchot, because he believed that some of the Roosevelt-Pinchot conservation practices had been "exercised far beyond legal limitation." Yet the record of the Taft administration for progressive measures and policies compares favorably with that of the Roosevelt administration. The achievements of Taft's four years in office included the Mann-Elkins Act; the eight-hour day for workers on government contracts; the establishment of the postal savings system and the parcel post; the creation of a separate Department of Labor (1913); the extension of the merit system to new branches of the civil service; the vigorous prosecution of illegal combinations in restraint of trade; and legislation reserving additional public land from private exploitation. Constitutional amendments for an income tax (the Sixteenth Amendment) and direct election of Senators (the Seventeenth Amendment) were also approved during his administration, though they owed more to a coalition of Progressive Republicans and Democrats than to the President.[7]

Indeed, these were the days when Cannon ruled as well as Taft. As Speaker of the House of Representatives, Joseph G. Cannon exercised enormous power in connection with the legislative process: he controlled the Committee on Rules, which determined the routine procedure of the House; he appointed all committees and designated their chairmen; and he had the power to recognize members who desired to speak from the floor and therefore could guide the course of debate. Cannon wielded these considerable powers in such fashion as to aid the conservatives and embarrass the Progressives. He was "Uncle Joe" – but it was rarely said with affection. In the spring of 1910, the insurgent Republicans rose in revolt against Cannon's dictatorial tactics. Aided by the Democratic minority, they passed a resolution (introduced by George W. Norris of Nebraska) which deprived the Speaker of his control over the Rules Committee. The following year the Democrats, now in the majority, denied the Speaker the right to appoint standing committees, thus establishing "representative government" in the House.

Taft's performance in foreign affairs was similarly mixed. A strong proponent of international law, he strove unsuccessfully to win Senate support of a series of arbitration treaties, but he also sent marines into Nicaragua. Whereas Roosevelt relied on a vigorous

[7] Burton, *The Learned Presidency*, p. 93.

diplomatic policy, Taft was inclined to use economic means to reach diplomatic objectives and he supported an unproductive program of "dollar diplomacy" in Canada, the Caribbean and the Far East.

In 1909 Taft's secretary of state, P. C. Knox, persuaded American financiers to join with British, French, and German bankers in a consortium to construct Hukuang Railroad in China. Three years later President Taft gave his approval to a more pretentious undertaking – a loan to the Chinese Republic in which American bankers were invited to participate. The investment of American capital abroad was described by President Taft as merely an effort "directed to the increase of American trade." He sincerely hoped that American dollars would help American diplomats maintain the balance of power in the Orient, thus perpetuating such American policies as the Open Door and the preservation of the territorial integrity of China. Prior to World War I, the growth of American foreign investments seemed to follow the pattern of European economic imperialism, but it was fundamentally due to an interest in overseas trade and rarely led to the attempt to impose political control over colonial possessions.

The antagonism to President Taft on the part of the Progressives, notably the Western insurgents, was accentuated by his ill-fated plan for reciprocity with Canada. In 1911, a reciprocity agreement was negotiated with Canada which provided for (1) free trade in primary foodstuffs, such as grain, vegetables, and eggs; (2) mutual reduction of tariff duties on secondary food products, like flour and meats; and (3) a slight decrease in the duties on manufactured goods. Despite the bitter opposition of the Western agrarian interests, who feared the competition of Canadian produce, the President succeeded in persuading Congress to approve the reciprocity agreement. But Taft's victory was fruitless, for the reciprocity issues caused a dissolution of the Canadian Parliament and the overwhelming defeat of Sir Wilfred Laurier, who had negotiated the agreement. Many Canadians interpreted Taft's interest in reciprocity as the first move in an American policy to bring Canada within the political and economic control of the United States. Taft failed to be re-elected in 1912 because of the defection of Progressives to Roosevelt, who ran on the Bull Moose ticket, and to Woodrow Wilson, the successful Democratic candidate. "As a man and as a real honest-to-God fellow Mr Taft will go to his grave with more real downright affection and less enemies than any. ... We are parting with three hundred pounds of solid charity to everybody, and love and affection for all his countrymen" (Will Rogers, 1930).[8]

[8] Paola Coletta, *The Presidency of William Howard Taft* (Lawrence, University

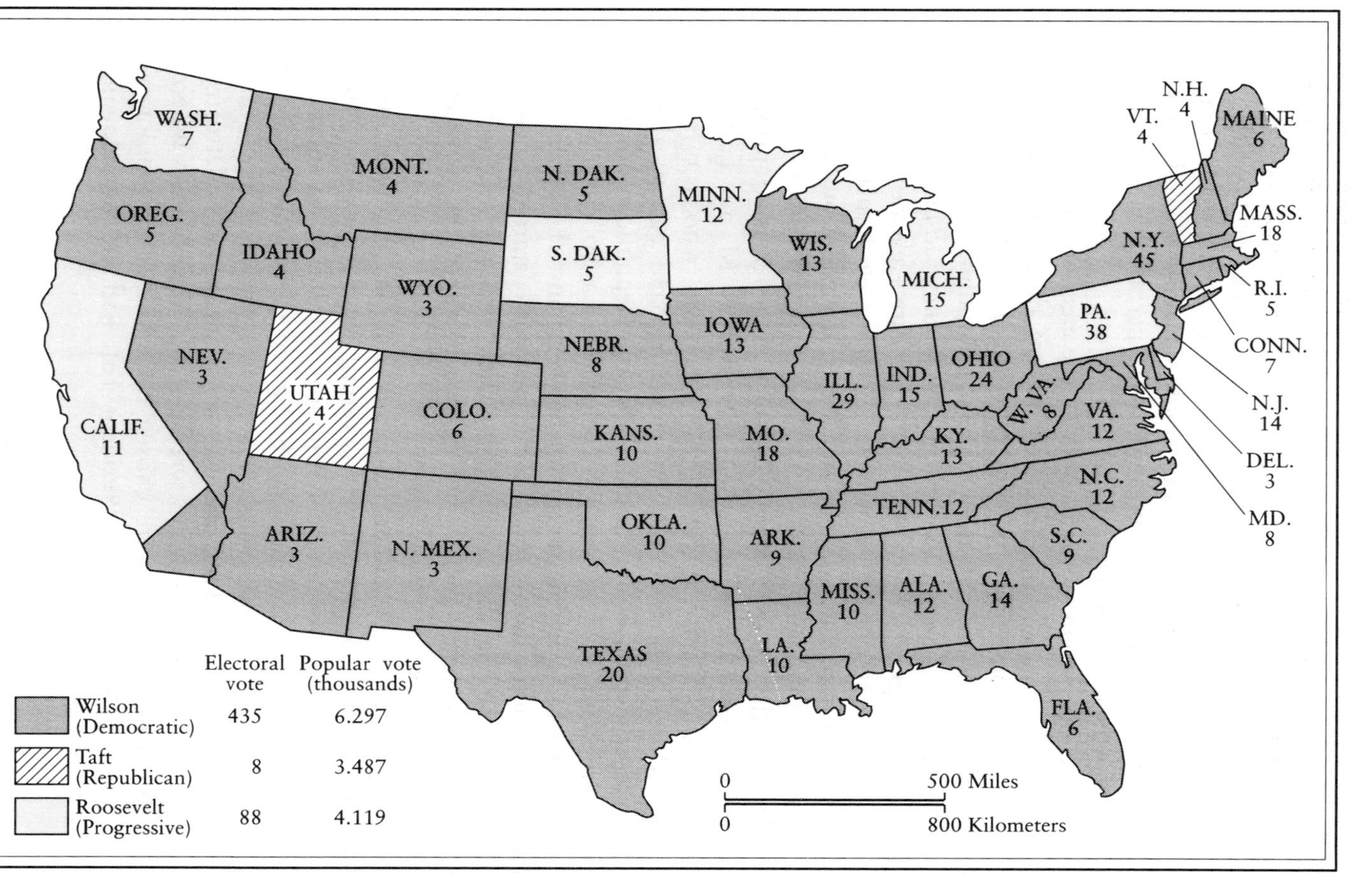

Map 6 The election of 1912.

Yet one aspect of Taft's policy is most typical of the age, an age that was becoming urban and industrial rather than rural and agrarian: the rights of labor unions. Labor union membership rose from less than 1 million in 1900 to almost 3 million in 1916 and – partly because of Taft's work on the War Labor Board – to 5 million in 1920. Taft saw himself as sympathetic to workers' rights and to strikes. But labor, he held, should enjoy no special privileges or immunities; no secondary boycotts were permissible. The growth of unions was not synonymous with progress.

From the standpoint of party politics the election of 1912 was of unusual significance; from the standpoint of the crusade for social justice it was confusing and indecisive. Following the insurgent Republicans' revolt of 1910 the Progressive Republican League, sponsored by several Republican senators in January 1911, announced the political program of Progressivism: (1) direct election of United States Senators; (2) direct primaries; (3) direct election of delegates to national nominating conventions; (4) state adoption of the initiative, referendum, and recall; and (5) a national corrupt practices act. At first the League merely advocated progressive principles, but in October 1911 it indicated that Robert M. La Follette of Wisconsin, the former governor of Wisconsin who was to vote against the declaration of war on Germany, and against the Versailles Treaty, would be its candidate for the Republican nomination against President Taft in the 1912 election. La Follette, who had won national fame by his successful battle against the power of the great corporations in his own state, promptly started a vigorous campaign to arouse the voters from their lethargy. Although an isolationist in foreign policy, he vigorously supported government intervention in the economy.

Although former President Roosevelt had been supporting the insurgent Republicans ever since his return from Africa in 1910, he refused to join the Progressive Republican League or to support La Follette. After weeks of indecision he agreed to become a candidate for the Republican nomination. Then came an unseemly scramble for delegates between Taft and Roosevelt, with La Follette trying to salvage something from the wreck of his high hopes. Wherever the Republican delegates were chosen by state conventions or were hand-picked by the "bosses," President Taft had the advantage, but

---

of Kansas Press, 1973); Alpheus T. Mason, *William Howard Taft: Chief Justice* (New York, Simon and Schuster, 1965); Henry F. Pringle, *The Life and Times of William Howard Taft*, 2 vols. (New York, Farrar and Rinehart, 1939), pp. 143–7.

in those states which permitted the voters to express their preference for the nominee, Roosevelt was clearly the choice. The national convention was controlled by the administration forces and proceeded amidst great confusion to grant Taft another nomination.

Roosevelt charged that the nomination had been "stolen" from him by irregular tactics. With evangelical fervor his followers undertook the task of forming a new party. On August 5, 1912, the Progressive party held its first convention in Chicago, where two months earlier its hero had been rejected by the Republicans. Roosevelt was nominated by acclamation, while Hiram Johnson of California was named for the vice-presidency. The schism in the Republican ranks was complete.

The Democrats meanwhile had also been engaged in a spirited contest between the conservative and liberal forces within the party. As the delegates assembled at Baltimore for the Democratic Convention, it was evident that no candidate for the nomination could control the convention. Champ Clark, Speaker of the House, had both conservative and liberal delegates in his following. The extreme conservatives were kindly disposed toward Governor Judson Harmon of Ohio and Representative Oscar Underwood of Alabama. The liberals had rallied behind Governor Woodrow Wilson of New Jersey, who described himself as a "Progressive with the brakes on." Speaker Clark would probably have been nominated had it not been for the influence of William Jennings Bryan. Although one of the delegates instructed to vote for Clark, Bryan dramatically denounced the "sinister influences" supporting Clark and on the fourteenth ballot switched to Woodrow Wilson, who was finally nominated on the forty-sixth ballot.

The Progressive and Democratic platforms frankly invited the support of those who were willing to enlist in the warfare against political and economic privilege. Even the Republican pronouncement could not be regarded as ultra-conservative. Roosevelt's "New Nationalism," which demanded governmental regulation of economic activity, was not really distasteful to Wilson, though he presented his "New Freedom" in the lofty phrases of economic liberalism. Both candidates were eager to offer some program to meet the social unrest of the times, but Taft seemed anxious to avoid recognition of popular discontent.

The overwhelming nature of the Democratic victory in November was largely due to the disruption of the Republican party. Roosevelt's popular following was amazing, for he had no regular organization and his most ardent supporters were amateurs in politics. Yet he carried six states with 88 electoral votes. Taft won only the 8 votes of Utah and Vermont. Wilson had 435 votes. The House and Senate were Democratic by wide margins.

For the next eight years Taft taught law at Yale (1913–21) and lectured widely, and during World War I he served as co-chairman of the National War Labor Board (1918–19). In 1921 President Harding appointed Taft to succeed Edward D. White as chief justice, a post he filled until his death. A gracious and genial person, on the bench Taft was generally conservative (though not reactionary) in his political and social views. His achievement as a jurist was his prolonged and tireless labor for judicial reform.[9]

Optimistic advocates of international conciliation believed that important progress toward world peace had been made during the first decade of the twentieth century. In January 1905, Roosevelt had presented to the Senate identical arbitration treaties with seven European nations. The Senate amended them in a manner which the President deemed undesirable, but two years later Secretary of State Elihu Root had similar treaties ratified, with requirements for Senate advice and consent. In 1911 Secretary of State Knox negotiated treaties with Great Britain and France providing for arbitration of any matters in dispute between the United States and these nations but the Senate refused to ratify the treaties.

The Franco-German conflict over the Moroccan crisis of 1905 was so ominous that Roosevelt exerted diplomatic pressure at both Paris and Berlin to secure agreement to the plan for an international conference. The subsequent meeting at Algeciras revealed the powerful influence of the United States as represented in the person of Henry White; the formula finally accepted by the conference for the international regulation of police, banking, and trade in Morocco did not differ materially from the proposals of Secretary Root.

Roosevelt hoped that the Second Hague Peace Conference in 1907 would take steps toward disarmament. He was disappointed in the results, however, for the delegates could not agree on specific proposals and adjourned after suggesting that a conference meet in London in 1908 to draw up an international code for naval warfare.

The so-called "peace movement" reached impressive proportions in the decade prior to the outbreak of World War I, as American philanthropists and public officials joined forces to arouse public opinion to the dangers of war in the new industrial age. In 1910 Edwin Ginn, a Boston publisher, endowed the World Peace Foundation with funds for research and publicity in the cause of international

[9] See Pringle, *William Howard Taft*.

conciliation. Andrew Carnegie, too, used his great wealth in various ways to promote public understanding of the evils of war and the means by which peace might be achieved. He established in 1911 the Carnegie Endowment for International Peace, and he provided the funds to erect stately public buildings to house the activities of various peace organizations, among them the Peace Palace at The Hague, and the Pan-American Union in Washington. The most eloquent arguments for a world peace program and for a stable world order under international law were voiced in the annual conferences held at Lake Mohonk, New York, in which President Taft and some of his associates were interested; but the high hopes of these enthusiasts were wrecked by the outbreak of war in 1914.

4 WOODROW WILSON'S "NEW LIBERALISM"

One of the most curious phenomena in the writing of recent American history is the failure of American historians to agree on a verdict on Woodrow Wilson. This is the more surprising since for many decades now American Presidents have been, in their varied and at times conflicting ways, world leaders. Isolationism is no longer fashionable, nor indeed tenable; those who in the past might have been its foremost advocates have recently been found on the Far Right, supporters of McCarthy, MacArthur, or of brinkmanship in varied forms. Historians, prompt to reflect the preoccupations of their own times – one has to understand the present, it is now fashionable to say, in order to understand the past – have in any event long been doubting the accuracy of isolationism as a description of American foreign policy. Honored when it suited its purposes, and binding as myth, it was ignored in 1798 and again in 1812; even its bible, the Monroe Doctrine of 1823, was accompanied by expressions of sympathy for struggling Greece; it was never honored except in lip-service in the Caribbean, in Latin America, or in the Pacific; and since 1898 it has been essentially discarded as a Great Rule. Alexander DeConde, in his *Entangling Alliance*,[10] has recently doubted whether the much-cited Washington or Jefferson texts were designed to be binding on posterity, and has suggested realistically that they were, like most state papers, meant for the day they were issued.

[10] Alexander De Conde, *Entangling Alliance: Politics and diplomacy under George Washington* (Durham, NC, Duke University Press, 1958).

Yet, sympathetic though the climate has become to idealism, and even to interventionism in foreign affairs, to liberal causes and crusading leaders, there has been no concerted effort to resurrect and worship Wilson as America's greatest international crusader. There has been little emotional appeal about the picture of the stricken warrior in his bath chair, watching after 1919 the wrecking of his efforts that spelt doom for his party and for the League of Nations, and thus made likely a second world war. When, from time to time, appeals have been made to regard him in these terms, they have been made by politicians rather than by historians. His own contemporary biographer, Ray Stannard Baker, did, of course, see him as hero. Something of this kind was attempted for a short period in 1941 and 1942,[11] and the centenary of his birth produced many tributes, particularly an admirable assessment in *The Virginia Quarterly Review* (Autumn, 1956), But, even then, no major claims for him were made. Why is there no Wilson legend?

The 28th president of the United States came from a theological and academic background. Born in the Presbyterian manse in Staunton, Virginia, in 1856, Wilson received the Ph.D. degree from the Johns Hopkins University in 1886. He remained a Southerner his entire life: "I am obliged to say again and again that the only place in the country, the only place in the world, where nothing has to be explained to me is the South." It was in fact only part of the truth. Although he was born in Virginia and grew up in Augusta, Georgia, he had among his British-born and Ulster-born ancestors some who lived in Pittsburgh and Steubenville, Ohio. His Southern patriotism, in David Burton's phrase, "was acquired rather than innate." As the first Southerner to enter the White House after the Civil War, his policies were national in scope and purpose. But it was in Dixie that he felt at home.[12]

As a college professor, Wilson was one of the founders of the discipline of political science in the United States and made significant contributions to the fields of comparative government and administration. He was a prolific academic and popular historian. He launched himself with an expanded PhD. thesis, *Congressional Government* (1885), still in print over a century later, and he followed it with a number of highly regarded and much-reprinted volumes, including *The State: Elements of historical and practical*

[11] Ray Stannard Baker, *Woodrow Wilson, Life and Letters*, 8 vols (Garden City, NY, Doubleday, 1927–39).
[12] Burton, *The Learned Presidency*, pp. 138–9.

politics (1889), a five-part *History of the American People* (1902), and *Constitutional Government in the United States* (1908). Appointed president of Princeton in 1902 – the first layman to hold the office – he transformed a venerable college into a world-class university, but conflicts over the reorganization of the social life of undergraduates and control of the graduate school caused him to resign in October 1910. Apart from preaching from a pulpit in his father's empty church, he had no special skill in politics, except as orator and publicist.

Meanwhile, Wilson had accepted the Democratic nomination for governor of New Jersey. With the backing of influential Democrats, including wealthy conservatives who believed he would stamp out radical Bryanism, Wilson won election as governor of New Jersey in 1910, and in 1911–13, as a forward-looking progressive, established a record which brought him to the forefront of national politics.

After his election in November 1910, he pushed through measures that put the state in the forefront of progressive reform. This success catapulted him into national prominence and led to his election as President on the Democratic ticket in November 1912. The Taft-Roosevelt forces were split; the Progressive party at their first convention in Chicago in August 1912 nominated as their presidential candidate by acclamation Theodore Roosevelt, in the same city where at the Republican convention Taft had been renominated – though not by acclamation. In the Electoral College, the votes were cast thus: Wilson 435, Roosevelt 88, Taft 8. Although a minority President, Wilson was in a remarkably strong political position when he assumed office. The Republicans were at loggerheads, a Democratic majority prevailed in both Houses, and Wilson's reforming zeal captured independent congressional support. Sensitive to the demands of public opinion, he secured passage of legislation that his collection of eloquent campaign speeches, *The New Freedom*, had envisaged. In fighting machine politicians he developed his own dignified but nonetheless ruthless brand of populism. He emerged as the hero of the notorious Democratic party convention at Baltimore in 1912, one of the longest, most dramatic, and fiercely contested ever held, at the end of which he beat the Missouri boss, James "Champ" Clark, decisively.

The Republican party had dominated American politics since the Civil War, and throughout Wilson's day it remained, in numbers of registered voters, much the larger organization. Until Theodore Roosevelt came along, the Republicans had chosen a series of nonentities. The Democrats had done little better, though in Grover

Cleveland they at least produced a man of some integrity. But Cleveland had had to contend with the destructive rivalry of the great orator William Jennings Bryan, whose pseudo-intellectual crankiness made him a favorite with Democratic militants, won him the party's nomination three times, and – for the same reasons – made him unelectable.

Bryan's last great service to his party, however, was to help secure Wilson's nomination, which at last gave the Democrats a candidate of outstanding ability. Moreover, as a Southerner of liberal views, he was able to construct, for the first time, the classic coalition of Southern conservatives and Northern and Western progressives that was to remain the Democratic mainstay until the end of the 1960s. But the Republican following was such that Wilson was able to win in 1912 only because Roosevelt's Bull Moose party split the Republican vote. Wilson scored a miserable 41.8 percent , the lowest for an elected President since Lincoln's 39.9 in 1860. Even in 1916, after a successful first term, he only just squeaked home against a poor opponent, and again with a minority (49.3 percent) of the votes cast.

Yet Wilson's victory in 1912 was a turning point in American political history. He successfully stole Teddy Roosevelt's Progressive clothes and gave back to the Democrats the political image they had possessed in the days of their founder, Andrew Jackson – identification with "the people." Not that Wilson was incapable of wheeling and dealing; quite the reverse. He rewarded Bryan by making him secretary of state, a hard-to-defend choice that smacked precisely of the "corrupt bargain" between Adams and Clay that had outraged Jackson and given birth to his Democratic party in the first place. All the same, the first Wilson administration, in putting through a successful and coherent plan of much-needed reforms, has remained the model of all Democratic Presidents ever since. The Republican split not only put Wilson into the White House but also gave him a Democratic Congress. This was good fortune, but the way in which Wilson, who never sat in Congress, made himself the undisputed leader of the Democrats in both houses and persuaded them – along with many Republicans, too – to enact the legislative program he laid down, is without parallel in American history.

After taking the oath of office, Wilson delivered a stirring inaugural address, summoning "all honest men, all patriotic, all forward-looking men" to join him in service to the nation. In his address, he itemized "things that ought to be altered," including the tariff, banking and currency, the industrial system, and agricultural policies. His seriousness was reflected in his decision not to hold the traditional Inaugural Ball.

A mild-mannered and shrewd Texan, Colonel Edward House, became the President's most influential adviser. Wilson admired him for his rare combination of idealism and administrative ability and turned to him constantly for confidential counsel. The choice of members of his Cabinet revealed to Wilson some of the difficulties in his path: his contacts with leaders of his own party were limited; he found it difficult to secure men trained in public office, for his party had long been out of power; there were political debts which had to be paid; the strength of the Democrats in the South tended to give that section undue influence in his administration. With the exceptions of W. J. Bryan (secretary of state), W. G. McAdoo (secretary to the Treasury), and F. K. Lane (secretary of the interior), the Cabinet appointees were not well known. Most of them, however, worked well under the President's forceful leadership.

In his collection of speeches and articles, *The New Freedom*, Wilson distinguished between his view of the State and TR's.

> You know that Mr Roosevelt long ago classified trusts for us as good and bad, and he said that he was afraid only of the bad ones. Now he does not desire that there should be any more bad ones, but proposes that they should all be made good by discipline, directly applied by a commission of executive appointment. ... All that it is proposed to do is to take them under control and regulation. ...
>
> Our purpose is the restoration of freedom. We propose to prevent private monopoly by law, to see to it that the methods by which monopolies have been built up are legally made impossible. We design that the limitations on private enterprise shall be removed, so that the next generation of youngsters, as they come along, will not have to become protégés of benevolent trusts, but will be free to go about making their own lives what they will.[13]

Whereas Roosevelt had stated his position earlier in 1910 at Osawatomie, Kansas –

> This New Nationalism regards the executive power as the steward of the public welfare. It demands of the judiciary that it shall be interested primarily in human welfare rather than in property, just as it demands

[13] Woodrow Wilson, *The New Freedom* (Garden City, NY, Doubleday, Page, 1913), pp. 194, 222.

that the representative body shall represent all the people rather than any one class or section of the people.[14]

– Wilson was explicitly opposed to doctrines of public welfare:

I do not want to live under a philanthropy. I do not want to be taken care of by the government, either directly, or by any instruments through which the government is acting. I want only to have right and justice prevail, so far as I am concerned. Give me right and justice and I will undertake to take care of myself.[15]

Wilson's New Liberalism was in practice a continuation on a more thorough scale of Theodore Roosevelt's own reforms. His enemy was the "invisible government" that dominated the country, especially the "money trust" of the great banking houses of New York. His attack concentrated on the tariff, on banks, and on the trusts. Unlike Taft, he brought pressure on Congress to counter the lobbyists who tried to block reductions in tariff rates. In the end, he successfully defied the protectionist principles of Republican tariff laws that had been in effect for sixty years; the Underwood Tariff of 1913 reduced duties, especially on foodstuffs and raw materials, and increased the duties on luxuries; it was a real attempt to lower the cost of living. It imposed a graduated income tax, as the Sixteenth Amendment permitted. The Federal Reserve Act of 1913 appointed a Federal Revenue Board to supervise the national banking system. The Clayton Antitrust Act and Federal Trade Commission listed and banned unlawful methods of trade competition, prohibited interlocking directorates and, in particular, exempted labor unions from antitrust laws. Other measures ensured minimum wages, improved conditions on American ships, and established the eight-hour day for railway workers. Further reforms were the La Follette Seaman's Act (1915), the Child Labor Act (1916) forbidding the transit in interstate commerce of products manufactured in establishments using child labor, and the Adamson Eight-Hour Act (1916).

Three attempts were made by the Wilson administration to meet the needs of the farmers. First, short-term credits. Provisions in the Federal Reserve Act permitted national banks to loan money on farm mortgages and authorized the rediscount of agricultural paper

[14] Roosevelt, *The Works of Theodore Roosevelt* (New York, Scribner's, 1926), vol. XVII, pp. 19–20.
[15] Wilson, *The New Freedom*, p. 198.

which was payable within six months (though neither of these provisions actually met the farmer's demand for long-term credits). Second, the Smith-Lever Act (1914). This Act granted federal funds to the states for farm extension work, under the joint supervision of the Department of Agriculture and state agricultural colleges. Third the Federal Farm Loan Act (1916). This measure created twelve Federal Land Banks which were empowered to make loans at reasonable rates to cooperative farm loan associations composed solely of farmers wishing to borrow on long-term mortgages. The Democratic party, till then predominantly Southern and states' rightist by inclination, became identified with the cause of "plain folk," with farmers and industrial workers.

These were major pieces of constructive statecraft. If Wilson as a Southerner was less prompt to identify himself with the cause of the black in which he was culpable, he pushed farther than ever before the federal government's concern with and responsibility for the living conditions of the people. The US federal government was *laissez-faire* no longer. Government meant freedom for all but power and privilege for a few; both parties came to accept a major role for the state. Even for Jeffersonian Democrats, the answer to big business seemed inevitably, if reluctantly, to be big government.

It is, by any standard, an impressive record. By the end of his first term Wilson had not only overcome the handicap of being the first Southerner in the White House since the Civil War, but also enjoyed a degree of personal respect, and indeed popularity, that far surpassed that of the still lowly regarded Democratic party.

The two years from 1912 to 1914 brought one particularly revealing example of Wilson's strength and weakness. The Mexican affair and the frontier war it produced were a dramatic foretaste of things to come. Wilson began his presidency with some impeccable liberal pronouncements. There was to be no emphasis on material or commercial motives, but on "the self-restraint of a really great nation which realizes its own strength and scorns to misuse it." He declared at Mobile, Alabama, in October 1913 that the United States would never acquire another square inch of territory at the expense of a neighbor. In keeping with this, he refused to recognize the Huerta regime in Mexico. It was, he believed, "government by murder." The step seemed bold and liberal. In fact, it ran counter to the advice of the accredited American diplomats in Mexico City and the practice of all the other powers. It led him to send unofficial and less expert emissaries such as John Lind, and it encouraged rivals to Huerta like Carranza and Villa; it fostered civil confusion in Mexico and border war for years along the Mexican frontier;

despite its intent, it led to the near-imperialist actions at Tampico and Vera Cruz. War itself was only averted by the intervention of the ABC Powers and the Niagara Falls Conference. And, by demanding the creation of "honest constitutional government" as a prerequisite to American recognition – teaching the world to elect good men, as he put it – a most dangerous precedent was set in the matter of recognition, which has marked American policy ever since – toward Russia in 1917, toward the Kaiser in 1918, and toward China in 1949. Since 1913, American policy and world affairs have been bedevilled by Wilson's didacticism.

Whatever their value as the high point of Progressivism in domestic politics, the first two years were far from happy as auguries of "moral imperialism" abroad. The policy was negative; and all it had to its credit was the check to dollar diplomacy in China. This left the situation in China all but unchanged, as Madame Chiang Kai-Shek stressed in her own writings. Mexico was left in civil confusion; and the Marines were in Haiti and the Dominican Republic.

5 WILSON AND FOREIGN POLICY

We are suffering here from hindsight, of course, if we assume that Wilson in 1912 was, in any major degree, concerned with foreign policy. He was not. A student and teacher of American constitutional history, his preoccupation was with the operation of government; and, as President, he expected to have to deal mainly with domestic problems. He had shown his skill as a party leader in New Jersey – at least, during his first few months in office – in putting through a considerable program of reform. His interest lay, apparently, in municipal government and education, in food and factory inspection, in workmen's compensation, hours, and conditions of labor, in banking reorganization and control through the Federal Reserve System, tariff reduction, support of labor organizations and federal aid to education and agriculture. This suggests that he was in the broadest sense a Progressive: but, in fact, he was a *laissez-faire* liberal – "The history of liberty," he said, "is the history of the limitation of the governmental power." There is little evidence of a passionate interest in Progressivism as a creed before his decision to run for governor. His speeches as president of Princeton were mainly on educational themes – and able and constructive speeches they were. Although it is often said that Wilson was in the situation of Pitt the Younger – a domestic reformer plagued after 1914 by questions of foreign policy – there is equally small evidence for this. As Harley Notter has shown[16], all the essentials of Wilson's thought on foreign policy had been formulated before he became President: the faith in constitutionalism, the dislike of big business in its operations at home and abroad, the belief that the United States could be a force for order and for morality in world affairs. But as yet these as principles were an implicit, not to say vague, part of the common political jargon of the day; and they were to be sorely tested. So, too, was the man's character.

Long before he became President, Wilson had campaigned for leadership, for authority and responsibility in government, against the anonymity of Congressional power: "Somebody must be trusted." The emphasis on personal authority was reflected in an authoritativeness of manner – an authoritativeness that hid flaws and dangers. The high-mindedness carried with it from the first a good conceit of itself; and it could repel. Raymond Robins, the Chicago Progressive who was later active in Russia, left the Democratic party in 1912 after a luncheon with Wilson, because he got the impression that Wilson felt "I'm a tremendous person and you don't seem to appreciate it yet." The fact was that Wilson came to politics too late – he was nearly fifty-four when he was elected governor of New Jersey – and he had not been a "mixer" as an academic. He had many of the characteristics of the South – a strong sense of honor and an unbending expectation that others would live by the same code as himself, a prickly integrity, devotion to good causes, and the luxury – more satisfying to himself than others – of plain speaking. With these characteristics he shared others also rooted in the planter's code: a quest in politics for victory rather than for agreement, a certain condescension in his personal attitudes, indeed a strongly personal view of politics as less a matter of ideals and causes than of triumph or disaster for himself. "A very virtuous man, and an obstinate one too," said the British diplomat Spring-Rice. House told a British friend that the only way to handle Wilson was: "Never begin by arguing; discover a common hate, exploit it, get the President warmed up and then start on your business." Integrity, as so often, was wrapped up with egotism; there was little charity for his friends, as House and his secretary Joseph Tumulty were to discover, and none for his enemies; his faith in himself was rooted in a Scotch-Irish Presbyterian background, a Calvinist acceptance of order (and of segregation) in

[16] Harley Notter, *The Origins of the Foreign Policy of Woodrow Wilson* (New York, Russell and Russell, 1965).

society, a certain patrician quality that was as much self-induced as native to the South. For the force that drove Wilson was nervous as well as inherited: he was never physically strong; aloof and shy, he needed reassurance and love – and found that they came more readily from women than men; the successful reformer who yet remained cold and lonely, he was from the first curiously vulnerable.

Nor were the qualities strictly intellectual. There were important gaps in Wilson's education: little knowledge of science, of art and music, or of languages. He confessed that, after becoming president of Princeton, he had no time for serious reading. His years from 1902 to 1910 were indeed political rather than intellectual: he saw himself as engaged in a "fight" with Dean West and with the Princeton clubs; and the campaign for governor hid the fact of academic escape and defeat. At Princeton there were clear educational issues at stake, and on them Wilson lost. He acted inconsistently and without finesse, and took defeat badly. Princeton asked for his resignation before the result of the election was known. And in 1910 Wilson was completely devoid of political experience and without any clear program.

Moreover, as a teacher, he had betrayed "unprofessional" qualities: he enjoyed the *réclame* of his oratorical skill with his big classes, but disliked work with small groups. He was never at ease in personal contact, with academics or with businessmen. His view of politics was heavily pedagogic and declamatory, in an age when mass persuasion, without benefit of electronics, was one of the great tests. He had practiced in his father's pulpit, haranguing the empty pews. The liberal journalist Herbert Croly spoke of "his halo of shimmering rhetoric." His view of a political campaign was that of a series of speeches; and his success as a speaker hid from him that oratorical triumph is only a small part of the game. He was gifted with words and could project himself easily. But Lincoln Steffens made a shrewd distinction between his "wisdom" and that of House, and thought the latter's – essentially a form of political "know-how" – far more patient and productive in the end. Wilson came to lean on House, soft-spoken and endlessly obliging – "an intimate man," Jonathan Daniels put it, "even when cutting a throat." By the same token, he later came to feel that it was this very skill of House's that had betrayed him at Paris.

Wilson saw himself less as a persuader than as a crusader, exhorter, and political evangelist. From this was derived, in part, his odd liking for Alexander Hamilton. The ideal was to be parliamentary: on the canal tolls question in 1913, he went so far as to threaten resignation unless Congress repealed the offending Act; in 1918, he sought a vote of confidence from the electorate. As student, teacher, and politician, he preached the role of the presidency as a unifying force in government. He appeared before Congress in person, reversing the tradition that had held for over a century. By this guidance of Congress and dramatization of himself as both legislator and executive, Wilson put through an impressive amount of legislation in the halcyon days of 1912–14. But these methods and achievements carried their own penalty. Wilson was reluctant to share responsibility. He was irritated by opposition. He scorned the advice of the military. By 1915 he had abandoned meetings with the press. His advisers in foreign policy were inexperienced; and all but Bryan were pro-British.

The appointment of Bryan to the secretaryship of state was in itself regarded as a matter for alarm, a reward for services rendered at the Baltimore Convention that seemed to confirm the President's lack of interest in the State Department. Bryan was discredited, both as man and politician: a teetotaler, a fundamentalist, an agrarian radical, and a party warhorse. His mind, said one cynic, was like his native Platte River, "five inches deep and five miles wide at the mouth." The Assistant secretary of state, Huntington Wilson, reported that

> From the first moment his waiting room was overflowing with political friends from all over the country seeking favor for themselves or their constituents. He was left hardly a moment for Department business and I even had to sign most of the mail for him. ... He had never been interested in diplomacy; and this made it not only difficult but actually impossible quickly to impart to him a conception of foreign affairs.

If together Wilson and Bryan made a number of good appointments, 29 of the 40-odd diplomatic chiefs of missions were changed within six months; and some distinguished career men – William Rockhill in Turkey, John B. Jackson in the Balkans, Arthur Beaupré in Cuba, William Russell in the Dominican Republic, and Percival Dodge in Panama – were removed. Wilson and Bryan got on happily together – more happily than might have been expected. The Canal Tolls exemption measure was repealed. Some 22 "cooling-off" treaties were signed. President and secretary were in accord in their attitude to dollar imperialism – the proposed six-power consortium in China was repudiated. But the cooling-off treaties were of slight importance; before he left the White House, Wilson was to reverse himself on the role of the bankers in China; and in the Caribbean the United States Marines intervened in ways that suggested that imperialism still flourished – the Roosevelt Corollary to the Monroe Doctrine was to be followed, it seemed, almost to the letter.

At the beginning of his presidency Woodrow Wilson was little concerned with foreign policy, but it was the irony of his public life that his presidential years were darkened by perplexing international problems. During his first term, he acted most notably as an anti-imperialist and advocate of human rights. He defended and protected the Mexican Revolution begun in 1910, sought to protect the infant Chinese republic against Japanese aggression, and brought home rule to the Philippine Islands and Puerto Rico. Wilson viewed the outbreak of war in 1914 as the result of European imperialistic rivalries and arms races, and sought to protect American neutrality against both British and German violations of American rights on the high seas. It was no easy or automatic alignment with Britain and France versus Germany. The German-American farmers, strong in Wisconsin, Illinois, and the Middle West, were the core of Progressive liberal voters.

In foreign affairs the difficulties beginning to come to a head in Latin America stemmed in part from inherited commitments, and culminated in partial protectorates in Nicaragua, Haiti, and Santo Domingo, which continued until well after Wilson's death. His naiveté in judging foreign relations in terms of Golden Rule Diplomacy had been evident from the moment he brought Bryan into his cabinet as secretary of state.

A spirited dispute between the United States and Great Britain over the Panama Canal alarmed Wilson early in his administration. The Tolls Act of 1912 had imposed a schedule of tolls upon all foreign vessels using the completed canal, but had provided that vessels of United States registry engaged in the coastwise trade should be exempt from toll payment. Great Britain contended that this was a violation of the "equality of treatment" for the vessels of all nations which the United States had promised in the Hay-Pauncefote Treaty. Wilson strongly urged repeal of the Act on the ground that the British interpretation of the treaty was correct. His attitude was probably determined by his desire to avoid trouble with the British in the Caribbean area, his feeling that cordial Anglo-American relations were a necessary prelude to Colonel House's mission to promote European peace, and his hope that, in return for repeal of the Tolls Act, Great Britain would support the American policy in Mexico; and the Act was repealed on June 15, 1914.

President Wilson's determination to "cultivate the friendship and deserve the confidence of our sister republics of Central and South

America" was the basis of his well-intentioned, if not highly successful, policy toward Mexico. The despotic regime of Porfirio Diaz (1876–1910) had been brought to a sudden close by the revolt of wealthy liberals and landless peons, under the leadership of Francisco Madero. From 1910 to 1913 Madero worked in vain to establish his program of reforms – the allotment of land to landless peons, the nationalization of the railroads, the extension of the suffrage, and the grant of provincial autonomy – until his efforts were ended by the revolt of one of his military supporters, General Victoriano Huerta.

Although 25 nations accepted Huerta as the *de facto* president of Mexico, Wilson refused to recognize the new regime on moral grounds, charging that it did not represent the will of the people and that it was responsible for the murder of Madero. Huerto retaliated with acts of reprisal on American citizens, culminating in the arrest of a squad of American marines at Tampico in April 1914. When the United States promptly seized Vera Cruz in order to prevent a shipment of arms from reaching Huerta, war seemed imminent.

To avert the outbreak of war, Argentina, Brazil, and Chile (the "ABC" powers) offered their good offices, which were accepted, They proposed the retirement of Huerta and the installation of a reform government. But the several weeks of deliberations were fruitless, since Venustiano Carranza, in revolt against Huerta, refused to sign the protocol to maintain peace and order. When Carranza, having seized power, gave promise of establishing an orderly government, President Wilson abandoned his policy of "watchful waiting" and accorded the new regime *de facto* recognition. But Carranza failed to restrain the swashbuckling Pancho Villa, who attacked foreigners and finally led a raid against Columbus, New Mexico. The United States, with Carranza's permission, sent a punitive expedition, under General John J. Pershing, into Mexico in 1916; but it failed to capture Villa and was withdrawn as war with Germany loomed in 1917.

In dealing with Mexico, President Wilson tried to introduce a strongly moral tone into the relations between his country and its neighbors. He insisted: (1) that the United States had no intention of acquiring any further territory in this hemisphere; (2) that peaceful negotiation rather than force should be the chief instrument of American foreign policy; (3) that no foreign government would be recognized if it came into power through violence; and (4) that the United States would maintain scrupulous honesty in its international relations.

Wilson's policy toward the Caribbean countries was less dangerously idealistic than his approach to the Mexican situation, but he was motivated more by a desire to promote the political and economic stability of regions close to American shores than to carry out a program of economic imperialism. A revolution in the Dominican Republic in 1916, which threatened the financial convention signed by Theodore Roosevelt in 1907, was the occasion for intervention by the United States and the assumption of political control. For nine years the provisional government, supported by American military forces, gave the natives the benefit of orderly administration despite their protests. It was not until 1924 that a new financial convention, superseding that of 1907, was signed and American troops were withdrawn as soon as ratifications had been exchanged.

When in 1915 Haiti's European creditors pronounced the republic bankrupt and threatened drastic action, the United States intervened and compelled the Haitian government to sign a treaty which established American control of customs, public works, and the constabulary. Native resistance to the subsequent military occupation caused frequent disorders, but American officials went forward with their work of building highways, improving sanitary conditions, and instituting financial reforms. Not until 1934 were the last United States troops withdrawn.

From 1912 to 1925 American marines were based in Nicaragua to protect the administration of Nicaraguan finances and to maintain political tranquility in the country. During this occupation the Bryan-Chamorro Treaty was negotiated (1916), by which the United States acquired a 99-year lease to the Corn Islands and permission to establish a naval base on the Gulf of Fonseca. The withdrawal of the marines in 1925 was followed by political insurrection, and two years later President Coolidge sanctioned another intervention for the purposes of protecting the lives and property of American citizens defending United States canal rights in Nicaragua, and enforcing the Central American treaty (1923), which pledged the Central American republics to deny recognition to any government which seized power by force. Having supervised new elections, the marines were withdrawn in 1929, save for a legation guard which left the country in 1933.

In 1917 the Wilson administration acquired for $25 million the Virgin Islands (Danish West Indies), which the United States had been endeavoring to purchase from Denmark for more than a decade. The chief motive behind the purchase seems to have been the desire to use the islands as a necessary naval defense for the

Panama Canal and the proposed canal through Nicaragua. The territory was placed under an appointed governor and granted limited self-government. In 1927 its inhabitants were made United States citizens.

One of the results of the policy of intervention, which went far toward converting the Caribbean into an American lake, was the widespread distrust of the United States in Latin America. Whether American activities were based upon a logical application of the Monroe Doctrine or were merely a manifestation of national self-interest, they were regarded by many publicists in South America as proof of United States desire to establish hegemony of the two Americas. It was not until after World War I that the United States slowly began to appreciate both the changed status of the Latin American republics and its new relations to them.

6 THE CHALLENGES OF INTERVENTION

Wilson's expertise lay in domestic reform. Within eighteen months of his entry into the White House, however, Europe became embroiled in World War I, and his name is associated with all the problems and tensions of the war to make the world safe for democracy.

To the dilemmas posed to the United States by the outbreak of war in 1914 there had been a precursor, in the War With Spain in 1898. In some measure this had been a domestic issue: Cuba had throughout the nineteenth century been a preoccupation of the United States. By 1898 American Cuban investments and trade exceeded $150 million, so when in 1895 a Cuban revolt against Spain broke out, it was hard to distinguish between selfish and humanitarian motives for intervening. It is inaccurate to ascribe the war to "imperialism"; the majority of American businessmen opposed it. Imperialism was less its cause than its consequence. However, the concern over investments was soon extended to protection of them, and to the wider aspects of diplomacy. On the outbreak of the Russo-Japanese War in 1905 Roosevelt warned France and Germany that if either power aided the Russians, the United States would support Japan. He mediated successfully in that war, and repeated the attempt in relation to Morocco at Algeciras in 1906.

Thus the declarations of American neutrality in 1914 were hard to sustain. In February 1915 Germany proclaimed that it would destroy every merchantman found in the waters about the British Isles. At once President Wilson replied that if this course caused the loss of American vessels or lives, the United States would hold Germany to "strict accountability." Three months later the British transatlantic liner *Lusitania* was sent to the bottom, with the loss of nearly 1,200 people, including 128 American citizens, and the United States blazed with resentment. There grew up also a steady American involvement in the European war – the chemicals and explosives industries, iron and steel, coal and metals boomed. By 1917, in loans and goods, the United States was committed tenfold to an Allied victory as compared to its investment in Germany. While there is no evidence that these economic pressures influenced Wilson, they certainly moved public opinion; by 1916 it was overwhelmingly anti-German. German propaganda was much less skillful than British, and Britain controlled the news channels across the Atlantic.

The President was narrowly re-elected in 1916, re-elected in part because of the slogan that he hit upon by chance: "He kept us out of war." Within five months of his victory he asked Congress to declare war. In January 1917 the Germans, expecting to starve Britain out in six months, announced the intensification of submarine warfare. Within a few weeks, five American vessels were sunk, and on April 2, Wilson appeared before Congress to ask for the declaration of a state of war. "The world," he said, in a phrase that rang round the globe, "must be made safe for democracy."

It is not too much to say that the United States won the war for the Allies. The deliberate and calculated gamble of the German government that in launching all-out submarine war, Britain could be destroyed before American reinforcements could be decisive, proved wildly wrong. By November 1918 there were almost two million American troops in France. By January 1918 Wilson's preoccupation was with the shape of the peace. In his Fourteen Points address in January 1918 he called for the abandonment of secret international understandings, a guarantee of freedom of the seas, the removal of economic barriers between nations, reduction of national armaments, an adjustment of colonial claims with due regard to the interests of the inhabitants affected and the rights of self-rule and of unhampered economic development for the nations of Europe. For his 14th point, Wilson reserved the keystone of his arch of peace: the formation of an association of nations to afford "mutual guarantees of political independence and territorial integrity to great and small states alike." The German request for an armistice was made precisely because of the liberal character of this initiative. Once again an American President, even though a participant in the war, was seen as above the storm, liberal and objective, the Man on the Mountain.

At this point Wilson made tactical mistakes. Indeed, by 1918 he was no longer a true spokesman for a majority of his countrymen. War-weariness and disillusion were spreading; in the 1918 elections Republican majorities were returned to both houses of Congress. In defiance of unbroken precedent, and against the advice of many of his own wisest colleagues, Wilson decided to attend the Peace Conference in person. In addition, he failed to place a leading Republican on his Peace Commission, a major error in judgment. When upon his return the President called a special session of Congress to consider endorsement of the Versailles Treaty and the League of Nations, he found acrimonious debate already under way and little prospect that ratification would be forthcoming. Wilson resorted to a tour of the country and a direct appeal to the people on the issue of the League of Nations, but made little progress, and he finally suffered a physical collapse from which he never recovered. In March 1920 the Senate rejected the treaty and the League covenant, committing the United States for years to come to a policy of isolationism.

7 WILSON: AN ASSESSMENT

There were other Wilsons. The young student was "Tommy" Wilson. The mature politician was Woodrow, with a taste for spats and pearl-colored trousers. The earlier Wilson was boisterous, joked, sang songs, and told stories brilliantly. Until his second term, Wilson retained this last gift: along with Lincoln and Reagan, he was the President who used the apt and funny tale to most effect. But he was also fond of women, highly sexed, even passionate, and capable of penning memorable love letters. His first wife, Ellen, was a proto-feminist, and their marriage a grand love affair. But it did not prevent Wilson from striking up, in due course, an acquaintance with a frisky widow, whom he met in his favorite vacation haunt, Bermuda. This developed into a liaison, which led in time to a bit of genteel blackmail. Ellen's death was nonetheless a bitter blow. But Wilson soon recovered and found a second wife, another merry widow, the 42-year-old Edith Bolling Galt, like Ellen an emancipated woman, who owned Washington's most fashionable jewelry store and was famous for being the first woman in the city to drive her own car. She was tall, junoesque, and "somewhat plump by modern American standards," as one of the President's secret servicemen put it. Having secured this statuesque lady, President Wilson was described by an associate as jigging dance steps on the sidewalk and singing the current vaudeville hit "Oh, you beautiful doll, you great big beautiful doll!"

This light-hearted Wilson, however, retreated into the shadows as his second term involved him in war and, eventually, failure. Another Wilson, aggressive and even bellicose, jostled for the spotlight with Wilson the moralist and world statesman. Like many prominent academics, Wilson had long possessed a talent for irritable abuse. During his second presidential campaign, he cabled the Irish-American leader, Jeremiah A. O'Leary, who had accused him of pro-British sentiments: "Your telegram received. I would be deeply mortified to have you or anybody like you vote for me. Since you have access to many disloyal Americans, I will ask you to convey this message to them." When, at the beginning of his second term, Wilson proposed a bill to arm merchant ships in response to the German U-boat campaign, a group of Senators started a filibuster, and Wilson issued a statement that made sensational headlines: "A little group of willful men, representing no opinion but their own, have rendered the great Government of the United States helpless and contemptible."

There was, in short, a mean streak in Wilson, and a tendency to resort to force when he felt his moral principles threatened. He tried to compel Mexico to conform to his democratic notions and sent General Pershing on a punitive expedition deep into the country that might well have ended in disaster or fullscale war. He intervened in Central America and the Caribbean more than any other President before or since. He was no pacifist; on the contrary. That being so, it is curious and tragic that he failed to take the United States into the European war in 1915, when the sinking of the *Lusitania* provided a valid pretext. Earlier American intervention might have shortened the war and prevented the fearful catastrophes of the years 1916–18, which changed the course of world history.

But here we come to the central paradox of Wilson: the way in which his moralism and his political pragmatism competed for mastery. During his first term, he developed an almost uncanny gift for perceiving the drift of US opinion and giving it form, rhetoric, and a moral rationale – for leading it firmly in the direction where it was edging anyway. This skill underlay the success of his legislative program. For the first two years of the Great War, Wilson saw that most Americans wanted to keep out, and that there was no prospect of winning re-election except on a peace platform. So, with some difficulty, he held the balance between the combatants, and campaigned in 1916 on an aggressively pacifist platform. He avoided the charge of being indifferent to what was becoming a horrific struggle by identifying the United States, in a lofty, vague, but impressive way, with the long-term interests of the entire world. "In the days to come," he ended his closing campaign speech, "men will no longer wonder how America is going to work out her destiny, for she will have proclaimed to them that her destiny is not divided from the destiny of the world, that her purpose is justice and love of mankind."

Hence for the first time – but by no means the last – the Democrats won an election on peace policy, and then proceeded to make war. Indeed, Germany's resumption of indiscriminate submarine warfare early in 1917 made US intervention more or less inevitable. But if Wilson did not exactly enter the conflict with relish, he did so nonetheless with great determination and thoroughness. He not only created a vast war machine but also penalized – some would say persecuted – those who opposed it, culminating in the first of America's modern witch-hunts, led by Attorney General Mitchell Palmer, perhaps the worst of Wilson's many bad appointments. Moreover, the kind of war Wilson chose to wage created for the first time a federal appetite for a growing share of the GNP, and it set up the institutions and devised the methods whereby that insatiable appetite has since been fed. It was another turning point in American history, for though big government went underground under Harding and Coolidge, it re-emerged under Franklin Delano Roosevelt and has strengthened ever since. As the pacifist Randolph Bourne warned Wilson at the time: "War is the health of the state."

Wilson, to do him justice, saw some of these dangers. To meet them, and to distance his American war aims from the (as he saw it) disreputable war aims of Lloyd George's Britain and Clemenceau's France, he devised the Fourteen Points and the League of Nations policy. But to wage war with all America's enormous resources, and at the same time to construct a peace that was not Carthaginian, was a difficult balance to maintain. It became more so as German behavior, up to and beyond the Armistice, led Wilson increasingly to distrust and despise the enemy. Hence Europe came to occupy all Wilson's attentions and energies. Therein lay his, and the world's, tragedy. It was not that most Americans did not support the war, or Wilson's efforts to make a just peace. The evidence suggests that, properly led, Americans would have done all that Wilson could reasonably have required, including participating in a world security organization. But his obsession with the affairs of Europe, and his actual – quite unnecessary – presence there during the Versailles negotiations, indicated that he had ceased to take note of what Americans were saying. He no longer intuited the American mood, then shaped and led it. Indeed, he did not lead at all: he commanded, and his commands were not obeyed.

The first sign of disaster came in the midterm elections of November 1918, which Wilson handled in a lackluster manner, and which produced a Republican Congress. Here was a clear signal to Wilson to bring the Republicans, who scented a revival in their fortunes, immediately into the peacemaking process and into the shaping of the postwar security plan. Wilson did no such thing. He had always tended to autocracy in foreign affairs. When Bryan resigned, he appointed a feeble official, Robert Lansing as secretary of state, and when even Lansing proved difficult, sacked him and put in his place a personal crony, a nonentity named Colby Bainbridge. He treated the new Senate majority leader, Henry Cabot Lodge, as an enemy, and of course he became one. It has long been apparent from the evidence that through the League of Nations Wilson was the architect of his own destruction. American membership – and thus an American involvement in Europe that in all probability would have prevented a second world war – might have been negotiated through Congress. But Wilson refused to compromise, or indeed to negotiate at all. He declined to make concessions that even the British, the strongest supporters of the League, would happily have accepted. As a result he got nothing, and the last, most disastrous, phase of American isolationism began.

Wilson's behavior was so far from his earlier ability to get Congress to enact contentious domestic legislation, and so contrary to the constitutional practice he taught in his books and lectures, that it suggests a rapid decline in judgment, itself the result of a physical deterioration. One of the merits of August Heckscher's study[17] is that he collates carefully all the medical evidence available on Wilson throughout his life. The evidence shows that from a comparatively early age he suffered from deep-seated, possibly inherited, circulatory problems. These produced a series of crises, one of which made him virtually blind in one eye, and which were plainly aggravated by overwork and strain. The President had great willpower, and could and did make extraordinary efforts to recover from these crises; but it is evident that for much of his second term he was unfit to hold office. Admiral Grayson, his personal physician, should accordingly have advised resignation, in the interests of both his patient and the nation. But he owed his rapid, and much resented, naval promotion to Wilson's patronage, and the last thing he wanted was to see Wilson quit the White House. The President's

[17] August Heckscher, *Woodrow Wilson* (New York, Scribner's, 1991).

deteriorating health made him irritable, resentful of criticism, and quite unwilling to dissipate any of his remaining energies on conciliating his opponents. His physical condition effectively cost him the battle for the League of Nations some time before a massive stroke at the end of September 1919 destroyed his remaining usefulness as a public servant.

What followed was a scandal, from which no one emerged with credit. Edith Wilson had, from the moment of her second marriage, taken a close interest in the presidential power structure. She had helped to oust Wilson's chief crony, Colonel House, and had stripped Tumulty, his secretary, of much of his influence. She now engaged with Grayson in a conspiracy to conceal from Congress and the public the true state of the President's health and his incapacity to conduct the nation's business. This involved play-acting in which the helpless invalid collaborated, insofar as he was able, when anxious Congressmen were brought into his bedroom. It also involved Mrs Wilson's taking many executive decisions herself, and forging her husband's signature on public documents. The fraud should have been prevented by Lansing; but he proved pusillanimous, and, even when sacked, failed to expose it. The man who had the right and duty to take over, Vice-President Thomas R. Marshall, also avoided his responsibility. Marshall was a singularly unambitious man, quite content with his humdrum role. Thus, in effect, an unelected woman governed America, insofar as it was governed at all, for the last year and a half of the Wilson presidency.

The stricken Wilson made a limited recovery, oddly enough surviving his unfortunate Republican successor, Warren G. Harding, and dying in 1924. His widow lived on until after John F. Kennedy, another President handicapped by serious illness, had entered the White House. In the meantime, the world paid a heavy price for Wilson's obstinate refusal to admit the political consequences of his physical state.

To return to the original theme: the learned man in the White House. Of the three, the last was learned, if not quite a scholar. David Burton's is one verdict; Paul Johnson's is another. Perhaps they are not far apart?

Roosevelt, Taft, and Wilson should be linked to the three remarkable men who came to the presidency after the retirement of Washington. Adams, Jefferson, and Madison are a necessary reference point in any consideration of the learned presidents who introduced the high office to the twentieth century. The three latter-day chief executives were themselves deeply aware of the power of the office. As close students of the American past they appreciated the promise inherent in the minds of Adams, Jefferson, and Madison, and they deplored the nineteenth-century developments by reason of which that promise went unfulfilled. They consciously proposed to continue to exercise the great powers of the office, while at the same time restoring it to the level of honor and respect that had obtained one hundred years before their time. Their personal ambitions and sense of national purpose combined to return an intellectual dimension to a position that had become, at various times, a prize, a sectional pawn, a political football, and a martyr's seat. Given their achievement, it becomes necessary to add that the promise they ably renewed met rejection, as it had in the preceding century. While they did not stand out as individuals of exceptional intellectual habit, as John Quincy Adams and Abraham Lincoln did during the long hiatus of the nineteenth century, it is still reassuring to record Herbert Hoover's literary accomplishments as well as his technological expertise, or Harry Truman's mastery of the facts and no small part of the meaning of the American past. If such efforts failed to sustain the intellectualism of the country's early decades, at least one or more of these men come through to us as perhaps touched by the fire of their predecessors.[18]

Cathedocracy, or rule from the teacher's chair, the exercise of power by scholars, is a tempting theory of government. Is it not logical that the most learned should take the most important decisions? Cathedocracy worked well, for instance, in traditional Jewish societies. But, then, those were mere self-governing enclaves in Gentile states. They did not have to take ultimate decisions of peace and war – there is no word for army in Yiddish. Dr Francia's Paraguay in the nineteenth century and Professor Salazar's Portugal in the twentieth were examples, albeit ruthless ones, of successful cathedocracies; both men ran their countries like highly disciplined academies, but only by isolating them from the contemporary world and at the price of storing up trouble for their successors.

At first glance, no country could be more remote from cathedocracy than the United States, with its strong democratic and egalitarian instincts. Yet many of the Founding Fathers had an academic bent. Books as much as battles helped to create the new Republic, and scholarly interpretations of its constitution by learned judges have shaped much of its subsequent history. American society has always revered education, not least in its higher reaches, and college presidents are, or were until recently, among the most respected groups in the country.[19]

Yet what happens when a professor/college president actually takes over? The triumph and tragedy of Woodrow Wilson (1856–

[18] Burton, *The Learned Presidency*, Preface.

[19] Reviews of Heckscher, *Woodrow Wilson*, by Paul Johnson, *The American Spectator* (Nov. 1991).

1924, and President 1913–21) is one of the most instructive stories in the whole of American history, and the appearance of August Heckscher's scholarly, thorough, and dispassionate biography provides an opportunity to draw some of its lessons.

Wilson came of Scots or Irish Calvinist stock on both sides of his family. His forebears struck roots in the South, which left some traces on his public persona, but his culture was essentially British-American. The statesman he most admired was the great reforming Liberal, William Ewart Gladstone.

> Wilson's career ... holds many lessons. One is that intellectuals sometimes make successful rulers: a man who teaches the art of government can also practice it. Cathedocracy can work, at least in peacetime. But governing is a two-way street. Wilson began to make mistakes when he stopped listening, when he continued to lecture but ceased to converse, a corruption of power from which all rulers are liable to suffer – Margaret Thatcher is a recent example – but which in his case was catastrophically accelerated by illness. Hence, not the least of the lessons is the need for objective medical supervision of anyone who holds as much lawful power as an American President. I say objective because the political supervision of a ruler's health is open to the strongest objections: for example, following Lenin's first stroke, it was Stalin who got the Central Committee to appoint him medical superintendent of Lenin's well-being, a maneuver that led directly to the final breach between the two men.[20]

There is another conclusion. Just as over 200 years the growth in power of the presidential office is one of the most striking features of the American story, so it is also clear that that office-holder is vulnerable: to assassin's bullets, to political intrigue, and to amphetamines. And in an age when publicity is endless and unforgiving, it is clear how prone the office-holders are to ill-health, to scandal-mongering, to sinfulness and to the making of mischief – their own and other people's.

[20] Johnson, ibid.

7
World War I

1 CAUSES OF THE WAR

World War I (1914–18) had threatened to erupt on several occasions during the first decade of the twentieth century, when a precarious balance was maintained by two sets of alliances: the Triple Alliance, or Central Powers (Italy, Germany, and Austria-Hungary), and the Triple Entente (Great Britain, France, and Russia). Late in June 1914, a Serbian revolutionary, Gabrilo Princip, assassinated the heir to the throne of the Dual Monarchy, Archduke Franz Ferdinand when he was visiting Sarajevo, a mainly Muslim-peopled city on the edge of Bosnia, one of Austria-Hungary's eleven component nations. Princip was one of the Black Hand, a small group of Serbian nationalists. Ironically, the Austrians had discovered a Glasgow shipyard worker who, having lost a job at home, was employed in the Trieste shipyards, who bore a striking resemblance to the archduke; they had almost completed training him to appear on ceremonial occasions as a substitute for the archduke, but as it happened, the archduke decided to go to Sarajevo in person. So there is a moral legacy: had a deputy gone and been killed instead of the real archduke, would the Austrian government have dared admit to the subterfuge? Would it have made any difference – except to the victim? As it was, the Glasgow worker went back home – and once war broke out there were jobs aplenty on the Clyde, since Britain as well as Austria and Germany needed battleships.

Austria retaliated against the Slavic threat by making such demands on Serbia as virtually to end its independence, thereby making a general war inevitable, and declared war on Serbia on July 28, 1914. Russia, with hegemony in the Slavic world, mobilized her army.

Lest it be caught between two enemies, Germany declared war on Russia (1 August) and on France (3 August), and struck first at France through Belgium, whose neutrality she and the other powers were bound by treaty to respect. On 4 August Great Britain declared war on Germany, and the first global war had begun. (Turkey and Bulgaria later joined the Central Powers. Italy disregarded her alliance and in 1915 joined the Entente, as in the course of time did Romania, Portugal, Greece, Japan, and the US.)

The determination of Americans to stay out of Europe's embroilment was thoroughgoing, and it cut through political, sectional, racial, and class lines. It was given official sanction early in September 1914 when President Wilson proclaimed the neutrality of the US, thus invoking the long-standing tradition of neutral rights. Secretary of State Bryan announced that war loans to belligerents violated neutrality, but on October 15 the State Department quietly allowed such loans. President Wilson on September 7, 1915, permitted New York bankers to lend $500 million to France and Great Britain. By the time the United States entered the war American bankers had loaned the Allies $2.3 billion and Germany $27 million.

Of primary significance among the reasons for the entry of the US into the war nearly three years later is the fact that in general, from the start, American sympathies were predominantly with the Allies, and ultimately German provocations tipped the balance. In scores of ways, both tangible and intangible, and especially in national origins, the ties with England and France were strong. Relations were not cordial with Germany, a nation regarded with suspicion as militaristic and unfriendly to democracy. Thus to enter the war on the side of the Allies, however agonizing the decision, was conceivable. But pro-German sentiment was strong among the German Americans, many still German-speaking immigrants, concentrated in Illinois, the grain and milk belt of Wisconsin and Minnesota, and in the Dakotas.

Allied publicists, however, played up such provocations as Germany's violation of Belgian neutrality and the sinking of the *Lusitania*, and they created hatred by embroidering atrocity stories. By joining Canadian contingents or the French Foreign Legion thousands of young Americans gave psychological and material support to the Allied cause. The Allied blockade of Germany was so effective that within a year the US economy began to depend on the success of the Allies, and neither Congress nor public opinion looked upon armed merchantmen, transporting commodities and munitions to France and England, as "warships." As we have seen, considerable bank credits were extended. Yet in the end it was not propaganda, nor trade, nor loans that tipped the balance and led the US to declare war on Germany; indeed, the financial stake favored neutrality. America went to war in reaction to German submarine warfare.

The blockade that Britain and France enforced against Germany, although it violated neutral rights (and was constantly protested by the State Department), was an economic stranglehold which the Germans tried to break by the use of mines and submarines, with a resulting and steadily mounting toll of American lives. Wilson's "strict accountability" note on Germany early in 1915 therefore forced the issue.

After the sinking of the Lusitania in May 1915, in which over 100 Americans lost their lives, the US embarked on a series of notes to Germany insisting on American rights on the high seas, asking for reparations, and demanding that the Germans give up unrestricted submarine warfare, but received little satisfaction. Wilson's insistence on specific pledges brought about the resignation of Secretary of State Bryan, who was afraid it would precipitate war. It was not until February 16, 1916, that Germany agreed to pay an indemnity for the loss of American lives on the Lusitania – and by that time many other Americans had also lost their lives at sea.

With a presidential election approaching in 1916, Wilson sought to capture the vote of the militant element by outlining a program of military preparedness, while at the same time his managers campaigned under the slogan "He kept us out of war." He was re-elected but, rebuffed in his repeated appeals to the belligerents for a "peace without victory," he was then faced with Germany's decision to embark on unrestricted U-boat warfare – a decision taken because the German high command now discounted any additional aid to the Allies, believing that by destruction of merchant tonnage they could starve Britain out and win the war in six months. Diplomatic relations between Germany and the US were severed in February 1917.

The US could have stayed out of the war if the American people had been willing to suffer the consequences of a disastrous shipping embargo and surrender to German demands. But by the spring of 1917 the preservation of peace and honor seemed to the American public what Wilson declared, an "impossible and contradictory thing." It accepted his crusading slogan that the US should make "the world safe for democracy," and by joint resolution on 6 April 1917 Congress declared war on Germany. After a short but bitter debate, in which Robert M. La Follette made a four-hour speech opposing war, the Senate voted 82–6 for war, and the House voted 373–50 for war. In the House minority, 34 were from the Mid-West.

Charles Seymour emphasized the role of the submarine in causing America's entrance into the Great War:

Thus, from the point of view of material interests, there could be no comparison between the damage resulting to Americans from the Allied blockade and that from the intensive submarine campaign. If the latter were permitted, under protests comparable to those sent to the Allies, the result would be an almost complete blockade of American commerce, since shippers would not dare send cargoes and crew out to destruction. A clear illustration of the effect of the submarine campaign on American commercial, industrial, and agricultural interests was given by the congestion of our ports that followed the threat of submarine attacks in February and March 1917. Freights were snarled, goods were spoiled, business was menaced with a complete tie-up.

Even so, Wilson might not have taken his firm stand against the submarine if merely property rights had been threatened. He was always careful not to interpret national policy in terms of purely material interests. Despite the difficulties involved, the economic aspects of the diplomatic conflict with Germany might have been adjudicated. But the submarine warfare involved attacks upon American lives, whether sailors on merchants ships or passengers. To Wilson it seemed a war on humanity. Between property interests and human rights there lay a clear distinction. ...[1]

Accepting the fact of German disregard for American neutral rights, Harry Elmer Barnes argued that Britain was as responsible as Germany in such matters:

The United States could not have been more perfectly set up for neutrality than it was in July and August, 1914. President Woodrow Wilson was a lifelong and deeply conscientious pacifist. His convictions in this matter were not emotional or impressionistic, but had been based upon deep study and prolonged reflection. Moreover, he was married to a woman noted for pacific sentiments and firm convictions on such matters. She strongly backed up her husband in his pacific beliefs and policies. As Secretary of State, we had in William Jennings Bryan the world's outstanding pacifist ... England started out in 1914 by making a scrap of paper out of the Declaration of London governing contraband in war-time. Next, we proceeded to allow her to make use of armed belligerent merchantmen as if they were peaceful commercial vessels. England violated our neutral rights far more extensively between 1914 and 1917 than she did before the War of 1812, even to the point of flying the American flag.

[1] Charles Seymour, "American neutrality, the experience of 1914–17", *Foreign Affairs*, 14 (1935), p. 30.

> Wilson came to believe, however, that Great Britain was fighting for civilization and that so trivial a thing as international law must not be allowed to stand in her way. ...
>
> The net result ... was that we entered the World War in April 1917. We did so, even though there was no clear legal or moral basis for our so doing. If there ever was an instance in which the facts were clearly in accord with a neutrality policy it was in the spring of 1917. We should have fought both Germany and Britain or else neither. But the country went into war, with most of the citizens of the United States feeling that our self-respect and national honor demanded it. No other course seemed open to us.[2]

Richard Leopold assessed the mood of the country similarly:

> And so America went to war. There were no crowds in the street shouting "On to Berlin' as there had been in Paris in August, 1914. There was no violent rage, as there would be in December, 1941. There was no thought of territorial gain, as there had been in some quarters in June 1812 and May 1846. There was no expectation of an easy victory, as there had been in April 1898. The American people had not wanted this war and did not relish it any more than the English people would wish to oppose Hitler over Poland in September 1939. Both cases were marked by a calm resignation over the seemingly inevitable, by a reluctant conviction that there was no honorable alternative, and by a grim determination to get a dirty job over with as quickly as possible.[3]

2 THE WAR MACHINE

Thus began the gigantic task of converting US industry to a war footing at a time when the Allies were approaching exhaustion in munitions and commodities, and the effectiveness of German submarines was most complete. The Emergency Fleet Corporation immediately set out to build a "bridge to France," and was soon laying down two ships for every one sunk by U-boats. The government took over the railroads and the War Industries Board regimented the national economy to a degree never before known. Food and fuel were rationed. The cost of financing both US and Allied expenses was met by heavy taxation and by loans. (At war's end the total direct levy on US citizens amounted to $36,000

[2] Harry Elmer Barnes, "The World War of 1914–1918," in *War in the Twentieth Century*, ed. Willard Waller (New York, Random House, 1940), pp. 71, 73, 81–2.

[3] Richard W. Leopold, *The Growth of American Foreign Policy; A history* (New York, Knopf, 1962) pp. 336–7.

Plate 3 Newly arrived US troops debarking at the French port of Brest during World War I. (Library of Congress.)

million, a massive figure at the time.) Public opinion was mobilized by every means imaginable, for unless the nation as a whole believed that the war was both righteous and necessary, it would not have supported the curbs on personal liberties. Indeed, the degree to which "disloyalty" was punished by the Espionage Act of 1917 has never before or since been matched in American history.

The German high command had expected to win the war before American aid could adversely affect their military situation, but they misjudged the character of the American people and the organizational genius of such leaders as Bernard Baruch (War Industries), Herbert Hoover (Food Administration), and above all, Secretary of War Newton Baker, who within 18 months created an effective army of four million men, half of whom were transported to France. The navy immediately set out to make war on U-boats, and in June General John Pershing arrived in France with the first contingent of the American Expeditionary Force.

Yet the Allied fortunes grew worse as the year advanced. Unable to budge the German armies from the Hindenburg line, France was bogged down in a trench warfare of attrition. The Flanders offensive (June–November) by the British was indecisive. Following the Bolshevik Revolution in November, Russia was lost as a military ally, and masses of German troops were released for service on the western front. At the close of 1917 the Italians suffered disaster in the Caporetto campaign. The balance of strength on land clearly lay with the Germans.

But by the spring of 1918 effective US resources of manpower, finances, raw materials, and munitions had altered the picture, and by May, American troops were deployed in large numbers along the front. The initial American success at Cantigny (late May) was quickly followed by thrusts at Chateauthierry and Belleau Wood (June). The turning point of the war came in the second battle of the Marne (July), in which some 275,000 American troops were engaged. The first distinctively American engagement, at St Mihiel in mid-September (involving 550,000 American troops) preceded the final push, the Meuse-Argonne Offensive (26 September–11 November), the greatest battle in which US troops (1,200,000 of them) had ever been engaged. The fighting ended with the signing of the armistice on the last day of the Offensive, on 11 November 1918.

3 OTHER MOTIVES FOR WAR

Granted that both Britain and Germany violated American neutrality. Yet what were those American ships doing in a war zone besides asserting their neutral rights? They were carrying goods for Americans who were profiting from war sales. Charles C. Tansill suggested that profits from selling war materials greatly influenced American foreign policy:

Within a few weeks after the outbreak of the World War it became apparent to competent military observers that victory for either side would largely depend upon the possession of adequate supplies of munitions of war. The nation that labored under the greatest handicap in this regard was Great Britain, whose assistance to France in the early months of the war was sharply limited because of a glaring deficiency in effective artillery and in high explosive shells. Although the production of British factories could be rapidly increased there would remain an alarming shortage of supplies necessary for the conduct of successful warfare. The only means of meeting this situation was through the importation of munitions of war from neutral nations. European neutrals, however, soon placed embargoes upon the shipment of war materials, so the British Government was forced to look to America as the only important neutral that could supply her needs.

In America the rise of "big business" had produced a vast industrial organization that could fill war orders in an amazingly short time, and the very fact that this organization was severely suffering from a widespread business depression meant that these orders would receive special attention. It was not long before immense exports of American munitions were crowding British ports. In 1916 the value of American war supplies to the Allied Governments amounted to more than a billion dollars, and the intimate economic ties thus created served to supplement the sentimental bonds that had long attached America to the side of the Entente Powers.[4]

However, taking issue with the viewpoint that profits drove President Wilson to favor the Allies, Edward H. Buehrig contended that a threat to America's security forced Wilson into war:

The intent to remain neutral, which Wilson set out with in August, 1914 did not long remain uncompromised. Great Britain wielded vast economic power as a consequence of her large merchant marine and control over a great and productive empire. Reinforcing this gigantic economic complex in peacetime, and mobilizing it in wartime for political purposes, was the

[4] Charles Tansill, *America Goes to War* (Boston, Little, Brown, 1938), p. 32.

British Navy. For the United States to yield to this all-pervasive influence was the course of least resistance, and was the more attractive because any other action would have entailed serious economic sacrifice. Yet Wilson might have foregone the rewards of bending before British power had it not been for still another circumstance. For a hundred years Anglo-American relations had progressively improved, until by 1914 the accommodation between the two countries was complete. This state of affairs had for decades been the cornerstone of the security of the Western Hemisphere and was the underlying condition of the unprecedented freedom of action so long enjoyed by the United States. This is understood better today than it was then, but Wilson was not the man to disturb a relationship so significant and so firmly established. By the fall of 1914, therefore, the United States, both by omission and acquiescence, had set a course highly favorable to the British cause.[5]

4 DID WILSON HAVE A CHOICE?

There is yet another explanation of why the United States entered the Great War. Ernest R. May argued that President Wilson, having exhausted all other alternatives, had no other course but war:

> All of us saw Wilson's efforts to avoid conflict with the British and to prevent a German U-boat campaign as not only a rational but almost inevitable response to problems with which the President had to deal. The trade loss resulting from the Allied blockade was negligible. The gain from Allied war buying, on the other hand, meant the difference between prosperity and depression. Moreover, long before propaganda could have had any effect, Wilson estimated that 90 percent of the public was pro-Ally. When confronting the first German submarine decree, he had to recognize that it threatened the American economy. He also had to take account of the fact that a significant part of the public already felt outraged against Germany not just because of atrocity stories but also because of such acts as the violation of Belgian neutrality and the bombing of open cities. Charles Seymour and Arthur Link and I all stressed the importance of seeing Wilson's actions in perspective against those of the Allies and especially of the Germans. We pointed out that the British deliberately endeavored to keep American goodwill while the German government always discussed submarine operations in terms of war or peace with the United States. We endeavored to show ... that the American government was not making a series of absolute moral judgments but was choosing among the unsatisfactory alternatives available to it at given moments of time.[6]

[5] Edward H. Buehrig, "Idealism and statecraft," *Confluence*, 5 (1945), p. 257.

[6] Ernest R. May, *The Reconstruction of American History*, ed. John Higham (New York, Harper and Row, 1962), p. 192.

Concurring in the above, Arthur Link proposed that, failing to obtain peace as a neutral, Wilson sought lasting peace by making war:

It seemed for a moment that Wilson's bold stroke and secret negotiations [in late 1916] might succeed. The British government, for reasons still unknown, returned a favorable response to Wilson's overtures on January 26 [1917]. The Austro-Hungarian government soon sent secret feelers to the White House. Everything now depended upon the reply from Berlin. Bethmann was so excited by Wilson's secret appeal that he rushed to Pless to plead for a friendly response. It was too late to postpone the submarine campaign, for U-boats were already on the way to their stations. But the Imperial Chancellor did obtain permission to send a statement of moderate peace aims and an appeal to Wilson to persevere in his efforts for peace.

Events immediately afterwards led to an intensification rather than to an end to the war. But they need not have turned out that way. Wilson, to be sure, broke diplomatic relations with Germany on February 3, soon after the announcement of the new submarine campaign. But he was still as dead set against belligerency as ever. He clearly would have accepted a severe intensification of the submarine war, and he yielded to the growing American demand for war only after the Germans began to sink passenger liners and American merchantmen without warning, and only after the bungling Zimmermann telegram, proposing a military alliance between Mexico and Germany, had caused him to lose all faith in German good intentions. But in the end, when he made his final decision, it was the conviction that the war was in its last stages, and American participation would hasten its end, that most powerfully influenced the President to decide for belligerency.[7]

Whether the United States had any reason for entering World War I is clearly debatable. George F. Kennan offered one viewpoint worthy of consideration:

I would like first to say a word about the total results of these two world wars in Europe. These wars were fought at the price of some tens of millions of lives, of untold physical destruction, of the destruction of the balance of forces on the Continent – at the price of rendering western Europe dangerously, perhaps fatefully, vulnerable to Soviet power. Both wars were fought, really, with a view to changing Germany: to correcting her behavior, to making the Germans something different from what they were. Yet, today, if one were offered the chance of having back again the Germany of 1913 – a Germany run by conservative but relatively moderate people, no Nazis and no Communists, a vigorous Germany, united and

[7] Arthur Link, "Woodrow Wilson and peace moves," *The Listener*, (1966), p. 870.

unoccupied, full of energy and confidence, able to play a part against the balancing-off of Russian power in Europe – well, there would be objections to it from many quarters, and it wouldn't make everybody happy; but in many ways it wouldn't sound so bad, in comparison with our problems of today. Now, think what this means. When you tally up the total score of the two wars in terms of their ostensible objective, you find that if there has been any gain at all, it is pretty hard to discern.[8]

There is no evidence that Wilson judged the situation in Europe, on the outbreak of war in 1914, any more accurately than his countrymen. It was a war attributable to wicked men, to autocracy, and to the absence of genuinely democratic government, a war "whose causes cannot touch us." He shared the faith of the Progressives: man in America was a rational being, and war was barbarous; the American ethic was still a product of the farm, individualist, utopian, and non-military; its only imperialist philosopher thus far was a sailor, Mahan, not a soldier. Separated from, and superior to, the feuds of the Old World, the United States could and should stay out. As late as February 1916, Wilson described American neutrality as "a matter of conviction and of the heat." This viewpoint was not far from that of the *Chicago Herald*, which offered a vote of thanks to Columbus for having discovered America.

Despite the testing issues of the first few months of the war – the bombing of Rheims and the German invasion of Belgium, with their sharp impact on American opinion ("Germany has almost made England popular in America," said Spring-Rice in October), the disputes with Britain over neutral shipping, over contraband and the seizure of mails and the blacklisting of shipping firms – Wilson held to his faith in neutrality "in thought as well as in action." It came gradually to be reinforced by the hope that a free and neutral United States, growing in moral and material strength as the war dragged on, might in the end act, under his leadership, as an acceptable and impartial mediator.

It was to this end that Col. Edward M. House, Wilson's close adviser, was sent on his peace missions to Europe. When House, a far more realistic politician, returned in the spring of 1916 with the House-Grey memorandum, involving, if the proposed peace conference failed, a promise of American entry into war, Wilson retreated from such a step and added a cautionary "probably" to

[8] George F. Kennan, *American Diplomacy, 1900–1950* (New York, Mentor Books, 1952 edn), pp. 50–1.

House's commitments. As late as September 1916, Wilson was so irritated by Britain that he got authority from Congress to prohibit loans and restrict exports to the Allies if they did not change their policy. In January 1917, he still thought that the United States could and should remain aloof. Although it was hit upon by accident, Martin Glynn's slogan, "He kept us out of war," was a true statement. "Once lead the people into war and they'll forget there ever was such a thing as tolerance." If he lost this fight too, he fought hard and nobly for neutrality.

As always, the problem for the statesman was not the soundness of his aim but whether he could translate it into action: means, not ends, are the vital thing. If neutrality was the goal, how successful were the means? One difficulty here has often been cited – Wilson's anglophilia. His ancestry and his Presbyterianism, his training as constitutional historian and political scientist – a training that had not included the customary spell in Germany – his love for the Lake poets, all ministered to a pro-British feeling. He certainly disliked the arbitrary character of the German government and its militarism. Those who were close to him had no doubts about the depth of the private sympathy for Britain. "'You and Grey are fed on the same food, and I think you understand.' There were tears in his eyes, and I am sure we can at the right moment depend upon an understanding heart here." So Spring-Rice wrote to Britain's Foreign Secretary Grey on 8 September 1914. Of his advisers, only Bryan was strictly neutral, and he lacked the standing to make his neutrality impressive; in any case he resigned on the Lusitania question in May 1915. Walter Hines Page, the US ambassador in London, was more British than the British; Franklin Lane, Wilson's all-too-genial secretary of the interior, was a Canadian by birth; Robert Lansing, who succeeded Bryan, became more and more critical of Germany – though more critical, perhaps, in his retrospective writings than in his actual administration; House, by the spring of 1916 at least, if not much earlier, had come down on the British side.

But it is altogether too simple, and quite out of character, to see Wilson, the man of principle, finally falling victim to his own prejudices or those of his associates. He fought against these with Calvinist firmness. Alone they would never have determined his actions. Far more challenging than his pro-British sympathy was the dilemma presented by the situation in Europe, the succession of crises, the growing involvement. The theme of his career is this constant battle between ideal and reality, the all-too-wide gulf between his abstract principles and the difficulties and contradictions of the situation in which he found himself; and, on each occasion, it was his inflexible principles that were destroyed, and in the end the man with them. There was nothing wrong with the policy of neutrality, which clearly accorded with the wishes and economic interests of the majority of the American people. But, by restating in each crisis a position of principle, by giving no room to himself or to his emissaries to maneuver, he inadvertently steered his country closer and closer to a point at which no alternative but war would remain open to it. As he put it to Senator Stone in 1916, "I cannot consent to any abridgement of the rights of American citizens in any respect ... if in this instance we allowed expediency to take the place of principle, the door would inevitably be opened to still further concessions." This very firmness ministered to tension. The years from 1914 to April 1917 saw a succession of crises with common characteristics; they were invariably defined by him not as issues of peace *versus* war, but of morality *versus* expediency. Each time, of course, morality won; and each time war was remorselessly brought a step nearer.

The first step to perdition was the American note on "strict accountability," holding Germany responsible for any American vessels sunk or lives lost after she had proclaimed her submarine blockade of Britain in February 1915. The viewpoint was buttressed by the *Lusitania* notes in May, June, and July: submarine warfare violated the principles of international law, of humanity and justice; American citizens had a legal right to take passage on belligerent ships; international law provided for the safety of passengers and crew; any repetitions of the *Lusitania* sinking would be treated as an unfriendly act. Bryan's refusal to sign the second of the *Lusitania* notes and his resignation dramatized Wilson's dilemma. He was seeking to argue not only that the sea-lanes should be peaceful avenues for Americans on their own ships, but that their presence on unarmed belligerent ships should make those ships sacrosanct. There can be no question that submarine warfare violated international law; there is some ground for wonder that the *Lusitania* should have been given no convoy or protection by Britain in the war zone; it is probable that, as he claimed, the commander of U-boat 20 did not know the name of his victim until he saw it on the ship's bows as she was sinking. Nevertheless, all this said, the decisions of February and May–July 1915 made the final steps inevitable consequences. Wilson could have warned Americans against travel on the armed ships of belligerent powers; he could have ordered his own ships to avoid the war zones established by the belligerent; he could have swallowed whatever injuries or insults might have followed from such precautions. Such courses, however, were for him inconceivable, for American rights and honor were at issue; and on these there could be no compromise.

Not only American rights, but by 1916 the rights of all mankind were at issue. Had Wilson limited himself to defending Americans, and sought, ignobly perhaps, to keep them out of mischief, he might have averted war. But by 1916 he was taking a step beyond the question of submarine warfare and the role of neutrals, and he was presenting his arguments on it to the American people in new – and dangerously general – terms. The "preparedness" campaign of February 1916 – in part wished upon him by his party with an eye on Republican charges in an election year, in part a necessary warning lest House's mission fail – was put to the American people by one who now saw himself as a crusader for world causes. "There is something that the American people love better than they love peace." "There is a price which is too great to pay for peace." The words are repeated in speech after speech: "moral obligation laid upon us;" "there are ... rights higher and greater than the rights of trade and commerce. I mean the rights of mankind;" "we are in some sort and by the force of circumstances the responsible spokesmen of the rights of humanity." Wilson put the case for "an universal association" of nations at a meeting of the League to Enforce Peace in 1916 – sharing the platform, oddly enough, with Senator Henry Cabot Lodge. As late as January 1917, the hope was still for neutrality. But another Wilson was appearing, now voicing principles not only of national honor but of international order.

If Wilson contributed by his inflexibility to the ultimate declaration of April 1917, the responsibility for American entry rests squarely on the German decision to resume submarine warfare, and on the singular folly of appealing to Mexico in the Zimmermann Note. If German calculations on U-boats were made coldly, they were not well served by their Intelligence in the United States; Admiral von Holtzendorf doubted if a single American soldier would set foot in Europe. By 1917 it was the German government that was at once inflexible and rash.

Nor is there reason to assess the economic or propagandist pressures on Wilson. If the American economy was by 1917 in the broadest sense bound up with Allied victory, and if the pressures of Wall Street on public opinion and on Congress were considerable, there is little sign of financial pressures being brought to bear on Wilson. It was difficult enough for his closest Cabinet colleagues to influence him, much less Wall Street. "I rarely consult anybody," he told Ida Tarbell in 1916. And it is impossible to view the promoter of the Underwood Tariff, or of the Federal Reserve Act, as one ready to indulge in war to protect the investments of "privilege" and of "Other People's Money." Whatever the motives of Congress in 1917 – at least as seen from the standpoint of Senator Nye in 1935 – Wilson did not go to war to save the skins of bankers. Nor are the arguments of "Propaganda for War" any more convincing. It was the sound adage of the propagandists of World War II that no nation can be persuaded by propaganda to do something that it would not do anyway: all propaganda can do is to speed the process of conversion. The issues used by British propaganda between 1915 and 1917 – used very skillfully, it is true – were provided by Germany; Bernstorff put the "blame" squarely on the German Foreign Office, not on Parker or Wiseman, on the British Information Services nor Admiral Hall and his cipher experts. There were forces at work here in economics and public opinion but their importance has been exaggerated; and they certainly had little influence on Wilson himself.

5 THE PEACE SETTLEMENT

In his address to Congress on January 8, 1918, President Wilson proposed his Fourteen Points as a basis for the eventual settlement of the war. They were:

1 Open covenants of peace, openly arrived at
2 Freedom of navigation upon the seas in peace or war
3 The removal of all economic barriers and the establishment of an equality of trade conditions among all nations
4 Adequate safeguards given and taken that national armaments will be reduced to the lowest point consistent with domestic safety
5 A free, open-minded and impartial adjustment of all colonial claims, based on the principle that the interests of the populations concerned have equal weight with the equitable claims of the government whose title is to be determined
6 The evacuation of all Russian territory
7 Belgium must be evacuated and restored
8 All French territory should be freed and the invaded portions restored, and the loss of Alsace-Lorraine in 1871 righted
9 Readjustment of the frontiers of Italy should be effected along clearly recognizable lines of nationality
10 The peoples of Austria-Hungary should be accorded the freest opportunity of autonomous development

11 Romania, Serbia and Montenegro should be evacuated; occupied territory restored; and the relations of the several Balkan states to one another determined by friendly counsel along lines of allegiance and nationality
12 The Turkish portions of the Ottoman empire should be assured secure sovereignty, but the other nationalities now under Turkish rule should be assured an undoubted security of life and unmolested opportunity of autonomous development
13 An independent Polish state should be erected, including territories inhabited by indisputably Polish populations, which should be assured a free and secure access to the sea
14 A general association of nations must be formed under specific covenants for the purpose of affording mutual guarantees of political independence and territorial integrity to great and small states alike.

After the end of hostilities, Wilson insisted on taking his proposals to Europe in person. But his peace commission – General Tasker Bliss, Lansing, House, Henry White, and Wilson himself – was thoroughly unrepresentative; it included neither a Senator nor a major Republican – White, the sole Republican, was an ex-ambassador of small influence in Republican circles. Wilson took with him to Europe a cohort of advisers, many of them selected from the group known as the Inquiry, a vast army of specialists, many of whom were future academic administrators; and he needed a liner to carry them. There were distinguished figures in this intelligence service, from its head, Sidney Mezes of the College of the City of New York, House's brother-in-law, to its youthful secretary, Walter Lippmann; and they included some academic figures who then and later were to be among the outstanding men of their day: James Shotwell, Isaiah Bowman, Charles Seymour, and C. H. Haskins, to name only a few. It was Lippmann and the journalist Frank Cobb who drafted the "interpretation" of the Fourteen Points that became Wilson's working guide at Paris. Yet this assistance, expert though it might be, was not weighty in influencing the Senate or the House back home; and it was not particularly effective in quickly predigesting material for Wilson's use in Paris. Harold Nicolson has left a scathing indictment of Wilson and the American delegation at work in his *Peacemaking 1919.*[9]

With some of his advisers Wilson was to have sharp differences of opinion – as over Italy; and they did not save him from revelations of profound ignorance of history and geography. Somewhat

[9] Harold Nicolson, *Peacemaking 1919* (London, Constable, 1928).

casually, he had already "created" certain "new" countries, such as Czechoslovakia; he only afterwards learnt of the size of the German population in northern Bohemia. His faith in national self-determination was hard to translate into reasonable terms for the populations of Eastern Europe. He was never very certain about his Near Eastern geography; and he had a perennial difficulty over the location of Baghdad. If his confusion over the status of the Tigris-Euphrates Valley was in 1919 all too understandable – and reflected, be it said, the contemporary confusion in Baghdad itself – his frequent inaccuracies and vagueness augured ill for the bigger inquest ahead of him at home.

Knowledge of the idealism but vagueness of Wilson's approach, and of his somewhat amateur intelligence service, was perhaps among the reasons why Colonel House, who had spent a few months in Europe as his emissary, had urged him not to go to Paris in person. In House's view – and Seymour's – this was his supreme mistake. "He was the *God on the Mountain*," wrote House, "and his decisions regarding international matters were practically final. When he came to Europe and sat in conference with the Prime Ministers and representatives of other states, he gradually lost his place as first citizen of the world." House and Lansing both urged him not to attend – and House reported that his view was supported by Lord Reading, the British ambassador in Washington, and the French premier, Georges Clemenceau. This may well have begun the process of Wilson's own disenchantment with House himself; by March 1919 he came to discern and dislike House's own easy acceptance by the French and the British, to be sensitive about House's conferences with them, to feel that House was "giving away" all he had stood for.

Wilson's difficulties at Paris, however, were, in the last analysis, a matter of personality. He distrusted even his closest advisers; and, after his quick visit to the United States in February-March 1919, the distrust deepened. It brought a break with House; and in the end the break was complete. He refused to see House again after he left Paris and House never could discover why. As the conference progressed, he relied more and more on the rightness of his own judgment, and more and more drew on his own reserves for assurance. Henry White, once ambassador in Paris, was never used as an intermediary with Clemenceau. Wilson took the decision to send troops to Siberia without discussion with his secretary of war, Newton D. Baker – though Baker was his favorite Cabinet officer. The view that he had expressed on the *George Washington en route* to Europe, that he would be the only disinterested member of the Conference because he had no territorial demands to make or reparations to ask, grew in certainty as the months passed. None of his advisers could obtain specific or concrete statements from him. His frankness in stating his views, at the outset of an argument, made retreat difficult; for the retreat was always so much an abandonment of a very general principle. Anything other than firmness, however, became, in his eyes, a form of surrender. To bargain was to play a European – and an immoral – game. The British prime minister David Lloyd George described him as "a missionary whose function it was to rescue the poor European heathen from their age-long worship of false and fiery gods." This remained the fundamental tragedy in Wilson, a tragedy bound up with his own fineness of character and transparent honesty of intention – the belief, so close to naiveté, that there was a right in politics of which he alone was the champion. "Tell me what is right and I'll fight for it" was a dangerously simple view to bring to a war-torn world in 1919. Parliamentary politicians had long lost such illusions.

Moreover, Wilson was at a tactical disadvantage *vis-à-vis* Lloyd George, Clemenceau, and the Italian prime minister, Vittorio Emmanuele Orlando. They were wilier men than he; and they were certainly more adept in the ways of the *coulisses*. Wilson had the disadvantages of one over-dependent on the document and the printed word. He stayed up night after night wrestling with written material, in a constantly losing effort to keep pace with the problems that awaited him next day; his associates – whom he was prompt to see as enemies quite as tangible as the Germans – were far better trained in learning from conversation and from quick summaries, and were better acquainted with the nature of the problems themselves. He had only two stenographers at the peace conference, had made no plans for adequate secretarial staff, and made far from efficient use of the service House provided for him. Once again, Wilson had to draw on his reserves of nervous and mental energy. "The rest of us", said Lloyd George years later, "found time for golf and we took Sundays off, but Wilson, in his zeal, worked incessantly." Soon there came testiness and ill-concealed anger; in April came influenza and conversations through bedroom doors; occasionally there were evidences of utter tactlessness – in the failure to voice appreciation of the sufferings of Britain or France, the brusque refusal to visit the battlefields or devastated areas of Northern France, or the folly of the Fiume appeal to the Italian people over the heads of their chosen leaders. The errors have their own nobility – the high temper and will-power of an overworked and over-dedicated man, fighting against error and wickedness that he was prompt to see personified in those about him. The admirer of Bagehot refused to accept as binding on himself the master's respect for a liberal society as "a polity of discussion." For him, politics was an affair of *pronunciamentos*.

This, however, is not to say that Wilson failed at Paris. A critic might even argue that it was only his brusqueness and inflexibility that won any concessions from the selfish European politicians. He had not achieved all his Fourteen Points: but without them the Treaty would have been a great deal worse than it was. When the Treaty was signed on 28 June 1919, it included the following terms:

1 Germany was forced to admit her war guilt and was disarmed and forced to pay reparations.
2 France recovered Alsace Lorraine and was to occupy the Saar Basin for fifteen years. The League was to occupy the Rhineland (left bank) for fifteen years, while a 30-mile zone on the right bank of the Rhine was demilitarised.
3 Poland was created as an independent State and received Posen, part of Upper Silesia, and a corridor to the sea. Danzig became a free city.
4 German imperial possessions went to various Allied powers under the League mandate system.
5 The Covenant of the League of Nations determined that members of the League were each to have one vote in the General Assembly; a Council composed of representatives of Great Britain, France, the United States, Italy, Japan, and four other powers was to serve as the executive. A permanent secretariat was to sit at Geneva. According to Article X members were to preserve each other's territorial integrity, and Article XVI provided for economic sanctions against aggressors.

Wilson wanted a fixed amount of reparations to be agreed on, and a definite type of payment specified. There were to be no "punitive damages." He had been compelled to accept the inclusion of the cost of pensions in addition to direct damages; but he had at least succeeded in keeping the demands made on Germany short of the total costs of the war. By promising aid to France that the Senate later was to ban, he prevented the complete separation of the Rhineland from Germany, and the annexation of the Saar by France. He had the ex-German colonies "mandated" to the League, and thus probably speeded the process whereby they attained their ultimate independence. If he lost to the Japanese on Shantung, at least he extracted a promise of the eventual return of sovereignty over Shantung to China. If it was far from the idyllic hopes of December, the Treaty agreed on in May 1919 was, as Wilson put it to Ray

Stannard Baker, "the best that could be had out of a dirty past." This is what Charles Seymour has in mind when he refers to "the Paris education" of Wilson.

And, for Wilson, the gloom was offset by the creation of the League of Nations. It had been set up with astonishing ease by a Commission over which he had himself presided; the Covenant was drafted, and approved by a plenary Conference, before his visit to Washington was made in February; and to all the mounting problems of the period after March – consequent on what R. S. Baker described over-dramatically as the February "plot" – it was in the League that Wilson put his faith. The more difficult the issues to be resolved, the more there would be for the League to do. His very success here, contrasting with the battle of words with Lodge and the Round Robin of the dissenting Senators before he sailed back to Paris, brought both exaltation and exasperation. The Covenant became bound up with the Treaty and with the man – a symbol of his European achievement.

Despite Lodge and the die-hards, the attitude in Washington towards the League and the Treaty in July 1919 was not hostile. Most Democrats and most Republicans supported it; so did Taft and Root. There is no reason to doubt Seymour's view that "a few conciliatory gestures by the President would have sufficed to win the two-thirds vote necessary to ratification." But they were not forthcoming. He acted gracelessly and, in its eyes, unconstitutionally toward the Senate, and peremptorily towards its Foreign Relations Committee. On Colonel House's pressing, he gave a dinner to the Senate and House Committees; he thought it unsuccessful. Senator Brandegee said it was like wandering with Alice in Wonderland and having tea with the Mad Hatter. For Wilson there would be no changes in Covenant or Treaty – even though Grey brought evidence later that Europe would have been ready to accept any changes the Senate thought necessary. By September, Wilson saw the issue as sharp and personal, a battle between himself and Lodge. Once again, the people should be the judge. Once more, the liberal optimism held, and for the last time. "Whoever knew truth put to the worse in free and open encounter?"

On 3 September 1919 Wilson set out, against his doctor's orders, on his famous crusade in the West; 37 speeches in 23 days, and the last the greatest of all. "My clients are the children," he said. "My clients are the next generation." On September 10, the Senate Committee on Foreign Relations reported the Treaty to Senate with amendments and resolutions. Senate rejected all amendments but accepted a number of reservations.

On 25 September, at Pueblo, Colorado, when Wilson thought the tide was turning towards him in the country, he reached the limit of his nervous and physical strength. Brought back to Washington, he suffered a stroke on 2 October, and for seven and a half months conducted no official business. He was guarded with possessive, even perhaps over-zealous, devotion by his second wife, Edith Bolling Galt, whom he had married in December 1915. Only four or five people were allowed to visit him. So complete was the isolation that a Senate and House Committee had to insist on seeing him – the smelling Committee", as Wilson called it, led by one of his critics, the opprobrious Senator Fall.[10] Whatever the cause, however vigilant Mrs Wilson might be, there was no leadership from the White House; and there could be no compromise. He had been forced into compromises at Paris, and had emerged with some results to show. He might have done so once more in Washington, had he been fit. But, leaderless, his Democratic Senators held to an all-or-nothing attitude, enough, in alliance with the dozen irreconcilables in the Senate, to prevent the necessary two-thirds majority. This was not Lodge's fault, in November at least; he was for the Treaty, heavily amended. On November 6, Lodge proposed 14 reservations to the League Covenant, the most vital of which said that Articles X and XVI, which required involvement to stop aggression, would be binding only when Congress so directed. While the reservations did not seriously impair the League, Wilson opposed them because he felt that the United States had a moral commitment under Article X. On November 18, President Wilson instructed the Democratic majority in the Senate to vote against the Treaty with reservations. Wilson in particular opposed the reservation against Article X, which he considered the "heart of the Covenant." The following day the Senate rejected the Treaty with the Lodge reservations by the following vote: 39 Yea (35 reservationist Republicans and 4 Democrats) and 55 Nay (42 Democrats and 13 Irreconcilable Republicans). The Senate also voted against the treaty with five mild Democratic reservations and against it with no reservations.

When the Treaty came before the Senate again in March 1920 it had a majority, but this was seven short of the necessary two-thirds. Irony was added to tragedy by the fact that, in the end, the Treaty was defeated not by its enemies but by its friends.

[10] See Arthur S. Link, "Dr Grayson's predicament," *Proceedings of the American Philosophical Society* 138.4 (1994), p. 487. Dr Cary Grayson was Wilson's physician and friend; he recognized the acute state of the President's health, and in this note Link describes Wilson's condition.

The fault was hardly Wilson's, since he was *incommunicado*; he had made his contribution to the result, however, by his earlier intransigence. Lodge had contributed, by a political tactic that was quite remarkable; for it had succeeded by March 1920 in undoing what in November some 80 percent of Americans had wanted. And Lodge had done this by an uncanny skill in reading Wilson's mind, and assuming its inflexibility. Only an emissary close to Wilson's heart could now have acted as an interpreter of his obstinacy, his dedication, and his faith. But House was not permitted an entrance. The circle of friends was now very small. And the democracy that depended so heavily on the leader drifted under Harding towards isolation and Normalcy. For the next three years Wilson led a retired life, a crippled figure in a bath chair. He died on 3 February, 1924.

The defeat was that of Wilson and the League, far more than that of the Treaty of Versailles. Indeed, when in the end the United States made its peace with Germany by the Treaty of Berlin (August 1921), it did so by incorporating into that Treaty many of the less happy terms of the Treaty of Versailles. The United States accepted the decisions on colonies and reparations, on war-guilt and on the military occupation of Germany. What it rejected were, in fact, the more constructive aspects – the League and the International Labour Organization – although, here again, the reality was less disturbing than the myth, and to many League conferences it sent observers, and joined the ILO in 1934. What was rejected in 1919 and 1920 was Wilsonian idealism and Wilson's effort at justice, and the risky ventures of Article X. The United States was not acting from motives of a superior morality; it was being neither noble nor isolationist, but at best cautious, and at worst blindly vindictive. It, too, had cried for revenge against Germany; and by the terms of the 1921 Treaty it was quite as responsible as any other power, in law and morality, for the events that unfolded in Europe. All it had done was to weaken the one institution, which its own President had labored to build, that might have been able to control them.

One has then not to look far to understand the reasons for the lack of a Wilson legend. Failure alone would not prevent its growth – though, as with everything in politics, it is success that breeds admiration and anecdote. But legends are part of folklore; and Wilson remains not only an idealist who failed but a forbidding figure. His ways now seem cold, and his language stilted and pious. Even the efforts to present him as warm and human, dancing a jig on station platforms in the 1912 campaigns, coaching the football squad, composing limericks and telling dialect stories, read oddly in our own world, at once more folksy and more sophisticated. What fun there may have been was less in evidence after 1912, and especially after his first wife's death in 1914. The academic turned politician is seen to have been from the first more politician than academic; despite the record as student and as teacher, his range of learning was narrow, his tastes administrative rather than original. He made few contributions to his chosen field, domestic reform; what he voiced was familiar. He made no attempt to solve the racial question, or to check the Red Scare, caused largely by his own attorney general, Mitchell Palmer. The crusade against the special interests and against "privilege" was rooted in a faith in the judgment of the people that it is now harder to accept than it was then. He applied it lavishly, and sometimes disastrously, at the expense of other people's leaders in Mexico and Italy, in ways that showed a grave lack of patience and an incapacity to appraise political realities. There was an undercurrent of national pride in Wilson that marks him of the age of Burgess, Mahan, and TR: there was not so much to choose between the *New Nationalism* and the *New Freedom* – and neither of them was very new. After each initial success in his career – as professor, as governor, as President – came a reaction and some degree of failure. On each occasion he escaped and started afresh elsewhere. The ideals were of the highest: but each time the edifice crumbled in his hands.

The greatest defeat of all – over American entry into the League – is now seen in the light of our own experience since 1946 not to have mattered so much anyway; international organization is no longer seen as the great panacea for the world's ills. It is now generally agreed that, if Wilson was not the most culpable figure in the great debate in 1919, by his intransigence he made compromise impossible. And psychologists, as well as historians, have seen deep personal malaise in the man's loneliness, his frequent headaches, his need for women friends, the speed of his second marriage, the final break with House and Tumulty. He never lived at peace with himself, says Garraty. Some psychologists have argued that it was his personal maladjustment that bred the driving energy and ambition. "I want people to love me," Wilson said, "but I suppose they never will." The incapacity to elicit affection, for which he strove harder than most, is in the end the reason why there is here little material for legend.

This is, however, not the final verdict; for verdicts reflect our own age and our own needs. In 1941 Wilson was seen by Paul Birdsall as one who "With all his mistakes, ... emerges as the only man of real stature at Paris."[11] The case for intervention in 1917 is now made less in terms of Wilsonian idealism, British propaganda, or American bankers, than as a matter of sober self-interest, as by Lippmann and Buehrig. It is no longer seen as a matter for controversy; and Wilson's own anxious heart-searching is minimized – as is his long fight to keep the United States out of war. Wilson at Paris is judged by the now professional standards of cold war diplomacy, and in the light of the disillusion that now attaches to much international action. He thought that he had but to declare his truths for the people – in the United States in 1912 or 1916, in Germany in 1917, and in Italy in 1919 – to heed his call. Even for Clemenceau this was *noble candeur*. Today his idealism is even more clearly out of fashion. Yet few would challenge the man's integrity, his honesty, or his battle for what he thought was right. The criticisms made of him are primarily criticisms of method. Even his failure to realize what Salvador de Madariaga called "the dream of reason" – as, in the short view, a failure it must be described – has the elements of Greek or Roman tragedy about it. His career, like that of Coriolanus, is far nobler in its defeat than the success stories of many lesser men.

6 THE MESSIAH

What brought the United States into World War I was the German decision to resume U-boat warfare. That decision produced war, in part because of Wilson's stand on principle from February 1915. As late, however, as January 1917, he was hopeful of averting war. He might still have done so, had he been able to control one situation five thousand miles from American shores. The German decision of January 1917 might not have been made if the Russian Revolution had occurred two months earlier and had brought Germany victory on the eastern front. Coming when it did, however, with the United States indignant, and American lives being lost on the high seas, the Russian Revolution made it appear that the Allies – and their new associate – were fighting the battle of democracy against autocracy. And here, after the failure to keep his country neutral, was a new battle to fight and a new crusade to lead – the greatest of them all.

[11] Paul Birdsall, *Versailles Twenty Years After* (New York, Reynal and Hitchcock, 1941).

The decision to go to Paris in person in 1918 – about which there has been so much debate – was for Wilson itself a logical result of the decision to go to war in April 1917. If the world was to be re-made, it could only be done in Europe. And it was indeed only in the months in Paris, when he was almost at the end of his physical and nervous resources, that Wilson came to make any compromise with his principles. To Paris he went as a Messiah, cheered by returning troops as the *George Washington* sailed down the Hudson, fêted in London, Paris, and Rome, his image worshipped – for a time – in little shrines in Northern Italy. By the time of his return, though the crowds were out in Washington, so were his enemies in the Senate; the high idealism soon cooled in Europe and at home; and the Capitol was but dimly lit for his homecoming. The great test of Wilson, as negotiator, diplomat, and President, was his conduct abroad and at home from January to September 1919.

Hailed as saviour though he was on his arrival in Europe, Wilson was already a heavily committed politician. There was bitterness among Allied leaders that the German offer to negotiate had been made to Wilson; by his notes to the German government, it was felt, he had allowed a peace mood to develop in Germany that threw awry the careful plans of the soldiery for a knockout blow in the spring of 1919, and thus saved Germany from invasion and unconditional surrender. Germany itself was afterwards to make quite contradictory criticisms; that far from being saved, she was offered conditions that were not in fact fulfilled, that she had been lured into a false confidence in Wilson's ability to carry out his undertakings. Out of this came the myth that she was not defeated in the field. Wilson had even sharper troubles with the Allies. The basis of negotiations with Germany was the Fourteen Points speech of January 1918. Yet, until November, the Allies had treated these with scant respect and had refused to approve them. Lloyd George never accepted the second clause committing the Allies to the freedom of the seas; and Clemenceau insisted on reparations from Germany for war damage to civilian populations. It is even doubtful if, before the armistice, Clemenceau had ever read the Fourteen Points speech. Only on House's insistence had the Fourteen Points been accepted by the Allies as a basis for the armistice; and this approval had led to the so-called "Pre-Armistice Agreement."

Moreover, the awe in which Wilson was held by the European crowds was not shared by their more cynical leaders. Clemenceau's savage references to Wilson's piety and moralism are well known – "he speaks like Jesus Christ but he acts like Lloyd George" was only one of his pleasantries; Wilson's confreres in Paris were shrewd judges of a politician's strength and weaknesses; newspapers as sympathetic to Wilson as the London *Times* had already been speaking of "the reign of righteousness." And, by January 1919, there were many gaps in Wilson's political and personal armor. His ill-judged appeal for the return of Democrats in the Congressional elections of November 1918 had failed; the Republicans had a majority of two in the Senate; and the control of the Senate Foreign Relations Committee had passed into the hands of his bitter critic, Henry Cabot Lodge; it was possible for European politicians to see Wilson as one already repudiated at home.

8

Puritans in Babylon

1 THE BOTCHED CIVILIZATION

The veterans who returned from World War I might or might not have seen Paree; but whatever their heroism, they were restless and discontented men, with a taste for drink. They wanted to get back to the values they associated with "home;" they heralded a decade of malaise and mischief, of confusion and disillusionment: this was the Jazz Age.

Together with the uncertain triumphs of victory, the new psychology of Sigmund Freud, with its stress on man's animal nature and the importance of sex, persuaded many who had never actually read Freud to adopt what they called "emancipated" standards of behavior which Freud, himself a staid, highly moral man, had neither advocated nor practiced. Women in particular threw off the restrictions of the past. The "modern" woman, often called a "flapper," wore knee-length skirts, bobbed her hair, smoked cigarettes, and drank cocktails in public places – all examples of behavior that would have marked her mother or grandmother as a prostitute or wanton. For Ezra Pound it was a "botched civilization." The soldiers, said he,

> walked eye-deep in hell
> believing in old men's lies, then unbelieving
> came home, home to a lie,
> home to many deceits,
> home to old lies and new infamy;
> usury age-old and age-thick
> and liars in public places.[1]

[1] Pound, *Hugh Selwyn Mauberley* (1920)

One recurring theme of the 1920s was the Ku Klux Klan's vendetta against immigrants (especially if they could also be branded as anarchists), against Jews and against Catholics. Posing as guardians of public and private morality, the KKK persecuted gamblers, loose women, violators of the prohibition laws, as well as respectable persons who happened to differ from them on religious questions or who belonged to a "foreign race." The Klan professed to believe that the Pope intended to move his headquarters to the United States, that American bishops were stockpiling arms in their cathedrals, that Catholic traitors had already entrenched themselves in many branches of the government. The Klan also conducted crusades against unfriendly politicians and in some cases controlled the elections of governors and congressmen, as well as countless local officials. Since a considerable percentage of its members were secret libertines and corruptionists, the dark, unconscious drives leading men to join the organization are not hard to imagine. By the mid-1920s it claimed an enrollment of several millions, mainly in the rural Middle West.

Fortunately the very success of the Klan led to its undoing. Factionalism sprang up and rival leaders squabbled over the large sums that had been collected from the membership. The cruel and outrageous behavior of the organization roused both liberals and decent conservatives in every part of the country. Klansmen themselves began to worry about the misuse of Klan funds. And, of course, its victims joined forces against their tormentors. When the powerful leader of the Indiana Klan, a middle-aged reprobate named David C. Stephenson, was convicted of assaulting and causing the death of a young woman, the rank and file abandoned the organization in droves. It remained influential for a number of years, contributing to the defeat of the Catholic Alfred E. Smith in the 1928 Presidential election, but it ceased to be a dynamic force after 1924. By 1930 it had only some 9,000 members.

National morality was a problem which concerned not only the Ku Klux Klan. Other Fundamentalist-minded Americans wanted to save the nation from the moral disaster which they believed to be imminent. George E. Mowry recounted a few events in this "moral revolution" of the 1920s:

> The defenders of the old traditions and morals, the agrarian-minded social conservatives and the religious orthodox, did not let this complex series of radical innovations in American society go without an angry and persistent challenge. The spate of movies and books in which sex was free, easy, and explicitly shown was met with such a volume of state and local

censorship laws that the film industry decided to establish its own control of morals and manners in self-protection. But what the Hays Office, named after the former Postmaster General Will H. Hays, succeeded in doing with its "two feet on the floor" rules for bedroom scenes was to substitute the suggestive for the explicit. By requiring that virtue must triumph it also divorced the average movie from any connection with life. Book censors also took vigorous action, and in cities like Boston, where the new Catholics and the old Puritans were allied in the effort, even acknowledged literary masterpieces were denied a place in libraries or bookstores.[2]

By the mid-1920s, the nation read in awe of a religious Fundamental battle against the encroachments of the scientific age. Upholding his belief in religious freedom, John T. Scopes, a high school biology teacher, deliberately broke a Tennessee law which prohibited the teaching of evolution in schools. Representing rural America in the case, especially in the South and Middle West, was William Jennings Bryan, three-time losing candidate for President. In opposition was a noted defense lawyer, Clarence Darrow, an agnostic and American Civil Liberties Union attorney. Thus began a "duel to the death," as Bryan put it. In fact, as it happened, the death was his own, soon after the rural jury convicted Scopes and fined him one hundred dollars. Nevertheless, William E. Leuchtenburg cautioned against a simple interpretation of this event.

Yet the case was not simply a morality play between the good form of intellectual freedom and the evil spirits of obscurantism. In the Scopes trial, the provincialism of the city was arrayed against the provincialism of the country, the shallowness of Mencken against the shallowness of Bryan, the arrogance of the scientists against the arrogance of the fundamentalists.

The very faith in science, as C. E. Ayres pointed out, had reached the point where it had become "superstition, in another guise." In the 1920s the nation was captivated by radioactivity, even by more mundane matters like calories and vitamins; science, many people believed, was a universal balm that would answer every human need. ...[3]

From its very beginning, Bolshevik Communism found little public hospitality in the United States. Property-minded Americans viewed the Russian Revolution with displeasure. Seizing upon this national anti-Communist climate, super-patriots found Communism a useful

[2] George E. Mowry, *The Urban Nation 1920–1960* (New York, Hill and Wang, 1965), pp. 28–9.

[3] William E. Leuchtenburg, *The Perils of Prosperity, 1914–1932* (Chicago, University of Chicago Press, 1958), p. 221.

excuse upon which to blame America's domestic ills. The result was the Red Scare of 1919–20. On the surface an anti-Communist development, the episode was in reality a "ferocious outbreak of nativism," in the opinion of Stanley Cohen:

Rather, the Red Scare ... was brought on largely by a number of severe social and economic dislocations which threatened the national equilibrium. ... Runaway prices, a brief but sharp stock market crash and business depression throughout Europe, widespread fear of domestic revolt, bomb explosions, and an outpouring of radical literature were distressing enough. These sudden difficulties, moreover, served to exaggerate the disruptive effects already produced by the social and intellectual ravages of the World War and the preceding reform era, and by the arrival, before the war, of millions of new immigrants. This added stress intensified the hostility of Americans strongly antagonistic to minority groups, and brought new converts to blatant nativism from among those who ordinarily were not overtly hostile toward radicals or recent immigrants.

Citizens who joined the crusade for one hundred percent Americanism sought, primarily, a unifying force which would halt the apparent disintegration of their culture. The movement, they felt, would eliminate those foreign influences which the one hundred percenters believed were the major cause of their anxiety.[4]

Although anti-foreignism abated after the 1920s, anti-Communism did not, as Robert A. Rosenstone suggested:

Common among rightist groups, especially in the twentieth century, has been an anti-Negro, anti-Semitic, anti-foreign and often anti-Catholic ideology. Along with this, ever since the Russian Revolution, all extreme groups on the right have shared a militant anti-communism. For reasons that have never been satisfactorily explained, between the thirties and the late forties the feelings against Negroes, Jews, Catholics and foreigners seem to have receded from the panoply of acknowledged rightist beliefs. At least they were subsumed into an increasingly violent anti-communism. Thus Senator Joseph McCarthy, leader of a rightist crusade in the early fifties, was himself a Catholic, and two of his chief aides (Roy Cohn and David Schine) were Jews. Somehow these once-foreign elements had Americanized themselves, and they were able to join with older-stock Americans in a militant front against what they usually termed "atheistic communism." This is not to say that all anti-Semitic, anti-Catholic, anti-Negro "hate groups" disappeared from the American scene. But those that remain are truly part of a dwindling "lunatic fringe" and far less important in numbers,

[4] Stanley Cohen, "A study in nativism," *Political Science Quarterly*, 79 (1964), p. 59.

financial resources and influence than organizations like the John Birch Society, which concentrate solely on the menace of communism.[5]

Distaste for foreigners and for anarchism compounded in one ugly incident: the Sacco-Vanzetti case. In April 1920 two men in South Braintree, Massachusetts, killed a paymaster and a guard in a daring daylight robbery of a shoe factory. Shortly thereafter, Nicola Sacco and Bartolomeo Vanzetti were charged with the crime, and in 1921 they were convicted of murder. Sacco and Vanzetti were anarchists and also Italian immigrants. Their trial was a travesty of justice. The presiding judge, Webster Thayer, conducted the proceedings like a prosecuting attorney; he even referred privately to the defendants as "those anarchist bastards."

The case became a *cause célèbre.* Prominent persons all over the world protested, and for years Sacco and Vanzetti were kept alive by efforts to obtain a new trial. Vanzetti's quiet dignity and courage in the face of death wrung the hearts of millions. "You see me before you, not trembling," he told the court. "I never commit a crime in my life. ... I am so convinced to be right that if you could execute me two times, and if I could be reborn two other times, I would live again and do what I have done already." When, in August 1927, the two were at last electrocuted, the disillusionment of American intellectuals with current values was profound. Recent historians, impressed by modern ballistic studies of Sacco's gun, now suspect that he, at least, was actually guilty. Nevertheless, the truth and the shame remain, Sacco and Vanzetti paid with their lives for being radicals and aliens, not for any crime.

At the roots of the conflict between the provincial-minded and the cosmopolitan-minded urban inhabitants, between the farm and the city, lay a sense of frustration. In the view of Richard Hofstadter, Fundamentalists attempted to foist their anti-intellectual views on the enlightened;

> The 1920's proved to be the focal decade in the *Kulturkampf* [cultural battle] of American Protestantism. Advertising, radio, the mass magazines, the advance of popular education, threw the old mentality into a direct and unavoidable conflict with the new. The older, rural and small-town America, now fully embattled against the encroachments of modern life, made its most determined stand against cosmopolitanism, Romanism, and the skepticism and moral experimentalism of the intelligentsia. In the Ku

[5] Robert A. Rosenstone, *Protest from the Right* (Beverly Hills, Glencoe Press, 1968), Introduction.

Klux Klan movement, the rigid defense of Prohibition, the Scopes evolution trial, and the campaign against Al Smith in 1928, the older America tried vainly to reassert its authority; but its only victory was the defeat of Smith, and even that was tarnished by his success in reshaping the Democratic Party as an urban and cosmopolitan force, a success that laid the groundwork for subsequent Democratic victories.[6]

2 THE OHIO GANG

Rarely had the voters faced such a lackluster pair of presidential candidates as they did in 1920. Each of the two major parties, turning away from the late examples of a strong chief executive, nominated a political mediocrity from Ohio. For the Democrats, Governor James M. Cox offered the best alternative to the stricken but still ambitious President Wilson. The Republicans selected the weak, affable, but strikingly handsome Senator Warren G. Harding in order to break a convention deadlock. Harding had been editor of a newspaper in Marion, Ohio. He had served in the US Senate (1915–21), and was nominated for President by the Republican National Convention after a deadlock in the balloting between General Leonard Wood, who represented the Roosevelt faction, and Illinois governor Frank O. Lowden. He straddled on the issue of whether or not the US should join the League of Nations; in his campaign Harding pledged "a return to normalcy," whatever that meant. During the campaign, Cox talked as if he had lost his way in national affairs, and Harding relied almost exclusively on empty platitudes. "Why does he not get a private secretary who can clothe ... his 'ideas' in the language customarily used by educated men?" one Boston gentleman demanded of Senator Lodge, who was strongly supporting Harding. Lodge, ordinarily a stickler for linguistic exactitude, replied acidly that he found Harding a paragon by comparison with Wilson, "a man who wrote English very well without ever saying anything." Most Americans, untroubled by the candidate's lack of erudition, shared Lodge's confidence that he would be a vast improvement; the handsome senator at least showed Americans a warm smile and a friendly manner. In November 1920, that genial personality, along with a nationwide accumulation of grievances against the Democrats, gave Harding an overwhelming 61 percent of the popular vote, to become the 29th President of

[6] Richard Hofstadter, *Anti-Intellectualism in American Life* (New York, Vintage Books, 1963), p. 123.

the US. Cox and his running mate Franklin Delano Roosevelt carried no states outside the South.

An era, it seemed, had ended. America now had a passive, conservative President with no taste for reform, and no ambition for either national or international ventures. Promising the nation a return to "normalcy," Harding entered the White House with no apparent goals of any sort. Some observers concluded that he was trying to recapture the spirit of the McKinley years, when the chief executive had watched beningly while other people ran the country. They might better have cited the spirit of the Grant administration, for Harding allowed a swarm of greedy men to infest the government, to corrupt many of its offices, and to ruin his own reputation.

Despite appointments to his Cabinet of such men of standing as Charles Evans Hughes (State), Herbert Hoover (Commerce), and Andrew Mellon (Treasury), he opened the way to corruption by making what became known as the "Ohio gang" his confidants. Harry Daugherty (later dismissed) was his attorney general. Alfred Fall, a former Senator, headed the Department of the Interior. Both Fall and Daugherty, along with Edwin Denby (Navy) and others, were implicated in the notorious Teapot Dome oil scandal. They shared the President's taste for poker, liquor and women; and those who had been Senators continued to treat Capitol Hill as a club.

In an inconspicuous house on K Street, members of the "Ohio gang" with connections in the justice department sold immunity from federal prosecution. Charles Forbes, a chance acquaintance whom Harding appointed director of the Veterans' Bureau, fled the country in 1923 to avoid punishment for purloining millions of public funds meant for hospitals. When he returned after a two-year absence, he was tried and given a two-year prison sentence. Most sensational of all, a long Congressional inquiry in 1923 and 1924 exposed the bribes and backroom deals behind the private leasing of government oil lands on Teapot Dome in Wyoming and Elk Hills in California. For his part in the "Teapot Dome Scandal," Secretary of the Interior Albert Fall, whose lean frame, broad-brimmed hat and drooping handlebar moustache made him look for all the world like a Hollywood sheriff, became the first Cabinet officer in history to serve a jail sentence. Harding's close associate Attorney General Harry Daugherty, barely escaped being the second. By any index of morality or energy or ideology, the contrast between Harding's crowd and the administrations of Theodore Roosevelt and Woodrow Wilson could not have been more striking. Harding, who was naive but not himself corrupt, blamed his "God-damn friends." Demoralized by the betrayal of his friends, and humiliated by the inevitable exposure, Harding, though not officially involved, was under acute tension. He died of a heart attack on 2 August 1923, while in San Francisco returning from a trip to Alaska. Simple, friendly, and easy-going, he could not resist more unscrupulous wills, and his sudden death spared him from the aftermath of events which had revealed an administration both incompetent and corrupt.

By general consent Warren Gamaliel Harding has come to be considered the sorriest of American presidents, remembered chiefly for the scandals that came out after his death and for the mysteries that continue to surround his life. Yet other presidents have tolerated scandals without being branded by them, and one can scarcely maintain that Harding's administration was shot through with scandal when it included such men as Charles Evans Hughes, Herbert Hoover, and the elder Henry Wallace in the Cabinet, and the Harding-appointed chief justice William Howard Taft.

That J. F. Kennedy owed his election in 1960 to fraudulent vote counts in Texas and Illinois has been as little unsettling to the Thousand Days saga as has been the belated knowledge of his casual amours. The roguery of Jesse Smith, hanger-on of attorney general Harry Daugherty, was small-scale compared to that of Lyndon Johnson's Bobby Baker, and Harding at least repudiated Smith. In 1926, three years after the President's death, Harry Daughterty went on trial charged with conspiracy to defraud the government. He refused to testify on the grounds that, as former attorney for Harding, he might give self-incriminating testimony. The implication of his refusal was that he was shielding Harding.

The source material for this rich and juicy legend begins with three ghost-written books: *The President's Daughter*, by Harding's girl-mistress Nan Britton; the psychotic swindler Gaston Means's *The Strange Death of President Harding; and* Daugherty's own *The Inside Story of the Harding Tragedy*. Nan – assisted by an astute press agent – told in schoolgirl prose the story of her affair with Harding: their rendezvous in third-rate hotels, and the child she bore him that she claimed was conceived in the Senate Office Building. Daugherty's turgid apologia, actually written by the Rev. Thomas Dixon, the author of *The Klansman* (later made into the first film epic, *Birth of a Nation*), compared Harding to Lincoln. The Rev. Dixon's sister, May Dixon Thacker, a *True Confessions* writer and wife of a Southern evangelist, was responsible for Means's book, a book she later repudiated. In it Means wrote a detailed account of how Mrs Harding had poisoned her husband to save his reputation from impending ruin.[7] The President certainly was addicted to writing compromising letters to married women full of urgent (but unsuccessful) instructions that all such letters should be destroyed.[8]

Yet, perhaps unsurprisingly, the more solid accomplishments of Harding's White House years are too easily overlooked. Harding's most cherished wish was to be remembered for the naval disarmament conference that he called in November 1921. Though the war he hoped to avoid was not avoided, his conference did stop the construction of capital ships by the United States, England, and Japan for ten years and scrapped a number of warships already built or under construction. Harding, putting aside his usual flowery rhetoric, told the delegates of Britain, Japan, China, France, the Netherlands, Italy, and Portugal that "one hundred million, frankly, want less of armament and none of war." It was his shining hour.

Secondly, Harding's administration was the first to adopt a formal budgetary system, something the United States had lacked from Washington to Wilson. In a special message to Congress, Harding demanded and received authorization for a Bureau of the Budget. Though he had been elected on an anti-League of Nations platform, he sent a bombshell message to Congress demanding – if vainly – that the United States join the World Court. After inviting forty-one steel industry leaders to a White House dinner, he informed them bluntly that the twelve-hour day for steelworkers must go. When the leaders objected that it would dislocate the industry, raise costs, and require 60,000 unavailable additional employees, Harding insisted, and they were forced reluctantly to agree to an eight-hour day.

And third, Harding reopened jobs and offices that had been barred to blacks. Though long forgotten, his speech in Birmingham, Alabama, at the city's semi-centennial celebration, to an audience of 20,000 whites and 10,000 blacks, was the boldest defense of civil rights made by an American President since the Civil War. There in the Southern heartland he told his strictly segregated audience that democracy in the United States was a lie until the Negro was granted political, economic, and educational equality.

[7] *The President's Daughter* (New York, Guild, 1927); *The Strange Death of President Harding* (New York, Guild, 1930); *The Inside Story of the Harding Tragedy* (New York, Churchill, 1932).

[8] Samuel Hopkins Adams, *Incredible Era: The Life and Times of Warren Gamaliel Harding* (Boston, Houghton Mifflin, 1939).

3 BOOM – AND DEPRESSION

The world had never seen such a high level of material well-being as that which existed in the US during the 1920s. With only 6 percent of the world's population, the US had 60 percent of the world's telephones, and 80 percent of its automobiles; it consumed 75 percent of the available rubber, 65 percent of the raw silk, and 25 percent of the sugar. The US produced 40 percent of the world's coal, electric power, and iron ore, 25 percent of the wheat, 75 percent of the corn, 55 percent of the cotton, 50 percent of the timber, and 70 percent of the petroleum and oil products.

From 1909 to 1919 there had been a 10 percent increase in the national income in terms of material goods; from 1919 to 1929 there was a 90 percent increase. This 100 percent increase occurred mainly because industry became nearly twice as efficient, the output per man-hour in manufacturing industries almost doubling from 1909 to 1929.

The high level of foreign investments by the US also helped to stimulate the domestic economy. US loans abroad, especially the three billion dollars lent to Germany, were often used for the purchase of American goods, in particular such capital goods as heavy machinery and locomotives. By 1930 the US had approximately sixteen billion dollars invested abroad, over half in Canada and Western Europe.

The system of mass production for a mass national market depended upon a population with a purchasing power sufficient to buy and consume the ever greater number of commodities produced by an ever more efficient industrial plant. When, late in the decade, the population could no longer maintain its purchases, inventories of surplus goods began to pile up, the market became glutted, and the economic collapse of 1929 resulted. During most of the decade, however, advertising successfully stimulated effective consumer demand. This decade was the first great age of advertising; during it, all the now-familiar psychological techniques of encouraging the desirability of "keeping up with the Joneses" were developed: testimonials from such admired figures as top athletes, medical warnings calculated to frighten the consumer into buying, titillating suggestions on the themes of love and sex, and so on. The purpose of this vast advertising campaign – on which one and a half billion dollars was being spent annually by the latter part of the decade – was to convince the American people of the need to spend, in order to insure that the immense amount of goods rolling off the production lines would be consumed. This was no easy task, for the American people for the past 300 years had been following the maxims of Poor Richard, holding thrift as the supreme virtue; now, suddenly, the advertisers had to convince Americans to spend their income instead of saving it.

A second method developed in the 1920s for stimulating purchases was the system of consumer credit, especially in the form of installment buying. By 1926, 15 percent of the purchases of consumer goods was being financed by this method, and the resultant consumer debt exceeded three billion dollars.

Partly because of the expansion occurring in advertising and in consumer credit, the consumer industries enjoyed large booms in this decade. Naturally this boom stimulated the more basic industries, such as transportation and steel, but it was the producers of consumer goods that enjoyed the most remarkable growth.

The rapid growth of the automobile industry was one of the most important bases of the prosperity of the 1920s. Whereas in 1918 there had been 9 million cars on the road, in 1929 there were 26 million. In 1928 alone, 4 million autos and 500,000 trucks were sold. Nearly 400,000 workers were employed directly in the production of automobiles, and millions more worked in industries and occupations which supplied raw materials, or serviced cars, or were otherwise closely connected with the automobile industry. More than a billion gallons of gasoline were consumed annually, and the petroleum industry grew rapidly to keep up with the demand; the construction of new concrete highways across the nation stimulated the cement, gravel, and asphalt industries, and provided employment for thousands of people, from engineers to unskilled workmen. The truck branch of the automobile industry also became an important part of the American economy. By 1928 there were 3 million trucks on the road, and they had taken over the short-haul business. Trucks made possible the quick transportation of farm commodities to rail centers, whence they could be sent to mass markets; truck farming was especially stimulated in California.

The growth of the automobile industry was accompanied by the development in that industry of all the modern techniques of efficient mass production. Such techniques as centralization of management, specialized plants, specialization of labor within a plant, and fast-moving assembly lines which brought the work to the worker, were introduced into other industries as well. The automobile industry also developed a system of short working hours and relatively good pay, and it maintained strict company discipline, with no outside unions permitted.

Another great boom occurred in the radio industry, providing employment and income for thousands – producers, retailers, entertainers on radio stations, and so forth. The first radio station began broadcasting in Pittsburgh in 1920; by 1929 over a billion dollars was being spent annually on the purchase of radio sets.

Other consumer industries which greatly expanded during the 1920s were those which manufactured various appliances and gadgets for the household – electric refrigerators, vacuum cleaners, etc. The movie industry also enjoyed a rapid growth during the decade. After it settled down in Hollywood, it was an important stimulant to the prosperity of California. The cigarette industry also prospered during the 1920s. Soldiers in World War I began smoking cigarettes (rather than smoking cigars or pipes, or chewing tobacco) in training camps and in the trenches overseas, and the new popularity of cigarettes spread over the nation during the decade. The industry was further stimulated when women began to join the ranks of smokers in large numbers. The construction industry, too, was extremely active especially in building surburban dwellings, as the growth of the suburb in the US was made possible by the automobile. The construction of skyscrapers, as cities became more crowded, provided another great field for expansion.

Agriculture, however, remained depressed throughout the decade. Agriculture suffered from overexpansion to the point of recklessness. The inability of farmers to sell their products at a profit left them in turn unable to buy, and handicapped industry itself. Unlike the new industries, the older industries suffered. Industry as well as agriculture experienced overexpansion: iron, steel, lumber, copper, oil – every basic commodity – was overproduced, until by 1929 warehouses were filled with goods for which there was little or no demand.

The textile industry in particular was injured by a number of changes in the styles of both men's and women's clothing. The installation of efficient central heating plants, which permitted people to wear fewer and lighter clothes in winter, and the shift in styles to silk and artificial textiles, depressed the wool and heavy cotton industries. The short skirts and the generally skimpy clothing of the 1920s required less cotton and wool. (The wool industry was also adversely affected by the substitution of linoleum for coarse woolen rugs.) As a general geographical shift of the textile industry from the North to the South, which had been going on since the 1890s, accelerated rapidly in the 1920s, the industry declined, especially in New England. Hundreds of textile mills there were shut down, never to reopen, thus causing not only heavy capital losses but also widespread unemployment. The industry was attracted to the South by the cheapness of electric power and of labor, by the nearness to raw materials (in the case of cotton industries), by the extremely low tax rate at the state level, and by the lack of legislation protecting labor as well as the lack of unionization in Southern states.

Because of the severe competition now forthcoming from other sources of power – especially petroleum and water power – the coalmining industry too was depressed during the 1920's. Whereas in 1900 coal had furnished nearly 90 percent of power in the US by 1930 it furnished only 60 percent. In contrast, oil as a source of power furnished 6 percent in 1900 and 25 percent in 1930. Moreover, mine shafts had to be dug deeper and deeper in order to extract coal, so that the cost of mining continually increased. The resultant depression caused much unemployment.

During the 1920s many labor-saving devices were introduced and adopted by industry. These new machines helped to produce goods more efficiently, but they created a serious unemployment problem, and men left unemployed by such changes often had considerable difficulty in re-establishing themselves. There was no uniform, nationwide attempt to alleviate the problem of technological unemployment by shortening the hours of work. Further, business enterprises generally invested capital surpluses in plant expansion, rather than distributing them in the form of wages or dividends. This practice left labor unable to buy as large a share of consumers' goods as it might have if these surpluses had been distributed as wages. The Federal Reserve Board made it easy to borrow money for business expansion or speculation on the stock market. Throughout the prosperity of the 1920s the new system of installment buying contributed to the overexpanded credit structure of the nation, and increasingly large shares of the national income went into interest payments.

Of the many causes of the stock market collapse and the depression that followed, one of the most important was the saturation of the consumer-goods market by the continually expanding industrial plants of the nation. For example, by 1929 virtually every family in the United States able to afford an automobile had purchased one, so that additional sales had to be largely replacement sales. The complex network of industries which had benefited from the low prices and mass production inaugurated by the automobile industry also suffered. Similarly, sales of houses, radios, refrigerators, and innumerable other commodities had fallen off sharply by the time of the crash.

The market collapse on Wall Street in October 1929 was precipitated when the Bank of England raised interest rates to 6½ percent, in order to bring back to Britain British capital used for speculation on the New York Stock Exchange. Since there was no real basis for the high prices current on the Exchange there was nothing to cushion the panic of selling which followed. Prices on the Exchange fell as much as 80 percent, and within a month listings declined by 37½ percent.

The consequences of the stock market collapse were serious and widespread. Many factories closed down, and business and bank failures were common. Unemployment rose from 6–7 million in 1930 to 12–14 million by 1932. A worldwide depression followed the crisis in the United States.

The stock market crash had immediate repercussions in almost every foreign country. Private investors in the United States were unable to continue the loans they had been making to Europe throughout the 1920s, and as a result foreign purchases in the United States fell off sharply. Also, the declining price of silver made it difficult for Far Eastern nations to buy in American markets. With many nations seeking "autarchy" (economic self-sufficiency), international trade was seriously hindered. As political unrest grew with the deepening of worldwide depression, the question of whether unmodified capitalism could continue without ever-expanding markets to support it became increasingly pertinent.

4 A PURITAN IN BABYLON: CALVIN COOLIDGE

Had he lived, Harding might well have been defeated in 1924 because of the scandals involving his administration. But Vice-President Coolidge, unconnected with the troubles and not the type to surround himself with cronies of any kind, seemed the ideal man to clean out the stables and restore honest government. When Harding's death in August 1923 made him President, Coolidge moved quickly to neutralize the effects of the Harding scandals, control the party machinery, and secure the 1924 Presidential nomination for himself. After he replaced Attorney General Daugherty with the eminently respectable Harlan Fiske Stone, dean of the Columbia Law School, the Harding scandals ceased to be a serious political handicap for the Republicans. In November 1924, Coolidge was easily elected, receiving 54 percent of the popular vote and 382 electoral votes, to 136 for Democrat John W. Davis and 13 for Progressive Robert M. La Follette. His victory seemed to confirm both the appeal of his public image and the popularity of the conservative policies that he claimed were responsible for a growing national prosperity.

Calvin Coolidge was a Vermont man, educated at Amherst, who had practiced law in Northampton, Massachusetts, before entering state politics. He served two terms as governor (1919–20) and brought himself fame by using militia to suppress the Boston police strike: "There is no right to strike against the public safety by anybody anywhere any time." It is likely that this maxim and its implication of high Toryism won him the nomination for the Vice-Presidency. Coolidge, silent Cal, was untouched by the scandals. He succeeded Harding on 3 August 1923 and was elected in his own right in 1924.

Coolidge soon became the darling of the conservatives. His admiration for businessmen and his devotion to *laissez-faire* knew no limit. "The man who builds a factory builds a temple," he said in all seriousness. "The Government can do more to remedy the economic ills of the people by a system of rigid economy in public expenditure than can be accomplished through any other action." Andrew Mellon, whom he continued in office as secretary of the Treasury, was his ideal and mentor in economic affairs.

In domestic affairs Mellon, multimillionaire banker and master of the aluminum industry, dominated the Harding and Coolidge administrations. Mellon set out to lower the taxes of the rich, reverse the low tariff policies of the Wilson period, return to the *laissez-faire* philosophy of McKinley, and reduce the national debt by cutting expenses and administering the government more efficiently. In principle, his program had considerable merit. Wartime tax rates, designed to check consumer spending as well as to raise the huge sums needed to defeat the Central Powers, were undoubtedly hampering economic expansion in the early 1920s. Certain industries such as chemicals, silks and rayons, and toys, which had sprung up in the United States for the first time during the Great War, were suffering acutely from German and Japanese competition now that the fighting had ended. Rigid regulations necessary during a national crisis could well be dispensed with in peacetime. And efficiency and economy in government are always desirable.

Mellon, however, carried his policies to unreasonable extremes. To reduce the national debt he insisted that the Allies repay the money they had borrowed to the last dollar, not seeing that protective tariffs on European products would deprive them of the means of accumulating dollar credits to meet their obligations. Mellon also proposed eliminating inheritance taxes and reducing the tax on high incomes by two-thirds in order to stimulate investment, but he opposed lower rates for taxpayers earning less than $66,000 a year, apparently not realizing that economic expansion required greater mass consumption as well. Mellon actually suggested increasing the tax burden on the average man by doubling certain excises, raising postal rates, and imposing a federal levy on automobiles. By freeing the rich from "oppressive" taxation, he argued, they would be able to invest in risky but potentially productive enterprises, the success of which would create jobs for ordinary people. Little wonder that Mellon's admirers called him "the greatest secretary of the Treasury since Alexander Hamilton."[9]

Although the Republicans had large majorities in both houses of Congress, Mellon's proposals were too drastically reactionary to win unqualified approval. Somewhat half-heartedly, Congress did pass a Budget and Accounting Act (1921), creating a director of the Budget to assist the President in preparing a unified budget for the government, and a comptroller general to audit all government accounts. A general budget had long been needed; previously Congress had dealt with the requirements of each department separately, trusting largely to luck that income and expenditures would balance at year's end. The appointment of a comptroller general enabled Congress to check up on how the departments actually used the sums granted them.

Mellon's tax and tariff program, however, ran into stiff opposition from Middle-Western Republicans and Southern Democrats, who combined to form the so-called "Farm Bloc." This alignment was essentially economic. The revival of European agriculture was cutting the demand for American farm produce just when the increased use of fertilizers and machinery were boosting output. As in the era after the Civil War, farmers found themselves burdened with heavy debts while their dollar income dwindled. In the decade after 1919 their share of the national income fell by nearly 50 percent. The Farm Bloc represented a kind of revival of populism, economic grievances combining with a general prejudice against "Wall Street financiers" and rich industrialists to unite agriculture against "the interests."

A man like Mellon epitomized everything the Farm Bloc disliked. Rejecting his more extreme suggestions, it pushed through the Revenue Act of 1921, which abolished the wartime excess-profits tax and cut the top income tax rate from 73 to 50 percent, but raised the tax on corporate profits slightly and left inheritance taxes untouched. Three years later Congress cut the maximum income tax

[9] William A. White, *A Puritan in Babylon* (New York, Macmillan, 1938).

to 40 percent, but reduced taxes on lower incomes significantly and raised inheritance levies. The Farm Bloc also overhauled Mellon's tariff proposals, placing heavy duties on agricultural products in 1921 while refusing to increase the rates on most manufactured goods. Although the Fordney McCumber Tariff of 1922 granted more than adequate protection to the "infant industries" (rayon, china, toys, and chemicals), it held to the Wilsonian principle of moderate protection for most industrial products. Agricultural machinery and certain other items important to farmers remained on the free list. The act also authorized the President, upon the recommendation of the Tariff Commission, to raise or lower any rate by as much as 50 percent. However, the changes made under this provision by Harding and Coolidge were all trivial.

Although Congress blocked many of his proposals, Mellon did succeed in balancing the budget and reducing the national debt sharply. The first director of the Budget, Charles G. Dawes, a Chicago banker, cut the requests of the departments drastically; government expenditures fell from $6.4 billion in 1920 to $3.3 billion in 1922 and a low of $2.9 billion in 1927. Throughout the 1920s the national debt shrank an average of over $500 million a year. So committed were the Republican leaders to retrenchment that they even resisted the demands of veterans, organized in the politically potent American Legion, for an "adjusted compensation" bonus. Arguing, not entirely without reason, that they had served for a pittance while war workers had been drawing down high wages, the veterans asked for grants equal to a dollar a day for their period in uniform ($1.25 for time overseas). Congress responded sympathetically, but both Harding and Coolidge vetoed bonus bills in the name of government economy. Finally, in 1924, a compromise bill granting the veterans paid-up life insurance policies was passed over Coolidge's veto.

The business community heartily approved the policies of Harding and Coolidge, as indeed it should have, since both were uncritical advocates of the business point of view. "We want less government in business and more business in government," Harding pontificated, to which Coolidge added the slogan: "The business of the United States is business." Besides pushing a reluctant Congress as far as it would go on tax and tariff matters, Harding and Coolidge used their executive powers to convert regulatory bodies like the Interstate Commerce Commission and the Federal Reserve Board into pro-business agencies.

In foreign affairs, Coolidge accepted the guidance of his secretaries of state, Charles Evans Hughes and Frank B. Kellogg, and continued the search for improved international relations through mechanisms operating outside the League of Nations. Among his administration's diplomatic achievements were the Dawes Plan for scaling down German reparations, the Stimson accords for pacifying Nicaragua, and the Kellog-Briand Pact outlawing war.

While in 1924 Coolidge won the Republican nomination easily, the Democrats, badly split, required 103 ballots to choose a candidate. The Southern, dry, anti-immigrant, rural pro-Klan and Protestant wing had fixed upon William G. McAdoo, Wilson's secretary of the treasury (and his son-in-law). The Eastern, urban, centre and Catholic elements supported Governor Alfred E. Smith of New York, child of the slums, himself a Catholic, who had compiled a distinguished record in the field of social welfare legislation. The Democrats' difficulties were compounded by their "Two-Thirds Rule," dating from the 1830s, which required the Presidential nominee to obtain the votes of two out of three delegates at the national convention, unlike the Republican procedure that required only a simple majority. While the Two-Thirds Rule might ensure that the eventual nominee had wide support within the party, it was also a recipe for obstruction, making it possible for a determined minority to block rivals even if they could not nominate their own champion. It had, for example, taken 46 ballots in 1912 and 44 in 1920 to select a candidate, and there were distant memories of 1860 when the convention had to adjourn after 57 fruitless ballots without a party standard-bearer, and the rival factions each subsequently nominated its own man. After 17 days of disastrous and futile politicking and no less than 103 ballots, in New York City's convention, the party compromised on John W. Davis, a conservative corporation lawyer closely allied with the Morgan interests. Dismayed by the conservatism of both Coolidge and Davis, the aging Robert M. La Follette, backed by the Farm Bloc, the Socialist party, the American Federation of Labor, and numbers of intellectuals, entered the race as the candidate of a new Progressive party. The Progressives adopted a neopopulist platform calling for the nationalization of railroads, the direct election of the President, the protection of labor's right to bargain collectively, and other reforms. La Follette stressed the perennial monopoly issue; his chief objective, he said, was to remove "the combined power of private monopoly over the political and economic life of the American people."

The situation was almost exactly the opposite of 1912, when one conservative had run against two liberals yet been swamped. Coolidge received 15.7 million votes, Davis 8.4 million, La Follette only 4.8 million. In the Electoral College, La Follette won only his native Wisconsin, Coolidge defeating Davis by 382 to 136. In all its alarms and crises conservatism was clearly the dominant mood of the entire country, not merely of the business classes. Beyond this many factors explain the Democrats' confusion at their Madison Square Garden convention in 1924. Although Al Smith four years later secured the nomination, that outcome neither gave him victory against Hoover, nor reconciled the irreconcilables: religion, Prohibition, the Klan, sectional animosities, the urban-rural divide. Their problems would a decade later be solved by the cripple who managed in 1924 to get to the rostrum to nominate Al Smith as the "Happy Warrior": Franklin Delano Roosevelt.

In 1927 Coolidge announced that he would not run for president again, and in March 1929 he returned to Northampton. There he busied himself with writing his autobiography and a daily newspaper column entitled "Thinking things over with Calvin Coolidge."

Throughout his tenure, Coolidge remained a remarkably popular president. But the Great Depression brought his policies into disrepute, and most historians now regard him as having been overcomplacent and inactive, lacking in vision, and ill-equipped to deal with the country's emerging problems. In the conservative 1980s he became a hero in some quarters, but scholarly revisionism has been limited largely to more positive assessments of his rhetorical, political, and public relations skills.

The primacy of business is the most likely reason for Davis's selection as Democratic candidate in 1924, not a distaste for Smith's Catholicism. It was not until JFK's victory in 1960 that religion ceased to be a factor, and it is easier now to judge Smith's failure, first for the nomination, and then in 1928 as candidate, than it used to be. Richard Hofstadter's verdict is still relevant, and accurate:

> The prime fallacy in the popular view of the 1928 election lies in noticing only what Smith lost from the religious issue and ignoring what he may have gained. Of course the number of voters who were decisively influenced by the religious issue is something that eludes exact measurement. But it is vital to remember that there are two such imponderables to be considered: not only the number of voters who voted against Smith but also the number who voted for him because of his religion. Smith's Catholicism, a grave liability in some areas, was a great asset in others. He made about as good a showing as could have been expected from any Democrat that year.[10]

[10] Richard Hofstadter, "Could a Protestant have beaten Hoover in 1928?" *The Reporter*, 22 (Mar. 1960), p. 30. Cf. Paul A. Carter, *The Twenties in America* (New York, Thomas Y. Crowell, 1968), and John D. Hicks, *Republican Ascendency 1921–1933* (New York, Harper, 1960).

Moreover, rural sentiment and mores clashed with the realities of urban life. Controversies arose over public support of prohibition laws and the acceptance of teaching evolution in public schools. This clash of values, however, was not necessarily responsible for Al Smith's nomination failure in 1924, than his election defeat in 1928. Moreover, to stereotype persons of rural or urban backgrounds as having rural or urban values often proves misleading.

The famed Kansas editor, William Allen White, in a letter to Supreme Court Justice Louis D. Brandeis, expressed a similar opinion two months after the 1928 election:

> The people were not in a rebellious mood this year, but I think thousands of western progressives balked at Smith, first because he was going too fast and second because he zigzagged on the wrong side of traffic on prohibition; and third because he represented a strange, unfamiliar, and to many narrow minds, an abhorrent tendency in our national life. Partly it was religion that symbolized the distrust. But I think it was chiefly an instinctive feeling for the old rural order and old rural ways, the tremendous impact of a desire for the good opinion of the old lady next door. I think inevitably in this century we shall see another moral censor than she, new moral standards. But still the old order holds fast in spite of our urban and industrial development.[11]

5 HERBERT HOOVER

Herbert Clark Hoover (1874–1964), 31st President of the US, was born at West Branch, Iowa, and graduated from Stanford University in 1895. Until 1914 he engaged in a worldwide mining and engineering career, earning a fortune which enabled him thereafter to devote himself to public service. A Quaker, as chairman of the US Commission for Relief in Belgium (1915–19), he won wide recognition for his humanitarian efforts, and Wilson appointed him to the critical post of US Food Administrator during World War I. His administrative skill in insuring the feeding of America's near-bankrupt allies, as well as themselves, was credited as a major contribution to winning the war.

As secretary of commerce under Harding and Coolidge (1921–8), Hoover persuaded large firms to adopt simplification and standardization of production goods and a system of planned economy.

[11] *Selected Letters of William Allen White*, 1899–1943, ed. Walter Johnson (New York, Henry Holt, 1947), p. 290. Cf. Walter Lippmann, *Men of Destiny* (New York, Macmillan, 1927), p. 8.

Esteemed as a moderate liberal, in 1928 he received the Republican nomination for President. His easy defeat of his Democratic rival, Alfred E. Smith of New York, by an electoral vote of 447 to 87, is largely attributed to the fact that the election year had been unusually prosperous. Smith was, however, the first Irish Catholic and lifetime New York East Sider to be the choice of a major party. He was a Tammany man with a strong record for securing progressive welfare laws, and a "wet" during the days of Prohibition; in the 1928 election he got no support in the South or the West.

Few informed persons in the spring of 1929 chose to read the signs pointing to the massive stock market crash of October, and Hoover's announcement that "in no nation are the fruits of accomplishment more secure" reflected a judgment shared by most of the nation. As the country drifted into the Great Depression, the government adopted measures that proved inadequate to stop the increasing number of commercial and farm failures, the rising number of the unemployed (12 million or more by 1932), and a sharp decline in foreign trade.

As a matter of fact Hoover, more than any other depression President in American history, had taken steps to try to bring recovery. But he had functioned largely through giving aid at the top to prevent the further collapse of banks and industries, and the concentric rings of further collapses and unemployment which would then ensue. Also he had continued to pin his faith upon voluntary action. He felt that too great federal intervention would undermine the self-reliance, destroy the "rugged individualism" of the American people, and that it would create federal centralization, thus paving the way for socialism. It was not until June 1932 that he approved a measure permitting the Reconstruction Finance Corporation to loan $300,000,000 for relief purposes.

The President's exhortations had little effect, and business retrenchment became common. In October 1930, Hoover established a nonpartisan Committee for Unemployment Relief. Through this committee he sought to stimulate and coordinate private relief for the unemployed, but again he confined himself to exhortation and cajolery, for he was opposed to any direct attempts by the federal government to turn the economic tide.

In 1930 the growing unemployment problem was aggravated by a severe drought in the lower Mississippi valley. In many mining communities of West Virginia, near-starvation conditions prevailed, but Hoover remained unalterably opposed to any kind of federal dole. He urged the states to solve their own problems, but was willing to lend federal money to private enterprise or to the Red Cross to handle the relief problem.

The Congressional elections of 1930 made it clear that the failure of the Hoover administration to take decisive action had lost it the support and confidence of the people. The Senate was now composed of 47 Republicans, 46 Democrats, and one Farmer-Laborite, and some of the Republicans were no supporters of Hoover's policies. The Democrats gained control of the House of Representatives when 219 Democrats, 214 Republicans, and one Farmer-Laborite were elected. Although a round robin to the President signed by former Democratic Presidential candidates (including Alfred E. Smith, James M. Cox, and John W. Davis) offered the support of the Democratic party to the President, the attempt to call off politics in the face of the depression failed. The Democrats were naturally aware of the opportunity to return to power which would be theirs in 1932, and they gave little real cooperation to the President.

It finally became overwhelmingly clear that if the President did not take positive steps, the economic structure of the nation might collapse. The states lacked adequate resources to solve the unemployment problem, and the administration, however unwillingly, was forced to act. The measures it adopted were to determine the pattern of much of Franklin Roosevelt's New Deal legislation. These measures represented a startling departure from precedent; in all the nation's depressions, major and minor, the government had done virtually nothing but wait for business to recover by itself.

The administration first attempted to bring relief by creating jobs on government work projects. In his annual message to Congress of December 8, 1931, Hoover urged that all governmental agencies engaged in construction work be consolidated into one "Public Works Administration directed by a public works administrator." The President advocated self-liquidating public works projects as sound business investments: the Democrats favored direct federal aid to individual states. His recommendation was ignored, but Hoover continued to urge the building of post offices and other federal structures in order to create jobs and aid business.

Hoover viewed the large intergovernmental debts as an important obstacle to the international trade which he believed essential to the prosperity of farmers and manufacturers. European nations were unable to buy American goods so long as their credit was impaired, and most of them eagerly accepted the one-year moratorium on intergovernmental debts on the principal and interest of their obligations.

Lacking direct federal aid, local and state agencies taxed and borrowed to the limit; but the unemployment relief they were able to provide was inadequate, and finally, toward the end of the Hoover administration, the federal government began making loans directly to the states. The Reconstruction Finance Corporation, which handled these loans, also made federal money available to banks, railroads, agricultural credit agencies, and life insurance companies. Hoover still clung to the fiction that the government was not in the business of unemployment relief, but the government could not reasonably expect repayment of the money it was "lending" to states and counties, and the aid which it alone could give was vital to prevent starvation among the unemployed.

In the last year of Hoover's administration, federal receipts totalled about 2,000 million dollars, and expenditures were over 5,000 million dollars. As revenues decreased and expenditures increased, it became clear that the government was committed to a policy of deficit financing. In the attempt to raise more money for relief measures, appropriations for the army and navy were drastically cut. As a further money-raising measure, Hoover advocated the enactment of a federal sales tax; but the Democratic support necessary to pass such legislation was not forthcoming, a federal sales tax being considered too hazardous politically.

Few Presidents have ever faced more melancholy prospects for re-election, and Hoover's defeat at the polls in 1932 by F. D. Roosevelt, who received more than 57 percent of the popular vote (electoral vote 472 to 59), was a mandate for change. The final months of Hoover's term were tragic. During that interim period a "lame duck" session of Congress was virtually controlled by the Democrats, and President-elect Roosevelt refused to jeopardize his New Deal program by joint action with the defeated President. The fact is however, that Hoover had anticipated certain New Deal measures, and his Reconstruction Finance Corporation even became a major anti-depression engine for Roosevelt.

Hoover returned to public affairs when he headed the Hoover Commission (1947–9, 1953–5), which was empowered by Congress to advise on reorganizing the executive branch of the government. A man of intelligence, integrity, and humanitarian principles, with administrative skill of the highest order, as President he envisioned an "American system," as he termed it, in which *laissez-faire* methods could be balanced by economic planning. He had a long wait for recognition of his economic statecraft.

6 PROHIBITION

Despite Coolidge's squeaky-clean image, the Coolidge-Hoover era was sleazy too: it was the Prohibition and boot leg decade. The Volstead Act (National Prohibition Enforcement Act, 1919) was designed to enforce the Eighteenth Amendment to the US Constitution, by defining as intoxicating liquor any beverage containing more than one-half of 1 percent of alcohol. It was female in its inspiration, the legacy of the puritanical Anti-Saloon League founded in 1893; the enemy was the demon drink, seen especially as a menace when the armed services returned from Europe, and felt that they had much to celebrate. By the time the Volstead Act became federal law, most of the states had been "dry" for years. By 1914 14 states had adopted prohibition; by 1919, the number had risen to 26. Even many temperance advocates had opposed the extension of federal power necessarily involved in national prohibition, but with the outbreak of World War I, the Anti-Saloon League was able to win passage of various federal prohibitory laws as part of the war effort, either to protect the morals of servicemen or to conserve grain for nutritional purposes. Thus, the principal effect of the Volstead Act was to extend the wartime measures to peacetime. The federal government took its task seriously, made annual appropriations of more than 10 million dollars to circumvent rum-running, and in the decade 1920–30 made over 500,000 arrests and secured some 300,000 court convictions.

But drinking continued. Speakeasies replaced the corner saloon, home-brewing and bootlegging became established practices, and night clubs made illegal liquor operations fashionable. Large urban populations, especially among middle-class citizens who could afford high liquor prices, sabotaged the laws to an extent not matched since the North had nullified the fugitive slave laws nearly a century earlier. Calls for repeal of the Eighteenth Amendment began as early as 1923. Political parties could not avoid the troublesome issue. By 1928 the "wets" were in control of the Democratic party; its presidential candidate, Alfred E. Smith, lost the election to Herbert Hoover, who genuinely tried to encourage "an experiment noble in motive and far-reaching in purpose." But after the Wickersham Commission set up by Hoover reported in 1931 that in effect prohibition laws were unenforceable, the country was in a mood to repeal an Amendment that tended to breed disrespect for law in general.

If one man was notorious in this era it was the legendary gangster "Scarface" Al (Alphonse) Capone. He was more than notorious,

Plate 4 "Beware of Tangling Alliances": cartoon by Nelson Harding showing the President juggling affairs of state while rendered helpless by having to enforce Prohibition.
(Library of Congress.)

but publicity-addicted and even in his way a tourist attraction. He was big, handsome, and expensively attired. He was born in Brooklyn in 1899 and loathed being called Italian. His Neapolitan parents were dirt poor – he was their fourth son in a family of nine. His schooling was reasonable enough, although, at fourteen an ungovernable temper caused him to fell a teacher, receive a caning, and stalk out. His remaining education was on the streets among the kid gangs of the neighbourhood: these were of varied nationalities – Irish and Jews the fiercest – and Al, growing to hefty size, was never troubled by a ghetto complex. At sixteen he was recruited by Frank Loele (now Yale) into the Five Pointers, his first adult gang.

From bartender in a seedy Coney Island dive he graduated to bouncer – combining "the mass to bounce authoritatively and the intelligence to do it with tact." He was a fearsome fighter, receiving his scarred face at eighteen when his temper exploded against a man with a knife. At nineteen he married the Irish Mae Coughlin a few weeks after the birth of their only son; it was his greatest good fortune, for she was loyal to the end, though, in her own words, he broke her heart.

Rising fast in this sleazy hierarchy, Capone again boiled over, giving such a brutal beating to a rival gang member that he was marked out for revenge. So Yale put through a call to Johnny Torrio, head of a big Chicago gang, who had his eye on the promising twenty-year-old, and Capone and family were spirited from New York to the capital of the underworld. Torrio was cool and systematic; he became Capone's mentor, laying the foundations for spectacular success.

The lunacy of Prohibition and the corruption of officials and police gave Capone all he needed. He rose and rose; he expanded bootlegging and prostitution to the Chicago suburbs, and dealt ruthlessly with rival gangs who got in the way. Murders were commonplace and juries lethally threatened. Torrio gradually combined the many large and small gangs under his experienced hand, for the greater good of all; on his eventual retirement, after a near-fatal shooting in 1325, Capone became king, frequently challenged, but always surviving intact. In 1927 he earned 100 billion dollars.

Capone reserved his greatest contempt for politicians, mayors, aldermen and police of all ranks, for their corruption and hypocrisy, and the ease with which he bought them. And they seem, indeed, infinitely more contemptible than the honestly wicked gangland boys. He was sent down for eleven years by tough judge Wilkerson for tax evasion. He served two in a notoriously hard Atlanta jail (eight to a cell) and then became one of the first convicts in the newly-opened dreaded Alcatraz. By now he had tertiary syphilis, caught from one of his own prostitutes; his life was a hell of advancing disease and the hatred of fellow prisoners for his refusal to join rebellions. He was determined to win remission for good conduct, and he did, being freed to his family and a Baltimore hospital in 1939.

His last years at his Florida home, cradled by the faithful Mae, were quiet and pitiable. He was spared final madness and died from cardiac arrest on January 25, 1947, still only 48.[12]

[12] Robert J. Schoenberg, *Mr Capone* (New York, Robson, 1993); Andrew Sinclair, *Prohibition: the era of excess 1933* (London, Faber, 1962); Laurence Bergreen, *Capone, The Man, The Era* (London, Macmillan, 1994).

In 1932, the Democrats came out for repeal of Prohibition. Their overwhelming electoral victory encouraged Congress to pass the Twenty-First Amendment, repealing the Eighteenth, on February 20, 1933. On March 22 the Volstead Act was amended to permit the sale of 3.2 percent beer and wine. Once the Twenty-First Amendment was ratified the following December, the Volstead Act became void.

By the passing of the Twenty-First Amendment, much of it at FDR's urging, the Eighteenth Amendment was repealed. Thereafter the issue was decided by state or local option.

9

FDR and the New Deal

1 ROOSEVELT THE MAN

Franklin Delano Roosevelt (1882–1945), 32nd President of the United States, was born in Hyde Park, New York, the only child in an affluent patrician family, Roosevelt was educated at such citadels of the Northeastern establishment as Groton School, Harvard College, class of '04, and Columbia Law School. But law practice bored him, and he early embraced a career in politics. Two influences shaped his public career: his distant kinsman Theodore Roosevelt, whose niece Eleanor he married in 1905, and Woodrow Wilson, whom he served as assistant secretary of the navy during World War I.

When he was President, Roosevelt confessed to Louis Howe that he was a "juggler," a man who would "mislead or tell untruths" in his own self-interest. This becomes especially apparent in Roosevelt's relationship with Secretary of the Navy Josephus Daniels. Roosevelt was Daniels's assistant secretary in World War I, a role he hated: "The simple fact was he thought no man should be his chief, that things were in their proper order only when he was at the head of the list." Roosevelt tried to distance himself from his "quaint and unpolished" superior, so he was cordial to Daniels's face, but contemptuous behind his back. Finally, Franklin K. Lane, secretary of the Interior, rebuked FDR; "You should be ashamed of yourself. Mr Daniels is your superior and you should show him loyalty or you should resign your office." Roosevelt did not resign, but he tried to restrain himself and even learned to admire the way Daniels protected his power against the admiral's attempts to usurp his authority.

In 1920 Roosevelt was the Democratic candidate for Vice-President in a Republican year. Struck down by poliomyelitis in 1921, he never recovered the use of his legs, though with braces and cane, buoyant determination, and the cooperation of the press, he managed in subsequent years to convey the illusion of mobility. Encouraged by his wife, he returned to politics, and in 1928 was elected governor of New York.

On March 8, 1933, retired Supreme Court justice Oliver Wendell Holmes celebrated his ninety-second birthday. Late that afternoon, President Franklin Delano Roosevelt paid a visit to the grand old man. For Roosevelt, Holmes was the living embodiment of American history: from his grandmother, Holmes had heard stories of the British occupation of Boston during the Revolution; Holmes himself had known Ralph Waldo Emerson; he had been wounded three times in battle during the Civil War; and he had been named to the Supreme Court in 1902 by Franklin's cousin, Theodore Roosevelt. Over tea, the President and the justice discussed boxing and American history. After Roosevelt left, Holmes rendered his verdict on the new President. "A second-class intellect," he said, "but a first-class temperament!"

Roosevelt's legendary "million-vote smile" often concealed a private uneasiness that he felt with men and women who were not of his class. In the case of Irish Catholics, for example, he could not refrain from a kind of "jaunty patronization" in public: more than once he began his speeches with "Fellow Dimmycrats," speaking in a mock-Irish brogue. FDR's attempts to make people forget his privileged background were not always successful. He liked to call everyone he met by his or her first name, and during his presidency he made a particular point of addressing European royalty by their given names – George and Elizabeth of England, Martha of Norway, Juliana of the Netherlands. Yet, while FDR was affecting a certain universal, democratic chumminess, he was to them all – kings, queens, senators, secretaries, servants – 'Mr President.'

The New Deal, though sometimes contradictory in detail and uneven in impact, restored national morale and remolded the landscape of American life. In particular, it established the responsibility of government to maintain a high level of economic activity, to provide for the unemployed and the elderly, to guarantee workers unions of their own choosing, to prohibit anti-social business practices, to protect natural resources, and to develop the Tennessee valley and other undeveloped regions.

Though some, especially in the business community, hated "that man in the White House" as a "traitor to his class", the voters returned him to office by a landslide in 1936. But ill-advised effort in 1937 to overcome judicial vetoes of New Deal legislation by enlarging the Supreme Court broke his political stride, and the forward thrust of the New Deal had come to an end by 1938.

2 TAKING POWER

In 1932, at the bottom of the Great Depression, Roosevelt defeated Herbert Hoover in the Presidential election. A quarter of the labor force was out of work, the economy in collapse, and the nation in despair.

Both President Hoover and Governor Roosevelt had carried out extensive programs of speech-making during the campaign. The President defended his party's protective tariff, farm relief, and economic recovery policies, and denounced the proposals of the opposition as demagogic appeals. Roosevelt stressed the "new deal" for the "forgotten man" without clearly indicating the specific measures of his program. He accused the Republicans of seeking prosperity by conferring favors on the "special interests" and stressed the government's responsibility to promote the well-being of the great masses of its citizen. His party's platform was unusually brief and specific, committing the party to repeal of the Eighteenth Amendment (the Prohibition Amendment) and "continuous responsibility of government for human welfare."

FDR's campaign was masterly. The keynote was his acceptance speech, in which he denounced "the economic royalists." In his last speech, at Madison Square Gardens, he declared roundly; "I should like to have it said of my first administration that in it the forces of selfishness and lust for power have met their match. And I should like to have it said of my second administration that in it these forces have met their master." The applauding roars were deafening. His campaign song was "Happy Days are Here Again." He radiated confidence. "I pledge you, I pledge myself to a New Deal for the American people." The only thing we have to fear," he said in his Inaugural, "is fear itself." The result at the polls was an unprecedented majority for the Democrats. President Hoover carried only six states with 59 electoral votes.

Between Roosevelt's election and his inauguration, economic conditions steadily worsened. Roosevelt was inaugurated on March 4. (The Twentieth Amendment, which provided for the inauguration of succeeding Presidents on January 20, did not go into effect until the following October.) When he took power he had no coherent program. Confronted by an emergency to which no one knew the answer, Roosevelt saw the national government as the instrument of the general welfare and experiment – the method of democracy.

The "New Deal" was a phrase hit upon by a speech-writer, a merger of Theodore Roosevelt's "Square Deal" and Woodrow Wilson's "New Freedom." FDR had no coherent view of economics or foreign affairs – except repeal of Prohibition and the federal operation of the Muscle Shoals project, from which came the Tennessee Valley Authority. The sharpest of all his speeches in the campaign was that made to the Commonwealth Club of San Francisco, in which he stressed that the purpose of his crusade was to adapt existing economic organizations to the service of the people, and that the safety of an individual's personal savings was inseparable from the rights of property. The New Deal would be an attempt to make capitalism work. When asked what he believed in, the President-elect said: "I am a Democrat and a Christian." He was not the author of a welfare state, but a supreme improvisor. When he met J. M. Keynes, he did not understand him, and Keynes thought him an economic illiterate. There was no coherence, nothing but programatic ambiguity. As Rex Tugwell, the professor of economics at Columbia who became one of the President's "Brain Trust" put it years later, "The New Deal does not deserve the reputation it has gradually gained. Roosevelt does."

Moreover, in view of the interregnum that then held between the election (November 4, 1932) and the taking of office (March 4, 1933), FDR worsened matters by his indecision. Hoover was convinced that America's recovery was closely dependent on the rest of the world. He supported the plan for a World Economic Conference, which met after he left office, and which Roosevelt refused to attend and – in the end – sabotaged. Hoover also took the initiative in securing a one-year moratorium on intergovernmental debts.

Indeed, despite the Hoover administration's pride in rugged individualism, it made heroic efforts to stay the collapse. It is too little remembered that a year after the stock market crash of 1929, the American people returned a House of Representatives and a Senate that were still Republican in allegiance. Hoover urged on businessmen and on state governments increases in construction. Four months before the crash, the Agricultural Marketing Act authorized the Federal Farm Board to create a Grain Stabilization Corporation and a Cotton Stabilization Corporation; they went out into the market and bought up commodities in an artificial effort to maintain prices, and they spent half-a-billion dollars in doing so.

In January 1932 the Reconstruction Finance Corporation (RFC) was set up, with a capital of 500 million dollars, later increased almost to two billion dollars, with authority to loan money to banks, insurance and building companies, public and private agencies. It saved many a tottering company and bank from collapse.

On similar lines, the resources of the Federal Land Banks were increased to give help to farmers, and the Home Loan Act of 1932 was authorized to create not less than eight nor more than twelve Home Loan Banks to extend emergency credit to home owners. A case indeed can be made that it was Hoover, not Roosevelt, who was the originator of the New Deal. Certainly the Reconstruction Finance Corporation, the Home Owners Loan Corporation and the Federal Emergency Relief Administration extended what Hoover in his hesitant way had begun. FDR had no doubts – before his election. He criticized Hoover not for his inactivity but for his recklessness: "the most reckless and extravagant past that I have been able to discover in the statistical record of any peacetime government, anywhere, any time." Asked what he would do, he said that he would slash government expenditure and balance the budget.

The central explanation for the financial collapse was the weakness of the American banking system, which was not a new phenomenon: 6,987 banks had failed in the decade of the 1920s; there were 2,294 failures in 1931 and 1,456 in 1932. Of all of FDR's early measures, the most important was the nationwide bank moratorium of March 6 and the Emergency Banking Act of March 9, by which the banks which were members of the Federal Reserve System might open under license. Savings bank deposits up to 5,000 dollars were insured. None of this involved economic theory. What it called for and called forth was confidence. The powers of the Federal Deposit Insurance Corporation were extended in 1935, and the Securities Exchange Commission was set up in 1936 to regulate securities exchanges. FDR could easily have asked for the nationalization of the banks, and Congress would almost certainly have supported him. But he was a conservative, not a radical – at least in 1933. Raymond Moley of Columbia, who had – inaccurately – expected to be FDR's right-hand man, said later that capitalism was saved by FDR in a period of eight days.

By 1935, hearing the thunder on the left (from Huey Long in Louisiana and from Upton Sinclair and Francis Townshend in California), Roosevelt moved to absorb it in what was a second New Deal.

No one, of course, can minimize the New Deal achievement, and least of all FDR's contribution to it – by his confidence, by his magnetic voice and "fireside chats," by his political acumen and his readiness to experiment. He had such popular support that he could push through in his first 100 days a mass of legislation, some of it contradictory, much of it unplanned: a slashing of government costs, legalization of 3.2 percent beer, the setting up of the Civilian Conservation Corps and the Tennessee Valley Authority, and considerable emergency banking measures, much of it drafted by Hoover's Treasury officials.

3 THE HUNDRED DAYS

In March 1933, the initiative clearly lay with the man in the White House and his team. And his team included an impressive if unorthodox cabinet. As secretary of the Treasury, the President chose William Wooden, a Republican until 1928, a firm conservative but Roosevelt admirer who took ill in 1934 and was then replaced by Henry Morgenthau, a neighbor and a close friend of the President, and a firm New Dealer. Cordell Hull, the veteran Congressman from Tennessee and ardent low tariff advocate, went to the Department of State. The Department of the Interior was first offered to Hiram Johnson of California, and when he refused it went to Harold Ickes, the contentious and aggressive Bull Mooser who became and stayed a friend of Roosevelt through the years. Frances Perkins, the first woman to hold a Cabinet office, was secretary of Labor, and Henry Wallace, whose father had held the same post in both the Harding and Coolidge administrations, was secretary of agriculture. In the background and on the sidelines stood the Brain Trust which included, in the early days, financier Bernard Baruch, the labor leaders Sidney Hillman and William Green, Rex Tugwell, Judge Sammy Rosenman (Sammy the Rose), Adolf Berle and, not least, Raymond Moley from Columbia University.

Congress, called into special session on March 9, 1933, proceeded to enact a series of measures which President Roosevelt deemed essential. It was a remarkable period – the "Hundred Days" of cooperation between the legislative and executive branches of the government.

The emphasis in the Hundred Days legislation was primarily on relief and recovery and only to a lesser degree on reform. Some of these relief measures began where the Hoover administration had left off, but they were different, not only in size, but in spirit and character. Hoover, as we have seen, believed that the federal government should give relief only after private agencies and local governments proved inadequate; he was therefore slow to react to the needs of the unemployed during the depression. The Roosevelt administration was not so conservative; after the crisis had deepened so seriously by the spring of 1933, it abandoned its campaign promises of government economy and a balanced budget, and engaged in a program of deficit financing in order to provide federal relief. Roosevelt believed that relief was not the province of private charity, as Hoover believed, but rather a matter of society's duty.

The first" New Deal had some major features. Runs on banks had forced most of them to suspend operations. Fearful that the banking system was on the verge of collapse, President Roosevelt declared a bank holiday (March 5–9, 1933) which closed all national banks and other banking institutions affiliated with them. Congress quickly passed the Emergency Banking Act, giving the President power to reorganize insolvent national banks. In April 1933, the United States went off the gold standard, while a month later the President was authorized to inflate the currency by adding $3,000,000 in new treasury notes, or by reducing the gold content of the dollar up to 50 percent. At the same time the government began purchasing gold at home and abroad at high prices, thus seeking to devalue the dollar still further. The financial measures did not succeed in raising prices, while security holders lost heavily. But foreign trade was stimulated by dollar devaluation, which lowered the price of American goods abroad. The Glass-Steagall Banking Act of 1933, designed to prevent future collapse of the private banking system, forbade banks to engage in the investment business, restricted the speculative use of bank credits, and expanded the Federal Reserve system to banks previously excluded. Its most popular provision created the Federal Deposit Insurance Corporation (FDIC) to insure all deposits up to $5,000. The "Truth in Securities" Act (1933) required that all securities offered for sale in interstate commerce be registered with the Federal Trade Commission, that each issue contain accurate information allowing the buyer to judge the soundness of the corporation, and that the directors be held criminally liable for any false information. By the Securities Exchange Act (1934) all stock exchanges were required to obtain licenses from the Securities and Exchange Commission (SEC), which was given broad powers to regulate their activities. The power of registering securities was also transferred from the Federal Trade Commission to the SEC.

In May 1933, the Federal Emergency Relief Administration (FERA) was created to assist the state in caring for the unemployed. It was authorized to match funds with state and local governments in distributing aid to the jobless. A dramatic recovery measure was the creation in March of the Civilian Conservation Corps (CCC), providing work for unemployed young men. They were used in national parks and forests and in reclamation projects in wilderness areas throughout the nation.

The New Deal also attempted to encourage private enterprise. The Reconstruction Finance Corporation (RFC), originally set up by the Hoover administration, was given new powers in 1934, when it was authorized to grant loans to industries as well as to railroads and banks. In all, 11,000 million dollars was loaned before 1936, most of the money being returned shortly afterwards. Home building had shrunk to a negligible point by 1933, while many home owners were unable to keep up their mortgage payments. To remedy this situation three measures were passed: the Home Owners Loan Corporation (HOLC) (1933) was authorized to loan money to mortgage holders faced with the loss of their property, saving the homes of more than a million persons; the Federal Housing Administration (FHA) (1934) was empowered to insure mortgages issued by private concerns for construction purposes; and the United States Housing Authority (1937) assisted local governments in slum-clearance projects and the building of low-cost housing.

To stimulate industry, the National Industrial Recovery Act was passed, which set up the National Recovery Administration (NRA), headed by the blustery General Hugh Johnson. Manufacturers were encouraged to draw up codes of fair business practices, to raise prices and to limit production by agreement. Workers were to be protected by minimum-wage and maximum-hour regulations, and were guaranteed the right to "organize and bargain collectively through representatives of their own choosing" – an immense stimulus to the labor and union movement. Hundreds of codes were drawn up – not all of them effective. This famous "Clause 7a" became the basis of the labor movement; to maintain the right of collective bargaining with employers, yet another agency, the National Labor Board, was set up, with Senator Wagner of New York as chairman.

This program was neither a happy nor a successful experiment. The codes were drawn too hastily; they often failed to consider the complexity and wide geographical distribution of American industry; they were usually drawn up by the major employers, who inserted clauses protecting monopolistic practices like price-fixing and quotas, practices which were made possible by Congress's express exemption of NRA agreements from anti-trust laws. Small producers

Plate 5a During the Depression shanty towns known as "Hoovervilles" sprang up around major cities. Housing projects like this one in Harlem,

Plate 5b here being officially accepted by Mayor La Guardia of New York, formed part of Roosevelt's New Deal. (Library of Congress.)

Plate 6 Under the New Deal, the Farm Security Administration commissioned a number of photographers to document the appalling agricultural conditions. Children as young as six years old were expected to help with cotton-picking, as Dorothea Lange's portrait shows.
(Library of Congress.)

were handicapped and wage increases for employees were offset by higher prices. Wage requirements gave efficient, mechanized concerns an advantage, and small concerns survived only by disregarding the Codes. The general was prompt to attack "chiselers" and "eye-gouging and ear-chewing in business." Whatever spirit of cooperation was bred under the symbol of the Blue Eagle was largely destroyed by his impetuosity and gruffness. He was persuaded to resign after a year in office: the Agency initials, said the disenchanted, stand for "No Recovery Allowed." In 1935 the whole experiment ended when the Supreme Court declared in the Schechter Case that it was unconstitutional. Congress applied code control to the bituminous coal industry and again the Supreme Court intervened (*Carter* vs. *Carter Coal Co.*).

The Codes, however, did achieve important results. The agreements ended the centuries-old problem of child labor in industry. They established a system of judicial regulation of wages and hours.

Within a year the United Mine Workers expanded from 150,000 members to 500,000, and 10,000 automobile workers and 10,000 steel workers joined unions.

The Roosevelt program of agricultural recovery rested on two foundations: to ease the debt burden of the farmer and to raise prices through crop control. A Farm Credit Administration was created to refinance farm mortgages at low rates, to advance money for current needs, and buy back foreclosed property. By 1936 the FCA had lent 3,700 million dollars. The Resettlement Administration established "subsistence homesteads" in many communities.

Under the Agricultural Adjustment Act (1933), farmers who agreed to restrict their output were compensated out of money raised from taxing processors of agricultural commodities, like flour millers or meat packers. Farmers were paid to sow grasses on untilled land to provide cover for top soil and prevent dust storms. Farmers ploughed under cotton and wheat acreage, killed millions of pigs, and destroyed part of the tobacco crop. The Agricultural Adjustment Administration (AAA) made contracts with cotton growers to withdraw about two-fifths of their acres from cultivation. Similar agreements were made with other producers. The program, says Richard Hofstadter, represented "organised scarcity in action." Farm crop prices rose rapidly, and thanks to higher prices and benefit payments, the farmers' cash income rose from $\$4\frac{1}{3}$ billion in 1927 to $7 billion in 1935. City dwellers complained of the rising cost of food, so the New Deal created the Federal Surplus Commodities Corporation (1933) which distributed surplus foods among welfare recipients. In 1936 the Supreme Court killed the AAA by its decision in *US* vs. *Butler*. Congress then passed the Soil Conservation Act by which the federal Treasury was to make benefit payments to cooperating farmers for retiring exhausted land, preventing erosion and rotating crops.

While Congress was enacting the various laws that constituted a recovery program, it was also considering long-range reforms – legislation to deal with serious problems only indirectly related to the economic depression. The Tennessee Valley Authority Act (TVA) of 1933 marked the triumph of Republican Senator George Norris of Nebraska, who had long sought to place the power resources of the Tennessee River at the disposal of the people. It created an independent public corporation to develop the economic and social well-being of an area embracing parts of seven states and including the power project at Muscle Shoals. Through construction of dams, power plants, and transmission lines, many farms and villages in the Tennessee valley were supplied with electric current at low rates. Important by-products of the Authority's work were the production of nitrogen fertilizers, plans for flood control, and the improvement of navigation on inland rivers. (TVA power aided atomic research at Oak Ridge after 1945). In all, these measures provided relief work for over four million people and spent over a billion dollars. New Dealers believed that where possible it was better to provide relief by works projects rather than by the laying out of a cash dole.

The New Deal program was remarkable in containing a provision for artists. Roosevelt himself developed the idea that unemployed artists should be put to work at something which they could do and like to do, and decided that there must be public places where paintings were wanted. This was part of the whole general idea behind the Public Works Administration (PWA) – that the program should be fitted into the particular talents, needs and desires of each individual.

However, all of these measures could be described as primarily designed for relief. The PWA was designed not only to provide relief but to promote recovery. Under it, $3 billion were appropriated for a program of public works, administered by Harold Ickes, the honest, blustering secretary of the interior – though the driving force here was left-inclined Harry Hopkins. By 1936 under its auspices, 1,497 water works, 883 sewage plants, 741 highway improvements, 263 hospitals, 166 bridges, and 70 municipal power plants had been built, and over 500 million dollars had been spent on school buildings. Artists were called in to decorate with murals all these schools, hospitals, and buildings; writers were commissioned to publicize the government's programs; and musicians were formed into touring orchestras to bring music into out-of-the-way places that had heard little before. One of the most impressive by-products of the New Deal was in fact its stimulus to writers, artists and sculptors by the commissions it gave them. The Federal Writers' Project produced over 1,000 publications, including 51 state guides.

The 150 volumes in the "Life in America" series ranged from the moving *These Are Our Lives* to *Baseball in Old Chicago* and embraced a notable series of ethnic studies, including *The Italians of New York*, *The Hopi*, *The Armenians of Massachusetts*, and *The Negro in Virginia*. The projects, under the guidance of state directors such as Vardis Fisher in Idaho, Ross Santee in Arizona, and Lyle Saxon in Louisiana, reflected the fascination of the 1930s with the rediscovery of regional lore, the delighted recapture of place names – Corncake Inlet, Money Island, Frying Pan Shoals – and the retelling of long-forgotten tales of Indian raids. The Project made use of the talents of established writers such as Conrad Aiken, who wrote the description of Deerfield for the Massachusetts state guide, and "new" men like John Cheever and Richard Wright, whose "Uncle Tom's Children" received the *Story* magazine prize for the best story by a FWP writer. Commercial publishers were happy to print most of the guides, and many of them sold exceptionally well. Congress in 1939 abolished the Federal Theater Project and allowed the other projects to continue only if they found local sponsors who would bear 25 percent of the cost. The Federal Writers' Project proved its popularity when, to the amazement of its critics, every one of the forty-eight states put up the required amount.[1]

By 1939 it could be claimed that Public Works projects had been instituted in all but three counties of the United States. Obviously this program was advantageous to those it helped and advantageous also to Roosevelt's reputation. But it also was characterized by remarkable freedom from graft and corruption. Despite the vast sums passing through innumerable hands, FDR could proudly boast that the New Deal had "no Teapot Dome."

Recovery, however, in the long run, mattered more than relief. The essence of the first New Deal – the heavy legislative program of the years from 1933 to 1935 – lay in four major areas: currency reform, a stimulus to the capitalist system, and basic reforms in agriculture and industry. Industry benefited from the NRA; farmers benefited from the AAA; labor got little perhaps other than Clause 7a of the NRA and the Wagner Act, and this had not been very successfully enforced on employers – but they gave him their support and their affection. The unemployed benefited in the form of cash doles or work relief. The Democratic party benefited most of all, since Roosevelt manufactured an unusual alliance of the big cities, the poor, the Deep South, the TVA, and blacks throughout the country. He gave them success and a cause, if not a creed. Some of his supporters backed him not because of his policies but because of the enemies he had made: from the beginning there were those behind the New Deal who were hostile to the trusts, to the monopolists, to the money-changers in the temple, to the economic royalists. But more than all this, FDR gave Washington DC, and the country, faith in itself. The city was transformed from a placid and leisurely Southern town into a breezy, sophisticated and metropolitan center. "Come at once to Washington," Senator La Follette, son

[1] William E. Leuchtenburg, *Franklin Roosevelt and the New Deal 1932–40* (New York, Harper and Row, 1963), p. 127.

of "Fighting Bob," telegraphed to Donald Richberg, the Progressive of twenty years before, "Great things are under way." Judge Harlan Stone of the Supreme Court noted that "Never was there such a change in the transfer of government." And Norman Davis, who had known the President when he was the debonair young undersecretary of the navy of 20 years before, met a mutual friend on the White House steps. He said to him: "That fellow in there is not the fellow we used to know. There's been a miracle here."

Roosevelt was a master conciliator, the arch political manipulator. If he had an objective it was a return to the lost world of the 1920s, before booms and slumps destroyed the prosperity that capitalism brought. For this purpose Roosevelt, the Brain Trusters, and the Democratic politicians in general wished to win and hold the support of a diverse coalition: of conservative Southern Democrats, of the labor groups on the left, of the big-city machine politicians, of the antimonopoly Western wing with its folk memories of Bryan and Populism. Each of these and other groups had to obtain something from the New Deal, and no single one could get everything it wished. The President had to walk a tightrope between them all, and use it also to bind them all to him and to his cause. Or, to use another analogy, he had to keep his ear close to the ground – even if sometimes grasshoppers jumped in.

4 IN PERSPECTIVE

But what did it all cost, and how successful were the two New Deals?

The cost was appallingly high. Direct relief cost 4 billion dollars by 1935, 16 billion by 1940. Hopkins boasted of spending 5 million dollars in his first two hours in office. He is said to have said; "We will spend and spend – and elect and elect." The WPA, however, claimed to provide at one time or another jobs for 3½ million people – about one in three of the unemployed – and to construct 660,000 miles of roads, 77,000 new bridges, 285 new airports, and an uncounted number of post offices. In doing all this, it created a bureaucracy, especially in the NRA, with 576 basic codes and 189 supplementary codes shaped – which was in 1935 held to be unconstitutional anyway.

It was appallingly wasteful, especially in agriculture. Farmers ploughed under countless acres of cotton and wheat, killed six million pigs and destroyed much tobacco at a time when city dwellers stood in food queues. By deliberately causing scarcity, however, prices rose and farmers' incomes with them.

The measures were a mass of economic contradictions. Some were inflationary, others deflationary. Salaries of government workers were cut by 25 percent in the first weeks of the New Deal; even veterans' payments were slashed. But the prompt devaluation of the currency and deficit financing were clearly inflationary. Where the farmers were concerned, it was an economy of scarcity; but for the TVA and the WPA it was an economy of abundance. The TVA was in fact a form of state socialism, involving social as well as economic planning, low-cost housing and public health services. For the banks, no nationalization; for the TVA it was the state as planner and director. In the NRA and the Agricultural Adjustment Act there were artificial restrictions on production and the acceptance of monopolies; at the same time, monopoly was curbed by the SEC. It was in all a system almost of national socialism. In his first two years FDR all but totally ignored the outside world and was indifferent to its problems. Part of the recovery was due to planning, part to enormous public spending and subsidies, part to a prodding of industry that came close to direction. If the blacks moved to support Roosevelt's policies, they got only modest recognition. In the vast majority of cases, the New Deal agencies deferred to local custom in granting jobs and determining living conditions. The TVA model towns were for whites. The NRA allowed blacks to be paid less than whites. Racial segregation was still customary, whatever Eleanor's urgings, and FDR rarely spoke out for blacks.

Nor, if the ending of unemployment was the goal, was it successful. Unemployment stood at 13 million early in 1933, and in 1938 stayed stubbornly at 10 million out of a total workforce of 50 million. Not until 1943 did it drop to 2 million – the effect not of the New Deal but of World War II. And the work in CCC camps and WPA projects was often menial, and demanded little skill. WPA became known as "We Piddle Around."

Neither did the New Deal prevent waves of strikes and "sit-ins." Despite the extension of social security, the labor movement split into two: the American Federation of Labor (AFL) and the CIO. There were spectacular strikes among car workers in 1937, but the struggle for union recognition was long, bitter, and often violent. Union membership grew from 3 million in 1933 to 8 million in 1939 and to 13½ million in 1943.

The instruments of central planning – the AAA, NRA – did not last; there was no nationalization, and little centralization. What did emerge were federal regulatory agencies. They did little to cope with the problems of the inner city or of the condition of the blacks; and they created power in Washington, which became a Mecca to the planner and the bureaucrat, while weakening initiative in the states and cities.

Nor did the coming of the Social Security Act of 1935 dramatically introduce any new regime. It was not strictly "welfare" as yet, since money for unemployment compensation and old age pensions came mainly from the private sector, ultimately from recipients. The government itself provided no money; it was still an insurance system, not a "dole." When old-age pensions began in 1940, only 20 percent of workers qualified. Benefits varied from 10 dollars to a maximum of 85 dollars a month, which was well below subsistence. There were no payments for health insurance or for disability. Until 1939 the government did not assist widowers or survivors. Provision was small and patchy. It was not yet a welfare state but a capitalist society, with the state constructing and operating railroads. It accepted some obligations, however, for the less fortunate. It was no longer a *laissez-faire* world.

Rex Tugwell, who had reason to be discontented, having been dropped, was critical of what had not been done. "Unless I am mistaken," he wrote later, "painful reorganizations are still to be gone through. The compulsion this time is not cold and hunger; it is a rising revolution of technology, which demands even more insistently the institutions of great management. Those institutions ought to have been perfected in 30 years of experience, instead of being smothered in the tangles of a system more accurately called a non-system."[2]

Never before in American history had either a party or a man won so overwhelming a victory as did Roosevelt and the Democratic party in the election of 1936. He won 60 percent of the popular vote and carried every state but Maine and Vermont – "As Maine goes, so goes Vermont" became a popular Democratic jibe. He had no less than 523 electoral votes against 8 for the Republican candidate, Alfred M. Landon of Kansas. The Democratic party won tbree-quarters of the seats in the Senate and four-fifths of those in the House. He carried with him to victory a host of other Democrats: the party won 39 of the state governorships, and three other states were won by Farmer-Labor party candidates of a New Deal type. Only six states returned Republican governors; and the combined vote of Socialist and Communists was less than 300,000. It seemed as though this was a triumph not only for a man and his party but for the Democratic system. His critics – and he was now

[2] Rexford Tugwell, *The Democratic Roosevelt* (New York, Doubleday, 1957), p. 302.

as hated as he was admired – pointed, however, to the scale of the national debt, which in 1936 had reached 34 billion dollars, to the steady interference with business enterprise, to the rise in the strength of labor organizations, particularly the CIO, and to the growing power of the man in the White House. Despite these criticisms, and despite the scale of the radical and rabble-rousing sentiments of Huey E. Long of Louisiana, of Dr Francis Townsend in California and of the Rev. Charles Coughlin, or perhaps because of them, Roosevelt and the Democrats had campaigned on their massive legislative record and treated their victory as a popular mandate. The way seemed clear for the announcement of a Third New Deal.

The Democratic platform of 1936 was outspoken and eloquent –

> We hold this truth to be self-evident that government in a modern civilisation has certain inescapable obligations to its citizens, among which are: 1. Protection of the family and the home; 2. The establishment of a democracy of opportunity for all people; 3. Aid to those overtaken by disaster.

To this now conventional New Dealism, Roosevelt added the famous remark expressing the new militancy of 1936: the promise to "rid our land of kidnappers, bandits and malefactors of great wealth." In his second Inaugural, delivered in January 1937, he called attention to "One-third of a nation ill-housed, ill-clad, ill-nourished" and made clear that the New Deal would continue. It was a statement of a broad and coordinated plan of social and economic reform.

The high hopes of 1936 were, however, to be disappointed. Very little legislation was passed in 1937 and the legislative achievement for 1937 were only partial and meagre. The attack on the malefactors of great wealth led to the establishment of a joint Congressional-Executive committee to gather evidence on monopolistic trends. It was rich in documentation but feeble in achievement. The extension of social security was postponed, and was indeed not enacted fully until the advent of President Truman's Fair Deal. And, not least, the attack on the Supreme Court brought a split between those who trusted and those who distrusted the President, and did great harm to the Democratic party and to Presidential-Congressional relations.

Nevertheless, some important economic reform measures were enacted in these years. In 1936 the Securities Exchange Commission was given new responsibilities under the Public Utility Holding Act, by which all utility companies were compelled to register with the

SEC and to give it full information on all their operations. The Commission was now to see that each company limited its activities to a single well-integrated system, unless control of the two or more of them was necessary to economical management and was confined to neighbouring geographical areas. But this "Death sentence law" against holding companies did of course add to the bitter antagonism towards the President and many utility corporations fought it with tooth and claw. Nevertheless, it was upheld by the Supreme Court in 1938 and was genuinely effective. In 1937 the Rural Electrification Administration (first set up in 1935) was given extended powers. It was not authorized to build its own power generating plants but to encourage the formation of cooperative groups of farmers who would buy electricity from existing sources. It soon found that many farming communities were hungry for electricity. By 1944 nearly 1,000 farmers' cooperatives for this purpose had been set up and electricity lines were winding into remote communities from Vermont to Oregon.

In 1925 only 4 percent of the country's farms had electricity. By 1940 it was 25 percent. In 1937 the United States Housing Administration was established. Federal aid was provided to local and state governments for the building of low-cost housing. If again the program was not as successful us the ardent New Dealers had hoped, by 1939 300 housing projects had been begun. Again in 1937 the Farm Security Administration was set up. Under it, long-term credit at low interest rates was extended to tenant farmers, so that they could purchase their own farms. A system of short-term loans was also provided, to help farmers pay off outstanding mortgages and also to meet emergency needs caused by drought, floods, dust storms, and insect plagues. But, as with the USHA, this program fell short of the expectations in Roosevelt's original program for enhancing the economic position of farm tenants. The second AAA was enacted in 1938 and replaced the Act of 1933 that the Court had declared unconstitutional. It provided that the secretary of agriculture could fix the acreage for basic crops each year and establish "marketing quotas" to restrict the sale of surpluses; that in bad years the AAA would grant farmers "parity payments" sufficient to offset the difference between the low price and the price their produce would have commanded before World War I; that farmers who adopted anti-erosion practices should be given conservation payments; and that the government would provide storage space and loans for surplus crops to assure an "ever normal granary." The measures failed to reduce the 1939 crop, while in subsequent years demands from war-torn Europe outbalanced supply.

And in 1938 the Fair Labor Standards Act was passed: Congress's answer to the recommended program for the regulation of hours and wages. (A similar bill had been defeated in June 1937, being the first major New Deal bill to be rejected by Congress.) National standards of a 44-hour maximum week and a 25-cent hourly minimum wage were established for industries engaged in interstate commerce. These standards were gradually raised until they became, in 1940, a 40-hour week and a 40-cent hourly wage. Over 300,000 workers received increased wages and/or shorter hours under this law in 1937. This was a major reform, but even so, it had been watered down from the original bill presented to Congress, and had only barely been passed.

The President now clearly had enemies. In a Jackson Day Dinner in 1936 he dwelt on the comparison with Jackson, and used the phrase that the people loved him "for the enemies he had made." He was ready now to identify his own enemies. Some of them had been his friends and allies. "The old Roosevelt magic has lost its kick," Hugh Johnson said, and with malice, in the spring of 1938. "The diverse elements of his Falstaffian army can no longer be kept together and led by a melodious whinny and a winning smile." There was nothing new to the hatred of him by the rich. And there was little new in the publicity that his family received, the attacks on his children, the charge in the *Saturday Evening Post* that his son James had exploited his family connections to obtain insurance business, all the spite, gossip, and amusement occasioned by Eleanor Roosevelt's daily columns in the press. People in America, as Mr Dooley once said, "build their triumphal arches out of brick so that they will always have something handy to throw at the hero when his moment of decline comes." Opinion polls in the spring of 1938, however, still showed that eight out of ten Americas liked FDR as a personality. They showed also that the blacks, the poor in general, the ranks of labor and the unemployed were for him enthusiastically. The Southwest as a section was 98 percent for him personally, But fewer than half of those polled expressed support for his economic goals, and more than half were either opposed to them or uninformed on them. Of five major economic groups – the blacks, the poor, the lower middle class, the upper middle class, and the prosperous – all but the first two showed majorities against his methods. Running through this opposition there was now a genuine streak of fear at his apparent bid for political power. Half of those polled thought that he had too much power, and as a consequence of dictatorship in Europe there was a great deal of talk of the danger of dictatorship at home. On Capitol Hill, this sentiment took the form of distaste for his controversial legislation, distaste for government by crises and talk of crises, and in particular distaste for the non-elected zealots who surrounded him, do-gooders, academics, and economic pundits, running a "Phi Beta Kappa Tammany Hall."

This mood affected his own party. There was clearly now an anti-New Deal group, including Vice-President Garner, and Senators like Josiah Bailey of North Carolina, Harry Byrd of Virginia, Millard Tydings of Maryland and Royal Copeland of New York. The violent battle over the Supreme Court as a result of its opposition to the New Deal programme had helped to split the party for the first time since the beginning of the New Deal. Senators Wheeler and Carter Glass, formerly leaders of the New Deal programme, went over to the opposition and subsequently felt free to vote against other legislative proposals made by or for Roosevelt. They were followed in this action by other New Deal supporters. The Court battle also lost Roosevelt the influential backing of several progressive Republicans, including Senators Norris, Johnson, and Borah, who had previously supported the domestic policies of the New Deal. The myth of Roosevelt's invincibility was shattered, and the remainder of his 1937 program was jeopardized.

To this difficulty there has to be added the impact of the recession of 1937. There had been a slow steady upswing of the business cycle from 1933 to 1937, but suddenly, in the late summer of 1937, a reversal set in which has been termed the Roosevelt Recession. In part it was due to Federal cutbacks in the spending program, especially in WPA budgets, in part by the government's apparent distrust of business. During this business decline, which lasted for twelve months, stocks dropped, the national income dwindled, unemployment rose, and industrial production fell off. The New Deal was caught unawares, and its leaders did not understand what the trouble could be, for there had been none of the stock market speculation, overproduction, or overexpansion of credit which had preceded the crash of 1929. The recession was a challenge to Roosevelt for a number of reasons. It seemed clear that the New Deal had not gone far enough. Despite the alphabet of agencies, the mass spending and the mass liberal and radical waves of protest, there were still over 7 million unemployed. The National Resources Committee, an executive fact-finding agency, revealed that 59 percent of all American families had annual cash incomes of less than $1,250, and 81 percent of less than $2,000. If the goods of the New Deal were not only prosperity but some measure of distributive justice – and many of its advocates made this claim –

it had failed to reach them. Progressivism was not enough, said Rex Tugwell, "It was in economics that our troubles lay." There was an obvious need, once again, for the President to spend his way out of adversity. But by 1938 not all his advisers were agreed on this. There were those such as Henry Morgenthau, Jr who wanted to balance the budget and made plain their demands for government economy. There were those such as Thurman Arnold campaigning for an attack on the economic royalists and the busting of the trusts. And there was the most influential of all, Harry Hopkins. There were rising stars too: products of Harvard Law School and protégés of Felix Frankfurter, in the eyes of Hearst's newspapers "The Iago of the Administration:" shy Ben Cohen from Muncie, Indiana; the bubbling Tommmy Corcoran, "Tommy the Cork," adept at Irish jokes and good with his accordion; William O. Douglas, the sandy-haired ex-professor, now chairman of the SEC, who was later to become a Supreme Court judge and live a long and much-married life; and Robert Jackson. To Hugh Johnson, they were "White House Janizeries." Among them all the President dickered. His friends pleaded for a reassertion of his moral leadership. "Mr President," wrote Henry Wallace, "you must furnish that firm and confident leadership which made you such a joy to the nation in March 1933." What finally moved the President was the steady drop in the stock market, especially in the spring of 1938 – a drop from the previous September that was the sharpest the country had ever known. In mid-April he moved and put forward to Congress a three billion dollar public works spending program; and he carried the same message to the nation in a long fireside chat. Two weeks later he launched a thorough study of the concentration of economic power in American industry, and the effect of that concentration on the decline of competition. Washington recognized the signs. By 1938 the phrase was: "Moley is in opposition; Tugwell is in the city planning business; Hugh Johnson is in a rage."

Paradoxically, the New New Deal suffered from the fact that the Democrats enjoyed an excessive majority in Congress. It is an axiom of American, or of any democratic, politics that when no substantial organized political opposition is ready to step in and take over from the party in power, the incentive for party unity in the latter is lacking. In 1937 the Republican party, like the Federalist party in 1816, had almost collapsed. The Republicans who had survived the New Deal landslide were, with some exceptions, undistinguished figures incapable of directing an effective political opposition. With no obvious need for unity in the diverse

Democratic coalition, many dissident Democrats, especially from the South, who hated Roosevelt more than they hated their Republican opponents, began to form a working coalition with Northern Republicans against the Roosevelt bloc. The group was often joined also by some middle-class liberals, who were tired of reform and even fearful of the consequences of what they had already done to further the New Deal program.

As the Congressional elections of 1938 drew near, it was clear that the President intended to seek to discipline his large but divided party. The Postmaster General, James Farley, "the man with the beckoning finger" who had "managed" the 1932 and 1936 campaigns advised him that the wisest course of discipline would be closer consultation between the White House and Capitol Hill, and a more skillful use of patronage. It was clear indeed that there was a wide gap between the White House and the Hill and increasingly less consultation between the two branches of the federal government. But Farley's advice was ignored. In Georgia, Maryland and New York the President openly supported candidates who were trying to unseat the sitting members. He wanted, he said, to get rid of those who deep in their hearts did not believe in New Deal "principles." In Kentucky he threw his influence on the side of Senator Barkley (later to be President Truman's Vice-President), who was fighting desperately against the energetic Governor ("Happy") Chandler. In state after state he sought to purge anti-New Deal Democrats from Congress by appealing directly to the people for their defeat. In this he was in fact imitating his one-time hero Woodrow Wilson, who had similarly intervened in the Congressional elections of 1918. He met, in fact, the same result. In the South, where the need for it was greatest, the purge met with a sorry defeat. Senators Walter George of Georgia, Millard Tydings of Maryland, "Cotton Ed" Smith of South Carolina, and others easily won re-election; thus even before the Republican victory in the 1938 Congressional elections, it was clear that the New Deal was in deep trouble.

It is true that there were still overwhelming Democratic majorities in both Houses after November 1938. The Republicans lost 24 of the 32 Senate seats in the contest. Blacks, Poles, Italians and the unions were now solidly Democratic. But there were nevertheless striking Republican gains; 8 in the Senate and 81 in the House, and 13 new governorships. In New York Governor Herbert Lehman, the brilliant vote-getter, only just managed to defeat the youthful Republican candidate Thomas E. Dewey. In Ohio the Republican John W. Bricker defeated the Democratic governor, and Robert Taft defeated a capable New Deal Senator, Ian Black. Democrats lost control of the state government of Pennsylvania. In Michigan Governor Murphy was punished for his alleged tolerance of sit-down strikes and in Connecticut Governor Cross was punished for his intolerance towards them. It was not only the Democratic party that was suffering; the candidates the President supported were defeated and the candidates he denounced as "Copperheads" were triumphantly nominated. There were indeed only two exceptions, in Kentucky where Senator Alban Barkley was renominated and in New York City where Representative John O'Connor was narrowly defeated. Although Democrats retained control of both Houses, their majorities in 1938 were so reduced that for the first time in five years the Republican party could operate as an effective minority.

There was a further reason for the decline in the President's reputation. It is true that the New Deal had conspicuously given some measure of recognition to the unions. But economic recovery and the growing union strength encouraged a division in the ranks of labor and produced a wave of public alarm at union power. Unskilled Workers, long excluded from the American Federation of Labor, found a leader in pugnacious John L. Lewis, the bitter and beetle-browed president of the United Mine Workers, who maintained that unions should be organized along industrial rather than craft lines. When the AFL refused to support him in his view, he formed the Committee for Industrial Organization, the CIO, to organize the steel and automobile industries. He won his first victory when the United Automobile workers, a CIO union, used a sit-down strike to force recognition from General Motors in November 1936.

In 1937, United States Steel, led by Scots-born Philip Murray, was similarly induced to accept the CIO as a bargaining agent for its own employees. Electrical workers and longshoremen, lumber workers and glass workers were organized, and the textile unions' leaders – Sidney Hillman and David Dubinsky – emerged as powerful political figures. By the fall of 1937 the CIO had 3,700,000 members against the AFL's 3,600,000, and in November 1938 the two organizations split. The President sought successfully to arbitrate between them. John L. Lewis for his part was highly critical of what he called the excessive loyalty of most union leaders to the President. In the CIO, Communist infiltration won some influence for members or for friends of the Communist party like Harry Bridges of the Longshoremen of the West Coast. The strength of the labor movement and the character of Lewis as its leader were proving to be a source not of strength but of weakness in the uneasy Democratic coalition.

In January 1939, Roosevelt, concerned about the threat of world war, called a halt to his domestic reform program. What he said then, concerning the world crisis of 1939, is remarkably applicable to the United States more than five decades later:

> We have now passed the period of internal conflict in the launching of our programme of social reform. Our full energies may now be released to invigorate the processes of recovery in order to preserve our reforms, and to give every man and woman who wants to work a real job at a living wage. ... But this is of paramount importance. The deadline of danger from within and from without is not within our control. The hour-glass may be in the hands of other nations. Our own hour-glass tells us that we are off on a race to make democracy work, so that we may be efficient in peace and therefore secure in national defence.

How then does one assess the New Deal as a whole? It is of course clear that Roosevelt was first and last a supreme politician and that his various experiments were based primarily on considerations of political opportunism. Richard Hofstadter has called him "The patrician as opportunist." It can certainly be argued that the New Deal had no consistent policy or far-seeing plans; that the President's major desire was to win the support of the majority by giving to each group in the country enough of what it wanted. He had no coherent plan to replace the capitalist system; his role was that of the genial arbiter, the deft political manipulator. If he had an objective, it was a return to the lost world of the 1920s, the restoration and revival of the capitalist system.

From this point of view it is clear that Roosevelt and the Brains Trusters and the Democratic politicians in general wished to win and keep the support of a coalition of voters capable of carrying an election. The Democratic party could not afford to move so far in any one direction, either to the left or right, as to alienate any of the many diverse groups that composed the party. The conservative Southern Democrats, the labor groups on the left, the big city machine politicians, the antimonopoly Western wing of the Bryan tradition – each of these and other groups had to obtain something from the New Deal, and no single one could get everything it wished.

In general, the New Deal followed the political philosophy, expressed by Vice-President Garner in 1938, that it was foolish to talk of dividing the nation into two opposing political camps, progressive and conservative, because any party in America which serves the nation must necessarily be a coalition of diverse interests. It was in large part the failure of the Republicans to take more diverse and progressive elements into their party during this period that caused them to lose elections. Given this philosophy, based largely upon the nature of the party system in America, the New Deal was neither left nor right, and Roosevelt may be said to have pursued a zig-zag course in accordance with the conditions of political wind and weather. In the 1932 campaign he criticized Hoover for extravagance. In 1938 he charged that he had failed to spend enough to fight the Depression. Consistency is a rare and non-political quality.

But if the theory of political opportunism is partially valid, this theory fails to recognize that actually there were consistent policies and a philosophy underlying the New Deal. One important aspect of the New Deal was its essential humanitarianism; in addition to being a superb political opportunist, Roosevelt was a twentieth-century humanitarian. He loved people, in the concrete and not in the abstract, and was deeply interested in their problems and needs, their psychological quirks, their liabilities and potential. No person, great or modest, escaped his interest and concern; like President Jackson, he considered himself a tribune of the people, one having a responsibility to all the groups in the community. His interest in "the forgotten man" was shown by the provisions in the WPA program for occupational groups such as artists and writers, not usually considered in such government programs, and by other programs to benefit minority groups such as tenant farmers, who exerted no direct political power, or the 12 million blacks in the US (though in this case political strategy may have played a part along with Roosevelt's undoubtedly sincere interest in the needs and desires of a relatively suppressed minority group), and the youth of the nation (though here again his genuine interest, which his wife shared, may have been joined with the realization that most young people eventually reached voting age). As Frances Perkins once stated, Roosevelt's central belief was that people mattered, and he hated those who would deny people their basic individual rights and a position of human dignity in society.

Roosevelt was a political realist who had come to see, as had many others in this period, that in the twentieth century, political stability rested upon economic security; political and social democracy, that is, was impossible as long as there were conditions of mass unemployment and widespread want in the midst of potential plenty. It is significant that in his famous Four Freedoms speech of January 1941, FDR added to the two negative "liberal" and Jeffersonian freedoms of worship and the press, which are rights against interference from the government, two new and positive freedoms – from want and fear – which concern the right of protection against economic insecurity and military aggression. He accepted here that there lay an obligation on government to secure both these positive freedoms; that government was no longer best which governs least. There was more to it than James Madison or Thomas Jefferson had foreseen. In a fireside chat of 1938, he stated that democracy had disappeared in many other nations of the world because the people had grown tired of hunger and insecurity while their governments did nothing, and that they had chosen to sacrifice liberty in return for something to eat. He believed that a government must accept the responsibility of providing economic security for its people if social and economic democracy was to be preserved. On a smaller scale, the Hoover Administration had begun gradually and reluctantly to move in the same direction, but the New Deal accepted government responsibility for general welfare cheerfully and vigorously, and executed it in full measure. By 1938 Roosevelt's thinking had taken a new direction. He was seeing his enemy clearly now and some would call him a traitor to his class in doing so. Private power, he said, was "stronger than the democratic state itself." In the United States "a concentration of private power without equal in history is growing" which is "seriously impairing the effectiveness of private enterprise." Indeed, that private enterprise "is ceasing to be free enterprise and is becoming a cluster of private collectivisms." And "Big business collectivism in industry compels an ultimate collectivism in government."

Given this recognition of government responsibilities and of its range, the New Deal sought to create an economic balance between the different major economic groups of the nation, so that by protecting and aiding them in a significant way, the natural operation of the economy would be restored. Business was aided by the NRA, and by the reciprocal-trade program, which stimulated world trade and increased America's share of the world market. The farmers got the AAA and FSA. Labor was given the NLRA and the Fair Labor Standards Act. The unemployed were given the work and relief projects, and with others, they shared in the benefits of the social security program. These programs of support were based not on political opportunities alone, but on the basic theory that by the subsidizing of each group, the whole economy would operate more efficiently.

Reacting in part to the rise in the twentieth century of Big Business and Big Labor, the US under the New Deal turned to Big Government, paralleling a similar development in other nations of the Western World. With this the economic center of the US shifted from New York to Washington DC as the federal government increasingly took over a major, perhaps the primary, role in the directing of American economic life. After a tour of the US in 1935 Sir Josiah Stamp wrote: "Just as in 1929 the whole country was Wall-Street conscious, now it is Washington conscious." The government became at once the partner of business, making loans through the RFC, and also the competitor of business, through the TVA. A myriad of new powers were taken on by government. It began to manage and manipulate the currency; it became the nation's largest banker, not only making business loans through RFC but also making loans for housing and slum clearance projects through HOLC and to farmers through FSA; it became the nation's largest insurance salesman, through its social security program and the insurance program for servicemen during World War II; it engaged in the manufacture and sale of electric power, fertilizers and other products, under the TVA; it stored agricultural surpluses; it subsidized American drama and fine arts under WPA; it enlarged the program for the conservation of natural resources begun under Theodore Roosevelt. Taxing, spending, lending, building, regulating – all became the functions of Big Government.

Economic collapse and the resulting insecurity acted as at least one major cause of the rise of Big Government. Another significant cause was World War II, under the pressures of which the government undertook price control, regulation and allocation of raw materials, and other controls over the whole economy. Thus the wartime needs accelerated the trend precipitated by conditions of economic insecurity. And there is truth in the thesis that the depression was destroyed not by the New Deal but by the preparation for war.

The practice of deficit financing, by which the government spent more than it took in in taxes, was a major part of the New Deal. In this, New Dealers operated on the theories of the British economist John Maynard Keynes, who held that during a depression the economy would be stimulated by the injection of mass purchasing power at the lowest level. Thus government money would be put into the hands of farmers and laborers, so that they could consume the surplus products of industry and agriculture.

The enormous increase in the public debt since just before World War I may be shown by the following list:

1916	1.2	billion	1933	22.5	billion
1920	23.5	"	1945	26.0	"
1929	17.0	"	1950	280.0	"

World War I caused an increase in the public debt from slightly over $1 billion to over $23 billion. This latter figure was reduced by over $6 billion through the economy measures of the 1920s, but in the depression years of Hoover's administration, the debt again increased, by over $5 billion. The eight years of the New Deal saw an increase of some $25 billion, although this increase resulted in large part from the expenses of the rearmanent and defense program of 1939–41. The years of World War II caused the astonishing increase of over $210 billion, and five years later, because of the cold war, the debt had risen by $20 billion more. Thus, however costly the New Deal might have seemed to contemporaries, the cost of World War II caused an increase in the public debt which was more than eight times that of the cost of the New Deal. It is war, rather than social progress, which is expensive. And, unlike war, the New Deal did not destroy life but maintained it and enhanced its opportunities.

The pronouncements of certain New Dealers and the relative speed with which the program was executed gave it the appearance of a revolution. In fact it was in essence conservative. Most New Deal acts had deep roots in American history – in the reform movements of the nineteenth century such as the populist movement, and in the progressive era of Theodore Roosevelt and Woodrow Wilson. It is the administrations of Harding, Coolidge and Hoover, not the New Deal that now appear as aberrations from the American economic stream. The New Deal did not attack capitalism, but saved it; by reforming capitalism it warded off socialism. From one point of view it can be seen as a failure. It was unable to secure full economic recovery for the nation. Unemployment remained a problem, and production never neared capacity until World War II. It did, however, restore national self-confidence; it caused a re-assertion of faith in democracy; and in the United States it gave the democratic system a firm push in a plebiscitary and executive direction. The New Deal, and its creator, permanently altered the nature of the presidency, and of American government. FDR not only gave energy to government but in an age of dawning public awareness of and involvement in public affairs, he gave to its activities not only vividness but drama. The word charisma had to wait for a television age, but he had it in abundance. It was as if there were a man, and an operator, in the White House who had an extra dimension, and a special zest for life. Rex Tugwell said that he was

> not a made President, but a born one ... No monarch ... unless it may have been Elizabeth or her magnificent Tudor father, or maybe Alexander

or Augustus Caesar, can have given quite that sense of serene presiding, of gathering up into himself, of really representing, a whole people. He had a right to his leeways, he had a right to use everyone in his own way, he had every right to manage and manipulate the palpables and impalpables. ... He had touch with something deeper than reason. ...[3]

Arthur M. Schlesinger Jr has a deeper insight into the personality and the inner loneliness of the man:

The public face, all grin and gusto, had been carefully cultivated at Groton and Harvard; illness had made it second nature. But behind the cordiality and exuberance there remained an impassable reserve which many reconnoitered but none could penetrate. The relentless buoyance was less an impulse of the soul than a mark of cheer to the world, in part spontaneous enough, but more a defense against pity without and discouragement within. ... Underneath there remained the other man – tougher than the public man, harder, more ambitious, more calculating, more petty, more puckish, more selfish, more malicious, more profound, more complex, more interesting. ... Detachment endowed him with a capacity for craftiness in politics and for calculation, sometimes even for cruelty, in human relations. Those who loved him best he teased most mercilessly. Nearly everybody was expendable.[4]

Another verdict is that of his son, Elliot. He sees that his father was, first and last, an opportunist, and that the ambition began early. In part it is the story of the poor little rich boy cushioned by affluence, by the best education a proud parent could buy, at Groton and Harvard, and by the chaperonage even at Harvard of a doting mother who was to reign over him and his wife in the White House itself.

History must record that he led the greatest social revolution the free world has ever known. He inaugurated a system of governmental responsibility for every citizen that has been accepted by each succeeding Administration. He built a military machine with an incredible productive capacity. He was the progenitor of the United Nations, who served his country fearlessly, and with remarkable compassion. There have been differences in the character of Presidents and the Presidency in recent years, but few improvements.

[3] Tugwell, *The Democrat Roosevelt*, p. 302. See Bernard Sternsher, *Rexford Tugwell and the New Deal* (New Brunswick, NJ, Rutgers University Press, 1964); Rexford Tugwell, *The Brains Trust* (New York, Viking, 1968).

[4] Arthur J. Schlesinger, Jr, *The Crisis of the Old Order* (Boston, Houghton Mifflin, 1957).

I believe that April 12, 1945, when Father died, marked the day when morality in government began to pass from the picture. The downhill road carried us into Vietnam and the abyss identified as Watergate.[5]

5 THE VERDICT

By 1939 the farmer's income was twice that of 1932. The National Recovery Act had shortened working hours, raised wages, and recognized trade unions. The Wagner Act was evidence of a new attitude towards organized labor. The Works Progress Administration financed new building projects. The federal government even brought in social security benefits for unemployment and old age – always thought of before this as "state" not "federal" matters.

These measures set the country on the road to recovery. Roosevelt's measures were not socialist, although many of his opponents described him as a "Red," and worse. His job, as he saw it, was to revive the capitalist system – which had produced so high a standard of living in the past – by using federal funds to prime the pump, and to start the economy moving again. He had to inspire in Americans a new faith in themselves; all that America had to fear, he said, was fear itself.

He was successful; and he not only revived the economy but enormously extended the power and impact of the presidency. He also won over to the Democratic party many of the poorer groups, especially the blacks. Next to Lincoln, who freed the slaves, F. D. Roosevelt and his wife Eleanor, a notably generous and sympathetic person, were idolized by American blacks and by many working-class people.

To summarise, Roosevelt's success stemmed from a number of factors; FDR built and retained his winning coalition by keeping the issue initiative by launching and fighting hard for a steady stream of policy proposals, even though he knew many of them would lose in the Congress. He knew that many items which passed the Congress would be declared unconstitutional by the Supreme Court. But he kept the nation speaking about his proposed solutions for the great problems facing the United States. He reduced what was left of the Republican party simply to reacting and complaining about what he was proposing. Thus the Republicans lost their credibility as an alternative vehicle for governing.

[5] Elliot Roosevelt and James Brough, *A Rendezvous with Destiny; The Roosevelts of the White House* (London, W. H. Allen, 1978).

Roosevelt kept his coalition together by giving each element of it frequent, solid reasons to stay aboard. No ally was taken for granted. To the extent that he could, Roosevelt ran each ensuing election on the central themes of his 1932 success. Specifically, he attempted to pit the always more numerous "have nots" in society against the "haves." Even today, the "liberal" political coalition lineally descended from FDR tries to convince people that conservatives are on the side of only those people who are rich, while the "liberals" are working for everyone who is not rich. As long as that argument was persuasive, the liberal coalition remained the normal governing majority.

Roosevelt used legislation, his administrative powers, and the prestige of his office to build the political power of the key elements of his coalition, particularly organized labor. Changes made in labor law during the 1930s gave long-lasting advantages to the growth of monopoly union power. Today the political power of unions is such that, in most areas of the United States, Democratic candidates are wasting their time and money if the unions are against them.

Roosevelt cheerfully used confrontation with his opponents in order to motivate his coalition. Once he announced a draconian regulation of prices that could be charged by businesses across the country. Sewell Avery, president of Montgomery Ward, one of the largest corporations in the country, announced that he would keep Montgomery Ward prices as low as he could and that he would ignore Roosevelt's price-fixing regulations. Roosevelt could simply have filed a legal action against Sewell Avery and Montgomery Ward, but he didn't. Instead, he sent federal officers into Sewell Avery's office. They picked Avery up from behind his desk and dragged him off. Of course, Roosevelt thoughtfully informed the news media, so there were many dramatic pictures of the president of a major corporation being hauled away.

Roosevelt almost cheerfully accepted the most intense unpopularity with a smaller number of Americans in order to achieve unique popularity with the majority of Americans. It is possible to describe him as both the most popular and the least popular President in our century. That is to say, a greater number of Americans revered Roosevelt more than any other President of our century, and a greater number loathed and despised him.

We should not forget that FDR built a stable, winning coalition while the Great Depression raged all during the 1930s. Economic prosperity, or his lack of success in creating it, proved largely irrelevant to his political success.

Nor did Roosevelt's coalition lack mutually antagonistic elements. It contained most of the Jewish population, most of the devoutly Catholic urban ethnics, and most of the Southern Protestants who regarded the Roman Catholic Church as the Whore of Babylon. It was home to liberal intellectuals who abhorred racial segregation, but also to Ku Kluxers and to labor unions with "white only" membership restrictions. These and other polar elements submerged their differences sufficiently to govern together in coalition for two generations.

With the New Deal, the Democrats became the party of government, both as the majority party – holding the White House or both houses of Congress between 1932 and 1980 for all but four years – and as the party that set out to use government, whether to steer the economy, provide for welfare, or act as "countervailing power" for the have-nots against the haves. With World War II, the Democrats became internationalists, and in 1948, Dixiecrats aside, the party of civil rights. Modern Republicans were the opposition, the party of fiscal caution, isolationism, and free enterprise, unfettered but not necessarily unaided by government. Between 1932 and 1980 there were 48 years of a normal governing majority operating under the label of the Democratic party. During that period, the coalition initially set up by Roosevelt controlled either the Congress or the White House or both for all but two years. Only in the first two years of the Eisenhower Administration did the Republican party control both the White House and Congress. Franklin Roosevelt proved to be thus far the most successful president of the twentieth century. His new, normal governing majority lasted far beyond his lifetime.

For 40 years, the Democrats were the party that reached out and gathered people in, while the Republicans were the party that turned inward and kept people out. Democrats had in Roosevelts or Biddles old wealth, as well as new money in Harrimans and Kennedys, not to mention raw political talent in Johnsons or Humphreys, who started out with next to nothing at all. Considering the party's ambition to reconcile irreconcilables, it is astonishing it showed such vigor for so long.

At its height, the party was an elite coalition of financiers, lawyers, and industrialists, linked particularly with corporations on government contract or doing business abroad; it included university-trained specialists and administrators, purged of Marxists or socialists; it rallied a reformist, anti-Communist union leadership; it worked, in parallel, with Eastern or "moderate" Republicans who accepted the Liberal Consensus. Neat as all this sounds, the

Democrats also depended for voting strength until the 1960s on the segregationist wing of the party in the South, a reminder of the doctrinal untidiness of American parties.

From Franklin Roosevelt's time, modern conservatives have defined themselves as opponents of the Democratic Idea. Reconciled to being unable to capture the government for any length of time, let alone control it, modern conservatives concentrated instead on trying to limit its scope. Unlike conservatives in Europe, where working-class politics is strong, their American counterparts have tended to concentrate fire on "big government."

Repeated rout of conservative Republicans at the polls before the late 1970s concealed conservative strength. While it is right to treat the long period from the New Deal to the late 1960s or early 1970s as one in which Democrats and Republicans, once in office, subscribed to the Democratic Idea, the conservative opposition was far from ineffective. It set limits on how far the Roosevelt-to-Johnson, and perhaps even the Nixon, version of welfare capitalism could stray from the supposedly true American path of individualism and free enterprise. After 1938, a coalition of Northern Republicans and Southern Democrats brought an effective end to Roosevelt's social reforms. Truman Democrats would not push through national health insurance. Democrats saw their job not as controlling but as reinvigorating the economy. Public ownership, state direction of investment, or serious economic planning – accepted features of welfare capitalism in Western Europe or Japan – were not elements of the Democratic Idea. The social democratic, not to mention the socialist, tradition has not flourished on American soil.

The Democratic Idea, conceived during the depression, took its strength from the long course of economic expansion which began with production for war in the 1940s and peaked during the Vietnam War in the mid-1960s. By the late 1970s, when the Democratic Idea seemed to be withering away, it was obvious to all that nobody had simple ways of recovering steady growth with manageable inflation. So long as this had lasted, expansion of the federal government was not seriously questioned, except by conservative Republicans. When it ended, doubt and rejection crowded in from all sides.

FDR's very political success made his threats to traditional arrangements more ominous. So did the progress of events in Europe, where dictatorships continued to make gains at the expense of democracy. And so did a subtle shift in the stated goals of the New Deal. In the First and even the Second New Deal – in NRA and AAA, deposit insurance and social security and even the Wagner

Act – the beneficiaries were the great mass of Americans, land-owning farmers and upwardly mobile city-dwellers whose plans had been frustrated and hopes dashed by economic collapse. In the second Roosevelt term the beneficiaries were depicted increasingly as those on the bottom or somewhere near the bottom of the economic ladder – a group with which only a small percentage of the voters identified.

Just after the 1936 election, Gallup reported that only 15 percent of those with an opinion wanted the second Roosevelt administration to be more liberal than the first, 50 percent wanted it more conservative, and 35 percent wanted it about the same: no mandate here for the new departures suggested in Roosevelt's campaign speeches and his inaugural address. Yet by a 65 percent to 35 percent margin, respondents said they would "vote for Franklin Roosevelt today."

Undercutting the landslide even more was the recession that began in the fall of 1937, the first downturn in the economic cycle since the beginning of recovery from the depths of 1933. Unemployment rose from an annual average of 7.7 million in 1937 to 10.4 million in 1938. That was not as high as the 12.8 million of 1933, but it was still five times higher than any figure in the 1923–29 period, and unemployment would not decline below the 7 million level until after World War II began.

"I see millions," cried Franklin Roosevelt, "denied education, recreation, and the opportunity to better their lot and that of their children. I see millions lacking the means to buy the products of farm and factory and by their poverty denying work and productiveness to many other millions. I see one-third of a nation ill-housed, ill-clad, ill-nourished." At his rain-streaked Second Inaugural on January 20, 1937, Roosevelt was making his intentions clear. He wanted to build a stronger, larger federal government to stimulate the economy and redistribute income and wealth. He wanted the nation to go farther down the road it had embarked on in June 1935.

It was against this background that in February 1937 Roosevelt unveiled his proposal to pack the Supreme Court. He was frustrated because the Court had ruled unconstitutional so many New Deal laws and because, despite the advanced years of many justices, he had completed a four-year term without having the opportunity to fill a single vacancy – the only President between Woodrow Wilson and Jimmy Carter thus deprived. Some of the Court's decisions on New Deal measures may have seemed sensible in retrospect – NRA, for example, was surely "delegation running riot" and had exhausted its political support before the Court killed it – but in others the Court did seem to invalidate popular legislation by using a definition of interstate commerce which was straight out of horse-and-buggy days. Attempting to preserve a field in which Congress could not act, the Court found itself drawing lines which made no sense and making distinctions which seemed to almost all thoughtful people to make no difference: jurisprudence running riot. From the turn of the century through the days of Chief Justice Taft, the court had sometimes been attacked as an instrument of the rich because the justices had felt a duty to make sure that activist legislation passed by inexpert legislatures did not violate constitutional limitations. But until 1935 the abstract principles enunciated by the Court had seldom found their way into political discourse or threatened to overturn widely popular laws which were at the center of political debate. As 1937 began, important laws – the Wagner Act, the Social Security Act, and the second AAA – seemed threatened by the Court. Roosevelt evidently felt he must act.

Yet what he did came as a surprise to almost everyone, and the instant reaction of many politicians was negative. One reason was his disingenuousness. He proposed not a constitutional amendment to overturn the Supreme Court decisions he disagreed with, but a simple law to allow him to name up to six new justices, one for each incumbent who failed to retire after reaching the age of 70. Congress had changed the number of justices in the nineteenth century, and one of the four conservative stalwarts on the Court, Justice James McReynolds, had proposed years earlier the appointment of new judges on the lower federal courts when an incumbent refused to retire at seventy. But Roosevelt, concentrating on secrecy, had failed to enlist his normal political allies. Henry Ashurst of Arizona, grandiloquent chairman of the Senate Judiciary Committee, had recently denied vehemently that the President favored packing the court; and Hatton Sumner of Dallas, Texas, chairman of the House Judiciary Committee, told his companions in Vice-President Garner's car as they were being driven back to the Capitol after Roosevelt's announcement, "Boys, here's where I cash in." Liberal Democrats like Burton Wheeler and Wyoming's Joseph O'Mahoney, progressive Republicans like Hiram Johnson and George Norris, were opposed; these were all politicians whose careers had been imperiled by their devotion to civil liberties, and the proposal to overturn Court decisions by political might stuck in their craw. Wheeler, for example, had been savagely criticized when as United States attorney in the turbulent mining city of Butte, Montana, he had refused to cooperate with Attorney General Mitchell Palmer's Red Raids in 1920; he remembered how in "the hysteria of the First World War, I saw men strung up. Only the federal courts stood up at all, and the Supreme Court better than any of them. Not as well as they should have, but better than the others." At a Senate Judiciary Committee hearing in March 1937, Wheeler read a letter from Chief Justice Charles Evans Hughes conclusively refuting Roosevelt's charges of inefficiency and delay in the Court's activities.[6]

In fact, the issue was simply whether the Court's power to overturn laws should be limited by "dilution" (or the threat of dilution) of its membership. What Roosevelt really wanted, of course, was for the court to change its reasoning and quit overturning New Deal laws. On that issue, public opinion as measured in polls seemed to be with him. But on the procedural question of limiting the Court's powers Americans were dubious. In November 1936, Gallup had found that a 59–41 percent majority of those with an opinion agreed that the Supreme Court should be "more liberal in reviewing New Deal measures," but a majority of exactly the same size opposed "limiting the power of the Supreme Court to declare Acts of Congress unconstitutional." In February 1937, Gallup showed a 53–47 percent majority of those with an opinion opposed "President Roosevelt's proposal to reorganize the Supreme Court;" and a week later, only 30 percent said Congress should pass the Roosevelt plan, while 23 percent said it should be modified and 39 percent said it should be defeated. Even if most of those with no opinion were pro-Roosevelt, as the President himself sensibly assumed, it was clear that the voting public remained unconvinced of the merits of the court-packing proposal.

If the politicians and the public were nonplused, the justices may have been affected. On April 12 the Court surprised many by upholding the Wagner Act, with Hughes and Owen Roberts joining the usual liberal bloc of Louis Brandeis, Harlan Stone, and Benjamin Cardozo. On May 18, Justice Willis Van Devanter resigned, and on May 24 the Court upheld the Social Security Act. All these events undermined the court-packing bill, since it seemed now that New Deal legislation would be safe without it. Roosevelt still lobbied furiously. But on the day of Van Devanter's resignation the Senate Judiciary Committee defeated the bill 10–8, and all the energetic efforts of majority leader Joseph Robinson, an Arkansas conservative

[6] Studs Terkel, *Hard Times: An oral history of the Great Depression* (New York, Pocket Books, 1978), p. 163.

who had been promised the first new seat, availed nothing. On July 14, Robinson suddenly died; court-packing had died some time before.

Was the court-packing bill a drastic political mistake? It can be argued that it achieved many of Roosevelt's goals; that without it the Supreme Court might have overturned the Wagner and Social Security Acts (it had difficulty distinguishing them from laws it *had* overturned) and the elderly conservative justices would have stayed on the Court, threatening any New Deal legislation passed in the second term (Van Devanter was joined in retirement by George Sutherland in January 1938 and Pierce Butler in November 1939). But even if these premises are granted, it is plain that Roosevelt paid a high political price. He split the congressional Democratic party, which despite its huge majorities passed little New Deal legislation in 1937 and 1938. He eroded his own credibility inside Washington and out; plainly he had not been frank about why he wanted the bill. An impression was etched deep in the public mind that Roosevelt was trying to evade all traditional restraints on presidential and political power. Already politicians were asking whether Roosevelt should and would seek a third term – not questions usually asked about American Presidents who had just won their second. Already people were noticing that "reliefers" gave New Deal Democrats a greater percentage of their votes than did any other group – proof to some that government money was being used to buy Roosevelt votes. Although the percentage of Americans who were pleased that Roosevelt had been reelected in 1936 remained as high as ever, the percentage who wanted to see him and his New Dealers given all the power they wanted had probably fallen well below 50 percent.

The administration's most venturesome initiatives failed. One was the reorganization bill, which would have put into effect the recommendations of the President's Brownlow Committee; the other was the Seven TVAs bill, which would have set up seven regional authorities, defined by river basins, as a basis for a sort of national economic planning. Together these bills amounted to what historian Barry Karl has called a Third New Deal. The Brownlow Committee called for centralizing national political authority by ending the independence of the federal regulatory agencies and creating a permanent planning board in the White House, which would have authority over regional planning boards set up all over the nation. As a resident of the White House who identified with the central government, and a son of the Hudson River valley who instinctively loved to organize programs by watersheds, Roosevelt naturally liked the Seven TVAs plan; and it seemed to meet certain obvious needs for control of natural disasters, such as the floods which had devastated the Ohio River valley in early 1937 and the Dustbowl which had been developing in the valleys of the Mississippi's tributaries farther west. But other politicians hated these bills and the ideas they represented. They did not want experts or White House appointees deciding where dams would be built and post offices established: they wanted to make those politically crucial decisions themselves. To them, the idea of national planning seemed increasingly to mean rule by unaccountable intellectuals. Congress kept putting into administration bills provisions cutting the salaries of men like Harry Hopkins and requiring all officials above a certain salary level to be confirmed by Congress. Father Coughlin and newspaper chain owner Frank Gannett campaigned strenuously against reorganization, which was called the "dictator bill" often enough that Roosevelt issued an announcement which included the odd statement; "I have no inclination to be a dictator. I have none of the qualifications which would make a successful dictator." Yet a 45–44 percent plurality of Americans agreed that "Roosevelt has too much power." The reorganization bill was passed in 1939 only after it had been stripped of all its revolutionary centralizing features, and the Seven TVAs bill never passed at all.

In fact, the main effect of these proposals was to increase the apprehensions that politicians and many voters already had about the New Deal. In November 1938 when Hopkins's WPA still had 3–4 million people on the payroll, he was quoted by Frank Kent as saying that the administration would "tax and tax, spend and spend, elect and elect." Hopkins denied saying anything of the sort, and Kent refused to name his anonymous source (it turned out to be a theatrical producer who was a racetrack companion of Hopkins). But the story struck a chord (Arthur Krock of the *New York Times* told a congressional committee that "it was a most logical statement of what Mr Hopkins might have said" – a peculiar standard of journalistic integrity), and it became a staple of Republican oratory. Ronald Reagan, a four-time Roosevelt voter, was still quoting it in the late 1980s.

6 THE GREAT DEBATE: US FOREIGN POLICY

It is hard for us, accustomed to the important role played in the world by the United States since 1945, to realize that until December 7, 1941, when Japanese bombs were dropped on Pearl

Harbor, the United States preferred isolation to intervention in European affairs. The isolationists were able to prevent American entrance into the League of Nations in 1919, to delay and hamper close cooperation with it, to keep the United States out of the International Court of Justice, and in 1935–6 to draw up a series of Neutrality Acts which prevented stern action against nations which attacked others.

The United States is isolated by geography; isolationists claimed that it could easily be defended against attack, and they considered European entanglements with suspicion. The United States, they argued, can be economically self-sufficient, and does not need a policy of Free Trade. The United States is a mixture of races, and should be given time to fuse its many peoples into one, to find its own special character and culture.

Internationalists rebutted the argument about geography. After the development of swift modern fleets of air power, the ocean was no longer a barrier but a possible path of conquest. The cotton-growers of the South, the wheat-growers, dairy-farmers, and cattle-raisers of the Middle West, were dependent on Europe for the marketing of their surplus crops. The United States depended equally on foreign nations for its tin, nickel, tungsten, chrome, rubber, coffee, tea and tropical drugs, and increasingly for extra supplies of oil. The practical stoppage of immigration in the last generation, and the steady progress of Americanization, had, they contended, largely solved the problems of absorbing the immigrant. But, above all, there were two chief arguments against isolationism, one historical and one practical.

The historical argument held that the United States has always valued the promotion of democracy more than sterile isolationism. The United States has repeatedly been ready to denounce tyrannies and dictatorships, and to take practical measures against them. Franklin D. Roosevelt was simply following a long American tradition when in the years 1935–40 he made it plain that the United States had a vital interest in the survival of democratic freedoms abroad, in face of the threat from Hitler. President Kennedy tapped the same strain of concern and idealism when he committed the United States to aid to Latin America and when he identified himself in 1963 with the people of West Berlin in his famous speech there ("Ich bin ein Berliner"). This identification with freedom and democracy, the distaste for imperialism (whether that of Britain in America in 1776, or in India in 1930, or Suez in 1956, of Spain in Cuba in 1898, or of Russia in Cuba in 1962), these are noble and persistent themes throughout the American story.

The practical argument was one which time soon proved correct. Briefly, the internationalists held that peace could never be preserved by being negative like the isolationists. Peace must be organized and protected by a system of collective security. They argued that the United States would always he drawn into any world war, as it had been drawn into the Napoleonic Wars (the American "War of 1812") and World War I. Its only real safety lay in trying to prevent any new world war from breaking out; and this could be done only if it gave its full aid to a world organization like the League of Nations.

Isolationism won its biggest victory in 1919–20 when the Senate refused to allow the United States to join the League of Nations. Nevertheless the United States took an active part in European affairs. It sponsored the Washington Conference of 1921–2 to cut down naval armaments. It tried to solve the war debts problems of the 1920s. It was a small group of Americans who tried, in the Kellogg-Briand Pact of 1928, to "outlaw war." But the depression revived isolationism. Americans felt that all their energies were required for domestic problems. A wave of economic and political nationalism swept over the globe. The depression brought Hitler into power in Germany, overthrew the last hopes of the liberal, anti-military party in Japan, and strengthened reaction in Fascist Italy. Americans, anxious to remain at peace, reacted to this change in atmosphere by retreating into their storm-cellars.

By 1935 it became plain that new wars were breeding both in Asia and Europe. Congress wished at all costs to keep America from being involved. Hence the rigid "neutrality legislation" of the years which banned the sale of military goods to all countries at war. President Roosevelt strongly opposed such legislation; and the dramatic series of Axis aggressions in Europe and Africa and the threats from Japan finally convinced all far-sighted Americans that they could keep aloof from the common democratic cause only at their peril. It became plain that Roosevelt was right in criticizing the Neutrality Acts, which prevented the United States from assisting weak nations under attack.

The demonstration was complete when Hitler's allies, the Japanese, struck at Pearl Harbor, the American base in the Hawaiian Islands, in 1941, two years after Hitler had attacked Poland and started World War II. The United States found itself for the first time in its history assailed by powerful foes on both the Atlantic and the Pacific flanks. The attack on Pearl Harbor ended isolation for any realist.

World War II was a godsend to American liberals. The New Deal had been dead since 1937, torpedoed by its fundamental failure to effect an end to depression and its increasingly annoying meddling with traditional patterns of American life. Congressman Charles Halleck of Indiana predicted in 1936 that the "social experimentation and reckless extravagance of the New Deal are on the way out because the common sense of the American people is reasserting itself." A "conservative coalition" of Republicans and Southern Democrats blocked almost all of President Roosevelt's initiatives at least until the foreign policy crisis of 1939–41, brought about by the wars in Europe and the Far East. What happened between 1941 and 1945 was an expansion of the national state so vast as to be virtually irreversible.

In December of 1943 the President told the press that "Dr New Deal," who was a specialist in internal medicine, had given way to "Dr Win-the-War," an orthopedic surgeon. Soon after, speaking to a group of reformers, the New Deal poet laureate Archibald MacLeish lamented: "Liberals meet in Washington these days, if they meet at all, to discuss the tragic outlook for all liberal programs, the collapse of all liberal leadership and the defeat of all liberal aims."

What prompted his lament as well as FDR's change of physicians was a Congress which kept cutting back on New Deal programs. Wartime Congresses were made up of men with formidably conservative leanings, and while they usually authorized money, agencies, programs, regulations, and taxes to fight the war, they also looked upon some of the sillier, outdated, unworkable, and visionary New Deal programs with budget-chopping eyes. During 1942 and 1943 the Civilian Conservation Corps, the Works Progress Administration, and the National Resources Planning Board – visible agencies all, from early on in the New Deal – got the axe. Farm Security and Rural Electrification Administrations were cut back. Expansion of social security was put on hold. Federal aid to education, national health insurance, and regional TVAs got nowhere.

It falls to the President, as commander-in-chief, to take war-winning initiatives, and FDR ran a New Deal War. That is, his initiatives included crisis regulation the scope of which no American could have dreamed of even as late as 1939. It included four main elements: price control (Office of Price Administration – OPA), rationing, command over production (War Production Board), and control of labor (National War Labor Board). Taken together they represented a bewildering interlocking complex of agencies, and they resulted in a command economy that differed only in tone and details from totalitarianism,

By 1943 government boards and agencies could (and did) tell Americans how much they could drive, what they could manufacture and how much, whether they could change jobs, raise rents, eat beef, or stay on the streets at night. Government built housing and tore it down, reorganized the entire automobile industry, created aluminum companies, and withheld new tires from trucks carrying objectionable items like booze, cigarettes, and Orange Crush. In Oklahoma, which was still a Prohibition state, the OPA demanded that all speakeasies post ceiling prices for bootleg whiskey.

Further, the war rid New Deal liberalism of its most obvious enemy: a large chunk of big business was by 1945 married to big government.

Take Henry J. Kaiser. This paunchy, jowly, duckwaddling, table-pounding, oath-swearing package of pure energy took a sand and gravel business and made it into "an organization that combined the merits of a Chinese tong, a Highland clan and a Renaissance commercial syndicate with all the flexibility and legal safeguards of the modern corporation." In the 1930s Kaiser built dams (Boulder, Grand Coulee, and others), and during the war he built ships – Liberty ships, small aircraft-carriers, tankers, troop ships, destroyer escorts, landing craft – all on a cost-plus basis. In 1943 he garnered 30 percent of the national production total, over $3 billion in contracts. Roosevelt wanted fast production, and Kaiser gave him speed; once he built a Liberty ship in 14 days. His ships didn't last very long, and they didn't work very well, but he could produce so many that the war machine couldn't grind them up as fast as he could spit them out. When the big steel companies fell short of delivering the materials he demanded, he borrowed $106 million from the RFC and built the Fontana steel plant, at no risk to himself.

The war also occasioned a tax structure that threatened to abolish profits and that provided the indispensable base for future liberal social experimentation. As much as Roosevelt played the class game during the depression, as much as he tried to "soak the rich," he never got a revenue bill that matched his appetite through Congress until 1942. Even then Congress for the most part insisted on acting responsibly and taxing the citizens directly, rather than resorting to the administration's funny money schemes of unlimited borrowing and confiscating business revenues. But there was an "excess profits" tax, and payroll deductions became mandatory, and the rate for personal incomes over $150,000 was 90 percent.

Once again this was a matter of acceleration rather than point of origin. The war did not create politicization: basic Progressive-liberal ideas did. The New Deal nurtured politicization, and World War II brought it to maturity. One of the war's most significant doctrines is especially pertinent to this part of the discussion: compulsory military service.

The Selective Service Act of 1940 was the nation's first peacetime draft. It was passed after the fall of France and after a terrific political struggle in the United States Congress, which was in many ways the last political gasp of the isolationists. According to one biographer, James T. Patterson, Taft summed up his vigorous opposition: the draft is like roulette. Furthermore, a series of veterans' buyouts collectively known as the "GI Bill of Rights" largely removed the issue from postwar politics. Any veteran became entitled to generous help in adversity. The GI Bill was to transform American higher education; it also cemented the state's control over its youth in place. The classroom replaced the foxhole. Government could take opportunity away, and government could also restore it; since the sequence went in that direction, compulsory service did not surface as an issue again until the Vietnam quagmire recalled it.

Meanwhile the universities which would benefit from the GI Bill had become militarized in the war. Professor Merle Curti wrote: "The federal capital became the intellectual center of the nation." Government promoted research, enlisted scholars, and proved that both "were as necessary to war as to peace." Militarization of the intellect promoted politicization of the universities, perhaps the single most important social consequence of the entire war.

Through the National Defense Research Committee and the Office of Scientific Research and Development (OSS) the government sponsored thousands of (mostly short-term) projects in hundreds of universities and colleges. The most celebrated was the Manhattan Project, which produced the atomic bomb, but that was only the tip of the iceberg. Less visible were the thousands of academic intellectuals who flocked to the war effort. And less visible too were the thousands of "social scientists" – economists, sociologists, political scientists, psychologists, anthropologists – whose war-related research brought them into the government orbit.

But there is a more significant side to the story. Until World War II it was an unwritten law of the universities that academic freedom in part depended on the ability to steer clear of the nation-state and its nosy bureaucrats. The war altered that. Add four background factors, and by 1945 the stage was set for the conversion of the university into virtually an arm of the national state and its liberal agenda: (1) the war generation remained in control of postwar universities, and impressed future generations with their new-found importance; (2) the GI Bill provided a new source of almost endless funding for postwar academic expansion;

(3) the Progressive-liberal agenda had always included the dream of nearly universal education funded by the public; (4) most academic people shared the liberal-Progressive outlook.

One casualty was the emphasis on teaching. Prior to World War II the function of the American college and university had been to pass on our common memory through teaching. This did not mean that faculty members did no research; it meant that they knew that their first responsibility was to their students, and that their research was strictly subordinated to their teaching. The war allowed the liberal emphasis on *process* to emerge at the heart of the university function. Problem-solving research, the university as agent of and guide to change, students as *method*-learning creatures, rather quickly took the place of the old emphasis on substance, reflection, culture, and memory.

Academic entrepreneurs appeared: grant-getters, doing result-oriented, short-term research projects that could be published. Since their patronage came from outside (government and foundation money), these entrepreneurs gained leverage in their universities to define "contact hours," "teaching loads" and other elements of piecework.

Rewards and standards shifted away from the ideal of teaching, service and commitment to the academic *community*, and especially away from loyalty to school. The new academic nation was discipline oriented, professional rather than institutional, institute-making, arrogant enough in its access to money that it created an academic star-system, first in the sciences but ultimately in economics, business schools, and even humanities.

And it is crucial to understand that these changes put the universities in the service of the liberal-left agenda: social experimentation, economic planning, the growth of the state, destruction of absolutes, hostility to traditional religion – in general, an adversarial relationship with traditional American values and culture. It was all based, to a large extent, on unlimited access to taxpayers' money, but operated without accountability to taxpayers' values.

Total war also politicized the Constitution, or rather it completed the politicization that Roosevelt began when he tried to pack the Supreme Court in 1937. The Congress and the American people decisively rejected that attempt, so vigorously that the episode threatened to stop the New Deal in its tracks. But by use of his "emergency powers," FDR later managed to politicize the Constitution and alter it forever in the direction of national and executive power.[7]

[7] John Willson, "World War II, the great liberal war," *Imprimis* (May, 1992).

7 ELEANOR

Eleanor Roosevelt was the niece of President Theodore Roosevelt and closer to that ebullient figure than was FDR: the Oyster Bay clan seemed more regal – until 1933 – than the Hyde Park Roosevelts, despite the grand dame ways of Sara Delano. Eleanor Roosevelt was as a girl rebuffed by her extrovert and charming mother because she was plain, gauche, always older in manner than her years and intensely shy. She idolized her father but he was addicted to drink and other temptations and saw little of her. In any case, both parents had died by the time she was ten. It was a miserable childhood and she never threw off her high seriousness, her self-consciousness about what she thought her own unattractiveness, and her expectation of being a subject for amused ridicule.

Consequently the love affair and marriage with her brilliant cousin Franklin, handsome and cavalier, with wealth, jest and a winning smile – itself seen as a major political asset as early as 1905 – transformed her. Her wedding, when she was twenty and her groom twenty-two was a national festival. The bride was given away by the President, recently re-elected in the 1904 landslide; and indeed the couple were forgotten in the bustle that surrounded the great man – of whom a friendly cynic said that in any case the President always wanted to be the bride at every wedding he attended and the corpse at every funeral. The years from 1905 to the last year of World War I were years of happiness: four boys and a girl were born; and her husband, first active in New York politics as a state Senator (1910–13) was from 1913 to 1920 assistant secretary of the navy, as Uncle Teddy had been in his time. The portents were promising. If the young FDR seemed something of a lightweight, it nevertheless seemed likely that he would follow in Teddy's footsteps: the governorship of New York and in due course perhaps even the White House, as indeed he did. His wife was compelled dutifully to be a socialite, to give big parties, to tour the country and to overcome not only her fear of the sea but of almost everything else. In the process she was transformed. But he brought a problem with him from the start. His mother lived with them – always. Even in the White House it was his mother who acted as hostess: Mrs James Roosevelt.

But there were two shattering experiences ahead. The second in time was her husband's polio at Campobello in 1921, which left him thereafter with his legs paralysed. It is clear that the man, physically strong, was prone to chills and was throughout that summer both over-active and yet thoroughly tired; a less active man might well have had more resistance to the disease. Its effect was absolutely shattering, then and afterwards, for the man and the marriage. The essential fact thereafter was that this man, hitherto jovial and restless, moved now, when he moved at all, with his legs in steel braces. If after 1921 there was a new Eleanor, there was also a new Franklin. The gaiety, the zest, the twinkle were still there, but now as a mask, and as a banner. There was also now a psychological strength, a steel in the mind as well as on the legs. And the smile was now for use.

But before this, in 1918, Mrs Roosevelt had discovered her husband's affair with Lucy Mercer, her social secretary, and this was her first ordeal. This was, says Joseph Lash, "the flame whose heat hastened and fixed the change from private into public person. Franklin's love for another woman brought her to total despair, and she emerged from the ordeal a different woman."[8] There was a family conference but in the end talk of a divorce was dropped, in part because of the children, in part because Lucy Mercer was a Catholic, in part because Sara Delano Roosevelt, Roosevelt's formidable mother, opposed it, and in part no doubt because a career would have been put at risk.

From this there came the new Eleanor, the do-gooder, speaking, writing, broadcasting, seeking in endless outside activity a balm for her wounded spirit. After her husband's polio, her restlessness could be presented as a political embassy for her stricken husband, playing the role of his eyes and ears, but this was not the original motive. Eleanor Roosevelt wanted to be a personality, it seems, in her own right, and according to Lash she was able thereafter to render her husband only "a service of love."

Clearly Mrs Roosevelt was transformed, to the point that by 1940 there was talk of running her for the presidency if the third-term tradition was too strong for FDR himself. Her activity was all but overpowering – through his years as governor of New York, for instance, she insisted on spending two and a half days a week teaching at a private girls school, Tadhunter – and highly remunerative: $500 a month for a 750-word piece for the North American Newspaper Alliance; $1,000 a month for a monthly column "I Want you to Write me" in *The Woman's Home Companion*, radio talks at $3,000 each, serial rights for *My Day, This Is My Story*, and not least for *Babies, Just Babies* – the last of which was

[8] Joseph Lash, *Eleanor and Franklin: The story of their relationship based on Eleanor Roosevelt's private papers* (London, Deutsch, 1972).

a butt for caricature, as were her newsreel appearances as a dress model, which usually produced hysterics in cinema audiences. In 1938 she earned $60,000 from these activities: this was "do-goodism" put to mercenary use, and if it made her all too familiar as a face it was a source of much criticism.

She was criticized in verse as well as prose. One McTavish wrote:

> Dear Madam: Pray take this tae mean
> A kindly counsel for a freen
> That ye hae reached the White House door
> 'Is just because the folk were sore.
> Noo, though ye talk an' thought ye write
> Fair words wi' brilliant sapience dight
> Tis better far for ye, I ken
> To curb the tongue an' eke the pen.

With all this the press had a field day. Admiral Byrd at the South Pole, it was said, had set a place for her at supper in case she dropped in; and a child who heard the Robinson Crusoe story knew that the footprints in the sand were those of Mrs Roosevelt. The *New Yorker* cartoon was very popular, in which two startled coalminers look up and say "Good Gosh, here comes Mrs Roosevelt." In fact it was almost true. When she went down a mine in miner's overalls, Sara wrote to her son: "I hope Eleanor is with you this morning; ... I see she has emerged from the mine ... That is something to be thankful for."

In the process she became – inevitably – a crusader; a glutton for punishment and for causes. She became an advocate of the rights of the black, of the young, of women. She pestered her husband – usually at breakfast or at the end of the day and at the end distractingly – with suggestions, with views, and with people. And the man retreated still more behind his braces and his smile. He needed – desperately needed – help and understanding. He had to look for them elsewhere, and got them from his daughter Anna, from Missy Le Hand, from Princess Martha of Norway and perhaps at the end from Lucy Mercer (then Lucy Rutherford) at Warm Springs. But one reading of Joseph Lash's book suggests that the barrier between husband and wife was as much of Eleanor's as of Franklin's making. And Lash wrote from an insider's point of view. He had met Mrs Roosevelt when he was an army sergeant in Guadalcanal, which the First Lady visited in 1943 on a tour of the Pacific. As a political left-winger and activist, he was and remained an admirer. She became curiously possessive and jealous when men

Plate 7 Eleanor Roosevelt with Madame Chiang Kai-Shek, February 1943. (Library of Congress.)

like Hopkins, having reached FDR through her friendship, became more his man than hers – jealous and, oddly, surprised, as if she really thought she was as important as he was. She was so pure, so noble, so dedicated that any criticism of her seems ungracious and almost treasonable. Yet she was also so dedicated as to be a bore, so generous with her own energy that she asked too much of others, one of those salts of the earth who could be a sore trial to their friends. Americans then and now would call her a "lovely person."

Lash's book offers a psychological interpretation of why one First Lady threw herself into the great game of politics. Despite all her activity, she did not get very far inside. The President clearly gained immensely in the early years from his wife's zest, her knowledge of people and places, her sometimes highly sentimental and emotional liberalism, her obvious wish to do good. But it is also clear that if he was unfaithful in 1918 – though the evidence is far from clear – he was made to pay a high price for it.

On FDR's death in 1945 Mrs Roosevelt still had 17 years to live. Her admirers and detractors – and there were as many of the latter as of the former – believed that she would gradually fade from public view. Henry Morgenthau told her how upset he was that when he had gone to the White House he had not even been recognized. "Don't you know," she told him, "that if you are out of the limelight three days they will forget you?"; and then she added "They will forget me too." They did not. Indeed, there were those like Frances Perkins, Roosevelt's secretary of labor, who were never fully reconciled to the contrast between the silence that surrounded their activities and the notoriety that still continued to attend Mrs Roosevelt. Miss Perkins was the more critical because, as she put it, "Eleanor Roosevelt did not even have an intellectually tidy mind." And Westbrook Pegler continued to attack "Eleanor the Great," "the Widow," "the Gab." As far as he was concerned she was "a coddler of communists and she lived off the tax payers' largesse." The facts were that Mrs Roosevelt, before her husband's death, had become in her own mind a distinct and public figure. She believed that she had made a success of a professional career outside as well as inside the White House and that she had done it on her own. Accordingly, she continued to be active in a host of good causes, notably in the United Nations. She was, in Arthur Schlesinger Jr's words, "a tough old bird" and people tangled with her at their peril, from Harry S. Truman in the White House to Cardinal Spellman in New York. When she was seventy-five and her husband had been dead sixteen years, she was voted "America's most admired woman" – more popular than Jackie Kennedy, Queen Elizabeth, or even Madame Chiang Kai-shek. Even at that age her professional income totaled more than $100,000 a year, of which lecture fees alone brought in over $33,000 and her general journalism $60,000. As she wrote in that year "When you cease to make a contribution you begin to die."[9]

[9] Joseph Lash, *Eleanor: The Years Alone* (London, Deutsch, 1972).

In fact, Eleanor was not the relict of a great man but the surviving partner of a great firm. She had developed, in her long battles with Franklin, a special role as the custodian of executive morality, a role she perpetuated as moralist to a secular society; but she also developed some sense, watching her husband, of how to mix principle with politics to make policy. When he died she took on his role, as best she could, and added to it her own; again and again, in Lash's stories, she displays the kind of charm, flattery, ruthlessness and compromise that were foreign to her public performances before, but which she learned from the Master. It was no wonder she was formidable; she was continuing on her own, though on a reduced scale, the most successful political act the country had seen.

She must have missed, nevertheless, the special relationship with immediate power she had enjoyed so long, and, in a sense, she tried to establish it again. She was not madly for Adlai Stevenson at first, but she was thrilled by his speeches in the 1952 campaign and for the rest of her life she cared more for his advancement than anyone else, certainly including himself. She carried the fight into 1960, when she pressed him to try for a third nomination against all the odds; she led his losing candidacy at the Convention, and cost him the post of secretary of state which he would have had if he had supported Kennedy instead of doing what Eleanor wanted.

Stevenson was unlike Franklin in almost every way, and Eleanor, in this new partnership, was unlike what she had been. The 1956 campaign, when Stevenson lost to Eisenhower a second time, was a personal as well as a political disaster. He ducked the chance to lead the fight for racial equality, which the Supreme Court had begun two years before with its famous desegregation decision; he chose moderation and politics instead, and lost a great part of his liberal reputation. Eleanor, surprisingly, pushed him this way, and defended his strategy of compromise in her columns and speeches.

Recent revelations of Eleanor's relationship with Lorena Hickok, a reporter with whom she became intimate in 1932, have already begun to reveal the private Eleanor to modern readers. Many readers know from these revelations that older stereotypes of her – as prim Victorian wife and mother, as fearless and peripatetic activist for liberal causes – scarcely begin to capture her complexity. Even so, the illuminating material in Lash's book[10] adds much that was previously unknown. The letters tend to support the statement by Arthur Schlesinger Jr that Eleanor Roosevelt was "the most liberated woman of the century."

[10] Joseph P. Lash, *Eleanor: The years alone*; *Love, Eleanor* (New York, Doubleday, 1973).

10

World War II

1 THE END OF ISOLATION

World War II ended a period not only of isolation and neutrality but of internationalization: an age of Pax Americana maintained, in Secretary of State Charles Evans Hughes' words, "not by arms but by mutual respect and goodwill and the tranquilizing processes of reason." The objectives in the 1930s were clear: to circumscribe the impact of the Soviet Union, to forestall and control the potential resistance of colonial areas, to pamper and cajole Germany and Japan, and to secure from Britain practical recognition of the primacy of Washington in any Anglo-Saxon collaboration. Foreign policy was also a recognition that the US was in the midst of a great depression and of high unemployment. For foreign countries, "Let them solve their own problems" was the attitude. In fact, to insure that no Americans became involved in foreign issues, Congress enacted a series of Neutrality Acts between 1934 and 1937, to prevent a repetition of the events that had brought America into World War I. The nation remained more isolationist than ever. The Neutrality Act of 1937 was designed to go into effect whenever the President proclaimed the existence of a state of war. It forbade American citizens to export arms and munitions to a belligerent, to loan money to a belligerent, or to travel on belligerent ships. A special clause (expiring May 1, 1939) empowered the President to prohibit the export of articles other than arms and munitions, unless the buyer paid cash and took the goods away in his own vessels (the "cash and carry" plan). To further satisfy the isolationists, the Act empowered the President to establish combat zones into which American ships could not go.

Then, in the late 1930s, American foreign policy began to change with public opinion. General N. Grob and George A. Billias outlined this shift:

> The outbreak of World War II in Europe in 1939 proved to be an important turning point in the development of American foreign policy. Domestic concerns such as the great depression and mass unemployment receded into the background as the fear of war swept over the country. Unlike Woodrow Wilson, Roosevelt refused to ask his countrymen to remain neutral in thought as well as action. "This nation," he told the American people in a fireside chat in September, 1939, "will remain a neutral nation, but I cannot ask that every American remain neutral in thought as well." From the very beginning of hostilities, Roosevelt's hope was to offer as much military aid to the Allies as he could without going to war. Upon presidential urging, Congress repealed the arms embargo that was then in effect because the two year cash-and-carry clause of the neutrality act of 1937 had expired. The fall of France in the spring of 1940 intensified Roosevelt's desire to rebuild America's military forces and to give Britain all aid short of war. In 1941 the program of military aid to the Allied cause was expanded considerably by the Lend-Lease Act that was passed in March. By the summer of that year, the United States was involved in an undeclared naval war with Germany, as American naval forces assumed the responsibility of protecting shipping in the western half of the North Atlantic. The most dramatic gesture of American sympathy for the British cause came in August of 1941, when Roosevelt and Churchill met off the coast of Newfoundland and agreed to a joint statement on mutual war aims. Known as the Atlantic Charter, the document not only spelled out the hopes of the two leaders for a better world, but referred specifically to "the final destruction of the Nazi tyranny" as a war aim.[1]

The paradox of these events is that none erased isolationism completely, not even the naval warfare between American ships and German submarines. Only after Japan attacked the United States at Pearl Harbor did the Roosevelt Administration abandon its fictional neutrality and the public strongly support military involvement.

World War II was, in fact, two separate wars. In the West, Hitler had two aims: the first, to seize all of Europe and North Africa so that he could dominate the Mediterranean; and the second, to wipe out Communism and eliminate the Jews. His ally, Mussolini, had his own aims: domination of both the Mediterranean and the Balkans.

[1] Gerald N. Grob and George Athan Billias, *Interpretations of American History: Patterns and Perspectives*, vol. II (New York, Free Press, 1967), p. 384.

As for the Allies, both Britain and France fought to preserve their countries and to stabilize Europe. Roosevelt's aim was broader: the destruction of Nazism and the establishment of democracy throughout Europe. The Soviet aim was to drive out the Nazis and emerge strong enough to continue Communization of the world.

In the Far East the Americans fought to rid themselves of a foe who some thought threatened their Pacific island possessions and their own West Coast. In addition, they were eager to aid Chiang Kai-shek's China. Some Americans also felt it was a good time to eliminate Japan as a serious economic rival. But Japan saw it differently, and posed a major military as well as economic threat.

Late in 1940 the Japanese government became a member of the Axis when it signed a ten-year pact with Germany and Italy which gave the Asiatic power a free hand to establish its new order in Greater East Asia. During 1941 the Japanese militarists, now in complete control, regardless of the ministry of the moment, grew more truculent. They interfered in the political and economic affairs of Thailand and Indochina, ruthlessly pressed the war against China, staged a naval demonstration in the gulf of Siam, and seized the Spratly Islands, only seven miles from the Philippines.

However, the Japanese government kept up a pretense that it desired to reach a peaceful settlement of all outstanding differences between the United States and Japan. Admiral Kichisaburo Nomura, the Japanese ambassador to the United States, tried in vain to convert Secretary Hull to the idea of an *entente cordiale* between the two nations in the Pacific. He demanded that the United States recognize Japanese control of China. After the extreme jingoist, General Tojo, became premier in October 1941, Saburo Kurusu came to the United States as a special envoy on a mission of peace; but the peace which he offered meant that the United States would be expected to abandon China to its fate, to recognize the dominance of Japan in its "Co-prosperity Sphere for Greater East Asia," and to reopen trade in all commodities which the Japanese desired. Secretary Hull made counterproposals for the United States, including the withdrawal of Japan from China and Indo-China, a multilateral nonaggression pact in the Far East, and support of the Chinese republic.

On December 7, 1941, while Nomura and Kurusu were still discussing with Secretary Hull the possibilities for a peaceful settlement in the Pacific, Japanese airmen carried out a "sneak attack" on American warships and defense installations at Pearl Harbor in the Hawaiian Islands, inflicting heavy damage. On the same day, Japanese forces attacked the Philippines, Guam, Hong Kong, and the Malay Peninsula. Next day, December 8, 1941, President Roosevelt asked Congress to declare that a state of war existed between the United States and the Japanese Empire. Three days later Germany and Italy declared war upon the United States – thus saving President Roosevelt from the risk of incurring the opposition of German-Americans by asking Congress to declare war on Germany first.

2 THE US ENTRY INTO WAR

Neither Japan nor America would have come to the brink of war except for the social and economic disruption of Europe after World War I and the rise of Communism and Fascism. These two sweeping forces brought about the tragedy of war between Japan and America. Unfortunately, both countries were inept negotiators driven by paranoiac fear – Japan, by fear of Communism from both Russia and Mao Tse-Tung, and America, by fear of the "yellow peril."

After learning that the Japanese army had pushed into Indochina, FDR froze all Japanese assets in America. In consequence, not only did all trade with the United States cease, but the fact that America had been Japan's major source of oil imports now left Japan in an untenable position. A war that could possibly have been avoided broke out because of mutual misunderstanding and language difficulties, along with Japanese opportunism, irrationality, pride, and fear, and American racial prejudice, distrust, ignorance of the Orient, self-righteousness, and pride.

Bitter political controversy had clouded the issue of war or peace in America. The interventionists, convinced that the nation's future safety depended on its helping to crush the aggressor nations, had in March 1941 pushed through Congress the Lend-Lease Act committing America to unlimited aid, "short of war," to the enemies of the Axis. Lend-Lease bypassed the Cash and Carry policy under which the US had sold armaments to Britain since November 4, 1939 – for by the summer of 1940 Britain was finding it hard to pay for supplies. By the end of the war, Lend-Lease aid would total some $51 billion. Despite the Neutrality Acts of 1936, the United States would be the "arsenal of democracy."

The opponents of intervention included strange bedfellows: the right-wing America Firsters of Charles Lindbergh, Senator William E. Borah, the German-American Bund, the "American peace mobilization" of the Communist and Labor parties, and the traditionally isolationist Mid-West, which, though sympathetic to Great Britain and China, wanted no part of a shooting war. This was especially so among the German-speaking folk of Wisconsin and Minnesota. Some of these domestic tensions eased when the Republicans in 1940 nominated as their Presidential candidate an internationally-minded Indiana businessman, Wendell Willkie; Roosevelt still moved cautiously – 50 destroyers were sent to Britain in September 1940 in the Destroyers-for-Bases deal. He won his third term convincingly in November by 449 to 82 in the Electoral College, 27 million to 22 million in the popular vote.

The bombs at Pearl Harbor on December 7, 1941, and the destruction of 19 ships and 150 planes together with the loss of 2,335 American lives, brought Americans together; but the honeymoon ended when Roosevelt put the blame for Pearl Harbor on the commanders in Hawaii, Admiral Husband Kimmel and General Walter Short. To quell protests the President appointed Supreme Court Justice Owen Roberts to head a Pearl Harbor inquiry. It found Kimmel and Short the principal culprits. Rather than ending the dispute, this stirred vigorous protests, which resulted in several minor inquiries followed by major army and navy inquiries in the summer of 1944.

There was evidence, for instance, that President Roosevelt knew as early as December 4, 1941, that Japanese carriers were approaching Pearl Habor. According to the testimony of Captain Johan Ranneft, naval attaché of the Netherlands in Washington, he was informed by US Naval Intelligence on December 2 that two Japanese carriers were halfway between Japan and Hawaii. Four days later they were some 300–400 miles from Pearl Harbor. He reported this to his government and wrote the details in his war diary. Of course, where the carriers were going and for what purpose was unclear.

Roosevelt had been assured by Marshall that Oahu was the strongest fortress in the world and any enemy task force would be destroyed. The President, therefore, took a calculated risk and lost. This was understandable, but if he instigated a cover-up, as some evidence indicates, that was a serious offense. Perhaps the whole truth will never be known.

3 FRANKLIN D. ROOSEVELT AND WINSTON S. CHURCHILL

Only days after Pearl Harbor, Winston Churchill, Lord Beaverbrook, and a selection of British military leaders steamed out of the Clyde on a new warship, the *Duke of York*, and made the slow voyage in North Atlantic winter weather to see the President in Washington. As Robert E. Sherwood recorded, the food at the White House improved noticeably in Churchill's honor, and drink flowed more freely. Churchill's map room was installed across the hall from his bedroom, and since he used his bedroom as his Washington office a novel traffic of British Embassy personnel and staff officers now enlivened the normally quiet family floor of the old house – whence James and Dolley Madison had fled the British in the War of 1812.

What really mattered for the future, however, was that the British and American war leaders now progressed from mutual liking and respect to warm intimacy. Churchill stayed no less than two weeks at the White House, for there was much to do. Daily he and the President spent hours together, often alone with Hopkins, then acting as Roosevelt's secretary of commerce and administering Lend-Lease aid. Almost daily they lunched together alone with Hopkins; and in the evening there were little parties, for which Roosevelt would perform his ritual of making the cocktails himself, and the Prime Minister would then wheel the President to the dinner table in his light, mobile chair. Nor was that all. Going to bed early and waking early was Roosevelt's habit, rigidly adhered to in normal times; but Churchill's habit was to do the opposite, and temptation led Roosevelt to alter his usually sacred schedule. He was tempted because he could not bear to miss the late-evening talk between Hopkins, so incisive and so laconic, and Churchill, with his grander periods, his flashes of wit, and his sudden pounces on the past to illuminate the present.

Roosevelt and Churchill were of very different natures, as Sir Isaiah Berlin pointed out in his messages home while stationed in Washington during World War II. Churchill, with his enormous historical reading and his position as leader of an Empire on its downward slope, was in essence an historical pessimist with too much heart and courage to accept defeat; whereas Roosevelt, with his provincial though sophisticated origins, his far narrower and more specialized historical knowledge, and his old-fashioned religious faith, was an unquenchable optimist, whose optimism might even have been dangerous if it had not been tempered by his enormous political experience and his almost unfailing political realism.

No wonder, then, that each of these two sometimes doubted the judgment of the other, Churchill thinking Roosevelt too superficial and naively hopeful, Roosevelt thinking Churchill too influenced by the wicked ways of the older world he came from and spoke for. The real wonder is that two great leaders with such immense power and such strong egos should have enjoyed one another so much in these weeks they had together in Washington in the grim time after Pearl Harbor.

Churchill went to Anacostia on his first wartime visit early in 1942 deeply afraid that Roosevelt might give total priority to defeating the Japanese, as would certainly have seemed politically necessary to a President of smaller stature. Instead, Roosevelt entirely understood that by defeating Adolf Hitler, Japan would also be defeated, whereas defeating Japan and its ramshackle new empire would still leave Hitler in control of most of Europe. Hopkins and the American chiefs of staff also saw the priorities in the same way, so the talks in Washington got down to detailed business without long abstract arguments. Many decisions of great future import were therefore taken, for example raising the targets of all forms of American munitions production to astronomical levels, which at first seemed impossibly unpractical to Churchill.

Yet the most far-reaching result of this remarkable Washington reunion of the two allies was the unspoken decision of Roosevelt and Churchill to be close friends forever after. The friendship was the cornerstone of the Western Alliance throughout the war, never interrupted by the differences their correspondence reveals, or dimmed by any of the subsequent meetings.

Franklin Roosevelt was, and remains, a hero to the British. During his rise to power Britain was detached from, and ignorant of, American internal politics to an extent that is not easily imaginable today. The Atlantic in the 1920s and 1930s was still very wide. The majority, even of the politically involved and informed, never crossed it. Very few did so frequently. The bitter internal controversies of Roosevelt's first term and a half therefore passed largely over British heads. There was little awareness of the enmity which he aroused among his moneyed opponents, or of the fluctuations of policy and uncertainties of delegation which flowed from his charismatic character. He appeared as a strong and accepted leader of a united people, almost above the politics at which he was in fact such a determined and skillful player. The result of his second election in 1936, mostly for the wrong reasons, would have been more accurately guessed in Britain than by many in America.

And it mostly gave pleasure and reassurance. At a time when the war shadows were again beginning to lengthen over Europe, it seemed better that the first President since Woodrow Wilson whose name at least was a household word should be confirmed in office. The fact that his first term had been almost entirely lacking in any internationalist initiatives was largely passed over. He was there; he had a great name; and he seemed to be handling the post-depression economy with more success than his British contemporaries. Moreover, with each six months that went by, with each advance of Hitler and with each faltering of the governments of Britain and France, the need for America, symbolized by Roosevelt, became greater, and so there increased the determination to believe, sometimes against the evidence, that he would eventually save the democracies. When, in 1941, Churchill quoted the lines of Clough, familiar to many as a Victorian hymn, he was merely expressing, in a peculiarly evocative form, a thought which had been strongly present in many minds for several years past:

And not through eastern windows only
When daylight comes, comes in the light,
In front the sun climbs slow, how slowly,
But westward, look, the land is bright.[2]

Yet, looking back, it is clear that Roosevelt's path to full involvement in 1939–41 was a much slower and more twisted one than had been President Wilson's approach in 1917. It was not until the meeting with Churchill that he became fully persuaded of the need to join not only the War in the East, but also that in the West.

As American resources were marshaled and unleashed, the disparities of power between the Allies became clearer, however undiminished might be Churchill's own stature and however rich his blarney. Churchill foresaw, moreover, that the American commitment had to go beyond victory, if Europe were to be rebuilt and Britain to recover some economic strength. Roosevelt, on the other hand, clearly envisaged American withdrawal after the job was done – like Truman after him. In particular, Roosevelt made plain his unwillingness to police France, Italy, and the Balkans: "After all, France is your baby and will take a lot of nursing in order to bring it to the point of walking alone." Unquestionably, however, it was Roosevelt, even with his blind spots, who had the wider world vision. The Atlantic Charter, the "Four Freedoms," even the United Nations (Roosevelt's own patented phrase) gradually came to alarm Churchill: he put his trust in crowns and thrones whereas Roosevelt placed his faith in nations and peoples. The remarkable thing in retrospect is that the unreconstructed imperialist and the

[2] Arthur Hugh Clough, "Say Not the Struggle Nought Availeth," in *An Anthology of World Poetry* (London, Cassell, 1929), p. 1109.

international idealist managed to walk together in harmony for so long.

4 GERMANY

Hitler had been wounded by gas in 1918, and had resolved that if he recovered his sight, he would abandon his goal of becoming an architect and enter politics. One night, like Saint Joan, he heard voices summoning him to save his country. All at once, as he recorded in *Mein Kampf*, "a miracle came to pass." He could see! He vowed he would become a politician and "bring Germany from the depths of despair to the greatness she deserved."

Like millions of frontline troops, Hitler believed that Germany had been betrayed by those back home – strikers, malingerers, Jews, politician, profiteers. They had forced the generals to surrender and accept the unjust and shameful Versailles Treaty. Soon he became convinced that the greatest enemy to his crusade for a new Germany was Communism, which he believed had been engendered by Jews. Antisemitism had flourished throughout Europe for centuries, and Hitler found many adherents. Obsessed by his dream of cleansing the Continent of Jews he became a warped archangel. He had intended the elimination of Jews to be his great gift to the world; ironically, it would lead instead to the formation of a Jewish state. He became the leader of Germany's largest party, the National Socialist party (NSDAP) and was appointed Chancellor of Germany in January 1933 by the 86-year-old and failing President Hindenburg. It was the beginning of the Third Reich. On Hindenburg's death in August 1934 Hitler became Führer.

Hitler's plan to seize all of Europe had been set into motion on March 7, 1936, when he sent troops into the demilitarized Rhineland in violation of earlier treaties. The British did not seriously consider taking action and the French feared to do so. Ironically, the Führer had given orders to retreat if challenged by the French; thus, his occupation of the Rhineland was accomplished by default. Then followed moves into Austria, where he was greeted with enthusiasm, and into Czechoslovakia. Finally, on September 1, 1939, his forces invaded Poland. This at last brought a declaration of war from Britain.

As Poland was about to fall, the opportunistic Russian leader Joseph Stalin occupied the eastern half of the country. On September 28, Stalin and Hitler signed a non-aggression treaty. With his rear thus protected, Hitler made plans to invade the West, and in May

1940 sent troops across the borders of Belgium, Holland, and Luxembourg. Caught by surprise, the British and French were soon overwhelmed. The survivors of a British expeditionary force escaped across the English Channel and the French capitulated on June 22.

Now Hitler prepared to turn on his ally, Stalin, and so become the master of all Europe. When massive air raids on England and Scotland failed to subdue the British, he sought to bring them to the negotiating table by capturing Gibraltar. This would not only keep the Royal Navy out of the Mediterranean, thus ensuring Hitler's takeover of North Africa and the Middle East, but drastically lengthen British lifelines to the Far East. Britain would be forced to surrender and become a silent partner in Hitler's crusade against Jewish Bolshevism. All he needed was General Francisco Franco's permission to transport troops through Spain. But to his dismay, the Spanish dictator, though he seemed to agree, kept stalling. He did nothing, thus saving Gibraltar for Britain. Besides fear of aligning himself with a possible loser, Franco had a compelling personal motive: he was part-Jewish.

This setback was followed by another when Italy's Benito Mussolini, who so far had avoided going to war, attempted to seize the Balkans and failed. Hitler felt compelled to do so himself before his attack on Russia could safely be launched; this forced him to postpone that invasion for at least a month. It finally began as Operation Barbarossa on June 22, 1941. Great advances were made until early October, and then sleet turned into snow and the mud froze. The cold intensified, and Field Marshal Gerd von Rundstedt radioed Hitler that his troops must retreat or "they will be destroyed." Instead, the Führer ordered the attack to continue and was caught completely off balance on the night of December 4, when the Soviets launched a massive counter-offensive. Hitler not only lost Moscow, but appeared destined to suffer Napoleon's fate in the winter snows of Russia.

The declaration of war by the US on Japan in December 1941 had thus been preceded by events in the Atlantic and on the European front. But the US had made moves of its own. On April 9, 1941, an American-Danish agreement allowed the United States to occupy Greenland for defensive purposes; on April 24, 1941, the US Navy began patrolling to protect convoys in the Atlantic Ocean as far as longitude 26° west. When, in violation of their treaty, Germany invaded Russia on June 22, 1941, President Roosevelt promised aid to Russia. And on July 7, 1941, the United States made an agreement with Iceland to establish bases on the island to prevent German occupation.

A major step in cooperation with the Allies was the Atlantic Charter (August 14, 1941). President Roosevelt and British Prime Minister Winston Churchill met secretly on August 9–12 at Argentia Bay, Newfoundland, and listed their postwar aims for the world:

1 No territorial aggrandizement;
2 Self-determination for all nations;
3 Easier channels of commerce and access to raw materials;
4 Freedom from want and fear;
5 Freedom of the seas; and
6 Arms reduction.

The two leaders took a major, though happily unannounced, decision, which was to become even more important in December: that the war against the Nazis would have priority. By December the US was in principle as heavily committed in the British struggle against Germany as it would become in its own war in the Pacific. On September 11, 1941, President Roosevelt ordered United States naval ships to shoot at sight at German submarines in American defense waters after the *USS Greer* had engaged a German submarine on September 4. And on September 16, 1941, the US Navy began to escort convoys of merchant ships from Newfoundland to Iceland. Between October 17 and 30, 1941, German submarines torpedoed the *USS Kearny*, killing 11, and sank the *USS Reuben James*, killing 100. Congress allowed the arming of all merchant shipping.

5 THE RESOURCES: ALLIED AND GERMAN COMPARED

In a passage in his history, *The Second World War* (1950), Winston Churchill wrote that after the entry of the US into the war, the defeat of Germany, Italy, and Japan was "merely the proper application of overwhelming force." By 1944 the combined Allied strength against Germany was three to four times greater. Moreover, Germany was without key material resources. The country was self-sufficient in only four items, while the Allies had between them sufficient stocks of all but one vital commodity, rubber.

By 1942 Germany had access to much of Europe's resources, as well as to that of western Russia. It had, however, difficulty in reaching resources outside Europe. For the Allies it was the reverse;

their problem was translating potential resources into forces on the battlefield. German grand strategy throughout the war showed a preoccupation with acquiring further resources, reflected in such decisions as the push for the Caucasus oilfields in southern Russia in 1942, while the Allies' preoccupation was with expanding industrial output and creating a global transport system.

The differences in education and work skills between the belligerents were not sufficiently marked to offset the impact of their population figures: Great Britain and the US with 49 million and 131 million respectively, had only relative difficulties in finding sufficient numbers of skilled workers for their expanding industries. Germany, with a population of only 70 million, suffered from a marked labor shortage, partly offset by the seven million workers from occupied countries who had arrived in the Third Reich by 1944, their status varying from that of genuine volunteers to outright slavery. By D-Day, about 40 percent of Allied prisoners of war (largely those from the Soviet Union) were also working directly or indirectly in German arms production.

The United States and Canada were net food exporters, particularly of wheat, and suffered no major food problems. Although always a net food importer, Great Britain could just about feed itself by rationing and increased agricultural production, as long as it also had access to overseas supplies. But prewar Germany was self-sufficient only in potatoes, and occupied Europe could not feed itself. Germany was fed at ration rates by progressively depriving the occupied countries through a system of quotas, fixed prices, and rationing that amounted to 25 million metric tons of food extracted from occupied Europe by 1944. As a by-product of the food shortage, Germany also suffered shortages in animal fats, leather, and wool, which were partly reduced by the invention of artificial fertilizers from nitrogen after the Allies cut off their supplies of nitrates from South America.

The basic fuels for industrialized societies in the 1940s were bituminous coal and crude oil. In 1944 the Allies controlled or produced about 66 percent of the world's coal. Germany and occupied Europe had considerable coal reserves, but production was hampered by passive resistance in the occupied countries. Estimated coal production for the major belligerents between 1939 and 1945 is as follows:

Germany	2,420,300,000 metric tons
Canada	101,900,000
Great Britain	1,441,200,000

Soviet Union	590,800,000	metric tons
United States	2,149,700,000	
Allied total	*4,283,600,000*	*metric tons*

Apart from its obvious use as fuel for power stations, furnaces, and domestic purposes, coal was also used in the manufacture of explosives, synthetic rubber, medicines including aspirin and the sulfa drugs, and methane gas. The Germans also put considerable effort into converting coal into synthetic oil by combining it with hydrogen.

Petroleum oils and gasoline were the single biggest German deficiency during the war, a fact that at times formed the basis for both German and Allied strategies. In 1944 the world's major oilfields were in Texas, Venezuela, and the Soviet Union, with the oil wealth of the Middle East still largely unexploited, and the allies controlled about 85 percent of the world's oil output. The only source of oil to which the Germans had access was the Ploesti oil fields in Romania. The estimates of oil either produced or imported by the major belligerents between 1939 and 1945 reflects this Allied advantage:

Germany	45,000,000	metric tons
Canada	8,400,000	
Great Britain	90,800,000	
Soviet Union	110,600,000	
United States	833,200,000	
Allied total	*1,043,000,000*	*metric tons*

From 1943 onward the Ploesti oil fields were subject to a bombing campaign by the US Fifteenth Air Force, while German synthetic oil plants formed a major target for US Eighth Air Force bombers.

The standard measure of industrialization in the 1940s was the level of production of iron ore and crude steel. In these the Allies had a significant, but not overwhelming, advantage over Germany, which imported over two-thirds of its iron ore, mainly from neutral Sweden. Iron ore production between 1939 and 1945 is estimated as follows:

Germany	240,700,000	metric tons
Canada	3,600,000	
Great Britain	119,300,000	
Soviet Union	71,300,000	
United States	396,900,000	
Allied total	*591,100,000*	*metric tons*

The figures for crude steel, which was produced by recycling scrap metal as well as directly from iron ore, are as follows for the period between 1939 and 1945:

Germany	159,900,000 metric tons
Canada	16,400,000
Great Britain	88,500,000
Soviet Union	57,700,000
United States	334,500,000
Allied total	*497,100,000 metric tons*

Aluminum, produced from bauxite but also obtained from recycling scrap metal, was most commonly used in aircraft and engine parts. German potential reserves of bauxite and aluminum scrap within Europe during World War II were fractionally greater than those available to the Allies. Nevertheless, Allied superiority over Germany in aluminum production between 1939 and 1945 almost equaled that in steel, although on a smaller scale:

Germany	2,142,300 metric tons
Great Britain	236,500
Soviet Union	283,500
United States	4,123,200
Allied total	*4,643,200 metric tons*

The largest deposits of bauxite then known lay in Dutch and British Guiana (modern Surinam and Guyana respectively), beyond German reach, although the world's largest producer of bauxite was actually France.

Of the less important industrial metals, Germany during the war could obtain only 70 percent of its zinc requirements (chiefly from France and Sweden,) 40 percent of its lead requirements, and 10 percent of its copper requirements. The Allies suffered no significant shortages in these metals, with the largest deposits being found in Australia and Mexico, the United States, and Canada respectively. One important, but not vital, Allied shortage was in tin, owing to the Japanese occupation in 1942 of British Malaya and the Dutch East Indies (parts of modern Malaysia and Indonesia respectively), where most of the world's reserves lay. However, the near impossibility of transporting bulk products from Japan to Germany meant that the Germans also suffered a shortage of tin.

A major German problem was a shortage in ferro-alloys, the comparatively rare metals essential for improving the hardness, lightness, or quality of steel for specialized machinery and weapons. Canada by itself manufactured almost all the world's chrome, either producing it itself or obtaining it from neutral Turkey, and most of the world's manganese, together with such rare metals as molybdenum, vanadium, and platinum, and the micas (naturally occurring silicates of aluminum) used in electrical equipment. In South Africa the Allies also controlled the main source of the world's gold and diamonds which had important industrial applications apart from their commercial value.

The Japanese occupation of British Malaya and the Dutch East Indies also cut the Allies off from almost all the world's rubber, giving the Axis a theoretical advantage in this crucial commodity. Throughout the war, rubber tires for vehicles were strictly rationed by the Allies. But again, it was virtually impossible for Japan to supply Germany with rubber. Commercial rubber also needed to be vulcanized by the addition of sulfur. The world's largest sulfur deposits were found in the United States, and although Italy had substantial sulfur deposits, Germany suffered once more from a serious shortage. Both sides managed to produce synthetic rubber substitutes during the war.

This massive disparity in resources between the Allies and Germany has led historians to a degree of economic determinism in their view of World War II. As long as the three major Allies remained at war, and as long as they committed no major political or strategic blunders, then, without a miracle, the defeat of Germany was indeed inevitable. By D-Day most senior German officers had also accepted this view, and regarded the war as virtually already lost.

6 OPERATION BARBAROSSA AND THE PROGRESS OF THE WAR

Previously classified documents in Russian military archives have divulged that Operation Barbarossa, the German invasion of Russia in June 1941, may have claimed the lives of nearly 49 million men, women and children. This "global loss," which includes those who died from hunger and disease and takes into account the drop in the birthrate after the war, is more than double the 20 million figure which has been the accepted total for 30 years.

The revised estimate of the Russian losses from the "Great Patriotic War of the Soviet Union," from 1941 to 1945, is the result of recent research: the new evidence of the devastating impact of the German offensive is produced in a book to mark the 53rd

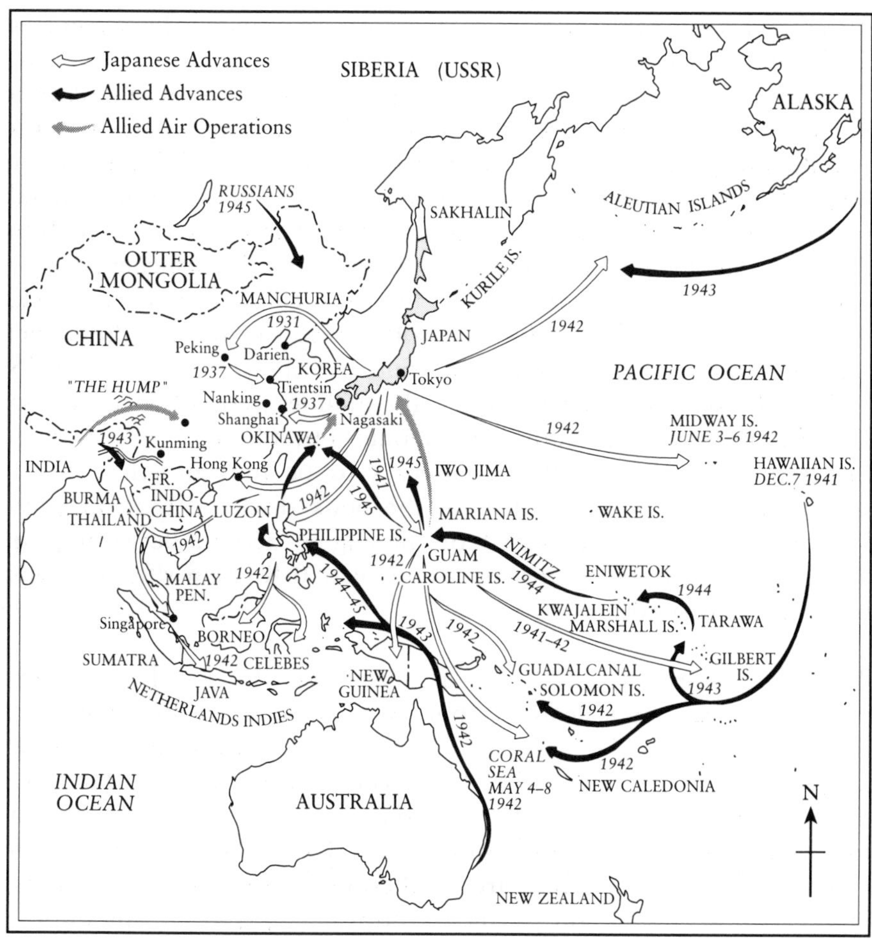

Map 7 World War II: the war in the Pacific.

anniversary of the beginning of Hitler's Operation Barbarossa on June 22, 1941, when German tanks rolled into the Soviet Union to begin a "war of annihilation and racial extermination."[3] After studying the archives, including the 1939 population figures, not publicly available until very recently, John Erickson uncovered a consensus among Russian experts of total war losses of more than 48 million. Taking into account the "actual wartime loss," the wartime "birth deficit" of unborn babies set by some at 10 million –

[3] John Erickson and David Dilks, *Barbarossa, the Axis and the Allies* (Edinburgh, Edinburgh University Press, 1994).

as well as the lower postwar birthrate due to the shortage of males, Erickson said the new total figure represented 23 percent in Soviet human resources.

According to the 1939 census figures, the Russian population immediately preceding the war was 197.1 million. Given natural population growth, the level should have risen to 212.5 million by 1946, but it was only 168.5 million, and by 1950 it had climbed to only 178.5 million. Erickson concluded: "The figure of 20 million military and civilian deaths was announced by Khrushchev, but it was just plucked out of the air for political convenience. Since *glasnost* (introduced by Mikhail Gorbachev, the former President) there has been a great clamour to find out the real figure." Of 35 million Russians called to arms, eight million were killed in action and 18 million were wounded. About 800,000 women served in the Red Army, but their fate appears to be unrecorded.

One statistical work studied for the book disclosed that 631,008 Red Army officers were killed or missing in action. Between June 1941 and June 1943, almost one-third of 670 Russian rifle divisions had been destroyed,

The whole Western world was astonished at the speed of the Japanese advance after Pearl Harbor. Within eight weeks Japan had secured the entire Malay Peninsula. The great British naval base of Singapore fell on February 15, 1942; three weeks later the Japanese had overrun the Netherlands East Indies and by early May British forces had retreated across Burma into India. Japanese bases on New Guinea and in the Bismarck and Solomon Islands were growing in strength. When 43,000 Japanese troops landed 135 air miles north of Manila, General MacArthur withdrew the bulk of his US-Filipino forces to Bataan Peninsula and the adjoining island of Corregidor. After a bitter struggle the defenders of Bataan were driven back, and MacArthur was ordered to fly to Australia. On April 7, more than 76,000 survivors on Bataan surrendered, and a month later General Jonathan Wainwright, MacArthur's replacement, surrendered the remaining troops in the Philippines. Shortly after the Japanese secured the Philippines their forces far to the north moved into the Aleutian Islands, occupying Attu, Agattu, and Kiska, which they held for more than a year before American forces ousted them in 1943.

In the most crucial sea battle of the war at Midway Island, US Navy and Marine airmen sank four carriers on June 4, 1942. America now controlled the Pacific. The Japanese commanders had fought the battle too carefully. In contrast, Rear Admiral Raymond Spruance, bold at the right moment, had launched his strike early.

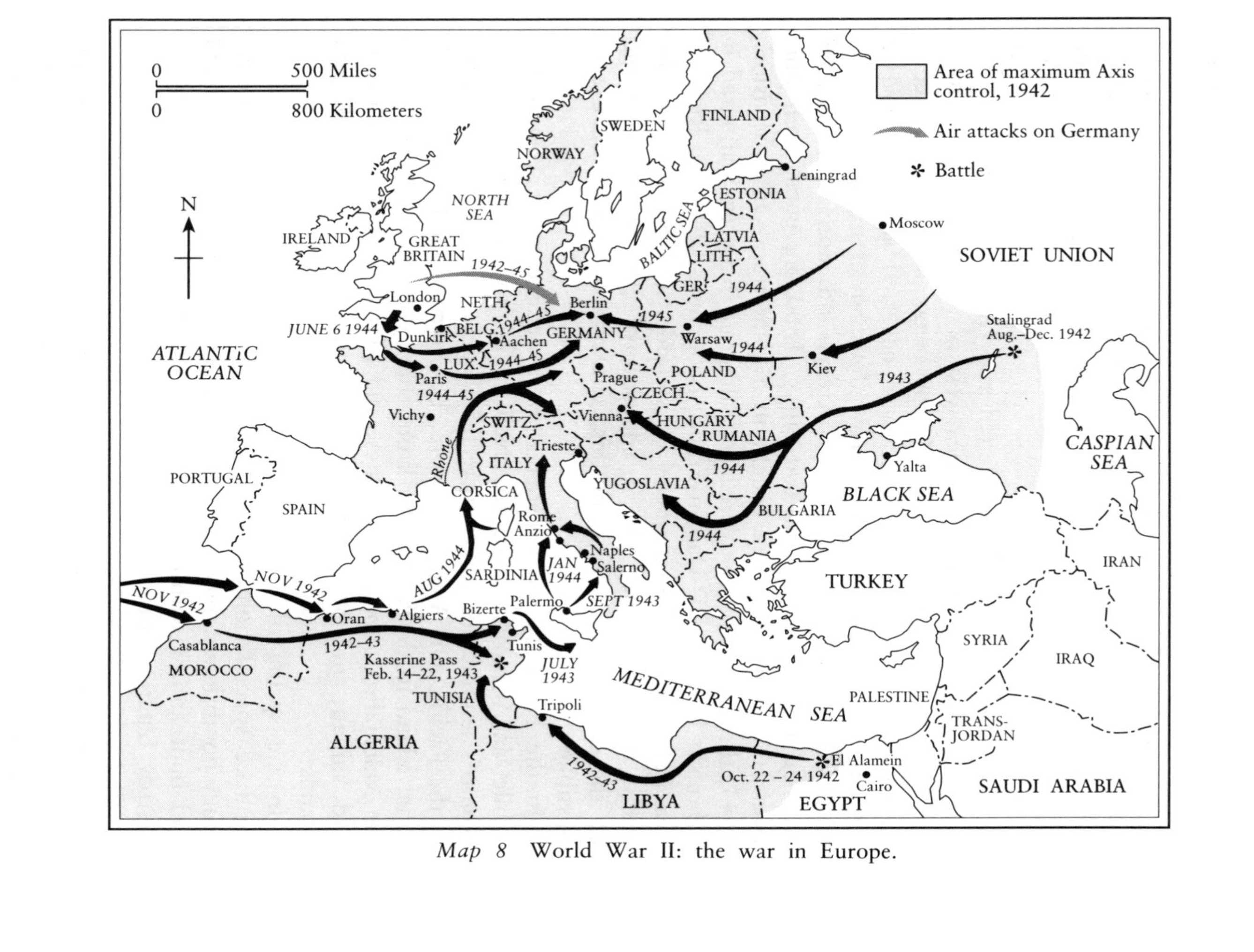

Map 8 World War II: the war in Europe.

The spring of 1942 saw almost no change in Germany's military situation. The eastern front remained stagnant, and General Erwin Rommel was not quite ready for a new offensive in North Africa. Still determined to crush Russia, Hitler ordered a drive into the Caucasus, but rains held it up until June. Then, encouraged by an early success, the Führer made another mistake. He decided to mount a major attack on Stalingrad, an industrial city on the Volga, while continuing the drive to the Caucasus. By mid-September double victory seemed certain – and then the Soviets' defense abruptly stiffened.

When fresh British forces halted the German offensive in the Middle East at Alamein, 80 miles west of Alexandria, in October 1942, Rommel and the Afrika Corps began a retreat that never halted. An even more critical reversal occurred at Stalingrad. On November 22, two arms of a tremendous Soviet pincer movement encircled the entire German Sixth Army, and more than 200,000 German troops along with 100 tanks, 1800 big guns, and more than 10,000 vehicles were caught in a giant trap. On February 2, 1943, the Germans capitulated at Stalingrad. Between Stalingrad in February 1943 and D-Day in France on 6 June 1944, the Russians lost 5.3 million combatants, 49,000 tanks and 30,000 planes – but in June 1944 they were holding down 200 German divisions on the eastern front. Without this, D-Day would never have been possible.

In the Far East the Americans were advancing on two fronts. While MacArthur slogged across New Guinea toward the Philippines, Nimitz's amphibious forces were leapfrogging from island to island in the Pacific. On August 7, 1942, US Marines landed on Guadalcanal Island in the Solomons. From the Solomons they moved into the Marshalls, Gilberts, Carolines, and Marianas; they took Guam and Saipan, and prepared for the reconquest of the Philippine Islands.

In the spring of 1944, American airplane factories began to produce special bombers (B-29s) designed for long flights with heavy bomb loads. Based on airfields in China, which Chinese labor had built almost without tools, these Superfortresses undertook to destroy Japan's industrial centers.

While the United States moved northward and westward across the Pacific Islands, the Chinese kept up their heroic resistance. They were heartened by increasing air support from General Claire Chennault's forces and by the campaign of Chinese and American troops to reopen the Burma Road. At the same time British Empire forces were gradually clearing the Japanese out of Burma.

There were impressive American victories. MacArthur, who had landed on Leyte in October 1944, had cleared the island of defenders by January 12, 1945. While he continued to advance toward Luzon, marines were wiping out the Japanese on the tiny but important island of Iwo Jima.

The war in Europe was marked by the Russian victory at Stalingrad a few weeks after the British Eighth Army victory at Alamein. In the spring of 1943, commanding the exercise Operation Torch from Gibraltar, General Eisenhower's US First Army invaded North Africa on the coasts of French Morocco. The British commander, Bernard Montgomery (Eighth Army), and the American Fifth Army under Mark Clark, led an invading army from North Africa into Sicily, and then at Anzio invaded Italy itself in September 1943. The Italians overthrew Mussolini, who was captured and executed.

During 1943 the British and American navies conquered the submarine and opened the sea lanes to the transport of troops and supplies. By June 1, 1944, Secretary of War Henry L. Stimson stated that more than two million American troops were in Great Britain awaiting the moment for invasion of that part of Europe which lay behind Hitler's Atlantic Wall.

7 OPERATION OVERLORD: THE SECOND FRONT AND THE BEGINNING OF VICTORY

In the judgment of many historians, Operation Overlord owed more to Roosevelt than to any other man. General George C. Marshall, the US Army's chief of staff, with the support of Secretary of War Stimson, championed it vigorously, but Churchill put many obstacles in its path. Although British historians maintain that Churchill strongly favored the cross-Channel attack, and he put himself on record many times to this effect, Churchill devoted a large part of his diplomacy to fostering operations that would have postponed Overlord. As a result, American planners believed that Churchill's real intent was to mount the cross-Channel assault, if at all, only after Russian successes had taken the risk out of it. That view explained to them why Churchill repeatedly insisted that the best place for the Allies to fight was in the Mediterranean, even after the grueling Italian campaign had demonstrated that the northern Mediterranean coast was anything but the "soft underbelly" of Europe. In the face of his energetic and repeated efforts to delay or derail Overlord, a weaker American President might well have given way.

Fortunately for the Allied cause, Roosevelt accepted Marshall's argument that the quickest road to victory in Europe began at the Channel coast of France. American planners were agreed that the war could not be won without invading Germany itself and that operations in the Mediterranean would only delay coming to grips with the core of German strength. Even so, in 1942 FDR sided with Churchill, who wanted to take North Africa before, or probably instead of, attacking German forces in France. Although Marshall opposed Operation Torch as a wasteful diversion, politically there was no getting around it – as even Marshall would concede many years later.

Roosevelt's problem was that Americans were much angrier with Japan than with Germany. At the time of the American entry into the war, Germany had done little damage to the United States, whereas the Japanese had bombed Hawaii and seized many American possessions. (A Gallup poll released on December 20, 1944, found that 13 percent of respondents favored exterminating the entire Japanese population; another, released on 10 June 1945, after the Nazi death camps had been photographed by newsreel cameras and shown in movie theaters, found that 82 percent of Americans believed the Japanese were more "cruel at heart" than the Germans.) These powerful emotions, tinged in some degree by racial animosity, put immense pressure on Roosevelt to concentrate the war effort on Japan. To compound his difficulties, army planners were working on a cross-Channel attack, codenamed Roundup, that would not take place until May 1943. Marshall did advance Operation Sledgehammer, an ill-considered emergency plan to land a few divisions in France during 1942 to take some of the heat off Russia. But even if executed, which fortunately it was not, the troops involved would have been largely British.

If all went as the US Army proposed, therefore, American soldiers would sit out the first 18 months of the war against Germany, during which time public opinion might force Roosevelt to move instead against Japan. However, Roosevelt was committed to beating Germany first, a strategy arrived at in secret talks between British and American military representatives while the United States had still been neutral. To protect that strategy, he decided that Americans had to engage German ground forces at the earliest possible date. Accordingly, on July 25, 1942, FDR ordered his military chiefs to plan for an invasion of North Africa by 30 October.

Operation Torch could not be launched until November 8, and progressed sluggishly after that because Hitler decided to hold North Africa and poured men into Tunisia. Thus when Roosevelt and

Churchill met at Casablanca with their chiefs of staff in January 1943, the cross-Channel operation was receding into the future. Marshall fought hard at Casablanca for a cross-Channel attack (Roundup) but, as he had feared, the North African campaign took too long and was not finished until after Roundup's target date had passed. Further, the great Allied buildup in Africa made an invasion of Sicily inevitable, as the men and machines assembled at such great cost could not be allowed to remain idle. Sicily was so close to the mainland that Italy also would be invaded, from sheer momentum as much as a desire to knock Italy out of the war. Contrary to Churchill's wishes, though, there would be no further large-scale operations in the Mediterranean.

At the next Big Two summit meeting, the Trident Conference in Washington that began on 12 May 1943, FDR and his chiefs insisted that the cross-Channel attack had to be the next big step after Italy and that it must take place in 1944, not 1945 or even 1946 (as suggested by General Alan Brooke, chief of the Imperial General Staff and, after Churchill, the most formidable British commander). With the Americans united against them, the British backed down, accepting 1 May 1944 as the date for D-Day of what was now code-named Overlord. This British retreat was less than it seemed, for Churchill had many arrows left in his quiver and would shoot them all at Overlord before he was finished.

At the November Sextant Conference in Cairo, just before the Teheran Conference, the British argued that Operation Buccaneer, a proposal to invade the Andaman Islands off Burma, must inevitably delay Overlord. Then when the Big Three – Roosevelt, Churchill and Russian leader Joseph Stalin – met for the first time at Teheran during November-December 1943, Churchill spent days arguing for more peripheral campaigns. Finally, on 30 November, worn down by the resistance of Roosevelt and Stalin, and with the British chiefs having agreed to it, Churchill once again accepted Overlord. Stalin then ensured its success by promising to launch a Soviet offensive timed to prevent Germany from reinforcing its French garrison with troops withdrawn from the eastern front (an offensive that actually began on 23 June – late, but not fatally so.)

On 5 December in Cairo, Roosevelt made what has been deemed one of his most important and best decisions of the war: General Dwight D. Eisenhower would command Overlord. General Marshall, who very much wanted the job, was the sentimental favorite of most American leaders. He had built the US Army up from scratch and deserved the opportunity to lead it in its greatest battles. According to Marshall, Roosevelt in breaking the news to him said:

"I feel I could not sleep at night with you out of the country." This was tactful, and perhaps true as well, but in the view of many historians, Roosevelt judged Eisenhower to be better qualified to lead the most critical Allied attack of the war. Marshall, though a brilliant staff officer, had never commanded troops in battle, while Eisenhower was a veteran of three amphibious invasions. His unique experience and growing skill were significant Allied assets. Of major importance was the fact that he was liked and trusted by the British, an essential requirement for combined operations.

Sentiment aside, it made little sense to put the untried Marshall in charge of Overlord. Nor was there much to be said for making Eisenhower chief of staff, which was to have been his job when Marshall left it, since the army was already being led by the greatest chief in history. Keeping the right men in the right jobs was Roosevelt's second most important contribution to Overlord, and may have been a crucial one, since Marshall's inexperience would have brought additional risk to an operation that was by its very nature hazardous. Roosevelt took the prudent course and history would justify it.

Subsequently Roosevelt's main task would be to keep Churchill from putting off Overlord for the sake of various Mediterranean schemes that he persisted in promoting. As the campaign in Italy bogged down, Churchill railed against the "tyranny" of Overlord, since the troops being sent to England to prepare for it would, to his mind, be better employed in the Italian campaign – which he apparently hoped would make Overlord unnecessary. Roosevelt bent over backward to accommodate Churchill. When Allied planners proposed to outflank the German Gustav Line by landing behind it in Anzio, there were too few LSTs (Landing Ships, Tank) available to ensure success. Roosevelt arranged for 56 LSTs, scheduled for Britain and Overlord to be kept in the Mediterranean. This made it possible to invade Anzio on 22 January 1944, but prompt German counterattacks bottled up the American troops, and Anzio became another stalemate leading to renewed British demands.

Churchill began insisting that Operation Anvil, landings on the Mediterranean coast of France in support of Overlord, be canceled or put off. In this, too, he would fail. Roosevelt had promised Stalin, who regarded Anvil as an essential complement to Overlord, that the French Riviera would be invaded. Eisenhower, worried about supplying the Allied armies in France, wanted its southern ports. But there were still not enough LSTs to go around, so it was finally decided that Anvil would have to wait until landing

Plate 8a UN troops taking part in the D-Day landings

Plate 8b Their Supreme Commander, General Eisenhower, with the US 101st Airborne Division before take off for Normandy. (Library of Congress.)

ships could be released from Overlord and sent to Italy to pick up the assault troops.

Another of Roosevelt's contributions to victory was the tactical bombing of French rail and road targets in preparation for Overlord. Inevitably, French civilians would be killed as a result of these sorties. Although most Free French leaders accepted them as part of the price of liberation, Churchill and his advisers were afraid that French resentment over these casualties would become a serious problem. On this issue Roosevelt remained adamant, informing Churchill on 11 May 1944 that he would not support any limitations on the military that would jeopardize Overlord or cause additional Allied losses. He was vindicated here as well, since French civilian casualties proved to be much lower than Churchill feared, while the bombing itself was sensationally effective. There was no French backlash afterward.

In the early hours of June 6, 1944, United Nations troops, on orders from their supreme commander, Dwight D. Eisenhower, left their bases in Great Britain and crossed the Channel to storm the French beaches in Normandy. Preceded by airborne paratroopers and protected by an awesome bombardment from the huge battle fleet, they soon established beachheads and, with the aid of the air forces, connected their landings into one battle front. The invasion of Europe on D-Day was the greatest amphibious operation of any war to date. It required 10 divisions, and used 11,000 ships which had assembled in the weeks before in a vast armada moored from the Wash to South Wales. Seven thousand aircraft were deployed overhead. On D-Day itself, 150,000 men left the South of England, and in the next two weeks one million men followed. Ten thousand were killed on the first day. Within 12 weeks of these successful landings, the Allied armies had conquered Normandy, overrun Brittany, chased the Germans north of the Seine, and assisted the French Forces of the Interior in liberating Paris. In August new landings were made with slight loss, on the Mediterranean coast of France near Marseilles. On August 26, General Eisenhower announced that the Seventh German Army had been destroyed and warned the residents of Alsace, Lorraine, and Luxembourg that they would soon be in the path of the retreating Nazis. The Battle of France had been won.

The Germans did not expect an invasion on June 6, 1944. Rommel was at home in Herrlingen, near Ulm. Informed of the invasion by telephone, he reached Reims by afternoon, where he gave the order to throw the Twenty-first Panzer Division into battle. Though stationed right on the coast, it had not yet been deployed by the army group's chief of staff, Major-General Hans Speidel, because the situation long remained unclear. In the night of June 6 Rommel arrived at his headquarters and took command. His beach barriers proved inadequate in the face of the Allied landing as superiority in matériel overwhelmed the operational and tactical planning of the German staff. Allied firepower (naval armament and bombardment) permitted little but tactical countermeasures.

The day before the Allies' great offensive began on July 18 at Caen, starting the breakout from the landing zone, as Rommel was returning to La Roche-Guyon from the headquarters of Panzer Group West, his car was by hit by the cannon of a British Spitfire, severely injuring him. He was taken to a hospital in France, and on August 8 returned to Herrlingen. Thus he missed further combat in the west, as well as the conspiracy of July 20, 1944. On that day Colonel Claus Count Schenk von Stauffenberg brought a bomb to the Führer's headquarters in East Prussia; its explosion was to set off a coup attempt, which, however, was defeated the same day. Speidel, Rommel's chief of staff, was involved in the plot, many of whose participants had hoped for the cooperation of the popular field-marshal. Stauffenberg's cousin, Lieutenant-Colonel Caesar von Hofacker, had sounded Rommel out; Rommel's answer is not known, but Rommel was not informed about the assassination attempt itself. He no doubt hoped to come to terms with his old adversary Montgomery, now leading the British Twenty-first Army Group in France. Verbally, and in a letter of July 15, Rommel had attempted to win Hitler over to negotiations, but he always met with abrupt rejections. Hitler's court took prompt action against the conspirators; most were executed, and Rommel himself came under suspicion. On October 14, 1944, when two generals appeared at Rommel's house in Herrlingen and offered him the alternatives of poisoning himself or facing the Nazi tribunal, he chose the former. Rommel received a state funeral, at which Field-Marshal von Rundstedt delivered the eulogy. The cause of death was kept secret. In this shabby way Hitler rid himself of his most prominent military leader.

After D-Day Roosevelt's main task was to keep Anvil, renamed Dragoon, on schedule. This he did, though of all his struggles with Churchill, preserving the timetable for Dragoon was one of the hardest. Numerous messages passed between them for weeks after D-Day, the prime minister using every argument he could muster to block, or at least minimize, Dragoon for the sake of operations in Italy. Not until after July 1, 1944, when Churchill made his last attack on Dragoon did Britain finally give way. Dragoon took place on August 15 and contributed significantly to the Allied victory in France. German resistance just west of the Rhine proved to be surprisingly determined but was overcome by Allied military power. In December 1944, the Germans mounted an offensive that created a huge bulge in the Allied lines: the Battle of the Bulge. After yielding some valuable ground, the American and British troops stood firm. One young American general, Anthony McAuliffe, when the Germans pressed him to surrender gave the simple but memorable reply: "Nuts!"

While incessant bombing pounded the German railroads into rubble, the American First Army reached the Remagen Bridge, crossing the Rhine southeast of Cologne. On March 8, 1945, the first troops crossed the river and moved into the interior of Germany.

For the next two months the United Nations armies in the west advanced steadily, while the Russians cut through Austria and closed in on Berlin. Hitler and other Nazi high officials, aware that the end was near, either committed suicide or went into hiding. On May 7, at Reims, France, a representative of the German general staff (which had taken over after Hitler's death) accepted the terms of "unconditional surrender." V-E Day was announced to an expectant world.

Roosevelt was felled at his desk in the "little White House" in Warm Springs, Georgia, at 13.15 on April 12, 1945. He was pronounced dead of a massive cerebral hemorrhage at 15.35. Though he did not live to see it, he knew at the time of his death that victory in Europe was near. Overlord had done its work, and so too had Roosevelt by making the great venture possible.

In one area, which turned out to have no military significance, Roosevelt met defeat. FDR disliked Charles de Gaulle, the leader of the Free French, and insisted that until elections were held, Eisenhower should govern liberated France. The British Foreign Office strongly opposed the decision, feeling that de Gaulle would take charge in any case, but Churchill, having fought Roosevelt on so many matters, declined to make an issue of it. All the fuss was for nothing. While de Gaulle was given no part to play in Overlord, he could not be kept from visiting Normandy on D plus 6. He was rapturously received by the populace and left behind one of his officers to look after civil affairs. No more was heard of AMGOT (Allied Military Government for Occupied Territory), which Roosevelt had intended to rule France. The legacy in peacetime was de Gaulle's bitterness towards Churchill. When he became President of France, he did his best to thwart Britain's entry into the European Economic Community, with consequences that are still with us. What eventually emerged as the European Union was originally in essence a Franco-German economic federation.

8 POLITICS

During the preconvention primaries for the 1944 election, Wendell Willkie, who had lost to Roosevelt in 1940, came to the conclusion that he could not again secure the Republican nomination. His position in the party, however, was still strong, and he used his influence to counteract the isolationist views of such Republicans as Colonel Robert McCormick of the Chicago Tribune. Those who were reluctant to make any positive commitments concerning the role of the United States in the postwar world probably would have preferred Governor John W. Bricker of Ohio or Senator Robert A. Taft, also of Ohio as the party nominee. They yielded, however, to the apparent popularity of Governor Thomas E. Dewey of New York and nominated him with but one dissenting vote in the convention, which was held at Chicago in June. Governor Bricker was unanimously chosen for the second place on the ticket.

When the Democrats assembled in Chicago in July, they knew that President Roosevelt was willing to be nominated for a fourth term. This they proceeded to do on the first ballot, though the opponents of a fourth term cast some 96 votes for Senator Harry F. Byrd of Virginia. Most of them came from Southern delegations. The drama of the convention came in the fight of Vice-President Wallace for renomination. Though he led on the first ballot, his defeat was finally brought about by an understanding between certain Southern delegates and the leaders of several powerful political machines in Northern cities. Senator Harry Truman of Missouri was named in a stampede on the second ballot.

More than 45,531,000 Americans voted on November 7, 1944, giving President Roosevelt a plurality of slightly over three million votes. In the electoral college the President had 432 votes to 99 for Governor Dewey. The greatest Republican strength was in rural counties. Roosevelt's sudden death on April 12, 1945, elevated Vice-President Truman to the presidency.

Even before World War II Congress had created the House Committee to Investigate Un-American Activities (May 26, 1938) to investigate Fascist, Communist, and other organizations. On June 27, 1940, President Roosevelt revived by proclamation the Espionage Act of 1917. The Alien Registration Act (Smith Act, June 29, 1940) required the registration of all aliens and tightened laws for deportation. The Act also made it illegal to advocate or teach the overthrow of any government of the United States by force or to organize a group dedicated to such a purpose. On February 19, 1942, President Roosevelt authorized the secretary of war to exclude persons from restricted military areas. As a result the Secretary removed 110,000 Japanese or Japanese-Americans from the West Coast to relocation camps in the interior during February-March 1942. The Supreme Court in *Hirabayashi* vs. *United States* (1943) upheld military curfew rules on the West Coast and in *Korematsu* vs. *United States* (1944) upheld the relocation program which ended on January 2, 1945.

9 THE WAR IN THE PACIFIC, 1941–1945

On December 8, 1941, the Japanese bombed the Philippines, Wake Island, Guam, and Midway, the same day as the Pearl Harbor attack. (The date differs because of the International Date Line.) On December 10, the Japanese sank the British capital ships *Prince of Wales* and *Repulse* in the South China Sea. They captured Guam, Wake, and Hong Kong between December 13 and 25.

Within eight weeks Japan had secured the whole Malay Peninsula, including Singapore, and within another month had overrun the Netherlands East Indies; by early May British forces had retreated across Burma into India. Under the command of General Douglas MacArthur, American and Filipino troops heroically defended the Bataan peninsula and the fortress of Corregidor until resistance was no longer possible; MacArthur transferred his headquarters to Australia (February 22), but his men under General Jonathan Wainwright held Corregidor until May 6, 1942. By the early autumn of 1942 the Japanese had occupied one million square miles of territory, including, far to the north, the Aleutian Islands (occupying Athu, Agattu, and Kiska, which they held until 1943).

The first defeat for the Japanese came between May 4 and June 6, 1942. At the Battle of the Coral Sea, the United States checked the Japanese advance in the southwestern Pacific by sinking or damaging three Japanese carriers (May 4–8). A month later the fleet prevented the Japanese conquest of Midway Island by destroying four Japanese aircraft carriers in the Battle of Midway (June 3–6). These battles marked a turning point in the war in the Pacific, and within two months the United States was on the offensive.

The first American advance in the Pacific came in the Solomon Islands, where Marines landed on Guadalcanal and other islands on August 7, 1943. The Japanese sank four Allied cruisers in the Battle of Savo Island, near Guadalcanal (August 9), but four American naval victories (between August 23 and November 15), in which the Japanese lost two battleships, kept Japanese reinforcements at a minimum. The Japanese abandoned Guadalcanal on February 9, 1943. For the next two years the story in the western Pacific is of the Japanese avoiding battle, and of their steady loss of island after island. General MacArthur, and Admirals Chester Nimitz and William Halsey, advanced from the Solomons into the Marshalls, Gilberts and Marianas; they took Guam (July 1944) and Saipan and prepared for the reconquest of the Philippines.

Allied forces under Lord Louis Mountbattan and US General Joseph W. Stilwell (recalled October 18, 1944, after bitter disagreements with Chinese ruler Chiang Kai-shek), took Myitkyina, Burma (August 3, 1944) and enabled the Allies to open the Ledo Road to China by the end of the year. The capture of Mandalay on March 20 and of Rangoon on May 3, 1945, completed the reconquest of Burma.

The United States began Superfortress (B-29) air attacks on Japan with a raid on Kyushu from bases in China (June 1945), and the raids continued until the end of the war. In the Battle of the Philippine Sea (June 19–20, 1944) the Japanese lost three aircraft carriers and several hundred planes and suffered heavy damage to battleships and cruisers. When General MacArthur's forces invaded the island of Leyte in the Philippines (October 20), the Japanese made one last naval attack. In the Battle of Leyte Gulf, one of the greatest naval battles of all time, the United States sank 3 battleships, 4 carriers, and 10 cruisers, and eliminated the Japanese fleet as a factor in the war. The United States invaded Luzon on January 9, 1945, and captured Manila on February 24. American casualties in the Philippine campaign amounted to about 60,000.

Between February 19 and June 21, 1945, the approach to Japan took place: United States Marines captured the island of Iwo Jima after a month of heavy fighting and casualties of 20,000. On April 1, the United States invaded Okinawa in the Ryukyus and had conquered the island by June 21. Many of the 50,000 American casualties were the result of Japanese suicide airplane (*kamikaze*) attacks.

Since 1930 research had been going on into the production of nuclear energy. Ernest O. Lawrence constructed the first cyclotron in 1930, making it possible to smash atoms. Enrico Fermi, who came to the United States in 1939, and others in Europe and the United States, carried out experiments between 1935 and 1939 in producing nuclear energy by splitting Uranium-235 atoms. When Arthur H. Compton, Fermi, and others produced the first controlled chain reaction in unseparated uranium in Chicago in December 1942, it pointed the way toward the atomic bomb. On May 1, 1943, the Army Corps of Engineers under General L. R. Groves took over the so-called "Manhattan Project" to develop the bomb. American and British scientists under Dr J. R. Oppenheimer finally produced a bomb at Los Alamos, New Mexico and exploded it at Alamagordo, NM, on July 16, 1945.

After Okinawa was occupied on July 12, the defeat of Japan was inevitable. Convinced that a direct attack on the four main islands of Japan would be too costly, President Harry S. Truman ordered the dropping of atomic bombs on Hiroshima and Nagasaki. The first bomb was dropped on Hiroshima on August 6; the second was dropped 3 days later on Nagasaki. Both cities were virtually obliterated. At an imperial conference Emperor Hirohito announced that the time had come to bear the unbearable. On August 15, 1945, he informed his people over a nationwide radio hookup that Japan was surrendering. Japan signed the surrender documents on board the USS *Missouri* on September 2.

10 THE COST

Within a year after Pearl Harbor the US produced 47 billion dollars' worth of war material, including 32,000 tanks, 49,000 airplanes, and 8,200,000 tons of merchant shipping. The manufacture of many peacetime commodities was either curtailed or prohibited in order to facilitate war production, but the net income of American corporations rose from $17,000,000 in 1940 to $28,000,000 in 1943.

Organized labor generally refrained from strikes and jurisdictional disputes during the first year of the war. When labor strife did flare up in 1943, Congress finally passed the Smith-Connally Bill, prohibiting strikes in plants which were working on war contracts and authorizing the President to seize plants where labor disturbances impeded defense production. American labor, however, scarcely needed such legislation to spur it on to great efforts. Its production record from 1940 to 1944 surpassed any previous record in the nation's history. At the same time, average weekly earnings rose from $25.20 to $46.08, while the length of the working week also increased from 38.1 to 45.2 hours. With the approval of the War Shipping Board, Henry J. Kaiser demonstrated the possibilities of the prefabricated vessel, which could be constructed in 78 days or less. Speed made possible the "victory fleet" which kept the service of supply more than adequate after the first few months of war.

Between January 1940 and January 1943, the appropriations for national defense and war amounted to approximately $220 billion, or slightly more than the cost of government from George Washington's Inauguration to 1940. From 1941 to 1945 the national debt rose from about $47 billion to $247 billion. By the second year of the war it was estimated that war's daily cost to the American people was $1.15 for every man, woman, and child in the population, while receipts from taxes were scarcely 40 cents per person. Successive tax bills were designed to increase the proportion of the cost of the war which would be met through taxation. This was accomplished by lowering the individual exemptions, thus adding millions of new taxpayers to the lists, increasing the rates of the normal tax and surtax on incomes, and virtually confiscating all corporate earnings which represented excess profits from the war. Congress finally accepted in 1943 a plan to place collection of federal income taxes on a pay-as-you-go basis (suggested by Beardsley Ruml, who was then treasurer of Macy's department store.)

Despite the increased revenues from taxes, the government relied upon war savings stamps and war bonds to meet the bulk of the war costs. Prior to July 1945, the Treasury Department conducted seven successful war bond drives with total subscriptions of $61 billion.

Financing the war

	1941	1943	1945
Federal expenditures ($ billion)	13.3	79.4	98.4
Federal expenditures for major national security ($ billion)	6.0	63.2	81.2
Federal receipts ($ billion)	7.1	22.0	44.5
Federal receipts from individual and corporate Income taxes ($ billion)	3.5	16.3	35.1
Federal debt ($ billion)	49.0	136.7	258.7
Gross National Product ($ billion, 1929 prices)	138.7	170.2	180.9
Wholesale commodity price index (1926 = 100)	87	103	106
Unemployment (millions)	5.6	1.1	1.0

There were, of course, human costs too. The numbers of those who died speak for themselves.

Casualties in World War II
(000)

	Total mobilized	Killed or died	Wounded
United States	16,113	407 [a]	672 [b]
China	17,251	1,325 [c]	1,762
Germany	20,000	3,250	7,250
Italy	3,100	136	225
Japan	9,700	1,270 [c]	140
USSR	– [d]	6,115	14,012
United Kingdom	5,896	357	369

[a] 292,000 of these were killed in battle.
[b] The United States also had 124,000 captured.
[c] Killed in battle only; China, 1937–45.
[d] Total mobilization figure, including civilian population, unavailable.

11

Harry S. Truman and the Cold War

1 THE SON OF THE MIDDLE BORDER

To tell the story of Harry S. Truman is to realize why Americans still have faith in the Lincoln myth, "from log cabin to White House," why they believe that "it can happen here." It is the story of a very ordinary American, born in the small town of Lamar, Missouri, close to the geographical center of the 48 states, Kansas City. He was literally and metaphorically, a man of Independence, since his home became his wife's birthplace, the small Missouri court-house town, six miles east of the spot where the Kansas River joins the Missouri – indeed, his wife Bessy Wallace lived her 97 years in the same house there except for the years in Washington, DC. He was, at least geographically, a son of the Middle Border. Harry Truman's roots were in the Civil War borderlands. His grandmother Young remembered how a Union general had stopped at her Missouri farm in 1861, seizing 15 mules and 13 horses, shooting 400 hogs, and forcing her to make biscuits for the raiders until her fingers blistered, while the future President's mother cringed under the table.

Truman, born in 1884, less than 20 years after Appomattox, was a bookish child who loved to play the piano and read widely in American and classical history. After high school he worked as a bank teller and then helped manage his Grandfather Young's family farm in Grandview, ten miles south of Kansas City. He joined the new Kansas City National Guard unit in 1905. His eyesight was so poor that it made him averse to games – it prevented his applying for West Point and embarking on a military career. His taste in youth was for music, but not for book-learning; on becoming a Senator in 1934 he enrolled for evening classes in Washington University. His career until he was 50 ran through a steady course of failures, on the farm, in oil, in haberdashery. He was a small farmer, dogged by a mortgage; he made so little money that as late as 1940, when he was a Senator, the mortgage was foreclosed, and his mother turned out with her furniture. After serving as a captain of field artillery in France during World War I, he ran a haberdashery business, which collapsed in 1921, attended Kansas City School of Law (1923–5), and, with the backing of the Democratic boss T. J. Pendergast, entered Kansas politics.

The Trumans were always in politics. Harry Truman's father, John, was a country road overseer at a time when road-building was just being undertaken seriously by local governments. He was allied with the Goats, the Jackson County Democratic faction which was headed by Alderman Jim Pendergast and opposed by the Rabbits, led by Joe Shannon. (These factions, led by Tom Pendergast and his son and by Frank Shannon, were still contesting elections in Kansas City in 1944.)

Truman was one of the Pendergast machine, and thus a member of a notoriously efficient group who controlled political appointments and rewards, paving and building contracts in Kansas City, Missouri. Pendergast served a term of imprisonment in Leavenworth for tax evasion – the non-payment of taxes as a federal offense was and is one of the few crimes that permits federal probing of state and local budgets (as with the case against Al Capone.) Truman's oil venture failed; so did his store. Truman was presiding judge of Jackson County (1926–34) when he was elected to the US Senate (1935–44), where he achieved national prominence as head of the very effective and immensely industrious Senate Committee investigating wartime government expenditures. In 1944 he was his party's candidate for Vice-President and took office with President F. D. Roosevelt. He replaced Henry Wallace who had served as Vice-President during the war, but was thought too left-wing in the pro-Russian years; at the Democratic convention, though, Wallace led on the first ballot, but Truman won on the second, thanks to an alliance of Southern delegates with northern Democratic political machines.

At 40 Truman was unemployed and uncertain of the future. At 61 he was the President of the United States. "Who the hell is Harry Truman?" asked Admiral Leahy on being told by FDR that Truman was to be his running mate in the 1944 campaign. The question had been asked before.

What success Truman won in politics seems to have been due to three factors. The first was luck – "the luckiest buzzard I ever knew" – the luck of the failure in oil: "Dave, maybe I wouldn't be President if we'd hit." It was the failure of his drapery store which pushed him into politics. The second was his apprenticeship in the Pendergast machine, where he developed those qualities of camaraderie and of folksiness that are indispensable to recognition in American public life. As a veteran he spoke the tough language needed on the Middle Border; his tastes were for poker and straight bourbon. If he lacked Roosevelt's political flair and his capacity as spellbinder, his plebeian qualities were nearer to America's grass roots than that rich patrician grace bred on the Hudson River. It was the Kansas City machine which put Truman into the Senate in 1934, where for the first term he seemed indeed "the Senator for Pendergast," but where in his second he showed industry and skill in heading the committee investigating national defense, which made his name.

And third, if he was nominated for the Vice-Presidency in 1944 because he was a more neutral figure than Wallace or James Byrnes, it was also with a clear recognition by the bosses that before long he would probably be in the White House. If he was with the machine on questions of patronage, he was for Roosevelt on policy. Though he had not the style of the master, his democracy was as genuine as Andrew Jackson's.

2 THE PRESIDENT: 1945

When Roosevelt died in April 1945, Truman succeeded to the presidency at a most critical period in the nation's history. He said that he felt as if the moon, the stars, and all the planets had fallen on him. But he soon showed an old soldier's decisiveness. Truman rapidly replaced Roosevelt's Cabinet with one of his own choosing, mainly from his former colleagues in the Senate. Deeply concerned over the grave international situation, he paid special attention to the State Department; James F. Byrnes, long a Senator for South Carolina, became secretary of state. He guided foreign policy until 1947, when General George C. Marshall, whom Truman greatly admired, succeeded him. Truman continued his predecessor's policies until the war's end, however, and attended the Potsdam Conference of July 1945, at which, Clement Attlee, the British Labour leader, replaced Churchill, and the Allies made postwar plans; and at the end of the war in August 1945, he gave his attention to the responsibilities that the US had inherited as the richest and most powerful of nations. To curb the spread of Soviet influence, in March 1947 he enunciated the Truman Doctrine and in July 1947 implemented the Marshall Plan for economic recovery in Europe. Diplomatic relations with the Soviet Union became increasingly strained when the Russian blockade of Berlin was answered by the Berlin airlift in 1948–9.

Cabinet changes were numerous during the Truman years, as the President sought efficient assistants who could also be politically helpful. With the death of Chief Justice Stone, Fred H. Vinson of Kentucky, then secretary of the Treasury, was named chief justice of the Supreme Court. President Truman called his Missouri friend, John W. Snyder, to Washington to be secretary of the Treasury. In 1947 Truman issued a Loyalty Order to oust from executive departments persons whose activities or associations were disloyal to the United States. A Loyalty Review Board was created to carry out this policy.

An Act of 1947 revised the line of succession to the presidency. The Speaker of the House and the president *pro tempore* of the Senate were placed next in line after the Vice-President; Cabinet officers followed in order of rank. The Twenty-second Amendment, passed by Congress in 1947 and ratified in 1951, prohibited any future President from being elected for more than two terms.

After months of rather bitter debate among the representatives of the armed services, Congress created a Department of Defense by a merger of the War and Navy Departments. In 1947 President Truman named secretary of the Navy James V. Forrestal as head of the new department. At the same time secretaries were designated for the army, navy, and air force interests within the Defense Department. The draft, which had been allowed to lapse for a year, was re-established by the Selective Service Act of 1948, which provided for the induction of enough men to provide an adequate defense establishment.

The problem of administering the conquered nations – Germany and Japan – and of guiding their people into normal relations with the Western world proved to be a long and difficult task. Conquered Germany was divided into zones of occupation, assigned to the military forces of the United States, the Soviet Union, Great Britain, and France respectively. Secretary Byrnes and his associates slowly formulated the general principles underlying American policy. As announced at Stuttgart, Germany, in September 1946, it provided for the long-term military occupation of the defeated country but promised that the German people would be assisted in their efforts to find an honorable place among the free and peace-loving nations of the world. The tremendous task of working out the details of this assistance fell upon the shoulders of General Lucius Clay and his associates in the Military Government until May, 1949, when John J. McCloy was appointed first United States civilian High Commissioner to the new Federal Republic of Gerrnany and also military governor of the United States occupation zone.

Ruling through Emperor Hirohito of Japan, General Douglas MacArthur tried to start the Japanese people along the democratic way. By July 1947, the General was able to announce that Japanese military forces had been disarmed, demobilized, and absorbed in peaceful pursuits and that Japan's remaining war potential was completely neutralized. In that year a new constitution was adopted, providing for democratic elections and limiting the powers of the emperor.

It was agreed that North Korea was to be occupied by the Soviet Union, South Korea by the United States. A Communist administration gained control in the north, and a republic, with Syngman Rhee as first president, was established in the south. By mid-1949 all occupying forces had been withdrawn.

The process of framing satisfactory peace treaties proved to be tortuous and tedious. Procedural difficulties developed in the Council of Foreign Ministers of the four great powers – the United States, the Soviet Union, Great Britain, and France. As tension increased between East and West, it became impossible to continue a joint policy toward former enemy nations. In 1947, after more than a year of negotiations, the Council of Foreign Ministers concluded peace treaties with Italy, Romania, Hungary, Bulgaria, and Finland. The treaties provided for reparations, demilitarization, and territorial adjustments. It was not until 1955 that a peace treaty was signed with Austria, restoring that nation to full sovereignty and prohibiting economic or political union with Germany.

Progress toward a peace treaty with Germany proved even more difficult because of the impasse over economic and political terms between the Western powers on one side and the Soviet Union on the other. In 1948 the Federal Republic of Germany – comprising the occupation zones of the United States, Great Britain, and France – was proclaimed. In May, 1952, these nations, acting without the concurrence of the Soviet Union, authorized their foreign ministers to sign a convention with the Federal Republic which restored its independence and recognized it as an equal partner in the West European alliance. Full sovereignty was restored to West Germany in 1955. Meanwhile, East Germany, under Soviet control, was proclaimed the German Democratic Republic and kept isolated from the West. The occupation of Berlin remained divided between East and West.

In 1951, a peace treaty with Japan, prepared under the direction of John Foster Dulles (then Republican adviser to the State Department), was signed by 49 nations; the Soviet Union refused to sign. This treaty restored Japan to full sovereignty but stripped her of her former empire. At the same time the United States and Japan signed a bilateral defense treaty.

3 THE HOME FRONT

On the home front rising prices soon brought widespread demands for wage increases, and an epidemic of strikes. The President sought to keep price controls, as an anti-inflationary measure, but it was an uphill struggle. When wages lagged behind prices, workers turned to the strike to compel employers to meet their demands. During 1946 approximately 1,650,000 people were on strike. United States Steel and General Motors plants were idle for months. The steelworkers settled on February 15, and Walter Reuther, after asking Truman to intervene to get the United Automobile Workers (UAW) members more money, accepted a similar settlement with General Motors on March 13. But then the United Mine Workers struck in the coalfields on April 1. At the time most factories and homes depended on coal for fuel, and by May the steel and auto companies were cutting back production and Chicago was cutting back on its use of electricity. On May 13 John L. Lewis sent the coalminers back to work for ten days, but two railroad unions struck on May 23, and the miners went out again on May 25. Truman went before Congress seeking a law to allow drafting of strikers, but the railroad unions settled as he was speaking and the bill was stopped in the Senate. In June, Truman vetoed the Case bill to restrict union power – a measure similar to the Smith bill passed by the House in 1941 and the Taft-Hartley bill which would be passed in 1947.

The government won in the courts, after the union had struck against government operation of the mines, and Lewis agreed to a compromise contract with the mine owners.

In an attempt to reduce the number of industrial disputes and to curb "unfair" labor practices, Congress passed the Taft-Hartley Act, over President Truman's veto, in 1947. Unions were placed under supervision so far as their finances and their relations with non-union laborers were concerned. Union officers were compelled to sign affidavits that they were not members of the Communist party. Concerning strikes, the law provided (1) that unions and management had to give 60 days notice of a decision to terminate a labor contract, and (2) that the government could secure an injunction postponing for 80 days any threatened strike or shutdown which might endanger public health or safety. The Act prohibited the closed shop, unfair practices of labor unions (e.g. "featherbedding" and excessive initiation fees), and union contributions to federal political campaigns.

4 THE VICTORY OF 1948

Truman's victory in the election of 1948 resulted in a political upset that confounded the professional forecasters of election returns. At the Republican national convention, held in Philadelphia on June 21–24, the supporters of Taft, Stassen, and Vandenberg were unable to find any plan which could prevent the nomination of Governor Thomas E. Dewey of New York, who had been the unsuccessful Republican standard-bearer in 1944. The Democrats, meeting at Philadelphia on July 12–15, somewhat reluctantly accepted President Truman as their candidate after Dwight D. Eisenhower, then president of Columbia University, had made it clear that he was not available. Some conservative Southern Democrats, who opposed President Truman's civil rights program, formed the States' Rights Democratic party (Dixiecrats) and nominated Governor J. Strom Thurmond of South Carolina. The extreme left-wing faction of the Democratic party organized a Progressive party and chose Henry A. Wallace as its candidate.

Neither Governor Dewey nor his running mate, Governor Earl Warren of California, was inclined to be specilic about the issues confronting the country. Just what a Republican victory would have meant in terms of domestic policies remained unclear. President Truman, strongly supported by his vice-presidential candidate, Senator Alben Barkley of Kentucky, proposed that the New Deal be continued and that the idea of the "welfare state" be translated into more effective legislation. He called his program the "Fair Deal."

Though President Truman ran behind his ticket in many Democratic districts, he carried 28 states with 304 electoral votes. Governor Dewey won 16 states with 189 votes, while Governor Thurmond received 38 votes from 4 Southern states. Wallace received no electoral votes.

Both before and after the election the President emphasized extension of social security benefits to more wage earners, provision for national health insurance, increased funds for public housing and slum clearance, and federal aid for schools. In an attempt to establish equality of civil rights he supported federal laws against lynching and for equal job opportunities. Yet few of his Fair Deal proposals outlining his domestic program for the ensuing four years were enacted. A coalition of Republicans and Southern Democrats prevented the passage of much of the "welfare" legislation; and a stubborn filibuster led by the Dixiecrats in the Senate defeated the civil rights program. Congress was also reluctant to carry out the President's campaign pledge that the Taft-Hartley labor Act would be repealed, and overrode his veto of the Taft-Hartley Act and of the McCarran-Walter Immigration Act of 1952. On the other hand, though Congress failed to accept the major provisions of President Truman's "Fair Deal" program, it enacted several measures which had the strong support of the administration. A minimum-wage bill increased the standard from 40 to 75 cents an hour. An appropriation of more than $2,700 million was voted for slum clearance and low-rent housing. By executive authority, Truman desegregated the armed forces and federally-supported schools. In the session of 1950 the Social Security Act (originally passed in 1935) was modified to include new groups of wage-earners and to provide old age pensions for many who were self-employed.

In 1949 Truman supported NATO, the first US peacetime military alliance; he devised the Point Four Program for backward nations; and when the Communists attacked Korea in June 1950, he secured armed intervention from the United Nations. He declined to seek renomination in 1952, and retired to private life.

5 THE TRUMAN DOCTRINE AND THE MARSHALL PLAN

Like President Monroe – but with more accuracy – Truman gave his name to a major feature of US foreign policy. And unlike James Monroe (for whom John Quincy Adams did most of the work), it is fair to acknowledge the President's role as statesman. The Truman Doctrine was the legacy of British weakness, and of its slow postwar withdrawal from the Middle East and the eastern Mediterranean.

The Doctrine was the name appliecl to the anti-Communist principle of foreign policy enunciated by President Truman in a message to Congress at a time when Greece and Turkey were in danger of Communist subversion. Had Britain not intervened earlier, Greece would certainly have become a Communist state. Truman recognized that underlying the struggle for power between the Soviet Union and the Western democracies, led by the United States, was the knowledge that an atomic war could bring doom to mankind; and in March, 1947, he asked Congress to approve a program of large-scale aid for the peoples of Europe who were then trying to maintain a democratic way of life in a world that seemed to be surrendering to Communist totalitarianism. In that message he stated, "I believe that it must be the policy of the United States to support free peoples who are resisting attempted subjugation by armed minorities or by outside pressures." He requested (and received) an appropriation for military and economic aid to countries whose political stability was threatened by Communism. The chief instruments of the Truman Doctrine were NATO, the Marshall Plan, and the Point Four Program which offered to raise the economic level of underdeveloped countries. Communists attributed the Cold War to the Truman Doctrine and its adjuncts. Western spokesmen attributed the salvation of Greece, Turkey, and in a sense, Yugoslavia, to the Doctrine.

Nevertheless, like President Monroe, HST had his henchman and chief of staff, General George Marshall. George Catlett Marshall (1880–1959), after graduation from Virginia Military Institute in 1901, served in the US Army for 43 years, during World War II as chief of staff (1939–45), and after 1944 as a general. He was expected to be the field commander in the invasion of Europe in 1944, but FDR felt that he was too precious as an overall administrator and strategist to risk. In December 1945 General Marshall was sent on a major mission as ambassador-envoy to end the Chinese civil war, but he succeeded only in bringing about a brief truce. Failing to unite the Kuomintang and the Reds, he withdrew, angrily denouncing both sides for bad faith. Even generous US military aid could not thereafter save Chiang from defeat.

President Truman selected Marshall as his secretary of state in 1947, and, in his commencement address at Harvard in June 1947, Marshall proposed the European Recovery Program, or "Marshall Plan," to rebuild the economy of western Europe, which had been ravaged by war. His direction of that program was recognized in 1953, when he was awarded the Nobel peace prize. He remained secretary of state, until 1949, and for a year held office as secretary of defense, in 1950–1.

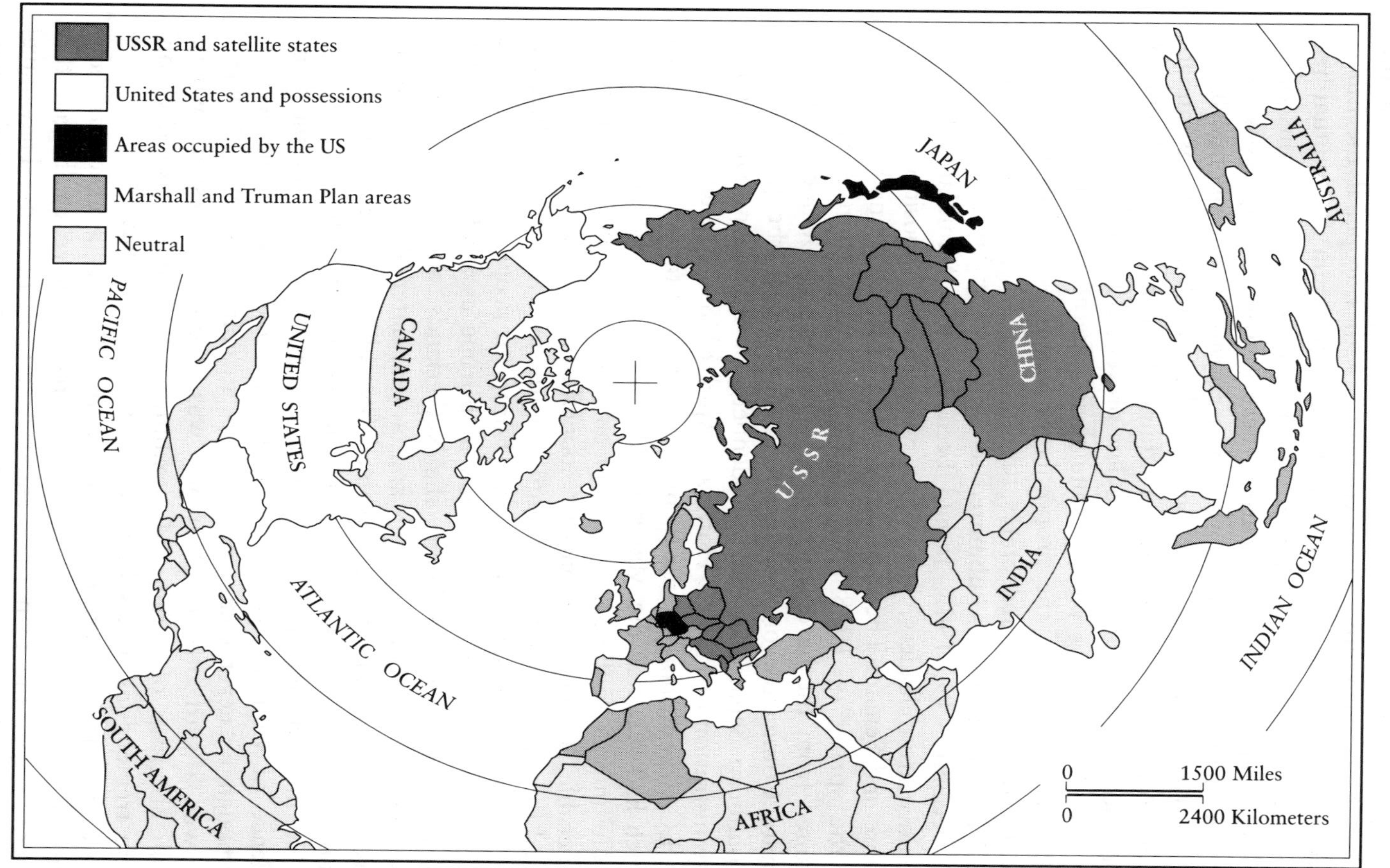

Map 9 The Cold War line-up. In 1945, American policy-makers believed that Russian-American cooperation was possible and desirable. Soon afterward, various conflicts lined up the two powers and their dependencies and allies into separate camps.

In June 1947, Secretary of State Marshall pointed out that the United States was anxious to cooperate with Europe, if the European nations were ready to formulate a program for mutual reconstruction. Sixteen western European nations accepted this offer and sent representatives to Paris, where a corps of experts worked out the details for international cooperation along economic lines. The Soviet Union, however, viewed the Marshall Plan as an attempt to interfere in the internal affairs of other states, and refused to participate. Ultimately, the Soviets prevented Poland and Czechoslovakia from taking part, despite their eagerness to do so.

By October 1947, the proposals were sufficiently specific to be submitted to the United States for approval. A proposal to enact the Marshall Plan was submitted to Congress by President Truman on December 19, 1947. It had been carefully formulated by the administration leaders, but it met with strong opposition in both House and Senate. The modified version which was finally accepted in the spring of 1948 (the Economic Cooperation Act, ECA) resulted from the hard work of Republicans and Democrats in the Senate Committee on Foreign Relations, under the guidance of Republican Senator Arthur Vandenberg of Michigan. During the administration of Paul G. Hoffman (April 1948 to September 1950), the ECA spent more than $10 billion in Europe to aid the countries which had accepted the Marshall Plan.

The impact of the Marshall Plan on European countries was soon noticeable. It spurred economic cooperation among them and stiffened their resistance to Communist aggression, meeting its objective of "restoring the confidence of the European people in the economc future of their own countries and of Europe as a whole." In 1949 the Benelux states – Belgium, the Netherlands, and Luxembourg – established a customs union; and a year later Robert Schuman, foreign minister of France, obtained favorable consideration for his plan to internationalize the steel industry of the Ruhr.

No military leader in US history has more fully won the confidence of Congress or of the Presidents under whom he served. Although he never commanded troops in combat (in World War I he was a staff officer), Marshall was a soldier-statesman whose brilliant grasp of detail and flexibility in administrative decision were tremendous assets in peace as well as in war.

At the time, Americans perceived the Plan as a generous subvention to Europe. But revisionist historians have challenged the assertion that the plan represented American altruism. They have argued that the export of dollars to Europe kept the United States from backsliding into depression by providing a market for US capital goods. The Marshall Plan, according to revisionists, allowed the United States to remake the European economy in the image of the American economy. The plan promoted European economic integration and federalism, and created a mixture of public organization of the private economy similar to that in the domestic economy of the United States. This reorganization of the European economy provided a more congenial environment for American investment.

6 CHINA AND KOREA

The governments of many Asiatic countries were harassed after World War II by the infiltration of Communism. In the Republic of the Philippines Communist-led "Huks" spread terror; Indochina was split asunder by Communistic subversion; in Malaya, Burma, Indonesia, Siam, and other areas the Communists threatened established governments.

When General Marshall became secretary of state in 1947 he recommended the withdrawal of the remaining military and naval forces of the United States stationed in China, maintaining that support of Chiang Kai-shek's regime would require more men and materials than the American people could supply. However, United States economic aid to Nationalist China continued until its defeat on the mainland. When Chiang Kai-shek fled the mainland of China and set up the Nationalist government on the island of Formosa, the United States promptly recognized the Formosan regime as the true government of China (January 1949). China proper was now controlled by the Communists, whom the American government refused to recognize. The United States guaranteed the safety of Formosa from external aggression by the Chinese Communists.

After World War II, Korea, which had long been dominated by Japan, was divided into two parts along the 38th parallel. Free elections under the United Nations resulted in the creation of the Republic of Korea, with Dr Syngman Rhee as president. Dr Rhee was an ardent nationalist, who hoped some day to incorporate North Korea into the Republic of Korea.

On June 25, 1950, North Korean troops, supplied with Russian equipment and led by Russian-trained officers, crossed the 38th parallel and attacked South Korea. This unprovoked assault was regarded by many in western Europe and the United States as the signal that the so-called Cold War was moving into the stage of

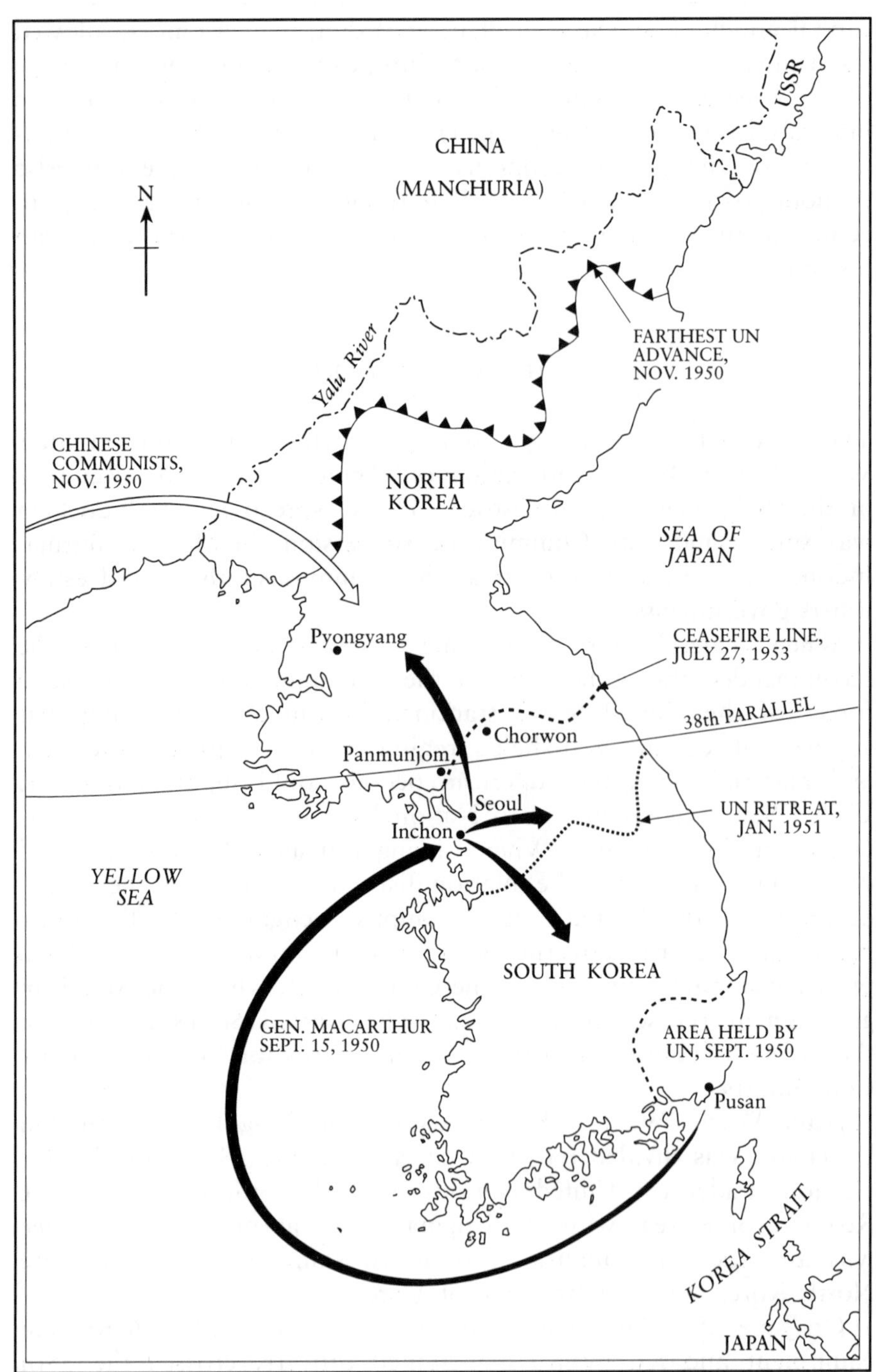

Map 10 The Korean War.

Plate 9 General Douglas MacArthur watches the naval bombardment of Inchon from his command ship during the Korean War, September 15, 1950. (Library of Congress.)

widespread military hostilities. The Security Council of the United Nations (with the Russian delegate absent) branded the North Korean invasion as an act of aggression and approved the use of force to punish the aggressor. On the same day that Communist forces invaded South Korea, President Truman ordered General Douglas MacArthur into the area, and the United Nations supported the move with forces supplied by 15 other nations. Fighting centered mainly on the 38th parallel, the previously negotiated division between North Korea (industrial and Communist) and South Korea (primarily agricultural).

The successful attack of the North Koreans drove the South Koreans and Americans back nearly to the tip of the peninsula and the defense perimeter of Pusan; but the triumphant amphibious landing at Inchon, near the 38th parallel, made possible the northward drive of the United Nations forces to the Yalu river, the boundary between North Korea and China. By November 1950, the United Nations forces had broken the North Korean attack and had driven the invaders in retreat across the 38th parallel. Meanwhile, Communist China had moved large troop concentrations to the Manchurian border. Early in December, 1950, these troops crossed into Korea, apparently with the determination to defeat the United Nations forces and drive them from the Korean peninsula. General MacArthur wanted to launch an all-out counteroffensive against the Chinese Communists, attacking them on Chinese territory.

Frequent disagreements between General MacArthur and the Truman administration over the way in which the war in Korea should be conducted caused an open rupture in April 1951, when the President relieved MacArthur of his command for disobeying an order to clear policy statements through the Defense Department. On his return to the United States, MacArthur was hailed by some as a hero, but many seemed to agree with President Truman that the real issue was the subordination of the military to civil authority and that the drastic action was necessary in order to prevent the Korean fighting from developing into a third world war. MacArthur was replaced in Korea by General Matthew B. Ridgway.

In June 1951, after the Communist troops had been checked by UN forces, Russia suggested that it would be possible for discussions between the antagonists in Korea to lead to a ceasefire. Negotiations between the two truce teams began but made very slow progress – the main point of contention being the forcible repatriation of prisoners of war, the UN seeking freedom for a POW to choose where he went.

The UN naval and air forces maintained control of the seas and skies of the combat zone, with American strategic bombing reaching a zenith in mid-1952. The command was led by General Ridgway until May 1952, and thereafter by General Mark Clark. The US Eighth Army which was the principal ground force of the UN Command, was headed by General James Van Fleet and then by General Maxwell Taylor.

The armistice signed in Panmunjon on July 27, 1953 resulted in a cessation of hostilities and a prisoner exchange, but it left the peninsula divided close to the 38th parallel and actually satisfied none of the belligerents. No peace was ever made.

The Korean War was a civil war that was a legacy of the Japan-versus-USSR conflict that had preceded and then become part of World War II. It was for the US the last "old-fashioned" war where strategies, tactics, and weapons were concerned. Eventually 1.8 million Americans would serve in Korea, of whom 54,200 were killed, 103,300 wounded and 8,200 missing in action. After the cessation of hostilities, the Republic of Korea (South) signed a mutual defense treaty with the US, and North Korea allied itself with Communist China.

Because of their appalling human and property losses in the war, both Koreas underwent slow rehabilitation. North Korea remained a staunchly Communist state, though more closely aligned after 1953 to Peking (Beijing) than to Moscow. South Korea developed into a prosperous, if politically divided, country with strong economic and security links to the United States.

The consequences of the war for the United States were manifold. Desegregation of the Eighth Army during the Korean operations was a milestone for blacks in the American military establishment. McCarthyism fed on public discontent with the conduct of the war. Dissent grew as the war became protracted and indecisive, contributing to the 1952 presidential triumph of General of the Army Dwight D. Eisenhower, the first Republican in the White House in two decades. The Korean hostilities prompted the United States to strengthen its military commitment to NATO. The war also hastened the signing of the Japanese peace treaty, the formation of SEATO, and the creation of American security pacts with Japan, Australia, New Zealand, and the Philippines.

From the start of the Korean fighting, the Truman administration escalated military assistance to the French in the Vietnam War and then sent aid and advisers to the fledgling Republic of South Vietnam. The US assumed that global Communism was monolithic and that Moscow was dictating the aggression both in Korea and in Vietnam. In the later American involvement in Vietnam, as in Korea, the US government was never able to delineate clearly the currents of nationalism, Communism and imperialism that seemed to flow into one another.

7 THE BEGINNINGS OF THE COLD WAR, AND REACTIONS AT HOME

Despite the alliance of the USSR with the US and Britain during World War II, tensions between the Communist states and the democracies arose sharply after 1945. Some states were split into free and Communist: as in Korea, between South and North. In some the government was unpredictable, witness Yugoslavia then and after Tito. Some were divided for postwar administrative purposes, as in Germany and Austria (witness the film *The Third Man*, set in a Vienna that was administered jointly by the four Occupying Powers.)

In the summer of 1948 the Soviet Union stopped all rail and road traffic between Berlin and the western German occupation zones. The Western powers, led by the United States, responded by keeping an air corridor open between their zones in Germany and their respective sections of Berlin, along which they could fly cargoes of food, fuel, and other supplies into the city. For 10 months and 23 days the Berlin airlift was maintained, demonstrating the determination of the Western powers not to be forced into a policy of appeasing the Soviet Union. Finally, the Russians agreed to terminate the Berlin blockade in return for a Western agreement to lift the counterblockade and to arrange an early meeting of the Council of Foreign Ministers. This compromise became effective on May 12, 1949.

Some observers felt that the change in Russian policy marked by the calling of a meeting of the Council of Foreign Ministers had in part been induced by the success of Western diplomats in formulating and signing (on April 4, 1949) the North Atlantic Security Treaty (North Atlantic Pact). Twelve nations on either side of the Atlantic – including Great Britain, France, Belgium, the Netherlands, Norway, Canada, and the United States – adopted a defensive pact whereby they would regard an aggressive attack upon any one of their number as an attack upon all.

The defensive pact was given form in the North Atlantic Treaty Organization (NATO) and in December, 1950, President Truman called General Eisenhower from his post as president of Columbia University to be Supreme Commander of the Western forces in defense of Europe. For more than a year Eisenhower built carefully but rapidly the structure of the military forces of the Western world and won wide support for a political, as well as an economic, union among the states of western Europe. When he decided to enter politics in 1952 he was succeeded by General Matthew Ridgway, who had been commander of UN forces in Korea. General Alfred M. Gruenther succeeded Ridgway in 1953, and he in turn was succeeded in 1956 by General Lauris Norstad. In December, 1957, the first NATO heads-of-government meeting was held in Paris. The representatives agreed that NATO should stockpile nuclear missiles and announced plans for closer economic and political cooperation.

But at home, as well as in Europe, all was not well. Prosperity appeared to depend in substantial part on exports for which foreign countries could not pay; and on an armament program which increased an already staggering tax burden. The individualism and the opportunity of an earlier America seemed to have faded; and some felt that the United States had suddenly grown old. Predictions of disaster were common; the fear of Communism – despite the value of Russia as victorious ally – was all too real.

Early in World War II, when Stalin was the ally of Hitler, the Roosevelt administration had taken action against American Communists, sending Earl Browder to prison for passport fraud. At the time, American Communists were denouncing Roosevelt as a warmonger and World War II as an imperialist affair. After Germany invaded Russia, the Communists shifted ground, becoming interventionist and viewing the conflict as a "people's war." Browder (now out of jail) supported the war effort after Pearl Harbor, saying that Communist and capitalist nations could work together. But the party line changed again after the war. Browder was deposed for his cooperative stand, and the American Communists (under William Z. Foster and Eugene Dennis) became violently opposed to capitalism and to American foreign policy.

As feeling against Russia increased in the United States, American Communists came to be regarded with increasing alarm by the American people. Congress and the President launched investigations. Some government officials were dropped or allowed to resign after loyalty checks. The Justice Department issued lists of "subversive organizations", groups that had been founded or used by Communists. The Taft-Hartley Act required labor leaders to swear that they were not Communists. Several cases hit the headlines. There were convictions on charges of perjury (Harry Bridges, the longshoreman labor leader, and Alger Hiss, formerly a high official in the State Department); contempt for refusing to answer questions asked by Congressional investigators (ten Hollywood writers, among others); espionage (Judith Coplon, a Justice Department employee, and Valentin Gubitchev, a Russian employed by the United Nations); violation of the Smith Act of 1940, i.e. plotting to overthrow the government by force (Eugene Dennis and ten other Communist party leaders). Americans were particularly disturbed to hear of spy activities, as when Harry Gold, an American scientist, confessed to helping Dr Klaus Fuchs, a British citizen, supply Russia with information about the atomic bomb. (Russia achieved an atomic explosion in 1949.) Feeling against such people was heightened by disclosures of Soviet espionage during the war and by the conviction of former State Department official Alger Hiss, charged with handing over secret documents to Communist agents.

In 1950 Congress passed the Internal Security Act (McCarran Act), over President Truman's veto. This law required the registration of Communist and Communist-front organizations. It also provided for the deportation of Communist immigrants and prohibited the immigration of anyone who had been a member of a totalitarian organization. (Certain exceptions were permitted by 1951 amendments for those who had been forced to belong to such organizations).

The McCarran-Walter Act, passed in 1952 (also over Truman's veto), revised the immigration laws. It maintained the quota system but ended racial bars and gave priority to persons with needed skills and to relatives of United States citizens. It placed additional restrictions on the immigration and naturalization of Communists and Communist sympathizers.

Former Communists, persons who had associated with Communists, and persons suspected of radical tendencies became the objects of public and private investigation throughout the country. Many of them were dismissed from their jobs on what seemed to be insubstantial evidence. The government "loyalty" investigation was extended to federal employees who for any reason could be considered security risks, and a number were dismissed on that ground, though very few were discovered to have been Communists. The most spectacular Red hunt was conducted by Senator Joseph R. McCarthy of Wisconsin, as chairman of a Senate committee on un-American activities. McCarthy's charges, which eventually included the Eisenhower administration, resulted in his being censured by a bipartisan Senate resolution for conduct unbecoming a Senator.

The Supreme Court upheld the constitutionality of the Smith Act on the ground that the Communist conspiracy was a "clear and present danger;" but it narrowed the application of the law to persons who had actually advocated forcible overthrow of the government. Other Supreme Court decisions, in 1957, held that the investigating powers of Congress were restricted to specific functions of Congress and that FBI files used as evidence in loyalty cases must be produced in court.

Anti-Communist activity was not confined to government channels. Communists and pro-Communists who had gained influence in the labor movement were voted out of office. The Congress of Industrial Organizations (CIO) expelled Communist-dominated unions (1949–50) and set up new unions to take over the field. There were campaigns to get Communists out of religious and veterans' organizations and out of minority group associations. A New York Episcopal clergyman lost his post because of the activities of his son and coworker. The regents of the University of California required employees to swear that they were not Communists. There was a flood of books by former Communists, reciting the evils of Communism, and Hollywood began turning out anti-Communist movies. *The Iron Curtain* and *Conspirator*, to give two examples, were in sharp contrast with *Mission to Moscow* and *Son of Russia*, pro-Soviet pictures produced during the war years, when Russia and the United States were cooperating.

The American public wholeheartedly endorsed the efforts of the FBI to round up Russian spies. The overwhelming majority of Americans also approved of the bipartisan anti-Russian foreign policy developed after 1946, and of the steps taken to prevent Communists from getting control of unions and other American organizations. At the same time, many citizens were disturbed by the tendency of some anti-Communists to identify everything they disliked with Soviet Russia. Ambitious and unscrupulous politicians gained the spotlight by making wild and reckless charges. Ultraconservative newspaper columnists and radio commentators suggested that socialists and Communists were virtually identical, and that socialists included all who advocated public housing or socialized medicine. David Lilienthal and other thoroughly loyal officials were harassed by investigations, so much so that many able private citizens were reluctant to enter public employment. Even some who were strong foes of Communism and of Russian expansion were denounced as "Reds" – religious leaders with liberal beliefs, CIO and AFL officials, and liberal intellectuals.

12

Ike, the Supreme Commander

1 DWIGHT D. EISENHOWER

General Dwight David Eisenhower (1890–1969), 34th President of the United States (1953–61), was born in Texas, but reared in Abilene, Kansas. After his graduation at West Point, he served as an instructor in US Army camps, was graduated from the Army War College, and eventually became General Douglas MacArthur's chief of staff in the Philippines. By the time the US came into World War II Eisenhower had, after General Marshall, an unmatched administrative experience; and, indeed, after the massive exercises of Walter Krueger's Third Army in Louisiana in 1941, when he was chief of staff, he had more command and planning experience than any senior American soldier. His remarkable ease of manner and his skill at man-management, and the qualities of even more sophisticated colleague-management (product maybe of years as a football coach?), made him a natural and wise choice for command. In 1942 he was given command of US headquarters in England. He commanded the US forces which landed in North Africa in November of that year (Operation Torch), and the next February he was placed in command of all the Allied forces in Africa. His success in the invasion of Sicily and Italy led to his appointment as chief of the Allied invasion forces in Europe at the end of 1943. In this capacity he directed the invasion of France in June, 1944, and the liberation of western Europe (Operation Overlord).

Eisenhower was recognized for his diplomatic as well as military skill, and served as US representative in the Allied military government in Germany until he succeeded General George C. Marshall as US Army chief of staff in November 1945. This position he held until he was appointed president of Columbia University in 1947. In December, 1950, he was called by President Truman to become Supreme Commander of the Western Forces in Europe.

In 1951, on leave of absence from Columbia, he served as Supreme Commander of NATO until he resigned to campaign in 1952 as Republican nominee for the presidency against the Democratic candidate, Adlai E. Stevenson.

2 THE REPUBLICANS IN POWER

Both major party conventions in 1952 were exciting, because the delegates were unusually free to reach decisions as the proceedings developed. The Republicans nominated General Eisenhower after a spirited revolt of many delegates against the supporters of Senator Robert A. Taft of Ohio, who seemed to have control of the convention committees. Senator Richard M. Nixon of California, who was presented as a fighter against Communist infiltration in the civil service received the nomination for Vice-President. Equally dramatic were the proceedings of the Democratic convention in which the willing candidates – Kefauver of Tennessee, Russell of Georgia, Barkley of Kentucky, Harriman of New York, Kerr of Oklahoma – lost to Governor Adlai Stevenson of Illinois, who insisted that he was being drafted. For its vice-presidential candidate, the convention turned to Senator John Sparkman of Alabama, hoping thus to overcome the disaffection of some of the Southern Democratic leaders.

Governor Stevenson, with rare literary skill, tried to fix the voters' attention on the costly struggle which would be required to overcome the threats of war, poverty, and tyranny. However, he could not overcome the personal popularity of General Eisenhower, or escape the Relublican charge that the Democrats had condoned corruption in executive departments. Perhaps the most effective oratory of the campaign was Eisenhower's simple promise: "I will go to Korea." Voters hoped he could thus end the war.

When the results were declared, the Republican candidates received 442 electoral college votes to 89 for their opponents. Eisenhower received the largest popular vote ever polled to that time (34 million), a sweeping personal victory.

The landslide proportions of this victory did not carry over to the Congressional vote, however. The Republican majority in the House was large enough to provide for party control, but the Republican margin in the Senate was dependent upon Senator Wayne Morse of Oregon, who had supported Stevenson as an "Independent Republican" and who later defected to the Democratic camp. To be successful, the administration's legislative program required support from conservative Democrats as well as from Republicans.

President Eisenhower sincerely hoped to elevate the "tone" of politics, for he had strong faith in his countrymen's ability to make the right choices if they had the facts. His Cabinet included several supporters of Senator Taft, named in an effort to repair the damage which had been caused by the fight in the nominating convention. The new Cabinet position of secretary of health, education, and welfare went to Oveta Culp Hobby of Texas, who became the first woman of her party to serve as a Cabinet member. John Foster Dulles, a New York lawyer and close friend of Governor Thomas E. Dewey, was named secretary of state at a time when international problems were acute. (He had previously been an adviser to the Truman administration.)

The Eisenhower administration disappointed those conservative Republicans who wanted a frontal attack on the New Deal and Fair Deal laws. Actually the moderates in both major parties had accepted the principle that the federal govermnent is responsible for the welfare of its citizens, and legislation signed by President Eisenhower in 1954 added almost ten million persons to the lists of those who were entitled to receive social security benefits, and increased the payment levels. In 1955 the minimum wage in covered employment was raised to $1.00 an hour.

In the area of civil rights, the issue of extending equality of public treatment to blacks divided the nation along sectional rather than party lines. President Eisenhower and his advisers were joined by many Northern Democrats in the movement to extend civil rights. After long Congressional debate a bill was passed in the summer of 1957 which empowered the federal government to seek court orders, if necessary, to guarantee the individual's right to vote in any state in the Union. A bipartisan Civil Rights Commission was appointed by President Eisenhower to examine abuses of civil rights and to make recommendations for new legislation.

In May 1954, the Supreme Court, presided over by Chief Justice Earl Warren, former governor of California, handed down a momentous decision on the segregation issue in the public schools. This ruling reversed a decision of 1896 (*Plessy* vs. *Ferguson*) that "separate but equal" facilities were constitutional. Later in the same year, in the case of *Brown* vs. *The Board of Education of Topeka,* the Court unanimously held that the maintenance of "separate but equal" schools for blacks – which was the practice in 17 states – violated the Fourteenth Amendment. "Separate educational facilities," said the Chief Justice, "are inherently unequal." Implicit in the ruling was the Court's understanding that enforcement would require careful planning over a considerable period of time. The Eisenhower administration encouraged the several states to work out their own plans.

In September 1957, the Board of Education of Little Rock was prepared to admit to high school eight carefully selected black students. Governor Faubus, insisting that violence would break out if the students were admitted to classes, used the Arkansas National Guard to bar them from the school building. President Eisenhower responded by ordering federal troops into Arkansas to protect the students as they carried out their studies in the school year 1957–8. He maintained that the action of Governor Faubus violated the law of the nation.

In a number of Southern states legislation was passed to allow the governors to close schools under orders to integrate. During 1958–9, schools in Little Rock and in several Virginia communities were closed by such action. However, decisions by state and federal courts required the reopening of some of these schools on an integrated basis. Progress toward integration was most notable in border states such as Maryland and Kentucky. Schools in Washington, DC (where a separate Supreme Court decision involved the Fifth Amendment), were also desegregatecd.

Neither a heart attack in September 1955 nor an operation for an intestinal ailment in June, 1956, could deter President Eisenhower from seeking a second term. He and Nixon opposed Stevenson and Senator Estes Kefauver of Tennessee. Eisenhower polled 457 electoral votes to Stevenson's 73. The overwhelming endorsement of the President, however, did not apply to his party. The Democrats recaptured both the House and the Senate and won a majority of the governorships that were at stake.

After his re-election, President Eisenhower began to exert pressure on Capitol Hill for his legislative program. Since the Democrats controlled Congress, bipartisan support was necessary for those measures that were enacted into law. In the case of the proposed Pentagon reorganization (1958), the President secured virtually the bill he wanted, putting the defense secretary in direct command of the armed forces and giving him explicit authority to assign weapon development among the various services. The Act also provided for a director of research and engineering (under the defense secretary) to be in control of defense research projects.

At President Eisenhower's request the reciprocal trade program was extended at periodic intervals. The longest extension – four years – was enacted in 1958. This law authorized tariff cuts up to 20 percent below prevailing rates. The President was permitted to reject Tariff Commission recommendations for higher rates unless he was overridden by a two-thirds vote of both houses of Congress. President Eisenhower was less successful in his urging of an adequate mutual security program; the appropriations authorized by Congress for this purpose were usually below his minimum standards. However, the basic policy of granting economic, technical, and, if necessary, military aid to countries whose defense was deemed vital to the containment of Communism remained unchanged.

Amendments to the Social Security Act passed in 1958 raised the benefits and tax rates for old age survivors, and disability payments. They also increased the amounts of federal grants to the states for maternal and child welfare and public assistance projects. Aid to farmers was continued by means of flexible price supports for basic products (a departure from the Democratic policy of fixed supports). In 1958, Congress authorized the expenditure of $887 million over a four-year period for education purposes. State school officials were asked to come to Washington to draw up plans for the use of these funds.

During the fall of 1957 and the first half of 1958, the United States was confronted with the most serious economic recession since World War II. Retail sales and industrial production declined sharply, and the number of unemployed rose to more than five million in the spring of 1958. To help overcome the recession, the Federal Reserve Board reduced its discount rate and the margin requirements for stock transactions; Congress authorized large expenditures for public works, including interstate highway construction; and President Eisenhower urged increased consumer buying. By the end of 1958, the nation was well on the road to economic recovery.

In 1955 the AFL and the CIO had merged into a powerful 15-million-member organization. During 1957–8, investigations by a Senate committee disclosed corrupt financial practices by some high union officials. Under its Code of Ethical Practices, the AFL-CIO launched a house-cleaning drive and expelled some unions, including the International Brotherhood of Teamsters. Labor continued to benefit from cost-of-living wage increases and welfare programs that unions had secured from a number of industries. However, by November 1958, 19 states had enacted "right-to-work" laws, under which a worker could not be barred from a job for refusing to join a union.

The career of Frederic Morrow, the first black man to occupy a senior post in the White House, reflects the difficulties that faced an able black man in public life in the 1940s and 1950s. The son of a Methodist minister, Everett Frederic Morrow studied at Bowdoin College in the late 1920s but failed to get a degree, and was a field secretary for the National Association for the Advancement of Colored People before joining the US Army Field Artillery in 1942. Entlisting as a private, he left as a major in 1946 and went to work for CBS studying in his spare time at Rutgers University, where he eventually took a doctorate in law.

Morrow had entered politics as a consultant to Eisenhower's 1952 campaign, for which he took leave of absence from his job as a writer for CBS News. He so impressed Sherman Adams, Eisenhower's chief of staff, that Adams promised him a job on the White House staff and urged him to resign from CBS while awaiting appointment. It was to be the first of many broken promises. Morrow found himself living on his savings while he waited for a call from the White House that did not come until July 1955. Even then, it was to be another three years before he was formally sworn in and Eisenhower, who usually attended such ceremonies, ostentatiously stayed away.

Life in the White House during the Eisenhower era was not easy for Frederic Morrow. Although formally ranked as an administrative assistant to the President, he was usually mistaken for a servant at official functions and was largely excluded from the decision-making process. Regarded by fellow blacks as an "Uncle Tom" and coldly snubbed by his white colleagues (in social terms Washington was then very much a Southern city) Morrow endured five years of frustration before being freed from his ordeal by John F. Kennedy's victory in the 1960 presidential election.

In September 1958 Morrow was named as administrative officer for special projects, dealing almost exclusively with civil rights. It was a position he had hoped to avoid because, as he wrote in his journal, the White House was handling civil rights "like a bad dream," refusing to take action on the racial violence which was exploding across the South. Morrow later turned his journal into a book, *Black Man in the White House*, published in 1963. This, with its account of the color prejudice in the Eisenhower administration, did not endear him to the Republican leadership.

On leaving the White House, unlike most white men in a similar position, he found it impossible to get an executive post in private industry. "It still shocks many captains of industry," he said at the time, "when a Negro seeks a job on the executive level, even though he dealt with them directly as part of his official White House assignment." Eventually, though, he did succeed in breaking through the racial barriers. In 1964 the Bank of America, then the largest privately owned bank in the world, made Morrow an assistant vice-president at its international subsidiary on Wall Street. He retired as senior vice-president in 1975 after writing a second book, *Way Down South Up North*, then went to work for the Educational Testing Service which sets examinations for most of America's schoolchildren.

3 POSTWAR AMERICA

As they entered the second half of the twentieth century, Americans were enjoying great material prosperity. National income was enormous, well over $200 billion a year. Employment was high, around 60 million. Farmers were doing well, working men – thanks to the war – were obtaining some of the security which they had long desired. Improved educational opportunities, especially grants for veterans, were making it possible for an increasing number of Americans to satisfy their ambition to enter the professions. Business earnings were at peak levels. Americans had more mechanical conveniences, more cultural opportunities, more leisure than before. Women and minority groups met with less discrimination than in earlier periods. At long last, Americans were learning to conserve their natural resources. On the world front, the United States had more naval and economic power than any other nation; and America was becoming a great scientific and cultural center. If atomic energy discovered in part because of war needs could be put to peacetime use, still greater gains might lie ahead. As President, Eisenhower was able to work easily with Congress, even though it was predominantly Democratic for six of his eight years in office. He promoted a vast national highway program, conspicuous for its 40,000 miles of "interstates" gradually displacing the "M" network that had been a feature of the coast-to-coast network. The Highway Act of 1956 – with only one opposing vote in Congress – authorized a $32 billion project. The Act came at a time when the highway lobby's interests coincided with the high point of America's postwar love affair with the automobile. By the 1960s, three-fourths of urban commuters traveled to work in their own automobiles, and between 1956 and 1969 urban highway mileage increased from 36,000 to 56,000 miles. High-speed metropolitan expressways increased from 8.2 percent of the total urban highway mileage to

34.6 percent. The Highway Act paid fully 90 percent of the cost of the interstate highways and 50 percent of other federally-aided road construction.

By creating the interstate highway program, the federal government facilitated the suburbanization of commerce, industry, and services, as well as the suburbanization of residential housing. Once the lower-priced land outside city limits became accessible, companies could also consider other suburban advantages, such as room for up-to-date one-storey factories, spacious parking lots, lower property taxes, and easier recruitment of management and professional staff intent upon raising children in a suburban environment. Completion of the Capital Belt way surrounding Washington DC in 1962 brought about 800,000 new residents to its bordering communities during the following decade, as well as a dozen regional shopping centers catering to their needs. Tam O'Shanter industrial park near Chicago was placed on what had been a championship golf course. Volkswagen Corporation located its factory for the Rabbit model amid the green rolling hills of Allegheny County near Pittsburgh. Some 800 small silicon chip and semi-conductor plants sprang up during the 1970s in the industrial parks in California's Santa Clara County.

The St Lawrence Society was state-financed. President Eisenhower liberalized the social security laws. It was, in John Kenneth Galbraith's term, "the affluent society:" with televisions and electronic computers, new rocketry and the space program. The nation, with 6 percent of the world's population, produced nearly half the world's goods – and most of its inventions.

Yet, in the midst of plenty, Americans were gravely concerned about the future. The rise of Soviet Russia, the threat of Communism, the horrors of atomic war, bore heavily upon Americans in an age when isolation had become impossible. In the one world of 1950, domestic prosperity no longer seemed enough. It now appeared that no nation was secure while distress and want haunted other sections of the globe.

4 COLD WAR DIPLOMACY

After World War II, Poland, Hungary, Czechoslovakia, Romania, Bulgaria, and Albania had fallen under dictatorial control from Moscow. An attempted revolt in Hungary in 1956 was crushed by the USSR. Moreover, Russian Communist influence penetrated Malaysia, Burma, Thailand, Indonesia and China itself. As fear of

Communism grew in the West, both major powers – US and USSR – formed groups of allies or satellites in support.

In 1955, the United States took the lead in forming the South East Asia Treaty Organization (SEATO). This was not a firm military alliance like NATO, but its members – the United States, the United Kingdom, France, New Zealand, Pakistan, the Philippine Republic, and Thailand – agreed to work together for security against external aggression. In 1954 the United States signed a Mutual Security Treaty with Nationalist China providing for mutual aid in the defense of Formosa and the Pescadores. When, in 1958, Quemoy and other offshore islands were shelled from the Communist-held mainland, the United States convoyed supply ships to these islands.

President Eisenhower quickly put into effect his campaign promise to visit Korea. Though not directly related to the truce negotiations at Panmunjon, his military inspection signified the desire of Americans to end the war. A truce was finally signed in July 1953, fixing a line of demarcation between the Northern Communist state and the Southern republic and providing for repatriation of war prisoners on a voluntary basis.

In July 1954, the pressure of Vietnam Communist forces led to a conference held at Geneva by the foreign ministers of 19 nations, including the United States. This conference settled upon the 17th parallel as the dividing line between Communist North Vietnam and Southern Vietnam, which became a republic. There was after the end of the war in Korea a six-year spell of peace, thanks to the system of alliances thwarting the USSR. For the Cold War strategy of Secretary of State John Foster Dulles was to ring the Communist states with groups of American allies: the North Atlantic Treaty Organization (NATO) in western Europe, the Australia, New Zealand and United States military alliance (ANZUS) in the Pacific, and the Baghdad Pact group of America's then Middle East "satellite" states, principally Iran, Pakistan, Turkey, together with the UK.

There were growing problems in the Middle East. With the waning of British and French influence after World War II, the United States was confronted by heavier responsibilities in that part of the world. The intense nationalism of Arab peoples formerly under European domination created difficult problems. Arab leaders, especially the Egyptian dictator, Colonel Abdul Gamal Nasser, soon learned that they could play the Soviet Union against the United States and thereby win concessions from both sides.

Trying to forestall Soviet influence in Egypt, Secretary of State John Foster Dulles had promised that nation financial aid in building the Aswan Dam to secure electric power from the River Nile. However, in 1956 Nasser's request for a large loan was turned down by the United States and Great Britain, precipitating the Suez Crises. Nasser quickly seized and nationalized the Suez Canal. Without informing the United States of their plans, Israel, Britain, and France successfully invaded the Canal area. When Britain and France blocked action by the Security Council, the General Assembly of the United Nations acted promptly, with both the United States and the Soviet Union pressing for a withdrawal of foreign forces from Egypt. The withdrawal was made and the UN sent an emergency force to patrol the area.

In March 1957 Eisenhower asked Congress to grant funds for economic and military aid to help friendly Middle East nations to preserve their independence, and to permit the use of US forces to resist armed Communist aggression there, in what became known as the Eisenhower Doctrine. On this basis, troops were sent to the Lebanon in 1958. The policies also, as *quid pro quo*, assured oil supplies to the US.

In an attempt to ease international tensions, the leaders of the United States, Great Britain, France, and the Soviet Union met in a summit conference at Geneva in July 1955. The Soviet Union was represented by Nicolai Bulganin, who had become premier following the death of Stalin in 1953; he was replaced in 1958 by Nikita Khrushchev. President Eisenhower made a daring proposal for mutual aerial inspection of military installations in all parts of the world; but this proposal was unacceptable to the Soviet Union, and so the conference merely generated for a brief time a spirit of good will.

In May, 1959, as the sessions of a foreign ministers' conference of the Big Four in Geneva became more bitter, President Eisenhower dramatically turned to personal diplomacy. Khrushchev accepted an invitation to visit the United States in September, and Eisenhower agreed that he would journey to Russia at a later date. The exchange of visits was hailed as a prelude to a summit conference of the Big Four.

Early in December 1959, President Eisenhower set out on a goodwill tour to Europe and Asia. Although his trip to Japan had to be canceled because of political unrest there, his tour seemed on the whole immensely successful in arousing the people of many countries to an awareness of his determination to preserve the peace of the world. In Paris he conferred with British Prime Minister Harold Macmillan, French premier Charles de Gaulle, and the West German Chancellor, Konrad Adenauer; and it was agreed that

Khrushchev should be invited to a summit conference in the spring of 1960. However, just before the leaders of the United States, Great Britain, France, and the Soviet Union were due to meet in Paris for the conference, an American U-2 reconnaissance plane was brought down by the Russians hundreds of miles within their borders. Khrushchev and his associates promptly used the plane incident, and the capture of the pilot, Francis Powers, as an excuse to wreck the conference and to rescind Eisenhower's scheduled visit to Russia. Their attacks on the President and his countrymen were obviously designed for propaganda purposes, but the meaning was clear – the Cold War between East and West would be intensified.

During the summer of 1960, the Soviet Union tried to take every possible advantage of political and economic crises in the Caribbean and in Africa. Soviet agents established close contact with the revolutionary government of Fidel Castro in Cuba, and Castro belligerently announced that he would use Russian rockets to fight off his enemies. Alarmed by the threat of Communist intervention in Cuba, the United States accused the Castro government of subversive policies at a meeting of the Organization of American States in Costa Rica in August, 1960. The OAS foreign ministers approved the Declaration of San José, which condemned the intervention or threat of intervention of any extracontinental power in the affairs of the American republics. Secretary of State Christian Herter, successor to John Foster Dulles, interpreted the action of the San José Conference as "a clear indictment of the Castro government."

In Africa, as the Republic of the Congo, newly independent of Belgian political control, tried to establish a responsible government, many Congolese refused to accept the authority of Premier Patrice Lumumba. The efforts of a police force authorized by the United Nations to maintain law and order were not entirely successful. Premier Lumumba repeatedly threatened to use the power of the Soviet Union to secure his own objectives. The United States insisted that the troubles of the new Republic should be settled in the UN. Yet it was apparent by September 1960 that the Soviet Union might use the Congolese disturbance to weaken the UN and to bring the Cold War into a strategic area of the African continent.[1]

[1] John Lewis Gaddis, *The Long Peace: Inquiries into the history of the Cold War* (New York, Oxford University Press, 1987); Walter La Faber, *America, Russia and the Cold War 1945–1984* (New York, Kropf, 1985); Louis Halle, *The Cold War as History* (New York, Harper and Row, 1967).

5 I LIKE IKE

Eisenhower's two-term presidency, scorned at first by liberals and specialists as unresponsive and lethargic, came to be seen later as an example of holding the line against contemporary political and social forces. Only with great reluctance did he force the racial integration of Little Rock's high school in 1957; he ended the war in Korea, and he pacified the storm-clouds raised by Senator Joseph McCarthy. He won comfortably, again defeating Adlai Stevenson in 1956, carrying all but seven states (457 electoral votes against the Democrats 73, or 35.6 million popular votes against Stevenson's 26 million).

Eisenhower contained the Republican right wing, winning it over to internationalism, while pursuing Cold War policies that largely continued the Truman legacy. He and his secretary of state, John Foster Dulles, dealt with conflicts in different parts of the world, most notably Southeast Asia, via mutual security treaties and covert military intervention. The Eisenhower-Dulles policy departed from the Truman-Acheson focus on Israel, now an independent state, promoted US-Arab understanding as well as a barrier against the USSR via the Middle East Treaty Organization (METO: Turkey, Iran, Iraq, Pakistan, and Britain) or the Baghdad Pact, and distanced itself from British-French economic interests as a rebuke to Britain and France's Suez policy and fiasco. The US courted Egypt's support by offering the prospect of America's assistance in building the great hydro-electric dam at Aswan on the Nile. They were cautiously wary of Soviet leader Nikita Krushchev and his overtures toward détente.

Eisenhower did not have much success in his efforts to trim the military budget, the central concern of his farewell address on January 17, 1961. He left a deficit of over $500 million. Facing the three successive Congresses controlled by the Democrats – the first President to do so – he could manage few new departures in domestic policy. But he had managed to keep intact the major reforms and institutions inherited from the New Deal and, at the same time, to produce three balanced budgets. The leadership that seemed timid and uncreative at the time was later described by historians as adroit management of a not-so-placid decade.

John Foster Dulles (1888–1959), Wall Street lawyer and secretary of state, grandson of one secretary of state (John Foster) and nephew of another (Robert Lansing), served Eisenhower in that capacity from January 1953 until his death from cancer in 1959.

As international lawyer and senior partner in the prestigious Wall Street firm of Sullivan and Cromwell, he built a modest reputation in the 1920s as an authority on the tangled issue of Allied war debts and German reparations. Long an unreconstructed Wilsonian, Dulles opposed American involvement in Europe in the 1930s on the grounds that the victors of 1919 had ignored Woodrow Wilson's call for "peaceful change" and sought only to preserve the harsh features of the Versailles settlement.

Dulles emerged during World War II as draftsman of the UN Charter in 1945, and as the principal lay spokesman for the Federal Council of Churches in its effort to promote the proposed United Nations. At the same time, as a protégé of New York governor Thomas E. Dewey, he was also emerging as a leading proponent of the foreign policy views of the eastern wing of the Republican party. Senator Arthur Vandenberg and he were the architects of post-war bipartisan foreign policy. By the late 1940s he was a Republican adviser, and later consultant, to the Truman administration and in that capacity negotiated the Japanese peace treaty in 1950–1.

But by 1952 partisanship and policy differences led him to become one of Harry S. Truman's and Dean Acheson's (US secretary of state 1949–55) most acerbic critics, especially on Far Eastern policy. His well-publicized article in *Life* magazine condemned the containment policy of the Truman administration as merely a negative attempt to restrain Soviet expansionism and demanded a new policy of boldness that would restore the initiative to the United States. During the 1952 campaign he called stridently not only for the "rollback" of Soviet gains in eastern Europe but also for the "unleashing" of Chiang Kai-shek.

As secretary of state, Dulles was often portrayed as the stern Presbyterian moralist who made speeches condemning atheistic Communism and threatening "massive retaliation." To many contemporaries he seemed the very model of a "cold warrior," and a moralist. To them also he seemed the true architect of US foreign policy, against a President who was but a *roi fainéant*. The records have belied the journalistic interpretation. Ike was in fact much more active, despite his ileitis. Dulles was shrewd and thoughtful; he did recognize the changes taking place in post-Stalinist Russia, and was prudent and cautious on atomic issues. And despite the repeated crises over Suez, Dien Bien Phu and the Lebanon, Dulles was adept at crisis management.[2]

[2] Dean Acheson, *Power and Diplomacy* (New York, Atheneum, 1962); Allen Dulles, *The Craft of Intelligence* (New York, Signet Books, 1962); Norman

Eisenhower, however, was far more than the conciliator with a ready smile that the cynics of the 1950s and 1960s made of him, and he resented the image of a "do-nothing" that was manufactured of him. There were tensions: the strains that long absence brought to Ike and his wife Mamie, the difficulties he later encountered with Marshall and with Truman when he moved towards politics, and the difficulties he found in handling academics in his short "reign" as president of Columbia University. But Eisenhower's was an unbroken success story. He never experienced defeat, either in war or in two presidential elections. And he never did anything wrong (which is not to say that he did not make serious errors of judgment). Even the celebrated "affair" with his English chauffeuse, Kay Summersby, seems, in Stephen Ambrose's considered view, to have amounted to no more than holding hands. He was, in fact, an absolute straight arrow, nurtured on the home, mother, and Bible prescriptions of small-town America.

Montgomery, who had little regard for Eisenhower's generalship and often disagreed with him, found that "He has the power of drawing the hearts of men towards him as a magnet attracts the bit of metal. He merely has to smile at you, and you trust him at once."

Other qualities included remarkable skill at poker (of which Montgomery would not have approved) and, surprisingly, a hot temper – what MacArthur described as "Ike's damned Dutch temper." Like that other famous soldier-president, George Washington, Eisenhower had an early brush with a fruit tree. In Washington's case the tree, a cherry, was chopped down with an axe and the offence admitted to his indignant father. Eisenhower's tree, an apple, had a different impact on the future President's formative years.

Refused permission at the age of ten to go "tricking and treating" on Hallowe'en, he rushed out and thumped the tree until his fists were a bleeding mass of torn flesh. Eisenhower was hauled away from the tree by his father and handed over to his mother, who as she bandaged his hand noted that "He that conquereth his own soul is greater than he who taketh a city." He remembered the occasion as "one of the most valuable moments of my life."

The temper flared again in Washington during the early days of America's involvement in the war, when General Marshall told him

---

Graebner, *The New Isolationism: Politics and foreign policy since 1950* (New York, Ronald Press, 1956); Christian Heron, *Towards an Atlantic Community* (New York, Harper, 1963); Henry Kissinger, *The Necessity for Choice: Prospects of American foreign policy* (Doubleday, Anchor Books, 1962).

he was going to remain deskbound in the capital. The fury was fleeting and Marshall changed his mind. Later, in Britain, it was noted at press conferences that his face reddened with anger when he spoke of the Nazis.

Criticisms of his generalship have focused on his broad front strategy in the advance to the Rhine and his failure to accept British advice and occupy Berlin before the Russians got there. The differences were so great over the need for a thrust to Berlin that by the end of the fiighting Eisenhower was no longer talking to Montgomery.

Perhaps Eisenhower was "weak", tending to be, as Field Marshal Sir Alan Brooke put it, "an arbiter balancing the requirements of competing allies and subordinates rather than a master of the field making a decisive choice." But would a more ruthless general have held together the alliance so successfully?

A veteran of long service to his country, Eisenhower came to high office as an attractive new personality with an internationalist outlook in foreign policy and a middle-of-the-road orientation in domestic affairs ("Moderate Republicanism"). During his eight years as President he delegated much of his party responsibility to Vice-President Richard Nixon, and a large part of foreign policy to Secretary of State John Foster Dulles.

As a soldier Eisenhower had a quick, clear understanding, human insight, and wide experience of the nation and the world. As President, he was able to work with Congress, predominantly Democratic for six of his eight years in office, with noteworthy cooperation. In domestic affairs he promoted a vast national highway program, liberalized the social security laws, and aided urban renewal. With Dulles as his representative in foreign affairs he ended the Korean War, initiated SEATO, and revived rapprochement with Latin America through the Organization of American States.

13
JFK, LBJ, and Vietnam

1 THE KENNEDY FAMILY

The line between criminal and tycoon is a narrow one. Consider the career of Joseph P. Kennedy, father of President John F. Kennedy. He was born in East Boston in 1888, the grandson of an Irish immigrant. The President's was a tightly knit family, his father a liquor merchant turned state senator, who married Rose Fitzgerald, daughter of Boston's garrulous mayor, John F. Fitzgerald, known to those who liked him as Honey Fitz. The marriage endured until his death, despite the couple leading separate private lives. Joe and Rose almost came to the point of formal separation after she had borne five children in six years, but she returned, fortified by the consolations of her religion and frequent shopping trips abroad. Joe was generous with her, and he could afford to be. In the 1920s he made one fortune after another, always setting the trend – liquor, automobiles, movies. On Wall Street he found it easy to play the market, boosting stocks with his allies until the moment came to unload them on the gullible. He wanted to make this easy money fast, he said, "before they pass a law against it."

Then he bought an ailing British film company, FBO, and moved on, to Hollywood, where he became a big producer of low-budget films, learning techniques of publicity he would never forget, and losing his head to the movie queen Gloria Swanson. At the height of their affair Kennedy had flaunted Swanson, even taking her on an Atlantic crossing with his wife. Nearly 50 years later Rose Kennedy was still ingenuous about the trip, telling the biographer Doris Kearns that "I knew I never had a thing to worry about, and I only felt sorry for poor little Gloria."

Kennedy *père* remained an avid pursuer of women – an hereditary trait. "He was a big, handsome, well-muscled, charming guy," his former aide Harvey Klemmer recalled. "He liked women and women liked him. But he regarded them as a kind of food – to be consumed." His staff were expected to procure for him; a chore which was repeated for his second son. Neither the dignity of ambassadorial office, when he became the US ambassador in London, nor the self-respect of late middle age ever got in his way. His sons became used to him as a sexual competitor. "The ambassador prowls at night," Jack would warn girls visiting the Kennedy estates at Palm Beach and Hyannisport. The role of the sexual predator was one he handed on to his older sons, Joe Jr and Jack. "You must remember," says Jack's friend William Walton, who visited the compounds often in the 1940s and 1950s, "there was no tradition of monogamy in that family."

That was true for the sons, but Kennedy went to extreme lengths to protect his daughter's virtue. Kathleen Kennedy told her startled suitor John White that her father had a dossier on him, and that she had to report her doings to him each day. Joe relished the control that his money gave him. He was generous and loving, but he found it hard to let go. Even when his second son was a US Congressman, Joe methodically worked through his staff until he found one who was prepared to be his eyes and ears in Washington. As the sons progressed through school and Harvard and toured the world at his expense, Joe kept up a barrage of advice and encouragement, pressing their letters on his friends. Trust funds were settled on them at an early age. They never needed to work in his enterprises, and they may never have fully known what these were. It was not always easy to find out.

In the 1920s, rumor had it that the older Kennedy was a bootlegger, importing and selling illicit liquor. Doris Kearns, the only historian to have access to Kennedy's papers, found scant evidence there to support the claims made by, among others, the gangster Frank Costello and Meyer Lansky, of large underworld deals. But Kennedy went into the Prohibition era with large stocks of liquor from his father's stores, and on the day it ended he had three lucrative franchises for British whisky and gin, a company to import them, and a network of retailers already in place. It was the work of a man who knew well where the subterranean rivers of illicit booze had run during Prohibition, but kept the knowledge close. His papers guard it still.

In any event, the liquor profits were a mere aperitif for the fortune Kennedy made on Wall Street. In February 1929, with the market still rising in response to the election of Hebert Hoover, Kennedy began to sell out, for cash or bonds. Arthur Poole, the last survivor of his financial team in the 1920s, remembers the incredulity of Kennedy's boardroom colleagues at Paramount Pictures when he told them that their stock was overvalued, and that he proposed to sell it short in the market. "They all said, 'Don't do that; you'll lose your shirt. Things are doing wonderfully well.'"

By selling short (borrowing the stock, selling, waiting for the price to fall and then buying back at a far lower price the stock to be returned), Kennedy took the Paramount share price down from $35 to $6. When the October crash came, Kennedy was one of the few who kept his shirt, and more.

This was an unlikely background for a public man, but Joe Kennedy saw no incongruity. He sensed that the response to the crash would bring a greater role for governments, and he became Franklin Roosevelt's ardent supporter, raising $200,000 for the 1932 presidential campaign. He correctly saw that Roosevelt would save capitalism, not destroy it, and would have been happy, he said, to gamble half his fortune on the New Deal if that meant he could keep the other half. He wanted power as well as security, but the reformers around Roosevelt were suspicious of him. Roosevelt had been in power two years before Joe was given a job, and it was greeted with howls of protest in Washington. The poacher was asked to turn gamekeeper, and chair a new Securities and Exchange Commission to regulate Wall Street. It would mean policing the very practices out of which his own fortune had come, and he did it with alacrity. "He knew which way these jokers worked, you see," recalls Frank Wardrop, then editor of the *Washington Times-Herald*. "So he thought he could sort them out. And he did."

Always a man of prodigious appetites, he now wanted power for himself. In a ghosted book titled I'm For Roosevelt, the self-styled "Father of Nine" disclaimed personal ambition and called for four more years of FDR. The President rewarded him with warm words and a second-rank appointment, outside the Cabinet. He was made chairman of the US Maritime Commission, charged with the regeneration of America's merchant marine. Kennedy was unabashed. "It's not what you are, but what people think you are," he always said. And he made sure that the commission's economic survey secured dramatic publicity in the newsreels and newspapers of media magnate William Randolph Hearst. One of the men who turned it out for him, Harvey Klemmer, was astonished to find it "treated like the second coming of Christ." No opportunity was lost to build up his achievements in his two government posts, and he now craved another. By the end of 1937 Roosevelt had three years to run in his second and (it was assumed) final term. Kennedy dreamed of succeeding him – as the first Catholic President.

There was one post which offered both social status for the brash Irish-American outsider and a high international profile, ambassador to the Court of St James. Kennedy lobbied hard for it, through FDR's worldly son Jimmy, who had already done him favors in securing British liquor franchises. Kennedy did not expect to stay long. His style was to move in, analyze, recommend, and move on, with profits and/or publicity augmented. Eighteen months in the embassy might be the perfect coronet for the public career of Joe Kennedy, contender for the Democratic nomination in 1940. Instead, his London years were to bring disaster.

The posting began well, in March 1938. "The regular diplomats were absolutely terrified of Joe," the embassy secretary Page H. Wilson recalls, "but the press went absolutely ape over the entire family. I don't think there was a day in a month that there wasn't a photograph of the Kennedy family." Teddy opened the Children's Corner at the Zoo. Even their unfortunate eldest daughter Rosemary was presented at Court and appeared in the newsreels. Joe Jr, Jack, and their sister Kathleen cut a swathe through London society.

The only problem was Hitler. When Joe Kennedy arrived in London, Hitler's designs on Austria and Czechoslovakia were apparent for all to see. They gave Kennedy few qualms. He had no desire to see his country embroiled in any kind of European war, and the best way to avoid it, he argued, was to follow through the appeasement policies of Neville Chamberlain. The two became a mutual admiration society, with Kennedy privy to Cabinet secrets in exchange for his support in public speeches.

The ambassador had no faith that the British cause would prevail in a war with Germany, and for ancestral reasons he had little faith in the British Empire. He saw it like a business problem. Germany, if you believed the estimates of Colonel Lindbergh, as Kennedy did, was now the stronger military power. It would be better to cut a deal than be taken over. The moral case against the Nazis meant little to him. Harvey Klemmer, whom he had brought from the Maritime Commission, knew him to be a casual antisemite ("Individual Jews are all right, Harvey, but as a race they stink – look what they did to Hollywood.") Now Klemmer's reports back from Germany on the repression of the Jews were dismissed. "They brought it on themselves," Kennedy said, and in a confidential meeting with the German ambassador, Von Dirksen, he said that he "understood our Jewish problem completely." After the *Kristallnacht* outrages, Kennedy's views changed, but up to the outbreak of the war he hoped desperately that the Germans could somehow be bought off. Nor did his tone change thereafter. Home on a visit in East Boston (not a notably pro-British locality), he said, "There's no place in this fight for us." The three months that elapsed before he made a tardy return to London allowed British resentment to come to the boil.

Kennedy had tried hard to be popular in Britain, and he unfailingly complimented the nation's tenacity, even if he thought it doomed. Now his stock had fallen. A "Kennediana" file circulated in the Foreign Office, recording Joe's rumored words and deeds. He told more than one journalist his dismissive view of Winston Churchill, the new power in the British government: "Never trust a man who is always sucking on a whiskey bottle." As Churchill established his own correspondence with Roosevelt, and the President tried to keep his options for aiding the democracies open, Kennedy was first sidelined, then undermined.

The Kennediana file contained allegations that Joe was playing the stock market, using his insider knowledge. No one knew for sure how much information he had on British plans to liquidate American security holdings to raise cash for war supplies. Klemmer remembered him on the phone from his English country retreat, yelling instructions down the phone to Johnny Burns, who handled his stocks in New York, but not the stocks involved. The mud stuck. He was "a very foul specimen of double-crosser and defeatist who thinks only of lining his own pocket," said Lord Vansittart, the senior Foreign Office figure most clearly identified with opposition to appeasement. And his business dealings were insensitive. When he had come to Britain he had kept his whiskey company, Somerset Imports, in full operation. Klemmer, the attaché from the Maritime Commission, was charged with commandeering precious cargo space on the perilous convoys for the ambassador's whiskey. "Using the prestige of the embassy," he remembered, "we got space for 200,000 cases, and it got so bad that a friend in the Ministry of Shipping came to see me and said, 'You'd better go easy because one of his competitors is threatening to raise a question in Parliament about the improper activities of the American embassy.' So we pulled our horns in a little after that."

In their eagerness to trap Kennedy, the British security services had his phones bugged. Embassy cars were stopped on a pretext and covertly searched. The chargé d'Áffaires, Herschel Johnson, was bombarded in Kennedy's absences with dark hints about the leaking to the Germans of the ambassador's cables to Washington.

The ambassador's fury was palpable. He had to admit to Roosevelt that their secret correspondence had been filched and decoded; he could not guarantee the security of the embassy's communications. He had been neatly stitched up by Churchill, who could feel sure that the most dangerous opponent of American involvement in the war had been discredited.

Joe Kennedy now ached to return to his family back home. Roosevelt was bullied and threatened. When the night bombing of London began, the ambassador took himself at 4 p.m. each day to a rented mansion in the country. The ruling circles which had welcomed him and been charmed by his vibrant children began to shun him. The present Duke of Devonshire, whose older brother Billy Hartington was to marry Kathleen Kennedy in 1944, remembers that "when he pushed off to somewhere in Surrey to avoid the bombing we didn't think much of that, no. We thought if we could face it and not think much of it, so could he."

He returned home for good in October, telling Klemmer that he was going back to tell the American people "that that crippled son of a bitch in the White House is going to drag their kids into the war." He did no such thing. When the Boeing Clipper touched down at the New York terminal, he was whisked away with Rose to see the President, encouraged to pour out his frustrations, cajoled and flattered.

No one knows quite how the Roosevelt magic worked, but Kennedy went out and paid $320,000 of his own money for radio time. He urged the nation to stay out of war, mentioned his own "nine hostages to fortune" – and endorsed Roosevelt. His wilting political career might have been saved even then, but a few days later he blew it away forever with some remarks in Boston which he thought were off the record. "Democracy all done in Britain, maybe here" was the headline. It was Kennedy who was all done. His daughter Kathleen phoned her friends: "Please cheer Dad up. He thinks his life is over."

The foreboding with which Kennedy had greeted the war was personally justified. At first he could play the patriarch at home. "He's always presented as a stupid money making capitalist," remembers the artist William Walton. "Well, he was all those, but he was also very bright, and quite intellectual in many ways. Not the conventional picture. Nor was his role in the family. He was home more than I expected. And he had a far greater role in his children's lives than their mother did."

Joe's plans for the family were boundless; again, they were destroyed when America went to war. His eldest son, Joe Jr, to whom he had transferred all his political hopes, was blown to pieces over East Anglia on a secret bombing mission. His daughter Kathleen married Lord Hartington, a Protestant, to the great anguish of Rose, whose simple piety decreed that mixed marriages were made in hell. Within weeks, Hartington too was killed in action. In another cruel twist, Joe had had his daughter Rosemary lobotomized in 1941, neither consulting Rose nor telling her afterward what had gone wrong. Rosemary survives in body to this day, but the pretty, gentle creature whom the family had cherished in their competitive midst was gone.

Jack, the detached, ironic second son, was injured in the Pacific but survived to become the family standard-bearer. Joe submerged his own ambitions, and even his personality, in Jack's campaigns. By 1957, Joe was estimated to be one of the dozen richest men in the United States. He did good works for charity, often anonymously, and he would go anywhere – even deep into the underworld – to help his second son become President.

When that bright day dawned, Joe Kennedy was on the rostrum as the Inaugural Parade rolled by. As the President passed, Joe raised his hat to the young man who had always puzzled him, and Jack Kennedy rose awkwardly in the limousine to doff his own hat in reply. The older man could be forgiven for a moment of melancholy. Twenty years before it had been his hour, and he had failed the test. But the family had captured the castle in the end.

2 JFK AND CIVIL RIGHTS

Born in 1917, John Fitzgerald Kennedy, the 35th President, who was assassinated in Dallas, Texas, in November 1963, was not only the youngest President in American history and the first Roman Catholic to be elected President, but he promised to be one of the greatest. He was indeed a charismatic figure: he was Irish-American, he was rich, he was Harvard-educated, he was a liberal and a thinker as well as a man of action. He won a first-ballot nomination at the Democratic party's Los Angeles convention in July 1960 and then pulled off what proved to be an essential political coup by selecting Senator Lyndon B. Johnson of Texas as his running mate. Kennedy's electoral college margin of 303 to 219 against Richard M. Nixon was won with little more than a 100,000-vote plurality out of nearly 69 million cast; the margin was especially narrow in Cook County, Illinois (Chicago). At the age of 43, he became the youngest man to reach the White House.

Civil rights became Kennedy's major domestic preoccupation as President, and aided by his brother Robert, the attorney general, he strove hard to ensure equal rights and equal opportunities for black people. The name JFK gave to his program was "The New Frontier." On March 6, 1961, an executive order established the President's Committee on Equal Employment Opportunity for firms with government contracts. Within the first 10 months his Administration began 14 voting-rights cases under the Civil Rights Act of 1957, compared to 9 cases between 1957 and 1960. On May 14, black and white Freedom Riders were attacked when testing segregation barriers in bus terminals in Birmingham, Alabama. In September, the Interstate Commerce Commission prohibited segregation both on interstate buses and in terminals.

On August 27, 1962, the Twenty-fourth Amendment, banning the poll tax requirement in federal elections, was sent to the states; it was ratified by January 23, 1964. On September 30, President Kennedy sent 3,000 federal troops to the University of Mississippi to stop a riot and secure the admission of James H. Meredith, the first black student at the university. On November 24, he issued an executive order banning discrimination in federally-assisted housing.

In April 1963 Martin Luther King began to lead mass demonstrations in Birmingham, Alabama, to desegregate the city. Police met marching blacks in Birmingham with fire hoses and police dogs in May of that year. Kennedy threatened, but never sent troops. On June 11, Governor George Wallace barred the registration of two black students at the University of Alabama, but gave way when Kennedy federalized the Alabama National Guard. On the same day, in a television address, President Kennedy referred to civil rights as a "moral issue" and strongly supported a civil rights Act. The following day, Medgar W. Evers, a leader of the NAACP in Mississippi, was shot from ambush and killed in Jackson, Mississippi. On August 28, 1963, a massive civil rights march took place in Washington DC, and Martin Luther King gave his "I have a dream" speech at the Lincoln Memorial. On September 15, efforts to integrate schools in Birmingham led to violence. Bombing of a Sunday school killed four black girls; it was the 21st such bombing in Birmingham in eight years.

It was after JFK's death, but as a legacy, that on July 2 1964 The Civil Rights Act became law. The terms (1) expedited law suits over voting rights; (2) barred discrimination in public accommodations (the Supreme Court upheld this section in *Heart of Atlanta Motel* vs. *United States*, 1964); (3) authorized the attorney general to institute suits to desegregate schools; (4) barred discrimination in any program receiving federal assistance; and (5) set up an Equal Employment Opportunity Commission.

The passing of the Act was marked by black riots caused by ghetto living, unemployment, and hatred of the police, which erupted in Harlem (July 18–22), Rochester, NY (July 24–25), Jersey City (August 2–4), Chicago (August 16–17), and Philadelphia (August 28–30). On August 4, three young civil rights workers were found murdered near Philadelphia, Mississippi. The FBI arrested 21 people in connection with the murders. In October 1967, seven were convicted of conspiracy to violate a person's civil rights.

On February 21, 1965, Malcolm X, formerly eastern leader of the Black Muslims, was shot and killed in New York City. Elijah Muhammed, leader of the Black Muslims, who had ousted Malcolm X, denied any connection with the murder. In March, a civil rights march took place from Selma to Montgomery, Alabama, to encourage greater black voter registration. On August 6, the Civil Rights Act of 1965 became law, with the following terms: (1) literacy tests were to be suspended in any county that used the test to disqualify voters and had a voter turnout of less than 50 percent of its eligible population (Alabama, Georgia, Louisiana, Mississippi, South Carolina, Virginia, and parts of Arizona and Idaho were included in this category); (2) federal voting examiners would then be sent to register voters; (3) the attorney general was empowered to proceed against discriminatory state poll taxes. The Supreme Court upheld the Act in *South Carolina* vs. *Katzenbach*, 1966.

3 JFK AND FOREIGN POLICY

Kennedy's grand design in Europe was an attempt to extend the European Economic Community (or Common Market) by the adherence of Britain and the Scandinavian states, and to help it to become a political community. It was hoped that this would lead to the development of the Atlantic Alliance into a balanced partnership between two more or less equal elements – equal at least in population and economic potential – United Europe and the United States. The weakness of the "equal partnership" theme of the Kennedy administration was that the virtual supremacy of the United States in its nuclear weapons made any real equality of rights and duties within the Atlantic Alliance impossible.

At the same time, Kennedy worked for a thaw in the Cold War. Although on guard against further Soviet expansionism, he improved relations between the Soviet Union and the United States in 1963 by a treaty banning the testing of nuclear devices in the atmosphere, and by easing the most acute tensions over Berlin. On August 5, 1963, the nuclear Test Ban Treaty was signed, by which the US, the USSR, and Great Britain agreed not to test nuclear weapons in the atmosphere. On August 30, the US and the USSR opened a "hot line" communications link to lessen the risk of accidental war. France, which had exploded its first nuclear bomb in February 1960, did not sign the treaty.

Indeed, in 1963–5 President de Gaulle of France adopted an independent anti-American foreign policy: he

1 signed a cooperation treaty with West Germany (Jan. 22, 1963);
2 vetoed the admission of Great Britain to the European Common Market;
3 opposed American plans for a NATO nuclear force;
4 having already developed France's own nuclear bomb, refused to sign the nuclear test ban;
5 gave diplomatic recognition to Communist China;
6 opposed American participation in the Vietnam War; and
7 insisted (Sept. 1965) that NATO withdraw all troops and bases from France by 1967.

Cuba, within 90 miles of the Florida Keys, and with which the US had felt involved since "liberating" it from Spain 50 years before, brought the Cold War close to American shores. In April 1961, JFK's attempt to free Cuba from Fidel Castro's grip by launching an invasion of "friends" (US-sponsored Cuban exiles), became a fiasco at the Bay of Pigs, which heightened tension in the relations between Cuba and the US. On October 14, 1962, a second and far more dangerous crises occurred. The US discovered that the Russians were installing missile sites on Cuba with a range covering most of the US. On October 22, President Kennedy ordered the USSR to withdraw its missiles and imposed a quarantine by naval blockade on Cuba. On October 26, with a possible nuclear war threatened, Khrushchev offered to remove the missile bases if Kennedy would promise not to invade Cuba. On October 28, Kennedy and Khrushchev agreed on the substance of Khrushchev's offer to withdraw the armaments. Finally, on November 21, Kennedy lifted the blockade after the USSR had given assurances that the missiles had been removed.

From the beginning of its history the United States has been concerned with South America. President Kennedy in 1961 committed his country to a ten-year plan of economic and social development

Plate 10a Cuban Missile Site.
(Library of Congress.)

Plate 10b President Kennedy calls the USSR's bluff during the Cuban missile crisis of October 1962; the missiles were dismantled.
(Library of Congress.)

of Latin America; and in May 1961 Congress passed appropriations of $500 million for general aid, plus a further $100 million in loans to help Chile recover from the disastrous 1960 earthquake. It was estimated that the whole ten-year program (which the President named *Alianza para el progreso* or "Alliance for Progress") might cost some $13,000 million. This aid was made conditional on the willingness of the Latin American governments to carry out social reforms – in particular, land reform and adequate taxation of the rich. While outwardly grateful, some Latin Americans resented these political strings; others doubted whether this attempt to impose social democracy from without could be successful.

John F. Kennedy was responsible for the US becoming aware of black Africa. Colonialism was in flight, and Kennedy was squarely behind those who had won or were about to win their freedom. Washington during this period was wide-eyed in its hopes for democracy in Africa. It was generous in its grants of aid and technical assistance and engaged in covert intervention to prevent the new nations from tying themselves to the Soviet Union.

During this period the independence of black African nations emboldened the black power movement in the United States. The example and the rhetoric of the new governments encouraged black Americans, just as black power in the United States subsequently helped stimulate the rise of a black consciousness movement in apartheid-ridden South Africa. In many ways the ideological forebears of the African movements of independence and black power were the same: both Marcus Garvey's back to Africa crusade of the 1920s and the Pan-African Congresses of the 1920s–1940s. Many of the Africans who led the Congresses and later became national leaders in West Africa had been schooled in the United States and had incorporated its social and political values.

No greater contribution to strengthening the bonds between America and Africa was crafted than by Kennedy's Peace Corps, which from its inception forged strong people-to-people ties between two very different cultures. By 1989, 3,000 volunteers were living in 27 African countries.

Since the Kennedy era, US aid levels have dropped dramatically, to $850 million of non-military aid in 1989. Some of Kennedy's successors, like Presidents Richard M. Nixon and Gerald Ford, aligned the United States with Portugal (which had colonies in Africa until 1974–5) and South Africa. Although major efforts were made during the presidency of Jimmy Carter to wrest Namibia from South Africa and assist Rhodesia's transition to independence as Zimbabwe (in 1980), President Ronald Reagan's administration had markedly cool relations with black Africa. Nearly all the nations on the continent perceived the United States during this period as pro-South Africa and at best ambivalent about the freedom struggle there.

4 CAMELOT

When you ask an American what it is about the Kennedys which still intrigues the nation, they usually reply with something like; "They're our royal family, you should understand."

On the face of it, that explanation is ludicrous. John Kennedy was President for just two years and ten months. Bobby Kennedy was cut down while pursuing the presidential nomination in 1968 before he could submit to the national electorate. The youngest brother, Edward Kennedy, is an effective member of the US Senate, but on account of his legendary boozing and philandering, he is viewed as a lightweight figure outside his home state of Massachusetts. JFK's assassination was shocking in that it cost the country someone so young, so full of promise, so selfconsciously forward-looking. It was the crime of the century, and it has since come to be viewed as a crime against that generation which came of age, and fought, in World War II. Yet, there is still a weird discrepancy between the intensity of the continuing national mourning – the sheer size of the Kennedy phenomenon – and JFK's relatively small real legacy. His legislative record was unremarkable. He was slow to move towards passing a civil rights bill, and his presidency coincided with some of the ugliest scenes of overt racial hatred the country had seen (or has seen since). Then there were foreign-policy disasters, like the bungled Bay of Pigs invasion.

Over three decades, the image of national renewal under Kennedy, the generational aspect of torches being passed, has been assiduously promoted, not least by the Kennedys themselves. The Kennedy presidency was supposed to represent a new era, but in many respects it marked the end of an old one.

Aside from the endless replay of footage from Dallas, most of the recurring images on television of that time reflect prosperity and glamor, economic self-confidence. There are frequent TV "repeats" of the black-tie concerts in the White House, of his beautiful wife Jackie (later Mrs Onassis) and the picture-perfect children, and even that famous film of Marilyn Monroe, breathless (and tipsy), singing "Happy Birthday, Mr President." By contrast, the fleeting images of the Lyndon Johnson presidency which make their way onto television screens today show civil unrest, racial protest, and, of course, Vietnam. It is true that much of the civil turbulence first emerged in the Kennedy era, and that Kennedy himself often sounded like President Clinton today with his dire warnings about stagnating living standards. But Americans still associate Kennedy with prosperity.

A recent study of Kennedy[1] presents an unusual but plausible portrait of those years in the White House. The author argues that Kennedy was an adequate but scarcely inspirational chief executive, who made his share of mistakes but was usually saved by a natural intelligence and an irrepressible personal charm. Kennedy is presented not as a megahero, nor as a fiendish sexual predator – the two extremes portrayed in some biographies – but as an astute politician, hiding behind a glamorous veneer. Kennedy was, of course, the first American President to understand the power of television, and to know instinctively how to exploit it.

Americans like to see a certain style in the White House, and they want their Presidents somehow to fit that great office, and to look like winners. That is why they quickly tired of Jimmy Carter with his woolly cardigan and the turned-down thermostat, and why they liked the way the Reagans seemed to relish their eight years in the White House. Even those who hated the Reagans enjoyed being appalled by their vulgar Hollywood friends.

Highlights of Kennedy's most famous speeches are carved into the stone surrounding his grave in Arlington. Those rhetorical flourishes about bearing any burden for the cause of freedom suggest a governing class at one with itself and certain of its mission, and a people still feeling rich after the explosive economic growth of the 1950s. America is rightly judged an optimistic nation, but Americans are also a nostalgic people. When they look back to the Kennedy era, they think of wealth, certainty, and their national virtue, a brief pause before the world suddenly became a nastier place, which it remains.

JFK's rash sexual conduct put his presidency at risk, not least the reputation for prudence, loyalty, compassion, and integrity that has come to be seen as the hallmarks of the men who were Washington's successors. Politicians should not be held to unreasonable standards, and they can sometimes grow in office, as JFK did, but while good character is not a sufficient condition for office, it should be considered a necessary one. The press has a responsibility

[1] Richard Reeves, *President Kennedy – Profile of power* (New York, Bantam paperback, 1963).

to examine questions about character; in the Kennedy years, it failed, seduced by the glamor and the sycophants that the Kennedy millions bought. The press treated JFK as one who could do no wrong. By contrast, they hounded Richard Nixon.

With the death of Jacqueline Onassis in 1994, two questions raised themselves more strongly than ever. Why did the American press never report Jack Kennedy's compulsive promiscuity? American newspapers are biased towards respectability. Most of all they protect their readers. Styling themselves "family newspapers," they ruthlessly reveal scandals of the boardroom but not the bedroom. They are far less political in news coverage than the British press, and (even the *New York Times*) very much anchored to the city where they are based – as they must be to pull in the huge local advertisements on which their revenues depend. And they know their audience is by and large puritanical in outlook. The reason why Kennedy's affairs were ignored was not the liberal press's sympathy for his policies but the public's own aversion to reading about it. In the era before the sexual revolution, presidential indiscretions were never reported.

The lesson that American papers are reluctantly learning from Britain is that sex is political news. They must learn the lesson, however, not to boost falling circulations but to honor their own sexual equality laws. Sex is now recognized as power that can be abused. Sexual harassment legislation, according to John Finney, former Washington editor of the *New York Times*, now lecturer in media at Georgetown University, is presenting a terrible problem for the serious American newspapers of the kind he believes in. "We don't like gossip and scandal unless verified," he says. But, under today's new ethos, to refuse to print allegations unless these get to court is tantamount to depriving victims of access to the press unless they are rich enough to hire lawyers. The press's self-restraint therefore serves to shelter those in power.

The advance of information technology also now yields up evidence of the kind that can be aired in court, such as records of phone calls giving the destination and length of each one. In the early. 1960s, Kennedy's women were not talking to the press, let alone gathering up their taped conversations and going to court, bankrolled by his political opponents.

But JFK's was not the only Camelot of the 1960s: the 1960s was the "peace and love era." This was in part the product of affluence: many of its followers were children of affluent middle-class families. But parents watched in bewilderment as their children dropped out of college, burned their draft cards, grew their hair long and joined free-living communes where drink, drugs, and sex were readily available. Some of the members of this (so-called) "family" were devil-worshippers, and some were murderers. Much of their language was incoherent.

Some saw the "high priest" of this cult as Charles Manson. In August 1969 Manson and some of his acolytes tortured and then murdered the film star Sharon Tate, the wife of Roman Polanski, and eight other randomly selected Hollywood victims, in a vicious and senseless crime. Manson was found guilty of murder after a trial that was itself for weeks a TV drama, and he is still serving a prison sentence in Corcoran Prison, California. The crime brought alarm to the Establishment. From being a weird and charismatic figure, Manson is now, it seems, aged sixty and a mildly crazed nonentity; it appears that he will never be released. He has been described as "The Man Who Killed the Sixties."

The story is uglier even than this. Only two years before the Tate murder, Manson had been released from prison, where he was serving a sentence for a number of murders. He formed and led a "group marriage" commune and preached race war. Alarmed by the emergence of the militarily organized Black Panthers, he expected the US to become torn by racial conflict, and planned to blame the Sharon Tate killing on blacks. He himself in 1969 was no young student; he was 35, and had spent 17 years in jail. But the society in which he caused so much alarm was torn not only by the fear of race war, but by the reality of the war in Vietnam, against which there were hundreds of protests, notably at Kent State University and in California, and where drugs were too easily available. Only a few months before both Robert Kennedy and Martin Luther King had been assassinated; Woodstock – a farm in the Catskills where in August 1969 a quarter of a million young people gathered – had become synonymous with vice and violence, as well as rock 'n' roll and the fateful Rolling Stones concert had taken place at Altamount.

There was yet a further "Camelot". In July 1969 the Apollo mission landed two astronauts on the moon: Neil Armstrong and Buzz Aldrin – a remarkable achievement, another great myth come true.

The space race was a by-product of the arms race, which was part of the Cold War fallout from Hitler's war; Soviet-American conflict by scientific proxy, "our Germans versus their Germans," as Tom Wolfe put it in *The Right Stuff*. With American rocketry under the tutelage of Wernher von Braun, Saturn V was the direct descendant of the V-2 flying bomb. The cost was tremendous; but the competitive edge it gave the West was huge. Forget Teflon and lightweight aluminium foil, the real spinoff of the space program was the research and development of computer systems that could be trusted to function even on the dark side of the moon. The lunar program was the genesis of the revolution in information technology, though the commercial development of it turned out to be a small step for America and a giant leap for Japan.

With the race over, the exploitation of space technology is now back where it started with Sputnik and Telstar, close to home. Space itself remains the final frontier.[2]

5 LYNDON B. JOHNSON

President Kennedy was succeeded by his Vice-President, the Texan, Lyndon B. Johnson. A native of the hill country of Texas, Johnson appeared to his enemies as a stereotypical Texan: large, crude, egotistical, manipulative, and overbearing. Although a remarkably resourceful Congressional leader, he could not shake the popular view that he was a wheeling-dealing political operator.

He earned a degree from South West Texas State Teachers College in 1930, taught school in Houston, served as a Congressional aide in Washington, and became Texas director of the National Youth Administration, a New Deal agency. Elected as a Democrat to the House of Representatives in 1937, he served until 1949, and then moved to the Senate. Johnson rose quickly in the upper chamber, becoming majority leader in 1955. In that capacity he developed a well-earned reputation for hard work, attention to detail, and great skill at reconciling varied interests. President Johnson was an experienced politician who believed strongly that problems can be settled if men will reason together. He described his task as that of building in the United States "The Great Society;" he pledged the support of his Administration to a "war against poverty" and to a policy of aid for "the forgotten fifth."

Thanks mainly to profitable investments in radio and television, Johnson was wealthy, but he identified with poor people, including African-Americans and Hispanics, and he greatly admired the liberal programs of President Franklin D. Roosevelt. When he reached the

[2] Andrew Chainik, *A Man on the Moon: The voyages of the Apollo astronauts* (London, Michael Joseph, 1980); Tom Wolfe, *The Right Stuff* (New York, Farrar, Straus and Giranx, 1983).

White House, he resolved to broaden and expand the New Deal – to create what he called the Great Society. Using all his political talents to the full, he secured approval in 1964 of the War on Poverty program and the first significant civil rights legislation since the 1870s.

After a landslide victory over Republican Barry Goldwater in the 1964 presidential election, he pressed successfully for a wide range of liberal programs, including Medicare (health insurance for the elderly), Medicaid (care for the welfare poor), federal aid to elementary and secondary education, more liberal immigration laws, the creation of the National Endowments for the Arts and Humanities, and a federal guarantee of voting rights. Thanks in good part to Johnson's extraordinarily able leadership, much of the agenda of modern American liberalism finally became the law of the land.

Many of these programs, however, evoked criticism. Medicare and Medicaid, although important to millions of people, proved to be much more expensive than proponents had anticipated. Partly because of cutbacks in funding, the War on Poverty fell far short of expectations. The civil rights law, while promoting legal equality, did not address the socioeconomic problems of African-Americans. Aggressive neo-conservatives counterattacked in the 1970s and 1980s, keeping American liberalism on the defensive.

Although President Johnson was less interested in foreign policy than was his predecessor, during his administration the Alliance for Progress moved from the stage of planning of Kennedy's day to the point where practical progress was possible. Johnson withdrew the US from the multilateral force, the NATO-nuclear-fleet concept that he inherited from the Kennedy administration, and foreign aid was put on a more hardheaded basis. New bridges of culture and trade were extended toward eastern Europe. The policy towards China was modified under the fresh slogan of "containment without isolation." And the Communist conquest of South Vietnam, which seemed imminent not long before, now seemed unlikely. With almost half a million men involved, the Vietnam War remained the major problem of the Johnson administration, and the major moral dilemma of the American people. As anti-war protests increased, the liberal spirit of the early 1960s waned, and the President became secretive and stubborn.

In 1968 Johnson began at last to listen to new advisers. He announced that he would not run again for President and that he was encouraging peace talks in Paris. But he refused to make significant concessions, and the war continued. When Johnson left office in January 1969 he was tired, despondent, and unpopular with the majority of the American people. He returned to his ranch in Texas, where he died four years later.[3]

6 VIETNAM

The war in Vietnam was in part the legacy of US support for France in its effort after 1945 to restore its empire in Indochina, and in part anxiety in 1945 and after at the spread of Communism both in Europe and Asia. Dictatorial communism was seen as Russian and Chinese in origin, and fear of it dominated American foreign policy from the presidency of Dwight D. Eisenhower to that of Ronald Reagan. Having triumphed in World War II, the US had a strong sense of moral rectitude and of material confidence. Any Communist anywhere – abroad and at home – was seen as the enemy. The appeasement of Fascism in the 1930s was seen as the cause of World War II; there must be no repetition. The enemy must be contained, and "containment" had become a jargon word for American foreign policy under Truman and "Ike."

Vietnam had a prelude in Korea. Each country was divided into North (Communist) and South. In Vietnam, Ho Chi Minh and the Vietmin front had been in power since 1941, and had the support of Communist China. They were ardent Vietnamese nationalists who fought first to rid their country of the Japanese and then, after 1945, to prevent France from reestablishing its former colonial mastery over Vietnam and the rest of Indochina. Harry S. Truman and other American leaders, having no sympathy for French colonialism, favored Vietnamese independence. But expanding Communist control of Eastern Europe and the triumph of the Communists in China's civil war made France's war against Ho seem an anti-Communist rather than a colonialist effort. When France agreed to a quasi-independent Vietnam under Emperor Bao Dai as an alternatiive to Ho's Communist forces, the United States decided to support the French position.

The American conception of Vietnam as a Cold War battleground largely ignored the struggle for social justice and national sovereignty occurring within the country. American attention focused primarily on Europe and on Asia beyond Vietnam. Aid to France in Indochina was a *quid pro quo* for French cooperation with

[3] Paul K. Conkin, *Big Daddy from the Pedernales: Lyndon Baines Johnson* (Boston, Twayne, 1986); Allen J. Matusow, *The Unraveling of America: A history of liberalism in the 1960s* (New York, Harper and Row, 1984).

America's plans for the defense of Europe through the North Atlantic Treaty Organization. After China became a Communist state in 1949, the stability of Japan became of paramount importance to Washington, and Japanese development required access to the markets and raw materials of Southeast Asia. The outbreak of war in Korea in 1950 served primarily to confirm Washington's belief that Communist aggression posed a great danger to Asia. And subsequent charges that Truman had "lost" China and had settled for a stalemate in Korea caused succeeding Presidents to fear the domestic political consequences if they "lost" Vietnam. This apprehension, an overestimation of American power, and an underestimation of Vietnamese Communist strength locked all US administrations from 1950 through the 1960s into a firm anti-Communist stand in Vietnam.

President Dwight D. Eisenhower increased the level of aid to the French but continued to avoid military intervention, even when the French experienced a devastating defeat at Dien Bien Phu in the spring of 1954. Following that battle, an international conference at Geneva, Switzerland, arranged a ceasefire, and provided for a North-South partition of Vietnam until elections could be held. The United States was not a party to the Geneva Agreements and began to foster the creation of a Vietnamese regime in South Vietnam to rival that of Ho in the North. Eisenhower enunciated the "domino theory," which held that, if the Communists succeeded in controlling Vietnam, they would progressively dominate all of Southeast Asia. With support from Washington, South Vietnam's autocratic president Ngo Dinh Diem, who deposed Bao Dai in October 1955, resisted holding an election on the reunification of Vietnam. Despite over $1 billion of US aid between 1955 and 1961, the South Vietnamese economy languished and internal security deteriorated. Nation-building was failing in the South, and, in 1960, Communist cadres created the National Liberation Front (NLF), or Vietcong as its enemies called it, to challenge the regime of President Ngo Dinh Diem.

President John F. Kennedy concurred with his predecessor's domino theory and also believed that the credibility of US anti-Communist commitments around the world was imperiled in 1961. Consequently, by 1963 he had tripled American aid to South Vietnam and expanded the number of military advisers there from less than 700 to 20,000.

In 1964, with a presidential election approaching, Lyndon B. Johnson did not want to be saddled with the charge of having lost South Vietnam. On the other hand, an expansion of US

Map 11 Southeast Asia and the Vietnam War.

Plate 11 US soldier in Vietnam.
(Library of Congress.)

responsibility for the war against the Vietcong and North Vietnam would divert resources from Johnson's ambitious and expensive domestic program, the Great Society. A larger war in Vietnam also raised the risk of a military clash with China. Using as a provocation alleged North Vietnamese attacks on US Navy vessels in the Gulf of Tonkin in August 1964, Johnson authorized limited bombing raids on North Vietnam and secured a resolution from Congress allowing him to use military forces in Vietnam. These actions helped Johnson win the November election, but they did not dissuade the Vietcong from its relentless pressure against the Saigon government.

During 1965 direct US involvement progressively increased. Toward the end of the year American strength reached a level of 165,000 men and was expected to rise shortly to 300,000. The US casualty toll during the last week in November (240 Americans killed and 470 wounded) exceeded the weekly average during the Korean War, but the Communist drive had been checked, it seemed. The cost was now annually reckoned in billions, and sentiment against this large commitment was expressed by "peace parades" in several cities. The US objective, however, was to prove that US troops could not be thrown out by the North Vietnamese, that South Vietnam could not be taken by military means, and that North Vietnam should negotiate on these terms. By 1967 almost 500,000 US troops were engaged, aided by an air bombardment of North Vietnam that surpassed the total tonnage dropped on Germany, Italy, and Japan in World War II.

Following the Communist Tet offensive of January 1968, American leaders began a slow and agonizing reduction of US involvement. Johnson limited the bombing, began peace talks with Hanoi and the NLF, and withdrew as a candidate for re-election. His successor, Richard Nixon, announced a program of "Vietnamization," which basically represented a return to the Eisenhower and Kennedy policies of helping Vietnamese forces fight the war. Nixon gradually reduced US ground troops in Vietnam, but he increased the bombing; the tonnage dropped after 1969 exceeded the already prodigious levels reached by Johnson. Nixon expanded air and ground operations into Cambodia and Laos in attempts to block enemy supply routes along Vietnam's borders, and traveled to Moscow and Beijing for talks that proved abortive.

To Nixon, World War III had begun before World War II was over, and it was being fought in the Third World. Since 1945, there have been 120 wars in which 10 million people have been killed. Except for Greece in 1947 (and had only aid and not troops gone there, it too would now be Communist) and the Falklands in 1981, all of these wars began and were fought in the Third World. Nixon quotes B. H. Liddell Hart: "If you want peace, understand war." He adds: "If we want peace, we must also understand the Third World, because it is there that an incident is most likely to occur that would lead to War between the US and the Soviet Union." He does not quote him, but he echoes throughout the exhortation of Theodore Roosevelt: "Speak softly, but carry a big stick." In his own books, Nixon is remorseless in his emphasis that, after Vietnam, came: Laos, Cambodia, and Mozambique in 1975, Angola in 1976, Ethiopia in 1977, South Vietnam in 1978, Nicaragua in 1979. The lessons are there for all of us, and not only Americans, to read.

In January 1973, thanks largely to the efforts of Nixon's secretary of state Henry Kissinger, the United States and North Vietnam signed the Paris Peace Agreement, which provided for the withdrawal of all remaining US forces from Vietnam, the return of US prisoners of war, and a ceasefire. The American troops and POWS came home, but the war continued. Nixon termed it "peace with honor," since a separate government remained in Saigon, but Kissinger acknowledged that the arrangement provided primarily for a "decent interval" between US withdrawal and the collapse of the South, inevitable without US aid. In April 1975 North Vietnamese troops and tanks converged on Saigon, and the war was over.[4]

The domestic consequences of the war were equally profound. From Truman through Nixon, the war demonstrated the increasing dominance of the presidency within the federal government. Congress essentially defaulted to the "imperial presidency" in the conduct of foreign affairs. Vietnam also destroyed credibility within the American political process. The public came to distrust its leaders, and many officials distrusted the public. In May 1970, Ohio National Guardsmen killed four Kent State University students during a protest over US troops invading Cambodia. Many Americans were outraged, while others defended the Ohio authorities. As this tragic example reveals, the war rent the fabric of trust that traditionally clothed the American polity. Vietnam figured prominently as a cause of inflation, wrecked the Great Society programs, and emphasized the generation gap. The Vietnam War

[4] George C. Herring, *America's Longest War: The US and Vietnam 1950–1975* (Garden City, NY, Doubleday, 2nd edn, 1986); Richard M. Nixon, *No More Vietnams* (London, W. H. Allen, 1986); *Richard Nixon, The Memoirs* (New York, Grosset and Dunlap, 1978); *Six Crises* (New York, Doubleday, 1962).

brought an end to the domestic consensus that had sustained the US and its economy since the end of World War II.

Why did the United States lose the war? Some analysts singled out media criticism of the war and anti-war activism in America as undermining the will of the US government to continue fighting. Others cited the restrictions placed by civilian politicians on the military's operations or, conversely, blamed US military chiefs for not providing civilian leaders with a sound strategy for victory. These so-called win arguments assume that victory was possible, but they overlook the flawed reasons for US involvement in Vietnam. Washington had sought to contain international Communism, but this global strategic concern masked the reality that the appeal of the Communists in Vietnam derived from local economic, social, and historical facts. The US response to Vietnamese Communism was essentially to apply a military solution to an internal political problem. America's infliction of enormous destruction on Vietnam served only to discredit politically the Vietnamese whom the United States sought to assist.

The Vietnam War, the nation's longest, cost 58,000 American lives. Only the Civil War and the two world wars were deadlier for Americans. During the decade of direct US military participation in Vietnam beginning in 1964, the US Treasury spent over $140 billion on the war, enough money to fund urban renewal projects in every major American city. Despite these enormous costs and their accompanying public and private trauma for the American people, the United States failed, for the first time in its history, to achieve its stated war aims. The goal was to preserve a separate, independent, non-Communist government in South Vietnam, but after April 1975, the Communist Democratic Republic of Vietnam ruled the entire nation.

Moreover, although Article 1 section 8 of the Constitution provides that "Congress shall have Power ... to declare war," no Congressional declaration preceded Lyndon B. Johnson's commitment of half a million men to combat in Southeast Asia. Johnson and his successor, Richard Nixon, insisted that the August 1964 Tonkin Gulf Resolution, in which Congress urged the commander-in-chief to "take all necessary measures to repel any armed attack against the forces of the United States and to prevent further aggression", and the many appropriation Acts in which the legislature provided funds for the armed forces, gave them whatever Congressional authorization they needed to conduct combat operations in Vietnam. Critics of their policies countered that because Congress had not declared war, they were behaving unconstitutionally. Some also accused the United States of waging a war of aggression in Vietnam and argued that anyone who participated in this conflict would be subject to punishment under principles established at the Nuremberg war crime trials. These split the nation and confronted the Supreme Court with some of the most difficult issues that it faced between 1965 and 1975. The Court ducked the toughest of these questions: the constitutionality of the war itself. While declining to order an end to the fighting, however, it provided a surprising degree of protection to anti-war protesters, expanding significantly the number of men who could gain exemption from military service as conscientious objectors.

7 ROBERT KENNEDY

Robert Kennedy, brother of the murdered President, was shot in the head by Sirhan Sirhan, a Jordanian immigrant, as he walked through the kitchen of the Ambassador Hotel in Los Angeles a few minutes after midnight on June 5, 1968. He died 25 hours later. He was 42 and had just won the Democratic presidential primary in California.

Victory was by no means assured for Kennedy. Within his own party he faced an uphill battle for the nomination against Vice-President Hubert Humphrey and the powerful Democratic party apparatus controlled by President Johnson, whose loathing for Bobby had reached the level of "no holds barred." Then, in the November election, there would have been the formidable figure of Richard Nixon, who went on to beat Humphrey by an eyelash in the popular vote. Yet the Kennedy dreamers still fantasize that had Bobby become President, there would have been no Nixon, no Watergate, and therefore no need for Carter, maybe not even for Reagan or Bush. And it is quite likely that, given such mammoth publicity, Robert Kennedy would have won both the Democratic nomination and the presidency; it is equally clear that he would have been a strange and unusual President.

Even if Kennedy had won, he would have faced serious obstacles. As a Vietnam dove, he would have wielded far less leverage in peace negotiations with Hanoi than the hawkish Nixon, who resumed bombing North Vietnam and invaded Cambodia to force the Communists to the bargaining table. On the domestic front, Kennedy would have struggled to govern. His commitment to civil rights had generated widespread hostility in the South. And how would he, a devout Roman Catholic, father of ten children with an eleventh on the way when he died, have coped with the controversy over abortion that became a dominant political issue within a few years of his death?

Nor was Kennedy a political saint. Indeed, he could be cold and ruthless. He promised Senator Eugene McCarthy that he would not compete for the presidency in 1968, yet he jumped into the race as soon as McCarthy had come within six points of defeating Johnson in the New Hampshire primary.

So what was it about Kennedy that caught the imagination, that drew mobbing crowds to his open convertible as he stood on the back seat using both arms to shake the forest of hands reaching up to him? The surname was magic, of course, for those who wanted to resurrect the legend cut down nearly five years earlier by President Kennedy's murder in Dallas. But there was more to it than that.

Kennedy was a mix of opposites, by turns shy and confident, abrupt and friendly, cautious and reckless, realist and idealist. But his courage was unalloyed. He was devoted to his brother Jack, eights years his elder, and had immense physical and moral courage. He forced himself to be a tough guy, against his own natural instincts, and because the Kennedy image and his dominant father required it. Shy and reticent as a youth, smaller and less coordinated than his brothers, a tag-along who learnt slowly, he threw himself into things, and suffered. He always had to prove himself – as swimmer, as footballer, as 50-mile hiker, and even (though he had no head for heights) as mountaineer. Life was always challenging.

Arthur Schlesinger, in his biography of Robert Kennedy, gives a view informed by an insider's knowledge.[5] He writes as "a great admirer and devoted friend," but this does not preclude the occasional note of criticism and rebuke, portraying the frailty as well as the valor. Schlesinger makes two claims for Robert Kennedy as a man: first, that he grew with his experiences and went on growing, and second, that he was a Representative Man of his age, in Emerson's phrase, "one who embodies the consciousness of an epoch." There is some truth – but not the whole truth – in both assertions. Of his growth there is no question. He began, aged 24 and fresh from an undistinguished record at Harvard and the University of Virginia Law School, as special counsel to Senator Joe McCarthy's Committee hunting out Communists. He owed the job, as so much else, to his father's intercessions with McCarthy.

[5] Arthur M. Schlesinger Jr, *Robert Kennedy and His Times* (New York, André Deutsch, 1978).

He was always merciless as prosecutor, apt to ignore constitutional rights, and from the first hungry for headlines. The conviction of righteousness, the fanaticism for virtue, gave him a proneness to vault over gaps in the evidence; in fact, as Schlesinger admits, to put ends before means. The same qualities of dedication, and an unexpected capacity as organizer and administrator, were revealed in his role in his brother's successful campaigns, for the Senate in 1952 and for the presidency itself in 1960. John Kennedy valued his brother's qualities as troubleshooter and hatchet man. He needed somebody who could say "No," a crackdown man, an expendable scout on distant frontiers, so that no unpopularity would ever be visited on himself. "Little Brother is watching you," was the phrase used in Democratic HQ. Bobby accepted the role – though at times it hurt. When his brother appointed him, against much advice, attorney general of the US at the age of 34, his lack of judicial experience was naturally a subject for scorn. The President treated it flippantly – "I can't see that it's wrong to give him a little legal experience before he goes out to practice law." Bobby objected to the remark and Jack said that he was just kidding. Bobby did not like it because, he said, "You weren't kidding yourself. You were kidding me."

He never lost the killer instinct. When he moved to serve Senator McClellan on the Rackets investigation, and as attorney general in his brother's Presidency, his vendetta against labor leaders like Jimmy Hoffa of the Teamsters Union became notorious; he believed that Hoffa had misused $9 million of union funds and had beaten and probably murdered opponents. In pursuing Hoffa, he pursued his Chicago henchmen like Joey Glimco and Sam Giancano (the latter a friend of Frank Sinatra). He saw labor racketeers as men who had betrayed a priesthood. As one Teamster put it, "Jimmy and Bobby both deserve one another." This was a Catholic radical, more puritan than John, more committed, more temperamental, and with a very low boiling point. Until 1960, however, the image he acquired was that of the fearless young crusader exposing rackets and organized crime, rather than the lover of the underdog. The interest in civil rights came late – since it could rock political barges in the South. Yet by 1968 his constituency was the poor, the black, and the young, and with them in a strange, almost non-verbal way, he identified. Jack Kennedy attacked injustices because he found them irrational, says Schlesinger, Bobby because he found them unbearable. The sight of people living in squalor appalled JFK, but like FDR before him, he saw it from without. Robert had a growing intensity of personal identification with the victims of the social order. He had in 1968 no clear program and essentially one set speech, always ending with a quote from Shaw that his brother had used: "Some men see things as they are, and say why? I dream of things that never were, and say why not?" He sought the lost romance of the Kennedy years, to capture now for himself the power and the glory, and the magic; he sought it in the only constituency left open to him – the very young, the bobbysoxers, the universities, the discontented, the desperate. Impelled by the pain of Dallas, to pain in others he responded. The campaign of 1968, improvised and emotional, was – in Schlesinger's words – a "movement beyond liberalism." His face was his platform, his name was his slogan. The concern seemed to cynics to be the perpetuation of the dynasty rather than the service of a cause. The strategy was to nominate him on the streets. But he did go into desperately poor Southern and Central Valley homes, pick up ill-nourished children twisted with rickets and ugly with sores, and nurse them, the tears pouring down his cheeks. The image was not by that point merely contrived. The emotions were clearly real, even desperate, on each side. On the night of Martin Luther King's murder, two months before his own, he strode into a black ghetto of Indianapolis against the advice of police and made an impromptu speech:

> For those of you who are black and are tempted to be filled with hatred and distrust against all white people at the injustice of such an act, I can only say that I feel in my own heart the same kind of feeling. I had a member of my family killed. But we have to make an effort in the United States to understand, to go beyond these rather difficult times.

The crowd went home quietly. Indianapolis, unlike many other cities, was spared a night of race rioting.

We can accept then that he grew, even if he had a lot to grow away from: his father's rampant individualism, his own McCarthyite period, his lack of interest in civil rights before and even after 1960, since it would lose Southern votes, his use of wiretapping and bugging and other violations of due process of law as attorney general. When as attorney general he sent Nich Katzenbach to the University of Mississippi to ensure the admission of black student James Meredith, his final words were "If things get rough, don't worry about yourself. The President needs a moral issue." There is that continuing ugly side of Bobby Kennedy's personality, expressed in the verdict of one-time family intimate Gore Vidal:

There are flaws in his *persona* hard to disguise. For one thing, it will take a public relations genius to make him appear lovable. He is not. His obvious characteristics are energy, vindictiveness and a simpleminded-ness about human motives which may yet bring him down. To Bobby the world is black and white, Them and Us. He has none of his brother's human ease, or charity. He would be a dangerously authoritarian-minded President.

Although born to privilege, Robert Kennedy was developing a persona to challenge the *status quo* of American politics on behalf of the afflicted to a degree unseen since the Civil War. His way might well have led to dreadful divisiveness or, given time, might possibly have coalesced into a new era of social justice.

8 EDWARD KENNEDY

There was still another brother, Edward Kennedy, the present Senator, and the subject of a highly controversial and much-criticized book by Joe McGinniss, *The Last Brother*.[6] His story is as colorful as that of any of his clan. During a weekend outing in Martha's Vineyard in July 1969 he drove his car off a bridge to Chappaquiddick. In it as passenger was Mary Jo Kopechne, a 28-year-old Kennedy staffer and aide; she was drowned. Kennedy's failure to call the police and the variously changing stories he and his aides put out destroyed confidence in the man who at 26 had come close to being drafted to run for President at the Chicago convention in 1968. Before the accident, he had been seen as sure to be the Democratic nominee in 1972, and not just by Nixon, who after 1960 was steadily haunted by the Kennedys. The prospect and the fear died at Chappaquiddick; and with it the promise of yet another Kennedy. Edward (Teddy) Kennedy has been an active liberal legislator; he is still popular and widely respected at home, and was a keen supporter of Michael Dukakis in the 1988 campaign. Until the deaths of his brothers, he had been a practical politician and no more dreamy-eyed liberal; he then took up the liberal causes and prooccupations with the poor which had been the focus of Robert Kennedy in the last year or two of his life. But Teddy's interest in moral arguments cannot now but seem unseemly in the light of his own lifestyle. He is now too old for a new career – and older than were his brothers when they died.

[6] New York, Simon and Schuster, 1993.

9 ASSESSMENTS: JFK AND LBJ

With the exception, perhaps, of FDR, JFK is the most fully chronicled and most dissected of twentieth-century American public figures. In 1988, Thomas Brown calculated that there were then already over 200 books dealing wholly or partly with him.[7] Two of these are excellent and admiring portraits by participants in the administration who were also friends. Already a historian of Presidents, Arthur M. Schlesinger Jr used a ringside seat to advantage. He salutes the grace, youthfulness, and sense of style that marked Kennedy and is full of intimate detail (though not including information about JFK's private sexual encounters). Theodore C. Sorensen was closer to JFK than was Schlesinger and knew him longer; along with the President's brother Robert, Sorensen became the President's *alter ego*, and was his chief speechwriter and speech-thinker. He was "there" for the major events – the Bay of Pigs, the Cuban Missile Crisis, the Nuclear Test Ban Treaty – and thus provides fresh primary source material along with the Camelot-style "gush."[8] The most complete and fairest biography is Herbert Parmet's two-volume survey.[9] Parmet is fair, noting the President's medical problems and recognizing that his style in a world-television age served as model for many young people. But such is the detail in all of these studies, and so much the quantity of revelation, that it is clear that the myth of Camelot was from the start a remarkable piece of imagination and illusion.

Harris Wofford provides an insider's view that is distinctly critical.[10] Himself a former Civil Rights activist and an ex-Associate Director of the Peace Corps, Wofford makes clear how cool, calculating and Machiavellian the Kennedy presidency was. The machine was primed by the millions of a doting and himself devious father, manned by ruthless operators. There was from neither of the brothers any passionate conviction over civil rights until very late in the term; and even then it was always a calculating concern. This is well portrayed here in the long account of how JFK was persuaded

[7] Thomas Brown, *JFK: History of an image* (Bloomington, Indiana University Press, 1988).

[8] Arthur M. Schlesinger Jr, *1000 Days* (Boston, Houghton Mifflin, 1965); Theodore C. Sorensen, *Kennedy* (New York, Harper, 1965).

[9] Herbert Parmet, *Jack: The struggles of John F. Kennedy* (New York, Dial, 1980) and *JFK: The presidency of John F. Kennedy* (New York, Dial, 1983).

[10] Harris Wofford, *Of Kennedys and Kings* (New York, Farrar, Straus and Giroux, 1980).

to make his famous phone call to Coretta King in 1960, showing a personal concern that some believe won him black votes – and victory – in the election. Bobby Kennedy's ruthlessness, a carefully nurtured plant, came, after all, by way of Joe McCarthy's investigative committee, and his was the cutting edge of the team in 1961.

Wofford is interesting, also, in his probing of the transformation in Bobby after November 1963. He attributes it less to the horror of the events in Dallas than to his awareness that, since there were covert attempts planned to assassinate Castro, John Kennedy's murder may have been indirectly at Castro's orders, and that in one sense, brother had been responsible – however indirectly – for the death of brother. In a mind that was intensely puritan, this might well have wrought the changes that led to the half-demented hunger for crowds and for suffering and the curious evangelism behind his own campaign for the presidency in 1968, until he too was struck down.

Again, Wofford is explicit in his charges of the involvement of John F. with Mrs Exner, of the President's sexual aberrations, and of the possible links with Giancana and the Mafia. However discreetly hinted at, this is a sordid tale: at Camelot it was not the king who erred. To this Wofford adds some embarrassing touches in describing how the President would summon members of the Special Forces to show their prowess at weekends at Hyannisport, and in recalling his request to the CIA to find in their ranks the nearest man to James Bond. This is not the world of Tennyson but of Sapper's Bulldog Drummond. That First Inaugural was, after all, a call to arms; but at times the trumpet hit very false notes. In this court a man was measured less by ability than by cleverness, by which Wofford calls the Bloomsbury syndrome. It does not produce respect for the system.

Opinion moves quickly in the US–and academic opinion quite as quickly as any other. Indeed, if we are seeking to explain and understand contemporary American discontents, we ought after stressing the violent and emotional character of its history to consider the role of the intellectuals. For much of contemporary criticism of the political scene in the US is due quite simply to the alienation of the American intellectual from the Johnson and Nixon regimes; this is indeed the real *trahison des clercs*. Vice-President Spiro Agnew was right to draw attention to it, though by doing so he became even more a target for academic scorn. Among the mandarins, there have been many more critics then admirers of recent Presidents. And it has to be recognized that the central distorting fact in the last decades has been the veneration of many academics for JFK, for his youth, his charm, his image as fellow-intellectual, his style as a cool and philosophic Harvard man, ennobling and edifying politics by entering the arena; he seemed a better-looking and younger edition of Adlai Stevenson without any of his hesitations, at once relaxed and radical. Indeed, to many intellectuals his appearance of Machiavellian skill was as captivating as his charm; safely cushioned from the hazards and insecurities of political life, academics are quick to admire what they see as dexterity in politicians. The horror and shock of his assassination has drawn a screen between the truth about JFK and the image. The facts are that Kennedy made a rare mess of the Bay of Pigs; he admitted it, and his frankness in doing so ("Success has a thousand fathers;" he said; "failure is an orphan") won him an applause which few other unsuccessful politicians would ever have received. Indeed, the failure led Khrushchev to think him an innocent, and by October 1962 there was a tougher President to confront the second Cuban crisis. But he came through that by threatening the use of force. His handling of Congress was far from skillful. Only toward the end – and that largely because of his brother's passion – was he coming to show a real concern with civil rights. But the indentification of the academic liberals – and they are a large colony, with 1,800 universities as their base – with the Kennedy legend, their acceptance of the Camelot myth, is more than a piece of self-deception, and more than just a search for glamor and nobility in public life. It hides, and is in danger of distorting, two fundamental truths about the Kennedy and Johnson years.

"Let every nation know, whether it wishes us well or ill, that we shall pay any price, bear any burden, meet any hardship, support any friend, oppose any foe to assure the survival and the success of liberty." The assumptions were outgoing, and belligerent; the parallel was far more with Theodore Roosevelt than with FDR. There was to be $20 billion for the Alliance for Progress. There was to be support for the Grand Design in Europe. And free men – everywhere – were to be supported, not only in America and Europe but in Asia. It was Kennedy who began the escalation of the war in Vietnam and who in March 1961 authorized secret raids against North Vietnam. In May 1961 he despatched then Vice-President Johnson to Vietnam with orders to "encourage" President Ngo Dinh Diem to ask for US ground troops. Diem resisted American pressure at first, arguing that their presence would violate the 1954 Geneva Agreements and open his administration to criticism as a puppet government. But in October 1961 Diem made the solicited request, and Kennedy began a quiet, steady build-up of combat forces. (I recall spending the summer of 1961 doing research in the Yale Library, and meeting savage and repeated criticisms of a Britain that seemed to be letting the side down by its unwillingness to help the US with troops in Vietnam, and by its policy of "appeasement" in Malaya.) The Pentagon papers show clearly that Kennedy and his advisers first conspired with South Vietnamese military plotters against President Diem, then backed away from an active role and, in the end, stood by and allowed the coup against him to take place. Over this story of the real Kennedy – power-conscious, ruthless and opportunistic – the assassination has cast the glamor of a King Arthur, the glow that never was on sea or land.

But there has been as a consequence of the hypnosis of the liberals a second and still more serious miscarriage of justice. Lyndon Johnson, despite his spell as Senatorial leader and legislator and despite his own line of descent from FDR – he was an Old New Dealer rather than a New Frontiersman – was seen from the first as vulgar by contrast. Southwest Texas State Teachers' College – though far more typical than Harvard – seemed a long way from Cape Cod. Witness the disappointment of frustrated academics-turned-presidential-advisers like Eric Goldman; witness the resignations of Kennedy men through 1964. It was largely this sustained campaign of personal denigration spreading into the press and the media that undermined Johnson's confidence and drove him in 1968 not to stand again. The hero of 1964 became the villain of 1968. He stepped up the war in Vietnam as JFK would equally have had to do. But he also put through Congress, by personal skill and presidential leadership a social revolution that is matched in legislative range only by FDR's. In any assessment of contemporary America this record ought to be weighed in the scales. His Civil Rights Act prohibited racial discrimination in public places or under any federal aid program. The Appalachia Redevelopment Bill made grants for the construction of 3,350 miles of roads, for health facilities and vocational schools, for land improvement and the development of timber and water resources in the Southeastern states. His education Bill authorized for the first time federal funds ($1,300 million in the first year) for the general improvement of elementary and secondary schools, and extended aid for the first time to parochial schools, mainly Roman Catholic. His Medical Care-Social Security Bill ended a 20-year struggle fought over the highly contentious topic, "socialized medicine." The law provided for a health-care insurance program under social security for persons aged 65 and over, and increased social security pensions. His Voting

Rights Bill, the second important civil rights law in two years, directed the attorney general to take court action against the poll tax, suspended literacy tests, and provided for the registration of voters by the federal government whenever necessary. The Department of Housing and Urban Development Bill established a new Cabinet post and federal department for the purpose of improving metropolitan areas. And the Immigration Bill provided for the gradual elimination of the national origins quota system which had made it difficult for Southern Europeans and Asian immigrants to enter the United States. Under the new proposals (first enforced in 1960) visas are issued on a first-come, first-served basis, and the preference for British and Northern European immigrants is at an end.

Why, with this record, visit such scorn on LBJ and treat with long and deferential silence the locust years of Dwight D. Eisenhower? President Johnson might be a wheeler-dealer, prompt to say "Let me make the deals and I care not who makes the ideals." But by making deals he put some ideals on the statute book, which is the art of politics. He built on Kennedy foundations, but there is to his credit, in the records of the 89th Congress, an impressive legislative achievement; he did more for civil rights than any President since Lincoln.

Lyndon Baines Johnson is one of the most controversial of Presidents. He saw himself as a New Deal protégé charged to carry out the domestic and foreign policies to which JFK had committed himself before his assassination. Moreover, he sought to prove that a Southerner could implement a domestic reform program. His biographers have brought very different emphases to their studies, many of them highly critical. Robert A. Caro sees Johnson as manipulative, domineering, sycophantic, aggressive, secretive and opportunistic. But he also salutes his dedication to and success in securing progress on civil rights.[11] Until Caro's project is complete, it is proper to recognize Vaughan D. Bornet's *The Presidency of Lyndon B. Johnson* as far the most balanced comprehensive treatment.[12] Bornet is complimentary on civil rights, critical on Vietnam, and especially critical of LBJ's readiness to deceive in foreign policy. But his summing up is masterly:

[11] Robert A. Caro, *The Years of Lyndon Johnson*, vol. I, *The Path to Power* (New York, Knopf, 1982); vol. II, *Means of Ascent* (New York, Knopf, 1990).
[12] Vaughan D. Bornet, *The Presidency of Lyndon B. Johnson* (Lawrence, University of Kansas Press, 1983).

The presidency of Lyndon B. Johnson will inevitably be remembered – and ought to be – for the characteristics of its central figure; for the unintentional but substantial damage that it did with some catastrophical policies abroad and erroneous policies at home; and especially for the many worthwhile changes it embedded deeply in legislation, in the lives of millions, and in American society.

We need, I think, a long rest from Camelot. It is probable that these years will not stand the test of history as well as they caught the imagination of contemporaries. The Kennedys cultivated artists and writers, and they reaped a rich dividend of fame and fortune. They attracted intellectuals, who wrote them up lavishly, and speech-writers, who enshrined their words – JFK's more than Bobby's – in splendid prose. But the crude LBJ did more in practice than all the Kennedys and Kings put together. The sad fact is that the best are not always the brightest, nor the brightest the best.

14

The Civil Rights Movement

1 TOWARD CIVIL RIGHTS: 1900–1945

The early twentieth century was a low point for black civil rights. The Jim Crow laws in the South became more severe, and although lynchings were less frequent than in the 1890s, they still averaged over 60 a year between 1900 and 1920. The period ended with the worst outbreak of interracial conflict in American history to that point, as thousands of black soldiers who had served their country in World War I returned home demanding additional rights. Many of these riots took place in the North, for the migration of black people from South to North grew rapidly after 1900, with net migration rising from 186,000 in 1900–10 to 1,322,000 in 1940–50. The most serious riot took place in Chicago in July 1919, killing 23 blacks and 15 whites.

During the 1920s a new spirit of independence began to flourish, particularly in Harlem, typified in the writings of the black poet and novelist Langston Hughes. In the 1920s the South built more schools for blacks than in all previous years, and by 1930 there were 15,000 blacks with college degrees. In 1921, Marcus Garvey outfitted a steamship line to carry blacks back to Africa. At its height, Garvey's African Zionist Movement had 500,000 members, but it collapsed when Garvey went to jail for swindling.

The depression of the 1930s hit the black harder than any other group, particularly the black sharecropper. Roosevelt's New Deal farm programs often forced blacks to leave the farm and move to the city slum, but New Deal relief measures helped them to survive the depression. White Congress of Industrial Organizations (CIO) labor leaders treated blacks more fairly than had any labor organizers in the past. Blacks, traditionally Republican, went over to the Democratic party and helped form Roosevelt's urban coalition. Of 15 black wards, 4 went to Roosevelt in 1932, 9 in 1930, and 14 in 1940.

The 1930s also witnessed the continued growth in effectiveness of the NAACP, which grew from 50 local chapters to 599 between the two world wars. Concentrating on legal rights and aided by brilliant black lawyers such as Thurgood Marshall, later a Supreme Court justice, and Hamilton Houston, the NAACP struggled to make the Fourteenth Amendment a reality. In 1930 the Association put enough pressure on the Senate to block confirmation of President Hoover's Supreme Court nominee, John H. Parker, an opponent of black suffrage. Two years later Nathan R. Margold, head of the NAACP legal defense committee, decided to attack the principle of "separate but equal" education. He did not succeed, but he laid the legal foundation that ultimately led to the desegregation decision of 1954.

While attempting to achieve civil rights reform, the NAACP experienced a sharp internal struggle over ideology. William E. B. Du Bois headed the faction that by the 1930s had become thoroughly disillusioned at the prospects of reform within the American economic and political system. He proposed that blacks voluntarily segregate themselves from that system and turn instead to Marxism. Immensely impressed with his visit to Russia in 1927, Du Bois believed that if blacks sided with Communists, their combined force could topple a capitalistic order already reeling from the Great Depression. The National Negro Congress, founded in 1935 by Ralph Bunche and E. Franklin Frazier among others, was a step toward organization of a black proletariat. More conservative leaders of the NAACP such as Roy Wilkins, Walter White, and Martin Luther King, Sr, disagreed strongly with this approach. Pointing to the success of the CIO in advancing the interests of black laborers, they were not prepared to abandon capitalism or white America. Eventually they forced Du Bois out of the NAACP and into the Communist party.

Despite the hardships of the depression years, the election of Franklin D. Roosevelt as President in 1932 heralded great advances for black Americans. As President, Roosevelt did more than any of his predecessors. Blacks were included in nearly every phase of his administration, and some achieved high federal posts. The economist Robert C. Weaver, for example, headed the President's informal "Black Cabinet." Roosevelt's highly publicized refusal to sign an anti-lynching bill in 1938 for fear of losing the support of Southern

Democrats should be seen in the broader perspective of his entire record. Summing it up, *Crisis* reported that "for the first time in their lives government had taken on meaning and substance for the Negro masses."

Between 1938 and 1944, the NAACP entered a series of suits to gain blacks the right to vote in Southern primary elections and to attend public graduate schools. In *Missouri ex rel. Gaines* vs. *Canada* (1938), the Supreme Court ordered Missouri to admit blacks to the state university law school in the absence of other provisions for their legal training. In *Smith* vs. *Allwright* (1944) it held that exclusion of blacks from Texas primary elections was a violation of the Fifteenth Amendment.

The movement of blacks to the North, slowed by the depression, speeded-up during World War II as blacks went to work in defense plants. 920,000 blacks served in World War II, 7,768 of them officers, and some military segregation practices were given up.

On June 25, 1941, after blacks threatened to march on Washington, President Roosevelt issued Executive Order 8802, declaring that there should be no discrimination in employment in defense industries or government. His order also created the Fair Employment Practices Committee (FEPC) to investigate complaints of discrimination. In 1944, the "GI Bill of Rights" provided extensive educational benefits for soldiers returning from World War II, and in 1946 President Harry S. Truman set up the President's Committee on Civil Rights.

2 DREAMERS OF THE DREAM

The American Dream is too often seen as a phrase for African-Americans only. Not so. It was of course the theme of Martin Luther King in his address on August 28, 1963, from the steps of the Lincoln Memorial to some quarter of a million protesters who had thronged into Washington as the climax of the many demonstrations of that year; but it was the goal of all immigrants, whatever the color of their skins, and had been from their beginnings. For blacks, it had and has a legion of meanings, as the careers of some of its major exponents witness – Frederick Douglass, W. E. B. Du Bois, Martin Luther King Jr and Thurgood Marshall among them.

Frederick Douglass

Frederick Douglass (1818–1895), abolitionist, writer, and orator, was the most important black American leader of the nineteenth century. Born Frederick Augustus Washington Bailey on Maryland's Eastern Shore, he was the son of a slave woman and, probably, her white master. He never knew his father. Upon his escape from slavery at the age of 20, he adopted the name of the hero of Sir Walter Scott's *The Lady of the Lake*. Douglass immortalized his years as a slave in *Narrative of the Life of Frederick Douglass, an American Slave* (1845), which recounted how he was mobbed and beaten for expressing his views. He worked as agent and lecturer for the Massachusetts Anti-Slavery Society. This and two subsequent autobiographies, *The Narrative of the Life of Frederick Douglass* (1855) and *The Life and Times of Frederick Douglass* (1881), avowedly written as anti-slavery propaganda and political revolution, are regarded as the finest examples of the slave narrative tradition and as classics of American autobiography. During a two-year stay in Britain, he earned enough money to buy his freedom. He had imitators: William Wells Brown told his *Narrative* (1847), wrote a novel, *Clotel* deriving from the Sally Hemings story, and a play, *The Escape*, both of them portrayals of slavery. A year later came another runaway's story, that of Henry Bibb, who escaped in 1837, and wrote *A Narrative of his Life and Adventures*.

Douglass's life as a reformer ranged from his abolitionist activities in the early 1840s to his attacks on "Jim Crow" and lynching in the 1890s. For 16 years he edited an influential black weekly, the *North Star*, and achieved international fame as an orator and writer of great persuasive power. In thousands of speeches and editorials he levied an indictment against slavery and racism, provided an indomitable voice of hope for his people, embraced anti-slavery politics, and preached his own brand of American ideals. In the 1850s he broke with the strictly moralist brand of abolitionism led by William Lloyd Garrison; he supported the early women's rights movement; and he gave direct assistance to John Brown's conspiracy that led to the raid on Harper's Ferry in 1859.

His Fourth of July speech in 1852 is famous: "This Fourth of July is *yours*, not *mine*. You may rejoice, *I* must mourn," he declared. Then he accused his unsuspecting audience in Rochester, New York, of mockery for inviting him to speak and quoted Psalm 137, where the children of Israel are forced to sit down "by the rivers of Babylon," there to "sing the Lord's song in a strange land." For the ways that race has caused the deepest contradictions in American history, few better sources of insight exist than Douglass's speeches. Moreover, for understanding prejudice, there are few better starting points than his definition of racism as the product of a "diseased imagination."

Douglass welcomed the Civil War in 1861 as a moral crusade against slavery. During the war he labored as a propagandist of the Union cause and emancipation, a recruiter of black troops, and (on two occasions) an adviser to President Abraham Lincoln. He viewed the Union victory as an apocalyptic rebirth of America as a nation rooted in a rewritten Constitution and the ideal of racial equality. Some of his hopes were dashed during Reconstruction and the Gilded Age, but he continued to travel widely and lecture on racial issues, national politics, and women's rights. In the 1870s Douglass moved to Washington DC, where he edited a newspaper and became president of the ill-fated Freedman's Bank. As a stalwart Republican, Douglass was appointed marshal (1877–81) and recorder of deeds (1881–6) for the District of Columbia, *chargé d'affaires* for Santo Domingo and minister to Haiti (1889–91).

Douglas was a symbol of his age and a unique voice for humanism and social justice. His life and thought speak profoundly to the meaning of being black in America, as well as the human calling to resist oppression. Douglass died in 1895, a heroic and complex man. The various editions of his *Autobiography* are a reflection of and a commentary on the dramatically changing condition of African-Americans since the mulatto's escape from slavery in 1838.[1]

W. E. B. Du Bois

William Edward Burghardt Du Bois (1868–1963) is just as heroic and even more complex a figure. Historian, sociologist, writer, and civil rights activist, he was the foremost black intellectual of the twentieth century. Born in Great Barrington, Massachusetts, Du Bois knew little of his father, who died shortly after his birth, but he believed himself to be the descendent of a French Huguenot and an African slave. Born after the end of the Civil War and thus "free," and of handsome appearance, he could have "passed" as a white man. He chose to identify himself with the black cause and to advocate complete economic, political and social equality for

[1] Benjamin Quarles, *Frederick Douglass* (Washington, DC, Associated Publishers, 1948); Waldo E. Martin, *The Mind of Frederick Douglass* (Chapel Hall, NC, University of North Carolina Press, 1984).

black Americans. For, as he said, "the problem of the twentieth century is the problem of the color line in the relation of the darker to the lighter races of man in Asia and Africa, in America and the islands of the sea." Educated at Fisk University (1885–8), Harvard University (1888–96), and the University of Berlin (1892–4), Du Bois then embarked upon a 70-year career that combined scholarship and teaching with lifelong activism in liberation struggles.

Du Bois taught at Atlanta University from 1897 to 1910, when it was an undergraduate school, and returned as a professor in the graduate school from 1933 to 1944. Several of his most important works were written while he was there. Atlanta owed its beginnings to the work of the Reverend Frederick Ayer and his wife, who came to the city in 1865. In collaboration with blacks already engaged in self-help, they established the enterprise that was to become Atlanta University. It started in late 1866 as a school, with Edmund Asa Ware, a young Yale graduate, as principal. In 1867 it was chartered as Atlanta University. Several of the early leaders of Atlanta University were Yale graduates, and they developed the college program on the model of Yale and Harvard. Its first degree class graduated in 1876, though there had been preparatory and teacher training graduates previously. Among its most distinguished graduates were James Weldon Johnson, author, scholar, and diplomat; Walter White, author and civil rights pioneer; and Fletcher Henderson, composer, arranger, and originator of the big band tradition. In 1929 Atlanta University became the graduate school in a consortium which included the two undergraduate schools of Morehouse College, for men, and Spelman College, for women. Both Morehouse and Spelman had been founded under the patronage of the American Baptist Home Mission Society. Later the consortium was extended to take in Clark College and Morris Brown College.

Interspersed with Du Bois' teaching career at Wilberforce and Atlanta University were two stints as a publicist for the NAACP, of which he was a founding officer and for whom he edited the monthly magazine, *Crisis*. For a time he was the ally of the outspoken William Monroe Trotter, also a Harvard man, and editor-publisher of the strong-minded black paper, the *Guardian*. Together they opposed "The Tuskegee gang," the compromisers whose allegiance was to the ever-ameliorative Booker T. Washington. Du Bois resigned from the NAACP in June 1934 in a dispute over organizational policy and direction. He believed that the depression dictated a shift from the organization's stress on legal rights and integration to an emphasis on black economic advancement, even if this meant temporarily "accepting" segregation. But after teaching at Atlanta

University, he returned in 1944 as head of a research effort aimed at collecting and disseminating data on Africans and their diaspora and putting issues affecting them before the world community. Renewed disputes with the NAACP caused him to be dismissed in 1948.

During the 1950s Du Bois was drawn into leftist causes, including chairing the Peace Information Center. The center's refusal to comply with the Foreign Agents Registration Act led to his indictment with four others by a federal grand jury in 1951. All five were acquitted after a highly publicized trial, but the taint of alleged Communist association caused him to be shunned by colleagues and harassed by federal agencies (including eventual revocation of his passport) throughout the 1950s. In 1961, Du Bois settled in Ghana and began work on the *Encyclopedia Africana*, a compendium of information on Africans and peoples of African descent throughout the world. Shortly thereafter he joined the American Communist party and became a citizen of Ghana, where he died in 1963.

During Du Bois's prolific career he published 19 books, edited four magazines, coedited a magazine for children, and produced scores of articles and speeches. Perhaps his most outstanding work was *The Souls of Black Folk* (1903), a poignant collection of essays in which he defined some of the key themes of the African-American experience and the dominant motifs of his own work; but also influential are his *John Brown* (1909) and *The Black Flame* (1957–61). His *Autobiography* appeared posthumously in 1968.

He clashed on occasion with other black leaders over appropriate strategies for black advancement, notably with Booker T. Washington (whose strategy of accommodation and emphasis on industrial education for blacks he rejected) and Marcus Garvey (whom he considered a demagogue, although they shared a commitment to Pan-Africanism and the liberation of Africa). Du Bois's own approach was an eclectic mix of scientific social analysis, which led him eventually to Marxism and a romantic evocation of the poetry of black folk culture, which is reflected in his nationalist sympathies and Pan-Africanist organizational efforts. He sought to advance "the talented tenth," the blacks' own elite of leaders. Above all Du Bois sought to place African-American experience in its world historical context. Out of this mix evolved his dual projects of building an African socialism and publishing a unifying work of scholarship on the African diaspora.[2]

[2] Manning Marable, *W. E. B. Du Bois: Black Radical Democrat* (Boston, Twayne, 1986); Elliot Roderick, *W. E. B. Du Bois, Propagandist of the Negro Protest* (New York, Atheneum, 1968).

Booker T. Washington

In antithesis to Du Bois there arose a collaborationist view, of which the Tuskegee Institute and Booker T. Washington became the symbols. Born in Virginia about 1856, Booker Taliaferro was the son of a black slave and a white father. Booker and his family moved to Malden, West Virginia, immediately after the Civil War. There he worked in the salt and coal mines by day and attended school by night. In 1872, driven by the desire for an education, he made his way to the Hampton Normal and Agricultural Institute nearly 300 miles away by walking and hitchhiking. His tuition was paid by a friend of the headmaster, but he had to work as a janitor to earn his room and board. When he finished his course in 1875 he returned to Malden. He taught school, took an active part in community life, and began the study of law in the informal fashion of the day. His was already a remarkable achievement.

In 1878 he went to Washington DC, and studied at Wayland Seminary. By this time he seems to have adopted the surname of Washington. A year later he was called back to Hampton to speak at the commencement as a postgraduate. His performance apparently inspired the founder and director general Samuel Chapman Armstrong to invite him to join the faculty. After teaching the night class for a time Washington became the prefect for a group of American Indian students. In 1881 he founded Tuskegee Normal and Industrial Institute in Alabama, which quickly grew into a major institution. In his controversial Atlanta Exposition address (1895) he formulated the ideas of racial conservatism, frankly accepting segregation. "The opportunity to earn a dollar in a factory just now is worth infinitely more than the opportunity to spend a dollar in an opera house." He felt that segregation was a temporary tactic and believed that if the blacks would make themselves economically indispensable and concentrate upon learning the crafts, acquiring homeownership, and entering business whenever profitable, then social equality would follow.

His policies won him extraordinary gifts from philanthropists, and even Southern legislative grants for black schools, and he became the spokesman for his race before Presidents as well as the great industrialists. Younger blacks, especially the intellectuals like W. E. B. Du Bois, while agreeing with Washington upon the need for vocational education for the black masses (for which Tuskegee was a symbolic center), attacked his neglect of higher education for the "Talented Tenth," and his unwillingness to embark upon any program of agitation for civil rights. His numerous books include a classic autobiography, *Up from Slavery* (1901), and *The Story of the Negro* (1909). Tuskegee's task was seen as providing (in a rigidly segregated society) competent black teachers and businessmen who could educate black communities in practical affairs. Washington was succeeded as principal in 1915 by Robert Noton. The work of G. R. Carver as its director of agricultural research helped point the way toward diversified farming in the South.

For many, the dreams came true outside law courts – among authors, poets, and historians: Langston Hughes, John Hope Franklin, Paul Laurence Dunbar, Claude McKay, James Baldwin, Benjamin Quarles, and Melvin Tolson. Three who found fame sought refuge in exile: Richard Wright, Frank Yerby, and Eldridge Cleaver. Many become distinguished on the stage, like Paul Robeson, athlete, actor, singer, and scholar, whose father had been a runaway slave before becoming a Presbyterian minister. The list of celebrities is long and includes Shirley Verrett, Ethel Waters, Leontyne Price, Grace Bumbry, Marion Anderson, Jessye Norman, Sidney Poitier, Ray Charles, Sammy Davis Jr, Duke Ellington, and Dizzy Gillespie. It also includes "the most famous man in the world" – his phrase – Muhammad Ali, formerly Cassius Clay, whom expert opinion places as the third great boxing champion of this century after those two boxing heroes, Joe Louis and Sugar Ray Robinson.

The number and contributions of artists, performers, and civil rights activists are daunting. They have greatly enriched and extended American culture: from the blues, ragtime, spirituals, and worksongs to Scott Joplin and Leadbelly, from Louis Armstrong to operatic performances of great distinction. For many, their role has been combative; some have gone into exile, three were assassinated – Medgar Evers, the NAACP leader in 1963, Malcolm X in 1965, Martin Luther King in 1968. Some were founders of schools and colleges: Tuskegee, the Hampton Institute in Virginia and its related American Missionary Association educational endeavors, Atlanta University, Howard University, Lincoln University.

For the African-Americans of today the dream penetrates every aspect of life: politics, employment, sport – and irrespective of rank or status. The great Joe Louis, for example, called at the White House in June 1938 before defending his world heavyweight title against the German boxer Max Schmeling, and President Roosevelt declared: "These are the muscles that are going to defeat Nazism in this world." Louis won by a first round knock-out, mainly concerned to prove he was the better man, not to score propaganda points. Two years earlier, in the Berlin Olympic Games, Hitler had sulked when a superb black athlete, Jesse Owens, won four gold medals – but the man acclaimed as a symbol of the free world returned home to an America where blacks were second-class citizens. When Cassius Clay was refused service in a white restaurant he threw away the light-heavyweight gold medal he had won at the Rome Olympics in 1960; later he became Muhammad Ali, and after nine successful defenses of his world title was stripped of it because he would not go to Vietnam – "the real enemies of my people are right here," he said. And it was in the 1968 Olympics in Mexico City that sprinter gold medallist Tommie Smith gave his black power salute on the podium, the first time an athlete had made such a defiant political gesture on the world stage.

3 MARTIN LUTHER KING

The American struggle for racial equality did not begin in the 1950s. It was heralded by the speeches and writings of Frederick Douglass, who escaped from slavery in 1838 and helped organize two black regiments in the Civil War; by the courage of Harriet Tubman, the slave, who acted as a "conductor" on the "Underground Railroad;" by the hesitant proclamations of Abraham Lincoln; by the advocacy of W. E. B. Du Bois, the Harvard-educated historian, who campaigned against the conservatism and "Me-too" ism of Booker Washington for ignoring the higher education of "the Talented Tenth" who provided leaders for the black race, and who went on to found the NAACP; and by the post-World War II litigation efforts of Supreme Court justice Thurgood Marshall.

Still, it is not inappropriate to characterize the period from the mid-1950s until about 1970 as a unique watershed in the civil rights struggle in the United States. When the seamstress Rosa Parks refused to step to the back of an Alabama bus on 1 December 1955 – thus inspiring the successful Montgomery bus boycott – a decade and a half of civil rights protests were sparked that forever changed the American social fabric. Mrs Parks explained that her refusal was "a matter of dignity; I could not have faced myself and my people if I had moved." The young preacher whom the boycott brought to prominence, Martin Luther King, Jr, believed that the civil rights movement was an attack on "man's hostility to man." Encouraging widespread boycotts, freedom rides, and sit-ins to protest segregation, King stressed that one who breaks an unjust law openly and with a willingness to accept the penalty, expresses "the very highest respect for the law." For him the Declaration of Independence has always represented a "declaration of intent rather than of reality."

Martin Luther King Jr can be seen as the most significant of the black non-violent leaders; born in Atlanta, a student at Morehouse College in Atlanta, he then studied at Boston University, where he deepened his understanding of theological scholarship and of Mahatma Gandhi's non-violent strategy for social change.[3] He became pastor of Dexter Avenue Baptist Church, Montgomery, Alabama, and president of the newly formed Montgomery Improvement Association. As the boycott continued during 1956, King gained national prominence for his exceptional oratorial skills and personal courage. His house was bombed, and he and other boycott leaders were convicted on charges of conspiring to interfere with the bus company's operations. But in December 1956 Montgomery's buses were desegregated when the Supreme Court declared Alabama's segregation laws unconstitutional.

In 1957, seeking to build upon the success in Montgomery, King and other black ministers founded the Southern Christian Leadership Conference (SCLC). As president, King emphasized the goal of black voting rights when he spoke at the Lincoln Memorial during the 1957 Pilgrimage for Freedom. He traveled to West Africa to attend the independence celebrations in Ghana, and toured India, increasing his understanding of Gandhi's ideas.

King was seen in the media as the blacks' preeminent spokesman, but he was too pacifist-minded a leader for some Southern black college students. In 1960 they launched a wave of sit-in protests, and founded the Student Non-Violent Coordinating Committee (SNCC). In April 1960 King became the target of criticisms from SNCC activists. Even his joining a student sit-in and his subsequent arrest in October 1960 did not allay the tensions. (After his arrest, presidential candidate John F. Kennedy's sympathetic telephone call to King's wife, Coretta Scott King, helped attract crucial black support for Kennedy's campaign in 1960.) Conflicts between King and the younger militants were also evident when SCLC and SNCC assisted the Albany (Georgia) movement's campaign of mass protests in 1961–2. The SCLC protest strategy achieved its first major success in 1963 when the group launched

[3] Martin Luther King took a PhD at Boston University in the 1950s. Around this, however, there is controversy. There is some evidence that much of his work was plagiarized, and that this was covered up for him by his tutors. See Theodore Pappas (ed.) The Martin Luther King Jr Plagiarism Story (Rockford Institute, Ill.).

Plate 12a The March on Washington culminates at the Lincoln Memorial, where Martin Luther King declared: "I have a dream ...".

a major campaign in Birmingham, Alabama. Highly publicized confrontations between non-violent protesters, including schoolchildren, on the one hand, and police with clubs, fire hoses, and police dogs, on the other, gained Northern sympathy. The Birmingham clashes and other simultaneous civil rights efforts prompted President John F. Kennedy to push for the passage of new civil rights legislation.

In 1963, clashes between unarmed black demonstrators and police with attack dogs and fire hoses generated newspaper headlines throughout the world. Subsequent mass demonstrations in many communities culminated in a march on August 28, 1963, attracting more than 250,000 protesters to Washington DC. Addressing the marchers from the steps of the Lincoln Memorial, King delivered his famous "I have a dream" oration. "I have a dream," he said, "that one day this nation will rise up and live out the true meaning

Plate 12b Martin Luther King with Malcolm X, one-time eastern leader of the Black Muslims.
(Library of Congress.)

of its creed – 'We hold these truths to be self-evident, that all men are created equal'."

During the year following the march, King's renown as a non-violent leader grew, and in 1964, he received the Nobel peace prize. Despite the accolades, however, King faced strong challenges to his leadership. Malcolm X's message of self-defense and black nationalism through the Nation of Islam or "Black Muslims" expressed the anger of Northern urban blacks more effectively than did King's moderation, and in 1966 King encountered strong criticism from black power proponent Stokely Carmichael. Shortly afterward, white counterprotestors in Chicago physically assaulted King during an unsuccessful effort to transfer nonviolent protest techniques to the North. Nevertheless, King remained committed to non-violence. Early in 1968, he initiated a "poor people's campaign" to confront economic problems not addressed by civil rights reforms. As urban racial violence escalated, FBI director J. Edgar Hoover intensified his efforts to discredit King, and King's public criticism of American intervention in the Vietnam War soured his relations with the Johnson administration. When he delivered his last speech during a bitter sanitation workers' strike in Memphis, he admitted: "We've got some difficult days ahead, but it really doesn't matter with me now, because I've been to the mountaintop." The following evening, April 4, 1968, he was assassinated by James Earl Ray.

After his death, King remained a controversial symbol of the civil rights struggle, revered by many for his martyrdom on behalf of non-violence and condemned by others for his insurgent views. In 1986 King's birthday, January 15 became a federal holiday.

The assassination of Martin Luther King indicated that violence outdid non-violence. Both SCLC's protest strategy and SNCC's organizing activities were responsible for major Alabama protests in 1965, which prompted President Lyndon B. Johnson to introduce new voting rights legislation. On March 7 an SCLC-planned march from Selma to the state capitol in Montgomery ended almost before it began at Pettus Bridge on the outskirts of Selma, when mounted police using tear gas and wielding clubs attacked the protesters. News accounts of "Bloody Sunday" brought hundreds of civil rights sympathizers to Selma. Many demonstrators were determined to mobilize another march, and SNCC activists challenged King to defy a court order forbidding such marches. But, reluctant to do anything that would lessen public support for the voting rights cause, King on March 9 turned back a second march to the Pettus Bridge when it was blocked by the police. That evening a group of Selma whites killed a Northern white minister who had joined the demonstrations. In contrast to the killing of a black man, Jimmy Lee Jackson, a few weeks before, the Reverend James Reeb's death led to a national outcry. After several postponements of the march, civil rights advocates finally gained court permission to proceed. This Selma to Montgomery march was the culmination of one stage of the African-American freedom struggle. Soon afterward, Congress passed the Voting Rights Act of 1965, which greatly increased the number of Southern blacks able to register to vote. But it was also the last major racial protest of the 1960s to receive substantial white support.

By the late 1960s, organizations such as the NAACP, SCLC, and SNCC faced increasingly strong challenges from new militant organizations such as the Black Panther party. The Panthers' strategy of "picking up the gun" reflected the sentiments of many inner city blacks. A series of major "riots" (as the authorities called them), or "rebellions" (the sympathizers' term), erupted during the last half of the 1960s. Often influenced by the black nationalism of Elijah Muhammad and Malcolm X and by pan-African leaders, proponents of black liberation saw civil rights reforms as insufficient because they did not address the problems faced by millions of poor blacks, and because African-American citizenship was derived ultimately from the involuntary circumstances of enslavement. In addition, proponents of racial liberation often saw the African-American freedom struggle in international terms, as a movement for human rights and national self-determination for all peoples.

Severe government repression, the assassinations of Malcolm X in 1965 and Martin Luther King, in 1968 and the intense infighting within the black militant community caused a decline in protest activity after the 1960s. The African-American freedom struggle nevertheless left a permanent mark on American society. Overt forms of racial discrimination and government-supported segregation of public facilities came to an end, although *de facto*, as opposed to *de jure*, segregation persisted in Northern as well as Southern public school systems and in other areas of American society. In the South, anti-black violence declined. Black candidates were elected to political offices in communities where blacks had once been barred from voting, and many of the leaders or organizations that came into existence during the 1950s and 1960s remained active in Southern politics. Southern colleges and universities that once excluded blacks began to recruit them.

Despite the civil rights gains of the 1960s, however, racial discrimination and repression remained a significant factor in American life. Even after President Johnson declared a war on poverty and King initiated a Poor People's Campaign in 1968, the distribution of the nation's wealth and income moved toward greater inequality during the 1970s and 1980s. Civil rights advocates acknowledged that desegregation had not brought significant improvements in the lives of poor blacks, but they were divided over the future direction of black advancement efforts.[4]

King's activities were paralleled in the judgments in the Supreme Court. As de Tocqueville had noted in his *Democracy in America* hardly any political issue in the US failed in the end to require not only a judgment but a verdict from the Supreme Court; in this sense the nine old men, as FDR called them – now, more correctly, the seven elderly men and two middle-aged women on the Court – are the Supreme Government of the US. King's parallel as leader here was Associate Judge Thurgood Marshall.

4 THURGOOD MARSHALL

Thurgood Marshall was more than a lawyer; more than a judge. He was, above all, a crusader for common justice. In the long struggle for black civil rights in the United States few men have made a greater impact, even though the latter part of his career was steeped in bitter disappointment.

During 24 years as a Supreme Court justice (1967–91), Marshall fought racial and gender discrimination fiercely and was a determined upholder of liberal values. Among his more significant rulings were those stating that teachers could not be fired for speaking out truthfully on public issues, and that possession of obscene material within the privacy of one's home could not be made a crime. But for many years he was mostly a dissenting voice on the Supreme Court, for instance disagreeing sharply with the Court's ruling invalidating a plan for bussing pupils across school district lines to achieve racial integration and with its reinstatement of capital punishment. The most glaring of the inequities in the administration of the death penalty concerns the race of victims and defendants," he said in a speech in 1984. "A Negro who kills a white man runs a far greater risk of being executed than a white man who kills a Negro."

[4] Taylor Branch, *Parting the Waters: America in the King years, 1954–1963* (New York, Simon and Schuster, 1988); Clayborne Carson, *In Struggle: SNCC and the black awakening of the 1960s* (Cambridge, Mass., Harvard University Press, 1981); Hugh Davis Graham, *The Civil Rights Era: Origins and development of national policy* (New York, Oxford University Press, 1990); Steven F. Lawson, *Running for Freedom: civil rights and black politics in America since 1941* (New York, McGraw Hill, 1991); Coretta Scott King, *My Life with Martin Luther King, Jr* (New York, Holt Rinehart, 1969).

The younger son of an elementary schoolteacher and a Pullman car waiter, Marshall credited his father with his decision to study law instead of his original ambition to become a dentist. "My father turned me into a lawyer without ever telling me what he wanted me to be," he once said: "In a way he was the most insidious of my family rebels. He taught me how to argue, challenged my logic on every point, even if we were discussing the weather."

Rebellion seems to have been a family trait. His great-grandfather, who was captured in Africa and brought as a slave to Maryland's eastern shore, was said by Marshall to have won his freedom through his rebellious nature. "His more polite descendants like to think he came from the cultured tribes in Sierra Leone," he said. "But we all know that he really came from the toughest part of the Congo."

Marshall's mother pawned her wedding and engagement rings to help him attend Lincoln University, an all-black college in Pennsylvania, from which he graduated with honors in 1929. But his application to the all-white University of Maryland Law School was rejected on grounds of race, and he enrolled instead at the Howard University Law School in Washington. It was a slight that the young Marshall was soon to avenge. After graduating *magna cum laude* with an LLB degree in 1933, while working as counsel to the National Association for the Advancement of Coloured People in Baltimore, he compelled the law school that had rejected him to accept its first black student. No state law school south of the Mason-Dixon Line had ever been forced to do such a thing before. Thurgood Marshall was on his way.

In 1938 he became national counsel for the NAACP, and chief strategist in that organization's campaign to desegregate America's schools. He was a gregarious man and a lawyer of imposing presence. He traveled throughout the South creating a network of sympathetic lawyers to handle civil rights cases and instigate local challenges to segregated education.

The lower courts at that time were consistently upholding segregation. Marshall carried the issue to the Supreme Court, where he argued 32 cases on behalf of the NAACP and won 29 of them. Many felt that Marshall's efforts ranked with those of Martin Luther King. But Marshall was a scholar and traditionalist rather than an activist. He sought redress through the courts. When black militants queried his refusal to march at Selma, Marshall restated his faith in judicial gradualism. "I was there before you were born, and your father didn't have enough guts to go across the street. ... We've come a long way."

In *Smith* vs. *Allwright* (1944) Marshall persuaded the Supreme Court to invalidate the whites-only Democratic primary in Texas (which in effect applied to the election across the South) while in *Morgan* vs. *Virginia* (1946) the Court accepted his argument and forbade segregation on vehicles engaged in interstate commerce.

Marshall's greatest triumph came in 1954 when he won a unanimous decision in the case of *Brown* vs. *Board of Education of Topeka*. The court, under its chief justice, Earl Warren, ruled that "Separate education facilities are inherently unequal," thus overturning the "separate but equal" doctrine that had persisted in the United States since 1896. It was a verdict destined to have a profound effect on the whole of American society. The ruling, handed down at the beginning of Warren's tenure, determined that in the field of "public education, the doctrine of separate-but-equal has no place." Warren's painstaking and successful effort to forge a united front to overturn *Plessy* vs. *Ferguson* was surely the greatest of his many judicial accomplishments. The opinion, which drew on Warren's own sense of fair play and opportunity, emphasized that separating children "of similar age and qualifications solely because of their race generates a feeling of inferiority as to their status in the community that may affect their hearts and minds in a way unlikely ever to be undone." *Brown* was thus a bold move – even if it was a belated one, designed to rid the legal system of a court-created impediment to equality.

The *Brown* decision gave impetus to the demonstrations that began across the South in 1955. Robert L. Carter, former general counsel of the NAACP, argued that the desegregation ruling altered the status of blacks, who were no longer supplicants "seeking, pleading, begging to be treated as full-fledged members of the human race." Rather they were entitled to equal treatment under the law; the constitution promised no less. Therefore, *Brown*'s indirect consequences were dramatic. But most of the work – for both the Court and the civil rights activists – lay ahead.

The campaign on the streets was strengthened by the verdicts in the Court, so that the Supreme Court contributed significantly to the success of the civil rights movement in the 1960s. Martin Luther King, for example, acknowledged that the Court's determination that local laws requiring segregation on Montgomery's buses were unconstitutional, greatly rejuvenated his watershed community-wide boycott. Nonetheless, it is not too difficult to carry a reciprocal claim that the civil rights movement – over the longer course – contributed even more substantially to the development of the Supreme Court.

For the next seven years Marshall worked to ensure compliance with the new desegregation laws on a case by case basis. He fought, too, to eliminate racial discrimination in voting, housing, and public facilities. But in 1961 he left the civil rights battle to accept an invitation from President Kennedy to become an Appeal Court judge.

It was a tough decision to make. "I had to fight it out with myself," he said later. "But by then I had built up a staff – a damned good staff – and the backing that would let them go ahead. I've always felt the assault troops never occupy the town. I figured after the school decisions the assault was over for me. It was time to let newer minds take over."

The assault may have been over, but racial prejudice was not. Marshall's appointment to the bench was stalled for nearly a year by segregationists in the US Senate, before his confirmation in September 1962. The right wing had cause to worry. Once in place, Marshall confirmed their worst fears by strengthening constitutional safeguards against illegal searches and seizures, ruling that loyalty oaths for teachers were unconstitutional, and curbing the power of immigration authorities to deport aliens summarily.

With such a judicial philosophy, it was no surprise when President Johnson picked Marshall to become his solicitor general in 1965, and nominated him to the Supreme Court two years later as the first black justice. It was an act of political expediency at a time of acute racial tension, and produced a liberal majority on a court which had previously been split 5–4 in favor of conservatives. The broad underlying purpose of the Civil Rights Act of 1964 was to eliminate the pervasive discrimination against racial minorities that had long existed in American society. The two most important provisions of the act are Title II and Title VII, which provide federal administrative and judicial remedies against racial and other group-based kinds of discrimination in public accommodations and in employment respectively. The Supreme Court has interpreted the Act with reference to its broad underlying purpose and has resolved the major substantive and remedial questions under the Act in such a way as to maximize the protection afforded to racial minorities.

To be in the majority was a strange experience for Thurgood Marshall, and for some time he was uncharacteristically quiet. But with conservative appointments to the court by Presidents Nixon, Ford, Reagan, and Bush, he soon found himself fighting once more for liberal causes. But although he argued passionately against encroachments on individual liberty, against the death penalty and in favor of a woman's right to an abortion, Marshall found himself increasingly on the losing side. His frustration showed in dissenting judgments which became more embittered as the conservative hold strengthened, and in 1989 he accused the Supreme Court of being "in full-scale retreat from its long-standing solicitude to race-conscious remedial efforts directed toward deliverance of the century-old promise of equality of economic opportunity." In his last dissent, published on the day of his retirement, he roundly accused his fellow justices of overturning precedent for ideological ends. "Power, not reason," he said, "is the new currency of this Court's decision-making."

Nor did Marshall confine himself to comments from the bench. During the late 1970s and 1980s he publicly denounced the conservative trend of the Court at judicial conferences and Bar association meetings, and even broke with tradition to give a series of television interviews in which he accused President Reagan of having the worst record on civil rights of any American President. "I wouldn't do the job of dog-catcher for Ronald Reagan," he said.

His assessment of Mr Reagan's successor at the White House was not much more flattering. Asked his opinion of George Bush shortly before retirement, Marshall retorted: "It is said that if you can't say something good about a dead person, don't say it. Well, I consider him dead."

Failing health prompted Thurgood Marshall's retirement from the Supreme Court in June 1991, though he had always claimed that he would stay on the bench until he died. "Don't worry," he told a gathering of lawyers and judges in 1988, "I'm going to outlive those bastards." With the best of intentions, it was one promise he was unable to keep. When he retired in 1991, President Bush replaced him by Clarence Thomas. Marshall is said to have said, "If I die, prop me up and keep me voting." He died on January 24, 1993. Thurgood Marshall's eldest son, Thurgood Marshall Jr, was admitted to the Bar of the Supreme Court shortly before his father's retirement.[5]

[5] Randall Bland, *Private Pressure on Public Law: The legal career of Justice Thurgood Marshall* (Cambridge, Mass., Harvard University Press, 1973); A Tribute to Justice Thurgood Marshall, special issue, *Harvard Blackletter Journal* 6 (spring 1989).

5 ASSESSMENT

The modern African-American civil rights movement transformed American democracy. It also served as a model for other groups such as women's rights, Chicanos, gays and lesbians, the elderly, and many others. Continuing controversies regarding affirmative action programs and compensatory remedies for historically rooted patterns of discrimination were aspects of more fundamental, ongoing debates about the boundaries of individual freedom, the role of government, and alternative concepts of social justice.

The civil rights movement opened the modern era of race relations, yet it now seems to belong to a bygone time, when right and wrong itself was as stark as black and white. On May 17, 1954, a unanimous Supreme Court struck down racially segregated education in *Brown* vs. *Board of Education of Topeka*. Forty years later, that historic decision still reverberates through American life. The decision invigorated the nascent civil rights movement and, over time, changed not only law but attitudes, ultimately undermining broad popular support for state-sanctioned inequality. But today, despite the great economic, social and political progress for African-Americans that flowered from *Brown*, the divisions between white and black America are in some ways as jagged and intractable as ever. Today few leaders of any race place high priority on encouraging greater integration in housing or schools. Four decades after the decision, approximately two-thirds of African-American children attend schools that are majority black or Latino – largely because patterns of racial separation in housing remain immutable.

Brown also typified the conviction that the key to improving black lives was expanding civil rights and eliminating discrimination. But that belief has been corroded by a new generation of problems not clearly rooted in prejudice, and largely beyond the reach of legal remedies, the courts, and perhaps government policy of any sort: the loss of low-skill, high-wage jobs to automation and foreign competition, the rise in illegitimate births, and the crashing waves of violence and drug abuse immersing many inner cities.

Each of these changes has dulled the sharp moral clarity that defined the challenge of race relations in the age of *Brown*. The Jim Crow segregation laws offered a clear target for moral judgment and political activism; but today the source of blame, and the nature of solutions, for the enduring American dilemma of racial inequality have grown far more elusive.

"What *Brown* still correctly represents is that any inequality imposed by law is fundamentally unconstitutional," says historian David J. Garrow, author of the major biography of Martin Luther King. "But just because it is of great moral stature doesn't mean it is directly relevant to all questions today."

Brown's single achievement was to undermine the social legitimacy of state-sanctioned inequality. Overturning the 1896 Supreme Court decision that approved "separate but equal" public facilities for blacks, the unanimous court ruled in *Brown* that in education segregated facilities were "inherently unequal." The court followed with decisions striking down segregation in other public facilities, clearing the way for the 1964 Civil Rights Act that buried the last vestiges of Jim Crow, and outlawed discrimination in employment and education.

These laws did not extinguish racial prejudice. But over time, the legal standard of equal treatment under the constitution has widened into a consensus social standard. "The notion of a color-blind society is not just an accepted principle, it is a valued principle," says political pollster Geoff Garin. "If you think about where the country was 40 years ago, it's striking that in every major Southern city people watch the news every night delivered by an African-American anchor person and never think twice about it."

But whites have never accepted to the same degree the corollary of *Brown*'s logic – that integration in schools and other aspects of life was a positive good for society. Residential separation by race remains an obdurate force in American life: though some middle-class blacks have moved into formerly white suburbs, the overall level of segregation in cities like Chicago, Detroit, New York, Cleveland, and St Louis remains as great as 40 years ago, and in some Southern cities housing segregation is actually rising. Those housing patterns, combined with demographic trends like the powerful influx of Latino students, have undermined *Brown*'s promise in most urban school districts: according to a survey conducted in 1990, more than two-thirds of all black students attend schools that are primarily minority – the highest figure since 1968.

Against that backdrop of continued isolation, integration appears to be receding as a priority for blacks too. Some opinion surveys find increasing black support for militant nationalist and Separatist ideologies like that offered by Louis Parrakhan and the Nation of Islam. On college campuses, minority students now often seek affirmative segregation in separate dorms, student organizations and ethnically-based academic departments.

If faith in integration has waned since 1954, so too has faded the belief that ensuring civil rights is the key to narrowing the divide between blacks and whites. Though affirmative action and other legal strategies designed to expand minority opportunity have enlarged the black middle class, such programs offer less practical help to African-Americans trapped in poor neighborhoods. As Drew S. Days, solicitor general at the Justice Department, acknowledged in May 1994, even "massive enforcement" of all existing civil rights laws "would not alter significantly the lives of millions of black and other minority people who live at, or beyond, the margins of mainstream America." Even some sympathetic analysts view the continuing legal battles over discrimination – such as the legislative effort to ban the death penalty in jurisdictions where it is applied more heavily to minorities than to whites – as far less important than combating insidious cultural trends, such as the rise in illegitimate births and the explosion in gang-related violence.

In its *Brown* decision, the Supreme Court carefully avoided ruling that the constitution prohibited government from making any distinctions on the basis of race. But the decision was received as bearing precisely the message that all Americans, regardless of race, should be treated equally under the law. That standard shaped the landmark 1964 Civil Rights Act. But liberals have argued that government has to grant racial preferences in employment and education to produce "equality as a result," not "just legal equity." With that historic switch, *Brown*'s legacy became confused and contested. One of the briefs in the case suggested it was unconstitutional when government "confers or denies benefits on the basis of color or race." Now conservatives routinely cite that argument against the affirmative action plans that the civil rights movement promotes. "There has been this incredible flip-flop," says Linda Chavez, executive director of the US Civil Rights Commission under President Reagan. "The whole point of *Brown* and the civil rights movement was to make race irrelevant. Now we have come full circle."

As both candidate and President, Bill Clinton's instinct has been to leave undisturbed the liberal consensus behind affirmative action – seeking neither its expansion nor retrenchment. But in other respects, he is moving back toward the idea of common opportunities and standards that some see as *Brown*'s essence. Clinton's domestic agenda combines programs aimed at increasing opportunity without regard to race – such as job training and expanded tax credits for the working poor – with tougher enforcement of anti-discrimination laws in housing and credit, and calls for moral renewal and personal responsibility. As with *Brown* itself, many question whether those programs and exhortations are sufficient to bridge the chasm between white and black Americans, particularly those isolated in depressed inner cities. That mist of despair marks the starkest contrast from 40 years ago. For an earlier generation, the Supreme Court's majestic *Brown* decision illuminated a path to equality through the dismantling of segregation. Today, *Brown*'s beacon has dimmed, and nothing has entirely replaced its light.

Nevertheless, the ghetto has its compensations. Concentrations of urban blacks have provided political bases for an increasing number of black officeholders. Beginning with the election of Oscar DePriest from Chicago's Black Belt in 1928, and continuing with the elevation of Chicago's William L. Dawson, New York's Adam Clayton Powell Jr, and Detroit's Charles Diggs Jr in the 1940s and 1950s, a growing post-Reconstruction black presence was re-established in Congress. More recent advances have come on the state and local levels, with black mayors – beginning with Gary, Indiana's Richard Hatcher and Cleveland's Carl Stokes in 1967 – occupying center stage. Blacks, as in Virgina, have become state governors. These successes, however, have heightened black consciousness without demonstrably altering the conditions that called forth protest and political mobilization. Whether politicians shepherding their voters, black businesses catering to a concentrated black clientèle, ministers tending their flocks, or ordinary citizens occupying a zone of social familiarity, the ghetto has produced a class that could view its dispersal only with grave misgivings. There was thus irony in the freedom born of restriction. Alone, the forces emanating from within these increasingly complex black settlements could not determine the future development of the ghetto; there were larger economic, social, and political forces at work. And they rendered less clear, and perhaps more painful, the choices confronting urban blacks after World War II.

The increasing militancy of African-American politics during the 1960s after the Supreme Court verdict of 1954 was evident too. Perhaps the two most conspicuous personal examples of the militant and exotic were Muhammed Ali and Malcolm X.

Cassius Marcellus Clay experienced the racial restrictions that fueled the civil rights protests of the late 1950s and 1960s. As a youngster, he resented being named after a white man, albeit an abolitionist. When he read news of the 1955 racial murder in Mississippi of Emmett Till, a black youngster about his age, he reacted angrily, hurling stones at an "Uncle Sam Wants You" poster. He learned to box while a teenager, and his exceptional skills quickly became evident. By 1959 he had won a national Golden

Gloves championship. Following his success as a member of the 1960 US Olympic boxing team, he signed a professional contract with Louisville promoters and soon became a contender for the heavyweight boxing crown. Brashly outspoken about racial issues, he also bragged about his pugilistic ability, often proclaiming, "I am the greatest."

As he was perfecting his boxing and promotional skills, he became affiliated with the Nation of Islam, an all-black religious group, often labeled the "Black Muslims," led by Elijah Muhammad. He became close friends with the Nation's best-known spokesman, Malcolm X, but remained loyal to Elijah Muhammad after Malcolm's 1964 break with him. Recognizing that the Nation of Islam was notorious because of its advocacy of black self-defense and racial separatism, Clay kept his affiliation with the group secret until February 1964, when he defeated Sonny Liston and became heavyweight champion. He then announced his religious ties and stated that he had rejected his "slave" name in favor of the new name Muhammad Ali.

For a decade thereafter, Ali remained at the center of controversy. Many reporters and boxing officials continued to refer to him as Cassius Clay and some even demanded that his title be withdrawn. The hostility increased when he refused in 1967 to be inducted into the army, citing the fact that his religion forbade him from doing so. Government officials were unwilling to accept his claim that he was a lay Islamic minister, especially when he made clear his lack of sympathy for the war in Vietnam. "I ain't got no quarrel with the Vietcong," he explained. Although he indicated that he was simply responding to religious imperatives, Ali became a widely admired symbol of black pride and militancy because of his consistent unwillingness to back down in the face of threats from white authorities. Stripped of his title after being indicted for refusing induction, he was later convicted and sentenced to five years in prison. In June 1970, however, the Supreme Court overturned his conviction. In 1974, Ali gained further vindication when he defeated George Foreman and regained the title that had been taken from him.

Although Ali's activities in the years after 1974 were not as controversial as they had once been, he remained an internationally known public figure. After his retirement from boxing during the late 1970s, he developed Parkinson's syndrome, a condition that severely restricted his once extensive public speaking activities.[6]

[6] Muhammad Ali, with Richard Durham, *The Greatest: My own story* (New York, Random House, 1975); Henry Hampton and Steve Fayer, *Voices of Freedom:*

A pimp and hustler known by the nickname Detroit Red, Malcolm X – born Malcolm Little ("but my true family name I will never know") – discovered the Nation of Islam and its leader Elijah Muhammad in prison – where he went for burglary – and came out preaching separation from, and vengeance against, the "white devil." He was born in 1925 in Omaha, Nebraska, the son of a Baptist preacher who was a follower of Marcus Garvey. His father was slain by the Klan-like Black Legionaries; his mother had a nervous breakdown from which she never recovered; and the young Malcolm was put in a foster home but ran away for a life of crime. Muhammed's thesis that the white man is the devil with whom blacks cannot live had a strong impact on Malcolm. Turning to an ascetic way of life and reading widely, he began to overcome the degredation he had known. The argument that only blacks can cure the ills that afflict them confirmed for Malcolm the power of Muhammad's faith. He became a loyal disciple and adopted X – symbolic of a stolen identity – as his last name.

After six years Malcolm was released from prison. Later, he became the minister of Temple No. 7 in Harlem, his indictments of racism and his advocacy of self-defense eliciting admiration, as well as fear, far beyond the New York black community. Whites were especially fearful, recoiling from his sustained pronouncements of crimes against his people. While most contrasted him with Martin Luther King Jr, with whose philosophy they were much more at ease, white college students found ugly truths in his searing rhetoric of condemnation. Malcolm, however, grew increasingly restive as the Nation of Islam failed to join in the mounting civil rights struggle and became convinced that Elijah Muhammad was lacking in sincerity, a view painfully validated by corruption at the highest level of the organization. For his part, Muhammad seemed threatened by the popularity of Malcolm, whose influence reached even into the respected Student Non-Violent Coordinating Committee (SNCC), a pivotal force in the civil rights movement – hence, the organization's call for black power in 1966. Like Malcolm, SNCC looked to the independent nations of Africa as a source of inspiration and support. But SNCC failed to ground black power in the best of the nationalist tradition, and black nationalism was left in disarray even as its standard was being raised by the flower of America's black youth.[7]

An oral history of the Civil Rights Movement from the 1950s through the 1980s (New York, Bantam, 1990).

[7] Harold Cruse, *The Crisis of the Negro Intellectual* (New York, Morrow, 1967); Sterling Stuckey, *Slave Culture: Nationalist theory and the foundations of black America* (New York, Oxford University Press, 1987).

Malcolm's assertion that President John F. Kennedy's assassination amounted to "the chickens coming home to roost" led to his suspension from the Black Muslims in December 1963. A few months later he left the organization, traveled to Mecca, and discovered that orthodox Muslims preach equality of the races, which led him to abandon the argument that whites are devils. Having returned to America as El-Haj Malik El-Shabazz, he remained convinced that racism had corroded the spirit of America and that only blacks could free themselves. In June 1964, he founded the Organization of Afro-American Unity and moved increasingly in the direction of socialism. More sophisticated than in his Black Muslim days and of growing moral stature, he was assassinated by a Black Muslim at a rally of his organization in New York on February 21, 1965. Malcolm X had predicted that, though he had but little time to live, he would be more important in death than in life. The almost painful honesty that enabled him to find his way from degradation to devotion to his people, the modest lifestyle that kept him on the edge of poverty, and the distance he somehow managed to put between himself and racial hatred serve, in his autobiography, as poignant reminders of human possibility and achievement.[8]

National conferences on black power were held annually beginning in 1966. The increasingly radical and separatist resolutions agreed upon at these gatherings called for, among other things, a boycott of the military draft by blacks, self-defense training for black youths, the partition of the country into separate black and white nations and calls for reparation for the sufferings of slavery. But many others attracted to the concept sought to increase the numbers of black-owned businesses and black officeholders rather than pursuing extreme separatism. Black power advocates achieved only a few of their goals.

To Malcolm X the world was run by whites, and whites he saw as enemy. The Nation of Islam published "hate literature." But by the 1950s and 1960s there was another and a more complex world, that of the steadily desegregating South and Mid-South. To this there is a fascinating insight in the near autobiography of Henry Louis Gates Jr, *Colored People: A memoir.*

Gates, now a distinguished figure as chairman of Afro-American Studies at Harvard, was born in 1950 in tiny Piedmont, West Virginia; the elementary school he attended was integrated the year

[8] Malcolm X, with Alex Haley, *The Autobiography of Malcolm X* (New York, Grove Press, 1964).

before he entered first grade, the union at the paper mill nearby not until the end of his teens. His coming-of-age story is thus one of dramatic change in a small contained community that was swept by the forces of legislation, politics, and emotion from the distant world outside. Not all welcomed them. There were hunters and handymen in the hill country who had "carved out a dark-chocolate world" of their own; they clung to "colored" schools and churches as insurance of their dignity and independence, and they hated the younger blacks who would so readily abandon their world for the white one. But Gates does not forget that the pre-1950s was still a segregated world thick with humiliations, and he does not lament its passing.[9]

6 WOMEN'S RIGHTS

Throughout the last two centuries women too have campaigned for their rights; to vote, first, and later for equality of treatment in employment, in politics, and in their personal and social lives.

The immediate post-Civil War years proved a crucial period for women's rights. The controversial issue of black political rights – and debate over the Fourteenth and Fifteenth Amendments – quickly made women's suffrage the most prominent of women's demands. Elizabeth Cady Stanton (1819–1902) was the leading strategist, orator, philosopher, and publicist in her time of the movement for women's equality in the United States. The daughter of a wealthy conservative family in upstate New York, she married Henry B. Stanton, an abolitionist and lawyer and had seven children (the last born in 1859). She worked to pass landmark legislation in New York in 1848 that gave property rights to married women, and she was the prime mover behind the Seneca Falls convention for women's rights in the same year. In 1851 she met Susan B. Anthony (1820–1906), who had grown up in a liberal Quaker family in Massachusetts. She taught school, and as an unmarried woman she had became acutely aware of women's need for economic and personal independence. She worked actively in the temperance and abolition movements in New York. Unlike Elizabeth Stanton, who was then raising her large brood of children, Anthony was free to travel, speak, and organize during a long period when

[9] Henry Louis Gates Jr, *Colored People: A memoir* (New York, Knopf, 1994); cf. Robert Penn Warren, *Segregation* (New York, Random House/Vintage Books, 1957).

Stanton had to remain at home with her children. They formed a working partnership on behalf of women's rights that lasted for the rest of their lives and shaped the course of American feminism.

In February 1854, Stanton appeared before the New York State legislature in Albany on behalf of a state convention of women's rights advocates. Stanton and Anthony put a copy of the speech on every legislator's desk and printed 50,000 copies for distribution as tracts.

1st. Look at the position of woman as woman. It is not enough for us that by your laws we are permitted to live and breathe to claim the necessaries of life from our legal protectors – to pay the penalty of our crimes; we demand the full recognition of all our rights as citizens of the Empire State. We are persons; native, freeborn citizens; property-holders, tax-payers; yet are we denied the exercise of our right to the elective franchise. We support ourselves, and, in part, your schools, colleges, churches, your poor-houses, jails, prisons, the army, the navy, the whole machinery of government, and yet we have no voice in your councils. We have every qualification required by the Constitution, necessary to the legal voter, but the one of sex.

Stanton's view was simple:

We ask no better laws than those you have made for yourselves ... simply on the ground that the rights of every human being are the same and identical.

Susan Anthony endorsed the call:

It was we, the people, not we, the white male citizens, nor we, the male citizens; but we, the whole people, who formed this Union.

In 1866 women's rights leaders formed the Equal Suffrage Association to strive for both black and female suffrage, and joined a referendum campaign on these issues in Kansas in 1867. But in that state, male abolitionist support for female suffrage dwindled. Alienated from their former allies in the anti-slavery movement, Stanton and Anthony began to campaign independently. Through their publication *Revolution*, financed by the eccentric Democrat George Francis Train, they promoted a broad spectrum of women's rights – equal suffrage, equal pay, marriage reform, more liberal divorce laws, and "self-sovereignty." They denounced the Fifteenth Amendment, which enfranchised only black men and which other

Plate 13 "Mr President What Will You Do for Woman Suffrage?"
(Library of Congress.)

women's rights leaders endorsed. In 1869, two rival suffrage movements emerged: the New York-based National Woman Suffrage Association (NWSA) lea by Stanton and Anthony, which accepted only women and opposed the Fifteenth Amendment; and the Boston-based American Woman Suffrage Association (AWSA), which included men, and supported black suffrage as a step in the right direction. Among its leaders were Lucy Stone and Julia Ward Howe.

In the 1872 presidential election, Anthony led a group of women in Rochester, New York, to the polls to vote. Since women's suffrage was illegal, she was arrested and indicted. Before her trial in June 1873, Anthony traveled widely in upstate New York, giving a speech about the injustice of denying women the suffrage. She was ultimately convicted and fined, but she refused to pay the fine. No attempt was made to collect. In this speech, she argued that no Constitutional amendment was needed to "give" women the vote, because the Fourteenth Amendment – passed in 1868 – said that "all persons born or naturalized in the United States" were citizens and entitled to the rights of citizenship. Since women were persons and citizens, she insisted that they were fully entitled to vote.

The new woman's suffrage associations followed separate paths for two decades. The NWSA campaigned for a federal women's suffrage amendment, but made no progress. The AWSA published the *Women's Journal* and waged state campaigns, but lost all state referenda. By 1890 only Utah and Wyoming had enfranchised women. Although women had acquired partial voting rights (in local elections or school board elections) in 19 states, equal suffrage remained elusive.

Although suffragists won no major victories, the growing women's movement provided a potential constituency. The ranks of women activists increased in the Progressive Era with the emergence of new women's organizations devoted to reform. Such endeavors as the settlement movement, the National Consumers' League (1899), the Women's Trade Union League (1903), and the women's peace movement abetted the suffrage crusade. By taking part in public affairs, women reformers helped legitimize suffragist claims. Advocates of the ballot had always combined demands for sexual equality (women deserved the vote) with arguments based on sexual difference (women would bring special qualities to politics).

Despite the changing role of women in American society, as more women entered the workplace, became educated, bore fewer children, and spent less time caring for them, the movement met increased resistance from the liquor industry (which feared female support for prohibition) and the textile industry (which feared female support for restrictions on child labor). Beneath such practical concerns lay a more deeply felt anxiety about changing sex roles.

But the adoption of more vigorous tactics and the triumph of progressive reforms throughout the country, which made women's suffrage appear less radical, stimulated massive support for woman suffrage. In 1916, the Democratic and Republican parties both endorsed female enfranchisement; in 1919 Congress approved, and a year later the states ratified the Nineteenth Amendment, which granted women the right to vote.[10]

Reference to just a few of the women who by their own example, outside politics as such, furthered the cause of reform should be made here. Mary Lyon (1797–1849) founded the Mount Holyoke Female Seminary in 1837. This was the first true women's college, with its own campus, endowment, and a board of trustees committed to its continuation beyond the life of the founder. Pauline Wright Davis (1813–76) was the first American to use a model of the female anatomy while lecturing on physiology. She was also the founder in 1853 of *Una*, the first American newspaper devoted primarily to the cause of women's rights.

Maria Mitchell (1818–1889) was the first American woman astronomer, the discoverer of Mitchell's Comet (1847), the first woman elected to the American Academy of Arts and Sciences (1848), a member of the first faculty of Vassar College, the first woman elected to the American Philosophical Society (1869), and a founder of the Association for the Advancement of Women (1873). Mitchell explained her many achievements by saying; "I was born of only ordinary capacity but of extraordinary persistency." Don't you believe it.

Elizabeth Blackwell (1821–1910) was the first woman in the United States to earn an MD degree – in 1849, from Geneva (NY) Medical College, after having been turned down by Harvard, Yale, and most of the other medical schools in the country. In 1857 she founded the New York Infirmary for Women and Children; she played an important role in the establishment of the United States Sanitary Commission during the Civil War; in 1868 she founded the Women's Medical College in New York City. In later years she was a pioneer in sex education, writing *The Human Element in Sex* (1884) and campaigning against the double standard.

[10] Anne Firor Scott and Andrew MacKay Scott, *One Half the People: The fight for woman suffrage* (Philadelphia, Lippincott, 1975).

Antoinette Brown (1825–1921) studied theology at Oberlin College, but was not granted a degree because of her sex. (Oberlin finally gave her an honorary DD in 1908). However, in 1853 she was ordained as a Congregationalist minister, the first woman minister in the United States. She later became a Unitarian.

Myra Bradwell (1831–1894) founded (in 1868), managed, and edited the *Chicago Legal News* which soon became the most prominent legal journal in the West. She also qualified for admission to the Illinois Bar. When admission was denied because of her sex, she carried her case to the US Supreme Court, but lost. Finally, in 1882, she persuaded the Illinois legislature to pass a law banning the exclusion of anyone from any profession on the basis of sex.

Victoria Claflin Woodhull (1838–1927) in 1868 joined her sister Tennessee Claflin Cook (1846–1923), and together they became the first female New York stockbrokers. Victoria Woodhull was also (in 1871) the first woman to testify before a Congressional committee, on which occasion she campaigned vigorously for women's suffrage. In 1872 she was the candidate of the Equal Rights party for President of the United States.

Elsie De Wolfe (1865–1950) gave up a successful career as an actress to become the first woman professional interior decorator in 1905. Her "anti-Victorian" style, featuring bright colors and much light, was described in her book *The House in Good Taste* (1913). She is also said to have been among the first women to fly and to dance the foxtrot.

Alice Hamilton (1869–1970), another early woman doctor, created the field of industrial medicine and was a leader in publicizing the dangers of lead poisoning and other industrial hazards. In 1919 she became the first female professor at Harvard. (She was not, however, permitted to march at Commencement and was not even allotted her quota of faculty football tickets.) Her *Industrial Poisons in the United States* (1925) was the first textbook on this subject. Katharine Bement Davis (1860–1935), a pioneer in prison reform before World War I, conducted the first broad survey of women's sexual behavior, *Factors in the Sex Life of Twenty-two Hundred Women* (1929).

Ruth Benedict (1887–1948), anthropologist, developed the theory, particularly influential in the decades before and after World War II, that distinctive cultures produce people with one dominant type of personality. She was also, the first woman to become "the preeminent leader of a learned profession", a distinction symbolized by her election as president of the American Anthropological Association in 1947.

Sandra Day O'Connor (1930–) was appointed by President Reagan in 1981 as the first woman associate justice of the Supreme Court. Texas-born and Stanford-educated, she was a lawyer in practice before she served on the Arizona state senate (1967–74) and on the Arizona bench (1974–81). She began her tenure on the Supreme Court as a conservative, usually voting with Chief Justice William Rehnquist. But she steadily became an independent thinker. By 1990 she was the pivotal center vote in a Court then composed of four liberals and four conservatives.

Margaret H. Sanger (1879–1966) invented the term "birth control" in 1914 and founded the first birth control clinic in the United States in 1916. In 1921 she organized the American Birth Control League, forerunner of the Planned Parenthood Federation, and two years later opened the Birth Control Research Bureau, which became the model for hundreds of local birth control clinics.

The winning of female suffrage did not, however, mark the end of prejudice and discrimination against women in public life. Women still lacked equal success with men in those professions, especially the law, which provide the chief routes to political power. Further, when women ran for office – and many did in the immediate post-suffrage era – they often lacked major party backing, hard to come by for any newcomer but for women almost impossible unless she belonged to a prominent political family. Even if successful in winning backing, when women ran for office they usually had to oppose incumbents. When, as was often the case, they lost their first attempts, their reputation as "losers" made re-endorsement impossible. Nevertheless, the years after World War I saw some women politicians become active.

Belle Lindner Moskowitz (1877–1933), a shopkeeper's daughter born in Harlem, New York, spent her early career as a social worker on the city's Lower East Side. After her marriage in 1903, while her children were growing up, she did volunteer work until, by the 1910s, she had developed a city-wide reputation as an effective social and industrial reformer. Although considering herself an independent Republican, in 1918, the first year New York State women voted, because of Democrat Alfred E. Smith's reputation as an advocate for labor, she supported him for governor. From 1923 on, she ran his state re-election campaigns and guided the legislative enactment of his policies, all the while preparing the ground for his nomination by the Democratic party as presidential candidate in 1928. In that year, she directed national publicity for the campaign and served as the only woman on the national

Democratic party executive committee. Smith had offered her a number of government posts but she had refused them. She believed, and rightly so, that her work from behind the scenes would in the end give her more power than the holding of any bureaucratic, appointive office. Thanks to her, Smith, a man whose formal education had ended at the age of 13, was able to pursue his legislative program with enough success to become a viable presidential candidate. But because of her self-effacement, when Smith failed to win the presidency and then lost his party leadership role to Franklin Delano Roosevelt, her career was eclipsed along with his.

More famous than Moskowitz, Anna Eleanor Roosevelt (1884–1962) became known worldwide for the role she played as the wife of Franklin Roosevelt, four-term president during the Great Depression and World War II. Most portraits of Eleanor focus on her activities after 1933, when Franklin became President, until his death in 1945, when she became a United Nations delegate and moral force in world politics. What is less well known is that before FDR became President, even before he became governor of New York, she had accumulated a vast amount of political experience and influence in her own right.

Unlike Moskowitz, Eleanor Roosevelt was born into wealth and privilege, but endured an unhappy childhood. In 1920, her first venture into politics reached its first culmination when Franklin ran, unsuccessfully, for vice-president. By then their marriage was on shaky ground. Although in 1918 Eleanor had discovered Franklin's affair with Lucy Mercer, the couple had resolved to keep the marriage together. In 1921, Franklin was stricken with polio and withdrew from politics. Franklin's political manager and publicist, Louis Howe, convinced Eleanor to keep her husband's name alive by becoming active herself in women's organizations. Once involved in this work, Eleanor confirmed what she had discovered during her husband's earlier campaigns. She liked politics.

Eleanor's main interests were public housing for low-income workers, the dissemination of birth control information, the reorganization of the state government, and shorter hours and minimum wages for women workers. As a result, she became a well-known figure, almost as well-known as her husband, at both state and national level. But when her husband won the governorship in 1928, she gave up all activity. She knew where her duty lay – to become Albany's First Lady, not to hold office herself.

The first woman in the United States to hold Cabinet rank was Frances Perkins (1880–1965). Better educated than either Moskowitz or Roosevelt (she graduated from Mount Holyoke College), Perkins had a background similar to theirs. After working as a teacher and in a social settlement, she became secretary of the New York Consumers' League, a group seeking labor legislation to improve factory safety and health conditions for all workers. Although always known as "Miss" Perkins, she was married and bore one child, but her husband suffered from mental illness and was later unable to earn a living.

She was the first woman appointed to the New York State Industrial Commission (1919) and later she was the industrial commissioner of the state. In 1933, when President Roosevelt made her secretary of labor, she became the first woman member of a President's Cabinet.

Jeannette Rankin (1880–1973) became the first woman member of Congress when she was elected as Montana's sole member of the House of Representatives in 1916. Being a pacifist, she voted against declaring war on Germany in 1917 and was therefore not a candidate for re-election. In 1940, however, she was again elected to Congress. When she again voted against declaring war after Pearl Harbor, she became the only person of either sex to have voted against American participation in both world wars.

Ruth Bryan Owen (1885–1977), although benefiting politically from the fact that she was a daughter of William Jennings Bryan, was a pioneer in many ways. She was the first woman elected to Congress from a Southern state (Florida, in 1928) and the first woman member of an important Congressional committee (Foreign Affairs). In 1933, President Roosevelt named her minister plenipotentiary to Denmark, making her the first American woman to hold a high diplomatic post.

Mary (Molly) Dewson (1874–1962) was a pioneer in the mobilization of women as a force in partisan politics and as executives in the federal bureaucracy. She began this work during the 1928 presidential campaign of Al Smith, continuing it during Franklin Roosevelt's 1930 campaign for the governorship of New York, during his campaign for the presidency in 1932, and thereafter. As head of the women's division of the Democratic party, she was responsible for recruiting large numbers of women for government jobs and in training women campaign workers. After graduating from Wellesley College and holding some research jobs, she became superintendent of probation at the nation's first reform school for girls, then executive secretary of the Massachusetts Commission on the Minimum Wage. Never married, she maintained a lifelong partnership with a friend, Polly Porter, with whom she farmed in

Massachusetts and did suffrage and war work. Eventually, under the mentorship of Eleanor Roosevelt, Dewson moved into Democratic state and then national politics. Her personal ambitions remained severely limited, however.

Mary McLeod Bethune (1875–1955) became, after a long career as an educator, the founder of the National Council of Negro Women and then, in 1936, the first black woman to head a federal agency, the Division of Negro Affairs of the National Youth Administration. She was also a founder of the so-called "Black Cabinet," a group of New Deal officials working to persuade various government agencies to pay more attention to the interests of blacks.

In all these cases, however prominent the roles they played, none would have claimed parity with men in politics. Among the most politically adept of their generation, all of these women pursued political goals in the 1920s, but none as a man would have done. Moskowitz achieved an important advisory role but lost all her power at the fall of her mentor. Roosevelt sacrificed her own needs to those of her husband. Perkins reached high office but masked her strength and denied personal ambition. Dewson often put domestic happiness before career fulfillment and, like Perkins, downplayed her feminism. Others of their generation who had been leaders in the suffrage struggle acted similarly.[11]

Some of those constraints are still with us. Throughout the 1992 campaign, questions about women's appropriate roles in politics continued to surface. They dominated the controversies that swirled around Hillary Clinton, wife of Democratic presidential candidate, Bill Clinton. What role had she played in his years as governor of Arkansas? Why did she keep her maiden name when they were married? What was the quality of their married life together? Had she been a good mother or was she one of those career-orientated, ambitious feminists?

At its national convention in August 1992, the Republican party exploited popular doubts about Hillary Clinton's ability to operate in the traditional mode of the political wife. In an unprecedented move, convention organizers asked the wives of its candidates,

[11] Blanche W. Cook, *Eleanor Roosevelt*, vol. I (New York, Viking, 1992); J. Stanley Lemons, *The Woman Citizen: Social feminism in the 1920s* (Champaign, Ill., University of Illinois Press, 1973); George W. Martin, *Madam Secretary Frances Perkins* (Boston, Houghton Mifflin, 1976); Elisabeth Israels Perry, *Belle Moskowitz: Feminine politics and the exercise of power in the age of Alfred E. Smith* (London, Routledge, 1992); Susan Ware, *Partner and I: Molly Dewson, feminism, and New Deal politics* (New Haven, Yale University Press, 1987).

Barbara Bush and Marilyn Quayle, to speak. The shared theme of the women's speeches, "traditional" family values, sent our a clear message: political wives must adhere strictly to giving priority to their husband's careers.

The Democratic party response disturbed many feminists, but it was probably essential to victory. Hillary Clinton baked cookies and, in response to rumors that she was childless, trotted out her daughter Chelsea on every possible occasion. Still, when Bill Clinton and his running mate, Albert Gore Jr, made their victory speeches on election night, women heard some new words on national television. In describing their future government, for the first time in history both President and Vice-President elect included the category of "gender" as an important test of the diversity they envisioned.

A central issue in recent years has been abortion. Abortion has been practiced in the United States since the founding of the Republic, but both its social character and its legal status have varied considerably. Through the early decades of the nineteenth century, Americans regarded abortion primarily as the recourse of women wronged by duplicitous suitors or pregnant as the result of illicit relationships, though records exist of married women having abortions. Americans tolerated the practice, which had long been legal under colonial common law and remained legal under American common law.

In the middle decades of the nineteenth century several state legislatures began to restrict the increasingly common practice of abortion. Some lawmakers feared for the safety of women undergoing abortions. Others reacted negatively to what they considered indecent advertising. Concerned about falling birthrates, many opposed all forms of fertility control, not just abortion. But the greatest pressure for legal change came from the American Medical Association (AMA), founded in 1847.

Led by Horatio Robinson Storer, a Boston physician, the AMA and its affiliated medical societies worked in state capitals throughout the nation during the 1860s and 1870s to outlaw abortion at any stage of gestation, except when doctors themselves determined the procedure to be necessary.

The anti-abortion laws and legal decisions of the second half of the nineteenth century, though seldom and selectively enforced, drove the practice of abortion underground. Substantial numbers of women, especially immigrant women with limited access to other (also illegal) methods of fertility control, nonetheless continued to have abortions. Surveys conducted under the auspices of the AMA and the federal government confirmed the persistence of widespread abortion in the United States through the 1930s.

US involvement in the Vietnam War revived a claim made since the Revolution that men old enough to fight were also old enough to vote: in 1971 the Twenty-sixth Amendment lowered the voting age to 18. Alongside the campaign for the vote was a campaign for "the right to privacy," a code phrase for free choice for a women's right to choose not to have a child.

In January 1973 the Supreme Court in *Roe* vs. *Wade* ruled that women, as part of their constitutional right to privacy, could choose to terminate a pregnancy prior to the point at which the fetus reached a stage of development that would allow it to survive outside the womb. This ruling, and its subsequent refinements, effectively struck anti-abortion laws from state criminal codes and returned the United States, in a rough sense, to standards functionally similar to those of the early Republic. That ruling was one of the most controversial in the Courts history. "Roe" was Norma McGorvey, who was denied the right under Texas law to abort a fetus she did not want to bear. She sued the state, and the case came before the US Supreme Court. The Court had turned increasingly conservative after the retirement of Chief Justice Earl Warren, the deaths of liberal Hugo Black and moderate John Marshall Harlan II, and President Richard Nixon's appointments of Chief Justice Warren Burger and Justices Harry Blackmun, Lewis Powell, and William Rehnquist. Nonetheless, the Court ruled 7–2 that women had an unrestricted right to abort a fetus during the first trimester of pregnancy, but that the state had an interest in protecting the fetus after that, when it became "viable" or able to live outside the womb.

The opinion extended the "right to privacy" enunciated in *Griswold* vs. *Connecticut* (1965), in which the Court ruled that a state could not prohibit married couples from using contraceptives; this right to privacy was implied in the First Amendment guarantee of free speech, the Ninth Amendment's reference to "certain rights," and the Fourteenth Amendment's guarantee of due process of law. Blackmun wrote the majority opinion, with Rehnquist and Justice Byron White dissenting.

The ruling continues to cause controversy. Early in the 1980s, the "right-to-life" movement, with help from politicians such as President Ronald Reagan, pushed for a constitutional amendment prohibiting abortion except in cases of rape, incest, or a threat to the mother's life. Although anti-abortionists were unable to pass the amendment, they did secure a ban on federal and, in many cases, state financing of abortions. The Roman Catholic Church and many Protestant fundamentalist groups strongly opposed abortion. In response, women's groups such as the National Organization for Women stepped up their efforts to elect pro-choice candidates. The abortion issue had evolved into a "litmus test" for both liberals and conservatives and had become a trying issue for many political candidates and judicial appointees.[12]

The revival of feminism in the 1960s is often dated from the appearance of Betty Friedan's *The Feminine Mystique*. This 1963 bestseller found a receptive audience among middle- and upper-class women whose experiences Friedan captured. Founder and first president of the National Organization for Women, Friedan argued that most of the opinion-shaping forces of modern society were engaged in a campaign to convince women of the virtues of domesticity. By so doing, they were wasting the talents of millions. Women should resist these pressures, said Friedan. "The only way for a woman ... to know herself as a person," she wrote, "is by creative work."

Although her book was important for its challenge to the ideology of domesticity, other factors also contributed to the reemergence of feminism. Unprecedented numbers of married women were being drawn into the job market – albeit on unequal terms – as the service sector of the economy expanded and consumerism fueled the desire of many families for a second income. Both the growing numbers of women graduating from college and the availability of the birth control pill (which accelerated the already noticeable decline in the birthrate) further encouraged women's entry into the work force. By the early 1960s the contradiction between the realities of paid work and higher education, on the one hand, and the still pervasive domestic ideology, on the other, could no longer be reconciled. Equally important in sparking feminist consciousness were the oppositional movements of the 1960s, particularly the black freedom movement, which was a source of inspiration and a model for social change for second-wave feminists.

The new feminism emerged from two groups of educated, middle-class, predominantly white women. The National Organization for

[12] For abortion, see Kristin Luker, *Abortion and the Politics of Motherhood* (Berkeley, University of California Press, 1984); James C. Mohr, *Abortion in America: The origins and evolution of national policy, 1800–1900* (New York, Oxford University Press, 1978).

Women consisted mainly of politically moderate professionals; those who stressed women's liberation were younger, more radical women, and typically veterans of the black freedom movement and the New Left. For the former, John F. Kennedy's establishment of the President's Commission on the Status of Women (PCSW) in 1961 and Title VII of the Civil Rights Act of 1964, which prohibited employment discrimination on the basis of race, sex, religion, and national origin, were important catalysts for change. The PCSW, with Eleanor Roosevelt as chair, was charged with the task of documenting the position of American women in the economy, legal system, and the family. Its 1964 report uncovered such pervasive sex discrimination that many commissioners were shocked. Most states also convened commissions that similarly documented widespread sex discrimination.[13]

Geraldine Ferraro was typical of many of these new pioneers. She was the daughter of an Italian immigrant, and after a stint as legal secretary taught elementary school in Queens while attending Fordham Law School. Upon her graduation in 1960, she married businessman John A. Zaccaro. In 1974, her cousin Nicholas Ferraro, then district attorney of Queens, helped her get a job as an assistant district attorney. In this capacity, she headed a victims' bureau that dealt with child abuse, sex crimes, and crimes against the elderly. (She retained her maiden name in her professional life, she declared, to honor her mother).

At the Democratic National Convention in July 1984, presidential nominee Walter Mondale selected Ferraro as his running mate. When the convention confirmed his choice she became the first woman vice-presidential nominee of a major party. Reasons for Mondale's historic decision included Democratic hopes of capitalizing on a "gender gap" in voting patterns, pressure from the National Organization for Women to select a woman candidate, and sentiment within the party that such a candidate would signify equal opportunity for all. Democrats also hoped that as a Catholic and an Italian-American, Ferraro might appeal to blue-collar, ethnic voters who had been defecting to the Republicans in recent elections.

However, no sooner had the campaign started than a furor arose over whether Ferraro would reveal her family finances, beyond the income tax statements required by law. This meant a public airing

[13] Nancy F. Cott, *The Grounding of Modern Feminism* (New Haven, Yale University Press, 1987); Ellen Garol DuBois *Feminism and Suffrage: The emergence of an independent women's movement in America* (Ithaca, NY, Cornell University Press, 1978).

of her husband's business dealings before the press. Although Ferraro met the challenge with poise, the unexpected controversy did not help the Democratic cause in the campaign.

In the election, Republicans Ronald Reagan and George Bush defeated the Mondale-Ferraro ticket with 58.8 percent of the popular vote and an electoral college sweep. The Republicans also won 57 percent of women's votes. After the election, Ferraro returned to the practice of law. She never fully regained her status.[14]

There are happier stories of female adventures in politics. Two can be cited: from California, whose two Senators are both women, Dianne Feinstein and Barbara Boxer, both Jewish, both wealthy ex-stockbrokers, and the former a distinguished mayor of San Francisco for a decade. Feinstein is a conservative, Boxer, a liberal-leftist. Even more significant is California's Representative Anna Eshoo, who represents the heart of America's high-tech industry, the Silicon Valley, and yet who came from the life of a fulltime homemaker to defeat a Stanford law professor to win the seat.

Even more significant is the career of the Representative for Florida's seventeenth district, Carrie P. Meek. Her district, a black majority district, Liberty City in Miami, has a history of riots and violence. In her day a talented athlete and a graduate of the University of Michigan (where she went because Florida's graduate schools were then segregated), Carrie Meek is the granddaughter of a slave, but she has served on the Florida State Legislature and is now on the US House of of Representatives Appropriation Committee. Her story is, in its own way, a microcosm of American history.

[14] Geraldine Ferraro, *My Story* (New York, Bantam, 1985).

15

Nixon, Watergate, and Carter

1 THE 37TH PRESIDENT

Except for Herbert Hoover, no President elected in this century grew up in more difficult circumstances than Richard M. Nixon (1913–1994). His parents were Quaker and Methodist in background. He was born in a rustic Californian clapboard cottage which had no electricity, no running water, no wireless, no telephone, and no inside privy. He had a hard-scrabble childhood one step away from poverty, made difficult by a domineering father and saddened by the deaths from tuberculosis of two of his brothers. Strongest influence on him was that of his Quaker mother; she believed strongly in equality between the races and in peacemaking between nations. He told his friends that the real reason he wanted the presidency was to honor his mother's ideals. It was a promise he did much to keep. As President he desegregated Southern schools, he ended the war in Vietnam, he ended the draft, he saved Israel from annihilation, he brought China back into the family of nations, and initiated the process of détente with the USSR with a series of ground-breaking disarmament agreements.

Nixon's youth was marked by hard work in a family store, in his home town of Yorba Linda, a rural village 30 miles east of Los Angeles. He was unable to afford Harvard, so he went to less glamorous "schools." Following graduation from Whittier College (1934), the hometown Quaker institution, and Duke University Law School (1937), he practiced law in California, and in 1950 married Thelma (Pat) Ryan, a beauty, with a background as poor as his, but a qualified schoolteacher. As she put it herself, "We come from typical everyday American families that had to work for what they got out of life, but always knew that there was unlimited opportunity." Husband and wife shared the American dream. He served as a navy supply officer during World War II, and was elected to the House of Representatives in 1946. He became a Congressman by answering an advertisement that had appeared in 26 Southern California newspapers:

> WANTED: Congressman candidate with no previous experience to defeat a man who has represented the district in the House for ten years. Any young man, resident of the district, preferably a veteran, fair education, no political strings or obligations, and possessed of a few ideas for betterment of [the] country at large, may apply for the job.

The sitting member was a Democrat, Jerry Voorhis, who had been elected to Congress in the 1936 Democratic landslide. He was voted the best Congressman west of the Mississippi by Washington press correspondents. But the bankers and businessmen of his district, 12th Congressional district, saw him as the epitome of what was wrong with the hated New Deal. Nixon said that he thought he was a Republican because he had voted for Wendell Willkie in 1940 and Thomas E. Dewey in 1944 in the national elections. Moreover, he did not believe in the New Deal philosophy of "government control in regulating our lives."

The California Republicans found Nixon an almost ideal candidate. He projected the image of a clean-cut, hard-working, young (he was then 33 years old) go-getter. Moreover, he was politically naive and malleable – a fact that especially pleased Murray Chotiner, a Los Angeles lawyer, who had considerable skill in marketing candidates with a bagful of public relations tricks learned from Hollywood and the mass media. The Chotiner method featured the "smear," the device of associating an opponent with an unpopular position. In this case Nixon linked Voorhis with organized labor and organized Communism, though there was no factual evidence to support the charge. Newspaper and telephone ads implied that Voorhis had Communist sympathies, and Nixon repeated the charge in a public debate with Voorhis in South Pasadena. Nixon won comfortably. As a Congressman he showed similar instincts in serving on the House UnAmerican Activities Committee (HUAC), probing the activities of the Communist party and other illegal organisations.

In his years pre-World War II and during the war, he was not immoral but he was amoral. His political shrewdness was often undermined by his vindictiveness and his capacity for self-deception.

An intensely private person, "Pat" Nixon (who died in June 1993) found herself thrust into national prominence within two years of her marriage. When under attack for his use of a "slush" fund in the first Eisenhower presidential campaign in 1952, to which wealthy Southern Californian businessmen had contributed, the young Nixon, who was running for Vice-President, did not hesitate to exploit his wife. Not only, as he delivered his notorious "Checkers" television speech, in which he admitted fundraising and accounting for it, was she made to sit in camera shot with him in the studio; she was also the subject of perhaps the most mocked line in the broadcast – the one about her not possessing a mink coat but being the proud wearer of "a respectable Republican cloth" one.

Nixon's rise to power was largely the product of the post-World War II red scare. Elected as Congressman and active on HUAC in 1946, he convinced the House that Alger Hiss, a second-level New Dealer, had been a Soviet spy and, in 1950, persuaded California voters to send him to the Senate to continue his battle against subversives and "pink" Democrats. He used similar smear tactics in his election campaign against Helen Gahagan Douglas, the Democratic candidate, wife of actor Melvyn Douglas. To Nixon she was "The Pink Lady." His vitality and his right-wing tastes commended him as a vice-presidential possibility.

Elected Vice-President in 1952, Nixon served President Dwight D. Eisenhower dutifully for eight years. He tried to present himself as a statesman, but he never entirely lost the reputation of "Tricky Dick," and he lost races for President in; 1960 to John F. Kennedy, very narrowly, and for governor of California in 1962.

During the four years from 1960, while prospering as a corporate lawyer, he rebuilt his political base. On March 31, 1965, in the wake of the Tet offensive in Vietnam, President Lyndon B. Johnson announced that he would not seek re-election, and this prompted Vice-President Hubert Humphrey to announce his candidacy. In a stormy and riot-prone Chicago in 1967, Humphrey was nominated by the Democrats. The Republican race was less complicated. Nixon won the nomination, and he chose Governor Spiro Agnew of Maryland as his running mate. The ultra-conservative American Independent party nominated the segregationist Governor George Wallace of Alabama. Nixon won in November 1967 by 31,700,000 against 30,800,000 for Humphrey, and 9,400,000 for Wallace – all the last coming from the South.

Nixon's successful campaign for President in 1968 raised a central question: would he govern as a responsible conservative, in the fashion of his mentor Eisenhower, or as an irresponsible demagogue, in the mold of Nixon the campaigner. He proved to be both. Nixon in 1968 was a minority President, elected by the smallest percentage of the national vote (43.6 percent) since Woodrow Wilson's election in 1912 with 41.9 percent. Congress was hostile, as was the press – but there was nothing new for Nixon in that. But four years later, in 1972, even despite the Watergate scandal, Nixon won a landslide victory greater than those of any of the previous 36 holders of his office. In 1972 he won in 49 of the 50 states in the Union.

2 WATERGATE

In June 1972 President Nixon returned from his triumphant trip to the USSR, where he signed an arms limitation treaty with Russian premier Leonid Brezhnev. During his absence, a team of burglars employed by CREEP (The Campaign for the Re-Election of the President) and led by Gordon Liddy, burgled the Democratic party HQ in the Watergate building in Washington in order to "bug" the building; they were caught redhanded. Nixon knew nothing of it until it was over and he was not a party to its planning. In any event he won a landslide victory in the November 1972 election, and no burglary was required to ensure it. But afterwards he was involved in an elaborate cover-up, which was recorded in what became known as "the White House tapes." On these he can be heard saying to his chief-of-staff, H. R. Haldeman, Call the FBI and say "Don't go any further in this case, period!" He seemed thus to be seeking to hide the truth. This tape, when revealed, became known as "the smoking gun," and was seen as evidence not of Nixon's involvement in the burglary but of his part in a cover-up. Some might ask: What else is politics but a constant and intricate cover-up? And surely any leader would seek to protect his troops?

After his victory in 1972, Nixon promised a thorough investigation and accepted the resignations of several White House officials who were involved; he also agreed to the appointment of an independent special prosecutor, Archibald Cox. The President denied his own involvement, but when Mr Cox sought White House documents he had him discharged.

Among the evidence sought by Cox, and by the prosecutor who replaced him, Leon Jaworski, were the tapes that the President had made of his White House conversations with his advisers.

Aside from whether or not he was wise to have installed the taping system, his failure to turn it off while discussing the Watergate break-in and the resulting investigations, and failing that, his not having had the tapes erased, was an indiscretion of monumental proportions. Finally he had to release the tapes, and they contained statements clearly demonstrating that he had sought to conceal the truth. This "smoking gun" connecting him with the cover-up made his eventual resignation inevitable.

Much of the scandal was the result of news stories and gossip in the *Washington Post* and from the televized hearings of a Senate Select committee. The President claimed executive privilege, but this too appeared as a "cover-up."

The tangled web of scandals collectively known as Watergate dominated the attention of the country during the first seven months of 1974. Constitutional clashes between the executive and legislative branches and between the executive and judicial branches were given exhaustive coverage by the mass media. Confrontations were reported with accelerating frequency: charges and denials, subpoenas and claims of executive privilege and confidentiality, indictments and sentencings of Cabinet members and presidential aides. Senate and House probes ground on; prosecutors argued their cases in court. Edited transcripts of taped White House conversations, then the tapes themselves – with the unexplained gaps – were made public. Each day brought revelations of political immorality on a scale unprecedented in the American experience.

The increasing clamor for resignation or impeachment reflected the turning tide of opinion against the President who had been re-elected with the second largest electoral sweep in history. His Vice-President, Spiro Agnew, had already been forced to resign, pleading no contest to tax evasion charges. What brought about Nixon's own downfall was not merely the tapes of the conversations after the Watergate burglary, but a complex of schemes and misconduct at the highest levels. Some of the events predated the June 1972 break-in, some followed it, and all were damaging: the attempt to conceal staff responsibility for the theft; the earlier break-in at the office of Dr Lewis J. Fielding, the psychiatrist of Daniel Ellsberg, who had released the Pentagon Papers; the use of domestic surveillance and intelligence operations against political adversaries; the use of the Internal Revenue Service for political benefit; huge undisclosed campaign contributions by large corporations; the secret bombing of Cambodia; the President's questioned income tax returns; unwarranted federal expenditures for personal homes; the failure to cooperate with Congressional investigators and special prosecutors. Two years of "Watergate," of intensifying erosion of popular and Congressional support, led finally to the first resignation from office of a President of the United States.

On Thursday, August 8, 1974, at 9.00 pm, Richard Milhous Nixon, the 37th President of the United States, announced in a nationally televised speech that he would resign, effective at noon on August 9. Referring to his earlier repeated declarations that he would not leave office before his term expired, the President explained his decision:

> Throughout the long and difficult period of Watergate, I have felt it was my duty to persevere, to make every possible effort to complete the term of office to which you elected me.
>
> In the past few days, however, it has become evident to me that, I no longer have a strong enough political base in the Congress to justify continuing that effort. ...
>
> I would have preferred to carry through to the finish whatever the personal agony it would have involved. ...
>
> I have never been a quitter.
>
> To leave office before my term is completed is opposed to every instinct in my body. But as President I must put the interests of America first.
>
> America needs a full-time President and a full-time Congress. ...
>
> To continue to fight through the months ahead for my personal vindication would almost totally absorb the time and attention of both the President and Congress in a period when our entire focus should be on the great issues of peace abroad and prosperity without inflation at home.
>
> Therefore, I shall resign the presidency effective at noon tomorrow.

On the morning of August 9, 1974, the President bade farewell to his Cabinet and staff. The Nixon family left immediately for San Clemente, California, and did not attend the noon swearing-in of Gerald Rudolph Ford as 38th President. In September of the same year his successor, Gerald Ford, pardoned Nixon for all offenses he had committed or might have committed.

Bob Woodward and Carl Bernstein, the two reporters on the *Washington Post* subsequently published a book recounting the Watergate story, *The Final Days*. A more interesting and satisfactory book is Nixon's story: *In the Arena: A memoir of victory, defeat, and renewal;* it is his best "confessional."[1] *In the Arena* is Richard

[1] Bob Woodward and Carl Bernstein, *The Final Days* (New York, Simon and Schuster, 1975); Richard M. Nixon, *In the Arena: A memoir of victory, defeat, and renewal* (New York, Simon and Schuster, 1976).

Plate 14 The helicopter waits for ex-President Richard M. Nixon as his Vice-President, Gerald Ford, takes over after Nixon's resignation over Watergate. (Library of Congress.)

Nixon's strangest – and in some respects most interesting – book. His earlier books were built around specific themes: alerting the public to the dangers of Soviet expansionism, mapping out a strategy to deal with Gorbachev, or examining the nature of political leadership. By contrast, *In the Arena* seems unfocused – but it does give an insight into Nixon's view of politics. Nixon's starting point is that no one should embark on a political career unless he has a powerful sense of mission. "What separates the men from the boys in politics," he writes, "is that the boys seek office to *be* somebody and the men seek office to *do* something." Politics is, or ought to be, a high and honorable calling. Only if you are prepared to devote your life to a worthy cause should you contemplate a political career. But even if you are prepared to dedicate yourself to a great cause, Nixon cautions, politics might not be for you. For in recent years, politics has grown "more simplistic, less subtle, less thoughtful." The main reason for this change is television. "Any candidate," Nixon writes, "must learn to use television. He will be dismayed to find that whether he has had his hair blown dry may be more important than what he has between his ears. He may insist that he wants to be a legislator, not an actor. But unless he learns to be an actor, he will never have a chance to be a legislator."[2]

But television is not the only factor debasing the political process. The press is also culpable, he argued: "The press used to consider itself part of the fabric of society, with a shared stake in America's prosperity, the health of its institutions, and the success of its initiatives around the world. When they had to criticize, they did so as part of the team. But today the media consider themselves outside of and above society at large."

A third factor that has changed politics for the worse is the high cost of financing a campaign. Nixon estimates that, even taking inflation into account, it costs five times as much to finance a campaign for the House and Senate today as it did forty years ago. As a result, idealistic young Congressmen who come to Washington to do good are shocked to find themselves spending an inordinate amount of time "schmoozing with their PACs and

[2] Stephen E;. Ambrose, *Nixon: The education of a politician 1913–1962* (New York, Simon and Schuster, 1987), and *Nixon: The triumph of a politician, 1962–1972* (New York, Simon and Schuster, 1989); Garry Wills, *Nixon Agonistes: The crisis of the self-made man* (Boston, Houghton Mifflin, 1970); Roger Morris, *Richard Milhous Nixon; The rise of an American politician* (New York, Holt, 1990); Jonathan Aitken, *Nixon, A Life* (London, Weidenfeld and Nicolson, 1992).

fat cats at private cocktail parties." This deplorable situation leads Nixon to propose that the terms of House members be extended from two years to four. "This would mean that for at least two years of his four year term, a Congressman could be a Congressman rather than a perpetual candidate spending 75 percent of his time raising campaign funds and campaigning for re-election."[3]

The reason it is so important for a Congressman to be a Congressman is that only by diligently applying himself to his craft can he acquire the expertise necessary for leadership. And while there are obviously many areas in which a young Congressman can develop expertise, Nixon leaves little doubt that as far as he is concerned, foreign policy remains the crucial arena: "I have often said that the American economy is so strong it would take a genius to wreck it. But even a small mistake in foreign policy could bring destruction to the United States and even to the world." That is why a young politician who aspires to greatness must make American foreign policy his priority.

In discussing US foreign policy, Nixon quite reasonably focused on Soviet-American relations. And, as always, his comments are worthy of serious consideration. "Many observers," he writes, "now proclaim that the Cold War has ended. ... They are right to draw attention to the potential importance of the reforms inside the Soviet Union. But they overstate the extent to which these reforms have changed the fundamental structure of the Soviet system and the nature of Soviet foreign policy." For example, despite his commitment to "democratization," Mikhail Gorbachev has actually concentrated more power in his hands than any Soviet leader since Stalin. And the hallmark of his "new thinking" in foreign policy has been "shrewder tactics, not kinder intentions."

Nixon also focuses a good deal of attention on China. He is adamant about the danger of imposing harsh sanctions against the People's Republic of China in the wake of the Tiananmen Square Massacre: "Contact with the West represents a principal impetus for reform," he writes. "Isolating China with sanctions will close off a major stimulus for the economic reforms that have already improved the lives of the Chinese people and for the long-term political change that will lessen the repressiveness of the regime's rule."

How to handle the Russians and how to deal with the Chinese are complicated questions over which even the most astute scholars

[3] *In the Arena, passim.*

and policymakers might disagree. To a young politician, however, developing a general framework with which to approach foreign policy is far more important than staking out positions on specific issues. Nixon provides such a framework. He calls it "pragmatic idealism." Nixon's approach to foreign policy is idealistic in that he believes "our goal should be to make the world safe for freedom." As he explains it:

> We should engage in this cause not just for others but for ourselves. De Gaulle once said, "France was never true to herself unless she was engaged in a great enterprise." I have always believed that this was true of the United States as well. Defending and promoting peace and freedom around the world is a great enterprise. Only by rededicating ourselves to that goal will we remain true to ourselves.

But while remaining true to our high ideals, we should pursue them in a way that takes into account the world as it is, and not as we might like it to be. "In a perfect world, we would never resort to the use of military force, or align ourselves with countries with flawed human rights records. But the world is not perfect." Hence, we must temper our idealism with prudence, pragmatism, and a sense of the possible.

The greatest challenge to a politician, however, comes not from the dilemmas and complexities of foreign policy, no matter how important these may be. Rather, it comes when he loses an election, and is summarily cast out from the center of events to the periphery. It is then that his character faces its most severe test. Richard Nixon, of course, was no stranger to shattering defeats; and his account of how he coped with them is perhaps the most moving part of his book. "At some of the low points of the past," he writes, "I have been sustained by recalling a note Clare Boothe Luce handed to me right after Watergate first broke, when she was sitting next to me at a meeting of the Foreign Intelligence Advisory Board. It was St Barton's Ode: 'I am hurt but I am not slain: I will lie me down and bleed awhile – then I'll rise and fight again."[4]

There remains the savage scar on the presidency left by the revelations of the tapes, the slump in presidential style since the Kennedy era, the picture of a man improving his private homes at the public expense, the sleaziness that remains as the aftermath

[4] Ibid.

of Spiro Agnew's vice-presidency. There are the serious problems of control over campaign expenditure, in which indeed the Watergate affair began. President Ford, like every American President since Roosevelt, carried a heavy burden of responsibility that the Constitution never foresaw. An index of that burden was the size of his staff. Forty years ago President Hoover bequeathed to FDR three secretaries. Nixon's White House staff numbered several thousand – a bureaucracy within a bureaucracy, specialized, hierarchical, loaded with responsibility, loaded with hatreds, and dangerously out of touch with the public mood. As Professor Aaron Wildowski, dean of the Graduate school of Public Policy at Berkeley, has said, "Americans have come to demand more and more of government, and to trust it less and less." But this is a verdict that could be pronounced on all democratic governments on either side of the Atlantic.

3 THE US AFTER WATERGATE

American history is, of course, rich in scandals. They have affected almost every administration. They wrecked the administration of President Ulysses S. Grant. The circumstances surrounding the death of President Harding on his trip to Alaska remain mysterious, and that death seems directly linked to the revelations about Teapot Dome in Wyoming. But there is a major difference. The savage and sustained searchlight of publicity that in today's world probes and illumines every aspect of a President's activities, now makes all such intrigues difficult and probably makes corruption obvious, as soon as the first suspicion of it arises. The two-year campaign unleashed by the Watergate affair, and begun and developed brilliantly by the Woodward and Bernstein team on the *Washington Post*, was never therefore in essence a probe into Watergate, but from the outset a probe into the ineptness of the President's handling of it.

There was clearly a profound difference between Richard Nixon's White House and all its predecessors. Here was a loner, surrounded by figures drawn from an advertising rather than a political world, men who guarded him vigilantly – "the Berlin Wall," "the Potsdam Grenadiers." He was surrounded too by hidden tape-recording machines attached by miles of wire to concealed microphones in every room; at a footfall they would switch on, switching off only after an interval of silence. It was an alarming picture. And all of this information was apparently for history, suitably edited history, of course, with all expletives deleted. It would permit ultimately the production of a vast and costly record of the President's administration, and a record for sale. There was here a vast difference in the nature and the style of presidential authority from earlier Presidents. It was a crisis of a different dimension from any in the past. The sad fact is that Watergate reveals a slump in standards, but even more a slump in presidential political expertise.

But, after the agony was over, it became possible to assemble a tentative balance sheet. The Constitution stood the test. Impeachment – real impeachment – has only been used once, against President Andrew Johnson over 100 years ago. It did not come to that in Nixon's case. He was not impeached, but he was the first President to resign; he was also the first to be pardoned, by his successor, for possible offences against the US. He was the first President to nominate a Vice-President under the Twenty-fifth Amendment to the Constitution, which outlines how a President and Vice-President are chosen if normal electoral methods cannot be used, and which worked smoothly. Both Senate Committees and the House Judiciary Committee were seen in many sessions on TV and were seen as worried, responsible and honest in their processes. And there was a new President, Gerald Ford, who had been himself chosen by President Nixon to be his Vice-President ten months before: popular with Congress, where he was for 25 years a Michigan Representative for its fifth district, and standing the test of a massive probe into his financial and personal integrity.

One point does need emphasis. Henry Kissinger, President Nixon's ablest lieutenant, under constant attack himself, remained secretary of state, and in this sense the Nixon foreign policy continued into the Ford presidency. In an age marked by all but total scepticism about all aspects of politics, that foreign policy still seems to have had spirit and courage in it. Kissinger's statement on the role that his country would follow in international affairs during the Ford presidency was eloquent and hopeful: "In time of crisis, and at the conference table, America's military might is the fountain of our diplomatic strength ... Never forget that conciliation is a virtue only in those who are thought to have a choice." The United States would never, he said, accept strategic inferiority. Kissinger emphasized the strenuous but unavailing efforts the United States had made to reach nuclear agreement with Russia, and that until agreement was reached, American strategic strength would be maintained with unflinching resolve "at whatever cost or sacrifice." Nor should it be forgotten that with all Kissinger's expertise and flair, this foreign policy in its shape and vigor was Richard Nixon's achievement. Nixon went to Peking and Moscow; he sought to end the Cold War. That honor cannot be denied him. His first four years in the White House were distinguished and they should not be forgotten. But that said, there was relief in the US as the slow fight back to economic and political recovery got under way.

This is not to say that the legacy of Watergate is anything but one of bitterness. Watergate is, moreover, a reminder of the fantastic growth of government since 1787. Political intrigue is – gossip and newsprint apart – Washington's major, almost its sole, industry. There are now over three million civilian employees in the federal government, only one-tenth of 1 percent of whom does any President appoint. Each of the 535 Senators and Congressmen has lavish staffs, each Department has many officials – and there are thousands of official and many unofficial lobbyists, newshawks and media men seeking to influence and browbeat them. There are another 4 million in the 50 state governments and over 9 million in local governments. It is very difficult for a President as individual to direct this vast machine down any road that it does not wish to travel; it is a great Leviathan. More than this, Senators, Congressmen – and Judges – have got to the Hill by 544 distinct routes, from very diverse and distant constituencies, and they are hardly ever "pledged" to any doctrine or cause except their own careers. They often collect (if it is not always "earned") lavish resources; and they make up their own minds on each issue, so that a vast number of unstable alliances have to be manufactured to secure victory on each topic. It is easy for the President to seem to be "Enemy in chief;" as Nixon felt himself to be and indeed became. To many in the press he was and long had been *persona non grata*. For a boy who had come up the hard way, the defeats of 1960 (for the presidency), 1962 (governorship of California), and 1974 (Watergate) were hard to take.

4 HENRY KISSINGER

Richard Nixon attracted dedicated lieutenants, notably H. R. Haldeman, John Ehrlichman, and "Chuck" Colson, men of the Hard Right; and later Henry Kissinger. A German-Jewish refugee from Nazi Germany, Kissinger (1923–) rose to prominence as a Harvard University professor of government in the 1950s and 1960s. He then became the most celebrated and controversial US diplomat since World War II in the administrations of Richard M. Nixon and Gerald Ford. As Nixon's national security adviser he concentrated power in the White House and rendered Secretary of State William Rogers and the professional foreign service almost irrelevant by conducting personal, secret negotiations with North Vietnam, the Soviet Union, and China. He negotiated the Paris agreements of 1973 ending direct US involvement in the Vietnam War, engineered a short-lived era of détente with the Soviet Union, and opened frozen relations with the People's Republic of China. As secretary of state he shuttled among the capitals of Israel, Egypt, and Syria after the 1973 Middle East war.

A gregarious but manipulative man, Kissinger, seeking power and favorable publicity, cultivated prominent officials and influential reporters. For a while he achieved more popularity than any modern American diplomat. The Gallup poll listed him as the most admired man in America in 1972 and 1973. He received the Nobel Peace Prize in 1973 for his negotiations leading to the Paris peace accords that ended US military action in Vietnam. Journalists lauded him as a "genius" and the "smartest guy around" after his secret trip to Beijing in July 1971 prepared the way for Nixon's visit to China in February 1972. Egyptian politicians called him "the magician" for his disengagement agreements separating Israeli and Arab armies.

Kissinger's reputation faded after 1973. During the Watergate scandal, Congressional investigators discovered that he had ordered the FBI to tap the telephones of subordinates on the staff of the National Security Council, a charge he had denied earlier. Congress also learned that he had tried to block the accession to power of Chile's President Salvador Allende Goseens in 1970 and had helped destabilize Allende's Socialist party government thereafter.

Some of Kissinger's foreign policy achievements crumbled in 1975 and 1976. The Communists' victory in Vietnam and Cambodia destroyed the Paris peace accords, and détente with the Soviet Union never fulfilled the hopes Kissinger had aroused. By 1976 the United States and the Soviet Union had not moved beyond the 1972 Interim Agreement limiting strategic arms to conclude a full-fledged Strategic Arms Limitation Talks.

Kissinger became a liability for President Ford during the 1976 presidential election. Ronald Reagan, challenging Ford for the Republican nomination, and Democrat Jimmy Carter both assailed Kissinger's policy of détente with the Soviet Union for ignoring Soviet abuses of human rights and Moscow's greater assertiveness in international relations. Reagan complained that Kissinger's program offered "the peace of the grave." Carter accused him of conducting "lone ranger diplomacy" by excluding Congress and foreign affairs professionals from foreign policy matters.

Kissinger's flair for dramatic diplomatic gestures brought him fame, and it encouraged diplomats in the Carter, Reagan, and George Bush administrations to try to emulate his accomplishments. He failed, however, to create the "structure of peace" he had promised. By 1977 he had lost control over American foreign policy, and no one after him ever dominated the process as he had from 1969 to 1974.[5]

5 HUBERT HUMPHREY

Hubert Horatio Humphrey (1911–1978) was one of the most remarkable public figures of his time. But the goal he most desired, the presidency, eluded him. A Minnesota Democrat, a liberal in the New Deal tradition, he ran for President in 1960, 1968, and 1972, and seriously considered a fourth try in 1974. His first bid for the presidential nomination in 1960 was foiled mostly because of a primary loss in heavily Protestant West Virginia to John F. Kennedy, a Roman Catholic; the Kennedy victory resolved most of the fears of party leaders that Mr Kennedy's religion made him a risky candidate. Humphrey almost succeeded in 1968 when he was Lyndon Johnson's Vice-President. That was the only time he won the Democratic presidential nomination, and he lost to Richard Nixon by fewer than 500,000 votes. His defeat was due in large measure to his liberal friends deserting him because of his support of Johnson's Vietnam War effort. His comment was: "I was ready for it. I was prepared to be President. I knew what the country needed ... But I guess the country wasn't ready for me." Nor was it ready four years later, when he jumped into the primaries at the last minute, winning a few but losing the big one, in California, to Senator George McGovern (D-SD). Humphrey returned to the Senate in 1970, easily winning election to the seat vacated by Eugene McCarthy. His victory continued the Democratic-Farmer-Labor party domination of Minnesota that had begun with his 235,000-vote victory in 1948 over Republican Senator Joseph Ball.

Humphrey's liberalism as well as his political ambition had its roots in his South Dakota childhood. He was born on May 27,

[5] Seymour Hersh, *The Price of Power: Kissinger in the White House* (New York, Summit, 1983); Henry Kissinger, *The White House Years* (Boston, Little, Brown, 1979), and *The Years of Upheaval* (London, Weidenfeld and Nicolson, 1982).

1911, above the family drugstore in Wallace. His father was of Welsh extraction, a romanticist, a Democrat among Republicans and the idol of Hubert, his youngest son. His mother was Norwegian, stubborn, practical and domineering. As one biographer has said, Humphrey respected his mother but revered his father. That father, converted from Republicanism by the Mid-Western populist William Jennings Bryan, instilled the liberal principles of the time into his son. The writings of Woodrow Wilson and Bryan as well as Thomas Paine and Thomas Jefferson were thrust upon him, and politics – his father was later elected to the South Dakota Legislature – was a favorite dinnertime topic. Thus, Herbert Jr was well prepared for the New Deal principles soon to be expounded by Franklin Roosevelt.

The Humphreys were not poor by early twentieth-century Mid-Western standards. But they were not rich, and the depression struck as young Hubert enrolled at the University of Minnesota. Two years later, in 1931, he was forced to return home to help run the family drugstore, then in Huron. A year later, he went to pharmacy school in Denver, and received a degree in 1933.

In 1936, Humphrey and Muriel Buck were married. In two years, he was studying political science and economics at Minnesota, with Muriel helping support them with a $55-a-month job as a bookkeeper for a Minneapolis investment syndicate. He got straight As, was elected to Phi Beta Kappa, and won a BA degree in 1939, graduating *cum laude*. He also developed friendships in the crucible of liberalism that the university's political science department had became in the 1930s. These friends were to be the core of his advisers and supporters in the political fights ahead.

Humphrey spent a year earning a master's degree at Louisiana State University, and writing a thesis about the philosophy of the New Deal. He returned to the University of Minnesota and Macalester College, where he taught political science intermittently for three years. After his 1945 election as a mayor of Minneapolis, Humphrey not only closed the brothels and stopped the gambling, he also used the office to solve labor-management disputes, appoint the first municipal fair employment practices commission, and expand public housing.

His first effort at national politics came shortly after the Republicans won control of Congress in 1946. He traveled to New York City and, with a group of 19 other liberals including Eleanor Roosevelt, Herbert Lehman, and Walter Reuther, founded the ADA – Americans for Democratic Action – as a liberal but militantly anti-Communist political action group.

His election in 1948 to the Senate was a natural political step, and the Senate proved to be Humphrey's proper milieu. It was a place where he could vent his enormous energy, restlessness, and drive during the next 16 years.

Humphrey's reelection in 1954 and the gradual recognition of him as the leader of Senate liberals prompted Lyndon Johnson, then Senate Democratic leader, to approach him in 1955 about a working arrangement to hold the disparate parts of the party together. The approach came after Johnson had asked Humphrey to support him for the leadership position and Humphrey had turned him down, even though both knew Johnson was going to win. Johnson told Humphrey: "You're one of the fellows not playing both sides of the street. I want to work with you." This "working arrangement" lasted through the six years Johnson was majority leader and while he was Vice-President under Kennedy. And it lasted despite the 1956 Democratic convention when Johnson helped block Humphrey's open bid to be Adlai Stevenson's Vice-presidential candidate, and through 1960 when both Humphrey and Johnson were contesting Kennedy for the presidential nomination.

Back in the Senate, Mr Humphrey's stature as a legislator continued to grow. In 1964, he guided the Civil Rights Act through the Senate over Southern and conservative Republican opposition and won the respect of the losers within his party for his tact and humor throughout the long, bitter fight. Humphrey took on the civil rights job at the request of President Johnson and it was one of the factors that led to Johnson's choice of Humphrey as his running mate in 1964 over several senators, including Humphrey's longtime ally from Minnesota, Eugene McCarthy. The Johnson-Humphrey ticket rode to a landslide victory, but in many ways, it was the beginning of the end of Humphrey's presidential hopes. As he often said during his four years as vice-president, "I have a constituency of one." He served Lyndon Johnson well and loyally – so loyally that he lost his own identity in the process.

Although he privately opposed some points of Johnson's Vietnam policies, Humphrey was his most articulate spokesman for the increasingly unpopular war. Thus, when he became a candidate for the party's nomination for President in 1968, Vietnam was an albatross around his neck and one that he made little effort to remove. It was not in Humphrey's nature to turn on his President about Vietnam or any other issue, and he resisted the advice of some members of his staff and other Democrats to do that during the 1968 campaign. Many believed that the split in the Democratic party over Vietnam – Senator McCarthy, the anti-Vietnam candidate, endorsed Humphrey only a week before the election and then did so reluctantly – cost Humphrey the election.

The party split and the violence on Chicago streets during the Democratic convention set Humphrey's campaign back severely. Polls during the early fall indicated that Nixon would swamp him. But Humphrey worked tirelessly, and with third-party candidate George Wallace draining conservative votes from Nixon, he closed the gap in the final weeks of the campaign, but not enough to win. Although Humphrey returned in 1971 to the Senate, where he had served 16 years before his election as Vice-President, misfortune and disappointments continued to dog him. He died in 1978.[6]

6 H. R. HALDEMAN

The one thing no one ever accused H. R. Haldeman of was disloyalty. Almost everything else, but not disloyalty. His devotion to Richard Nixon, which began in 1948, was almost obsessive in its unswerving dedication to a man whom he saw as essential to his vision of a well-ordered American society.

The son of a successful California businessman, "Bob" Haldeman was educated at private schools and the University of California at Los Angeles before beginning a successful career with the J. Walter Thompson advertising agency. He became interested in Richard Nixon when watching the latter's performance on the Un-American Activities Committee in 1948, and offered to join his vice-presidential election campaign in 1952. That offer was refused, but Haldeman persisted, was hired as an advance man for the 1956 campaign, and from then on was rarely far from Nixon's side. When Nixon staged his political comeback in 1968 he assumed the role of campaign manager, using his advertising skills to sell the image of "the new Nixon" and orchestrating the campaign to keep the candidate as remote as possible from both the press and potentially unfriendly audiences. The success of that technique was soon to make Haldeman the *éminence grise* of the White House. But it also fostered the sense of remoteness and arrogance that was to lead to his own and his President's downfall.

[6] Carl Solberg, *Hubert Humphrey, a Biography* (New York, Norton, 1985); Hubert Humphrey, *The Education of a Public Man* (Garden City, NY, Doubleday, 1976).

Haldeman's grandfather had helped to found the Hollywood Bowl, and had been a member of the Better America Federation, an early anti-Communist organization. His mother had been named "Woman of the Year" by the *Los Angeles Times* in the 1950s. Having performed unremarkably in the state system of education, the young Haldeman was sent to a private military school for "straightening out." Here he imbibed "a zest for regimen and rigid command structure" that found further outlet when he was enrolled in the American Navy's wartime V-12 officer training program at Redlands, part of the University of California at Los Angeles. Haldeman led the campus Christian Science Organization and was president of Scabbard and Blade, the military fraternity. But he later denied that he had any political or ideological commitment when he moved on to the university proper: "I was a rah-rah college type."

Puritanically moral and a devout Christian Scientist, Haldeman enjoyed a reputation, rare in American politics, for financial incorruptibility. He neither smoked nor drank, and regarded those who did with a lofty and ill-concealed disdain. Where Nixon was concerned he was "the keeper of the gate," the President's guardian against almost anyone who tried to gain an audience, and his abrasive style won him few friends among the press or other workers at the White House.

With his flat-topped crewcut, Germanic name, and the verbal technique of a Marine Corps drill instructor, Haldeman soon gained the nickname of "the Iron Chancellor," after his appointment as assistant to the President in 1969. His loyalty, his lack of personal political ambition and rigid control over the White House staff, gave him an almost unprecedented concentration of power. It was a power he shared with John Ehrlichman and Henry Kissinger, forming a triumvirate which became known as "The Berlin Wall" around President Nixon.

"Every President," Haldeman once said, "needs an SOB." He accepted the role with enthusiasm, protecting Nixon not only from outside conflict but also from the President's own dark side, which Haldeman recognized could be petty, vindictive, and insecure. Though he claimed to have no interest in policy matters, he was known to delay implementation of Nixon's decisions when he considered them unwise, giving the President a chance to change his mind – which he frequently did. It was said by one White House insider at the time that "there is no policy that Haldeman is responsible for, yet there is no policy that he doesn't have a hand in somehow."

Given the intensity of his hero-worship, it was ironic that Haldeman should have been largely responsible for the downfall of the Nixon presidency. It was he who convinced Nixon to set up the White House taping system in 1970, urging that it would provide an unparalleled historical record of his presidency – which it did, all too well. If the tapes had not existed, or if their existence had not been revealed by one of Haldeman's protégés, Alexander Butterfield, there might have been no proof of White House involvement in the Watergate scandal and no move for impeachment. Haldeman always denied prior knowledge of the Watergate affair, which began in June 1972 when five employees of the Committee to Re-Elect the President (CREEP) were caught in the act of placing electronic eavesdropping devices in the headquarters of the Democratic National Committee. His first reaction, he once said, had been to ask: "Wire-tap the Democratic National Committee? For what?" But as the Senate hearings proceeded it became clear that he and other high-ranking White House officials had been deeply implicated in the cover-up operation, and on April 30, 1973, President Nixon announced the resignations of both Haldeman and Ehrlichman.

Haldeman continued to testify before the Senate, claiming that the Watergate scandal had not come to presidential attention before March 1973. Five years later, however, in his book *The Ends of Power*,[7] he was to say that President Nixon "initiated the Watergate break-in" and participated in its cover-up "from Day 1." It was his one lapse from unswerving support of the former President, and was said to have been prompted by Nixon's statement in a 1977 David Frost interview that he had been "too soft-hearted" in not firing Haldeman and Ehrlichman sooner.

On January 1, 1975, Haldeman was convicted on one count of conspiracy, one of obstruction of justice, and three counts of perjury before the Senate investigating committee. He was sentenced to from two-and-a-half to eight years' imprisonment, though this was later reduced on appeal to from one to four years. In the end he served just 18 months in the minimum security facility at Lompoc, California – known to its inmates as "Club Fed" because of its lax regime – and was released on parole in December 1978.

"Every President has to have his SOB," Eisenhower had told Nixon. "Bob" Haldeman played the part to perfection. If the grubbiest work was allotted to "Chuck" Colson, and the more subtle insinuations were left to John Ehrlichman, Haldeman had

[7] H. R. Haldeman, *The Ends of Power* (Boston, G. K. Hall, 1978).

no rival in administering the face-to-face humiliation. Where Nixon disliked confrontation, Haldeman proclaimed his talent for "chewing people out." Theirs, as Ehrlichman remarked, was a "true marriage."

In *The Ends of Power*, Haldeman suggested that his iron man image was cultivated, that in earlier manifestations he had been a particularly easy-going executive. If so, the transformation was perfectly realized.

"He sits 100 gold-carpeted feet down the hall from the Oval Office," noted *Newsweek*, "glowering out at the world from under a crewcut that would flatter a drill instructor, with eyes that would freeze Medusa." He impressed on his staff that he was a "zero defects" man.

"I rode them hard," Haldeman boasted, "made heavy demands on them for flawless work with no mistakes or excuses. I drummed into them the concept that anything can be done if you just figure how to do it and don't give up. I wouldn't take No for an answer." After Watergate, he spent 18 months in prison for perjury and the obstruction of justice.

7 NIXON: AN ASSESSMENT

Even while in semi-retirement, and now after his death in 1994, Nixon remains the most fascinating American politician of his time. An ambitious, intelligent, disciplined loner, Nixon cultivated no hobbies and had few close friends. Elected Vice-President in 1952, he served President Dwight D. Eisenhower dutifully for eight years, despite occasional humiliations. He tried to present himself as a statesmanlike "new Nixon," but, partly because memories of the old Nixon lingered, he lost races for President in 1960 and governor of California in 1962.

In domestic affairs, his record included, on the one hand, creation of the Environmental Protection Agency, expansion of the social security system, and advocacy of a Family Assistance Plan that guaranteed an annual income to the working poor; but, on the other hand, a weak civil rights record, sabotage of his political opposition, and emotional appeals to a "silent majority" who shared his resentment of the cosmopolitan elite. At home, most notable was his "new economic policy," introduced in 1971, which was designed to contain inflation, reduce unemployment, and correct the American balance of payments deficit, and which entailed the use of Keynesian measures previously eschewed by the Republican

President. The policy showed some success during 1972 in containing inflation, though not in reducing the balance of payment deficit.

His foreign policy record was similarly mixed. Nixon accepted modest curbs on the nuclear arms race, pursued detente with the Soviet Union, and opened relations with the People's Republic of China. But he also undermined the Marxist Chilean government and widened the Vietnam War by invading Cambodia before accepting truce terms in 1973 that he could have had in 1969. Abroad, the continuing policy of the President from the outset was the reduction of US involvement on the ground in Vietnam, and in excessive foreign entanglements generally – the "Nixon doctrine." By 1972, American ground forces had been reduced to comparatively small numbers after the massive escalations of President Johnson. Despite the renewal of air strikes against the North in April 1972, a ceasefire agreement was announced in January 1973. The de-escalation of the war was in part intended to contribute to another Nixon initiative, the normalization of relations with the People's Republic of China. After sending his aide, Henry Kissinger, to prepare the way, Nixon visited Peking in February 1972, thus reversing the longstanding American policy of non-recognition of the Communists.

The Watergate scandal was part of a broad campaign to sabotage political opposition. Although Nixon apparently had no advance knowledge of a break-in at Democratic National Committee headquarters in 1972, he subsequently obstructed an investigation of the crime. After fighting a two-year holding action, he faced impeachment by the House of Representatives and resigned on August 9, 1974. He accepted a pardon from President Gerald Ford and sank briefly into depression.

In the years that followed – in which he suffered from an attack of phlebitis in October 1974 that nearly killed him – he moved first to New York City and then to Park Ridge, New Jersey, in his quest for rehabilitation. Then, characteristically, he began to rebuild his reputation, primarily through books combining memoirs and foreign policy advice. As memories of Watergate faded, some commentators emphasized Nixon's intelligence, domestic reforms, and foreign policy successes. Never very penitent about Watergate, he grew persistently less so and in 1990 described the scandal as "one part wrongdoing, one part blundering, and one part political vendetta" by his foes.

But there is a dark side to his character, now embarrassingly preserved in the White House tapes. Watergate was a sordid and

Plate 15 Neil Armstrong and Buzz Aldrin became the first men to land on the moon, July 1969.
(Library of Congress.)

shameful mess, a terrible episode in a great career. If he had died – as he so nearly did – soon after his resignation, his obituary would have been an undiluted chorus of vilification. He could be vindictive about his liberal critics, and paranoiac. As it was, before his death in April 1994 he had 20 years as elder statesman, globe-trotting and speechmaking, wrote eight books on foreign policy and established the Nixon Center for Peace and International Relations. Longevity brought him serenity, acclaim as the US's leading foreign policy expert, and recognition, in George Bush's words, as "a true architect of peace."

And, for the record: in his presidency – thanks to the 400,000 staff who worked for NASA – 12 Americans walked on the Moon. This was a remarkable achievement. They found that it had no atmosphere and was "just dirt." The most fascinating sight was that of the Earth seen from the Moon; they thought that in full color it looked beautiful and was wonderful. It merits preserving.

8 GERALD FORD

Gerald Ford (1913–), 38th President of the United States, served in the House of Representatives from the Fifth District of Michigan beginning in 1949 and was elected minority leader in 1965. Under the provisions of the Twenty-fifth Amendment, President Richard M. Nixon chose him in 1973 to be Vice-President following the resignation of Vice-President Spiro T. Agnew. Upon the resignation of Nixon himself in the face of likely impeachment, Ford became President on August 9, 1974. He named as his Vice-President Nelson A. Rockefeller, former governor of New York, thus completing the only unelected presidential team in American history.

Ford had no clearcut political agenda, pledging only to end the "long national nightmare" provoked by the Watergate affair. A month after becoming President, he startled the nation by granting Nixon an unconditional pardon for any offenses he might have committed against the United States. A storm of protest arose, amid cries that a deal had been struck. No one has made the allegation stick, although Ford and Nixon were in constant negotiations before and after Ford took the presidential oath. Ford, keenly sensitive to the lingering suspicions, has insisted that his sole aim was to help heal the wounds of the nation. With poor timing, he announced only a few days after the pardon his amnesty proposal for Vietnam draft resisters and evaders. Unlike Nixon, they would have to meet conditions.

Ford presided over the evacuation of US personnel from Vietnam, which he ordered in April 1975. Because he was linked to this withdrawal, he was destined to have no notable strength in foreign affairs. Although he claimed credit for the Helsinki Accord in which the Soviet Union renounced its right to keep its states in line by military intervention, the true effect was to recognize at last Soviet domination of the Eastern Bloc nations. Possibly, however, the Helsinki Accord helped restrain the Soviet Union from intervening when citizens in Communist countries overthrew their governments in 1989.

In domestic affairs Ford's initiatives were few. A volunteer anti-inflation program, called by its acronym WIN (Whip Inflation Now), was widely derided as inadequate. When New York City fell into dire financial straits, Ford was unmoved. A now-famous headline in the *New York Daily News* – "Ford to City: Drop Dead" – helped underscore his apparent insensitivity to the national significance of the city's plight. In the presidential campaign of 1976, he aroused sympathy but not much support. In the election, his loss to Jimmy Carter was widely interpreted as completing the fall of the Nixon administration, for he had retained as his own staff most of Nixon's appointees.

Possessed of an open personality, Ford was perceived as a straight-shooter. He was "Mr Nice Guy," unpretentious but unimaginative. A splendid athlete (he had been an outstanding college football player), he sometimes seemed more comfortable talking about sports than about the intricacies of public policy. He could never live down Lyndon Johnson's cruel quips, which stuck like Velcro (for instance, "The trouble with Jerry Ford is that he used to play football without a helmet.")

Ford's wife, Betty, broke fresh ground for a First Lady by her forthrightness on controversial and personal matters. She championed abortion rights and the Equal Rights Amendment; expressed uncommon understanding for some of the new norms of young people's behavior, including premarital sex and the use of marijuana; and went public about her mastectomy, her drinking problem, and her entry into psychiatric treatment.[8]

Ford was deeply pained that he could not vindicate his presidency at the polls. He must remain satisfied to be remembered as a Congressional President whose historic role it was to clean up the dregs of the two most damaging episodes in the history of the modern White House, the Watergate affair and the Vietnam War.

Ford, and his Vice-President Nelson Rockefeller, were the the first to hold their respective offices without being directly elected to them. Ford's administration was significant for two main reasons: the first, that the Central Intelligence Agency and the FBI were found by the Justice Department to be implicated in the Watergate cover-up scandal.

The CIA, it was learned, had also infiltrated anti-war groups, joined in or originated plots to assassinate foreign political leaders, and conducted drug and bacteria experiments on unsuspecting Americans. The FBI was censured for such acts as violating civil rights while investigating dissident groups, engaging in partisan

[8] Betty Ford with Chris Chase, *The Times of My Life* (New York, Harper and Row, 1978); Gerald R. Ford, *A Time to Heal* (New York, Harper and Row, 1979); Edward I. and Frederick H. Schapsmeier, *Gerald R. Ford's Date with Destiny: A political biography* (New York, P. Lang, 1989).

politics, and conducting a campaign to discredit Martin Luther King, Jr.

For security reasons, the President initially sought to restrict Congressional inquiry. When the extent of the abuses became known, however, he attempted to curtail them and restore public confidence in the intelligence services. On November 2, 1975, William E. Colby was dismissed as CIA director and George Bush named in his stead. Secretary of State Kissinger was removed from the post of national security advisor. In February 1976 Bush was made chairman of a new intelligence operations coordinating committee under the policy direction of the National Security Council, and an independent oversight board of three was appointed. An executive order limited surveillance of American citizens. A sweeping reorganization of the FBI began in August, but Clarence Kelley was retained as director.

Even more important, however, was the President's statement on evacuation from Vietnam. With the military collapse of the Thieu regime in April 1975, President Ford ordered the evacuation of all remaining American personnel in South Vietnam. Reporting on his actions to the nation on April 29, he declared:

> During the past week, I had ordered the reduction of American personnel in the United States mission in Saigon to levels that could be quickly evacuated during emergency, while enabling that mission in Saigon to levels that could be quickly evacuated during emergency, while enabling that mission to continue to fulfill its duties.
>
> During the day on Monday, Washington time, the airport at Saigon came under persistent rocket as well as artillery fire and was effectively closed. The military situation in the area deteriorated rapidly.
>
> I therefore ordered the evacuation of all personnel remaining in South Vietnam. The evacuation has been completed. ...
>
> This action closes a chapter in the American experience. I ask all Americans to close ranks, to avoid recrimination about the past, to look ahead to the many goals we share and to work together on the great tasks that remain to be accomplished.

A threat to the life of President Ford was made on September 5, 1975, by Lynette Alice ("Squeaky") Fromme, aged 27, who pointed a loaded pistol at the President as he moved through a crowd in a park one hundred yards from the California State Capitol in Sacramento. A secret service agent, Larry Beundorf, jammed his hand over the .45-caliber pistol, preventing the weapon from firing. Later, it was found that the weapon's chamber was empty. Fromme, who described herself as a follower of convicted murderer Charles Manson, was charged with attempted assassination. She was tried in the US District Court at Sacramento before Judge Thomas Jamison MacBride, found guilty on November 26, 1975, and sentenced to life imprisonment.

On September 22, 1975, Sara Jane Moore, aged 45, fired a single shot at President Ford as he was leaving the St Francis Hotel in San Francisco. The bullet, from a .38-caliber revolver, missed him by five feet, striking a taxi driver, who was not seriously wounded. Moore was disarmed by Oliver Sipple, a former Marine, and police officers Tim Hettrich and Gary Lemos. Charged with attempted assassination, Moore pleaded guilty. Her plea was accepted December 16, 1975, by Judge Samuel Conti of the US District Court in San Francisco, and she was sentenced to life imprisonment. The day before the shooting, Moore had been arrested for carrying an illegal handgun, questioned by the Secret Service, and released after the weapon was confiscated. She had had ties with radical groups in Berkeley and had been employed by the Federal Bureau of Investigation as an informant.

In the election of 1976, Jimmy Carter, former Governor of Georgia, was nominated for the presidency on the first ballot at the Democratic party's Convention in Madison Square Garden, New York. His running mate was Senator Walter Frederick Mondale of Minnesota. President Ford was nominated on the first ballot for the presidency by the Republicans at their Convention in Kansas City, with Senator Robert Joseph Dole of Kansas as his running mate. The first public debate between an incumbent President and a rival candidate was held September 23, 1976. Under the sponsorship of the League of Women Voters, three network television companies pooled their resources to telecast President Ford and Jimmy Carter, the Democratic candidate, in a discussion of domestic issues at the Walnut Street Theater, Philadelphia. A second debate, on foreign policy, took place on October 6, 1976, at the Palace of Fine Arts Theater in San Francisco, and a third, unrestricted in subject, took place on October 22, 1976, at Phi Beta Kappa Hall on the campus of the College of William and Mary, Williamsburg, Va. Each debate was 90 minutes long and gave each candidate the opportunity not only to answer questions addressed to him by a panel of journalists, but to reply to his opponent's answers.

The first debate between vice-presidential candidates, also sponsored by the League of Women Voters, was held October 15, 1976, at the Alley Theater, Houston, Texas. The Republican vice-presidential candidate, Robert Dole, confronted the Democratic candidate, Walter Mondale, for 75 minutes of nationally televized debate on such issues as social programs and the nation's economy.

A response to the queries during the primaries concerning the relatively unknown Jimmy Carter is found in his book *Why Not the Best?* published in 1975: "I am a Southerner and an American, I am a farmer, an engineer, a father and husband, a Christian, a politician and former governor, a planner, a businessman, a nuclear physicist, a naval officer, a canoeist, and among other things a lover of Bob Dylan's songs and Dylan Thomas's poetry."[9] In the November elections, 40 million votes were cast for Carter, 39 million for Ford. Carter received 297 votes in the Electoral College (23 states plus the District of Columbia) against Ford's 240 from 27 states. One elector from Washington cast one of the state's nine electoral votes for Ronald Reagan instead of for President Ford.

9 JIMMY CARTER

Jimmy Carter (1924–), still active as a peacemaker (witness his visits to Ethiopia, Sudan, Liberia, and to Port au Prince to seek to settle the Haiti question in September 1994), is a remarkable man. He was the first President from Georgia; the first President to graduate from the US Naval Academy; the first President sworn in using his nickname; the first President inaugurated in a business suit; the first President to walk from the Capitol to the White House after his inauguration; and the first President to appoint two women to his Cabinet.

When James Earl Carter took office as 39th President of the United States in 1977 he inherited a nation divided by the social turmoil of the 1960s and disillusioned by the cynical political practices of the Nixon White House. Within minutes after his inauguration on January 20, Carter left his heavily armored limousine and, holding hands with his wife, Rosalynn, walked the parade route to the cheers of spectators. Later, their nine-year-old daughter Amy joined her parents in their walk. Carter's stroll down Pennsylvania Avenue seemed to symbolize the end of one era and the beginning of another. In retrospect, however, the Democratic victory in 1976 was a historical anomaly in an era of Republican domination of the presidency.

Carter, the son of a Georgia landowner and businessman, was part of the first generation of moderate Southern politicians who emerged in the aftermath of the civil rights movement. His term

[9] Jimmy Carter, *Why Not the Best?* (Nashville, Broadman Press, 1975).

as governor of Georgia (1971–5) was a modest success, marked by an emphasis upon governmental reorganization and aggressive actions to end racial discrimination. Still, it hardly seemed a springboard to the White House, and his announcement in December 1975 that he would seek the presidency evoked incredulity or amusement from most knowledgeable political observers.

But they underestimated Carter. American voters were disgusted by the Watergate revelations of corruption, and they responded warmly to the soft-spoken southerner with his perpetual smile and his often repeated promise: "I'll never lie to you." His moderate economic views, his commitment to civil rights, and his background as a Southerner helped him assemble a coalition of traditional Democrats, blacks, and Southern whites who had become increasingly alienated from the Democratic party. Carter narrowly defeated incumbent Gerald Ford with 50.1 percent of the vote.

Carter was helped by the selection of Walter Mondale as his running mate: a welfare state liberal, a protégé of Hubert Humphrey and very much a Washington insider – which Carter was not. In 1976 he carried almost all the South except Virginia and Oklahoma, and won also several big states in the Northeast: Massachusetts, New York, Pennsylvania, and Maryland. He won over 80 percent of the votes of blacks, who, thanks to the legislation of the Kennedy-Johnson years, were now all but solidly Democrat. Carter's victory symbolized the reconciliation of the races in the South and the acceptance by white Southerners of the civil rights revolution.

Taking a firm stand on the moral issue of individual rights, President Carter asserted that his foreign policy would be sensitive to the cause of freedom. The declaration was made in his inaugural address, and shortly thereafter his administration took steps to deal with the suppression of human rights. On January 2, 1977, the State Department charged Czechoslovakia with violation of the 1975 Helsinki agreement on human rights, and on January 27 it criticized the Soviet Union for its efforts to silence the dissident physicist Andrei Sakharov – criticism that led to sharp Soviet protest and threatened US–USSR relations and arms accords. On February 24 the United States reduced aid to Argentina, Ethiopia, and Uruguay because of violations of human rights. On March 17 the President discussed the rights issue in an address before the General Assembly of the United Nations.

In national as well as international politics, the President took direct action. Joined by Rosalynn Carter, he attempted to persuade state legislators to approve the Equal Rights Amendment as the disputed women's issue came to a vote in several states.

In April 1977 President Carter expressed his support for efforts to abolish the electoral college. He encouraged the attempt of Senator Birch Bhay (Democrat, Indiana) to obtain Congressional approval for an amendment repealing the Twelfth Amendment to the Constitution, which provides for presidential electoral votes based on state representation in Congress. Advocates of the controversial change hoped to substitute by 1980 a proposed Twenty-seventh Amendment, which would provide for direct popular election based on a national plurality.

But failures in domestic and foreign policy overshadowed these accomplishments. Carter had been elected as an outsider, and he often proved inept in dealing with his own party. He also seemed unable to mobilize public support for his policies of restraint and sacrifice. He was dogged, too, by events beyond his control: the energy crisis that triggered double-digit inflation, the fall of the Shah and the seizure of hostages in Iran, and the chill in Soviet-American relations following the Soviet invasion of Afghanistan. He had to invoke the Taft-Hartley Act and intervene in a long and bitter dispute in the mines. In retrospect, many of the crises Carter confronted were insoluble, but his style of hands-on management led a restive American public to hold him personally responsible for failure. The seizure of American hostages proved his final undoing. Americans' increasing frustration over the nation's inability to effect their release focused upon Carter. When an attempted rescue of the hostages ended in ignominious failure in 1980, his fate as President was sealed. He went down to a smashing defeat at the hands of Ronald Reagan.

There are a number of strands that explain "Jimmy" Carter. He was very much a Southerner; he was deeply religious; he was a graduate of the Naval Academy at Annapolis; and he had an unusual and thorough higher education including experience on nuclear submarines – unusual among Southern governors. He was determined – but did not succeed – to curb the growth of bureaucracy in Washington. He was much influenced by the teachings of the theologian Reinhold Niebuhr and constantly sought to emphasize the moral note, which came to mark his presidency. Even in foreign policy, human rights mattered. This was the reverse of Kissinger's *realpolitik*. Carter could with truth say that he had been honest to his campaign pledges: "I will never lie to you;" "It is a time for healing." Politics for him was a struggle for social justice, not a contest between lawyers. Perversely, therefore, whatever his Southern background, he was and remains in essence a Yankee puritan.

In practice, his cause was greatly assisted by his winning the support of Andrew Young, a former aide to Martin Luther King, whom he appointed US representative at the United Nations. A number of other black political leaders gave Carter their help, but this support was never total. He found promises easier to make than to fulfill. He was at his best mediating at Camp David. But his intentions were noble. Though no Supreme Court judgeships fell vacant in his term, he changed the face of the federal judiciary by appointing more women and more members of minority groups than any other President: there were 40 women, 38 blacks, and 16 Hispanics among his 262 appointments. Over 80 percent of them just happened to be Democrats, but Carter was very much in favor of affirmative action.

Nevertheless, Carter's administration was one of failure. He failed to produce the tax reforms and the welfare reforms he had campaigned to introduce. Despite the renown of his Camp David summit, he brought no permanent peace to the Middle East. Moreover, this post-Watergate President was personally embarrassed when his budget director and friend, the affable, able, and overweight Georgian Bert Lance, was forced to resign because of his failure to disclose personal financial problems, and compelled to leave business and politics and go back into the private sector.

Not all statesmen find life after power easy. But Jimmy Carter is perhaps the most successful retired head of state since Konrad Adenauer. In 1986 Carter founded the Carter Center of Emory University, an institution devoted to mediating international conflict and ameliorating health problems in the world's developing nations. In a departure from the usual quiet retirement of Presidents, Carter has played an active role in numerous diplomatic and domestic efforts after leaving office. The Carter Center, from its headquarters in Atlanta, has become one of the most respected champions of human rights, disease eradication, and child protection in the world, and frequently assists governments in the awkward transition to multiparty democracy. In retirement, the former President has become what he never could be in office; a true force for decency in international life.

Carter was hailed as a national hero on the success of his mission to Haiti in September 1994 – its code-word "Operation Uphold Democracy," more than 13 years after his reputation as a "wimp" helped to end his presidency in a massive election defeat. With his peacemaking deal in Haiti, Mr Carter rescued President Clinton's foreign policy for the second time in one summer (the first was his negotiation of a breakthrough in the nuclear standoff with North Korea). Carter could be forgiven for enjoying references to him as America's "greatest former President" and headlines hailing him as "Jimmy the Peacemaker." Even before the Haitian deal, he had been nominated for the Nobel Peace Prize, and must now be considered a strong favorite for the award.

11 NIXON NOSTALGIA

The most interesting taste in American politics today might be called Nixon Nostalgia. Nixon is not loved, but there is, increasingly, grudging admiration for the qualities that produced his durability as a public figure. And there is a recognition that his career reveals some truths about politics that Americans have been reluctant to take to heart. British readers may find all this intelligible, if not quite forgivable, when they read Stephen E. Ambrose's *Nixon: The education of a politician, 1913–1962.*[10] Ambrose is the author of a two-volume biography of Eisenhower, the best biographer of that complex, underrated man who understood, among many other things, the political advantage of being underestimated by the intelligentsia. It has been said that the best biographer is a conscientious enemy of his subject. That describes Ambrose as Nixon's biographer. He disliked Nixon when he began to write about him, but dislikes him less now. Ambrose feels some of the ambivalence the nation feels about Nixon.

Any American at least 60 years old cannot remember politics without Richard Nixon as a player. Nixon was a Congressman at 33, a Senator at 37. At 39 he was elected Vice-President, separated from the pinnacle of American politics only by the heartbeat of Eisenhower, who was to become the oldest man to serve as President until Ronald Reagan. Franklin Roosevelt is the only other person to match Nixon's record of running on a national ticket five times. More votes have been cast for Nixon for President than for any other person. And what is said of Margaret Thatcher's electoral successes can be said of Nixon's; they are encouraging evidence that even in the age of television (when, as an American wit has said, a political rally is three people clustered around a television set), a charming personality is not a necessary asset.

Americans have been educated about politics while watching Nixon's long education. Nixon was one of those compulsive campaigners whose careers have given rise to this axiom: anyone who

[10] See n.2 above.

has the consuming ambition and distorting passion necessary for the marathon run to the White House should, because of those qualities, be disqualified from holding the office.

One reason Ronald Reagan was a political force capable of carrying 93 states in 48 months is that he seemed so normal – so unlike Nixon. Three of the four Presidents who immediately preceded Reagan (Johnson, Nixon and Carter) were, to say no more, strange. They were driven men, working out private turmoils, anxieties and resentments in public action. The fourth President, the normal one, Gerald Ford, was an accident.

In a wired-up nation, where portions of the evening news programs are telecast from the President's front lawn, the President is a permeating presence in the nation's life. After Johnson, Nixon, and Carter, the nation wanted to feel comfortable in the presence of their omnipresent leader. They avidly embraced Ronald Reagan as a respite from strangeness, a chance for infectious serenity. But by Reagan's seventh year, the nation knew that serenity is not enough. They want to be comfortable with their President. But what if, as may have been the case since 1981, they have been comfortable with Reagan in part because he lacks the drivenness, the disturbing political energy needed to energize and control the government?

Nixon was nothing if not driven. But by what? Politics is mostly talk, much of it small talk with strangers, and Nixon never seemed to enjoy any of it. His career was the joyless pursuit not of joy but of one job after another. The playful element in politics – the exuberance of competition, the spontaneity and wit – is almost entirely absent from Nixon's story. For Nixon, politics was always work.

Nixon was an archetype of a phenomenon that is becoming too common for comfort, the young man who has never known, never desired and cannot imagine a vocation other than politics. There are two problems with such people. First, they know little about the everyday world of the average citizen, so they cannot easily empathize with people who are not similarly driven by public ambitions. Second, having only political skills, and deriving satisfaction only from the exercise of those skills, such people cannot contemplate losing.

But politics is a vocation unlike dentistry or manufacturing shoes. The ethic of politics, properly understood, requires a politician to be prepared to jeopardize his job by doing his job right. That is, from time to time a politician must say things that people do not want to hear and do things they are not pleased to have done. That is called leadership and it can be dangerous. After all, leadership has been defined as the ability to inflict pain and get away with it – short-term pain for long-term gain, but pain none the less. Young men, or men no longer young, who see the world as divided into just two realms, politics and the Void, find that the risks of leadership are intolerable.

On the other hand, the governance of a great nation requires a professional political class, a fact that Americans are tardy in facing. Americans cherish the idea of the "citizen legislator" who conducts public affairs while remaining essentially a private citizen. Americans do not take easily to the idea of the thoroughly public man. Nixon, who knew no profession but politics, was such a man.

The length of Nixon's stay on the stage made him one of the half-dozen largest figures of the postwar era. Were it not for the strength of his will, his drivenness, he would have been a minor footnote in the history of our times. Ambrose's first volume ends with what Nixon called his "last press conference," the one after he lost the 1962 California gubernatorial race. After losing to Kennedy in 1960, he ran in California two years later because that was what he did for a living – he sought political offices. Ambrose's closing sentence is: "as he drove away from his last press conference, he was already discussing his future."

And quite a future it proved to be. It included the most astonishing comeback in American political history – from the losses of 1960 and 1962 to the victories of 1968 and 1972. And there has been yet another comeback, from the role of national embarrassment that was caused by Watergate to the object of a strange, interesting nostalgia.

Since his death in 1994 there has been a distinct rehabilitation of Nixon's political reputation. Although a recent *Newsweek* poll showed that a vast majority of Americans still believed that Nixon's actions warranted his resignation, a growing number now believe that President Ford was right to pardon him. Similarly, revelations which have appeared recently in books and articles about "dirty tricks" carried out by other American leaders – notably President Kennedy and President Johnson – have caused many people to wonder whether Richard Nixon's behavior was much worse than that of his predecessors.

Another theme has been examination of the extent to which the lessons of the Watergate scandal have been learnt and absorbed by successive administrations or have been discarded and forgotten. For example, the federal governor is in the process of tightening up the Freedom of Information Act, under which journalists and others have been enabled to gain access to official documents previously closed to public scrutiny. At the same time moves are being made to loosen the tight controls placed on the Central Intelligence Agency (CIA) and the Federal Bureau of Investigation (FBI).

One of the most far-reaching reforms was the control imposed on election campaign financing to prevent "massive corruption and the abuse of power." However, there is now a widespread belief that this reform has not only reduced the influence of the main political parties but has also diverted money into the pockets of independent special-interest groups.

What of the cast of characters – the "plumbers," the "hatchet men," the "bagmen" – who took part in the scandal and who ended up in prison or in disgrace? Most now appear to be profitably exploiting their Watergate experiences. H. R. Haldeman, the White House chief of staff who served 18 months in prison for perjury and obstruction of justice, has written a book of his experiences and now runs a Los Angeles real estate firm. John Ehrlichman, President Nixon's chief domestic affairs adviser, who also served 18 months in jail, has written two political novels and his memoirs. John Dean, the White House counsel, and Gordon Liddy, the chief "plumber," make between $2,000 and $4,000 a time for lecture appearances. Mr Liddy also runs a private investigating firm which, appropriately, offers "anti-bugging sweeps" as one of its services.

Without condoning what President Nixon did (to cover up a political crime in order to protect his lieutenants), laying aside his considerable foreign-policy achievements, and laying aside equally the heady sermons on "morality-in-politics" preached by contemporary editorials in the New York and Washington press, White House politics are in a strange and worrying turmoil today. Watergate left a legacy behind: If the presidency became imperial with FDR, what happens to it when every President is seen not as Caesar but as Nero? Theodore White was right to say:

> Nixon has left behind a news system more powerful than ever – made so by its successful struggle with him. His hatred of the news system and his unrelenting effort to cripple, manipulate, deceive and coerce the leadership of that news system have provoked a counter-hatred which now has a life of its own. Will its suspicion of Richard Nixon be translated into a permanent suspicion of the Presidency itself?. The pursuit of Richard Nixon has made folk heroes of investigative reporters. But how much will the folklore of their triumphs inspire a new generation of editors and reporters to consider not only the Presidency but all government as a conspiracy against the people, to be ripped apart perhaps irresponsibly,

for years to come? If Nixon has bequeathed to his Presidential successors a permanently hostile news system, he has cursed them all. And he has also cursed all the men of House and Senate who might be found, by the press, of insufficient zeal in frustrating a President, any President, whether he merit it or not."[11]

White might have also asked why are some presidents treated with kid gloves (Eisenhower) or as glamor boys (JFK), and why are others (LBJ and RMN) persistently attacked? Why do the press make heroes of some (undistinguished) men and villains of other (undistinguished) men? There is in the Fourth Estate in America including its TV cameras, a massive capacity to deride. They now do it to the man in the White House whoever he is, surpassing themselves in the clever remarks and the snide and icy wisecracks that have been their major industry since 1965. If there is a real breach of faith with the American people it lies here, not only in the White House (if there at all), but in those who are themselves the makers of myths. Far from being the watchdogs of democracy, the men of the press are in danger of becoming its subvertors. *Quis custodiet custodes*?

[11] Theodore White, *Breach of Faith* (London, Cape, 1975), p. 337.

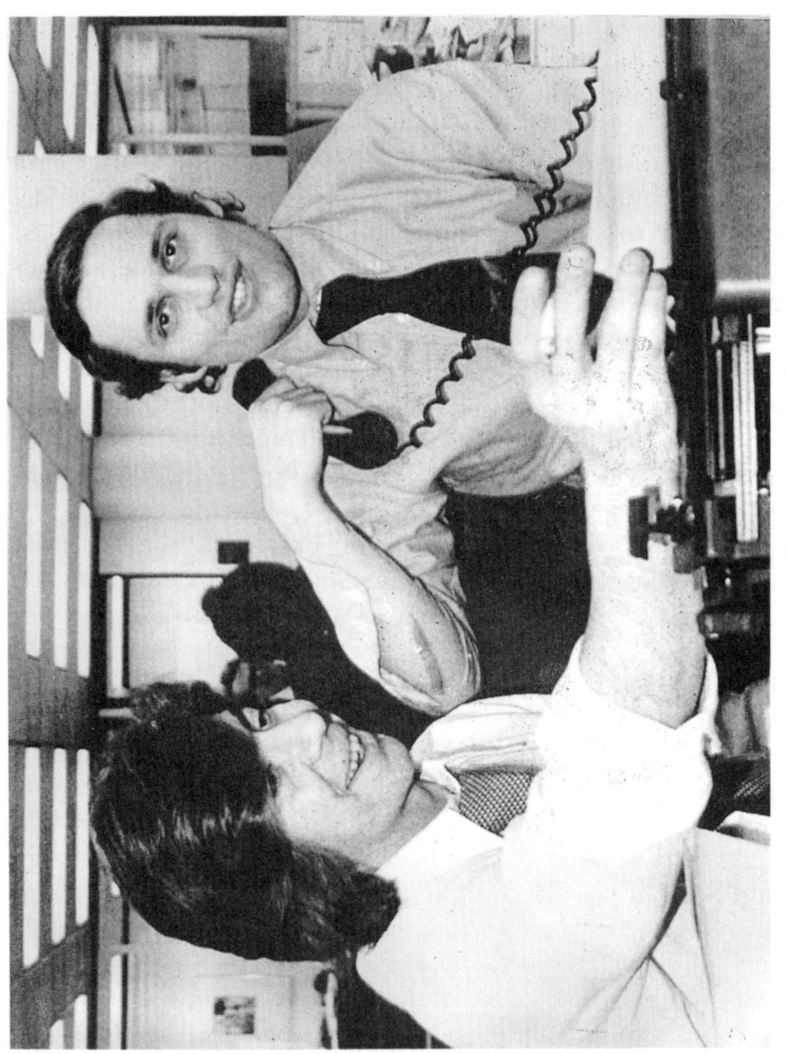

Plate 16 Carl Bernstein and Bob Woodward won a Pulitzer prize for their work in uncovering the Watergate scandal. (© Popperfoto.)

16

Ronald Reagan: The Man Who Won the Cold War

1 RONALD REAGAN

Ronald Reagan (1911–), 40th president of the United States, and an ex-liberal, built what was probably the most successful conservative coalition of the twentieth century, perhaps the most successful in American history, almost contemporaneously with Margaret Thatcher's reinvigoration of the British Conservative party across the Atlantic. Yet, conservative groups – alike in the US as in Britain – are not always led by the well-born, the bluebloods, the aristos. Reagan's story is, in fact, an up-to-date version of "log cabin to White House."

Though not born in the poverty that marked Lincoln's birth, Reagan was born in Tampico, Illinois, very near the wrong side of the tracks. His father, who liked his alcoholic refreshment, was unemployed in the depression; the son, like his elder brother, worked his way through an undistinguished Fundamentalist college, Eureka in Illinois, where he graduated in 1932 and where his chief interest was football. He counted himself lucky to get a job as a small-town radio sports reporter, which taught him to talk easily – and to invent and ad-lib when there were gaps to fill. He went to California and quickly established himself in the movies. Little affected by Hollywood glamor, Reagan aptly described himself as "Mr Norm;" he was familiarly known as "Dutch."

In these years, Reagan was a staunch Democrat. In World War II, he acted in government films. His physical presence, agility, and easy charm led to Hollywood in its expansionist age, and to some 50 films, in few of which was he especially distinguished. He became active in the Screen Actors' Guild, to serve it for six years as President, to become accustomed to its fierce union struggles – and, in the hothouse atmosphere of the postwar world, to become aware of a Communist attempt to "take over" the Hollywood unions. In this hectic apprenticeship, he lost his liberalism and became the close friend of those on the political right in Hollywood – James Stewart, Robert Taylor, Robert Montgomery, Clark Gable, to name a few. As presenter of General Electric's Sunday night television theater, he toured the company's plants through the country, and had a second political apprenticeship. He was by that time engaged on what he calls the rubber-chicken banquet trail, spreading the message of private enterprise and freedom in an open society; "For me, I think that service is to continue accepting speaking engagements, in an effort to make people aware of the danger to freedom in a vast permanent government structure so big and complex it virtually entraps Presidents and legislators." It was, of course, that activity that led him into active Republican politics, and in the end to the White House.

Reagan was unpretentious, honest and – mildly – anecdotal, ultra-discreet over the failure of his first marriage. There was no evidence of a vast political ambition, or of any great depth of political reading. When he quoted the great names, he called on the usual clichés of or from them. But he reached his views from his own direct experience; he was straight, uncomplicated – and owed no debts to anyone. In his early years in politics, he was a dedicated Democrat – as his father had been – and he voted, he confessed, four times for FDR. But after he changed his political views, leaving the Democratic party and becoming a conservative Republican, he was voted governor of California (1966) and in office strongly assailed big government; however, he enlarged the state budget and learned to compromise with Democratic legislators. Reagan won the presidential nomination in 1980, and defeated President Jimmy Carter in the election.

Intelligent but intellectually lazy, Reagan was prone to making groundless assertions that were often rendered as quips. More than any other modern President, he enunciated broad themes and then left day-to-day governance to subordinates. Personally he exuded friendliness, and, after an attempted assassination in 1981, he showed grace and bravery. These qualities facilitated negotiations with Congress, enabling him to hold together a coalition of Republican regulars, recently politicized evangelical Protestants, and disenchanted Democrats. Though affable to everyone, Reagan felt close only to a few old friends and to his wife, Nancy. Indeed, Nancy Reagan was said by White House watchers to have exerted greater influence on government operations than any previous First Lady.

Reagan reshaped American politics. While leaving intact such popular New Deal programs as Social Security, his administration gutted Great Society anti-poverty programs, accepted a deep recession in order to curb inflation, and sharply reduced income taxes in the higher brackets. Initially Reagan developed the unique SDI (Strategic Defense Initiative – "Stars Wars") program, supported the largest military buildup in American history, and denounced the Soviet Union as an "evil empire;" but in his second term he reached a détente with Soviet leader Mikhail Gorbachev.

His administration intervened briefly yet disastrously in the multi-sided Lebanese civil war, invaded Grenada, bombed Libya, and sponsored the Nicaraguan Contras, who were trying to overthrow the leftist government in that country. In 1985, Reagan authorized the sale of arms to Iran in an unsuccessful effort to free Americans held hostage in Lebanon; but he claimed not to know that subordinates were illegally diverting the proceeds to the Contras. When a Beirut newspaper released the story – in time for the off-year elections of November 1986 – "Irangate" became an international as well as a national scandal. Two days after the election US intelligence sources admitted that the story was true, and some eight days later Reagan admitted that he had known of the arms sale. A White House officer, Marine Lieutenant Colonel Oliver North, was investigated by Congress in a TV-covered probe. As a legacy of Irangate, Reagan's standing in the opinion polls fell from the high 60s in the summer of 1985 to 48 percent in December 1986.[1]

Reagan's most enduring legacy was perhaps his 372 appointments to the federal bench, including four to the Supreme Court. These included the first female associate justice, Sandra Day O'Connor, in 1981, and William Rehnquist as chief justice.

[1] Laurence I. Barrett, *Gambling with History: Ronald Reagan in the White House* (New York, Penguin, 1984); Lou Cannon, *Reagan* (New York, Putnam's 1982); Jane Mayer and Doyle McManus, *Landslide: The unmaking of the President, 1984–1988* (Boston, Houghton Mifflin, 1988); Ronald Reagan, *Reagan, My Early Life, or Where's the Rest of Me?* (London, Sidgwick and Jackson, 1981).

2 ECONOMICS

There was another factor alongside a strong foreign-policy stance to which Reagan attributed his success in national politics: his advocacy of supply-side economics and tax cuts. It fitted in with his own optimistic upbeat view of America if only the energies of the ordinary American people could be released, then they could overcome the problems that the United States faced. He was impressed that most of the conservative journals that he read – such as *National Review* or *Human Events* – were endorsing these ideas. In origin the ideas of Frederick Hayek, who for a time taught in Chicago, and of Milton Friedman, they became the language of Thatcherism, and formed the fashionable doctrines both in Britain and the US: the only way to enhance the performance of the economy was to improve its supply-side, by greater efficiency, to make markets better, to reduce costs and to increase competitiveness. It became increasingly clear that these were popular ideas with the electorate, which would gain Reagan votes in his campaign for the presidency. Once he had grasped this idea, he then became the Great Communicator of supply-side economics to a wider audience. In fact, it was Jack Kemp, then the Congressman from Buffalo, who was the first politician to try and spread the supply-side message, influenced by his conversations with people like Jude Wanniski and Arthur Laffer. In 1977 he introduced his Kemp-Roth Bill, calling for income tax cuts as an alternative to the Democrat budget.

In the United States the popularity of supply-side economics was first demonstrated in 1978 with the success of Proposition 13 in California, the idea of a spreading tax revolt; Republican candidates then found that using the tax issue in 1978 and 1980 brought success. Proposition 13 required the Government of California to reduce by more than half the tax on real estate. In the Presidential campaign in 1980, Reagan did very poorly in the Iowa caucuses. Then a TV blitz emphasizing tax cuts in the New Hampshire primary swept him to victory. That encouraged the campaign to make supply-side cuts a central theme of the 1980 elections. What began in California was imitated by Massachusetts, Arkansas, and other states.

Reagan was given considerable intellectual support and favorable public opinion from a number of think tanks. Spreading the same message, the American Enterprise Institute provided an institutional forum in Washington, DC, for monetarist ideas. The Hoover

Institution in California appointed Milton Friedman as a senior fellow. In Britain the Institute of Economic Affairs produced a short pamphlet by Friedman, *The Counter-Revolution in Monetary Theory*,[2] and brought him into touch with Thatcher. For supply-side economics, the American Enterprise Institute (AEI) gave a home to Jude Wanniski in 1977, which enabled him to write his book, *The Way the World Works*.[3] But most of the AEI economic establishment, including such notables as Herbert Stein, were very hostile to the conclusions of that book, and they made speeches and lectures attacking supply-side economics; so the AEI as a whole was not a center of supply-side economics in the late 1970s or in the 1980s.

Thus the supply-siders had to create their own institutions. One was the Institute for Research into the Economics of Taxation, formed in 1977 by Norman Ture. But that gained very little attention until the Heritage Foundation took it under its wing in 1981, and then gave its work a much higher profile in Washington. Ture contributed the chapter on the Department of the Treasury to the influential *Mandate for Leadership* report of the Heritage Foundation,[4] in which he summed up the case for supply-side tax cuts. He was appointed undersecretary for tax and economic affairs at the Treasury.

The President sought also to cut the size of government itself. By promising cuts in his defense program the President hoped to reduce the awesome figures of the federal budget deficit. The size of the government deficit, and the political difficulties of reducing it, however, ensured that once private and credit demand was added to the government's needs, interest rates were bound to rise. Interest rates stayed stubbornly high (10 percent against 20 percent in 1980), attracting short-term outside and mobile capital but delaying business revival. As a result unemployment stayed high, at 8.4 percent (though this was the lowest for two years). It was especially burdensome in some areas (for instance, the Middle West), among 16–24-year-olds, and among blacks. And there was (and remains) for the US, as for some British banks, a high exposure to Latin American debt problems.

In keeping with the fashion set by the White House, the new economic theology even had overtones of the Gilded Age. Much

[2] Milton Friedman, *The Counter-Revolution in Monetary Theory* (London, Institute of Economic Affairs, 1977).

[3] Jude Wanniski, *The Way the World Works* (New York, Basic Books, 1978).

[4] Norman Ture and Stuart Butler (eds), *Mandate for Leadership* (Washington, The Heritage Foundation, 1982).

more overtly than the supply-siders and the anti-tax theorists, Law and Economics stalwarts flirted with a neo-Darwinism that echoed Herbert Spencer and William Graham Sumner in its view that commercial selection processes in the market place could largely displace government decision-making. One intellectual frontiersman, Richard Posner, University of Chicago law professor turned federal appeals judge, even briefly suggested making a market for babies so it would be easier for couples to adopt. A second prominent Chicago legalist, Richard A. Epstein, leader of the movement's "economic rights" faction, deplored most government economic regulation as unconstitutional. "I oppose most of the legislation written in this century," he acknowledged in 1987. Posner and Epstein defined a remote ideological periphery, but they also confirmed the power of the mainstream conservative resurgence.

Most of the conservative theorists acknowledged their restatement of Adam Smith. The most important – and popular – of the theorists was George Gilder, in his *Wealth and Poverty*.[5] Gilder wrote what stands as the comprehensive theology of the Reagan era, relating conservatism to five central objectives. First was the importance of nurturing wealth ("a successful economy," wrote Gilder, "depends on the proliferation of the rich.") Next was his insistence that individual investment and production are inherently creative, echoing the notion that *supply* (capitalism) creates *demand*, thereby denying a Keynesian role for government:

> Supply creates its own demand. ... The importance of Says Law is its focus on supply, on the catalytic gifts or investments of capital. It leads economists to concern themselves first with the motives and incentives of individual producers, to return from a preoccupation with distribution and demand and concentrate again on the means of production.[6]

Gilder's third point was the need to curb government ("Since government has become a factor of production, the only way to diminish its impact on prices is to economize on it.") Gilder then hailed the unique and essential role of entrepreneurialism (entrepreneurs "are the heroes of American life"), and finally noted the critical importance of cutting upper-bracket taxes ("To help the poor and middle classes, one must cut the taxes of the rich.")

[5] George Gilder, *Wealth and Poverty* (New York, Basic Books, 1978).

[6] Say's Law – that supply creates demand – was named for the French economist Jean-Baptiste Say (1767–1832).

By the late 1970s inflation had increased tax discontent, and several economic theorists started talking about the central role of tax rates in the rise and fall of nations. Arthur Laffer, and his journalistic Boswell, former *Wall Street Journal* editorial writer Jude Wanniski, played the decisive role – the former with his Laffer Curve, insisting that beyond a certain point increased tax rates reduced rather than raised government revenue, and Wanniski with his book *The Way the World Works*, which publicized Laffer, and then proceeded to describe mankind's rise and fall so as to suggest that tax rates were the key to progress.

By 1987, when movement sympathisers Robert Bork and Douglas Ginsburg were nominated for the US Supreme Court, (though they were ultimately defeated), the relative acceptability of this part of their lexicon – markets, efficiency, competition – bespoke the country's shift away from the egalitarian and regulatory thinking of the 1960s and its brief Indian summer following Watergate.

In the election year of 1984, the President's critics, especially Democratic presidential aspirants like Walter Mondale, Gary Hart, or John Glenn, contended, however, that the only way to reduce the deficit was by tax increases and by cutting domestic spending – courses unlikely in an election year, and recommendations that would not help their own popularity. The President hoped that as taxes had been cut and as the recovery took place, the deficit would fall, and that no additional measures would be necessary until the elections were over.

The opposition, numerous but divided, was united in criticism of the size of the federal deficit, of nuclear weapons development, and of the role of the Marines in the Lebanon, and in criticism also of the President's conservative crusade to limit the size of the vast federal bureaucracy. Blacks were likely to register in greater numbers than before to support the Reverend Jesse Jackson's candidacy in the Democratic primaries, and to protest against budget cuts and new civil rights emphases. Farmers did not like the three years of low commodity prices and high interest rates. Trade unions, worried by falling numbers of members and by management requests for wage concessions (some of which were conceded), were likely to vote Democrat. And among women there was some evidence of a swing against Reagan, in what pundits now call the "gender gap." What the President had to do, like all his predecessors, was to manufacture afresh a winning coalition to give him enough support in the Electoral College to win – and win he did in 1984.

The Reagan economic boom was three times longer than the average post-1919 economic recovery. During it 20 million new jobs were created. The mean income of the poorest 20 percent of households rose 5 percent in real terms during the 1980s, and half the people who started the decade in the lowest group had moved up to a higher group by 1990.

George Gilder's tract of 1980, *Wealth and Poverty*, of which Reagan became an admirer, became a bestseller. The 1980s, in general, fully vindicated *Wealth and Poverty*'s social and economic arguments. This was the era when leftist dreams all collapsed in travesty. The mock-heroic youth of the 1960s emerged from schools sure that their nation was evil and owed them a living for their moral superiority, and capable of making no contribution to society except passing on their crippling creeds to future generations. The 1980s taught them the unwanted lesson that Marxist slogans, a sense of grievance, and a rhetoric of rights and "demands" are economically useless. Disdainful of science, enterprise, and other practical learning, they moved into law, teaching, and politics. Incapable of performing any useful task for a business, they thronged into the environmental movement; there they could harass businesses from a moral pinnacle without submitting to the humbling discipline of serving customers. They crowded onto the pulpits of the media and the academy in such numbers that a reporter or a professor often made less money than a garbage man. Seething at such obvious inequities of capitalism, they castigated the prosperous for "greed" and "workaholism."

Wealth and Poverty predicted the death of socialism. The 1980s were the decade when socialism died and left nothing but a bristling carcass of weapons pointed toward the West. It was the decade when tax rates were cut in 55 nations, following the success of that policy in the US, and revenues dropped in nearly all nations that raised their rates. It was the era when capitalism at last demonstrated conclusively its superiority as an economic system. It was the era when US economic growth rates, long lagging behind the rest of the world, surged ahead of Europe, Africa, and Latin America, and nearly caught up with Japan's for the first time since the early 1950s.

The 1980s also saw the longest peacetime expansion on record, with the highest rates of investment in capital equipment and the highest sustained rates of manufacturing productivity growth of any postwar recovery. During the 1980s, the US increased its share of global manufacturing output, global exports, and global production. Contrary to thousands of reports to the contrary, US balance sheets mostly improved, with debt as a share of assets dropping drastically for both businesses and households, as equity, net savings, and real estate values rose far more rapidly than indebtedness. Even government debt, as a share of GNP or in relation to real national assets, remained under control by historic and international standards.

After the tax rate reductions urged by *Wealth and Poverty* took effect in 1983 and 1984, total revenues at all levels of government rose some 9 percent a year in real terms, far faster than during the high-tax 1970s. During the 1980s recovery, industrial output rose nearly 40 percent, personal income 20 percent, and all segments of American society benefited from the creation of 22 million new jobs at rising real wages. Black employment rose 30.3 percent and Hispanic employment nearly 50 percent.

Unlike previous decades of growth, moreover, the American expansion of the 1980s came in the face of declining growth in Europe and Japan. Rather than being pulled ahead by faster development abroad, as in previous decades of growth, the US in the 1980s led the world economy. The greatest US triumph was the computer revolution, entirely a product of relentless discipline and entrepreneurial genius in capitalist nations. Computer industry revenues more than quadrupled; unit sales rose by a factor of hundreds; and computer cost-effectiveness rose ten thousand fold. At the end of the decade, US companies still held some two-thirds of the world market, and in critical software and leading-edge microchips their market share was above 70 percent and growing. In particular, the US led in using personal computers, with well over half of the world's 100 million PCs located in the US in 1990. The US still commands three times as much computer power per capita as the Japanese or Europeans.

This development, which impelled most of the world's economic growth during the decade, was also disastrous for the left. The left has always pinned its hopes on politics. The converging technologies of computers and telecommunications are radically reducing the power of politicians. An ever-increasing share of world wealth assumed the mobile form of information technologies, which – unlike the massive industrial systems of the past – are difficult to measure, capture, or tax. The computer age is an age of mind – elusive, and hard to control. This ascent of mind predicted in *Wealth and Poverty* is devaluing all the entrenchments of material resources and geography within the ken and command of politicians. As Mikhail Gorbachev has observed, the computer revolution was critical to the crisis of Communisms "We were among the last to understand that in an age of information science the most valuable asset is knowledge, springing from human imagination and creativity. We will be paying for our mistake for many years to come."

Nevertheless by every measure of prosperity, Reaganomics worked. Some 20 million new jobs were created. Inflation was brought under control. And inflation-adjusted income rose for all segments of the population. Much of the credit for this spectacular economic performance goes to the 1981 Economic Recovery Tax Act, which cut tax rates across the board for individuals and reduced the tax burden on business.

If policymakers want to restore economic growth, it seems that they should heed the following lessons of the 1980s:

1 Economic growth is the best weapon against poverty.
2 Economic growth is stimulated by low taxes, particularly low marginal rates.
3 The poor get richer when the rich get richer.
4 If the aim is to make the rich pay more actual taxes, cut their tax rates.
5 Raising taxes on the rich does not help the poor.
6 Increased Social Security taxes wiped out the benefits of Reagan's tax cuts for many Americans.
7 Hiking taxes does not lower the budget deficit, it raises it.

The Reagan boom was in large measure a legacy of the war economy, and it was most evident in California, with its aircraft plants and other key military industries. Wages climbed fast in the war years, not least on the West Coast. It was in California that the term "worker" took on new meaning. The Californian worker became an owner: first, of an automobile; then, soon enough, of a house (and then of a second automobile.) He began to think of civic life in the same way as any new property owner. He wanted stability, including one of its major props: moral decency. He wanted freedom from government intrusion, particularly high taxes. He wanted public policy to favor people like himself, people who had earned what they possessed. He wanted to take pride in what he had accomplished; and two of pride's most popular forms were official optimism and patriotism.

Of this new-style working class, which in function included many middle-class, Ronald Reagan became a natural spokesman: like many, he too had come up the hard way; like many, he was a California immigrant.[7] The prime beneficiaries were the top 5 percent of Americans, people who rode the cutting edge of the new technology

[7] Cf. Tom Wolfe "Head of the Class" in *National Review*, Aug. 5, 1988.

of autos, radios and the like, emerging service industries (including new practices like advertising and consumer finance), a booming stock market and unprecedented real estate development. As federal taxation eased, especially on the upper brackets, disposable income soared for the rich – and with it conspicuous consumption and financial speculation. Not the least prosperous were the lawyers: by 1988 the major law firms in the US probably counted fifty to sixty thousand attorneys. Of these over 40 years of age, probably half to two-thirds were millionaires.[8]

The Reagan boom has been called by George Gilder "Socialism's death rattle."[9] The collapse of Socialist/Communism in Russia and Europe has weakened its capacity to reinforce and buttress the embryo Socialist regimes, satellites and political parties in Cuba, in Latin America and the Caribbean, and in much of Africa. The map of the world is different.

Moreover, the American advance is technical. Over the last several years US firms have been expanding their global lead in the key technologies of the information age. Contrary to many false claims, US firms still produce half the world's microchips. The US share of global computer-software production has been increasing since 1982. At a time when value-added in information technology is moving toward software, microcomputers, and networks, US production of computer software, telecom products, and personal computers is between four and five times Japan's. With scores of new firms in microchips, bio-engineering, super-conductivity, and supercomputing, Reagan left a legacy of the largest and most rapidly growing generation of high-technology business start-ups in history.

Under Reagan, leading investors around the globe renewed their commitment to the US economy. US investors happily ended their feckless role as "net lenders" to the world, stopped pouring their money into Third World and Communist ratholes, and repatriated funds to the United States. Foreign investors also spurned their own economies and focused investment on America.

This capital flight from abroad and capital repatriation by Americans allowed the US to become the world's leading importer of advanced goods and equipment. Much decried by misinformed mercantilists and xenophobes, this influx of imports and investments was a thoroughly positive reflection of US success in integrating the world economy in the interests of Americans. With the US market

[8] Kevin Phillips *The Politics of Rich and Poor* (New York, Random House, 1990), p. 175.

[9] *National Review* Aug. 5, 1988, p. 36.

growing twice as fast as foreign markets, exporters to the US naturally outperformed US exporters to the rest of the world.

Ronald Reagan's legacy is a new epoch of American leadership in liberty and strength. Through his economic policies, Reagan brought the United States to world leadership among major industrial nations in all the key dimensions of economic growth: investment (51 percent growth), industrial production (30 percent growth), manufacturing productivity (26 percent growth), job creation (15 million new jobs), real per-capita income (18 percent increase), and technological innovation (a rising US market share in information technologies).

Defying a worldwide siege of economic stagnation, the Reagan boom was unique in the postwar era. By contrast, the US economic recoveries of the 1950s, 1960s, and 1970s all fed on faster growth abroad. During all these prior upturns, the US lagged behind Europe and Japan in all the key indices of expansion. During the Reagan era, the US surpassed Europe by a wide margin and caught up with Japan in rates of economic growth, and led the world in growth of investment and employment. Since Reagan assumed office, the US has been the only major industrial nation to increase investment as a share of GNP or to reduce unemployment.

Unlike the last US surge in job creation, in the 1970s, when productivity and real incomes declined, Reagan's world-beating employment boom was accompanied by a record six-year surge in manufacturing-productivity growth, a steady rise in per-capita income, and a striking increase in the quality of jobs.

From the beginning of 1983 through the end of 1989, real economic growth in the United States hit 3.8 percent per year – the Seven Fat Years. By 1990, GNP was 31 percent above 1982 in real, inflation-adjusted terms. Real disposable income *per capita* was 18 percent higher by 1990. The US economy added 18.4 million jobs.

What effect did tax cuts during the period have? Between 1980 and 1990, federal government receipts grew by 99 percent against GNP growth of 102 percent. From the low point in 1983 to the high point in 1989, tax receipts actually grew faster than GNP.

A comparison of purchasing power *per capita* in 1988 showed that the US still has the highest standard of living among developed nations, followed by Canada and Switzerland. West Germany ranked tenth and Japan twelfth.[10]

[10] Robert L. Bartley, *The Seven Fat Years* (New York, Free Press, 1992).

3 THE COLD WARRIOR

President Reagan, in retrospect, wrote:

> I took office in 1981 facing three urgent foreign policy tasks:
>
> To restore our nation's economic strength and help reinvigorate the world economic system after the blows of the energy shocks, spiraling inflation, and global recession.
>
> To restore our military strength after a decade when defense investment was neglected and the Soviet Union was allowed to overtake us in many crucial categories of military power.
>
> To restore this nation's dynamism and self-confidence as a world leader after the wounds of Vietnam and a period when our adversaries were emboldened and our friends disheartened by American retreat.
>
> With the support of the American people, and in a bipartisan joint effort between the President and Congress, we made headway in all of these areas. We put this nation back on the path of sustained economic growth with low inflation, resulting in the longest continuous peacetime period of economic expansion in our history. We achieved this by measures to ease the burden of government on the natural productive forces of our economy – by bringing inflation and interest rates down, by income tax rate reductions and a historic tax reform, and by reducing the regulatory burden. Around the world we see today a revolution in economic thinking, as developed and developing nations alike – even to some degree in the Communist world – are rediscovering that the wellspring of prosperity is the initiative and productivity of the individual, not the state. The United States remains the champion of a free, open, and fair international trading system. We have put forward major initiatives to lower trade barriers, promote economic development, improve monetary relations, and ease the problem of debt in the developing world.[11]

The collapse of Communism from 1989 to 1991 came as no surprise to Ronald Reagan. Throughout his career Reagan had emphasized the political, economic, and moral weakness of the Soviet Union, and the inevitable breakdown of the Marxist system if it were ever seriously challenged. Reagan spelled out his view of Communism in four speeches of astonishing prescience: his 1982 address to the British Parliament at Westminster; his speech before the National Association of Evangelicals in 1983; his appearance

[11] Ronald Reagan, "The US and the world in the 1990s," in Annelise Anderson and Dennis L. Bark (eds), *Thinking About America: The USA in the 1990s* (Stanford, Cal., Hoover Institution, Stanford University, 1988).

at the Brandenburg Gate of the Berlin Wall in 1987; and his talk under Lenin's statue at Moscow State University in May 1988. Of these, the speech to the evangelicals is best known: Reagan called the Soviet bloc an "Evil Empire" and referred to Communism as "the focus of evil in the modern world." These comments were widely derided at the time as the rantings of a Cold War ideologue. But to people living under the yoke of Soviet Communism, his words were all too obviously accurate – and they were words of hope. It was clear that the American President understood their plight and was not about to accede to their subjugation.

Today, after the people of eastern Europe and the former Soviet Union have thrown off the shackles of Communist rule, few doubt that the Soviet system was indeed an "Evil Empire" and that the world is better for its passing. If Reagan had done nothing more than proclaim this truth, while fashionable opinion was ridiculing it, he would stand vindicated before history. But the President did a great deal more than this.

In addition to stressing the evils of Communism, Reagan stressed its inherent weakness. In his view, the two were related, since in denying freedom the Communists not only engaged in tyranny, they also crippled the creative potential of the human spirit. Reagan firmly believed that freedom was both morally and materially superior to Communism. As he put it in his Westminster speech to the British Parliament:

> The decay of the Soviet experiment should come as no surprise to us. Wherever the comparisons have been made between free and closed societies – West Germany and East Germany, Austria and Czechoslovakia, Malaysia and Vietnam – it is the democratic countries that are prosperous and responsive to the needs of their people. And one of the simple but overwhelming facts of our times is this: of all the millions of refugees we've seen in the modern world, their flight is always away from, not toward, the Communist world.

Reagan described in the Westminster speech "the march of freedom and democracy which will leave Marxism-Leninism on the ash heap of history." He went even further in his address to the Evangelicals, where he predicted Communism's imminent demise. After attacking "moral equivalence" thinking, he called for a program of resistance to Soviet imperialism, and added: "I believe we shall rise to the challenge. I believe that Communism is another sad, bizarre chapter in history whose last pages even now are being written."

At the Brandenburg Gate, Reagan asked Mikhail Gorbachev to tear down the Berlin Wall, and expanded on his vision of history:

> In the 1950s, [he recalled] Khrushchev predicted, 'We will bury you.' But in the West today, we see a Free World that has achieved a level of prosperity and well-being unprecedented in all human history. In the Communist world, we see failure, technological backwardness, declining standards of health, even want of the most basic kind – too little food. Even today, the Soviet Union still cannot feed itself.
>
> After these four decades, then, there stands before the entire world one great inescapable conclusion: Freedom leads to prosperity. Freedom replaces the ancient hatreds among nations with comity and peace. Freedom is the victor.

Then, at Moscow State University, Reagan spoke of freedom's inevitable victory to the children of the *nomenklatura*:

> It's hard for government planners no matter how sophisticated, to ever substitute for millions of individuals working night and day to make their dreams come true. We Americans make no secret of our belief in freedom. ... Freedom is the right to question and change the established way of doing things. It is the continuing revolution of the marketplace. ... It is the right to put forth an idea, scoffed at by the experts, and watch it catch fire among the people.

Not long after, the idea of freedom caught fire among the republics of the Soviet Union.

Reagan's conviction that Communism was vulnerable was not simply theoretical. It was the essence of his foreign policy and defense strategy toward the Soviet empire. Reagan knew that the Soviet system could not command the allegiance of its captive peoples, and its economic system could not produce the goods required to shelter, feed, and clothe them. In any full-scale competition with the United States and other Western powers, therefore, Communism would be forced to choose between maintaining its empire and solving its many problems.

In contrast with prevailing liberal opinion, Reagan refused to negotiate with the Soviet Union from a position of weakness. He was not opposed to negotiations, and in his second term he was a very successful negotiator. But this was only after he had restored the strength of the American military, capitalized on American technological and economic advantages, assisted anti-Communist forces around the world, and reversed the West's posture of retreat. Reagan's strategic goal was to force the Soviets to choose: either to stand down from their continuing confrontation with the West, or face increasingly devastating pressures on the home front. He rejected accommodation with the Soviets, on the grounds that it would postpone their day of reckoning between their inherent domestic weakness and their globalist ambitions.

The President made these points frequently in his Cabinet meetings, "How long," he would say, "can the Russians keep on being so belligerent and spending so much on the arms race when they can't even feed their own people?" In his memoirs, he commented on intelligence updates about the condition of the Soviet economy in the early 1980s:

> The latest figures provided additional evidence that it was a basket case, and even if I hadn't majored in economics in college, it would have been plain to me that Communism was doomed as a failed economic system. The situation was so bad that if Western countries got together and cut off credit to it, we could bring it to its knees.

If economics were a major weakness of the Soviet system, he reasoned, it was a huge advantage for our own:

> The great dynamic success of capitalism has given us a powerful weapon in our battle against Communism – money. The Russians could never win the arms race; we could outspend them forever. Moreover, incentives inherent in the capitalist system had given us an industrial base that [meant] we had the capacity to maintain a technological edge on them forever.

The other side of the equation was for the United States and other Western powers to stop bailing the Soviets out of their economic difficulties through subsidized credit, one-sided business deals, and technology transfer. As Reagan observed, he wanted a coordinated Western policy in which "none of us would subsidize the Soviet economy or the Soviet military expansion by offering preferential trading terms or easy credit." He also wanted to restrain the flow of products and technology that would increase Soviet military capabilities. This was the principal motive behind the battle over the Siberian pipeline, and also behind the systematic effort of the Pentagon's office on technology transfer, to impede the flow of Western computers, precision machinery, microelectronics, and other militarily useful systems to the East. The coordinated effort (headed by Stephen Bryen) at the Department of Defense to curtail such transfers, both from the United States and from third world countries receiving our technology, was one of the great unsung successes of the Reagan era.

A vivid example of the Reagan strategy in action was the liberation of Poland, which presaged the disintegration of the other Communist regimes of eastern Europe. This was among the earliest of test cases for the President's effort to coordinate economic, technological, and diplomatic factors against the Soviets and their clients – and it turned out to be a momentous success.

In December 1981, the government of General Wojciech Jaruzelski declared martial law in Poland, cracking down on the protests of the Solidarity labor union headed by Lech Walesa. Here, indeed, was the face of the "Evil Empire," and it prompted a strong response from Reagan. The nature of that response was twofold: to provide material and moral support to Walesa's freedom movement, and to put the economic squeeze on Jaruzelski and his Soviet mentors.

In this area the President had a powerful ally. Reagan conducted this effort in concert with Pope John Paul II, himself a native of Poland, whom the President greatly admired and with whom he saw eye to eye concerning the Jaruzelski crackdown. The Administration shared intelligence data on the situation with the Vatican, making certain that their policies were on the same wavelength. The President conferred directly with the Pope, while others in the administration worked closely with Catholic Church officials.

The main elements of this strategy were to keep Solidarity alive through financial aid, clandestine radios, underground newspapers, and the like. Much of this was done jointly with the AFL-CIO, which had a strong and obvious interest in helping sustain the Solidarity union. At the same time, sanctions against the Polish regime – and against the Soviets – added to the pressure on the Communists. Administration opposition to the Siberian pipeline, and to other economic dealings with the Soviets, was integral to this campaign.

It was a carefully calibrated effort, designed to keep the opposition viable and the Communists on the defensive, without provoking the kind of violent clashes that had previously led to tragic outcomes in Poland, East Germany, Hungary, and Czechoslovakia. The object was to bring irresistible forces to bear that would exploit the political and economic weakness of the Communist regime – exactly as Reagan had envisioned in his many statements on the topic. Key players in the Polish drama included CIA director William Casey, National Security Advisers Richard Allen and William Clark, and Richard Pipes of the National Security Council.

In the end, Solidarity did survive, and the Jaruzelski government backed down in stages from its hard-line posture. In 1987, the Pope traveled to his native land, where he was acclaimed by millions of his co-religionists and countrymen, to give his personal backing to Solidarity. The days of Communist rule in Poland were numbered, and the other tottering dominoes of eastern Europe would soon follow in its wake – as would, eventually, the dictatorship of the USSR itself.

The battle over SDI was another important example of Reagan's strategy. Reagan thought that the US should exploit its technological advantages here, not unilaterally restrain them as most liberals were recommending. He favored SDI on its own merits because he wanted to move away from a deterrence strategy that relied on nuclear weapons. He was also convinced that US missile defenses would bankrupt the Soviet Union, and force it to abandon the struggle. This is essentially what happened. Even though Gorbachev himself attempted to contend otherwise (as in his book, *Perestroika*), considerable testimony from the Soviet standpoint confirms Reagan's judgment. Some of this appears in the reporting of Don Oberdorfer of the *Washington Post*, who closely tracked Soviet attitudes on Cold War issues from 1983 to 1987. On a 1984 trip to Moscow, for instance, Oberdorfer reported that when asked what were the most important questions facing the country, "nearly all of the 12 Soviet officials or journalists whom I met named the internal management or economy of the USSR." He quotes a former KGB official, assailing Reagan's policies, as saying, "You are trying to destroy our economy, to interfere with our trade, to overwhelm and make us inferior in the strategic field." Oberdorfer similarly quoted Soviet foreign minister Andrei Gromyko as telling former Senator George McGovern that Reagan and his aides "want to cause trouble. They want to weaken the Soviet system. They want to bring it down." Such concerns became more acute, Oberdorfer notes, when Mikhail Gorbachev came to power the following year: "Gorbachev and his new team were more conscious than their predecessors of the economic troubles of the country, induced in large part by massive military spending."

Plate 17 Ronald Reagan and Mikhail Gorbachev – the two "great communicators" – in Moscow's Red Square in 1988 (*opposite*).
(Library of Congress.)

These concerns were made official and overt at the Twenty-Seventh Party Congress of the Soviet Communist party in March 1986, which declared that "without an acceleration of the country's economic and social development, it will be impossible to maintain our position on the international scene."

The final straw for the Soviets, as the President foresaw, was SDI. Oberdorfer quotes Gorbachev advisor Aleksandr Yakovlev as saying, "We understood that it was a new stage, a new turn in the armaments race." If SDI were not stopped, "we would have to start our own program, which would be tremendously expensive and unnecessary. And this [would bring] further exhaustion of the country." For this reason, SDI became the focal point of US-Soviet negotiations, at Geneva in 1985 and at Reykjavik in 1986.

At Reykjavik, Gorbachev agreed to reduce by half, and eventually eliminate entirely, all intercontinental and intermediate missiles – but only on the condition that the United States abandon SDI. By all reports, Secretary of State George Shultz and others in the US delegation were more than willing to make the trade. Had Reagan been the passive creature popularly depicted, the offer would have been accepted on the spot, and SDI would have been eliminated. But Gorbachev – and just about everyone else – had greatly underestimated Reagan's comprehension of, and perseverance on, this issue. President Reagan understood the relevant factors concerning SDI just as well as, or better than, Gorbachev, and he was not about to trade it away, even for so enticing an offer as that extended by the Soviet leader. Since SDI threatened no one, Reagan realized that there was nothing incompatible with maintaining it as a defense while eliminating offensive weapons. So why insist on its removal?

Reagan also knew that the Soviets had a lengthy history of evading arms agreements. In a world devoid of missile defenses, and with everyone else disarmed, this meant that a power possessing even one offensive missile could exert irresistible blackmail. SDI was an insurance policy against that possibility, and Reagan was not about to give it up. As he put it:

> After everything had been decided, or so I thought, Gorbachev threw us a curve. With a smile on his face, he said, "This all depends, of course, on you giving up SDI." I realized he had brought me to Iceland with one purpose: to kill the Strategic Defense Initiative. He must have known from the beginning he was going to bring it up at the last minute. "The meeting is over," I said. "Let's go … we're leaving."

In global-strategic terms this was Reagan's finest hour – and arguably the one that conclusively won the Cold War for the West.

The President, going one-on-one with Gorbachev, not only avoided the trap set for him, but effectively turned the tables, strengthening rather than weakening the US commitment to SDI. Gorbachev must have known that he had gambled, and lost.

The loss had important economic consequences. As Chief of Staff Donald Regan, an important strategist for the President's early summits with Gorbachev, later put it: "To stay in the arms race, the Russians had to spend a lot more money because President Reagan had committed the United States, with all its wealth and all its technical capacity, to developing SDI, a defensive system that made the entire Soviet missile force useless.... This meant that Reagan had been dealt the winning hand."

Realizing that Reagan would not give up SDI or Western strength, Gorbachev soon began to abandon the struggle – as Reagan had predicted the Soviets eventually would. Indeed, the election of George Bush, who had been Reagan's Vice-President, was followed almost immediately by Gorbachev's December 1988 announcement at the United Nations that he was ordering a unilateral cutback of 500,000 men from the Soviet armed services and the withdrawal of some tank divisions from eastern Europe. Gorbachev himself put it this way in a luncheon with President Reagan and President-elect Bush: "I'm not doing this for show ... I'm doing this because I need to. I'm doing this because there's a revolution taking place in my country."

From a post-Cold War perspective, the main principles of the Reagan program may seem self-evident. Viewing the rubble of the Berlin Wall, the upheavals that have transformed eastern Europe, and the internal collapse of the Soviet regime, hardly anyone can doubt that Communism was indeed an "Evil Empire" and a failed economic system. Such points have been affirmed by the former leaders of the Communist world itself. Yet at the time Reagan was making these statements and pursuing these policies there was nothing self-evident about them. On the contrary, he was roundly attacked both for his general analysis of the situation, and for nearly all the specific steps he took in carrying out his policy – the defense buildup, INF deployments, aid to anti-Communist resistance forces, curtailment of technology transfer, SDI.

Even in the aftermath of the Communist collapse Reagan critics were reluctant to credit President Reagan with the accuracy of his vision or the correctness of his policy. Many discussions of the Communist débâcle completely ignore the impact of the Reagan strategy, attributing the demise of the "Evil Empire" to a change of heart on the part of the Communists or to unnamed forces that somehow brought about the toppling of the system. The collapse of socialism and Communism in Russia and eastern Europe has weakened Russia's capacity to reinforce and buttress the embryo socialist regimes and political parties in Cuba, Latin America, the Caribbean and much of Africa. The map of the world, thanks in part to Ronald Reagan, is now very different.

Reagan himself became a friend of Gorbachev. He knew that Gorbachev remained a dedicated Communist, but he thought the Soviet leader was different from his predecessors in sincerely wanting a better relationship with the Free World and in understanding many of the fallacies of Marxism-Leninism. Reagan frequently observed that Gorbachev was the first Soviet leader he had known who did not seek the establishment of a one-world Communist state. Reagan also felt that, although Gorbachev was not necessarily a believer, deep down the Soviet leader was influenced by his Christian upbringing.

Former British Prime Minister Margaret Thatcher knew Gorbachev and Reagan well. She said Gorbachev was a man we could do business with, but she didn't credit him with the collapse of Communism. That honor was due to Ronald Reagan, whose foreign policy accomplishments she summed up at a 1991 Heritage Foundation dinner in Washington: "He won the Cold War without firing a shot."[12]

4 MRS KIRKPATRICK

For the first term of the Reagan Presidency, Jeane Kirkpatrick played a key role in the development and the application of Reagan's foreign policy. It is a well-known fact that Ronald Reagan's interest in Mrs Kirkpatrick began when her now historic article, "Dictatorships and double standards," was brought to his attention. Ensuing personal conversations between the two only strengthened the bond between them with respect to the proper place of the United States in the world of nations.

It thus came as no surprise when Jeane Kirkpatrick became one of President Reagan's very early appointments at high level in government. She was appointed to the vital post of United States Permanent Representative to the United Nations (1981–5) and also to the Cabinet and National Security Council. Inevitably, by the

[12] Margaret Thatcher, *The Downing Street Years* (London, Harper Collins, 1993), p. 813.

nature of all three roles, she found herself deeply involved in foreign affairs. It is fair to say that her lifelong academic-scholarly interest in political science was brought to a splendid practical fruition in her ambassadorial status in New York and Washington.

Perhaps Mrs Kirkpatrick is best known in Britain because of the ambiguous position she took in June 1982 on the Falklands crisis. After supporting a British veto on the UN Security Council resolution condemning the British reaction to the Argentinian invasion of the Falklands, she then said that had instructions from Alexander Haig, then US secretary of state, arrived in time, she would not have condemned but abstained, indicating a certain ambiguity not only in her own position but in that of the American government. This ambiguity was not of her doing, yet it indicates the underlying ambiguity of the US when the interests of her long-time ally, Britain, conflict with those of the Third World, whose "arena" the UN has become.

Mrs Kirkpatrick was a professor of politics at Georgetown University in Washington, a resident scholar at the American Enterprise Institute – which is to the right of center in the American spectrum – and a Democrat when she came to the President's notice. She had, however, written widely and her articles expressed views he endorsed. This was especially true of her article in *Commentary* (November 1979) critical of Jimmy Carter's policies. She helped to found the Coalition for a Democratic Majority, a group of Conservative Democrats. Although in 1976 still a supporter of Jimmy Carter, she became critical of his foreign policy thereafter, and during President Reagan's campaign in 1980 she became a member of his foreign policy advisory board. On his victory in November 1980 she became his appointee as US Permanent Representative to the UN.

In her book *The Reagan Phenomenon*, Jeane Kirkpatrick collects addresses on a wide range of subjects inside the UN as well as outside it, and on each of them she is at once informed, incisive, and challenging.[13] Read at a sitting, they throw a fresh light on the significance of the change of direction in the US in 1980: that election was more than a change of President, but one of those elections that is truly a turning point – a "realigning election" in the jargon of the political science profession, similar to that of 1932 when Franklin Roosevelt was elected. It was evident not only in Reagan's own election but in the scale of Republican success

[13] Jeane Kirkpatrick, *The Reagan Phenomenon* (American Enterprise Institute, 1981).

in the Senate, giving it control of that body for the first time in more than two decades; in the defeat of many conspicuous liberal Democrats; and in the election of Republicans to state governorships and to state legislatures. There was a new grouping of interest blocs, a new Republican coalition similar to the reconstitution of the Democratic party at the onset of the depression. In Kirkpatrick's view, the 1980 election marked the end of the New Deal era in domestic affairs and the end of the Vietnam era in foreign affairs. It was the end of détente, and an indication that US foreign policy was a foreign policy of peace through strength and resolution.

A number of themes run through the book. Ambassador Kirkpatrick deals repeatedly with human rights and she rightly and courageously condemns the hypocrisy of much that is said on human rights in the UN.

> In my government's view, it is entirely appropriate that the agencies of the UN should condemn the spirit and the practice of apartheid and deplore its human consequences. But ... The human rights agencies of the UN were silent while three million Cambodians died in Pol Pot's murderous Utopia. The human rights agencies of the UN were silent while a quarter of a million Ugandans died at the hands of Idi Amin. The human rights organizations of the UN have been silent about thousands of Soviet citizens denied equal rights, equal protection of the law, denied the right to think, write, publish, work freely or to emigrate to some place of their own choosing.

It is a sad comment on the UN that recent American delegates such as Daniel Moynihan and now Jeane Kirkpatrick have had to say such things in the councils of the UN, but at least they have had the courage to do so. She, like her predecessor (now a Senator for New York), has not been afraid to stand alone. She is scornful of rhetoric about rights, emphatic about the value of constitutions and institutions rather than words.

In the book, she ranges widely, from Africa to Israel and repeatedly to the problems of Latin America. She identifies in a fresh and vigorous fashion the various power blocs in the UN, and not least the role of the new states in the NAM group, the Non-Aligned Movement. She is under no illusions. Even if the refugee program and the work of the specialized agencies of the UN are impressive, the organization is in "a profound and deepening crisis." Its denunciations are often matters of rhetoric and ritual. Its debates are intensely ideological. The US and Israel are always picked out for criticism, even though the US bears the cost of at least a quarter of the budget. Everything is predictable and politicized.

This is a stimulating and valuable book, the work of an activist and participant that nevertheless has about it the qualities of scholarship and objectivity.

But just as there is variety and diversity, there is also unity here. The unity springs of course from the author's long scholarly concern with national and international problems. But this unity is engendered also by Ambassador Kirkpatrick's extraordinary ability to fuse, to give creative union to the moral on the one hand and the strategic on the other. She believes deeply in the kind of values which have lighted up so much of America's history for more than two centuries. She has a passionate regard for human rights everywhere in the world, and writes of these repeatedly. She detests police states irrespective of ideological basis and seeks with every reasonable power to advance the cause of human rights even in those authoritarian nations with which the United States has and must have alliances or understandings of one kind or other. She is a pluralist in her view of the world, and knows full well that what is cherished politically in the United States is not now possible for all countries.

As a woman who has always believed in the primacy of words, Kirkpatrick took office in 1981 prepared to test thoroughly one of her favorite propositions: not only ideas but words, too, have consequences. From the outset she insisted that the rhetoric of delegates on the floor of the General Assembly be consistent with their privately expressed opinions and the national interests of their countries. When Kirkpatrick first began to call delegates on their behavior – in writing, on the telephone, or in person (which no previous US ambassador to the UN had done) – they complained loudly on the floor and to the press. Gradually, however, they came to see that the ambassador meant what she said. Those delegates who in private claimed to respect the US, and those delegates whose nations wanted and received assistance from the US, started one by one to match their public behavior with their private sentiments. Civility and moderation rose to levels unparalleled in recent memory.

Contrary to the high-minded assumptions of the UN's founders, world politics UN-style is a lot like old-style American urban politics – a matter of power, interests, skills, affections. As the ambassador liked to point out, the rough-and-tumble of Chicago or turn-of-the-century Jersey City makes a reasonably good model for understanding the dynamics of the UN (which helps explain why a portrait of Richard Daley hung on the wall of her office at the US Mission). Like any traditional big city mayor, Kirkpatrick knew when to cajole, when to twist arms. She traveled to places like Burundi and Rwanda and demanded "Why are you doing this? This is a terrible way to behave." Such unorthodox diplomacy paid off. In particular, the more moderate Third World delegations were encouraged in their moderation and now appear glad to play a more responsible role. Condemnation of the United States for its "imperialist" and "colonial" domination of Puerto Rico, another recurrent UN theme, came up neither in UN committees nor in the plenary sessions. Even more significant, Nicaragua withdrew an anti-American resolution when it could not round up sufficient votes for its adoption.

By UN standards, Kirkpatrick had done the impossible. Her willingness to state US positions forcefully and directly and at times to be confrontational paid dividends. She strengthened the US role at the UN, slowed the pace of attacks on Western values and institutions, and attempted to bring the UN back to the original purposes of its Charter. This contrasts sharply with the defeatist policies pursued at the UN by her Carter administration predecessor, Andrew Young and Donald McHenry. For example, Kirkpatrick declared to the UN that the US would no longer wear the "kick me" sign at the organization, and argued convincingly that those who use the UN as a political "playpen" demean the organization. She therefore set out not only to argue passionately and persuasively for US interests, concerns, and values, but also, and more importantly, to get the votes needed to actually win some key decisions within the organization. As such, the Kirkpatrick years at the UN left the US an important legacy and taught the US valuable lessons about how to conduct US diplomacy successfully in international organizations.

Kirkpatrick also identified a number of trends at the UN which not only work against US interests, but prevent the UN from fulfilling the worthwhile goals of its Charter. Among these trends were:

the use of the UN by the group of 77 [the Third World bloc] and the Soviet bloc to attack the free enterprise system in general, and multinational corporations in particular, as the source of the world's "economic ills";

the "globalization" of world problems by bringing local or regional issues to the General Assembly, forcing every nation to take a stand;

the UN's support for terrorist organizations and the elevation of those organizations, particularly the Palestine Liberation Organization (PLO) and Southwest African Peoples Organization (SWAPO), to quasi-member status;

a "double standard" by which the UN majority practices "selective indignation" over alleged human rights violations by the US, Israel, South Africa, and other Western states, while so often overlooking outrages committed by socialist and Communist countries.[14]

The striking characteristic of her stance was its toughness. On September 28, 1981, the so-called "non-aligned" countries issued a communiqué criticizing the US by name for a host of the globe's political and economic ills, Kirkpatrick promptly (October 6) sent a letter to most of the UN ambassadors of the non-aligned nations, expressing surprise and dismay at the communiqué, and asking each of them whether the statement actually represented the views of their country. The letter noted that the Soviet Union, which was conducting or supporting wars in Afghanistan, Cambodia, and Chad, was not mentioned even once in the document, while the US was condemned nine times. Many of the "non-aligned" delegates were dumbfounded that anyone would care what the communiqué said, or that any US official would even read such a document. When Kirkpatrick made it clear that the US was paying attention to what happens at the UN, many nations began acting more carefully when it came to offending Washington. Kirkpatrick had gotten the message across. Kirkpatrick and her team forcefully confronted the Soviets and their clients on their human rights abuses and their continuing effort to export war, revolution, and unrest. She also began to confront the Soviets on their abuses of the UN Charter within the UN secretariat.

Kirkpatrick and her deputies made equally strong statements on the Soviet war and occupation in Afghanistan and the Vietnamese aggression against the people of Cambodia. For the fifth year in a row in each case, the General Assembly voted to condemn the occupation of those countries by "foreign forces," without condemning by name the Soviets in Afghanistan or the Vietnamese in Cambodia. In 1984 Kirkpatrick successfully opposed Moscow's candidates for the non-permanent members of the Security Council. The Soviets sponsored Outer Mongolia and Ethiopia, but through the exercise of what one of Kirkpatrick's advisors has called "good machine politics," the UN successfully pushed the election of Thailand and Madagascar for the two vacant seats.

More important, perhaps, was Kirkpatrick's determination to expose Soviet use of the UN Secretariat as a base of espionage

[14] Jeane J. Kirkpatrick, *Defining a Conservative Foreign Policy* (Washington DC, The Heritage Foundation, 1993).

operations against the US and as a center for dissemination of Soviet propaganda. Kirkpatrick also brought to the attention of the UN Secretary-General and the media the fact that the Soviet bloc, through inordinate influence within the UN Secretariat, controlled important staff appointments and the daily agenda of UN conferences, agencies, and meetings.

During Kirkpatrick's years at the UN, Israel dominated the UN agenda. Of the Security Council's 88 sessions in 1982, for example, 46 were on issues related to Israel. In the 37th General Assembly in 1982 and its seven main committees, debates on the Middle East consumed over one-third of the delegates' time and led to 44 resolutions. The 39th General Assembly produced 36 Israel-related resolutions. Kirkpatrick made US firmness in the defense of Israel a focal point of her tenure at the United Nations. Not only did she work to ensure US opposition to attacks on Israel, but also with lawmakers in Washington, including Senator Robert Kasten and Congressmen Jack Kemp and Stephen Solarz, to enact legislation tying Israel's status within the UN to that of the US: if Israel were driven out, says the legislation, then the US would leave too.

Kirkpatrick enjoyed significantly more success than her Carter administration predecessors in holding down the growth of the regular UN budget. Even though the 39th General Assembly approved a revised appropriation for the current two-year budget (1984–5) of $1.61 billion, with the US and 16 other nations opposing the resolution, this budget still represents less than a 10 percent increase over the 1982–3 appropriation. Indeed, during Kirkpatrick's tenure at the UN, the average increase in the regular biennial UN budget has been around 13 percent. On the other hand, the average increase for the UN regular budget for the biennial 1978–9 and 1980–1, during the tenure of ambassadors Andrew Young and Donald McHenry at the UN, was approximately 30 percent. The reduction in UN regular budget growth in recent years derived significantly from Reagan administration economic policies, which virtually eliminated inflation in the US and strengthened the dollar throughout the world. Yet Kirkpatrick's effectiveness in articulating Reagan administration policies, and her tenacity in holding down UN spending, have played equally important roles.

In contrast to her predecessors, Kirkpatrick had the advantage of longevity at the UN. She served in the role of US Permanent Representative for longer than any other ambassador since Adlai Stevenson – 50 months in all, almost three times the average tenure of US representatives at the world body. This extended term allowed her to become more effective at the UN and in the Department of State.

Upon arrival at the UN, Kirkpatrick felt that she would have to overcome no small degree of bias against her as a woman. She has often said that whenever a woman is involved in non-traditional roles, she is likely to encounter certain kinds of discrimination. Kirkpatrick also soon found that she would have to overcome a legacy of acquiescence and timidity left by her predecessors. The Carter administration in particular allowed UN debate to depict the US as the principal source of instability and injustice in the world. The posture of UN ambassadors Young and McHenry seemed to signal to the world that the US was ready to abdicate its role as defender of the free enterprise system, of Israel, and of its other allies and friends. Young and McHenry were also reluctant to criticize Soviet and Third World human rights abuses. On numerous occasions, moreover, they indicated that the US was willing to join the UN majority in calling for the adoption of a long list of new "orders," most notably, the New World Information and Communication Order (NWICO), a UN blueprint for restricting press freedoms throughout the world.

Because of a policy characterized in part by defeatism and self-deprecation, the US found itself under attack, outvoted and outmaneuvered in the UN. The attacks against the US and the West continued for some time after Kirkpatrick arrived in New York. Realizing that these attacks were not going unnoticed outside the UN, however, Kirkpatrick strengthened the prevailing image of the US and eventually reasserted US moral and political leadership in the organization.

Jeane Kirkpatrick has demonstrated that the US need not always be defeated at the UN nor always on the defensive. She demonstrated too the continuing validity of key basic principles in the conduct of foreign policy:

that international relations depend above all on the relative power of nations;

that the power of international affairs is cumulative – the more you have, the more you get and vice versa;

that the relative position of the US and the Soviet Union depended in very important measure on US success in dealing with non-Communist nations in the world;

that US influence with other nations depends largely on hopes of gains and fears of losses; and finally that US effectiveness and power in organizations such as as the United Nations require absolutely that the US believe in itself and have confidence in its own values and experience.[15]

5 AN ASSESSMENT

Reagan's two-term presidency was remarkably successful. He ended the Cold War, and predicted – indeed accomplished – the collapse of Communism. His "biggest disappointment," he admitted, was his failure to cut federal spending, and to balance the budget. "I just didn't deliver as much to the people as I'd promised."

Happily for him, a President lives, first and last, from day to day, in what John F. Kennedy called "the drumfire of daily crises." His first tasks are to ensure that the laws be faithfully executed, that there is peace and order on the street, that American lives and property at home and abroad are secure, that his people can sleep quietly in their beds at night with no terrorist knocks on the door. This is enough, indeed much, to ask. But when American lives are threatened – moral questions or not – his duty is clear: he must protect them. Carter failed to do so in Iran in 1979–80, however hard he tried. Reagan moved fast in Grenada in 1983, and with success.

Foreign policy was Ronald Reagan's primary theme, in which he has always been consistent. His attitude towards the threat of Communism reflected his experiences as a young man in Hollywood. While he had always sought less government, tax cuts, and the reduction of federal power, these objectives were never at the expense of defense or vigilance in protecting American interests. On the day he took office the American diplomats in Teheran were freed, after a year's imprisonment. He vowed that nothing like that insult must occur again. He was outspoken in his criticism of Russian expansion in Afghanistan. He put Marines into the peacekeeping force in the Middle East in the belief that Syria, with its SAM-5s and SS21 missiles targeted on Israeli cities, was acting there as a Russian surrogate. He gave indirect airpower aid to Chad when Libya invaded, recognizing that Libya too was acting as a center where terrorists were financed and trained; US reconnaissance planes were regularly on patrol over the Gulf of Sirte. This world view, with the awareness that Russia could act by deputy, made

[15] Ambassador Jeane J. Kirkpatrick, Address to the American Farm Bureau Federation, Honolulu, Hawaii, Jan. 9, 1985.

him alert to the international threat that terrorism, as well as Communism, posed in the 1980s.

All of this reinforced his conviction that the nuclear defense program should continue, and that if there were to be nuclear arms reductions in US power and in NATO and Europe, which his diplomats sought at the Geneva talks, it must only be because the Eastern bloc would genuinely reduce its armaments in step with the West, and that any agreement reached be made from strength, not weakness. An arms control agreement with the USSR – yes, if possible; but not if in attaining it US security was itself imperiled. The horror of nuclear war was not in question. As a deterrent, however, it is its very horror that made it effective in securing peace.

By highlighting the evidence of Soviet expansion over the previous two decades, President Reagan managed to forge a bipartisan coalition on Capitol Hill. Since there were 243 Democrats elected in 1980 against 192 Republicans in the House of Representatives, he needed the support of some Democrats – usually drawn from the more conservative Southerners, the so-called "boll-weevils." In the 1982 elections, the House stayed firmly Democratic (269D to 166R). The President succeeded in "selling" his weapons program to Congress. From 1980 to 1983 the US defense appropriation rose by two-thirds, to $245 billion. The B-1 bomber program abandoned by President Carter was revived, the MX Missile was put into production, the target was set of a 600-ship navy.

The Democrats criticized the vehemence of the President's anti-Russian stand, and the dangers of a nuclear war if the two super powers became involved in a conflict over, say, a third country's policies in the Middle East or in Central America. More critical voices were heard from Congressmen about US involvement in Lebanon and the renewed alliance with Israel. The withdrawal of the US Marines from Beirut in February 1984, after suffering heavy casualties (246 dead, 150 injured) in a "peacekeeping" operation, was a blow to the President's prestige, and to the standing of his secretary of state, George Schultz.

The hostile view of Reagan's foreign policy is that he saw it all as an aspect of the East-West rivalry of the two superpowers; all questions usually summarized as Third World questions, or North-South questions, were for him only aspects of a continuing Cold War. To Liberals, Reagan was a John Wayne, or Davey Crockett, or Jim Bowie at the Alamo, a primitive, "trigger-happy" fire-eater. President Reagan was culpable here, in that during his campaign and after his election, his, and his first secretary of state Alexander

Haig's, rhetoric about the threats from Russia, and of the need for nuclear weapons for defense, produced waves of alarm, and activated the "peace" movements in Europe. American opposition to the Russian gas pipeline project lost it goodwill in Europe. And quick changes at the top (two secretaries of state and three national security advisers in three years) suggested uncertainty and jitteriness.

But the collapse of Communism in and after 1989 indicated Reagan's remarkable foresight and skill, with which few other Presidents can compare. Americans could walk tall again. In effect, Reagan transformed Russia from enemy to ally. Since the dialogue between Reagan and Gorbachev began, Russia shed the Soviet empire, dissolved the Soviet Union, agreed to sweeping cuts in conventional and nuclear forces, reduced military spending significantly, cast off the yoke of totalitarianism, and installed a democratically elected government. As a result, Russia can no longer be considered America's enemy. It is not yet, of course, an ally. Russia's leaders are taking a fresh look at the world, redefining Russian national security while at the same time struggling to keep their new democracy afloat. If they succeed, a new Russia can emerge. It can be a democratic Russia fully integrated into the West. If they falter, an assortment of ex-Communists, ultra-nationalists, and disgruntled military officers seems ready to return Russia to the militarism of the past 70 years. It is thus in America's interests to help Russia, the world's newest nuclear superpower, safely to make the transition from enemy to ally.

The price of peace, however, is always eternal vigilance. For, as the Cold War ended, chaos followed in the Soviet republics west of the Urals and in its neighbors. As the threat of nuclear war receded, conventional war made a comeback, often with the use of Soviet weapons; witness Dalmatia and Bosnia, Somalia, Cambodia, Afghanistan, and the Gulf. Moreover, weapons – rifles, machine guns, landmines and hand grenades – were available of ever greater potency and destructive capacity; many of them were formerly in Russian hands. Russia has over 18,000 nuclear warheads; its roughly 35,000 tanks make its land army Eurasia's most formidable. American security is tied inextricably to decisions made in Moscow and will remain so for the forseeable future. Whether Russia completes the transition from enemy to ally will depend on how its new leaders define their nation's national security requirements. Central, too, will be their success in demilitarizing Russian society, diverting resources from an all-consuming military-industrial complex, and bringing a smaller military firmly under civilian control.

Moreover, in November 1993 Moscow reversed a longstanding policy, agreed by President Leonid Brezhnev in 1982, which renounced first use of nuclear weapons and stated in a new military doctrine that Russia reserved the right to launch a nuclear attack first under certain conditions. General Pavel Grachev, the Russian defense minister, said the main focus would be to defend Russia and resolve regional conflicts. He said that, although Russia would not use nuclear weapons against any non-nuclear state which had signed the 1968 Nuclear Non-Proliferation Treaty, there were two exceptions; "The first is the case when a state which has an agreement with a nuclear state launches an armed attack on Russia, its armed forces and Russia's allies;" the second would be in the event of an alliance of a non-nuclear state and a nuclear state attacking Russia. "As for those states which have nuclear weapons, the doctrine says nothing," he said, implying Russia did not rule out first use of nuclear weapons against another nuclear state.

The new Russian military doctrine finally dropped the language of the Cold War – drafts in 1990 and 1992 implied that NATO was the enemy – but still indicates a desire to be a strong military power with a capability to intervene beyond Russia's borders. General Grachev said the post-Communist military would be geared towards controlling regional conflicts, which he described as the main threat to global stability: "The chance of them appearing in certain regions is growing. We must halt them earlier." His statement was seen as an attempt to consolidate support for the idea of the army as peacekeepers, asserting Russia as a strong regional power. The first stage of the new doctrine, which runs to 1996, will concentrate on creating more mobile armed forces, cutting manpower from 2 million to about 1.3 million, and completing the withdrawal from Eastern Europe.

6 THE REAGAN LEGACY

The 1980s were a second Gilded Age, in which many Americans made and spent money abundantly. Reagan's eight-year presidency had sparked the creation of 19 million new jobs. So many Americans had been making so much money that the term "millionaire" became meaningless. A Georgia marketing expert, Thomas J. Stanley, counted almost 100,000 "decamillionaires" – people worth over $10 million. Back in 1960 there hadn't been that many plain-vanilla *millionaires.*[16] In 1988, approximately 1.3 million individual Americans were millionaires by assets, up from 574,000 in 1980, 180,000 in 1972, 90,000 in 1964, and just 27,000 in 1953. Even adjusted for inflation, the number of millionaires had doubled between the late 1970s and the late 1980s. Meanwhile, the number of billionaires, according to *Forbes* magazine, went from a handful in 1981 to 26 in 1986 and 49 in 1987. As of late 1988, *Forbes* put that year's number of billionaires at 52, and *Fortune's* September assessment hung the billion-dollar label on 51 American families. No parallel upsurge of riches had been seen since the late nineteenth century, the era of the Vanderbilts, Morgans, and Rockefellers.

And it was equally conspicuous. Rising luxury consumption and social ambition prompted *New York* magazine to observe that for the third time in 125 years, "a confluence of economic conditions has created *arrivistes* in such great numbers and with such immense wealth that they formed a critical mass and created a whole new social order with its own new rules of acceptable behavior." A second circumstance was that wages – the principal source of middle- and lower-class dollars – had stagnated through 1986 even while disinflation, deregulation, and commercial opportunity were escalating the return on capital. Most of the Reagan decade, to put it mildly, was a heyday for unearned income as rents, dividends, capital gains, and interest gained relative to wages and salaries as a source of wealth and increasing economic inequality.

Meanwhile Reagean's critics described another country. In their eyes the 1980s were a last national fling with credit-card economics, a gaudy orgy of unprecedented domestic and international indebtedness, luxury imports, *nouveau riche* consumption and upper-bracket tax reduction, all indulged in with the greatest recklessness while beggars filled the streets and the average family's real disposable income declined towards a dimming future. So television audiences lost their early-1980s fascination with the rich; and many conservatives became defensive about great wealth, wanton money-making, and greed.

As always in US history, the economic changes were reflected in geography. The 1980s boom in the Boston-Washington megalopolis, coupled with hard times on the farm and in the Oil Patch, produced a familiar conservative economic geography – a comparative shift of wealth toward the two coasts, and toward income groups already well off.

[16] Thomas J. Stanley, *Marketing to the Affluent* (Dow Jones Irwin, Homewood, Ill., 1988).

The Reagan boom did not benefit the Middle West. In the thinly populated Dakotas, farmland lost $10 billion to $15 billion in value, a much sharper *per capita* decline. Estimates by the Conference Board suggested that the total value of farmers' land in the United States declined from $712 billion in 1980 to $392 billion in 1986. By 1988, however, prices were starting to reflate; but by 1988 fewer farmers could benefit from this recovery, as many had left their farms, voluntarily or through foreclosure. The US farm population dropped to under 5 million in 1987, down from over 6 million in 1980 and almost 9 million in 1975, as prosperous, larger farmers replaced poor, smaller ones. By 1987, speculators and other absentee investors accounted for about 31 percent of farm transactions, up from 23 percent in 1983. As landholdings concentrated, thousands of farmhouses were torn down, thousands of miles of fence ripped out. In autumn 1987 Don Paarlberg, a former senior official in the Eisenhower, Nixon, and Ford Agriculture Departments, feared a social revolution as he saw outside capital – from doctors, lawyers, businessmen, and wealthy investors – flooding in to buy up agricultural holdings as farmland prices stabilized. "We are drifting toward a structure of agriculture which approaches what we twice [after the Revolution and in the Civil War] previously rejected – a wealthy, hereditary landowning class, with new entrants almost ruled out unless they are well-to-do.

For 1988, income data showed a Middle West recovery, but it was most pronounced in the industrial Great Lakes area, where the devalued dollar had revived manufacturing. Though the Rust Belt was beginning to rejoin the "bicoastal economy," the small-town Great Plains remained devastated. In the meantime, the rise of the service industries was also redrawing the American economic map in historically familiar ways. Most of the benefits came within metropolitan areas, fairness, and social justice. Excesses in one direction have always bred a countermovement in the other direction, and the Reagan era certainly had its excesses.

Tax cuts certainly benefited many individuals, but at a grave price. Growing federal budget and trade deficits forced the United States to borrow heavily from overseas, and after 1985 the value of the dollar plummeted, resulting in an extraordinary realignment of world wealth and purchasing power – and possibly standards of living. For the first time in 70 years America had even become a net international debtor – an extraordinary transformation from the world's largest creditor nation to the world's largest debtor. Conservative insistence that it really did not matter rang increasingly hollow as US international indebtedness passed $269 billion at the end of 1986, reached $358 billion at the end of 1987, and was projected to exceed a trillion dollars by 1992. Between 1985 and 1987 the total national assets of the United States climbed from $30.6 trillion to $36.2 trillion, while those of Japan, just $19.6 trillion in 1985, soared to $43.7 trillion in 1987 an almost unimaginable transfer of relative wealth and purchasing power from the United States to Japan. Opinion polls showed that two-thirds of Americans worried that the US economy by the year 2000 would be dominated by foreign companies. One New York investment banker, Daniel Schwartz, managing director of Ulmer Brothers, even took unintended issue with the President of the United States over the future of the "Rust Belt." He told *Fortune* magazine that Japanese purchases might turn it into the "Sushi Belt".

The 1980s were the triumph of upper America – an ostentatious celebration of wealth, the political ascendancy of the richest third of the population and a glorification of capitalism, free markets, and finance. But while money, greed, and luxury had become the stuff of popular culture, hardly anyone asked why such great wealth had concentrated at the top, and whether this was a result of public policy. Despite the armies of homeless political leaders – even those who professed to care about the homeless – had little to say about the Republican party's historical role, which has been not simply to revitalize US capitalism but to tilt power, policy, wealth, and income toward the richest portions of the population.

In 1984, according to ABC News polls, young voters cast 57 percent of their ballots for Reagan. By 1988, despite the lack of any real effort by the Democrats to target and explain the relative economic decline of young Americans during the 1980s, turnout among 18– to 24–year-old voters declined and the Republican share of their vote for the President dropped to 52 percent. Even so, election-year and post-election polls found young voters much more Republican than the country as a whole, an irony in light of Reagan-era income trends. On economic grounds, the 18– to 24–year-old electorate was a vulnerable Republican constituency. But for the elderly, circumstances improved. During the early 1980s, as inflation-adjusted wages fell, retirees' pensions, especially Social Security, held steady or rose. Part of the explanation was that older voters were using political power to get more money.

By the time of the Democratic and Republican conventions in 1988, the boosterish style of the Reagan era – from entrepreneur worship to roller-coaster stock markets – was already yielding to a more restrained, centrist tone. That was clear in both parties. As summer turned to autumn each groped toward a different successor politics. George Bush presented himself as a low-key activist and reformer, casting an occasional well-bred aspersion toward those who did nothing but pursue money. Both candidates eschewed the values of the *glitterati*. Michael Dukakis, who originally styled himself as the architect of Massachusetts' economic "miracle," assumed a more populist stance by October, but by that time it was too late for him to benefit from Democratic themes of economic discontent.

The reality of the American economy during the 1980s contrasts sharply with much of the rhetoric. The facts show renewed industrial competitiveness and modest growth with equally modest economic gains for most Americans.

The nation did not, as some maintain, "deindustrialize." Real inflation-adjusted manufacturing output rose by 38 percent between 1980 and 1989, and manufacturing output as a percentage of GNP reached 22.6 percent by 1989, compared with 21 percent in 1980. The increase was not confined to consumer goods. Between 1967 and 1989, capital goods production (excluding defense and automobiles) rose from 28 percent to 38 percent of manufacturing production.

True, domestic-based manufacturing employment fell by 6 percent from 1980 to 1990, from 20.3 million jobs to 19.1 million jobs. But that reflected a surge in manufacturing productivity in many industries which enabled the US to be more competitive. US exports of manufactured goods grew by 90 percent between 1986 and 1992, compared with 25 percent for the other members of the Organization for Economic Cooperation and Development. And US manufacturing employment held steady at 30 percent of the world total through 1986.

There have been assertions that workers' average real wages began falling in the early 1970s. What actually happened was a slowdown in their growth, as well as a shift from money wages to more non-wage compensation such as Social Security contributions, health and life insurance, vacation days, and other fringe benefits. Non-wage compensation as a percentage of wages and salaries rose from just under 9 percent in 1960 to nearly 21 percent in 1990. Real total compensation (wages plus benefits), measured in 1959 dollars, rose from $9.61 per hour in 1959 to $16.60 in 1987 and settled at $16.25 per hour in 1990.[17]

[17] See Richard B. McKenzie, "America: what went right," Policy Analysis no. 172 (June 1, 1992), Cato Institute, Washington, DC.

By every measure of prosperity, Reaganomics actually worked. During the 1980s Americans did indeed enjoy an unprecedented economic boom. Reagan's Economic Recovery Tax Act of 1981 set the stage for this record expansion by reducing the tax penalty against business investments and sharply reducing, in three stages, income tax rates for individuals. Once the tax rate reductions were fully phased in, the economy took off.

Not only did Reaganomics produce the longest expansion in America's peacetime history, it did so while simultaneously reducing inflation, a feat that many economists believed could not be accomplished. Reducing marginal tax rates, along with regulatory relief and sound monetary policy, proved to be a potent prescription for an ailing economy. During the Reagan boom, inflation-adjusted GNP rose 32 percent and median family income hit record levels. Thanks to the creation of 20 million new jobs, the proportion of the US population holding jobs reached a new record of 63.1 percent.

Broad statistics, however, do not present a complete picture of the economic situation in the 1980s. The untold story is how low taxes benefited those Americans who traditionally had not enjoyed the fruits of the country's prosperity. Income levels for almost every demographic group had begun to decline sharply in the late 1970s; but once Reagan's policies took hold, the statistics reversed. Inflation-adjusted median household income for black Americans, for instance, jumped by 16.5 percent between 1982 and 1989, after declining by 10.2 percent between 1978 and 1982.[18] It was a hard act to follow.

Reagan is well-known for his description of Communism as an "evil" system. What is less familiar is his characterising "liberal" as "the dreaded L word." More than this: liberals were many, conservatives (especially ex-New Dealers) were few, especially the thinkers among them Indeed if there was a traditional style in American politics it was that of the "court" style, political philosophy as written by the insiders who were the lieutenants, speech-writers

[18] Economists continue to debate what year marks the beginning of Reaganomics. Many use 1981, since that was the year that Reagan actually took office. Others note that the budget for fiscal 1981 already had been signed into law by Jimmy Carter before Reagan was inaugurated; Reagan's first budget was for fiscal 1982. Some economists comment, however, that Reaganomics did not begin until 1983, the first year in which the tax rate reductions were fully phased in. There is no completely accurate answer to this controversy. What it is safe to say, and is supported by the statistics cited in this study, is that after beginning to decline in the late 1970s, most measures of economic well-being recovered in the early 1980s and improved dramatically throughout the decade.

and intimates of FDR, JFK, LBJ and Carter. The most typical of these was A. J. Schlesinger, Jr. He is a historian and political advocate whose ideas and activities have significantly influenced the shape and direction of American liberalism during the past fifty years. A central feature of his ideological perspective is his belief that American history has been marked by alternating periods of conservative and liberal dominance, which he has termed the "tides of national politics." It was a notion that he owed, in the first place, to his father, a distinguished historian himself. Throughout his career, Schlesinger has used the "tides of national politics" to defend the legitimacy and superiority of active liberal government and leadership.

His timing too allowed him to participate at a high level, as aide and as activist in the Kennedy menage. He learnt the importance of leadership and, in a television age, of the magic of, indeed the need for, charisma. Witness his *A Thousand Days*, *John F. Kennedy in the White House*, *The Vital Center: The Politics of Freedom*, and *The Bitter Heritage: Vietnam and American Democracy*.

In the first pages of *The Vital Center*, Schlesinger stressed the need for dynamic leadership in a democracy:

> I was born in 1917. I heard Franklin Roosevelt's first inaugural address as a boy at school, fifteen years old. Since that March day in 1933, one has been able to feel that liberal ideas had access to power in the United States, that liberal purposes, in general, were dominating our national policy. For one's own generation, then, American liberalism has had a positive and confident ring. It has stood for responsibility and achievement, not for frustration and sentimentalism; it has been the instrument of social change, not of private neurosis. During most of my political consciousness this has been a New Deal country. I expect that it will continue to be a New Deal country.

It is a safe deduction from the Reagan years to say that the US is no longer a New Deal country, though Reagan had no "courtly" lieutenant alongside him to chronicle his achievement.[19]

In November 1994, Reagan revealed that he was suffering from Alzheimer's disease, which affects the capacity of the individual to recall the past. In making his statement, he gave it a Hollywood twist: "I now begin the journey that will lead me into the sunset of my life," he wrote. "I know that for America there will always be a bright dawn ahead."

[19] Stephen P. Depoe, *Arthur Schlesinger, Jr., and ,the Ideological History of American Liberalism* (University of Alabama, Tuscaloosa 1994).

17

The Fragmentation of the Dream

1 INTRODUCTION

Americans can no longer assume that tomorrow will be better than today. Their traditional optimism has lost its economic and political roots. In the 1970s came the the industrial restructuring that swept over America's manufacturing centers, and enveloped the Rust belt, or "smokestack America." That old industrial base eroded in the face of greater foreign competition, and as a legacy of inefficient labor and management practices. In the recession of the early 1980s between June 1981 and January 1983, 4.2 million jobs were lost. During the presidential campaign year of 1992 such industrial giants as General Motors, General Electric, IBM, AT&T, Xerox, Unisys, DuPont, and TRW announced major reductions in plant and personnel. The "good jobs" that have traditionally provided the way up for Americans, offering opportunity to purchase homes and to send children to college, while giving health and pension protection for retirement years, are rapidly becoming relics of the past. Now, "temporary" jobs – those with no benefits, no security, and minimal wages – are the way of the future. When Clinton became President in 1992, the government projected that by the year 2000, there would be 35 million such "temp" jobs. Half of all workers, and two-thirds of all women workers, would fall into that category.

Compounding these long-term forces are five other factors. The first involves spending for defense. With the Cold War over by 1990 and the ranks of the permanent military establishment facing reductions of a fourth or more of its strength, a crucial underpinning that has sustained the US economy for nearly half a century

Plate 18 One man's experience of the American Dream. (Library of Congress.)

has been removed. This means further difficult restructuring of industry, and of the high-wage jobs that they carried, upon which a significant sector of the American economy rested, especially in California and the Mid-West. During Clinton's first months as President, other giants cut back drastically: Boeing, McDonnell Douglas, United Technologies, and Sears Roebuck.

The second factor involves the increasingly pessimistic attitudes of the people about their future, especially about the jobs they and their children can expect to have, and notably about the relations between black and white, and indeed among blacks themselves.

In a weekend speech of rare passion and spontaneity in mid-November 1993, President Clinton stood in the Memphis pulpit where Martin Luther King delivered his last sermon, and grieved at the "great crisis of the spirit gripping America today." In Washington alone, 16 blacks had died in the previous nine days, he said, one shot dead as he fled from gunmen with a year-old child in his arms; and Clinton quoted a *Washington Post* story about the capital's black teenagers planning their own funerals. He cited the hard facts that 37,000 Americans a year were shot dead, that gunfire was the leading cause of death among young men, and that 160,000 children avoided school daily for fear of violence. He declared that the great civil rights leader would be appalled if he could return today and see the violence, crime, and social disintegration that have turned America's predominantly black inner cities into killing grounds:

> He would say "I did not live and die to see the American family destroyed. I did not live and die to see 13-year-old boys get automatic weapons and gun down 9-year-olds just for the kick of it. I did not live and die to see young people destroy their own lives with drugs and then build fortunes destroying the lives of others."
>
> He would say "I fought for freedom, but not for the freedom of people to kill each other with reckless abandonment, not for the freedom of children to have children and the fathers of the children to walk away from them and abandon them as if they didn't amount to anything. I fought for people to have the right to work, but not to have whole communities abandoned ... I did not fight for the right of black people to murder other black people with reckless abandonment."

In 1968, the Kerner Commission, which had been set up to look into the causes of the urban riots of the 1960s, warned that America was "moving toward two societies, one black, one white – separate and unequal." Twenty-five years later, a report on the state of black America might arrive at a similar conclusion. For, in effect, there are now two black communities, the middle-class and the poor, and they too are separate and increasingly unequal.

The black middle class is a sizeable minority of the total black population. Estimated at around one-third, the proportion has remained unchanged for the past two decades. What has changed since the mid-1970s is the size of the economic gap between the black rich and the black poor. The top fifth of black families now have incomes which are on average 16 times larger than those in the bottom fifth; for whites, the ratio is 9 to 1. This enormous gulf has opened up because the black rich have become richer and the black poor have become poorer. Around 40 percent of black America lives close to or below the poverty line, and the position of that group has worsened relative to that of the worst-off whites. Yet the other 60 percent of African-Americans have seen their incomes rise faster than those of the top 60 percent of white earners.

The middle class has been the group that has most benefited from civil rights legislation and affirmative action, mainly because they had previously been the most economically disadvantaged by discrimination. Before World War II, 75 percent of black college graduates went into the ministry or education, because teaching and preaching were their only viable options. After the civil rights legislation of the 1960s, horizons were expanded, with immediate and dramatic effect. Seeing a black professor, lawyer, or doctor used to be as rare as sighting a puffin on the streets of London; that is no longer the case.

For the most part, the thriving of the black middle class delights whites. If some blacks are doing so nicely, they reason, America can't be that racist a society after all. And the black inner city poor can have nobody to blame for their plight but themselves. Whites like to think that the black middle class has more in common with the white middle class than with the black poor. There is a stereotypical image of the middle-class family, white or black, which features two cars parked in the drive of a two-story house, kids going off to college, and holidays spent skiing in the Rockies.

But this is a picture that distorts reality more by what it leaves out than by what it reveals. A white family and a black family might be comparable in material terms, but the chances are that they will also differ in important ways. They are, for example, unlikely to live on the same street; or even in the same neighborhood. The United States remains disgracefully segregated, and although this is particularly true for the black urban poor, most of whom live in areas that are 100 percent black, it also affects the middle class.

Moreover, though the black middle-class family and the white middle-class family might have the same income, the black middle-class family is more likely to have two breadwinners, both bringing home a salary of, say, $25,000. In contrast, the white middle-class family might have just one wage-earning adult, earning $50,000. Although there are now blacks in all occupations, for a black family more often than for a white family, a middle class income is likely to represent the sum of the wages of two solid blue-collar jobs.

On a middle-class income, the majority of black families have been able to migrate to the suburbs. This has provoked the accusation that they have abandoned and betrayed their less advantaged brethren in the inner cities. One of the country's leading sociologists, William Julius Wilson, argues that this exodus has severely undermined the value systems of those who are left. The middle class, he claims, were the bedrock of the community and provided important role models as well as essential contacts for those seeking to enter the workforce. It is an odd charge to lay at the door of the black middle class, who have quite understandably sought improved conditions in which to raise their families. No one seems to expect well-off whites to remain or settle in working-class white neighborhoods.[1]

But the most interesting fact about members of the black middle class is how alienated from mainstream society they remain and how their political and social views are often virtually indistinguishable from those held by the black poor. A survey conducted before and after after the acquittal of the police officers accused of beating Rodney King in 1993 showed that blacks with household incomes of over $50,000 were more disillusioned with the justice system, and with society as a whole, than were poorer blacks. Another poll in 1991 put this question: "Looking back over the last ten years, do you think the quality of life has gotten better, stayed about the same, or gotten worse?" Seventy percent of blacks with a college degree thought things had deteriorated, compared with just over half of those without a degree. And yet, in material terms, the quality of life for middle-class blacks has undoubtedly improved, while economic conditions for the poorest have deteriorated.

The third phenomenon is crime itself, as indexed in the size of the prison population. The prison population in the United

[1] William Julius Wilson, *The Declining Significance of Race* (Chicago, University of Chicago Press, 1978), *passim*.

States has passed one million for the first time. A survey by the Justice Department (October 1994) place. America second to Russia in its rate of incarceration and reflects decades of demands for tougher punishments.[2]

The study found that 1,012,851 men and women were in state and federal prisons on June 30, 1994, roughly the population of Phoenix, the country's eighth largest city. One out of every 260 American adults is behind bars, and blacks are jailed at seven times the rate of whites. In the first six months of 1994 the prison population grew by 40,000, an average of 1,500 new prisoners a week. This excluded the number of inmates in local jails, such as the infamous Rikers Island in New York, or those awaiting trial.

The level of imprisonment in the United States is more than 4 times that of Canada, 5 times that of England and Wales, and 14 times that of Japan. Experts say that the numbers reflect the higher rate of violent crime in America, and the too-easy availability of rifles and revolvers, and believe that the prison explosion is likely to continue with increased arrests for drug-related crimes. There has been a significant growth in those imprisoned for assault, robbery, drug and rape charges in the past two decades.

To the balance sheet, one has to add a fourth phenomenon: drugs and Aids, violence and gun culture. Gunshots now cause 1 of every 4 deaths among American teenagers, according to the National Center for Health Statistics. Bullets killed nearly 4,200 teenagers in 1990, the most recent year for which figures are available, up from 2,500 in 1985. An estimated 100,000 students carry a gun to school, according to the National Education Association. A survey released in 1993 by pollster Louis Harris contains alarming evidence of a gun culture among the 2,508 students he polled in 96 schools across the US. Fifteen percent of students 11 to 18 years old said they had carried a handgun in the past 30 days, 11 percent said they had been shot at, and 59 percent said they knew where to get a gun if they needed one.

But even the worst schools are safer than the streets, which is why summer is the deadliest season. For many teenagers, with their undeveloped sense of mortality and craving for thrills, gunplay has become a deadly sport. Not long ago, many Americans dismissed the slaughter as an inner city problem. But now the crackle of gunfire echoes from the poor, urban neighborhoods to the suburbs of the heartland. Miami has an equally bad record. More than 30,000 wanted felons are now on the streets in Dade

[2] *New York Times*, Oct. 17, 1994.

County alone, and people are losing patience with a revolving-door justice system that rotates criminals back onto the streets practically as fast as they are caught. Miami has the highest violent crime rate of any American city, and even former priests have been known to pack pistols in their briefcases. So far, however, the tourists are still coming, even if some may be thinking about packing a mercenary kit with their suntan lotion.

Adding to these problems is another factor: the "graying of America." The figures tell the story. In 1970 there were 20.1 million Americans aged 65 and older, but of them only 1.4 million were 85 and older. Twenty years later, the over-65 population had grown to 31.6 million. By 2030, that number will have increased to nearly 70 million. Of those, 8.4 million will be 85 and older.

Add to these demographics two other sets of figures: the rising costs of all health care and the increasing numbers of older people whose health care costs are far higher than those of younger Americas. To take the 1992 presidential campaign year as a base, the average amount then spent on health care for those under the age of 65 was $2,349. For Americans 65 and older, the average amount was almost four times higher – $9,125. Then consider the plight of those 37 million Americans – 15 percent of the entire population – who have no health insurance coverage, and the additional 72 million Americans who lack insurance coverage for prescription drugs. When all of these facts are combined, it is apparent that Americans are paying far too much for their health care and it is covering far too few. And the costs of each component continue to soar – and will keep on soaring until the entire system is reformed.

2 POPULATION GROWTH AND CHANGE

At the time of the first census in 1790 (there were then 14 states), the US had a population of nearly four million, of whom about 750,000 were colored. Ninety-one percent of the total had come from the British Isles: 82 percent English, 7 percent Scotch, 2 percent Irish. Of the rest, 5.6 percent were of German background, 2.5 percent Dutch, 0.6 percent French and 0.3 percent "other". This meant that the US was primarily a British nation, with all the faults and virtues of the English, and with a heritage of British political customs and ideals. (It has also meant that the pull of a common language and common customs has continued to influence American policy, helping, for example, to put the US on the side of the Allies in World Wars I and II. The presence of other national groups left scarcely a trace on national institutions in the US.) The total population of the US in the 1990 census was 248,709,873.

The colonial governments of the American colonies had been English-made, based on English political traditions, and it was only natural that the colonists should claim for themselves the rights and liberties for which the English people had fought since Magna Carta. They thought these were their rights and liberties as well, even though they resided in a new land. And in the sense that the American Revolution was based on the legal and political traditions which the British majority had brought with them, it can be said that it was not a revolution at all, but only a secession. By contrast, the French Revolution, and later the Russian, were great upheavals that worked fundamental changes in their systems of government; the American Revolution did not.

Walt Whitman exulted that the US was "not merely a nation but a teeming nation of nations." However, there are two ways of looking at the influence of "other national groups" on US culture: one view is that the US is a nation of Anglo-Saxons struggling to preserve its heritage against the hordes of foreigners; the other holds that the American nation is itself a blend of cultures, all of one piece, and that diversity is the pattern of America. This writer believes that the US is a new civilization, owing much to both Anglo-Saxon and other strains, to the influence of its great continental resources, and to the skills which have been brought or developed there. The US is not a great "melting pot" from which people have been poured into similar molds, but rather a "mixing bowl" or a "salad bowl" in which diversity is maintained. American traditions have been assimilated from many sources, but the sources stay distinct and are often visible. The covered wagon is German, the log cabin and the rail fence are Swedish. American life has been enriched by such diverse contributions as Santa Claus, minestrone soup, Paul Bunyan and Old Man River.

Nevertheless, the US, in its politics and its legal structure, is an English-based country. Unlike its mother-country, however, it is governed by a written 4,000-word document, interpreted by lawyers. Of those officers cited in the document, or its many amendments, the President (who is also commander-in-chief) is the most important, and can be re-elected once only. He has frequently been a state governor. Uneasily alongside him is a greedy, self-oriented Congress, in theory a legislative assembly.

Changes in the size and composition of a population depend upon birth rates, the excess of birth over deaths, and the net effect of immigration and emigration. The birth rate in the US began to decline early in the nineteenth century from its high point of around 55 (births per thousand persons per year). It dropped to 18 during the depression years of the 1930s, but the return of prosperity after 1945 and the baby boom that followed demobilization pushed it up to an average of 25 between 1947 and 1950. After 1958 the rate decreased, but the number of births per year still exceeded 4 million, the baby boom level, until 1965. During the early 1970s, the birth rate dropped further, reaching an all-time low of 14.8 in 1975 and 1976, but, as the baby boom generation reached reproductive age, the birth rate began to rise again, reaching 15.2 in 1978 and 16.1 in 1980.

The fertility rate – the number of children born per women of childbearing age – reached a post-1945 peak of 3.7 children per woman between 1955 and 1959, but had dropped to 1.8 by 1976. This trend away from large families had been under way between 1920 and 1950, but it speeded up after 1965. For white women, and probably non-white also, the decrease came entirely from the decline in births of three or more children. The rate per 1,000 women aged 15 to 44 for first and second births rose from 46 to 47, but for third or higher it dropped from 28 to 15. Numerous explanations have been offered for the upsurge of population growth during the late 1940s and 1950s and the population "bust" that followed the baby boom. The increasing sense after 1965 that the social, economic, and political condition, at home and abroad limited opportunities for future income probably contributed as much to the decline as improved birth control technology, changes in women's attitude towards their roles, and increases in employment opportunities for women. At the same time, increases in public awareness of problems caused by excessive population growth rates reinforced the other factors that contributed to limitations on family size. Oddly enough, at the time that fertility has been generally decreasing, there has been a rise in the birth rate for unmarried women of all ages. Rare in 1950, these births accounted for 8 percent of white births and almost one of every two non-white births at the end of the 1970s. Only a tiny part of this increase could be attributed to the rising proportion of births to women under the age of 20 who have historically had the highest percentages of out-of-wedlock births.

Death rates in the United States, at all ages, for both sexes, and despite race, stood lower in 1980 than they had in 1950.

Females had greater rates of decline than males and non-whites greater rates of decline than whites. Between 1940 and the mid-1950s, the spread of various new antibiotic drugs brought an unprecedented improvement, then the death rate leveled off until the late 1960s. Since about 1968 a new decline began in mortality rates, unusually rapid in infant and child mortality. The mortality improvements since the 1940s add up to an average increase in life expectancy at birth of almost 15 years, from 58.5 years in 1936 to 73.2 in 1977. Although the white life expectancy is still higher than all other races, the gap (after a widening in the 1954–68 period) has been more than halved (from 10.8 years to 5 years.) The death rate from diseases of the circulatory system has declined rapidly since 1965, although heart disease and cancer account for more than half of all deaths. Accidents and violence began to emerge as the greatest contributor to health costs by the end of the 1970s. In 1975, the economic cost of accidents and violence stood 62 percent higher than the cost of cancer and was 17 percent below the cost of all cardiovascular diseases.

But immigration has been much more important in the increase and movement of population than "natural" increase, and that immigration has been immensely varied. Further, that immigration has been accompanied by a striking internal mobility, notably of blacks from South to North, and equally notably of whites from inner cities to suburbs and "exurbs."

Despite its reputation as "the melting pot" of the world, most of the 50 million persons who have entered the United States since 1820 originated in Europe and most of them came from northern and western Europe (95 percent up to 1860 and 68 percent between 1861 and 1900); 58 percent of the 1901–30 immigration derived from southern and eastern Europe, but prejudice against these groups prompted Congress to pass restrictive legislation with national origins quotas in the early 1920s. Even before World War I, restrictive congressional legislation and treaties aimed at stopping the so-called "Yellow Peril" reduced Asian immigration to only 3 percent in the 1901–30 period. During the restriction period up to 1960, northern and western Europe, together with northern America and Latin America, provided 77 percent of all immigrants, and the average annual number admitted was about 132,000. From the 1920s to the 1950s, the racial make-up and the national origins of the population remained essentially stable, and the restrictions led to large reductions in total immigration, especially in relation to population.

During the 1960s and 1970s, significant changes took place in immigration to the United States. In large part, these changes followed the passage of the Immigration Act of 1965 which abolished national origins as the basis for quotas in favour of criteria such as labor skills and humanitarian concerns. Persons of Asian and Latin American origin accounted for over half of legal immigrants in the 1960s and nearly three-fourths of the 1971–4 period. From 1972 to 1976 Mexico, the Philippines, Korea, Cuba, India, Taiwan, and the Dominican Republic sent the highest numbers of immigrants to the United States, in that order. By 1977, the 462,000 net annual immigration amounted to 2.1 per thousand population, and in 1980 the number rose to 654,000 (2.9 per thousand), due to the Cuban and Haitian refugees admitted that year.

The illegal immigration of the post-1965 period received widespread attention in the press and stimulated congressional debate over changes in federal immigration policy. Estimates of the number of illegal aliens in the United States have ranged from 1 to 8 million. Official estimates made by the Immigration and Naturalization Service (INS) during the middle 1970s put the number at over 7 million, and the INS reported arresting and deporting between 600,000 and 800,000 per year during the same period. The Population and Reference Bureau, a private research organization, estimated in 1982 that of the projected 795,000 to 970,000 net annual immigration during the 1980s, half would enter illegally, primarily from Latin America.

Until about 1945, the American population carried out a significant long-term migration from rural to urban areas, including central cities of 500,000 or more. Since the end of World War II, the relative decline of the rural areas continued, but the large central cities experienced slower growth or in some cases decline. Suburban growth, though a familiar feature of American life long before the 1940s, assumed greater significance thereafter, as both smaller cities and urban areas outside city limits began to account for all of the relative growth of metropolitan places. Non-whites, however, kept moving to the central cities. Some 80 percent of the Mexican-American population made the shift from farms to central cities by 1970. (By 1980, 83 percent of the Spanish origin population lived in urban areas, including over 1 million Puerto Ricans in New York City alone). During the 1940s, 43 cities outside the South doubled their black population, compared to only two in the South, and during the 1950s, 1,457,000 non-whites moves out of the South. The 1960 census showed that for the first time more than half of American blacks lived outside the South.

Central cities showed a 48 percent increase in black population during the 1940s, compared to an increase of only 10 percent for whites. The non-white population of central cities rose from 10 percent in 1940 to 33 percent in 1950, and the black proportion increased to 58 percent in 1970. In 1980, because of a small increase in the proportion of blacks living in suburbs (black suburbanites still amounted to only 21 percent compared to 40 percent of the total population), 56 percent of the black population lived in central cities. The vast magnitude of this urban migration by black Americans led one demographer to conclude in 1964 that, "next to the worldwide population explosion, the movement of Negroes from the southern part of the United States has without a doubt been the greatest and most significant sociological event" of our country's recent history.

The American population as a whole became more urban, specifically metropolitan (living in places with central cities of 50,000 or more and their surrounding counties), between 1945 and 1970. In 1940 some 168 such places existed, with over half of the total population, and by 1970 their number had grown to 243 and they contained nearly three-fourths of the population. During the 1970s non-metropolitan areas grew faster than metropolitan areas. Due partly to the decentralization of manufacturing, this widely discussed "deconcentration" of the population also resulted from the development of recreation and retirement areas for the growing older population, the environmental movement, and the spread of the interstate highway network. Probably one-third to one-fourth of non-metropolitan growth can be attributed to suburban developments outside the official metropolitan boundaries used by the census-takers. Non-metropolitan population increases took place almost entirely in non-farm areas, so the phenomenon did not represent a "back to the farm" movement. The magnitude of the trend can be seen in a comparison of 1960s metropolitan growth rates with those of the 1970s. In the 1960s the metropolitan areas increased by 17 percent compared with 4 percent for non-metropolitan areas. During the 1970s the metropolitan areas experienced only a 9.5 percent growth, whereas the non-metropolitan areas grew by 15 percent and the country as a whole by 11 percent. Whereas two-thirds of the nation's total population growth during the 1970s occurred in metropolitan areas, during the 1960s these same areas had accounted for fully 92 percent of US growth. Despite the decline in the metropolitan growth rate, the nation continued to be metropolitan in 1980, with 165 million people, 73 percent of the population, in metropolitan areas.

Changes in the regional distribution of the population, historically an important consequence of the tendency of people to follow jobs, housing, retail shops, and roads, continued to shape the nation's development after 1945. The relative shift from the Northeast and North Central regions to the West had become a familiar story even before World War II. Between 1940 and 1970 the industrial expansion and urbanization of the West doubled its population and raised its proportion of the population from 11 to 17 percent. By 1980 the West contained 19 percent of the population, compared to the South's 33.3 percent (its largest share of the total since 1860), the Northeast's 21.7 percent, and the North Central region's 26 percent.

The Western United States (the states of California, Oregon, Washington, Arizona particularly) grew at a rate of 500 percent in population in the first half of the twentieth century, compared with a 67 percent increase in New England. The "Sunbelt" states of the South and West account for over 90 percent of the total population growth of 12 million between 1980 and 1985. Nationally, the US population increased by 5.4 percent in the period, but there were large growth rates in Alaska (29.7 percent), Arizona (17.2 percent), Nevada (16.9 percent), Florida (16.6 percent), Texas (15.0 percent), Utah (12.6 percent), and Colorado (11.8 percent), while Michigan, Ohio, Iowa, Pennsylvania, West Virginia, and the District of Columbia all showed a decline in population. The Western increase has been largely due to immigration from other parts of the country, especially as birth rates began their decline after the end of the postwar baby boom. The population growth of the South is largely due to natural increase; the movement of population there until recently has been more out than in.

California is an extreme example of population growth. Since 1900, it has jumped from 21st in size of population to 2nd. Witness in particular the growth of its cities. Since 1911, its representation in the House has leaped from 11 to 52. The fact that such California politicians as Nixon and Reagan, Warren and Knowland, have been prominent in national affairs is no accident.

Population growth has been accompanied by changes in the nature of the population. The age distribution, in particular, has been affected, the median age having shifted from 22.9 to 30.1 years since 1900. The proportion of people over 65 has doubled in the same period.

In cold, statistical terms, the survival of more children to a productive age means an increase in economic productivity, since there is less economic waste on children who fail to grow up. The US has only 6 percent of the Earth's population, but one half of its total production; these astonishing facts are connected with the further facts that 95 percent of all Americans who are born alive live to the age of 16, and 65 percent to the age of 60 or over. The strength of the US lies in its economic production, which is precisely due to its educated, healthy and capable population.

The new composition of the population has meant the appearance of the problem of the aged, who have special economic needs and desires of their own. The change in the family system, from being an economic unit to being a "filling station," has created a rootless, dissastisfied, and often impoverished group of senior citizens. This group's espousal of pension plans and other reforms has led some people to regard the aged as the truly radical people in US society.

Immigration is a familiar phenomenon – perhaps the most familiar phenomenon – in American society. What is less familiar is the extent of the internal movement. All Americans are mobile: indeed, almost restless. About 17 percent of Americans move house every year, and in 1970 it was estimated that just over a quarter of the population lived in a different state from the one in which they were born.

In regional terms, the main trend has been the move to the West. The pioneers who with rugged determination developed the country westwards are part of American legend, but their hard-won paths to the Mid-West and the Western coast have been followed, albeit more comfortably, by thousands and millions searching for the promised land of opportunity.

What is more, political power is moving, with the population, to the more conservative areas of the South and West and away from the cities of the Northeast, long bastions of New Deal liberalism. The reapportionment of the House of Representatives seats to take account of the demographic changes revealed in the 1980 Census led to a loss of 9 seats in the Northeast and 8 in the Mid-West, while there were gains of 8 in the South and 9 in the West (with Florida obtaining 4, California 2, Texas 3 extra seats). Rhode Island and New York both lost population, and with it, lost representatives. But while people have moved out of frost-belt city centers like Cleveland, Detroit, New York, and Philadelphia, the "Sun-belt" metropolitan areas have mostly grown at a prodigious rate, surpassing their already rapid growth rate in the 1960s.

Most people who move between states are looking for work or a warm place to retire. Labor migrants go to the new industries and services in the south and west, the elderly to Florida, the Ozarks and the southwestern states. Large-scale labor migration from the North Central states will in the medium term nullify advantages which created it: population density will rise, congestion, rents, and other costs increase, crime and racial tension will probably worsen as internal migration streams collide with immigration from abroad, especially when new Hispanic immigrants compete with blacks.

The Hispanic migration is the major part of Third World migration into the US; Mexican migration is from the only major Third World country which shares a border with the US, or indeed with any other Western industrial country. In the nineteenth century the US was safely isolated by sea and distance from its other sources of migration, making illegal migration much more difficult. The present migration, both legal and illegal, can only be controlled and regulated with Mexican help; as its strict control might incur Mexican hostility, it looks as though it will not be effectively controlled. Foreign policy complications are thus affecting immigration and the composition of the US population for the first time. Thus Mexican prosperity and stability is an American interest. Given its continuing economic distress, there will be a constant drain of Mexican talent to the US, legally or illegally. For example, in August 1982 the Immigration and Naturalization Service intercepted 78,000 illegal entrants, 16 percent more than in August 1981. Recent research suggests that less than one-third of illegal migrants from Mexico are apprehended. In 1982, however, Border Patrol Agents apprehended 819,900 deportable aliens of whom 795,400 were Mexican. In all, the INS made 1,251,357 arrests in fiscal 1983, and in 1984, arrests ran 10 percent higher.

From 1980 to 1990, the United States absorbed more than 8.6 million immigrants, mostly from Latin America, Asia, and the Caribbean – the largest influx since the 1920s. Sixty-eight percent went to just five states: California, New York, Texas, Florida, and New Jersey, with the foreign-born populations of 34 states increasing overall. California's foreign-born population rose from 15 percent to nearly 22 percent. Mexicans constitute 25 percent of these immigrants, their numbers in the United States doubling to 4.3 million during the 1980s. Except for Arizona, California, Illinois, New Mexico, and Texas, however, most states have more immigrants of other nationalities.

After a decade in the US, immigrants on average take home salaries comparable to those of non-immigrants. Rather than take jobs from Americans, immigrants tend to accept jobs that native-born Americans do not take. In 1980 immigrants represented only 3 percent of the population, but 23 percent took jobs as housekeepers and another 15 percent as servants. At the same time, however, a Census Bureau sample of 500 occupation categories includes only 30 in which immigrants hold more than 10 percent of the jobs.

If willingness to work is measured by labor force participation rates, immigrants compare favorably with the rest of the population. A study of labor force participation in California in 1990 found 81 percent of Latino men, 76 percent of white men, and 67 percent of black men, holding a job or actively seeking work. Only 20 percent of the immigrants who arrived between 1980 and 1990 earned more than $22,419 per year, the average income of US citizens between ages 25 and 54, but the gap closes as they remain in the United States. Immigrants who arrived before 1980 now earn on average only $2,000 less per year than other Americans.

3 IMMIGRATION – DREAM AND REALITY

America, the undiscovered and virgin continent, fired the imagination of Europe in a peculiar and unique fashion. The rumor of it stirred Shakespeare. Franklin, as epitome of its Natural Man, became part of the European Enlightenment; Rousseau, and for a while Thomas Jefferson, saw it as the *novus ordo saeculorum*. For Europeans like Coleridge and Priestley, for Du Pont de Nemours and Robert Owen, it was a place uncorrupted by power, congenial to experiments in human perfectibility, inhabited by a chosen people.

America was built by immigrants. To Plymouth Rock in the seventeenth century, to Ellis Island in the twentieth, people born elsewhere came to America. Some were fleeing religious persecution and political turmoil. Most, however, came for economic reasons and were part of extensive migratory systems that responded to changing demands in labor markets. Their experience in the United States was as diverse as their backgrounds and aspirations. Some became farmers and others toiled in factories. Some settled permanently and others returned to their homeland. Collectively, however, they contributed to the building of a nation by providing a constant source of inexpensive labor, by settling rural regions and industrial cities, and by bringing their unique forms of political and cultural expression.

By the time of the first census of 1790 nearly 1 million Afro-Americans and less than 4 million Europeans resided in the United States, The European population originated from three major streams; English and Welsh, Scotch-Irish, and German. From 1820 to 1975 some 47 million people came to the United States: 8.3 million from other countries in the Western Hemisphere, 2.2 million from Asia, and 35.9 million from Europe. The leading sources of immigrants between these dates were Germany, Italy, Ireland, Austria-Hungary, Canada, Russia/USSR, Britain, Mexico, the West Indies, and Sweden. The stream was relatively continuous from 1820 to 1924 with only brief interruptions caused by the Civil War and occasional periods of economic downturns such as the depression of the 1890s, the panic of 1907–8, and the Great Depression of the 1930s. World War II, of course, also greatly reduced the numbers immigrating. In fact, 32 million of the 35.9 million Europeans who came to the United States between 1820 and 1975 came prior to 1924.

Immigration on such a large scale resulted in greater ethnic diversity than ever before – or anywhere else. And yet the possibility of translating this uniqueness into permanent political form, making American society different from the rest of anguished mankind, died early, indeed died almost at conception. The ideal of a heavenly city on the plains, with a Nature that was more beneficent and generous than in the Old World, was imperiled at the start. Jefferson recognized it early enough. In his first comments on the Constitution, writing to Madison from Paris in 1787, he said that America would remain "virtuous" only while there remained vacant land. "When we get piled upon one another in large cities as in Europe we shall become corrupt as in Europe, and go to eating one another as they do there."

But the dream of a perfectible land dies hard. It is striking that so many discussions of the state of America today start with the questions "What has gone wrong?" Even in a secular age, a sense of Manifest Destiny is not deduced from sociological laws but treated as part of a providential plan. With boasts of great achievement goes the assumption that America could and should be judged by a special measuring rod.

In the state of American society today, many can be heard proclaiming the end of the American Dream. The country's worst critics – often its natives, rather than visiting Europeans – go further still: America is denounced as a nightmare society. Yet even here, the pride in country shows through, and shows in contradictory ways. Some Americans denounce their country as uniquely nightmarish – as if Hitler's Germany and Stalin's Russia were of no account in the history of this century. Other critics look ahead: America today is claimed to be the prototype of the nightmare existence facing European societies in the next century. The truth may be something different. Perhaps the idyllic America of an earlier era, to which the present is so unfavourably compared, is not a fact but a myth.

America was not only exceptional in origin but also exceptionally favored. In the late eighteenth century it had an extraordinary number of statesmen who were gifted in many senses. Its constitution-makers were men of ingenuity and good sense; they were, for their time, remarkably well educated. Its Presidents were either the Virginia dynasty – Washington, Jefferson, Madison, and Monroe – or their Yankee equivalents, the Adams family. These men brought to politics a high sense of personal responsibility and a sense of dignity and decorum worthy of the Senate of the Roman Republic. The majority of the Founding Fathers were graduates; four of them, Jefferson, Madison, and the two Adamses, were essentially scholars turned politicians. In Philadelphia a collection of scientists, architects and politicians made that city for a while as significant as Paris as a center of ideas and political programs. David Rittenhouse, the astronomer, Benjamin Rush in medicine, and painters like Benjamin West, John Copley, and the Peales were as significant as Madison and Jefferson.

There was more than a sense of optimism and of high adventure; there was also a sense that in the New World there was opportunity to discover new social and esthetic values, to formulate new laws, and virgin soil in which to plant new institutions. Jefferson was architect of much more than the Declaration of Independence and the University of Virginia. If, when he came to write his own epitaph, he gave pride of place to these and to the statute of Virginia for religious freedom, there were also his drafts for the Virginia Constitution for the Federal Bill of Rights, for the French Charter of Rights, the Kentucky Resolutions, the Ordinances for the West, the Notes on the State of Virginia, the notes of a coinage for the United States, standards of measurement for weights and coins – to name only a few. He was also architect of a charming eighteenth century country villa which, while smaller than its counterparts outside London and Vincenza, none the less offered those who called there the prospect of greater intellectual stimulus in the course of an evening's conversation.

With a polymath's concern for matching form and substance, Jefferson wished the architecture of the nation's capital buildings to express in stone and marble the ideals that he and his friends had tried to express in the words of the Declaration. After two wings of the Capitol building were finished, needing only the central dome to crown its classical grandeur, Jefferson wrote Benjamin Latrobe, the architect: "I shall live in the hope that the day will come when an opportunity will be given you of finishing the middle-building in a style worthy of the two wings, and worthy of the first temple dedicated to the sovereignty of the people, embellishing with Athenian taste the course of a nation looking far beyond the range of Athenian destinies."

The world in which the Founding Fathers moved had a certain unity. It was the ordered world of the New England towns or the Virginia plantations. It was a world in which movement was slow and communication difficult. It was a world of independent farmers. Some were also scholars, at home with Europeans of the Enlightenment; they were certainly no more isolated from new ideas than was Frederick the Great, condemned to life in a Prussian backwater, or Edward Gibbon, seeking education in an Oxford that was a century away from reform. Yet these men of the Tidewater also knew the problems of uncivilized lands. The trapper and the sharpshooter in his rude cabin were also part of their world. In the early years of the Republic the attraction shifted from exploring Europe to exploring the interior of an almost unknown continent. Thomas Jefferson advised young men no longer to go to Europe for an education. It was better to stay on native ground. He sent his private secretary, Meriwether Lewis, in company with William Clark, to explore the continent. The expedition not only crossed the Mississippi but also the wide Missouri and the vast Rockies, reaching the Pacific Ocean overland, instead of by the long sailing route. The reports they brought back opened vast new territories to knowledge and settlement. In the first decade of the nineteenth century the move west – away from Europe – began in earnest. Jefferson's ideal seemed within reach. America was to "stand with respect to Europe precisely on the footing of China. We should then avoid wars and all our citizens would be husbandmen."

Some Europeans agreed with the Jeffersonian dream. As early as 1782, Crevecoeur saw the Americans as Western pilgrims "who are carrying along with them that great mass of arts, science, vigor and industry, which began long since in the East." They would, in his phrase, "finish the great circle." The New World won the praise of de Tocqueville in the 1830s, and William Gladstone, notwithstanding his pride in Britain, thought its constitution one of the most providential acts in human history. Other Europeans agreed about the exceptional character of America, only to contrast it unfavorably with the civilization of the Old World. European visitors noticed many features that would be as true of the twentieth century as of the nineteenth: the passion for speed, the worship of size, the identification of success with money, prodigious meals, and preoccupation with the law – both making it and breaking it. They noted the vestiges of a Puritanical social and moral code, and were shocked by slavery. All disliked the prevalent tobacco-chewing and spitting habit. Charles Dickens described how he had to clean his fur coat repeatedly to remove the dried flakes of spittle from it. Another visitor thought the national emblem should not be the eagle but the spittoon. But the most frequent theme, then as now, was the ease with which weapons could be obtained, and police and politicians bribed. Duels were sometimes deliberate murders, and every Congressman went armed. A Southerner breakfasting at Willards Hotel in Washington, angered at an Irish waiter's service, stabbed him. The Dutch ambassador, who had just taken up his appointment, was having his first meal at a nearby table: "What peoples! If they do such things at breakfast, what won't they do at dinner!"

The wilderness, to many Americans proof of the country's status as Eden, was interpreted by many visitors as a token of barbarism. Mrs Trollope wrote in a distinctly un-Jeffersonian style of the Mississippi:

> ... now we glide
> Between the slimy banks; the horrent bear
> And bloated crocodile lie crouching there,
> Thy dark shores breath miasma: on thy breast
> The uptorn forest droops its leafy crest,
> Thy storm-crushed victims; none her strength can save
> That once hath dipped beneath thy fatal wave.
> This flood contemned of nature let me free –
> Turn here again, my bark, and seek the deep blue sea.[3]

[3] Frances Trollope, *Poems* (London, Black, 1898), p. 212.

Jefferson, the product of a settled Virginia, might also have turned his back on less admirable characteristics of the world of Kentucky, Tennessee, and points further west. This world was marked, in the words of James Paxton, by "abundance, idleness, Indians, Africans, isolation and whiskey."

In the 1820s and 1830s the distinctive character of American politics became recognized in Europe as a potential threat to established European ideas. Metternich, the great exponent of European conservatism after the downfall of Napoleon, expressed great alarm at the revolutionary potential of American political ideals, and the implications of the Monroe Doctrine. Writing to Nesselrode, the Russian Chancellor, in 1824, he said:

> These United States of America which we have seen arise and grow, and which during their too short youth already meditated projects which they dared not then avow, have suddenly left a sphere too narrow for their ambition, and have astonished Europe by a new act of revolt, more unprovoked, fully as audacious, and no less dangerous than the former. They have distinctly and clearly announced their intention to set not only power against power, but, to express it more exactly, altar against altar. In their indecent declarations they have cast blame and scorn on the institutions of Europe most worthy of respect, on the principles of its greatest sovereigns, on the whole of those measures which a sacred duty no less than an evident necessity has forced our governments to adopt to frustrate plans most criminal.
>
> In permitting themselves these unprovoked attacks, in fostering revolutions, wherever they show themselves, in regretting those which have failed, in extending a helping hand to those which seem to prosper, they lend new strength to the apostles of sedition, and re-animate the courage of every conspirator.
>
> If this flood of evil doctrine, and pernicious examples should extend over the whole of America, what would become of our religious and political institutions, of the moral force of our government, and of that conservative system which has saved Europe from complete dissolution?[4]

A half-century later, Bismarck paid ironic tribute to America's ability to be different, and survive, when he remarked that there "must have been a special providence looking after fools, drunkards and the United States."

Even before Bismarck spoke, Americans were beginning to wonder whether providence, or some other impersonal force, was not beginning to take them away from the Jeffersonian ideal. The

[4] Metternich, *Correspondence*, 4 vols, trans. from the German by A. B. Schmidt (London, Longman's, 1892), vol. II, p. 221.

real divide in American history was not the firing upon Fort Sumter, or Lee's surrender at Appomattox, but Andrew Jackson's boisterous inauguration in January 1829. At this point, the Democracy (or worse) of the Frontier displaced the older, settled world of the Virginia gentleman. Perry Miller has argued that the turning-point came in 1815. After the textile mills opened in New England, America was set to become a business civilization; capitalism and selfishness, rather than Indians and crude manners, were to be the new enemies. In 1898, when America went to war with Spain, it became, like the nations from which it had revolted, an imperial power. By this time, too, America could claim to be like any other industrial civilization – only more so. The absence of a feudal past meant there was no aristocratic class to challenge the claims of Mammon. Jefferson's dream was gone.[5]

The past is gone in a double sense. With greater awareness of American history, we can see that the America of Heine, like the America of Mrs Trollope, is a land that never was. The reality of the past is far more complex than any dream or nightmare could encapsulate. If the South had its intellectual aristocrats, it also had its Simon Legrees. If the North had grasping merchants, the same Yankee civilization also produced men who grasped and groped to find what transcended commerce, in a search for the soul of man. The frontiersmen were both incredibly brave and adventurous, and incredibly crude and violent.

A second reason for the disappearance of the dream is that at some point in the nineteenth century the line of continuity between past and present wore thin, then snapped. The pressures were multiple: expansion across a vast continent, the growth of industrialism, and, not least, the gathering-in of tens of millions of new immigrants from unfamiliar parts of the Old World. Previous chapters in this volume have emphasized how incomparable the American past is with the European past. My point is different, and perhaps more disturbing: the American past has now become largely irrelevant for an understanding of contemporary America too.

The first to voice criticism of Americans as cast in a single national mould was Horace Kallen, a Jewish-American philosopher. Writing in 1915, in an essay for *The Nation* entitled "Democracy Versus the Melting-Pot," Kallen argued that the melting pot was valid neither as a fact nor as an ideal. What impressed him was

[5] Perry Miller, *The New England Mind*, 2 vols (Cambridge, Mass., Harvard University Press, 1939, 1953).

the persistence of ethnic groups and their distinctive traditions. Unlike freely chosen affiliations, Kallen said, the ethnic bond was both involuntary and immutable. "Men may change their clothes, their politics, their wives, their religions, their philosophies, to a greater or lesser extent: they cannot change their grandfathers. Jews or Poles or Anglo-Saxons, in order to cease being Jews or Poles or Anglo-Saxons, would have to cease to be..." Ethnic diversity, Kallen observed, enriches American civilization. He saw the nation not as one people, except in a political and administrative sense, but rather "as a federation or commonwealth of national cultures ... a democracy of nationalities, cooperating voluntarily and autonomously through common institutions ... a multiplicity in a unity, an orchestration of mankind." This conception he came to call "cultural pluralism."

The civil rights revolution in the 1950s provoked new expressions of ethnic identity by the now long-resident "new migration" from southern and eastern Europe – Italians, Greeks, Poles, Czechs, Slovaks, Hungarians. The ethnic enthusiasm was reinforced by the "third-generation" effect formulated in Hansen's Law, named after Marcus Lee Hansen, the great pioneer in immigration history: "What the son wishes to forget the grandson wishes to remember."

Another factor powerfully nourished the new passion for roots: waning American optimism about the nation's prospect. For two centuries Americans had been confident that life would be better for their children that it was for them. In their exuberant youth, Americans had disdained the past and, as John Quincy Adams urged, looked forward to their posterity rather than backward to their ancestors. Amid forebodings of national decline, Americans now began to look forward less and backward more. The rising cult of ethnicity was a sympton of decreasing confidence in the American future.

The word "ethnicity" made its modern début in 1940 in W. Lloyd Warner's Yankee City series. From its modest beginning in that sociological study, "ethnicity" moved vigorously to center stage in popular discourse. The bicentennial of American Independence, the centennial of the statue of Liberty, the restoration of Ellis Island – all turned from tributes to the melting pot into extravaganzas of ethnic distinctiveness.

The pressure for the new cult of ethnicity came less from the minorities *en masse* than from their often self-appointed spokesmen. Most ethnics, white and non-white, saw themselves primarily as Americans. "The cravings for 'historical identity,' " Gunnar Myrdal said at the height of the ethnic rage, "is not in any sense a people's movement. Those cravings have been raised by a few well-established intellectuals, professors, writers – mostly, I gather, of a third generation." Few of them, Myrdal thought, made much effort to talk to their own ethnic groups. He feared, Myrdal added with a certain contempt, that this movement was only "upper-class intellectual romanticism."[6]

In 1974, after testimony from ethnic spokesmen denouncing the "melting pot" as a conspiracy to homogenize America, Congress passed the Ethnic Heritage Studies Program Act – a statute that, by applying the ethnic ideology to all Americans, compromised the historic right of Americans to decide their ethnic identities for themselves. The Act ignored those millions of Americans – surely a majority – who refused identification with any particular ethnic group. But with a Bicentennial approaching and worthy of salute, it was proper to recognize and preserve the evidence of black history, and to train those who would cherish it. Along with the civil rights bill, the political results were clear. Among blacks Kennedy won 68 percent and Carter 85 percent – the blacks were becoming Democrats and were getting to the polls.

The ethnic upsurge (it can hardly be called a revival because it was unprecedented) began as a gesture of protest against an Anglocentric culture. It became a cult, and today it threatens to become a counterrevolution against the original theory of America as "one people," a common culture, a single nation.

Attitudes toward Africa have changed markedly in the last 250 years. Alex Haley's compelling autobiography *Roots* helped create an audience for the tradition – though, as Ishmael Reed later observed, if Haley had traced his father's rather than his mother's bloodline, "he would have traveled 12 generations back to, not Gambia, but Ireland." The great stimulus was in fact less the civil rights revolution, which possessed its own momentum without benefit of Afrocentrism, than it was pride generated by the appearance of independent African states – for many American blacks a proof of racial virility, as the establishment of Israel was for many American Jews. The analogy is incomplete. Where Jewish-Americans can (or could until recently) look with pride on the achievements of Israel, African-Americans, hard put to find much to admire in contemporary Liberia or Uganda or Ghana, must instead seek moments of glory in the dim past.

[6] Gunnar Myrdal, *An American Dilemma: The Negro problem and American democracy* (New York, Harper's, 1942).

The glorification of the African past was accompanied by a campaign to replace Anglo "slave" names with African names, to wear African costumes, to replicate African rituals. LeRoi Jones, who had said in 1962 that "history for the Negro, before America, must remain an emotional abstraction," now saw Africa more concretely and changed his name to Amiri Baraka. As a result of the new Africanization have grown up black dormitories, black student unions, black fraternities and sororities, black business and law societies, black homosexual and lesbian groups, black tables in dining halls, in colleges and universities. Stanford University has "ethnic theme houses." The University of Pennsylvania gives blacks – 6 percent of the enrollment – their own yearbook. Campuses today, according to one University of Pennsylvania professor, have "the cultural diversity of Beirut. There are separate armed camps. The black kids don't mix with the white kids. The Asians are off by themselves. Oppression is the great status symbol."

Oberlin was for a century and half the model of a racially integrated college. "Increasingly," Jacob Weisberg, an editor at the *New Republic*, reports, "Oberlin students think, act, study, and live apart." Asians live in Asia House, Jews in "J" House, Latinos in Spanish House, blacks in African-Heritage House, foreign students in Third World House. Even the Lesbian, Gay, and Bisexual Union has broken up into racial and gender factions. "The result is separate worlds."[7]

Thus the era that began with the dream of integration ended up with scorn for assimilation. Instead of casting off the foreign skin, as John Quincy Adams had stipulated, never to resume it, the fashion is to resume the foreign skin as conspicuously as can be. The cult of ethnicity has reversed the movement of American history, producing a nation of minorities – or at least of minority spokesmen – less interested in joining with the majority in common endeavor than in declaring their alienation from an oppressive, white, patriarchal, racist, sexist, classist society. Ethnic ideology inculcates the illusion that membership in one or another ethnic group is the basic American experience.[8]

The result is that the US has turned full circle. "To separate [black children] from others of similar age and qualifications solely because of their race," Chief Justice Warren wrote in the school

[7] *The New Republic*, Jan. 11, 1988.

[8] Stephan Therstrom (ed.), *The Harvard Encyclopedia of American Ethnic Groups* (Cambridge, Mass., Harvard University Press, 1980); Thomas Sowell, *Ethnic America* (New York, Basic Books, 1983).

integration case in 1954, "generates a feeling of inferiority as to their status in the community that may affect their hearts and minds in a way unlikely ever to be undone." Yet in 40 years doctrine has completely reversed itself. Now integration is held to bring feelings of inferiority, and segregation to bring the cure.

The United States, as the saying goes, is "a nation of immigrants," but public opinion today is less receptive to the idea of more people seeking the American dream through immigration. In a July 1993 Gallup poll, 59 percent of those surveyed said immigration has been good in the past, but 60 percent said it is bad for the United States today.[9]

Immigration has become much more controversial in the past decade, probably for two principal reasons: first, the problem of illegal immigration has become more prominent as the ease of international travel has grown; and second, the influx of poorly educated immigrants with low skills from Mexico and Central America, as well as refugees from Indochina, has joined several social and poverty issues to the issue of immigration. The amnesty granted to illegal immigrants in 1986 has become a vehicle for the significant expansion of legal immigration, particularly under the "5th Preference" in the 1965 amendments to the immigration laws, which made family reunification the central objective of US immigration policy. Fewer immigrants now are granted visas on the basis of skills that would facilitate upward social mobility and help them become fully integrated into American society.

In general, however, the conclusion of the President's Council of Economic Advisers, which conducted an exhaustive study of the economic impact of immigration in 1986, still holds true:

> On the whole, international migrants appear to pay their own way from a public finance standpoint. Most come to the United States to work, and government benefits do not appear to be a major attraction. Some immigrants arrive with fairly high educational levels, and their training imposes no substantial costs on the public. Their rising levels of income produce a rising stream of tax payments to all levels of government. Their initial dependence on welfare benefits is usually limited, and they finance their participation in Social Security retirement benefits with years of contributions.[10]

[9] *The American Enterprise*, Jan./Feb. 1994, p. 97.
[10] *Economic Report of the President*, 1987, p. 233.

4 THE POLITICS OF IMMIGRATION

There are a number of facts which observers generally agree should be taken into account in evaluating any US immigration policy. The potential list is endless, but here are some major and salient points:

1 The United States shares a border with a large and growing Third World country, Mexico. In this regard it is unique among major countries in the free world. The population of Mexico was 80.5 million in 1986, with a doubling time of 28 years.

2 The US population was 250 million in 1990. It is increasing, but the birth rate is below replacement, as is that of Canada, Japan, and western Europe.

3 Legal immigration to the United States has increased in the last several decades and become increasingly Asian and Hispanic. From 1951 to 1960, 2.5 million people were admitted, 28 percent Asian and Hispanic; 3.3 million were admitted in the next decade, 48 percent Asian and Hispanic; an estimated 5.7 million immigrants were admitted in the years 1981–90, of whom over 75 percent were Asian and Hispanic. Between 1970 and 1980, the percentage of the population that was foreign-born (half of whom are citizens) increased from 4.8 percent to 6.2 percent , but was still half of what it was in 1910.

4 Markets are becoming increasingly international, and it is this international marketplace in which the United States needs to compete successfully.

5 The estimated number of illegal immigrants in the United States as temporary workers, cyclical workers, or permanent immigrants is far lower than many of the guesses presented to the public during debates on the legislation, and these estimates are sounder than is commonly believed. Estimates based on the 1980 census place the undocumented resident population at 2.5–3.5 million persons; this number may be increasing at 100,000–300,000 per year (though perhaps not at all in some years). Temporary workers are not included in these estimates. These numbers are lower than many higher, speculative estimates, which experts have found to have no basis in any available data.

6 As of 1983, 11 states (California, Connecticut, Delaware, Florida, Kansas, Maine, Massachusetts, Montana, New Hampshire, Vermont, and Virginia) and Las Vegas had employer sanctions legislation on

their books but had chosen not to enforce these laws. The Illinois and New Jersey legislatures had considered and rejected such legislation.[11]

Historians of immigration distinguish between the "First (mainly Spanish) immigrants" and the "Old Immigration", which began as a constant stream in the 1820s (mainly Irish, German, and Scandinavian) and reached its peak during the years 1840–80. The Irish, who arrived in immense waves, were abjectly poor peasants. The "New Immigration" from eastern and southern Europe developed in the 1880s; and a heavy flow at the turn of the twentieth-century from Russia, Poland, Austria-Hungary, the Balkans, and Italy concentrated sizable foreign-born blocs in the larger cities: Boston (Irish), New York (Jews, Italians), Chicago (Poles, Hungarians, Bohemians). Of the total US population in 1900 (76 million), more than 10 million had been born in Europe, and some 26 million were of foreign parentage. Most numerous were those who settled in New York.[12]

World War II transformed the view of immigrants. In 1921 and 1924 Congress passed, and Presidents Harding and Coolidge signed, laws which cut off most immigration from eastern and southern Europe. The visiting French demographer André Siegfried asked: "will America remain Protestant and Anglo-Saxon?" He understood better than most Americans that the Anglo-Saxon and Puritan stock were becoming a minority in what they had until then regarded as their own country. But few politicians were bold enough to oppose the immigration controls openly – even Al Smith only grumbled about them – and there was no move to repeal them. Even in the 1930s, with war in Europe in prospect, and when immigration slowed to a trickle, Congress still resisted any measure to allow refugees into the US.[13]

What of the post-World War II migration? In 1948 the immigration law authorized the admission of 205,000 European displaced persons, including 3,000 non-quota orphans, and the number was increased in 1950. The McCarran-Walter Act of 1952 codified US immigration laws, in general retaining the provisions of the 1924 Act on maximum immigration and the quota system, but removing

[11] Annelise Anderson and Dennis L. Bark (eds), *Thinking about America: The US in the 1980s* (Stanford, Hoover Institution, 1988), pp. 392–3.

[12] See Carl Wittke, *We Who Built America* (New York, Prentice Hall, 1939); M. L. Hansen, *The Immigrant in American History*, ed. A. M. Schlesinger (New York, Van Nostrand, 1941); and Oscar Handlin, *Immigration as a Factor in American History* (Cambridge, Mass., Harvard University Press, 1959).

[13] André Siegfried, *America Comes of Age* (London, Cape, 1972), vol. I, p. 3.

the ban against immigration of Asian and Pacific people. In 1965 the largest annual quotas applied to Great Britain (65,000), Germany (25,800), and Ireland (17,700). Other European quotas ranged from 6,500 (Poland) to 225 (Turkey). Asian and African national quotas were almost uniformly limited to 100. The total number admitted from all countries in 1965 was 296,697, about one-third of the number annually admitted in the peak decade 1900–10. In 1965 Congress enacted a new immigration law abolishing the national-origins quota system as of June 1968, thus wiping out racial discrimination in immigration.

The Immigration Act of 1965 abolished the discriminatory quotas based on national origins that had favored northwestern Europeans and substituted a system based on family preference. Only 170,000 people would be allowed to enter from the Eastern sphere and 120,000 from the Western, but relatives of individuals already in the US would be exempt from these quotas; once immigrants became citizens, they could bring their relatives and reconstitute their families.

Congress had anticipated that most immigrants would continue to be Europeans; but newcomers from Asia and Latin America quickly began to outnumber Europeans, with 3 out of 4 million immigrants coming from those areas in the 1970s. Between 1951 and 1965, 53 percent of all immigrants came from Europe and only 6.6 percent from Asia; but in the 12-year period after 1966 Europeans represented only 24 percent of immigration, and Asians, 28.4 percent. (Between 1965 and 1974, 75,000 foreign-born physicians entered the country in response to the increased need for medical services resulting from the establishment of Medicare programs.)

The leading sources of immigrants to the United States between 1976 and 1986 were Mexico, Vietnam, the Philippines, Korea, China/Taiwan, Cuba, the Dominican Republic, Jamaica, the UK, and Canada. A sizeable portion of the immigrants after 1965 were refugees – people with widely diverse skills and educational and cultural backgrounds. The largest refugee group, the Cubans, came in three stages. About 200,000, mostly well-educated and middle-class, had fled the island after the assumption of power by Fidel Castro in 1959; a second, more socially diverse, wave of over 360,000 came when they were allowed to leave the island in 1965; and, finally, about 130,000 – the "mariel group" – left when Castro permitted many working-class Cubans to emigrate in 1980–1. Some came to Florida in boats operated by relatives already in the United States. By 1980, Cuban-Americans made up the largest single nationality of the post-World War II refugee stream.

Indochina was the second major source of refugees after 1965. After the fall of Saigon in 1975, the United States immediately accepted 130,000 Vietnamese. As Communist power spread through Southeast Asia, sharply increased numbers of ethnic Chinese, Cambodians, and Laotians also sought asylum in the United States. By 1985, over 700,000 Indochinese had entered the country, many of them resettled with the help of churches and other sponsoring agencies rather than relatives and friends. Although large numbers of Vietnamese possessed skills and strong educational backgrounds, many Cambodians and Laotians were peasants who could not enter the American economy as easily. By 1985 Indochinese refugees in southern California, where most of them settled, were 15 percent less likely to be employed than the population as a whole and were relying on low-wage jobs and public assistance to survive.

The largest immigrant group after 1965 came from Mexico, averaging over 60,000 a year in the 1970s. After Congress in 1964 eliminated the *bracero* program, which had allowed the hiring of temporary workers from Mexico, there was a large increase in the number of undocumented (illegal) workers migrating to Texas and California to enter manufacturing jobs. In the 1970s employment expanded by 645,000 jobs in Los Angeles County, and about one-third of those openings were filled by Mexicans. By 1980 nearly 1 million aliens from Mexico were apprehended annually by the Immigration and Naturalization Service. But the influx continued, in large part because of the willingness of employers to ask the Mexicans no questions. In an attempt to stop this practice, the Immigration Reform Act of 1986 was passed. It imposed penalties on employers who hired illegal immigrants, but offered amnesty to those immigrants who had been in the United States continuously since 1982.

Not all immigrants after 1965 possessed the skills or the inclination to become entrepreneurs. Large numbers of Arabs entered Detroit auto plants; Mexicans in southern California moved primarily into the service economy; but Haitian immigrants in southern Florida in the 1980s encountered more serious problems of adjustment. Fleeing poverty and political repression, these Haitians, most of them under 30, were kept in government detention centers by Florida officials who feared they would become public charges. Even those who were free found it difficult to secure jobs, with few relatives to help and little in the way of skills or education. By 1985 about one-third of Haitian men in southern Florida were jobless. To survive in a strange land, they were forced to rely heavily on female household members who could earn a minimal wage or secure some form of public assistance.

By the 1980s the pattern of immigrant adjustment was a mixed one. Those with skills, education, and family connections frequently do reasonably well. The median family income of Cubans was nearly 30 percent higher than that of other Latin-American immigrants because they entered the well-developed Cuban-American economy in southern Florida. Asian immigrants arriving between 1970 and 1980 earned incomes that nearly equaled those of the native-born. On the other hand, Mexican-Americans forced into unskilled jobs in the service sector of the economy earned mean family incomes well below those of Asians and native whites.[14]

The American immigration situation is unprecedented in world history. The 1965 Immigration Act, which abolished the previous preference for Europeans, triggered an unexpected immigrant influx, predominantly Hispanic and nearly nine-tenths colored. Simultaneously, illegal immigration has soared. An estimated 9 million people arrived in the US in the 1980s, equaling the previous peak decade of the 1900s. About 15 million are expected in the 1990s. While American birth rates are, moreover, much lower than at the turn of the century, so the ethnic balance is shifting quickly. The proportion of whites fell from almost nine-tenths of the population in 1960 to less than three-quarters in 1990. Demographers calculate that America might cease to be majority white by 2050.

Much American political debate trembles with barely contained hysteria about race and ethnicity. To anyone who knows something of the history of nation-states in Europe, it is obviously no more possible to change the ethnic content of a polity without fear of consequence than to replace abruptly all the blood in a human body. Yet this is the experiment upon which America has embarked.

The rationale for the post-1965 immigration influx is that America is not a nation-state in the European sense. Instead, it is said to be an "idea," a political construct based on adherence to a written constitution, without any specific cultural, ethnic or linguistic content. That rationale is unhistorical. It would have astonished Theodore Roosevelt, President during the last great immigration influx, whose many books explicitly celebrated the link between the Anglo-Saxon invasion of England and their descendants' winning of the American West. When President Coolidge signed the legislation ending the last influx in the 1920s, he

[14] Nathan Glazer (ed.), *Beyond the Melting Pot* (Cambridge, Mass., MIT Press, 1973); David M. Reimers (ed.), *Still the Golden Door: The Third World comes to America* (New York, Columbia University Press, 1985).

explained his reason succinctly: "America must be kept American." Everyone knew what he meant.

Even in a country composed almost entirely of immigrants and their descendants, such policies have produced a backlash of fear and anger which threatens to become a hot national issue. Heavy majorities – around 70 percent in two polls in 1993 – favor reducing the flow of people through the Golden Door. Latinos, Indians, Pakistanis, Arabs and others – especially those who get into the country illegally – are unwelcome to Americans who find their cultures strange.

Indeed, the major reason for fearing a nationwide backlash is that illegal entries keep going up, despite government attempts to reduce them. The Immigration Control Act of 1986, which imposed criminal penalties on employers who knowingly hire illegal aliens, stanched the flow just briefly. Arrests by the US Border Patrol along the US–Mexican frontier dropped from 1.7 million in the year before the Act took effect, to 890,000 three years later. But the number has climbed back up to 1.2 million a year. As a rule of thumb, two or three illegals get away for every one who is caught, so the influx of aliens from Mexico alone might total 4 million a year – equal to the population of Philadelphia.

The sentiments of those who are against such open immigration are not entirely xenophobic. Many contend that at a time of slow job growth and pinched budgets for social services, America simply cannot accommodate a flood of the world's "homeless, tempest-tost." Bette Hammond, spokeswoman for a California group calling itself STOP IT – for Stop the Out-of-Control Problems of Immigration Today – suggests a rewrite of Lazarus: "If the Statue of Liberty could speak, she would say, 'Many of my people are jobless and homeless. My natural resources are fast disappearing from overcrowding and pollution, while my cities are full of crime. My domestic tranquility is a thing of the past.'"[15]

Like many national trends, the anti-immigrant backlash is appearing first and strongest in California. The nation's most populous state is the biggest lure for illegal immigrants, mainly Mexicans who sneak, run, and tunnel across the frontier in numbers far greater than the Border Patrol can possibly control. They then compete for jobs in a state that has suffered deeper employment losses than most during the long national recession and limping recovery. Or so say the critics; allies of the immigrants insist

[15] *New York Herald-Tribune*, Mar. 20, 1992.

they actually make the economy more competitive by taking low-wage, manual-labor jobs that Americans scorn.

In the Marin County town of San Rafael, north of San Francisco, "every day, a few hundred day laborers line the city streets," says Rick Oltman, leader of the Marin Immigration Reform Association: "They come here and live 15 or 20 in an apartment and work one day a week." Last week the city council shelved a plan to build a $175,000 job center for the day laborer. The center, says Oltman, "would just encourage more to come here."[16]

A bigger complaint is the cost of social services such as welfare, medical care, and schooling for immigrants and their children, who have no right even to be in the country. Assemblyman Richard Mountjoy puts the cost to California at $3 billion a year. Though some illegals pay taxes, he points out that the money goes mainly to Washington, leaving the states to supply the social services from inadequate federal reimbursements. "The state is broke," says an aide to Assemblyman Gil Ferguson. "We've had a multibillion-dollar deficit three years in a row, and yet we continue to pay medical benefits for these illegal immigrants. We take better care of them than of our own people."[17]

More than 20 bills have been introduced in the California legislature in 1994 to limit benefits to illegals. Mountjoy explains the strategy: the state cannot stop them from coming, because policing the borders is solely a federal responsibility. So "you have to stop the benefits of coming here: the educational benefits, the health care, the workmen's compensation." None of the bills has yet passed, though one has cleared the state senate. Two were defeated in early votes, but Mountjoy and his allies vow to keep trying to push them through. California tried again in Proposition 187 in the November 1994 election.

Elsewhere in the US anti-immigrant sentiment is widespread but less intense. Asked specifically by pollsters if they favor curbing immigration, most people say they do, but when presented with a general question as to what they consider the nation's most serious problems, only about 2 percent mention reducing immigration. Many people, too, have very mixed feelings. Even in California the most vehement opponents of illegal immigration profess the highest regard for those who come to the US legitimately and even view them as potential allies. "If you came here and obeyed the laws, then you should be on our side, because these

[16] *New York Herald-Tribune*, March 1993.
[17] Ibid.

people compete with the legal immigrant population," says Oltman, the Marin County leader. He adds that his own wife is an immigrant – from Belgium.

The politics of immigration has created strange alliances and oppositions. Liberal Democrat Eugene McCarthy and Conservative Democrat Richard Lamm favored restricting immigration, as does arch-conservative Republican Pat Buchanan. Polls by the Joint Center for Political and Economic Studies, a black "think tank", found that African-Americans were far more sympathetic than whites to the plight of Haitian refugees, but also far more worried than whites about competition from immigrants for jobs.

Although US immigration policy is irrational, the political establishment resists discussion of it. The reasons are various. Some will be familiar to British observers who recall MP Enoch Powell's famous "rivers of blood" speech against immigration in the 1970s, echoes of which have been voiced with reference to Mexicans in Los Angeles, Cubans in Miami, and Puerto Ricans along the Atlantic coast;[18] others reflect peculiar American pressures. We may be watching America heaping up its funeral pyre, to use Powell's phrase – or, perhaps, a launching pad to becoming the "first universal nation." Whatever it is, it looms increasingly large.

5 THE BLACK AMERICANS

I say to you today, my friends, that in spite of the difficulties and frustrations of the moment, I still have a dream. It is a dream deeply rooted in the American dream. I have a dream that one day this nation will rise up and live out the true meaning of its creed: "We hold these truths to be self-evident: that all men are created equal."

Martin Luther King,
Address at the March on Washington
August 28, 1963

The presence of black people in America has always cast a dark shadow across American professions of equality. No modern European societies had to live half slave and half free. Indeed, Russia freed the serfs – and faced an infinitely more complex economic problem in doing so – before the United States freed the slaves.

[18] Patrick Cosgrave, MP *The lives of Enoch Powell* (London, The Bodley Head, 1989).

Lincoln carried through Emancipation in 1863 only in those states at war with the North and as a military tactic, not from an absolute set of ethical convictions. The strange career of Jim Crow is a reminder that there has been nothing hypocritical in the eyes of many Americans about the status of America's blacks. For generations, many states maintained laws that defined their status as separate *because* unequal. It was a narrow band of intellectuals, living several removes from the largest concentrations of blacks and whites, who believed that Americans faced a dilemma in their race relations. In almost every generation, both whites and blacks have differed among themselves about the best form of race relations. Nor are the black Separatists of today unique in American history. Mormons, Fourierists, Mennonites, and settlers of foreign-language communities everywhere on the Prairies have also fought, usually unsuccessfully, to build a fence around their own plot of Eden.

But in an age of national dissatisfaction, there is danger that Americans as well as foreign observers will overlook the achievements of contemporary American society. Concurrent with the rise of anxieties about national policies many things were done, and done well, whether judged by American or European standards. And for many African-Americans history began only in 1954, and was mainly turmoil.

The affluence of America is taken for granted by Americans today, in a way that would not have occurred to a generation raised in the depression, whose first experience of economic laws taught them about scarcity rather than abundance. Europeans raised on the shortages of war and the austerity of reconstruction, as well as upon depression, still cannot take their eyes off the evidence of well-being in American society today. For example, Americans cannot be said to have a housing problem, when American housing (old or new) is judged against European counterparts. The only problem that Americans can claim is a problem of the people who live in houses in such a way that buildings with a solid fabric become slums long before their useful life need be ended. The basic problems of America today are those of a "post-affluent" society.

The "decade of discontent" of the 1960s also saw great advances in civil rights. The civil rights legislation passed by Congress with strong executive leadership went far beyond anything previously enacted in American history, and far beyond what a British government has yet seen fit to provide for British blacks. Notwithstanding the rhetoric of black militants, the majority of blacks are proud, and have incentive to be proud, of their American citizenship.

In the years after World War II, the suburbs whitened with the addition of families who could financially take advantage of post-war jobs and housing; the cities filled up with poor families of every complexion. The majority of the poor were white, but in the central cities the rapid darkening of the population gave the impression that poverty was a characteristic of black people; this fitted the prejudices of most Americans and facilitated the propensity of popular wisdom to blame urban problems on the victims of economic transformation.

Like the other 16 million Americans who gave up rural life for an urban existence, the 4 million blacks who flocked to the cities were redundant in the increasingly mechanized farms of the postwar South. Mechanization took place with remarkable speed, so that between 1940 and 1965 the proportion of blacks living on the land declined from one-half to one-fifth. Between 1958 and 1964 alone, the use of mechanical cotton pickers in the Mississippi River Delta area increased from 27 to 81 percent; the story was much the same in the upper South. Sometimes the black tenant farmers and sharecroppers moved to a Southern city, but most of them headed for six states outside the South: California, Illinois, Michigan, New York, Ohio, and Pennsylvania. Their destination was the cities in the largest metropolitan areas – and these were precisely the cities beginning to experience the highest rates of decline in manufacturing jobs. The black newcomers faced an unemployment rate double that of whites, for by the late 1950s they were moving into an urban economy on the decline.

In the summer of 1963, Martin Luther King delivered his "I have a Dream" speech to an estimated quarter of a million people who had converged on Washington. By the time of President Kennedy's assassination that autumn in Dallas, Southern politicians had already organized a dogged and time-consuming resistance. The following year, 1964, President Johnson, a liberal Texan and brilliant congressional strategist, helped by emotional reaction to Kennedy's assassination and to the bombing of a black church in Birmingham, Alabama, which killed four young black girls, was able to force the Civil Rights Bill through the Senate after 534 hours of filibuster.

Johnson's triumph was short-lived. Southern registration officials continued to use literacy tests and poll tax requirements in a blatantly discriminatory way. King and other civil rights leaders organized renewed registration drives and marches. In March 1965, Alabama police, under the command of "Bull" Connor, attacked peaceful demonstrators *en route* for Montgomery on the bridge at Selma, using tear gas, electrified cattle prods, night-sticks, and savage dogs. James Meredith was shot while leading another such march. The administration introduced a new Voting Rights Bill to throw the full weight of federal power behind black rights. In still-resistant areas of the South, the federal government would take over voter registration and would police the polling stations; the literacy test would be abolished, and poll tax requirements nullified. The bill became law in record time in August 1965, and thereafter in the South, after a century of struggle, blacks at last had that basic political right "without which all others are meaningless."

The revolution of rising expectations had not escaped the attention of Northern ghetto blacks. The disadvantages under which they struggled had been articulated by President Kennedy in 1963:

> The Negro baby born in America today, regardless of the section or the state in which he is born, has about one-half as much chance of completing high school as a white baby, born in the same place, on the same day; one-third as much chance of becoming a professional man; twice as much chance of becoming unemployed; about one-seventh as much chance of earning $10,000 a year; a life expectancy which is seven years shorter and the prospects of earning only half as much.

Five days after President Johnson signed the Voting Rights Act of 1965, the Los Angeles ghetto of Watts exploded into a week of black rioting, looting, shooting, and burning. The pattern was repeated in ghetto after ghetto in the next two "long hot summers." Few major Northern cities escaped outbursts of black frustration and rage. In 1968, the murder of Martin Luther King in Memphis triggered a new phase of outraged destruction. Parts of Washington DC resembled a blitzed city.

Meanwhile, young blacks in the North had become increasingly disillusioned with King's insistence on integration and Christian charity, which they found inadequate or irrelevant to their needs. The cry of Black Power, the title of one of Richard Wright's books, but first used by Stokely Carmichael (like Garvey, a West Indian) on a voter registration drive in the South in 1965, was enthusiastically taken up. The Black Muslim Movement, dominated since the 1930s by Elijah Mohammed in Chicago, recruited many disillusioned young blacks, among them Malcolm X and the young heavyweight boxing champion Cassius Clay. With its celebration of the non-white world, its program for forming a separate black nation in America, its contemptuous reversal of Christian myths – a white devil, for instance – and its insistence on Islamic asceticism and self-discipline, its rigor gave a new purpose to many young ghetto blacks lost in a chaos of drug addiction, crime, unemployment, truancy, or vice. In 1966, as a protest against pervasive police harassment and brutality, Huey Newton and Bobby Seale formed the Black Panther party in Oakland, California; a militant organization, visibly armed and rhetorically violent. Elsewhere, ghetto communities agitated for community control of education and welfare services. Black students demanded lenient admissions procedures to universities, and vocational training and the mounting of black studies programs in schools and colleges.

Increasingly, emphasis was placed on the separate identity of the Negro; indeed, the word "Negro" itself now became a term of abuse, betokening racial appeasement. Where Du Bois had once waged a battle to ensure that the word was written with a capital "N," now Baraka insisted on using the word "black" and the dominant tone was an aggressive assertion of cultural identity. Ironically, the Johnson anti-poverty program strengthened this movement by channeling money directly into the ghettos, thereby bypassing the conventional civil rights leadership.

Initially the new generation of young black leaders who emerged with heightened polemical styles concentrated on consciousness-raising, on a distinctive lifestyle, on confronting the black American with the question of his own authenticity. Du Bois's double consciousness was to be resolved in favor of blackness; "Black is Beautiful" was their early rallying cry. Yet, as their ideas developed, the essence of their message came to emphasize racial separation less than radical revolt. Indeed, individuals such as Eldridge Cleaver (*Soul on Ice*, 1968), Malcolm X (*The Autobiography of Malcolm X*, 1966), Bobby Seale (*Seize the Time*, 1970), Huey Newton (*Revolutionary Suicide*, 1973), George Jackson (*The Prison Letters of George Jackson*, 1969), and Angela Davis (*Angela Davis: An autobiography*, 1974) moved towards a class-critique of black problems.

Paradoxically, in the 1970s, while these radical and racial ideas were mulling, the black stake in the established American educational and political systems was increasing. The percentage of Southern blacks in all-black schools dropped from 58 percent in 1968 to 9.2 percent in 1972. By 1978, 2,200 blacks held political office in the South, compared with less than 100 before 1965.

Though significant discrepancies remained between black and white employment (13 percent black unemployment compared with 7 percent white in 1977), and though a black could still expect to receive a markedly lower income than a similarly qualified white, equal rights legislation forced on employers the onus of justifying the non-hiring of minorities. By 1976, black families had a median income of $9,252, an increase of 105 percent over the decade, though still $6,000 below the white median; 30 percent of all black families earned $15,000 or more, compared with 2 percent in 1966. The rise of the black middle class, an increasing number in white enterprises, occurred at a time of economic recession. In the South, more than half the eligible blacks were registered voters by 1978. Not only had Northern cities like Los Angeles, Cleveland, Detroit, and Washington black mayors, but so also had the leading Southern cities of Atlanta and New Orleans. Black students now constituted a higher proportion of the student body at the University of Alabama than at many Northern universities; the police force of McComb, Mississippi, known in the 1960s as "The Bombing Capital of the World," was now fully integrated; Selma had a Dr Martin Luther King Street. The easing of the burden of racism from the South brought relief to whites as well as blacks. Symbolic of the ending of that section's pariah status was the election to the presidency of Jimmy Carter, the first fully-fledged Southerner since the Civil War.

Curiously enough, these very real black gains in the 1970s, though founded on the liberal measures of the 1960s, took place at a time when racial conflict had been shifted out of the limelight. Nixon's policy was one of benign neglect. The trauma of Vietnam and then of Watergate distracted liberal consciences from the unfinished business of achieving racial equality. The problem of segregation in the North, where whites had left the inner cities for non-metropolitan suburbs, proved, however, far more resistant to change than did that in the South. The legally enforced solution of bussing to achieve racial balance in public schools led to violent white reactions in Boston in 1974. The recession and the financial crises of Northern cities threatened the welfare programs of poor ghetto blacks at the same time as their more fortunate brethren were joining the American middle classes. The general conservatism of the decade extended equally to the black community. The Black Panthers had been effectively destroyed by police bullets; the Muslims retreated from separatist doctrines. Bobby Seale became a Washington lobbyist; Eldridge Cleaver converted to Christianity; Amiri Baraka joined the ranks of radical conservatism as an orthodox Marxist. Alex Haley's *Roots* could hardly be described as revolutionary. There were even signs of a black re-immigration back to the South. While many problems remained, however, notably that of the poorest blacks – 26 percent of black families still earned less than $5,000 per year – the general prospect at the end of the 1970s was one of hope, compared with the despair felt by many blacks during the first century of "emancipation."

Another dream has haunted many African-Americans – the thought of the journey back to Africa. Jack E. White wrote of it in *Time* magazine, September 7, 1992:

> Everywhere I went, I felt a sense of kinship with the people I covered, who looked like long-lost friends and relatives back in the US. From the moment I set foot in Africa, I had a sense of having come home.
>
> But with time and greater knowledge, that powerful awareness of the genetic link between Africa and its lost children was alloyed with a more complex emotion: a realization of all that was lost when our unwilling ancestors made their transatlantic voyage. Our centuries in America have transformed black Americans into a Western people. The boxer Muhammad Ali, after visiting Africa, joked that he was glad "my great granddaddy caught that ship." The point is that whether or not we rejoice in the fact, our ancestors did come to America, and not many of us can ever go completely home again.

There has always been an understandable tendency among African-Americans to dismiss bad news about Africa as racist lies. During the late 1970s, for example, a certain civil rights leader tried to persuade black American professionals to lend support to Ugandan dictator Idi Amin. Reports that Amin had slaughtered tens of thousands of his people were brushed aside as inventions of the racist Western propaganda machine. The truth, of course, is that until Amin was chased into exile by Julius Nyerere's Tanzania, he was one of the most murderous tyrants the world has known. His country, once one of the most beautiful and prosperous in Africa, is still recovering from his depredations.

Until recently, it has been the fashion to explain away tyranny perpetrated by blacks against blacks across the continent, attributing it – sometimes correctly – to manipulation by former colonial powers or by Washington. Genocidal ethnic conflicts such as the vicious clan warfare in Somalia go largely ignored. Conversely, black Americans have directed enormous rage at the oppression of black Africans by white South Africans.

The gradual collapse of apartheid was brought about in part by international trade sanctions adopted by the US government because of relentless pressure from African-Americans led by Trans-Africa, a lobbying group based in Washington, and by the Black Caucus in Congress. There are signs that this victory may be ushering in a new, more mature relationship between African-Americans and Africa. Randall Robinson, Trans-Africa's executive director, is one of the orchestrators of this welcome change. He notes with justifiable pride that the imposition of sanctions on South Africa marked the first time black Americans significantly changed US foreign policy. Doing so instilled a new confidence in African-Americans about their ability to bring about change in this country, and in Africa as well.

Though it has been little noticed by the press, Robinson and like-minded black politicians and businessmen have been gradually doing away with the double standard that condemned oppression by South Africa's white regime, while ignoring oppression elsewhere on the continent. In 1990, a group including Robinson, Jesse Jackson, Coretta Scott King, and several black elected officials and labor leaders issued a statement calling for an end to the "violence and tyranny" inflicted by Kenyan President Daniel Arap Moi's one-party government. Robinson has since repeated the criticism in appearances before US congressional committees, adding Zaire's Mobutu Sese Seko and other African tyrants to the list.

Robinson points out that the end of the Cold War set the stage for a new and uncertain relationship between the US and Africa. Now that America is no longer engaged in a twilight struggle with the former Soviet Union, it no longer needs to prop up African despots like Mobutu to keep them out of the enemy camp. Thus the US is free to live up to its idealistic commitment to representative government by lending aid to the fledgling democratic and human rights movement that are springing up across the continent. The question is whether in a time of fiscal impecunity and crying needs in the newly independent countries of the old Soviet empire, the US will invest in the economic fledglings of Africa.

Robinson's hope is to add another arm to Trans-Africa's effort: a training school for young black foreign service officers and academics, who could become a permanent inside-the-system pressure group for increased US aid to Africa. But Robinson also points out that the effort cannot succeed unless African-Americans take a consistent moral stand regarding oppression throughout Africa. Like other black Americans who want to assist their motherland, he recognizes that they can succeed only to the extent that they accept Africa for what it really is – not by holding on to what they imagine it to be.

There is another African-American cause. Each summer, usually in Detroit, gather hundreds of African-American campaigners seeking financial redress for slavery. They cite parallels. The Sioux won compensation from the US government in 1980 for the seizure of their lands in 1877; Japanese Americans got damages for being locked up during the World II; and now a growing number of black Americans say that they should receive reparations for slavery.

The movement, which draws support from an array of black personalities from rap artists to Congressmen, wants the government to make good a promise made after the American Civil War to give freed slaves "40 acres and a mule." Campaigners say that that pledge is now worth $198,149 (£132,000) for every black American. About 1,000 activists gathered in Detroit in July 1994 to hold their fifth annual conference on reparations. Frustrated by the lack of progress, some descendants of slaves, such as Velena Conley, have decided to go it alone. The 70-year old former schoolmistress from Oakland, California, has filed a lawsuit against the US government seeking $110 million in damages for the enslavement of her ancestors. Adopting a different tactic, other reparationists have begun withholding income tax.

The reparationist movement has gained strength as blacks have become increasingly disillusioned with what they achieved in their struggle for civil rights in the 1960s. With black communities still beset by poverty and crime, reparations are seen as a new focal point in raising black consciousness. Dorothy Benton-Lewis of the Black Reparations Commission said recently: "Our ancestors had every single pay day of their lives stolen so that whites could be unjustly enriched. When they died, there was nothing to pass on to the next generation, and the next."

The reparations movement now counts among its supporters such luminaries as the former presidential contender, the Reverend Jesse Jackson, Martin Luther King's widow, Coretta Scott King, and the rap group Public Enemy. Spike Lee, the black filmmaker who directed the blockbuster *Malcolm X*, has pointedly named his production company 40 Acres and a Mule.

The issue of compensation for slaves and their descendants goes back to 1861, when two white abolitionists introduced Bills which would have given each slave 40 acres of confiscated land. But the measure was blocked.

There is debate about how any reparations could be paid. Some campaigners have suggested that black Americans should be tax-exempted, while others want land or a scholarship fund. Although in 1994 the claim was made to President Clinton, historians could in all frankness ask why the US government should be held responsible, since having fought a civil war that government officially ended slavery in the post-Civil War amendments to the Constitution, and after many were killed and maimed in that struggle. That apart, there is need for careful accounting. In many Northern states after the Declaration of Independence, slavery had ended (Pennsylvania in 1780, New York in 1799, New Jersey in 1804, and in Maryland free blacks outnumbered slaves, to cite but a few). Moreover, was it not the lords of the lash (Southern planters) and the lords of the loom (the Northern cotton manufacturer) who profited from the plantation economy rather than the federal government? Moreover, many slaves bought their freedom, or had it conferred in their masters' wills when they died – as with Washington and Jefferson. And many who became free men had learnt their skills as coopers and carpenters, blacksmiths and plumbers, in or near the Big House. Indeed, some blacks who became free became wealthy – and in turn, owners of slaves – witness Jehu Jones, the wealthy hotel owner in Charleston, or many a prosperous black entrepreneur in New Orleans, before and after the Civil War. Who pays whom? *Cui bono*? And to add irony to fact: Detroit, where such complainers gather, has a history of violence; it is a city that has more guns than people – Representative Barbara-Rose Collins, who has represented the 13th District of Michigan since 1990, is a member of the Shrine of the Black Madonna, a Pan African Orthodox Christian Church, and has been affected by crime herself, since her adult son was convicted of armed robbery. The 13th District coincides with Detroit's center city; originally the first automobile city in the US, now it is in decline, and prey to violence and arsonists, and in need both of effective gun control and – thanks to population movement out of it – redistricting. The Voting Rights Act, however, requires the preservation of black-majority districts even when they are demographically deserted. If there is any case for compensation for the wickedness of slavery, money could well be spent on the civic reform and rebuilding of Detroit.

6 CRIME AND VIOLENCE: THE GRIM STATISTICS

The troubles of today are not unique: they have their counterparts in earlier eras of the American story. If the 1960s found Vietnam, racial violence, the hippy culture and draft-dodging terrible problems, the 1950s found the beat generation and the witchhunting of Joe McCarthy equally distasteful and inexplicable. In the 1930s the depression drove many jobless emigrants to America back to their European origins. In the 1920s a number of American intellectuals left the United States in their own protest against its Babbitry, against the Ku Klux Klan and the judicial murder of Sacco and Vanzetti, making Paris for a while the intellectual capital of the United States. The 1890s might in retrospect seem to be the years of the full dinner-pail, but they were also the years of the Pinkertons and strongarm methods in strikebreaking, of Big Bill Haywood and the Wobblies, who did not stop short of dynamiting. The 1830s and 1840s found it hard to tolerate causes as diverse as the Mormons, the immigrant Irish, the Utopian New Harmony community and Elijah Lovejoy, the white abolitionist preacher. The outlaw, the eccentric, and the Utopian, the extremists of Right and Left, have a long history and a proud pedigree in America, north and south of the Mason-Dixon line. In American history the gun, rather than the Bill of Rights, has been "the great equalizer." Violence is a recurrent theme in the American story; it is, as Rap Brown said in 1967, "as American as cherry pie."

Crime rates have always been relatively high in the United States, which may have much to do with social values that stress individual achievement, wealth, and fame, without much regard to means or social cost. Still, the statistics should give pause to those who have not stopped celebrating the American Century. US rates for homicide and violent crime are four to ten times higher than those of western European countries and three times those of Canada.

A tidal wave of crime, which began in the 1960s, a decade during which crime rates more than doubled, continues to roll across America. Each year, about 6.6 million Americans become victims of murder, rape, robbery, or assault.[19] A murder occurs every 22

[19] Morgan O. Reynolds, "Crime pays, but so does imprisonment," National Center for Policy Analysis, *Policy Report* no. 149 (March 1990), p. 1, based on the National Crime Survey conducted annually by the US. Bureau of the Census for the Bureau of Justice Statistics.

minutes, a rape every 5 minutes, a robbery every minute, and an aggravated assault every 28 seconds.[20] About 29 million Americans each year are victims of arson, burglary, and larceny-theft.[21] A motor vehicle theft occurs every 20 seconds, a burglary every 11 seconds, and a larceny-theft every 4 seconds.[22] Eight out of every ten Americans can expect to be victims of violent crime at least once in their lives.[23]

Three decades after the passage of the Civil Rights Act of 1964 the situation of black Americans is arguably worse than it was three decades ago. In the face of massive (nearly 50 percent) unemployment statistics, the rotting of inner cities, and the abject collapse of the school system, minority youth especially turn to antisocial behavior and crime. The only response by federal and state governments, Republican and Democrat, to that increasing crime rate is an ever more costly penal system for which funds must somehow be found.

One-fifth of black men aged 16 to 34, and as many as three-fourths of black high school dropouts aged 25 to 34, had criminal records in the 1980s. In 1989 of all 16-to-34-year-old US men, 2 percent were in prison and another 5 percent were on either parole or probation.

Although blacks account for only just over 12 percent of the population, almost half of the 21,500 murders committed in the US in 1991 were of black people, 90 percent of whom were killed by other blacks, usually with firearms. Juvenile arrests for weapons law violations increased by 62 percent between 1987 and 1991, with black youths being arrested at three times the rate of whites. In addition to the murders, which in 1991 claimed more than six people a day under the age of 18, the Justice Department estimates that each year nearly one million teenagers are raped, robbed or assaulted, mainly by their peers. As they told the Rev. Jesse Jackson at countless school meetings in 1993, many black children regard possession of a gun as essential for their self-defense, just as rednecks do in the South. At one school in Washington,

[20] *Ibid.*; Federal Bureau of Investigation, *Crime in the United States, Uniform Crime Reports in the United States* (Washington, DC, US Department of Justice, 1992), p. 4.

[21] Reynolds, "Crime pays," p. 1.

[22] *Ibid.*; FBI, *Crime in the United States.*

[23] William J. Bennett, *The Index of Leading Cultural Indicators* (Washington, DC, Empower America, The Heritage Foundation, and The Free Congress Foundation, 1993), p. 2.

a boy upbraided Mr Jackson for naiveté about what it takes to survive in the streets. "I'm sorry, sir, this is 1993 not 1963," he said. "I don't know where you've been." Mr Jackson put his hand on the boy's shoulders and replied: "I've been to a lot of teenage funerals."

One can only guess at the effect all this has on black morale and self-esteem, but it is hardly conducive to optimism. Many black Americans still find comfort in their churches – a Gallup poll five years ago found that 75 percent of all blacks agreed with the statement that "religion can answer all or most of today's problem" – but now even the churches are losing credibility with their members, following allegations that church leaders in New Jersey took bribes from the Republicans to keep blacks away from the polls during the most recent gubernatorial election. One black Baptist pastor says parishioners now regularly call him to ask: "Reverend, how much money did you get?"

The fact of violence, and debate over its causes, are familiar today. It is especially now a norm in the cities, in Washington, Los Angeles, and New York City, and of gang *versus* gang. There are on average each year 2,000 murders in New York City, and a New York taxi-driver is killed every week.

Not since Chicago in the 1930s has a city been held hostage by such a large army of street gangs as Los Angeles. Los Angeles County has an estimated 130,000 gang members, with ever increasing firepower. (Of 20,000 weapons that disappeared from shops during the 1993 riots, only 3,000 have been recovered.)

More than 500 gangs, with some 80,000 known members, infest Los Angeles; the best known are the Bloods and the Crips, the two largest, predominantly black, gangs, and the most bitter of rivals. Bloods and Crips break down into small neighborhood sets, and it is not uncommon for one Crip group to fight another Crip group up the street, for Blood to fight Blood. There were 462 gang-related murders in 1988, 107 of them in South Central, 111 square kilometres of ghetto with a population of 500,000. Though the murder rate does not approach the carnage of Beirut or El Salvador on a *per capita* basis, it is higher than that of Belfast or Burma. The US Army has begun sending doctors to train in the emergency room of Martin Luther King Jr General Hospital in Watts, because there they can get 24-hour-a-day experience, treating the kind of gunshot wounds normally seen only in battle.

In the American Dream of a generation ago, suburban security was assumed. Not now. Take Dade County, Florida – i.e. Miami

– as example: it is now heavily fortified, a prey to fear and violence. In Hialeeh, Opa Locka, or any other blue-collar to middle-class neighborhood of Dade County, extravagant self-defense is on display. It goes in layers, from crude chainlink to floodlights and laser-beam alarms, telling stories of class and crime levels. It could be a cityscape from Mexico or Brazil.

The result is as far from the tranquil open-latch security of Britain's recent past as it is from the old American Dream of suburban contentment. Goodwill and a stable society were assumed, at least in rosetinted memory. But it is no accident that great stretches of Dade County should look like this. They are frontline evidence of what is known as the Brazilianization of America: the slide towards Third World extremes of wealth and poverty, the fraying of the Anglophonic, European consensus on the idea of what America means, and the failures of social organization writ large in crime figures.

From shotgun and dog to concierge, video-camera and alarm, the fortress mentality is digging ever deeper into the American Way. The rich and famous of Los Angeles build extravagant castles protected by everything short of vats of boiling oil. Private police forces of security guards patrol the lush streets of the fabled Beverly Hills zip-code with dogs and guns. Metal signs in the shape of police shields are posted along the walls of mansions and read: Caution. Armed Response.

"In the medium-to-luxury market," says Edguardo Defortuna, who runs a Miami estate agency, "what people are looking for is a gated *community*, with access only by residents and authorized visitors." The further up-market you go, the more discreet the security arrangements. The best security is in the gated community supported by the latest technology; video cameras to keep ever-vigilant watch, and computers with terminals at every security point to keep track of all who come and go. It would take a James Bond or a Viking raiding party to reach the family silver in Miami's hottest-selling locations, where state-of-the-art "smart card" entry keys are programmed, for instance, to admit the maid during her duty hours only.

7 THE SOCIAL MOSAIC

Crime pays in America. That is the harsh truth that the American liberal establishment cannot bring itself to face. The legal reforms of the 1960s and 1970s have undermined deterrence. The risk of arrest for robbery fell by two-thirds in the 1960s alone. By the mid-1970s, a young man in Chicago could be arrested 14 times on average before being imprisoned for the first time. Many states began to destroy all criminal records of offenders when they reached 18 which meant that teenagers could experiment with crime. Once they had started, of course, it was hard to stop. Indeed, there are even variations on matters of life and death. There is no national policy on the death sentence. Commit murder in Indiana and you may be put to death for it; murder across the line in Michigan and you do not take this risk.

The character of the American judiciary changes slowly, like a great tanker turning at sea. One by one the liberal justices appointed to the Supreme Court by Kennedy, Johnson, and, surprisingly, Nixon, have been replaced by conservatives, chipping away, with due respect for precedent, at the historic rulings of the Warren Court. In 20 years time the balance of justice will have shifted back from the criminal to the victim. The politically correct response to the Los Angeles riots is yet more social spending. This supposes the delinquency of ghetto life can be ameliorated by economic policies.

The system has arisen simply because the New York courts have become overloaded with cases. Some 250,000 are brought before the courts every year, but less than 1 percent are heard by a jury; the remainder are disposed of by the defendants pleading guilty in exchange for a greatly reduced sentence. Put like that, it sounds quite sensible; but the reality is very different. A fairer description would be to say that those who elect for trial by jury, and are then convicted, are given greatly increased sentences – almost as if they are being punished for bucking the system. Someone selling two dollars' worth of crack on the streets, for example, might expect one or two years if he pleads guilty and over 10 years if found guilty by a jury. Most people, inevitably, plead guilty.

Police brutality is endemic, but it does not follow that the whole system of law enforcement in America is biased against blacks. To some extent it discriminates in favour of blacks. The procedure of stacking juries, used to acquit the police in the Rodney King trial, is routinely employed by blacks as well. In Washington DC, where the majority of the population is black, the lawyers are able to choose the jury of 12 from a pool of 60. If the accused is black, "whitey" can go on home. A white called for jury service in a drug trial is likely to be dismissed on sight by defense lawyers. The result is that it is hard to convict a black in a Washington court for any offense – be it mugging, burglary, or homicide – in which the victim is white. Jury screening, in a society poisoned by racial animosity, works to the advantage of the criminal whatever the color of his or her skin.

In the meantime American bridges and highways are slowly falling apart, the public transportation system is increasingly unpleasant, when it is not positively unsafe, and health costs are rising remorselessly. Although the health insurance industry is enriched, the US has appalling health statistics and life expectancy compared with those of Europe, and somewhat worse infant mortality statistics than those of Cuba. New York City had infant mortality rates in 1991 resembling those of Shanghai. Tuberculosis has reappeared in the inner cities. A raging epidemic of AIDS has already killed more young males than the war in Vietnam did. Life expectancy of young black males in US cities is less than that of males in Bangladesh. This is the result of a combination of factors: lack of decent available jobs and of access to medical care; massive increase in the use of alcohol and drugs, with diminishing funds for rehabilitation, and the sheer increase in violent crime.

Little attention is paid to the politically irresponsible, demagogic, and absolutely appalling content of political campaigns in the United States. Americans seem to have quite lost the habit of treating politicians, particularly while campaigning, as adults, who should be taken seriously and held responsible for what they say. Campaigning is now an apolitical art form – better yet, a craft – an exercise in placing the right spin on exquisitely balanced cameo appearances, on monstrously expensive prime-time television spots. One should immediately add that it is an increasingly costly art form, accessible only to the rich and super-rich.

The political system dominated by the business community has been reinforced by the gross commercialization of all mass media and an absence of any political dialogue. A systematic depoliticization of politics has been proceeding in the United States for decades.

But there is concurrently a growing consolidation: of business, of agriculture, and of law firms too. The old founding families are being replaced by tough professionals. To become one of these, it helps in this land of equal opportunity to go to the right school and the right university, and not least in law to go to the right law school. The products are tough and aggressive – one of them was described by a Congressman as "the corporate embodiment of Jaws, the great white shark." And yet whatever the style, and whatever the language used by politicians, it is no longer the world of *laissez-faire*. Government is bigger than ever, and ever more intrusive.

The massive ethnic communities that make up the mosaic of American society cannot be adequately described as "minorities." There is, however, no "majority." The largest single identifiable ethnic strain are people of British ancestry – who make up just 15 percent of the American population. They barely outnumber German Americans (13 percent) or blacks (11 percent). Millions of Americans cannot identify themselves at all ethnically, due to intermixtures over the generations.[24]

The incomes, occupations, and unemployment rates of American ethnic groups are too different from one another to be described by any generalization. Moreover, it is as misleading in the economic area as in other areas to think of them as "minorities" who fall below some "majority," or national average, in socioeconomic terms. A number of ethnic groups exceed the national average in socio-economic status.

Family Income Index
(U.S. Average = 100)

Jewish	172
Japanese	132
Polish	115
Chinese	112
Italian	112
German	107
Anglo-Saxon	107
Irish	103
Total US	100
Filipino	99
West Indian	94
Mexican	76
Puerto Rican	63
Black	62
Indian	60

Source: US Bureau of the Census and National Jewish Population survey, 1993

Today, behind all the varied origins of the 250 million people, white and black, Hispanic and Oriental, Protestant, Catholic, Jewish, and all the rest, there is a rich and varied sameness. This is, they

[24] Cf. Thomas Sowell, *Ethnic America* (New York, Basic Books, 1981).

say, a maturing society and one that is now middle-aged in mood. It is increasingly integrated economically and culturally; the South is now part of the political mainstream; three national TV networks, nationally syndicated columns and news services, and the magnificent Interstate highways of the Eisenhower era, all make communication rapid, even instant. As part of the sameness, Main Street is everywhere, with Macdonalds, Kentucky Fried Chicken, and a Holiday Inn everywhere too. Less than 3 percent of the work force now work on the land; America's economy is now a service economy; government, health, and education between them account for one job in every three. Even in politics, the ward and the constituency matter less. As David Glancey, the Philadelphia Democratic leader, put it in 1980 "Today's precinct captain is the TV set."

There is considerable evidence that traditional ethnic "boundaries," the social borders separating groups from each other, have never really been obliterated. They still persist, and for reasons obvious to anyone familiar with the course of ethnic group formation and maintenance in the United States. "Ethnicity" – the measure of the individual's attachment to the group and its culture – survives in America because all of its ingredients – color, nationality, religion, language, and class – persist to one degree or another. Few would deny that racial discrimination still separates the dominant Anglo-Bourgeois whites from, roughly, 27 million blacks, 15 million Mexican-Americans, 2 million Asians, 3 million Puerto Ricans, 1.2 million Native Americans, and 1 million Cubans. Race remains a primary factor marking boundary divisions separating the population into discrete groups within the larger culture. It is the focal point of ethnic identity among individuals marked and set apart by reason of their genetic heritage.

The racial component of the underclass (it is overwhelmingly black) is partly a function of US history. The legacy of slavery, the Civil War and civil rights still weighs heavily upon black attitudes to white culture. Blacks were encouraged for three centuries to avoid assimilation. They have now had 20 years to reverse attitudes both among themselves and among whites. Ironically, it has been the success of some blacks in joining mainstream America which has intensified the predicament of others. The flight of the black middle class from the ghettos has left a more radically alienated community behind, with fewer role models to follow and less incentive to escape.

Add to this a changing economy where semi-skilled labour is becoming scarcer, and the picture begins to fill out. For generations, such work was the first step out of poverty to working-class respectability. Where such jobs exist now, they have moved out of the inner city. For those who remain in south Los Angeles or the south side of Chicago, the jump to the new breed of professional jobs is often too great for a single generation to make. The revival of the inner city on the backs of young professionals has also enforced a segregation between gentrified and ungentrified areas, and has further marginalized the poor.

More serious still is a collapse in traditional values. Illegitimacy rates in the underclass have doubled in 20 years. In some American cities, less than 25 percent of black children are born in homes with a father present. This has meant more than a decline in living standards; it has meant the loss of any sense of social authority among a generation. For these children, who have seen a real drop in their standard of living of 25 percent since 1977, failure rates at school are climbing. If the situation is to be saved, it has to be by reaching people whose closest idea of authority – a father – has never existed. White children born in 1980 can expect to spend a third of their childhood years in single-parent households; black children can expect to spend over half of their youth with only one parent. There has, moreover, been a huge transformation in just one generation: the corresponding proportions for the early 1950s were less than a tenth for white children, and less than a quarter for black youngsters.

As for marriage, divorce rates appear to have stabilized, but at an unprecedented level. About two-thirds of all first marriages are now likely to disrupt. Almost a quarter of first marriages will end within five years.

A growing number of children – now almost one in four – are born to unmarried women. The increase in illegitimacy has been striking. In 1951 the illegitimacy rate among whites was 1.6 percent ; by 1986 it had reached 15.7 percent. In 1909 W. E. B. DuBois recorded the percentage of illegitimate births among blacks in Washington, DC, for the years 1870 through 1907; it began at 19 and ended at 21. In 1986 it was 68 percent ; in Baltimore it has reached 80 percent. Among blacks nationwide the rate is 61.2 percent.

As if to compound this, drug use has been making dramatic gains in this group. (In the population at large, it is sharply declining.) Intravenous needles have had the added effect of spreading AIDS, now an epidemic in America. The development of more addictive drugs, such as crack, has above all broken single mothers. The proportion of women addicts at a major New York treatment center doubled with the arrival of the drug. Yet these mothers are the community's last defense against social catastrophe.

This is the climate in which a generation of Americans is now growing up. To call it a "culture of poverty" hardly captures the scope or the complexity of the crisis. It is a mix both of a decline in personal responsibility, and a cruel confluence of poverty, drugs, and economic change. For these reasons, it has challenged the customary positions of both Left and Right.

Liberals have rightly stressed an environment of despair, but were slow to recognize how their solution to poverty – the welfare state – contributed to its creation. Conservatives have been right to point out the need for personal responsibility, but unable to create it in the face of a culture almost beyond reach. Conservatives were also slow to see that economic growth alone could not solve the problem. In the 1988 election campaign, the issue hardly surfaced – there are no votes in the ghetto. The problems of the underclass – drugs, the family, welfare – were mentioned only in the context of the mass of prosperous America, where they do not exist. The only candidate honest enough to say that there was a crisis, Jesse Jackson, offered only pieties and was bypassed for the Democratic vice-presidential nomination.

Too late, the US Congress proposed a Bill which might do something to help. A national workfare scheme, mandating work even for women with children a year old in return for welfare, is a start toward providing some experience of normality and work for the new poor. Such schemes have already achieved some long-term success. Arkansas, Maine, Maryland, and Virginia have now reported gains in earnings for workfare recipients over a sustained six-year period.

Moreover, the tougher workfare proposals – which demand real work rather than training – have proved better in breaking the culture of poverty. In comparison with typical reductions of only 1 to 5 percent in welfare cases under "soft" workfare schemes (such as Michael Dukakis's in Massachusetts), Ohio's tough provisions have resulted in a 17 percent drop in female welfare recipients over a four-year period, and a 60 percent drop for families where a father is present.

But the difference between families headed by women and men – 17 compared with 60 percent – suggests the remaining scope of the problem. Family collapse among the very poor is tough to repair. Social breakdown is not amenable to quick fixes. But above all it is necessary to understand that the underclass is not essentially an economic problem. It is a cultural problem. It demands cultural, not economic, solutions: education and workfare from government, and a greater sense of responsibility and self-criticism from the community itself. That, at least, is what the American experience has taught.

8 THE ECONOMIC BALANCE SHEET

Donald Barlett and James B. Steele of the *Philadelphia Inquirer* did a thorough two-year probe of the rulemakers in Washington and the dealmakers on Wall Street, in a series subsequently published as *America: What Went Wrong?* Their conclusion, in "Rigging The Game," was as follows:

> Caught between the lawmakers in Washington and the dealmakers on Wall Street have been millions of American workers forced to move from jobs that once paid $15 an hour into jobs that now pay $7. If, that is, they aren't already the victims of mass layoffs, production halts, shuttered factories and owners who enrich themselves by doing that damage and then walking away.
>
> As a result, the already rich are richer than ever; there has been an explosion in overnight new rich; life for the working class is deteriorating, and those at the bottom are trapped. For the first time in this century, members of a generation entering adulthood will find it impossible to achieve a better lifestyle than their parents. Most will be unable even to match their parents' middle-class status. ....
>
> Look upon it as the dismantling of the middle class. And understand that barring some unexpected intervention by the federal government, the worst is yet to come. For we are in the midst of the largest transfer of wealth in the nation's history. It is a transfer from the middle class to the rich, and from the middle class to the poor – courtesy of the people in Washington who rewrote the rules.[25]

Barlett and Steele went on to list the six "rules" that they regard as governing the "game":

1 A tax system that is firmly weighted against the middle class;
2 Encouragement to companies to trim or cancel health care and pension benefits to employees;
3 The granting of subsidies to businesses that create low-wage jobs (which erode living standards);
4 The undermining of longtime stable businesses and communities;

[25] Donald Barlett and James B. Steele, *America: What Went Wrong?* (Kansas City, Andrews and McMeel, 1992), pp. 3, 4.

5 Rewards to companies that transfer jobs abroad and eliminate jobs in the US; and
6 A system that places home ownership out of reach of a growing number of Americans, and makes the financing of a college education impossible without incurring a hefty debt.

America's tax burden is only 30 percent of national output, the same as Japan's, which compares favorably with more than 40 percent in Britain, France, and Germany. American taxes feel high because they are visible, since there is no Value Added Tax (VAT). If such a tax were simply introduced without any compensating mechanism, it would be, in the parlance of Congress, "dead on arrival." Yet, the absurdity in the American tax system lies precisely in the absence of a substantial consumption tax, the result of which is a lopsided tax system, which depends for most of its revenue on income and direct business taxes. This means that savings are taxed, and hence investments. Dividends are effectively double-taxed. With few consumption taxes, except for state sales taxes, it is no wonder that America has a savings rate of 4 percent, the lowest among the Group of Seven countries.

But in terms of absurdity, nothing beats the tax imbalance between exports and imports. American exports are usually subject to consumption tax or VAT abroad, while foreign imports into the US are sold tax-free. Hence, the American tax system not only favors consumption over investment – an economic deficiency – but it favors foreign companies over American companies – an economic and political absurdity. The notion that Americans have a soft spot for voodoo economics is true even today.

Nevertheless, Michael Barone and Grant Ujifusa described the Reagan-Bush years as a decade of Americans at work: "And at work as never before. In 1980, 97.6 million Americans were employed; in 1990, 117.7 million were. That's an increase of 20 percent in a decade when population increased only 10 percent."[26]

Not only did more Americans work – more Americans worked harder:

In 1970 the American labor force worked 38.3 hours a week; in 1988, they worked 39.1 hours a week. The total hours worked by Americans every week rose from 3.0 million in 1970 to 3.8 million in 1980 and 4.5

[26] Michael Barone and Grant Ujifusa, *The Almanac of American Politics 1992* (National Journal, Washington DC, 1992).

million in 1988, almost a 50 percent increase in less than two decades time. Even the symbols of greed and wretched excess in the 1980s – Michael Millken, Donald Trump, Leona Helmsley, Ivan Boesky – worked long and hard. This was not a decade of leisurely playboys.[27]

But there has been – and will continue to be, according to current predictions – a radical change in the balance of the economy. The central economic fact is the slump in manufacturing. The US economy is expected to add 25 million new jobs between 1990 and 2005 – and practically all of them will be in the service sector.

Manufacturing employment will actually shrink somewhat during this period. As a result, the service sector – which ranges from retail shops and restaurants through computer and health care operations to local government – will account for 81 percent of all US wage and salary jobs in 2005, says an analysis of employment trends by Charles T. Bowman, chief of the industry employment projections division at the Bureau of Labor Statistics; it accounted for 70.5 percent of employment in 1975, and a bit more than 77 percent in 1990.[28]

Goods-producing has never been the US economy's principal employer, notes a CSI publication entitled "From Hamburger to High Tech: A Survey of America's Service Sector."[29] Until 1910, it says, most US workers were engaged in agriculture. Since then, services have gradually become the dominant sector, employing more than half the US workforce as early as 1920. As Barone and Ujifusa put it

> We have changed from a country in which there were just about equal numbers of fabricating and trading jobs to one in which there are twice as many trading as fabricating jobs, though this is not to say that manufacturing has disappeared. Quite the contrary: manufacturing in the early 1990s accounts for the same percentage of gross national product as it did in the early 1970s, but it takes fewer people to manufacture things; manufacturing processes have become more capital-intensive and economically efficient. That should not be too surprising: manufacturing has been getting more efficient and capital-intensive for at least 200 years, and we would not be richer today if it took as many man-hours to produce a ton of cast iron as it did in 1789.[30]

[27] Ibid.

[28] In *The Service Economy*, July 1993 (Washington DC, Coalition of Service Industries).

[29] Washington DC, Coalition of Service Industries, July 1993.

[30] Barone and Grant Ujifusa, *The Almanac of American Politics 1992*, Introduction.

Goods-producing industries, which include mining, construction, and manufacturing, will account for only 19 percent of wage and salary jobs by 2005, says Bowman's analysis; though they provided nearly 30 percent of all jobs in 1975 and almost 23 percent in 1990. However, while employment in manufacturing – the biggest component of goods-producing – will be shrinking, US manufacturers will actually be producing more because of increased productivity.

Of the more than 23 million new service jobs the US economy will create between 1990 and 2005, about five million will be in retail sales and restaurants, which generally pay lower wages than other service professions, says Bowman. The other new service positions, however, will be in better-paid professions. Health care will enjoy the biggest growth. This field is expected to add nearly 3.7 million employees, or one out of every six new US jobs, between 1990 and 2005.

Much of this growth relates to the need for well-paid technicians to operate and maintain the steady stream of increasingly sophisticated medical diagnostic and treatment equipment being developed, says Bowman. Perhaps the biggest factor driving the growing demand for medical services – and thus employment opportunities in that field – is the steady aging of the US population. More and more people in the United States are approaching the age when demand for medical services rises dramatically. Employment in residential health care services – primarily for the elderly – is growing at an average rate of 4.5 percent per year, says Bowman – faster than any other US industry.

State and local governments will add nearly 3.1 million new jobs during the period covered by Bowman's projections. More than half of these positions, 1.6 million, will be in public education, in response to the rapid growth of the school age population in some areas. Nearly 2.4 million new jobs will open up in business services between 1990 and 2005, while the economy will require about 1.3 million new managers and engineers over the same period.

Service industries analysts bristle at the popular misconception that service jobs are generally low-skill, low-wage positions. In an analysis prepared for CSI, economists Alan Sinai and Zaharo Sofianou flatly call this a myth. Retail positions, which account for about 21 percent of the total service workforce, are generally low-paid and pull down the average pay in the private service producing sector to $9.87 an hour, or $1.53 an hour less than the $11.40 an hour average in the manufacturing sector, the economists say. Service employees outside the retail trades, who account for nearly

53 percent of the entire US private industry workforce, earn on an average $10.99 an hour, just 41 cents less than the manufacturing average. Employees in some service sectors do substantially better than this. Health-care workers, for example, average $11.28 an hour; those in the transportation and public utility fields, $13.42 an hour. Some legal service employees earn as much as $14.95 an hour.

Pay in non-retail service fields has recently been growing faster than manufacturing wages, Sinai and Sofianou note, and for this reason they "could be higher than those in the manufacturing industry within five to six years." They also say that the economic value of such low-wage fields as retailing are not appreciated. These positions, they say, provide low-skill workers the opportunity to enter the labor force and earn income they otherwise would not have earned at all. Since many of these jobs are part-time, they allow students and parents of school-age children to gain work experience.[31]

President Bill Clinton is at present considering proposals to increase government spending in an effort to stimulate the economy. The "stimulus" plan is said to include at least $15 billion of new spending, most of which would be designated for public works spending. But the most likely result of these higher federal outlays, regardless of how the money is spent, would be a drop in the economy's performance. Record increases in federal spending and budget deficits did not help the economy during the Bush administration. There is no reason to think that expanding the size of the government will work any better for President Clinton.

If higher federal spending and larger budget deficits could stimulate economic growth, the economy would be booming today. In the four years from 1990 to 1994, federal spending increased by more than $340 billion. In 1994 alone, federal spending was expected to grow by more than $93 billion – not counting any spending which might be added by Clinton. The budget deficit, meanwhile, has jumped from $152.5 billion in fiscal year 1989 to a projected $327.3 billion for 1994. Rather than grow, however, the economy in this period experienced its weakest growth rate in more than 50 years. Nor has the increase in federal spending helped create jobs for American workers, the main goal of Clinton's planned stimulus package; unemployment climbed from 5.3 percent in 1989 to more than 7 percent in 1994.

[31] Coalition of Service Industries, March 1993.

The notion that higher federal spending generates economic growth is based on the Keynesian theory of economics, which was popular in the academic world prior to the 1980s. Under this theory, it is deemed to be total private and government spending that determines the economy's performance, especially in the short term. If the economy slows, Keynesians believe that policymakers can restore growth by increasing the budget deficit and thereby boosting total spending in the economy.

The Keynesian theory fell into disrepute in the 1970s when it became clear that high government spending and deficits were associated with slow economic growth and inflation – often called "stagflation" – and not with robust growth. Critics of the theory pointed out that, among other reasons, this was because Keynesians assumed that the money used for expanded deficit spending appears out of thin air. In the real world, however, every dollar of deficit spending requires the government to borrow one dollar from private credit markets. Rather than stimulate growth or increase total spending in the economy, deficits simply transfer resources from workers, consumers, and investors in the productive sector of the economy and put them under the control of politicians and bureaucrats. These officials tend to use the money less efficiently than the private sector would. The result is slower, not faster, economic growth and slower job creation.

If President Clinton approves $15 billion of additional deficit spending, this will simply crowd out $15 billion of private sector investment. World history suggests that is not very likely. Increased pork-barrel spending will please the interest groups on Capitol Hill, but it will not increase incentives to work, save, and invest.

Rather than increasing deficit spending, lawmakers should be slashing federal spending, so more of the nation's pool of savings will be available for investment in the productive sector of the economy. Private sector borrowing – which is used for such things as research and development, business investment, auto loans, and home mortgages – increases the economy's capacity to produce goods and services. And private investment makes possible the productivity increases that lead to rising wages and higher living standards for all Americans.

Clinton claims that spending increases will have a particularly beneficial impact if the money is spent on infrastructure. According to this theory, the economy's performance depends to a significant extent on how much taxpayer money is spent on roads, bridges, mass transit, government-financed research and development, education, and other programs that special interests have reclassified as public "investment." The evidence is very clear, however, that higher spending in these categories will not stimulate job creation and economic growth. The General Accounting Office, for instance, discovered that each job created by the "Emergency Jobs Act of 1983" cost the economy $175,000 in 1994's dollars. A 1979 study by the Office of Management and Budget found that infrastructure jobs cost between $136,000 and $384,000. Since an average of $40,000 is needed to create each private sector job, any government program that uses more than $40,000 to create a job will actually reduce the total number of jobs in the economy. Besides being a net job-destroyer, scholarly research has found that additional infrastructure spending does not increase private sector productivity.

In order to stimulate economic growth, the Clinton administration should copy the successful policies of John F. Kennedy and Ronald Reagan. Both Kennedy and Reagan triggered record economic expansions by slashing tax rates and reducing the burden of government spending. Both Kennedy and Reagan also favored free trade policies, resisting the siren song of protectionism. The pro-growth Kennedy and Reagan policies worked. The unemployment rate during the Kennedy expansion fell from 6.7 percent in 1961 to 3.5 percent in 1969, while Reagan's policies caused the unemployment rate to fall from 7.6 percent in 1981 to 5.3 percent in 1989.

Businesses are not charities; they create jobs when they expect that the revenues generated by an additional worker will exceed the total cost of employing that new worker, including government-imposed costs such as taxes and mandated benefits. If taxes, spending, regulation, and federal mandates are increased, some existing jobs will be destroyed and fewer new jobs will be created.

Like Presidents Herbert Hoover and Jimmy Carter, George Bush undermined economic growth by increasing the burden of government. Bush reversed President Reagan's successful policies, ending the longest peacetime economic expansion in American history. Ironically, Clinton's economic platform is similar – more taxes, higher spending, and increased regulation.

With federal spending already expected to increase by nearly $100 billion in 1994, the $15 billion of additional spending proposed by President Clinton will compound the damage already caused by a growing government share of the nation's economic output. Higher spending may produce economic growth on the university blackboards of Clinton's economic advisors, but it does not do so in the real world.

9 THE ENVIRONMENTAL MOVEMENT

Although the conservation movement of the first half of the twentieth century and the environmental movement that arose after 1950 had similar ideological roots, they had quite different objectives. The first emphasized natural resources as commodities to produce material goods; the second focused on resources – air, water, and land – that would enhance the quality of life.

The conservation movement grew out of a concern for the depletion of water, forests, minerals, and soils. Many deplored the rapid exploitation of these resources, fearing that they would soon be exhausted. They called for more efficient management to sustain the yield of renewable resources on a permanent basis and enable nonrenewable resources to last longer.

Key objectives of the movement were the construction of dams to conserve water for irrigation, navigation, and hydroelectric power production and, in the process, store flood waters and prevent flood damage; the management of forests on a sustained-yield basis; the reduction of soil erosion to foster permanent farm productivity; and the restoration of fish and game populations for fishing and hunting.

These policies emerged in the late nineteenth century, developed rapidly during the presidential administration of Theodore Roosevelt (1901–9), and took on new life in the 1930s during the presidency of Franklin D. Roosevelt, notably in the TVA project. In that decade funds to combat the depression were spent on large-scale dam and reservoir projects; the Civilian Conservation Corps constructed roads in the national parks and forests; fish and wildlife protection moved ahead rapidly.

Alongside but subordinate to these ventures was the movement to establish national and state parks in order to enhance the quality of the human environment by protecting natural areas. The first national park was Yellowstone (1872); after a number of other parks were created, the National Park Service was formed in 1916 to administer them.

The initial impetus for the environmental movement from the mid-1950s was the growing interest in outdoor recreation in a more natural environment. This led to the creation of the National Wilderness Preservation System (1964), the National Trails System (1968), and the National Wild and Scenic Rivers System (1968) and to a public purchase program in the Land and Water Conservation Act (1964). By 1989 the wilderness system, the most dramatic result of these measures, had reached 90 million acres.

These programs set a direction in resource management different from the conservation focus on efficient development of material resources. In wilderness areas no timber was to be cut and no roads built; wild and scenic rivers were to remain free-flowing with no dams built in them. The programs meant that resources were now prized for their aesthetic rather than their material value.

The environmental movement gave rise to a new appreciative use of wildlife as an object of observation rather than of hunting. This led to a federal endangered species program, nongame wildlife programs fostered by the states, a heightened interest in habitat for wild plants and animals, and a focus on biological diversity of wild resources.

In the environmental era a new interest arose in curbing pollution – first air and water pollution in the 1950s and 1960s and then the pollution from toxic chemical wastes in the 1970s and thereafter. A host of new laws, federal, state, and local, were intended to protect drinking water, contain the spread of pesticides and other toxic chemicals, and clean up the air, rivers, lakes, and oceans. These programs emphasized a healthy as well as an aesthetically pleasing environment. Environmental health policies had long stressed the purification of drinking water to prevent contagious disease. Now they were expanded to reduce exposure to pollution, including harmful chemicals in the workplace. One should note also the Highway Beautification Act of 1965, the campaign to ban billboards on interstate highways and the vast expansion of national park lands – doubled from the Carter administration forward.

Public support for environmental objectives grew steadily over the years, as charted by public opinion surveys and membership in citizen organizations such as the Sierra Club, the wilderness Society, the National Wildlife Federation, and the National Audubon Society. After 1970 many new organizations were formed, often to address specific problems such as scenic rivers, hiking trails, billboard removal, pesticide control, energy efficiency, mineral extraction on public lands, and solid waste management. These organizations expanded their activities from national legislative lobbying to include initiating legal actions and participating in administrative proceedings; in the late 1970s they began to work in electoral campaigns for members of Congress; and in the 1980s they became involved in state environmental affairs. This growth was a result of slow and persistent change rooted in the new attitudes, interests, and values of the American people.

Both the conservation and environmental movements focused on the management of public resources; hence they were deeply involved in the formation of public policy and debate over how land, air, and water should be used – for private or public objectives. But there were also differences. The conservation movement which arose out of the interests of technical experts and managers in reducing waste in production, had a limited popular base. The environmental movement, in contrast, arose out of broad public interests in improving the quality of life and thus had widespread support. It was an integral part of the increasing citizen participation in American public affairs during the last half of the twentieth century.

10 SUCCESS STORY?

The farmers' republic set up in 1787 on the eastern seaboard of an unknown continent, with a population of 3 million people and with only five towns of more than 10,000 folk, now stretches 3,000 miles from coast to coast, and has over 250 million people inside its borders, not all of them there legally. Its standard of living is the highest in recorded history – high and wasteful: it consumes 45 percent of the world's resources. American economic influence, directly over Canada, the Caribbean and the Philippines, and indirectly over Europe and Asia, is immense. Its defense interests span the globe, from Iceland to Vietnam, from Panama to the Antarctic. Its frontier now is in space itself, and its satellites girdle the earth.

Its story is one of unparalleled and very speedy success in which Americans can and do rightly take pride. They were from Davey Crockett's day a people given to boasting, to telling tall tales and recounting legendary exploits. Yet nothing is more worthy of pride than this story of material success, not because it is just a story of prosperity itself, or because of the skill and effort with which a vast continent has been mastered, but because all these were made possible by a democratic and open system of government, in which all men of whatever race or national origin were deemed to be free – or to be capable of freedom. The doubts of 1787 – whether republicanism and federalism could be successfully applied to an area as large and diverse as the original 13 states – have indeed been stilled. The Manifest Destiny of the people proved to be not geographic but ideological, not the West but the fact of freedom itself. The resources of land, environment, and people in mutual interaction have produced a new and distinct society.

The Founding Fathers built wisely, more wisely than they knew. But, despite that, it is also true that they would find it hard to recognize in highly urbanized contemporary America either the

Plate 19 Independence Day celebration, New York Harbor, July 4, 1986: the Argentine frigate *Levatard* joins many other vessels to honor nearly 100 years of the existence of the Statue of Liberty.
(Library of Congress.)

outlines or the characteristics of that idyllic agrarian community they sought to preserve and cherish. Perhaps they would conclude that all that can safely be said of the future, in America or elsewhere, is that it will always be different from the past.

To this, however, a number of codicils have to be added. Not all African-Americans live lives of total peace; some of the inner cities are no-go areas, and violence is a recurring theme in the American story, thanks largely to casual controls over the easy availability of guns. Again, the majority of Native Americans who survive are confined to reservations, where conditions are primitive. And, not least, democracy, however successful at home, has proved to be unsuitable for export. As a form of government it has been eminently satisfactory in the US for educated whites, best of all for those who live in cities where schools can easily be built, equipped, and supplied. It has not been suitable as an imperial tool, not in Vietnam nor any of the Caribbean republics. There the American republic has also been an empire, controlling the Panama isthmus and its canal, but unsuccessful in its self-appointed role as peacekeeper in Nicaragua, Cuba, or Haiti.

Moralism and populist politics are another legacy of American Independence. Men such as William Jennings Bryan and Tom Watson of Georgia, Gene Talmadge and Theodore Bilbo, Joe McCarthy and George Wallace are in each generation as much in the American grain as the Unitarians (or the latter-day non-Unitarian intellectuals) of Harvard. Any explanation of American politics has to pay as much attention to the evangelism of the Burned-Over District and the Bible Belt as to the cool and faded elegance of Beacon Hill. Populist politics is quicker to recognize enemies than allies; it is especially prompt to recognize or invent conspiracies. Yet the demand to know the truth because it is believed to be liberating, the demand for total freedom of speech, the idealism of Fighting Bob La Follette and the Wisconsin Idea of the early 1900s, this moralist politics is far more typical of the American grass roots and more truly democratic than anything taught in Ivy League colleges or New York City law firms. When President Kennedy consciously sought to surround himself by an elite, a praetorian guard of intellectuals, he was defying the American tradition. One of their legacies, the Vietnam War, is a monument to the fact that the people whom David Halberstam has termed "the Best and the Brightest" are not always the wisest when profound issues are at stake.

Another persistent theme of American history is revivalism and high emotion. The America of the Enlightenment was never far from the America of the Great Awakening as the writings and sermons of Jonathan Edwards testify. The tradition of Whitfield and Edwards, of Moody and Sankey, and of Billy Graham, also has a long pedigree. "The language of excitement," to use Reinhold Niebuhr's phrase. "is as important as the appeal to reason." If institutions are to be reformed, men also must be called to an individual salvation. Tocqueville noticed in America "a sort of fanatical spiritualism:"

In all states of the Union, but especially in the half-peopled country of the Far West, itinerant preachers may be met with who hawk about the Word of God from place to place. Whole families, old men, women and children, cross rough passes and untrodden wilds, coming from a great distance, to join a camp-meeting, where, in listening to these discourses, they totally forget for several days and nights the cares and business and even the most urgent wants of the body.

Professor Arthur Schlesinger Jr has summed the story up, but leaves it with a question:

The American synthesis has an inevitable Anglo-Saxon coloration, but it is no longer an exercise in Anglo-Saxon domination. The republic embodies ideals that transcend ethnic, religious, and political lines. It is an experiment, reasonably successful for a while, in creating a common identity for people of diverse race, religions, languages, cultures. But the experiment can continue to succeed only so long as Americans continue to believe in the goal. If the republic now turns away from Washington's old goal of "one people," what is its future? – disintegration of the national community, apartheid, Balkanization, tribalization?

"The one absolutely certain way of bringing this nation to ruin, of preventing all possibility of its continuing to be a nation at all," said Theodore Roosevelt, "would be to permit it to become a tangle of squabbling nationalities, an intricate knot of German-Americans, Irish-Americans, English-Americans, French-Americans, Scandinavian-Americans, or Italian-Americans, each preserving its separate nationality." Three-quarters of a century later we must add a few more nationalities to T. R.'s brew. This only strengthens his point.[32]

[32] Arthur M. Schlesinger, *The DisUniting of America* (New York, Norton, 1993), p. 118.

L'Envoi: America the Beautiful

Katharine Lee Bates (1850–1929) wrote "America the Beautiful" in 1893, and it was published in *The Congregationalist* in 1895. Bates revised the lyrics in 1904, and again in 1911 in her *America the Beautiful and Other Poems*. For most of her adult life Bates was a professor of English at Wellesley College. She was also an editor, wrote children's books, and published several collections of poetry. However, her lasting fame comes from her authorship of the memorable verses to "America the Beautiful." The song is widely admired, and it has often been proposed as a substitute for "The Star-Spangled Banner" as the national anthem.

O beautiful for spacious skies,
  For amber waves of grain,
For purple mountain majesties
  Above the fruited plain!
America! America!
  God shed His grace on thee
And crown thy good with brotherhood
  From sea to shining sea!

O beautiful for pilgrim feet,
  Whose stern, impassioned stress
A thoroughfare for freedom beat
  Across the wilderness!
America! America!
  God mend thine every flaw,
Confirm thy soul in self-control,
  Thy liberty in law!

O beautiful for heroes proved
  In liberating strife,
Who more than self their country loved,
  And mercy more than life!
America! America!
  May God thy gold refine,
Till all success be nobleness
  And every gain divine!

O beautiful for patriot dream
  That sees beyond the years
Thine alabaster cities gleam
  Undimmed by human tears!
America! America!
  God shed His grace on thee,
And crown thy good with brotherhood
  From sea to shining sea!

Chronologies

THE AMERICAN BLACK, 1900–1945

1903	Black leader William E. B. Du Bois published his essay "The Talented Tenth," calling on educated blacks to uplift their race, and his militant *Souls of Black Folk*, in which he demanded civil rights for blacks. Du Bois had broken with the moderate position of Booker T. Washington.
1905	At a conference at Niagara Falls in July, Du Bois and other militant blacks started the Niagara Movement, which called for an end to all racial restrictions.
1909	The National Association for the Advancement of Colored People (NAACP) was formed by blacks and white reformers. Du Bois became its chief black leader and for 22 years served as editor of *The Crisis*, which publicized lynchings and other anti-black atrocities.
1917	A race riot in East St Louis, Ill., killed 37.
1917–18	Some 360,000 blacks who had served in the war returned home demanding additional rights.
1919	25 race riots took place all over the US. In Washington, DC, white soldiers and sailors attacked black quarters. The most serious riot started in Chicago on July 27 and killed 23 blacks and 15 whites.
1920–30	The black "Renaissance" developed a spirit of independence in the 1920s, particularly in Harlem. Black poet and novelist Langston Hughes, who lived in Harlem, published *The Weary Blues* (1926) and *Not Without Laughter*

(1930). The NAACP grew from 50 local chapters to 599 between the two wars. Lynchings of blacks dropped to an average of 10 per year, 1921–45. The South built more schools for blacks in the 1920–30 decade than in all previous years.

1921 Marcus Garvey outfitted a steamship line to carry blacks back to Africa. At its height, Garvey's African Zionist Movement had 500,000 members, but it collapsed when Garvey went to jail for swindling.

1930–40 The depression hit blacks harder than any other group, particularly the black sharecropper. New Deal farm programs often forced blacks to leave the farms and move to city slums, but New Deal relief measures helped them to survive the depression.

White CIO labor leaders treated blacks more fairly than had any labor organizers in the past. Black voters, traditionally Republican, went over to the Democratic party and helped form Roosevelt's urban coalition.

1940 Richard Wright, one of the few blacks to join the Communist party, published his *Native Son*, which described the brutality of black slum life.

1940–45 The movement of blacks to the North speeded up during World War II as blacks went to work in defense plants. 920,000 blacks served in the war, 7,768 of them officers, and some military segregation practices were given up.

1941 After blacks threatened to march on Washington, President Roosevelt issued an Executive Order (June 25) declaring that there should be no discrimination in employment in defense industries or government, and creating the Fair Employment Practices Committee (FEPC).

1943 Roosevelt sent troops to Detroit on June 20 to quell a racial riot between blacks and whites that killed 34. On Aug. 1 blacks in Harlem rioted.

US EXPANSION IN THE PACIFIC AND LATIN AMERICA, 1887–1917

1887–9 US leased Pearl Harbor, Hawaii; US shared in Samoan protectorate.

1898 Spanish-American War: Cuba occupied, Hawaii, Puerto Rico, Guam, and the Philippines annexed.

1899	Filipino Insurrection initiated; Open Door policy announced; US annexed several of the Samoan Islands.
1990	Boxer Rebellion; "imperialism" was the presidential election issue.
1903	Hay-Herran Treaty: Colombia granted to the US a 99-year lease to build a canal across Panama at an annual rent of $10 million.
1904	Hay-Bunau-Varilla Treaty ratified, giving the US sovereign rights to a canal zone 10 miles wide across the isthmus at Panama, for $10 million down payment and $250,000 a year; the US received the right to keep order within Panama. Roosevelt Corollary to the Monroe Doctrine announced: the US took on "an international police power" in Latin America to prevent European states intervening to collect debts.
1910	"Dollar diplomacy" inaugurated in Latin America. US troops landed in Nicaragua to protect Americans; they remained there until 1933.
1914	Panama Canal opened.
1916	US intervened in the Dominican Republic, and in Mexico to try to end the civil war there.
1917	Puerto Ricans granted US citizenship and manhood suffrage.

THE US AND WORLD WAR I

1914–15	
Nov. 3– Mar. 11	British violated neutral rights by declaring the North Sea a war zone and proceeding to mine it. They also interfered with American mail, seized American ships, and on Mar. 11, 1915, blockaded all German ports. American protests were ineffective.
1915	
Jan. 28	German cruiser sank an American merchant ship carrying wheat to Great Britain.
Feb. 4	Germany proclaimed war zone around the British Isles and warned that neutral shipping in the zone would be in peril of submarines.
Feb. 10	US protested vigorously against the war zone and said it would hold Germany to "strict accountability" if American vessels or lives were lost.

Feb. 18	Germany announced that its submarines would sink enemy merchant vessels in the war zone without warning.
Mar. 28	One American killed when Germans sank the British ship *Falaba* in the Irish Sea.
May 1	Three more died when Germans by mistake torpedoed the American tanker *Gulflight*.
May 1	German embassy warned Americans by advertisements in New York newspapers that they sailed on Allied vessels at their own risk.
May 7	German submarine sank the British steamer *Lusitania* without warning off the Irish coast, killing 1,198 persons, of whom 128 were Americans.
May 10	President Wilson said in Philadelphia that a nation clearly in the right did not have to prove it with force: "There is such a thing as a man being too proud to fight."
May 13–July 21	The *Lusitania* notes. In the first note (May 13)), the US insisted on American rights on the high seas, reparations, and an end to German unrestricted submarine warfare, but Germany gave little satisfaction (May 28). The second note (June 9) demanded specific pledges; Secretary of State Bryan resigned, and Robert Lansing was appointed in his place. Neither the second nor third (July 21) notes brought a specific German response, but secretly the Germans ordered submarine commanders to spare passenger liners (June 6). On Feb. 16, 1916, Germany agreed to pay an indemnity for American loss of life on the *Lusitania*.
July 24, 1915–Jan. 11, 1917	American secret service agent seized documents proving that German Ambassador Count Bernstorff and Captain Franz von Papen, military attaché, were involved in sabotage. Von Papen and Austro-Hungarian Ambassador Dr Dumba were recalled. The US attributed two explosions with a loss of $55 million (1916–17) to the Germans.
Aug. 19, 1915	German submarine, violating orders, sank British passenger ship *Arabic* with loss of 2 American lives. On Oct. 5, German government promised that such an incident would not happen again.
Fall	From the fall of 1915 there was a growing German submarine menace. Efforts by German sympathizers, pacifists, and others to stop the sale of munitions failed; the Allies imported large quantities of munitions from the US. Total US exports to Great Britain and France rose from $754 million in 1914 to $2,748 million in 1916; exports to Germany fell from $345 million to $2 million in the same period.

1916

Feb. 8 — Germans declared that after Mar. 1 they would sink all armed enemy merchantmen without warning.

Feb. 22 — President Wilson sent Col. Edward M. House on first of two peace missions to Europe. The resulting House-Grey Memorandum stated that at an "opportune" moment, the US would propose a peace conference. If the Allies accepted but the Germans refused, the United States would "probably" go to war against Germany. Wilson endorsed the memorandum, but peace efforts failed.

Feb. 17– Mar. 17 — Congressman Jeff McLemore (Tex.) introduced a resolution asking the President to prohibit Americans from traveling on armed vessels. When Wilson refused, the House tabled the resolution (Mar. 7), and the Senate tabled one by Senator Thomas P. Gore (Okla.) to prohibit the issue of passports to Americans traveling on belligerent ships (Mar. 3).

Mar. 24 — German submarine torpedoed the unarmed French passenger ship *Sussex* in the English Channel, injuring several Americans and violating the *Arabic* pledge.

Nov. 7 — Woodrow Wilson reelected as President.

1917

Apr. 6 — US declared war on Germany.

May 18 — Selective Service Act called for registration of all US men aged 21–30 (amended Aug. 31, 1918, to 18–45). Of 24,234,021 men registered by Sept. 12, 1918, 2,810,296 were called for duty. National Guard was called up and many civilians volunteered; the total number of troops serving in the war was 4,791,172, of which 2,084,000 went overseas.

June 13 — General John J. ("Black Jack") Pershing, in command of the American Expeditionary Force (AEF), arrived in France; US 1st Division embarked for France.

July–Nov. — Elements of the 1st Division took positions in the front lines on Oct. 21. In Oct. and Nov. Austro-German forces routed an Italian offensive.

Nov. 7 — Nicolai Lenin led the Bolshevik Revolution in Russia and assumed control of the government. Bolsheviks made a separate peace with Germany by the Treaty of Brest-Litovsk (Mar. 3, 1918), which relieved Germany of the burden of a two-front war.

Nov. 24 — Leon Trotsky, Russian foreign minister, published the Tsar's secret treaties with the Allies, which revealed that

	the Allies had promised each other territorial gains after the war.
Dec. 7	US declared war on Austro-Hungary.
1918	
Jan. 8	President Wilson presented his 14-point plan for peace.
Nov. 9	After a revolution in Berlin, Kaiser Wilhelm II abdicated, and a German republic was proclaimed.
Nov. 11	Gen. Foch signed an Armistice with a German commission at Compiègne, France.

World War I Casualties
(*thousands*)

	Total mobilized forces	*Killed or died*	*Wounded*	*Prisoners and missing*	*Total casualties*
United States	4,791	117	204	5	326
Russia	12,000	1,700	4,950	2,500	9,150
France	8,410	1,358	4,266	537	6,161
British Commonwealth	8,904	908	2,090	192	3,190
Italy	5,615	650	947	600	2,197
Germany	11,000	1,774	4,216	1,153	7,143
Austria-Hungary	7,800	1,200	3,620	2,200	7,020
Total	58,520	7,707	20,293	7,187	35,187

THE US AND THE TREATY OF VERSAILLES

1918	
Nov. 5	Congressional elections. On Oct. 25, before he left the US for Europe, President Wilson appealled to the voters to return a Democratic Congress; but the Republicans captured both houses and began to claim that Wilson did not speak for the American people.
Nov. 18	Wilson announced that he would attend the European peace conference with a commission consisting of Col. House, Secretary of State Lansing, Gen. Tasker H. Bliss, and diplomat Henry White (the sole Republican).
Dec. 13	Wilson arrived in France and made a triumphant tour of France, England, and Italy that lasted until Jan. 1919.
1919	
Jan. 12–June 28	Peace Conference at Versailles, dominated by the "Big Four": Woodrow Wilson, Prime Minister David Lloyd George of Great Britain, Premier Georges Clemenceau of France, and Premier Vittorio Orlando of Italy.
Jan. 25	The Conference adopted the principle of the League of Nations.

Feb. 14	The Conference adopted the Covenant of the League of Nations provisionally.
Feb. 15	President Wilson sailed for the United States, arriving Feb. 24. On Feb. 26 Wilson met with members of the Senate and House committees concerned with foreign affairs and discussed the League of Nations.
Feb. 28	Senator Henry Cabot Lodge (Mass.) delivered his first speech against the League of Nations.
Mar. 2	37 Republican Senators and two Senators-elect signed a "round-robin" letter rejecting the League in its existing form.
Mar. 4	President Wilson defiantly defended the League of Nations in a speech at New York. On the following day, he sailed again for Paris.
Mar. 28–Apr. 30	The "Big Four" made final decisions on reparations and territorial terms amid bitter debate. The Allied leaders forced Wilson to concede several of his Fourteen Points; they in turn accepted amendments to the League Covenant exempting the US from the mandate system and excepting the Monroe Doctrine from the jurisdiction of the League.
June 28	Treaty of Versailles signed. The US and Great Britain signed a treaty with France in which they agreed to assist France if attacked by Germany, but the Senate never ratified the treaty.
July 10	Wilson submitted the Versailles Treaty to the Senate, where it was held up in the Foreign Relations Committee until Sept. 10.
Sept. 3–26	Wilson went on a Western speaking tour in which he defended the League before enthusiastic crowds. Republican Senators Hiram W. Johnson and William E. Borah followed him and spoke against the League. On Sept. 25, at Pueblo, Colo., after making his fortieth speech, Wilson collapsed and returned to Washington.
Sept. 10–Aug. 20, 1920	Austria-Hungary, Bulgaria, and Turkey signed peace treaties.
Sept. 10	The Senate Committee on Foreign Relations reported the Versailles Treaty to the Senate with amendments and reservations. The Senate rejected all amendments but accepted a number of reservations.
Oct. 2	President Wilson suffered a stroke that incapacitated him completely until Oct. 20. He held no Cabinet meetings until Apr. 13, 1920, and never fully recovered.

Nov. 6	Henry Cabot Lodge proposed 14 reservations to the League Covenant, which Wilson opposed. On Nov. 18 Wilson instructed the Democratic majority in the Senate to vote against the Treaty with reservations, and on Nov. 19 Senate rejected the Treaty with reservations by 55 to 39.
1920	
Mar. 19	Senate rejected the Treaty with 15 reservations, by 49 to 35. President Wilson still opposed any reservations.
July 2–Oct. 18	Congress by joint resolution terminated the state of war with Germany and Austria-Hungary, and on Oct. 18 the Senate ratified separate peace treaties with Germany, Austria, and Hungary.

FDR AND THE NEW DEAL

1882	FDR born Hyde Park, NY, Jan. 30.
1904	Graduated from Harvard University.
1907	Admitted to the Bar in New York City after studying at Columbia Law School.
1910–13	Democratic member of the New York Senate.
1913–20	Assistant secretary to the navy.
1920	Unsuccessful as candidate for vice-President.
1921	While holidaying at Campobello, stricken with polio, and never fully regained the use of his legs.
1924, 1928	Nominated Al Smith for President at the Democratic National Convention.
1929–33	Governor of New York.
1933–45	President of the US for three terms. After FDR's death, the Presidency was limited to two terms, so his was unique.

"First" New Deal

1933	
Mar. 4	First Inaugural: "The only thing we have to fear is fear itself..."
Mar. 5	4-day bank holiday closed all banks.
Mar. 9	Emergency Banking Act. Banks reopened after vetting. President took wide powers over money and banking.
Mar. 31	Unemployment Relief Act set up the Civilian conservation Corps to provide work for men aged 18–25.

May — Federal Emergency Relief Administration set up to provide grants to cities and states in need. Agricultural Adjustment Administration set up to restore farmers' purchasing power. Tennessee Valley Authority set up to build dams and power stations.

June — Glass-Steagall Banking Act separated commercial from investment banking and created the Federal Deposit Insurance Corporation.

National Industrial Recovery Act set up National Recovery Administration to draw up codes for competition, and to supervise a program of self regulation.

Nov. — Public Works Administration set up under Henry Hopkins to create jobs for the unemployed.

"Second" New Deal

1935

Apr. — Works Progress Administration set up imaginative projects: the Federal Writers' Project, Federal Theater Project, Federal Arts Project, and National Youth Administration.

July — National Labor Relations Act sponsored by Senator Robert Wagner (the "Wagner Act").

Aug. — Social Security Act passed. A Revenue Act increased surtax and estate duties. Soil Conservation and Domestic Allotment Act encouraged crop restriction.

The end of the New Deal

1937 — Supreme Court declared part of the National Industrial Recovery Act unconstitutional, as giving too much power to the President. FDR countered by proposing his "Court-packing bill" – to add a new member for each justice who did not retire at the age of 70. 1937 was the worst year for strikes between the stock market crash of 1929 and the end of World War II.

1938 — Agricultural Adjustment Act set marketing quotas for export crops. Fair Labor Standards Act established a minimum wage of 40 cents an hour and a maximum work week of 40 hours; it also forbade child labor.

1940 — In Nov. 1940 FDR became the first person to be elected for more than two presidential terms when he secured a majority of the popular votes against Republican Wendell Willkie.

1944 — In Nov. FDR won re-relection against Republican E. Dewey.

1945 — FDR died at Warm Springs, GA.

THE KOREAN WAR, 1950–1953

1950

Jan. 12	Secretary of State Dean Acheson announced that the US defense perimeter did not include Korea and Formosa.
Feb. 14	USSR-China 30-year mutual defense pact concluded by Stalin and Mao.
June 25	North Korean Communists invaded South Korea. The last US troops had been withdrawn from Korea a year earlier, and Soviet troops had left in 1948.
June 25	UN Security Council (USSR not present) declared North Korea the aggressor and demanded a ceasefire in Korea. The Council also called on members for military aid to repel the North Korean attack.
June 27	President Truman sent the US Seventh Fleet to the Formosa Straits to prevent the Chinese Communists from invading Formosa or the Nationalists from invading the mainland.
June 29	Truman ordered the US army into South Korea.
July 7	UN Security Council ordered a UN Command under a US Commander (Gen. Douglas MacArthur).
July–Aug.	North Koreans drove South Koreans and Americans to the Pusan beachhead.
Sept. 15	US counteroffensive began with the invasion of Inchon by sea.
Oct. 1	Allied forces crossed the 38th parallel.
Oct. 7	UN General Assembly called for unification of Korea.
Oct. 11	China warned that it might invade North Korea.
Oct. 27	Chinese troops were discovered to be fighting in Korea.
Nov. 7	The Joint Chiefs of Staff refused to let MacArthur bomb Chinese bases in Manchuria because they did not want to risk having the USSR enter the war.
Nov. 26	UN troops were turned back by Chinese counterattack after reaching the Yalu Valley.
Dec. 24	American troops were evacuated from the Hungnam beachhead.
Dec. 30	Truman rejected MacArthur's plan to use Chiang's troops in Korea.

1951

Jan. 25	The UN retreat halted south of the 38th parallel. By

	April 21, the UN forces had moved back across the parallel in many places, and the front was stabilized.
Mar. 24	MacArthur exceeded his authority and contradicted Truman by ordering the Chinese to surrender.
Apr. 5	Representative Joseph W. Martin, Jr, published a letter from MacArthur calling for a more aggressive policy in Korea.
Apr. 11	President Truman recalled Gen. MacArthur.
Apr. 19	Gen. MacArthur addressed Congress and called for all-out war in Korea.
June 27	After a two-month debate on foreign policy, the Senate committees investigating Asian policy urged a continuation of Truman's policy of limited war.
July 10	UN negotiators began truce talks in Korea, but problems such as that of the North Korean prisoners in the hands of the UN prevented a settlement for two years. Many of the prisoners did not want to return to North Korea, but the Communists insisted on compulsory repatriation.
Sept. 1	ANZUS Mutual Assistance Pact was signed by the US, Australia, and New Zealand.
Sept. 8	Japanese Peace Treaty was signed by 49 nations. The US was granted military bases in Japan.
1953	
July 27	Armistice of Panmunjon concluded after the Communists gave way on the question of compulsory repatriation; it provided for a demilitarized zone near the 38th parallel and called for a political conference, which has never been held.

JOHN F. KENNEDY

1961	
Jan. 20	In his Inaugural Address President Kennedy announced the arrival of a "new generation of Americans" to power, His Cabinet included Dean Rusk as secretary of state, Robert F. Kennedy as attorney general, and Robert S. McNamara as secretary of defense.
Jan. 30	President Kennedy called for heavy government spending to increase the growth rate of the gross national product and to reduce unemployment. He was the first President to subscribe fully to the ideas of the English economist John Maynard Keynes. Under Kennedy, administrative

budgets jumped from $81.5 billion (fiscal 1961, the last Eisenhower budget) to $97.7 billion (fiscal 1964). The national debt climbed from $289 billion to $313 billion, unemployment dropped from 6.7 percent to 5.2 per cent, and the gross national product grew from $520 billion to $629 billion. The 1960–1 recession ended Feb. 1961.

Mar. 1 Kennedy issued an executive order setting up a Peace Corps of volunteers to work in underdeveloped areas of the world. Congress made it permanent on Sept. 21.

May 1 Area Redevelopment Act provided $300 million to finance industrial or rural development where unemployment was high.

June 30 Housing Act authorized $6.1 billion for housing programs.

Sept. President Kennedy failed to get Congressional approval for a tax revision, a health care bill, a Department of Urban Affairs, and aid for secondary and elementary schools.

1962

Mar. 31 Steel unions and management agreed on contract terms with no price rise.

Apr. 10 U.S. Steel announced a price increase of $6 a ton, and most other steel companies followed suit.

Apr. 11 President Kennedy denounced the price increase and threatened anti-trust investigations.

Apr. 13 When Inland Steel and Kaiser Steel, under Administration pressure, announced that they would hold the line, US Steel and the others rescinded the price increase.

May 28 The stock market dropped abruptly. Some business leaders blamed the drop on lack of confidence in the Administration brought about by Kennedy's pressure on the steel companies.

July 17 The Senate tabled a bill to provide health care for the aged under social security proposed by Congressman Cecil King (Democrat, Cal.) and Senator Clinton P. Anderson (Democrat, NM). President Kennedy blamed the defeat on the American Medical Association.

Oct. 4 Trade Expansion Act gave the President great power to cut tariffs.

Oct. 14 US discovered that the USSR was installing missile sites on Cuba with a range covering all of Florida and much of the rest of the US.

Oct. 22 President Kennedy ordered USSR to withdraw its missiles and imposed a quarantine on Cuba by naval blockade.

Nov. 6 — In Congressional elections, Democrats maintained their position in Congress.

Nov. 21 — Kennedy lifted the blockade on Cuba after USSR agreed to dismantle missiles.

1963

Jan. — Kennedy proposed a tax cut, but it did not pass Congress.

Aug. 5 — Nuclear Test Ban Treaty: US, USSR, and Great Britain agreed not to test nuclear weapons in the atmosphere.

Nov. 22 — President Kennedy was assassinated by Lee Harvey Oswald, a former Marine and supporter of left-wing causes, in Dallas, Texas. Governor John B. Connally of Texas was also shot, but survived. Vice President Lyndon B. Johnson was sworn in as President on the presidential plane.

Nov. 24 — Jack Ruby, a Dallas night-club owner, murdered Oswald in the Dallas jail in front of television cameras. Ruby died of cancer in January 1967.

Nov. 25 — President Kennedy was buried in Arlington National Cemetery.

THE CIVIL RIGHTS MOVEMENT, 1945–1967

1945

July 1 — New York Fair Employment Law set up the first anti-discrimination commission.

1946 — President Truman creates Presidential Committee on Civil Rights.

1948

Jan. 12 — *Sipeul* vs. *Board of Regents of the University of Oklahoma* ruled that a state was not to deny a black person admission to its state law school on grounds of color.

Feb. 2 — President Truman proposed anti-lynching, anti-poll tax, anti-segregation, and fair employment legislation, but no laws were passed.

May 3 — *Shelley* vs. *Kraemer* declared that a state court could not enforce a racially restrictive covenant.

July 26 — Truman issued Executive Order 9981, barring segregation in the armed forces and discrimination in federal employment.

1950

June 5 — By the decision of *Sweatt* vs. *Painter*, a state could not keep a black person from its law school on the grounds that a black law school was available.

1953

May 4 — *Terry* vs. *Adams* held that segregated primary elections violated the Fourteenth Amendment.

1954

May 17 — In *Brown* vs. *Board of Education of Topeka*, the Supreme Court ruled, 9–0, that segregation in the elementary schools of Topeka violated the 14th Amendment, thereby ending the "separate but equal" doctrine of *Plessy* vs. *Ferguson*.

1955

May 31 — *Brown* vs. *Board of Education* (second decision) put responsibility on local officials for implementing the first *Brown* decision and kept jurisdiction in federal courts. School integration was to proceed "with all deliberate speed."

Nov. 25 — The Interstate Commerce Commission banned segregation of passengers on trains and buses in interstate travel. This ruling included railroad terminals but not bus terminals.

Dec. 5 — Montgomery, Ala.; blacks led by Rev. Martin Luther King, Jr, began a boycott against segregation on buses. It ended with a federal injunction (Nov. 13, 1956) against the segregation.

1956

Feb. 1 — The Virginia legislature declared the right of a state to "interpose its sovereignty" against the *Brown* decisions.

Feb. 3 — The Supreme Court ordered the University of Alabama to admit its first black student, Autherine Lucy, but she was expelled on Feb. 29 after a riot.

Mar. 11 — 100 Southern Senators and Congressmen issued a manifesto promising to use "all lawful means" to overthrow the *Brown* decisions.

1957

Sept. 9 — Civil Rights Act of 1957, the first since 1875, created a six-man Civil Rights Commission. District courts were authorized to issue injunctions to protect civil rights. Voting cases would be heard without jury.

Sept. — On Sept. 3 Gov. Orval Faubus called out the National Guard to prevent nine black students from entering Central High School in Little Rock, Ark. On Sept. 23 Faubus withdrew the troops after a federal court injunction. When the nine children approached the school,

	a riot broke out. On Sept. 24, President Eisenhower sent 1,000 paratroopers to Little Rock, the first federal troops in the South since Reconstruction. On Sep. 25, the black children entered school, but the schools were later closed until 1958.
1959	
Sept.	Prince Edward County, Va., closed its schools to prevent integration.
1960	
Feb. 1	A "sit-in" movement began in Greensboro, NC against segregation at lunch counters.
May 6	Civil Rights Act of 1960 made it a federal crime to transport dynamite across state lines in order to blow up a building. Federal courts could issue court orders enforcing black voting rights.
Nov. 30	Federal court in New Orleans enforced desegregation of the schools after riots took place in the city.
Dec. 5	*Boynton* vs. *Virginia* ruled that interstate bus terminals could not segregate passengers.
1961	
Mar. 6	An executive order established the President's Committee on Equal Employment Opportunity for firms with government contracts. Within the first 10 months the Administration began 14 voting-rights cases under the Civil Rights Act of 1957, compared to nine cases, 1957–60.
May 14	Black and white "Freedom Riders" were attacked when testing segregation barriers in bus terminals in Birmingham, Ala.
Sept.	The ICC prohibited segregation both on interstate buses and in terminals.
1962	
Aug. 27	Twenty-fourth Amendment banning the poll tax requirement in federal elections was sent to the states; it was ratified by Jan. 23, 1964.
Sept. 30	President Kennedy sent 3,000 federal troops to the University of Mississippi to stop a riot and secure the admission of James H. Meredith, the first black student at the university.
Nov. 24	President Kennedy issued an executive order banning discrimination in federally assisted housing.

1963

Apr. 3	Martin Luther King began to lead mass demonstrations in Birmingham, Ala., to desegregate the city.
May 2–7	Police met marching blacks in Birmingham with fire hoses and police dogs. Kennedy threatened but never sent troops.
June 11	Gov. George Wallace barred the registration of two black students at the University of Alabama, but gave way when Kennedy federalized the Alabama National Guard.
June 11	In a television address President Kennedy referred to civil rights as a "moral issue" and strongly supported a civil rights act.
June 12	Medgar W. Evers, a leader of the NAACP in Mississippi, was shot from ambush and killed in Jackson, Miss.
Aug. 28	A massive civil rights march took place in Washington, DC, and Martin Luther King gave his "I have a dream" speech at the Lincoln Memorial.
Sept. 15	Efforts to integrate schools in Birmingham led to violence. Bombing of a Sunday school killed four black girls; it was the 21st such bombing in Birmingham in eight years.

1964

May 25	*Griffin* vs. *Prince Edward County School Board* ruled that closing public schools to avoid desegregation was unconstitutional.
June 10	The Senate voted to close off the filibuster against the civil rights bill and passed it on June 19.
July 2	Civil Rights Act of 1964 became law. The terms (1) expedited law suits over voting rights; (2) barred discrimination in public accommodations (the Supreme Court upheld this section in *Heart of Atlanta Motel* vs. *United States* in 1964); (3) authorized the attorney general to institute suits to desegregate schools; (4) barred discrimination in any program receiving federal assistance; (5) set up an Equal Employment Opportunity Commission.
July 18–Aug. 30	Riots caused by ghetto living, unemployment, and hatred of the police took place in Harlem (July 18–22), Rochester, NY (July 24–25), Jersey City (Aug. 2–4), Chicago (Aug. 16–17), and Philadelphia (Aug. 28–30).
Aug. 4	Three young civil rights workers were found murdered near Philadelphia, Miss. The FBI arrested 21 in connection with the murders. In Oct. 1967, seven were convicted of conspiracy to violate a person's civil rights.
	Martin Luther King, Jr, awarded 1964 Nobel Peace Prize.

1965

Feb. 21 — Malcolm X, formerly eastern leader of the Black Muslims, was shot and killed in New York City. Elijah Muhammed, leader of the Black Muslims, who had ousted Malcolm X, denied any connection with the murder.

Mar. 21–25 — A civil rights march took place from Selma to Montgomery, Ala., to encourage greater black voter registration.

Aug 6 — Civil Rights Act of 1965 became law with the following terms: (1) literacy tests to be suspended in any county that used the test to disqualify voters and had a voter turnout of less than 50 percent of its eligible population (Alabama, Georgia, Lousiana, Mississippi, South Carolina, Virginia, and parts of Arizona and Idaho were included in this category); (2) federal voting examiners would then be sent to register voters; (3) the attorney general was empowered to proceed against discriminatory state poll taxes (the Supreme Court upheld the Act in *South Carolina* vs. *Katzenbach* in 1966).

Aug. 11–15 — Riots broke out in Watts district of Los Angeles.

Dec. — The percentage of blacks in school with whites in the 17 Southern and border states and in the District of Columbia rose as follows: 1957, 3 percent; 1960, 6 percent; 1963, 8 percent; 1966, 16 percent.

1966

May — Stokely Carmichael, president of the Student Non-violent Coordinating Committee (SNCC), introduced the concept of a unified black community ("Black Power"). Roy Wilkins, head of the NAACP, and Martin Luther King, head of the Southern Christian Leadership Conference, objected to the idea of Black Power, but Floyd McKissick of the Congress of Racial Equality (CORE) supported it.

June 6 — James Meredith was wounded by a sniper while making a "March against Fear" in rural Mississippi.

July — Rioting occurred in the black West Side of Chicago and the black section of Cleveland.

Sept. — A civil rights bill aimed at ending housing discrimination failed in Congress.

1967

Feb. — President Johnson again called for a civil rights bill to end housing discrimination, but none was passed.

May 29 — The US Supreme Court ruled unconstitutional an amendment to the California constitution that gave property

	owners the right to discriminate in the sale and rental of housing.
June 13	Johnson appointed Thurgood Marshall as the first black to serve on the US Supreme Court.
July	Severe riots in Newark, NJ (July 12–17) and in Detroit (July 23–27) left 63 dead. In the period 1964–7, outbreaks of racial violence occurred in 50 US cities.

THE VIETNAM WAR

1945

Aug.	Allied Commission, primarily British, arrived in Saigon to take control of French Indochina.
Sept. 2	Communist leader Ho Chi Minh set up the Democratic Republic of Vietnam (North Vietnam.)
Dec.	The British withdrew, leaving Vietnam in French hands.

1946

Mar. 6	France recognized the Democratic Republic of Vietnam as part of the Indochinese Federation and the French Union.
Nov. 23	Guerilla warfare between France and the Democratic Republic of Vietnam began.

1948

June 5	France established the state of Vietnam as part of the French Union (which included Cambodia and Laos). War continued between Vietnam and the regime of Ho Chi Minh.

1950

Feb. 7	The US recognized Laos, Cambodia, and Vietnam as independent states within the French Union.
Jan. 31	The USSR recognized the Democratic Republic of Vietnam under Ho Chi Minh.
May 8	The US began economic and military aid to the Vietnam government.
Dec. 23	The US drew up a mutual defense agreement with France, Vietnam, Laos, and Cambodia.

1954

Mar. 20	France asked for US military intervention.
Apr. 3	Secretary of State Dulles asked a group of Congressmen to support the use of American air forces in Vietnam, but his request was refused.

Apr. 26	A Geneva Conference began to determine the fate of Indochina with the US, France, Great Britain, the USSR, Communist China, Vietnam, the Democratic Republic of Vietnam, Laos, and Cambodia represented.
May 8	The besieged French garrison at Dien Bien Phu fell to the North Vietnamese. The defeat marked the end of effective French military strength in Southeast Asia.
July 7	Ngo Dinh Diem became prime minister of South Vietnam.
July 21	Declaration of the Geneva Conference, not signed by the US or Vietnam, divided Vietnam at the 17th parallel into the northern Democratic Republic of Vietnam and the southern Republic of Vietnam. Unification would depend upon elections, scheduled for 1956 but never held. France withdrew its troops.
Sept. 8	Protocol to the SEATO Treaty included Laos, Cambodia, and South Vietnam under the area protected by the Southeast Asia Treaty Organization.
Oct. 24	The US promised aid to South Vietnam.
1955	
Feb.	US military advisers began to train the South Vietnamese Army.
Oct. 26	The Republic of South Vietnam was established, and Ngo Dinh Diem was installed as President.
1960	
Dec. 20	National Liberation Front of Communists, peasants, and Buddhists opposed to Ngo Dinh Diem was set up in South Vietnam. The Viet Cong was the military arm of the NLF. By then, US military advisers to South Vietnam numbered about 350.
1961	
May 5	President Kennedy warned that the US was considering use of American troops in Vietnam.
Dec. 8	A US white paper warned that South Vietnam was in danger of Communist conquest from North Vietnam.
1962	
Feb. 7	US military forces in South Vietnam had increased to about 4,000; by December they numbered 20,000.
1963	LBJ inherited JFK's policy to defend South Vietnam against aggression from the North. His secretary of state, Dean Rusk, shared his "domino theory" – the loss of one country to Communism would be followed by others. "If the word gets around that the United States does not

	keep its promises then the world goes up in smoke – it is as simple as that," said Rusk.
1965	By the end of the year there were 165,000 US troops in Vietnam; casualties now surpassed those in the Korean War, and "peace parades" were held in a number of cities. By the end of 1967 half a million US forces were in Vietnam.
1968 Jan.	Communist Tet offensive. LBJ began peace talks with Hanoi and withdrew as a presidential candidate. Nixon announced a policy of Vietnamizations i.e. a return to the Ike and JFK policies of training Vietnam forces to fight the war, along with reduction of US ground troops (but increasing the air bombardments). Nixon also expanded air and ground operations into Cambodia to halt enemy supply columns. Nixon visited Moscow and Beijing for talks and sent Kissinger to Paris to conduct secret peace talks.
1973 Jan.	US and North Vietnam signed Paris Peace Agreement, providing for withdrawal of US forces and a ceasefire. Nixon called it "peace with honor," but the war continued.
1975 April	North Vietnam troops and tanks converged on Saigon, and the war was over.

PRESIDENTS OF THE USA, 1868–1988

1868	Ulysses S. Grant	Republican
1872	Ulysses S. Grant	Republican
1876	Rutherford B. Hayes	Republican
1880	James A. Garfield	Republican
1884	Grover Cleveland	Democratic
1888	Benjamin Harrison	Republican
1892	Grover Cleveland	Democratic
1896	William McKinley	Republican
1900	William McKinley	Republican
1904	Theodore Roosevelt	Republican
1908	William H. Taft	Republican
1912	Woodrow Wilson	Democratic
1916	Woodrow Wilson	Democratic
1920	Warrren G. Harding	Republican
1924	Calvin Coolidge	Republican
1928	Herbert C. Hoover	Republican
1932	Franklin D. Roosevelt	Democratic
1936	Franklin D. Roosevelt	Democratic
1940	Franklin D. Roosevelt	Democratic
1944	Franklin D. Roosevelt	Democratic
1948	Harry S. Truman	Democratic
1952	Dwight D. Eisenhower	Republican
1956	Dwight D. Eisenhower	Republican
1960	John F. Kennedy	Democratic
1964	Lyndon B. Johnson	Democratic
1968	Richard M. Nixon	Republican
1972	Richard M. Nixon	Republican
1976	Jimmy Carter	Democrat
1980	Ronald Reagan	Republican
1984	Ronald Reagan	Republican

POPULATION OF THE USA, 1870–1980 (in thousands)

1870	39,905
1880	50,262
1890	63,056
1900	76,094
1910	92,407
1920	106,466
1930	123,188
1940	132,122
1950	151,683
1960	179,992
1970	203,212
1980	223,313

Bibliographies

1 THE AMERICAN DREAM

Contributions to the Dream made by American philosophers and religious thinkers are effectively set forth by Sacvan Bercovitch, *The Puritan Origins of the American Self* (New Haven, Yale University Press, 1975); John K. Roth, *American Dreams: Meditations on life in the United States* (San Francisco, Chandler and Sharp, 1976); Paul F. Boller, Jr, *Freedom and Fate in American Thought: From Edwards to Dewey* (Dallas, Southern Methodist University Press, 1978); and Merle Curti, *Human Nature in American Thought* (Madison, Wisconsin University Press, 1980). A contemporary analysis of American attitudes toward human rights and the impact of those beliefs on foreign policy can be found in *American Dream, Global Nightmare* (New York, Norton, 1980) by Sandy Vogelgesang. Still in a philosophical vein, John W. Gardner seeks to nurture individual responsibility and social regeneration with *Morale* (New York, Norton, 1978).

Two earlier books, Stewart H. Holbrook, *Dreamers of the American Dream* (Garden City, NY, Doubleday, 1957), and Vernon Louis Parrington, Jr, *American Dreams: A study of American utopias* (New York, Russell and Russell, 1964), map "perfectionist" and reformist aspects of the Dream, which play a vital role in the tension between American aspirations and realities that has fascinated so many observers. For instance, A. N. Kaul's *The American Vision: Actual and ideal society in nineteenth-century fiction* (New Haven, Yale University Press, 1963) discusses Cooper, Hawthorne, Melville, and Twain as representatives of a recurrent dialectic in which "the actual and the ideal function in mutual critique." Marius Bewley's *The Eccentric Design: Form in the classic American novel* (New York, Columbia University Press, 1959) and Tony Tanner's *The Reign of Wonder: Naivety and reality in American literature* (Cambridge and New York, Cambridge University Press, 1965) also underscore the contrarieties in classic American literature, Tanner holding that a romantic "sense of wonder" was still dominant in American writing.

The 1920s and 1930s were critical decades for the Dream. In *The American Dream in the Great Depression* (Westport, Conn., and London, Greenwood, 1977), Charles R. Hearn defines the success myth as the "very essence of what we conceive America to be" and analyzes its permutations during that period. In *Nixon Agonistes: The crisis of the self-made man* (New York, New American Library, 1971), Gary Wills discusses the erratic fortunes of Richard Nixon's career as symptomatic of a more general disturbance within the Dream. Although it deals principally only with imaginative literature, David Madden (ed.), *American Dreams, American Nightmares* (Carbondale, Southern Illinois University Press, 1970) may be the best single book about the state of the Dream in this era. Madden's introduction puts the scene in historical perspective, Robert B. Heilman's essay defines "The American metaphor", and the other articles, by critics such as Leslie Fiedler, Maxwell Geismar, and Ihab Hassan, offer close analysis of how various authors have viewed the Dream in our time. Cf. also Daniel J. Boorstin's *The Image or What Happened to the American Dream* (New York, Atheneum, 1961); Oscar Handlin's *The Uprooted* (2nd edn, Boston, Little, Brown, 1973), and James Oliver Robertson's *American Myth, American Reality* (New York, Hill and Wang, 1980). It would also be remiss not to note that research on the Dream finds fertile soil in more widely disseminated cultural expressions. There is a useful brief guide, *The American Dream* (BAAS pamphlet no. 6, 1988), by Robert H. Fossum and John K. Roth.

There are a number of general works on American immigration, each of which offers a suitable starting point. In *American Immigration* (Chicago, Chicago University Press, 1960), Maldwyn A. Jones neatly surveys all aspects of the subject, while his *Destination America* (London, Weidenfeld and Nicolson, 1976) concentrates more upon the various immigrant groups and the problems of assimilation. Philip A. M. Taylor's *The Distant Magnet: European emigration to the USA* (New York, Harper and Row, 1971) is a carefully documented account of the immigration process from both the European and American vantage points; it is particularly informative about the Atlantic passage, as also is Terry Coleman's lively *Passage to America: A history of emigrants from Great Britain and Ireland in the mid-nineteenth century* (London, Hutchinson, 1972). Oscar Handlin's *The Uprooted: The epic story of the great migrations that made the American people* (1951; repr., Boston, Little, Brown, 1973), is a minor classic, written in a readable, almost novelistic style, which stresses the difficulties of adjusting to America. More recent writing has drawn a less gloomy picture, as notably in Stephan Thernstrom, *The Other Bostonians: Poverty and progress in the American metropolis, 1880–1970* (Cambridge, Mass., Harvard University Press, 1973), while Josef J. Barton, *Peasants and Strangers: Italians, Rumanians and Slovaks in an American city 1890–1950* (Cambridge, Mass., Harvard University Press, 1975), splendidly demonstrates the different patterns of assimilation possible even within the same ethnic group in Cleveland, Ohio. John Higham's *Strangers in the Land: Patterns of American nativism 1860–1925* (New Brunswick, NJ, Rutgers University Press, 1955) remains the most impressive analysis of American reactions to mass immigration.

Leonard Dinnerstein et al.'s useful text, *Natives and Strangers: Ethnic groups and the building of America* (New York, Oxford University Press, 1979) shows the contribution of a large number of immigrant groups throughout American history to the country's economic growth. Carl Wittke's *The Irish in America* (Baton Rouge, Louisiana State University Press, 1956) and William V. Shannon's *American Irish* (1963; rev. edn, New York, Collier, 1966) deal with the problems faced after arrival. Joseph Lopreato, *Italian Americans* (New York, Random House, 1970), discusses this group's development and problems with assimilation within America. Charlotte Erickson, *Invisible Immigrants: The adaptation of English and Scottish immigrants in nineteenth-century America* (London, Weidenfeld and Nicholson, 1972), reveals the tensions even British settlers faced in the nineteenth century. Nathan Glazer and Daniel P. Moynihan, *Beyond the Melting Pot: The Negroes, Puerto Ricans, Jews, Italians and Irish of New York City* (1963; 2nd edn, Cambridge, Mass., MIT Press, 1970) presents a sociological study of each of these groups.

Maurice Davie includes in his *World Immigration* (New York, Macmillan, 1936) a useful bibliography listing immigrant biographies and fiction. David Bowers presents a series of essays concerned with immigrant and American culture and institutions in *Foreign Influences in American Life* (New York, Peter Smith, 1952). In *The Rediscovery of the Frontier* (New York, Cooper Square, 1970), Percy Boynton discusses various literary aspects of the treatment of the frontier in fiction and includes a chapter on "The immigrant pioneer in fiction."

A useful book on the Scandinavian immigrant in literature is Dorothy Skardal's *The Divided Heart: Scandinavian immigrant experience through literary sources* (Oslo, Universitetsforlaget, 1974), which follows the implications of its title in terms of social history. Theodore Blegen's *Norwegian Migration to America, 1825–1860* (Northfield, Norwegian American Historical Association, 1931) is a standard work on its subject. For critical comment on O. E. Rolvaag, see Robert Steensma, "Rolvaag and Turner's Frontier Thesis," *North Dakota Quarterly*, 27 (1959), pp. 100–4, which discusses Rolvaag's attitude toward the frontier as "safety valve" and inspiration of democracy.

A wide variety of Italian-American authors and their works is discussed in Rose Green's useful text, *The Italian-American Novel: A document of the interaction of two cultures* (Rutherford, Fairleigh Dickinson University Press, 1974).

The most useful single text concerning Jewish life in America is Oscar Handlin's *Adventure in Freedom: Three hundred years of Jewish life in*

America (1954; repr. New York, Kennikat, 1971). Nathan Glazer's *American Judaism* (1957; repr. Chicago University Press, 1970), presents a short history of Jewish immigration to America and the changes to Jewish life which took place there. Louis Wirth's *The Ghetto* (1928; repr. Chicago, Chicago University Press, 1975), describes both the history and the psychological effects of the ghetto upon Jews in Europe and America. A most readable social history is *The American Jews: Portrait of a split personality* (New York, Paperback Library, 1969), by Jame Yaffe. A study combining immigration history and excerpts from first-person accounts of experience as an immigrant is Abraham J. Karp (ed.), *Golden Door to America: The Jewish immigrant experience* (Harmondsworth, Penguin, 1977).

Two excellent collections of documents on the black experience are Gilbert Osofsky, *The Burden of Race* (New York, Harper and Row, 1967), and Bradford Chambers, *Chronicles of Black Protest* (New York, Parent's Magazine Press, 1968). John Hope Franklin, *From Slavery to Freedom* (New York, Knopf, 1947), is a scholarly survey; Lerone Bennett, *Before the Mayflower* (Penguin Books, Baltmore, 1966), examines black history from a black journalist's viewpoint. Authoritative historical and social studies include Kenneth Stampp, *The Era of Reconstruction* (New York, Knopf, 1965); John Hope Franklin, *Reconstruction after the Civil War* (Chicago, University of Chicago Press, 1961); C. Vann Woodward, *The Strange Career of Jim Crow* (New York, Oxford University Press, 1957); August Meier, *Negro Thought in America 1880–1915* (Ann Arbor, University of Michigan Press, 1966); Elliott M. Rudwick, *Race Riot at East St Louis* (Cleveland, University of Illinois Press, 1982); Dan T. Carter, *Scottsboro* (Baton Rouge, Louisiana State University Press, 1969); Gilbert Osofsky, *Harlem: The making of a ghetto* (New York, Harper and Row, 1966); Gunnar Myrdal, *An American Dilemma: The Negro problem and American democracy* (New York, Harper, 1942); Kenneth B. Clark, *The Dark Ghetto: Dilemnas of social power* (New York, Harper and Row, 1965); E. Franklin Frazier, *Black Bourgeoisie*(New York, Collier, 1962); Stokely Carmichael and Alex Hamilton, *Black Power* (London, 1968); and C. E. Lincoln, *The Black Muslims in America* (Boston, Beacon Press, 1966).

Principal autobiographies include Frederick Douglass, *The Narrative of the Life of Frederick Douglass* (1855) and *The Life and Times of Frederick Douglass (1881);* Booker T. Washington, *Up from Slavery* (New York, Bantam Books, 1963) and W. E. B Du Bois, *The Souls of Black Folk* (1903). (Douglass's autobiographies, edited by Henry Louis Gates, Jr, and entitled *Frederick Douglass: Autobiographies*, have also been published by the Library of America, 1994); Martin Luther King, Jr, *Stride Toward Freedom* (New York, Harper and Row, 1964); Malcolm X, and Alex Haley, *The Autobiography of Malcolm X* (New York, Grove Press, 1964); Eldridge Cleaver, *Soul on Ice* (London, Cape, 1969); George Jackson, *Soledad Brother: The prison letters of George Jackson* (New York,

Coward-McCann, 1970); and Angela Davis, *Autobiography* (New York, Random House, 1974).

Important biographical studies are Samuel Spencer, *Booker T. Washington* (Boston, Little, Brown, 1955); Francis Broderick, *W. E. B. DuBois* (Stanford, Stanford University Press, 1959); Manning Marable, W. E. B. Du Bois, *Black Radical Democrat* (New York, Twayne, 1987); Edmund Cronon's life of Garvey, *Black Moses* (Madison, University of Wisconsin Press, 1955); Sally Belfrage, *Freedom Summer* (London, Deutsch, 1968); Theodore Rosengarten's oral history of a black sharecropper, *All God's Dangers* (New York, Vintage, 1974); and David L. Lewis, *Martin Luther King* (London, Allen Lane, 1970).

Among the leading novels by black writers are Charles Chesnutt, *The Marrow of Tradition* (1969); Claude McKay, *Banjo* (1929); Richard Wright, *Native Son* (1966); Ralph Ellison, *Invisible Man* (1952); James Baldwin, *Go Tell it on the Mountain* (1953); John A. Williams, *The Man Who Cried I Am* (1968); Ishmael Reed, *Yellow Back Radio Broke Down* (1972); Toni Morrison, *The Song of Solomon* (1977); and Alex Haley, *Roots* (1977).

A useful guide is the latest edition of *The Negro Almanac*, ed. Harold Ploski and Ernest Kaiser (New York, Bellwether).

2 RECONSTRUCTION

A number of volumes are useful on Reconstruction, notably those by C. Vann Woodward: *The Burden of Southern History* (New York, Vintage Books, 1960), and *The Strange Career of Jim Crow* (New York, Oxford University Press, 1957). One of the best treatments is that by Kenneth E. Stampp, *The Era of Reconstruction, 1865–1867* (New York, Knopf, 1965). Other useful volumes are: Arthur S. Link and Rembert W. Patrick (eds), *Writing Southern History* (Chapel Hill, NC, University of North Carolina Press, 1965); John Hope Franklin, *Reconstruction After the Civil War* (Chicago, University of Chicago Press, 1961); Paul D. Escott, *After Secession: Jefferson Davies and the failure of Confederate nationalism* (Baton Rouge, Louisiana State University Press, 1978); James E. Sefton, *Andrew Johnson and the Uses of Constitutional Power* (Boston, Little, Brown, 1980); Eric L. McKitrick, *Andrew Johnson and Reconstruction* (Chicago, University of Chicago Press, 1960); Eric Foner, *Politics and Ideology in the Age of the Civil War* (New York, Oxford University Press, 1980), and *Reconstruction: America's unfinished revolution* (New York, Harper Collins, 1988), also abridged as *A Short History of Reconstruction* (New York, Harper Collins, 1990); Allen W. Trelease, *Reconstruction: The great experiment* (New York, Harper Torchbooks, 1971); James M. McPherson, *Ordeal by Fire: The Civil War and Reconstruction* (New York, Knopf, 1982); W. E. B. Du Bois, *Black Reconstruction in America, 1860–1880* (New York, Meridien Books, 1964);

Albert Castel, "Andrew Johnson: his historical rise and fall," *Mid-Am*, 45 (1963), pp. 175–84; Bernard A. Weisberger, "The dark and bloody ground of Reconstruction historiography," *Journal of Southern History*, 25 (1959), pp. 427–47.

For the scalawags, see Otto H. Olsen, "Reconsidering the scalawags," *Civil War History*, 12 (1966), p. 314; and for the carpetbaggers, Jonathan Daniels, *Prince of Carpetbaggers* (Philadelphia, Lippincott, 1958) – the story of Milton Littlefield; and Richard N. Current, *Old Ihad Stevens: a story of ambition* (Madison, University of Wisconsin Press, 1942), and *Those Terrible Carpetbaggers: a reinterpretation* (New York, Oxford University Press, 1988).

3 THE GROWTH OF URBAN SOCIETY

The best study of Carnegie is John Frazier Wall, *Andrew Carnegie* (New York, Oxford University Press, 1970). A more concise and readable study, emphasizing his role in the growth of the steel business, is Harold C. Livesay, *Andrew Carnegie and the Rise of Big Business* (Boston, Little, Brown, 1975). The long and still controversial career of John D. Rockefeller is best studied in Allan Nevins, *Study in Power: John D. Rockefeller, industrialist and philanthropist*, 2 vols, (New York, Scribner's, 1953). This is a thorough study, expanded from an earlier edition (1940) as more papers became available. His is a vivid portrait. It covers the seemingly incredible span of Rockefeller's life from his boyhood and young manhood in the two decades preceding the Civil War to his death in the fifth year of the administration of Franklin D. Roosevelt. And on a second and also spacious dimension it covers Rockefeller's personal life, his benefactions and, of course, the story of Standard Oil. Nevins allows the color and drama to derive from his materials. In fact, it is hard to see how history could be better written. If Americans can be induced to read the history of any business enterprise, this is the one. Ida Tarbell, *History of the Standard Oil Company* (1904; repr. New York, P. Smith's, 1950) paints a different picture of the company, which – unlike Nevins – sees JDR as money-grubbing and miserly. *John D.: The Founding Father of the Rockefellers* (New York, Harper, 1980), by David F. Hawke, is the most recent and most balanced study: JDR emerges as far more complex than the man described by either Ida Tarbell or Allan Nevins.

Henry Ford is still a legendary figure. In his lifetime he was the fully acclaimed American tycoon, from the birth of the Model T in 1908. His later career – not least his antisemitism and his opposition to unionization – kept him secure in headline-catching. The most insightful account is that of Samuel S. Marquis, *Henry Ford: An interpretation* (Boston, Little, Brown, 1923), by an Episcopalian minister who served as head of the company's "Sociological Dept" when Ford experimented with welfare capitalism at the time of World War I. The fullest treatment is by Allan Nevins and Frank Hill, in three volumes: *Ford, the Times, the Man, the Company* (New York, Scribner's, 1954–63); *Ford Expansion and Challenge, 1915–1933* (1957) and *Ford: Decline and Rebirth 1933–1962* (1963).

Two useful studies of Edison are Matthew Josephson, *Edison* (New York, McGraw-Hill, 1959), a picture of a dedicated, intense inventor with immense drive, and Robert D. Friedel, *Edison's Electric Light: Biography of an invention* (New Brunswick, NJ, Rutgers University Press, 1986).

For finance, see Ron Chernow, *The House of Morgan: An American banking dynasty and the rise of modern finance* (New York, Touchstone Books, 1991).

For the years of the entrepreneurs, the most valuable source is a good social and economic history text. Harold U. Faulkner's most recent edition is one of the best of these: *American Political and Social History* (New York, Appleton-Century-Crofts, 1947). Alternatively, and immensely wide-ranging and readable, are Thomas C. Cochran and William Miller, *The Age of Enterprise: A Social history of industrial America* (New York, Macmillan, 1951), and E. David Cronon, *Government and the Economy* (New York, Holt Dryden, 1960).

Turning to urbanization, Charles N. Glaab and A. Theodore Brown, *A History of Urban America* (New York, Macmillan, 1967), is a survey of urban growth in America, while Blake McKelvey, *The Urbanization of America: 1860–1915* (New Brunswick, NJ, Rutgers University Press, 1963), examines the relationship of urban growth to other phases of American life. Lewis Mumford's *The City in History* (New York, Harcourt, Brace/World, 1961), is a lengthy synthesis of the city's role in civilization from its origins to its present; included is a 55-page bibliography. Other studies of the cities and their problems are A. M. Schlesinger, *The Rise of the City 1787–1898* (New York, Macmillan, 1933); Herbert G. Gutman, *Work. Culture and Society in Industrializing America: Essays in American working-class and social history* (New York, Knopf, 1976); William I. Thomas and Florian Znaniecki, *The Polish Peasant in Europe and America*, 2 vols (New York, Knopf, 1927), vol. I, pp. 207, 760; Harvey Zorbaugh, *The Gold Coast and the Slum: A sociological study of Chicago's Near North Side* (Chicago, University of Chicago Press, 1950); Richard Hofstadter, *Social Darwinism in American Thought* (Boston, Beacon Press, 1955); Richard Hofstadter (ed.), *Great Issues in American History: From Reconstruction to the present day* (New York, Vintage Books, 1969); Charles N. Glaab (ed)., *The American City: A documentary history* (Dorsey Press, Homewood, Ill., 1963); Christopher Tunnard, *The Modern American City* (Princeton, NJ, Van Nostrand, 1968); Allen M. Wakstein (ed.), *The Urbanization of America: An historical anthology* (Boston, Houghton Mifflin, 1970).

Some valuable and more recent studies include Robert Wiebe, *The Search for Order 1877–1920* (4th edn, New York, Hill and Wang, 1984);

James T. Patterson, *The Welfare State in America* (London, BAAS, Pamphlets in American Studies no. 7, 1981); William L. Barney, *The Passage of the Republic: an interdisciplinary history of nineteenth-century America* (Lexington, D. C. Heath, 1987); C. Vannn Woodward, *Tam Watson, Agrarian Rebel* (New York, Oxford University Press, 1966); Chester McA. Destler, *American Radicalism 1865–1901* (Chicago, Quadrangle Books, 1966).

4 THE PRESIDENCY IN THE GILDED AGE

For Ulysses Grant, the best introduction is his own *Memoirs* (1885–6). It has often been described as one of the great American books, though it was written when he was dying of throat cancer, and intended to repay heavy debts. It is clear and forceful. He recounts his boyhood in Ohio, and his education at West Point. Though Grant saw combat in the Mexican War, his view of the annexation of Texas was that it was a slaveholding conspiracy and that the conflict with Mexico was unjustified. Two-thirds of the book is devoted to the Civil War, with its two climaxes, Vicksburg and Appomattox. His 36 years of marriage are neglected, as are the post-Civil War years, including the presidency.

One of the best of the biographies is William S. McFeely, *Grant: A Biography* (New York, Norton, 1981). Grant had, says McFeely, "no organic, artistic or intellectual specialness." He had been a failure as farmer, clerk and businessman, but suddenly West Pointers were in demand. This book is, however, not especially sympathetic to the Civil War experience, and is a trifle flippant in style. More sympathetic is Bruce Catton's *Ulysses S. Grant and the American Military Tradition* (Boston, Little, Brown, 1954); it is brief and readable. Allan Nevins, *Grover Cleveland* (Chicago, Dodd, Mead, 1932) is thorough and well-researched study. For Bryan, there is a valuable and detailed 3-volume biography by Paolo E. Coletta, *William Jennings Bryan* (Lincoln, University of Nebraska Press, 1964–9). The best single-volume treatment is by Louis W. Koenig, *Bryan: A political biography of William Jennings Bryan* (New York, Putnam, 1971), but equally readable is Robert Cherny, *A Righteous Cause: The Life of William Jennings Bryan* (Boston, Little, Brown, 1985), who sees Bryan as a crusader for various causes: Free Silver, Peace, against Imperialism and Evolution.

There are three general surveys that are still worth reading: Matthew Josephson, *The Politicos 1865–1896* (New York, Harcourt Brace, 1938); idem, *The Robber Barons* (New York, Harcourt Brace, 1934); and Allan Nevins, *The Emergence of Modern America 1865–1877* (New York, Macmillan, 1927).

5 EMPIRE

There are a number of titles which deal with American imperialism and foreign policy: Henry F. Graff (ed.), *American Imperialism and the Philippine Insurrection* (Boston, Little, Brown, 1969); Robert F. Smith, *The United States and Cuba: Business and diplomacy, 1917–1960* (New York, Bookman Associates, 1960); J. Rogers Hollingsworth (ed.), *American Expansion in the Late Nineteenth Century*, American Problems Series (New York, Holt, Rinehart and Winston, 1968); Ernest R. May, *Imperial Democracy: The emergence of America as a Great Power* (New York, Harcourt, Brace/World, 1961); George H. Nadel and Perry Curtis (eds), *Imperialism and Colonialism* (New York, Macmillan, 1964); Julius W. Pratt, *The Expansionists of 1898* (Albert Shaw Lecture; Baltimore, Johns Hopkins University Press, 1936); and Richard W. Leopold, *The Growth of American Foreign Policy: A history* (New York, Knopf, 1962).

For George Armstrong Custer and the Indians see John Conway, *The Sioux Wars* (New York, Monarch Books, 1962); George Armstrong Custer, *My Life on the Plains* (New York, Citadel Press, 1962); William T. Hagan, *American Indians* (University of Chicago, 1964); David Lavender, *The American West* (New York, Penguin Books, 1969); Robert M. Utley, *Cavalier in Buckskin: George Armstrong Custer and the Western Military Frontier* (Norman, University of Oklahoma Press, 1988); Stephen E. Ambrose, *Crazy Horse and Custer: The Parallel Lives of Two American Warriors* (New York, Doubleday, 1975).

6 THE LEARNED PRESIDENCY

Originally, Henry F. Pringle wrote his biography of Theodore Roosevelt without too much involvement in the sources; but after the publication of *The Works of Theodore Roosevelt*, and the *Letters*, he brought out a revised edition, *Theodore Roosevelt, a biography* (New York, Harcourt Brace, 1931), but held that his judgments remained intact. He confessed, and with pride, that he had educated a whole generation into a picture of Teddy as a mixture of "adult greatness ... with the quality of being a magnificent child." Cf. Maton Keller, *Theodore Roosevelt, a Profile* (New York, Hill and Wang, 1967), and Arthur Link (ed.), *Woodrow Wilson, a Profile* (New York, Hill and Wang, 1968). Forty years after Pringle, William H. Harbaugh, in *Power and Responsibility: The life and times of Theodore Roosevelt* (Oxford, Oxford University Press, 1975), wrote the best and the most durable of the biographies of TR. Edmund Morris, *The Rise of Theodore Roosevelt* (New York, Coward, McCann and Geoghagen, 1979) is the first volume of a projected 3-volume study: it does not reach the presidency, but is well written. There are two excellent 1-volume treatments: John M. Blum, *The Republican*

Roosevelt (Cambridge, Mass., Harvard University Press, 1954), and David H. Burton, *Theodore Roosevelt* (New York, Twayne, 1972). See also David Burton, *The Learned Presidency* (New Jersey, Fairleigh Dickinson University Press, 1988).

Arthur S. Link has devoted a long career to Wilson scholarship and is editor of the Wilson papers (Princeton, NJ, Princeton University Press, 1966) and author of *Wilson*, 5 vols (Princeton, NJ, Princeton University Press, 1947–64). He is critical of Wilson's policies towards Latin America; he is valuable in showing how when Wilson took office, "The New Freedom" (breaking up large corporations with monopolistic powers) was modified into something closer to Theodore Roosevelt's "New Nationalism." Ray Stannard Baker was Wilson's Press Secretary at Versailles and is largely uncritical in *Woodrow Wilson and World Settlement*, 3 vols (Garden City, NY, Doubleday, 1922) and *Woodrow Wilson: Life and letters*, 8 vols (Garden City, NY, Doubleday, 1927–39). Alexander and Juliette George, *Woodrow Wilson and Colonial House: A personality study* (New York, J. Day, 1956), needs modifying in the light of Edwin Weinstein's *Woodrow Wilson: A medical and psychological study* (Princeton, NJ, Princeton University Press, 1981). There are two excellent briefer and less controversial treatments: J. M. Blum, *Woodrow Wilson and the Politics of Morality* (Boston, Mass., Little, Brown, 1956), and John A. Garraty, *Woodrow Wilson: A great life in brief* (New York, Knopf, 1956). See also Kendrick A. Clements, *Woodrow Wilson: World statesman* (Boston, Twayne, 1987); August Heckscher, *Woodrow Wilson* (New York, Scribner's, 1991); John M. Mulder, *Woodrow Wilson: The years of preparation* (Princeton, NJ, Princeton University Press, 1978); and Paul Birdsall, *Versailles Twenty Years After* (New York, Reynal and Hitchcock, 1941).

7 WORLD WAR I

Good general surveys of the period are: George E. Mowry, *The Urban Nation 1920–1960* (New York, Hill and Wang, 1965), and *The Era of Theodore Roosevelt 1910–1912* (New York, Harper and Row, 1958); Richard Hofstedter, *The Age of Reform: From Bryan to FDR* (New York, Knopf, 1955); and George F. Kennan (ed.), *American Diplomacy 1900–1950* (New York, Mentor Books, 1952).

For the issues raised by the US entry into war, see Woodrow Wilson, speech to Congress, April 2, 1917, *Congressional Record*, 65th Congress, First Session 55; Charles Seymour, "American neutrality: the experience of 1914–1917," *Foreign Affairs*, 14 (1935), p. 30; Harry Elmer Barnes, "The world war of 1914–1918," in Willard Waller (ed.), *War in the Twentieth Century* (New York, Random House, 1940); and Charles C. Tansill, *America Goes to War* (Boston, Little, Brown, 1938).

8 PURITANS IN BABYLON

For general studies of the period, see F. L. Allen, *Only Yesterday* (New York, Bantam Books, 1959); George E. Mowry, *The Twenties: Fords, flappers and fanatics* (Prentice-Hall, Spectrum, 1963); W. E. Leuchtenberg, *The Perils of Prosperity 1914–1932* (Chicago, University of Chicago Press, 1958); Andrew Sinclair, *The Era of Excess* (New York, Harper and Row, 1964); Gordon Craig and Felix Gilbert (eds), *The Diplomats*, vol. I, *The Twenties* (New York, Atheneum, 1963).

For Harding, see Charles L. Mee, *The Ohio Gang: The world of Warren Harding* (New York, Evans, 1982); Samuel Hopkins Adams, *Incredible Era: The life and times of Warren Gamaliel Harding* (New York, Houghton Mifflin, 1939); Andrew Sinclair, *The Available Man: The life behind the masks of Warren Gamaliel Harding* (New York, Macmillan, 1965); Robert Murray, *The Harding Era: Warren G. Harding and his administration* (Minneapolis, University of Minnesota Press, 1969); Francis Russell, *The Shadow of Blooming Grove: The one hundred years of Warren Gamaliel Harding* (New York, McGraw-Hill, 1968). For Coolidge, see Claude M. Fuess, *Calvin Coolidge, the Man from Vermont* (Boston, Little, Brown, 1940); Donald R. McCoy, *Calvin Coolidge* (Lawrence, University Press of Kansas, 1988); and William Allen White, *A Puritan in Babylon* (New York, Macmillan, 1938).

Probably the best biography of Herbert Hoover is by Eugene Lyons, *Herbert Hoover: A biography* (New York, Doubleday, 1964): a portrait of a principled, kindly, loyal man, betrayed by a fickle public. His shyness weakened his public relations, however; Lyons rejects the charges that he was callous, cold and humorless. A good and sympathetic picture of his Presidency is Martin L. Fausold, *The Presidency of Herbert Hoover* (Lawrence, University of Kansas Press, 1985). David Burner, *Herbert Hoover, A Public Life* (New York, Knopf, 1979), is an excellent account of Hoover as secretary of commerce, and holds that his accomplishments prior to the stockmarket collapse were considerable; had times been normal, he would have been an admirable reform President. Joan Hoff-Wilson, *Herbert Hoover: Forgotten Progressive* (Boston, Little, Brown, 1975), traces his liberalism and his compassion to his Quakerism; but sees him as inflexible, a "desperate ideologue." George Nash's biography is likely to be the definitive 3-volume treatment; two volumes are available: *The Life of Herbert Hoover* (New York, Norton, vol. I, 1983, Vol. II, 1988). Probably the warmest and most popular study is Carol G. Wilson, *Herbert Hoover: A challenge for today* (New York, Evans Publishing, 1968).

For crime, organized and otherwise, (and its wartime uses, notably via the Mafia in Italy), see Robert Kelly (ed.), *Organized Crime: A global perspective* (Lanham, Md, Rowman and Allanheld, 1986), pp. 68–77; Allen, *Only Yesterday*; Michael Woodiwiss, *Crime, Crusades and Cor-*

ruption: Prohibition in the US (London, Pinter, 1988), and *Organized Crime, USA* (BAAS Pamphlet, no. 19); F. D. Paley, *Al Capone, The Biography of a Self-made man* (London, Faber and Faber, 1966); Irving Stone, *Clarence Darrow for the Defense* (New York, Bantam Books, 1961); Burl Noggle, *Tea-pot Dome* (New York, Norton, 1965); and Andrew Sinclair, *Prohibition: The era of excess* (Boston, Little, Brown, 1962).

9 FDR AND THE NEW DEAL

There is a small library of highly readable books on FDR. Frank B. Freidel's 4-volume survey (Boston, Little, Brown, 1952–73), is based on monumental research and on a number of personal interviews. He criticizes the readiness to compromise, but doubts the usual view that it was the fight against polio that gave him his strength: Freidel argues that there was from the start a strong will and a sense of destiny. He stresses the importance of Roosevelt's years as governor of New York and his skill even then in calling on a "Brain Trust." The best study of Roosevelt as master politician is by James M. Burns, *The Lion and the Fox* (New York, Harcourt Brace, 1956). There are excellent 1-volume studies by Nathan Miller, *FDR: An intimate biography* (New York, Doubleday, 1983); by Geoffrey C. Ward, *A First-Class Temperament: The emergence of Franklin Roosevelt* (New York, Harper, 1989); by William E. Leuchtenberg, *Franklin Delano Roosevelt and the New Deal 1932–40* (New York, Harper, 1963); and by Rexford G. Tugwell, *The Democratic Roosevelt* (New York, Doubleday, 1957); and a 3-volume study by Arthur M. Schlesinger Jr, *The Age of Roosevelt*, 3 vols (Boston, Houghton Mifflin, 1957–60). Schlesinger's *The Coming of the New Deal* (Boston, Houghton Mifflin, 1958), is both friendly and magisterial. Ted Morgan, *FDR, A Biography* (New York, Simon and Schuster, 1980), is more critical; there was "a lack of frankness, a passion for manipulation, a mental and emotional shallowness, and a streak of vindictiveness." Two other useful bibliographical aids are: William J. Stewart, *The Era of Franklin D. Roosevelt: A selected bibliography of periodical and dissertation literature, 1945–1966* (New York, Hyde Park, 1967), and Richard S. Kirkendall, "The New Deal as watershed: the recent literature," *Journal of American History*, 54 (March 1968).

Two valuable studies of the New Deal itself are A. J. Badger, *The New Deal: The depression years* (London, Macmillan, 1989), and Roger Biles, *A New Deal for the American People* (Champaign, Northern Illinois University Press, 1991), both of which treat the topic thematically, looking in turn at agriculture, industry, labor, relief, women,and blacks. In general, early New Deal recovery agencies and the policies they followed have received an increasing amount of attention. The operation of the NRA in a particular industry is the subject of Sidney Fine's *The Automobile under the Blue Eagle: Labor, management and the automobile manufacturing code* (Ann Arbor, University of Michigan Press, 1963). Ellis Hawley has analysed the National Recovery Administration in the broad context of public attitudes toward concentration and competition in *The New Deal and the Problem of Monopoly: A study in ambivalence* (Princeton, Princeton University Press, 1966). The Roosevelt administration's agricultural policies also have been explored in some detail. The impact of the Agricultural Adjustment Administration upon landless farmers is evaluated in David E. Conrad's *The Forgotten Farmers: The story of sharecroppers in the New Deal* (Urbana, University of Illinois Press, 1965).

The creation of federal relief programs marked an important step in the development of the welfare state. Roy Lubove, in *The Struggle for Social Security, 1900–1935* (Cambridge, Mass., Harvard University Press, 1968), traces the origins of the old age pension system, and Arthur J. Altmeyer's *The Formative Years of Social Security* (Madison, University of Wisconsin Press, 1966) describes how the system functioned. One of the most popular relief ventures is explored by John A. Salmond in *The Civilian Conservation Corps, 1933–1942* (Durham, NC, University of North Carolina Press, 1967). Some of the problems that occur when relief is combined with support for the arts are considered by Jane D. Mathews in *The Federal Theater, 1935–1939: Plays, relief and politics* (Princeton, NJ, Princeton University Press, 1967), and by William F. McDonald in *Federal Relief Administration and the Arts: The origins and administrative history of the arts projects of the Works Progress Administration* (Columbus, Ohio, Ohio State University Press, 1969).

Franklin Roosevelt had great success in filling administrative posts with able and energetic men who have quite naturally attracted the interest of biographers. Searle F. Charles discusses the man most closely identified with welfare programs in *Minister of Relief: Harry Hopkins and the depression* (New York, Syracuse University Press, 1963). One phase of Henry Wallace's career is treated by Edward L. and Frederick H. Schapsmeier in *Henry A. Wallace of Iowa: The agrarian years, 1910–1940* (Ames, Iowa, University of Iowa Press, 1969), The contributions to reform of an important Brains Truster are analyzed in Bernard Sternsher's *Rexford Tugwell and the New Deal* (New Brunswick, NJ, Rutgers University Press, 1964). In *Senator Robert F. Wagner and the Rise of Urban Liberalism* (New York, Atheneum, 1968), J. Joseph Huthmacher examines the New York liberal who helped shape labor policy in the 1930s. The diaries of two New Deal officials have recently been published: John M. Blum, *From the Morgenthau Diaries*, 3 vols (Boston, Houghton Mifflin, 1959–67), and David E. Lilienthal, *The Journals of David E. Lilienthal*, vol. I, *The TVA Years* (New York, Harper and Row, 1964).

While Roosevelt was not the first President to draw advisors from the academic community, he did give scholars a large voice in the formulation of public policy. The role of social scientists in the development of the New Deal receive attention by Barry Dean Karl in *Executive Reorganization and Reform in the New Deal: The genesis of administrative management, 1900–1939* (Cambridge, Mass., Harvard University Press, 1963), and Richard S. Kirkendall in *Social Scientists and Farm Politics in the Age of Roosevelt* (Columbia, Mo., University of Missouri Press, 1966). Rexford G. Tugwell, in *The Brains Trust* (New York, Viking Press, 1968), offers quite different perspectives on Roosevelt's advisors. Tugwell's memoir provides a classic account of how Roosevelt's sense of the politically possible diluted broad-gauged proposals for economic reform.

Radical disillusionment in the 1960s soon produced sharp critiques of the New Deal. The most notable of these were Howard Zinn (ed.), *New Deal Thought* (Indianapolis, Bobbs-Merrill, 1966), see pp. xv–xxxvi; Paul Conkin, *The New Deal* (London, Routledge and Kegan Paul, 1968), and Barton J. Bernstein, "The New Deal: the conservative achievements of liberal reform," in *Towards a New Past: Dissenting essays in American history* (New York, Pantheon, 1967), pp. 263–8. See also Brad Wiley, "Historians and the New Deal" (Radical Education Project, Ann Arbor, n.d.), and Ronald Radosh, "The myth of the New Deal," in *A New History of Leviathan: Essays on the rise of the American corporate state* (New York, Dutton, 1972), pp. 146–87.

The free-market case against the damaging consequences of New Deal statism was most eloquently expressed by Milton Friedman, *Free to Choose: A personal statement* (New York, Harcourt Brace Jovanovich, 1980). Intellectuals on the right in the 1970s found the emphasis on New Deal limitations misguided. A vivid, detailed account of the Roosevelt years in the White House is in Michael Barone, *Our Country: The shaping of America from Roosevelt to Reagan* (New York, Free Press, 1990).

The most compelling personal testimony to the dramatic impact of the depression on individual lives is contained first in the oral history interviews collected by Studs Terkel in *Hard Times: An oral history of the Great Depression* (New York, Pocket Books, 1970), then in the life histories taken down in the 1930s by the Federal Writers' Project. Selections of these have been edited by Ann Banks, *First-Person America* (New York, Knopf, 1980), and by Tom Terrill and Jerrold Hirsch, *Such as Us: Southern voices of the thirties* (Chapel Hill, NC, University of North Carolina Press, 1978). Over 15 million letters from the public survive in the Franklin D. Roosevelt Library. Robert S. McElvaine studied a random sample of 15,000 of these and other letters to federal agencies for a study of working-class reactions to the depression: see his *Down and Out In The Great Depression: Letters from the forgotten men* (Chapel Hill, NC, University of North Carolina Press, 1983). A valuable study of blacks and the New Deal is Harvard Sitkoff, *A New Deal for Blacks: The emergence of civil rights as a national issue in the depression decade* (New York, Oxford University Press, 1978). The New Deal had racial limitations, Sitkoff admits, but argues that the younger New Deal liberals were part of the civil rights movement.

Two valuable works on foreign policy are Waldo Heinrich's *Threshold of War: Franklin D. Roosevelt and American Entry into World War II* (New York, Oxford University Press, 1988) and Robert Dallek's *Franklin D. Roosevelt and American Foreign Policy 1932–45* (New York, Oxford University Press, 1979).

On Eleanor Roosevelt, one of the best "inside" commentators is her friend Joseph P. Lash, who played an active part in Washington politics and died in 1987: see *Eleanor and Franklin: The story of their relationship based on Eleanor Roosevelt's private papers* (London, Deutsch, 1972), which won the Pulitzer prize for biography; and *Eleanor: The years alone* (London, Deutsch, 1972). More recently Lois Scharf's biography *Eleanor Roosevelt, First Lady of American Liberalism* (New York, Twayne, 1987) is a valuable addition to literature on the subject.

10 WORLD WAR II

For Hitler and the Third Reich, see Alan Bullock, *Hitler, a study in tyranny* (New York, Bantam Books, 1961); William L. Shirer, *The Rise and Fall of the Third Reich* (New York, Cross Books, 1964); T. L. Jarman, *The Rise and Fall of Nazi Germany* (New York, Signet Books, 1961); H. R. Trevor-Roper, *The Last Days of Hitler* (New York, Berkeley, 1960).

For the origins of the war and the war itself, see A. J. P. Taylor, *The Origins of the Second World War* (New York, Premier Books, 1963); Winston S. Churchill, *The Second World War*, 6 vols (New York, Bantam Books, 1962); Seymour Frieden and William Richardson (eds), *The Fatal Decisions* (New York, Berkley, 1963); Chester Wilmot, *The Struggle for Europe: World War II in the West* (New York, Harper and Row, 1963); John Erickson and David Dilks, *Barbarossa: The Axis and the Allies* (Edinburgh, Edinburgh University Press, 1994); and Dwight D. Eisenhower, *Crusade in Europe* (New York, Dolphin Books, 1962).

Bernard L. Montgomery's *Memoirs* (New York, Signet Books, 1959), and Jack Pearl's account of *General Douglas Macarthur* (New York, Monarch Books, 1969), are both of considerable interest, as is Omar Bradley's *A Soldier's Story* (New York, Popular Library, 1964).

For American espionage, see Stewart Alsop and Thomas Braden, *Sub Rosa: The OSS and American espionage* (Cambridge, MA, Harvard University Press, 1964), and Peter Grose, *Gentleman Spy: The life of Allen Dulles* (London, Deutsch, 1994).

11 HARRY S. TRUMAN AND THE COLD WAR

Probably the best single-volume, well-documented, and interesting presentation is William E. Pemberton, *Harry S. Truman: Fair Dealer and Cold Warrior* (Boston, Twayne, 1989). William P. Helm, *Harry Truman: A political biography* (New York, Duell Sloane, 1947) and Gene Powell's *Tom's Boy Harry* (Jefferson City, Mo., Hawthorn Publishing, 1948) are studies of HST's years in the Pendergast machine. Jonathan Daniel's *The Man from Independence* (Philadelphia, Lippincott, 1950) is a more balanced and favorable view, seeing HST as an "everyday man" who rose to the challenges of leadership. Beginning in 1975, the private presidential papers became available at the Truman Library, and more rounded studies emerged: see Harold F. Gosnell's big *Truman's Crises: A political biography* (Westport, Conn., Greenwood Press, 1980); Robert H. Ferrell's two volumes, *Harry S. Truman and the Modern American Presidency* (Boston, Little, Brown, 1983), and *Truman: A centenary remembrance* (New York, Viking, 1984), nd Richard L. Miller, *Truman: The rise to power* (New York, McGraw Hill, 1986), which is especially well-balanced and fair. For a useful guide to the economics of the Marshall Plan, see Robin Winks, *The Marshall Plan and the American Economy* (New York, Holt-Dryden, 1960). For a warm anecdotal and supportive family portrait see Margaret Truman's *Harry S. Truman* (New York, Morrow, 1972).

Perhaps the fullest – and the most thorough – treatment is that of the one-time White House reporter Robert Donovan, who produced a balanced "insider" portrait: *Conflict and Crisis* and *Tumultuous Years: The presidency of Harry S. Truman 1949–1953* (New York, Norton, 1983). In his first volume, *Conflict and Crisis*, Donovan lamented the development, by 1948, of an "overblown, zealous, and all too often crackpot alarm over communism." That domestic anti-communism, along with the threat of the Soviet Union abroad, remains the backdrop for Donovan's account of Truman's presidency after 1948. Yet Donovan doubts that another President could have done much better. Approvingly, he cites the views of David E. Bell, Truman's administrative assistant, who concluded, "there was nothing the Executive Branch could do that would successfully respond to the feeling of fear and frustration which was being played upon by McCarthy." Thereafter, Truman's most absorbing decisions involved Korea. Donovan, like other scholars, questions Truman's handling of the decision to intervene in Korea, but reminds us of the popular demand for a strong American stand against North Korea. In dealing with Truman's last two years as President, Donovan does not join those contemporaries who blamed the President for all the ills of the body politic. Yet, it is also clear from Donovan's account of these two years that Truman was fast losing his grip on important domestic problems. Political corruption grew to plague his administration – corruption that Truman was inept in trying to curb. As Republicans were to proclaim during the 1952 campaign, Communism, Korea, and corruption dominated American politics.

On the Cold War, see Norman A. Graebner, *Cold War Diplomacy, American Foreign Policy, 1945–1960* (Princeton, NJ, Van Nostrand/ Anvil Books, 1962); Christian Herter, *Toward an Atlantic Community* (New York, Harper, 1963); John Lukács, *A History of the Cold War* (Doubleday, Anchor Books, 1962); Reinhold Niebuhr, *The World Crisis and American Responsibility* (New York, Associated Press, 1968); Hugh Seton-Watson, *Neither War Nor Peace* (London, Praeger, 1963); William Appleman Williams, *The Tragedy of American Diplomacy* (New York, Dell, 1962); and Robin Winks, *The Cold War: From Yalta to Cuba* (New York, Macmillan, 1964), and *Cloak and Gown* (London, Collins Harvill, 1990); Jeff Broadwater, *Adlai Stevenson, the Odyssey of a Cold War liberal* (New York, Twayne, 1994).

12 IKE, THE SUPREME COMMANDER

The best biography is Stephen Ambrose, *Eisenhower*, 2 vols (London, Allen and Unwin, 1984), from which it is clear that the young Ike was given to rages, which he learned to control. From the first, Ike was ambitious, thin-skinned, stubborn, naive, culturally unsophisticated, and immensely likeable. Stephen Ambrose, *The Supreme Commander: The war years of General Dwight D. Eisenhower* (London, Cassell, 1971), is the most competent study of Ike's role in the war. A more critical biography is by Piers Brendon, *Ike: His life and times* (New York, Harper, 1986), which concentrates on the presidential years and their problems: Senator McCarthy, John Foster Dulles, Suez, Nixon, and the incessant golfing. Robert F. Burk, *Dwight D. Eisenhower: Hero and politician* (Boston, Twayne, 1986), is a briefer study, but has an excellent bibliographical essay. Other good surveys are: Peter Lyon, *Eisenhower: Portrait of a hero* (Boston, Little, Brown, 1974); Herbert S. Parmet, *Eisenhower and the American Crusades* (New York, Macmillan, 1972); and R. Alton Lee, *Dwight D. Eisenhower: Soldier and statesman* (Chicago, Nelson-Hall, 1981).

For a fuller bibliography and a revisionist view of Eisenhower, see Peter Boyle's *Update* in *The Historian* (London, The Historical Association), no. 43 (autumn 1994), pp. 9–11; and idem (ed.), *Churchill-Eisenhower Correspondence 1953–1955* (Chapel Hill, NC, University of North Carolina Press, 1990).

13 JFK, LBJ, AND VIETNAM

As early as 1988, there were already over 200 books dealing wholly or partly with John F. Kennedy (Thomas Brown, *JFK: History of an Image*,

(Bloomington, Indiana University Press, 1988). There are two excellent portraits by participants in the administration who were also friends: Arthur N. Schlesinger Jr, *1000 Days* (Boston, Houghton Mifflin, 1965), and Theodore C. Sorensen, *Kennedy* (New York, Harper 1965). In the same style, but without the sense of participation, is William Manchester, *One Brief Shining Moment: Remembering Kennedy* (Boston, Little, Brown, 1963), a coffee-table-style volume. The first attempt at a critical and original assessment was Gary Wills, *The Kennedy Imprisonment: A meditation on power* (Boston, Little, Brown, 1982). For Wills, it was power that drove all the Kennedys, and the symbol of their failure was Joseph's and John's private relations with women. Wills compares Kennedy to another assassinated leader, Martin Luther King, Jr, to JFK's disadvantage. The most complete and fairest biography is Herbert Parmet's two-volume survey, *Jack: The Struggles of John F. Kennedy* (New York, Dial, 1980), and *JFK: The presidency of John F. Kennedy* (New York, Dial, 1983). Harris Wofford provides a critical view in *Of Kennedys and Kings* (New York, Farrar, Straus and Giroux, 1980). For other views of Kennedy, see also Allan Nevins (ed.), John F. Kennedy, *The Burden and the Glory* (New York, Harper, 1964); Hugh Sidey, *John F. Kennedy, President* (New York, Crest, 1964); J. McGregor Burns, *John Kennedy, a Political Profile* (New York, Van Nostrand Anvil, 1961); Theodore White, *The Making of the President 1960* (New York, Pocket Books, 1962).

The biographers of that most controversial of Presidents, Lyndon Baines Johnson, have brought very different emphases to their studies. As Ronnie Dugger's title implies, his is a critical, even hostile, picture: *The Politician, The Life and Times of Lyndon Johnson: The drive for power, from the frontier to master of the Senate* (New York, Norton, 1982). In a study that does not reach the presidency, although he recognizes Johnson's compassion, he stresses LBJ's crudeness, his ruthlessness, and his vindictiveness. Power was the engine that drove him and it gave him, even in his early days, a fundamental hawkishness in foreign policy. By contrast, Doris Kearns, *Lyndon Johnson and the American Dream* (New York, Harper, 1976), is sympathetic.

In a recent study, Robert Dallek, *Lone Star Rising* (New York, Oxford University Press, 1991) describes with clarity and insight Johnson's almost literally unprecedented (and highly controversial) success – and domination – as the Senate majority leader between 1955 (when the Democrats recaptured the Senate) and 1960, when he left the Senate to become Vice-President. Perhaps the best brief treatment is Paul Conkin, *Big Daddy from the Pedernales: Lyndon Baines Johnson* (New York, Twayne, 1986); he is strong on Johnson's origins and background in the Texas hill country, and understanding of Johnson's civil rights and Great Society initiatives; "at least briefly, in the mid-60s, the federal government did try to be generous. Big Daddy saw to that." By contrast, Robert A. Caro is massively detailed, but critical, in *The Years of Lyndon Johnson*, vol. 1 *The Path to Power* (New York, Knopf, 1982), vol. II, *Means of*

Ascent (New York, Knopf, 1990). This is a life-and-times treatment. Vaughan D. Bornet, *The Presidency of Lyndon B. Johnson* (Lawrence, University of Kansas Press, 1983), is still by far the most balanced comprehensive treatment. See also Booth Mooney, *The Lyndon Johnson Story* (New York, Avon, 1964).

For Robert Kennedy, see Arthur M. Schlesinger Jr, *Robert Kennedy and His Times* (London, Deutsch, 1978).

14 THE CIVIL RIGHTS MOVEMENT

The impact of the New Deal on blacks is discussed in the following: Raymond Wolters, "The New Deal and the Negro," in John Braeman, Robert H. Bremner, and David Brody (eds), *The New Deal: The national level* (Columbus, Ohio State University Press, 1975), pp. 170–217; Nancy J. Weiss, *Farewell to the Party of Lincoln: Black politics in the Age of FDR* (Princeton, NJ, Princeton University Press, 1983); and Harvard Sitkoff, *A New Deal for Blacks: The emergence of civil rights as a national issue*, vol. I, *The Depression Decade* (New York, Oxford University Press, 1978). Manning Marable, *Race, Reform and Rebellion: The second Reconstruction in black America, 1945–1982* (London, Macmillan, 1984), offers a trenchant analysis of the civil rights movement in the context of wider American domestic politics. Harvard Sitkoff's *The Struggle for Black Equality, 1954–1992* (revised edition) (New York, Hill and Wang, 1989), is a useful account and assessment.

C. Vann Woodward's *The Strange Career of Jim Crow* (1955; 3rd rev. edn, New York, Oxford University Press, 1974) contains perceptive comments on the aims and objectives of (and the growing tensions within) the civil rights movement during the 1950s and 1960s. Catherine A. Barnes, *Journey from Jim Crow: The desegregation of Southern transit* (New York, Columbia University Press, 1983), provides a detailed account of the struggle to end segregated transportation in the South, and conclusively demonstrates that "federal action came in response to black protest and pressure." Southern opposition to the civil rights movement is treated by Numan V. Bartley, *The Rise of Massive Resistance: Race and politics in the South during the 1950s* (Baton Rouge, Louisiana State University Press, 1969). See also Anthony J. Badger's review essay, "Segregation and the Southern business elite," *Journal of American Studies*, 18 (1984), pp. 105–9.

Biographical and semi-biographical studies provide one exploratory avenue. The first truly thorough and scholarly biography of Martin Luther King was Stephen B. Oates's amply-detailed, well-researched and well-written work *Let the Trumpet Sound: The life of Martin Luther King Jr* (New York, Harper, 1982). Although its lack of a full bibliography and its use of notes only for quotations is annoying to researchers, it is and will remain for some time the most complete, balanced, and readable life of King. Frederick J. Downing, *To See the Promised Land: The faith pilgrimage of Martin Luther King, Jr* (Macon, Ga, Mercer University Press, 1986), offers a psychohistory based on the six-stage personality of James Fowler's faith development theory and on Erik Erikson's *homo religiosus*. As is the case with many psychohistorians, Downing pays especially close attention to the use of primary sources associated with early childhood and family experiences, and is less concerned with adult development and intellectual influences. His work is also marred by digressing at times into a study of Fowler's theory rather than of King's personality. Most recently, James A. Colaiaco's *Martin Luther King. Jr, Apostle of militant non-violence* (New York, St Martin's Press/London, Macmillan, 1988), has presented an interesting work of synthesis, less a biography than a study of King's non-violent protest campaigns, prepared from published sources by an intellectual historian.

The first biographer to provide at least a tentatively critical analysis of King, Lenwood G. Davis, *I Have a Dream: The life and times of Martin Luther King, Jr* (Chicago, Adams Press, 1969), raised some questions on the nature and adequacy of King's leadership but did not push them very far. Davis is well worth reading because of his careful depiction of the southern matrix in which King's personality and ideas matured. Davy's attempt at a critique is marred by continuous straining to demonstrate that King was forced slowly and reluctantly into his leadership positions by the pressure of events and by those around him. See also David L. Lewis, *King, a Critical Biography* (New York, Praeger, 1970).

The most significant books to appear on King study him in the context of his work with the Southern Christian Leadership Conference. David J. Garrow's *Bearing the Cross: Martin Luther King, Jr, and the Southern Christian Leadership Conference* (New York, Morrow, London, Cape, 1988), based on over 700 interviews and on FBI and CIA files, is the most complete study of King's leadership. Scholarly and balanced, it is the most informative portrait of the relationship of the man to the movement he headed. While its focus is primarily on King's political life and activity, it deals fully with his personality and interior struggles. David Garrow is also the editor of the 18-volume set *Martin Luther King, Jr, and the Civil Rights Movement* (New York, Carlson Publishing, 1989); Garrow's *Martin Luther King, Jr: Civil Rights Leader, Theologian, Orator*, is an invaluable collection of (previously published) essays and articles, drawn from an impressive range of periodicals. Aside from Garrow himself, contributors include Allan Boesak, James Colaiaco, August Meier, and three articles by Adam Fairclough, the most perceptive (and prolific) British commentator on King: "Was Martin Luther King a Marxist?," "Martin Luther King and the war in Vietnam," and "Martin Luther King, Jr, and the quest for nonviolent social change." David J. Garrow, Clayborne Carson, James H. Cone, Vincent G. Harding, and Nathan I. Huggins were the participants in a rewarding symposium, "A Round Table: Martin Luther King, Jr," published in the *Journal of American*

History, 74 (1987), pp. 436–81. See also John White, *Martin Luther King and the Civil Rights Movement in America* (British Association for American Studies, Stoke on Trent, 1991). Also of interest is *The Papers of Martin Luther King, Jr.*, edited by Clayborne Carson (University of California Press, 1994).

Unquestionably the best personal memoir is by Coretta Scott King, a widow's recollections that, however unscholarly and loyal, are enormously valuable for the detail they provide on King's family life and for the personal viewpoint they afford on events such as the Birmingham bus boycott and the freedom concerts in which she took an important role: *My Life with Martin Luther King Jr* (New York, Holt Rinehart, 1969, London, Hodder and Stoughton, 1970). Also of interest is Martin Luther King Sr's, *Daddy King: An autobiography* (New York, Morrow, 1980), in which Martin Jr appears in the role of successful son in a family committed to non-violent struggle for civil rights.

For more general studies of the civil rights movement, see Haywood W. Burns, *Voices of Negro Protest in America* (New York, Oxford University Press, 1963); Michael Dorman, *We Shall Overcome* (New York, Dell, 1965); E. Franklin Frazier, *Black Bourgeoisie: The rise of a new middle class in the United States* (New York, Collier, 1962); Martin Luther King, Jr, *Stride Toward Freedom* (New York, Harper and Row, 1964); Louis Lomax, *The Negro Revolt* (New York, Signet Books, 1964); Gunnar Myrdal, *An American Dilemma: The Negro problem and American democracy* (New York, Harper, 1942); Rhoda Blumberg, *Civil Rights, the 1960s Freedom Struggle* (New York, Twayne, 1990); Lerone Bennett, Jr., *The Shaping of Black America, The Struggles and Triumphs of African-Americans 1619 to the 1990s* (New York, Penguin, 1995); and Harvey Wish (ed.), *The Negro Since Emancipation* (Englewood Cliffs, Spectrum Books, Prentice-Hall, 1964).

General histories of women in the United States include Catherine Clinton, *The Other Civil War: American women in the nineteenth century* (New York, Hill and Wang, 1984); Carl Degler, *At Odds: Women and the family in America from the Revolution to the present* (New York, Oxford University Press, 1980); Gerda Lerner, *The Majority Finds its Past: Placing women in history* (New York, Oxford University Press, 1979); Anne Firor Scott, *Making the Invisible Woman Visible* (Urbana, University of Illinois Press, 1984); and Carroll Smith-Rosenberg *Disorderly Conduct: Visions of gender in Victorian America* (New York, Knopf, 1985).

Writings about domesticity and feminine culture include Ann Douglas, *The Feminization of American Culture* (New York, Knopf, 1977); Barbara Leslie Epstein, *The Politics of Domesticity; Women, evangelism and temperance in nineteenth century America* (Middletown, Conn., Wesleyan University Press, 1981); and Mary P. Ryan, *The Empire of the Mother: American writing about domesticity, 1800 to 1860* (New York, Institute for Historical Research and Haworth Press, 1982).

Many of the books on black women also examine women's lives in the South, since most black women until the end of the nineteenth century lived south of the Mason-Dixon Line. Elizabeth Fox-Genovese, *Within the Plantation Household: Black and white women of the Old South* (Chapel Hill, NC, University of North Carolina Press, 1988), illuminates class, gender, and race relations primarily in the South, but also in the ante-bellum United States generally. Other works include Dorothy Sterling, *We Are Your Sisters: Black women in the nineteenth century* (New York, Norton, 1984); Paula Giddings, *When and Where I Enter: The impact of black women on race and sex in America* (New York, Morrow, 1984); Jacqueline Jones, *Labor of Love, Labor of Sorrow: Black women, work and the family from slavery to the present* (New York, Basic Books, 1985); and Gloria T. Hull, Patricia Bell Scott, and Barbara Smith, *All the Women are White and All the Blacks Are Men, but Some of Us Are Brave: Black women's studies* (Old Westbury, NY, Feminist Press, 1982). Gerda Lerner edited a wide-ranging collection of black women's writings in *Black Women in White America* (New York, Pantheon, 1972). Bert James Lowenberg and Ruth Bogin, *Black Women in Nineteenth Century American Life: Their words, their thoughts, their feelings* (University Park, Pennsylvania State University Press, 1976), covers a narrower chronological span. Trudie Harris, *From Mammies to Militants: Domestics in black American literature* (Philadelphia, Temple University Press, 1982), and Judith Rollins, *Between Women: Domestics and their employers* (Philadelphia, Temple University Press, 1985), overlap somewhat in their focus.

There are many studies of the origins of feminism. Nancy Cott, *The Grounding of Modern Feminism* (New Haven, Conn., Yale University Press, 1987); Barbara J. Berg, *The Remembered Gate: The origins of American feminism* (New York, Oxford University Press, 1978); Bell Hooks, "*Ain't I a Woman?" Black women and feminism (Boston, South End Press, 1981); and Keith Melder, Beginnings of Sisterhood: The American woman's rights movement, 1800–1850* (New York, Schocken Books, 1977), all examine feminism and women's rights. Ellen Carol DuBois, *Feminism and Suffrage: The emergence of an independent women's movement in America, 1848–1869* (Ithaca, NY: Cornell University Press, 1978); Eleanor Flexner, *Century of Struggle: The woman's rights movement in the United States* (Cambridge, Mass., Harvard University Press, 1959); Aileen S. Kraditor, *The Ideas of the Woman Suffrage Movement, 1890–1920* (New York, Columbia University Press, 1965); and Anne Firor Scott and Andrew M. Scott, *One Half the People: The fight for woman suffrage* (Philadelphia, Lippincott, 1975), all focus upon the development of the women's rights movement and the fight for the vote. Abigail Scott Duniway, *Pathbreaking: An autobiographical history of the equal suffrage movement in the Pacific Coast states* (New York, Source Book Press, 1970), and Carrie Chapman Catt and Nettie Rogers Shuler, *Woman Suffrage and Politics* (New York, Scribner's, 1926), provide eye-witness accounts of the fight for the vote. Other studies of women political crusaders include Blanche Glassman Hersh, *The Slavery of Sex; Feminist abolitionists in America* (Urbana, University of Illinois Press, 1978); Alma Lutz, *Crusade for Freedom: women and the antislavery movement* (Boston, Beacon Press, 1968); Alan P. Grimes, *The Puritan Ethic and Woman Suffrage* (New York, Oxford University Press, 1967); Jack S. Blocker, "*Give to the Winds Thy Fears": The Women's Temperance Crusade* (Westport, Conn., Greenwood Press, 1985); and Ruth Birgitta Anderson, *Woman and Temperance: The quest for power and liberty, 1873–1900* (Philadelphia, Temple University Press, 1981).

The general topic of women and reform includes sexual, social, economic, and educational reform. Readers are directed to the following: Estelle B. Freedman, *Their Sisters' Keepers: Women's prison reform in America, 1830–1930* (Ann Arbor, University of Michigan Press, 1981); Barbara Kuhn Campbell, *The "Liberated" Woman of 1914: Prominent women in the Progressive Era* (Ann Arbor, Mich., UMI Research Press, 1979); Kathryn Kish Sklar, *Catherine Beecher: A study in American domesticity* (New York, Norton, 1973); Linda Gordon, *Woman's Body, Woman's Right: A social history of birth control in America* (New York, Grossman, 1976), Mari Jo Buhle, *Women and American Socialism, 1970–1920* (Urbana, University of Illinois Books, 1981); Karen J. Blair, *The Clubwoman as Feminist: True womanhood redefined, 1868–1914* (New York, Holmes and Meier, 1980); and Barbara Solomon, *In the Company of Educated Women: A history of women and higher education in America* (New Haven, Conn., Yale University Press, 1985).

The relationship between women and their families is the subject of Carl Degler, *At Odds* (New York, Oxford University Press, 1980); Herbert Gutman, *The Black Family in Slavery and Freedom* (New York, Pantheon, 1976); S. J. Kleinberg, *The Shadow of the Mills: Working class families in Pittsburgh, 1870–1907* (Pittsburgh, University of Pittsburgh Press, 1989); Virginia Yans McLaughlin, *Family and Community: Italian immigrants in Buffalo, 1880–1930* (Ithaca, NY, Cornell University Press, 1977); and Jacqueline Jones, *Labour of Love, Labour of Sorrow: Black women, work, and the family from slavery to the present* (New York, Basic Books, 1985). Elizabeth Pleck, *Domestic Tyranny: The making of American social policy against family violence from colonial times to the present* (Oxford, Oxford University Press, 1987), and Linda Gordon, *Heroes of Their Own Lives: The politics and history of family violence* (London, Virago, 1989), discuss the difficult subject of wife and child abuse.

In 1964 Senator Daniel P. Moynihan noted the prevalence of females among blacks who scored high on mental tests. See Miles D. Storfer, *Intelligence and Giftedness: The contributions of heredity and early environment* (San Francisco, Jossey-Bass, 1990), p. 13. Cf. Thomas Sowell, "Ethnicity and IQ," *The American Spectator*, Feb. 1995, p. 32–5.

Other useful studies published recently include Rhoda Blumberg's book *Civil Rights, the 1960s Freedom Struggle* (New York, Twayne,

1990); Claybarne Carson et al. (eds) *The Papers of Martin Luther King Jr.* (Berkeley, University of California Press, 1994); Lerone Bennett, Jr. *The Shaping of Black America, The Struggles and Triumphs of African-Americans 1619 to the 1990s* (New York, Penguin, 1995).

15 NIXON, WATERGATE AND CARTER

Richard M. Nixon's own books are of interest, especially *No More Vietnams* (London, Allen, 1986); *Richard Nixon* (New York, Warner, 1978); and *R. N.: Memoir of Richard Nixon* (New York, Grosset and Dunlop, 1978). There are many biographies: see Theodore White, *Breach of Faith, the Fall of Richard Nixon* (London, Cape, 1975); Robert Woodward and Carl Bernstein, *The Final Days* (New York, Simon and Schuster, 1975); Robert S. Parmet, *Richard Nixon and his America* (Boston, Little, Brown, 1990); Garry Wills, *Nixon Agonistes: The crisis of the self-made man* (Boston, Houghton Mifflin, 1970); Roger Morris, *Richard Milhous Nixon: The rise of an American politician* (New York, Holt, 1990); Earl Mazo and Stephen Hess, *Nixon, A Political Portrait* (New York, Harper, 1967); Stephen Ambrose, *Nixon: The education of a politician 1913–1962* (New York, Simon and Schuster, 1987); Stephen Ambrose, *Nixon: The triumph of a politician 1962–1972* (New York, Simon and Schuster, 1989); Fawn M. Brodie, *Richard Nixon: The shaping of his character* (Cambridge, Mass., Harvard University Press, 1983); William Costello, *The Facts about Nixon: A candid biography* (London, Hutchinson, 1960); Ralph De Toledano, *One Man Alone: Richard Nixon* (New York, Funk and Wagnalls, 1969); Charles P. Henderson Jr, *The Nixon Theology* (New York, Harper, 1972); James Keogh, *This is Nixon* (New York, Putnam, 1956); and Bela Kotnitzer, *The Real Nixon* (Chicago, Rand McNally, 1960). Theodore White, the historian of elections, turned from his usual quadrennial study to *Breach of Faith: The fall of Richard Nixon* (London, Cape, 1980).

For Kissinger, see Henry Kissinger, *The White House Years* (Boston, Little, Brown, 1979); *For the Record* (London, Weidenfeld and Nicolson, 1981); *The Years of Upheaval* (London, Weidenfeld and Nicolson, 1982); Seymour Hersh, *The Price of Power: Kissinger in the Nixon White House* (New York, Summit, 1983); Marvin Kalb and Bernard Kalb, *Kissinger* (Boston, Little, Brown, 1974).

For Carter, see Jimmy Carter, *Keeping Faith, Memoirs of a President* (New York, Bantam, 1982); Betty Glad, *Jimmy Carter in Search of the Great White House* (New York, Norton, 1980); William Miller, *Yankee from Georgia: The emergence of Jimmy Carter* (New York, Times Books, 1978). His character is well explored in David Kucharsky, *The Man From Plains: The mind and spirit of Jimmy Carter* (New York, Harper, 1977), and in Bruce Mablish and Edwin Diamond, *Jimmy Carter: A character portrait* (New York, Simon and Schuster, 1979). Both of these emphasize his evangelical ethos, along with his born-again experience. Also readable are James T. Wooten, *Dasher: The roots and the rising of Jimmy Carter* (London, Weidenfeld and Nicolson, 1978), the rather rambling work of a *New York Times* reporter who was himself once a Presbyterian minister. Two highly critical studies are Peter Meyer, *James Earl Carter: The man and the myth* (Kansas City, Sheed Andrews, 1978), and Victor Lasky, *Jimmy Carter: The man and the myth* (New York, R. Marek, 1979). For the political story, see Michael Barone, *Our Country: The shaping of America from Roosevelt to Reagan* (New York, Macmillan, Collier Free Press, 1990).

16 RONALD REAGAN: THE MAN WHO WON THE COLD WAR

The best place to begin is with Ronald Reagan's own delightful piece of autobiography, *My Early Life, or Where's the Best of Me?* (London, Sidgwick and Jackson, 1981).

There are many biographies of Reagan, the work of journalists, a number of them written during Reagan's governorship of California. The two most recent biographies attempt to explain Reagan and his politics by focusing on his childhood and by placing his life in a framework of the American social tradition. Robert Dallek's *Ronald Reagan: The politics of symbolism* (Cambridge, Mass., Harvard University Press, 1984) is a well-written and well-documented life, from childhood poverty to adult success; and Garry Wills, *Reagan's America: Innocents At Home* (New York, Doubleday, 1987) in a brilliant biography argues convincingly that to understand Reagan with all his contradictions is to go far toward understanding America. Wills says that Reagan does not just present a set of values, but embodies American values.

Former California governor Pat Brown's two Reagan biographies, *Reagan and Reality: The two Californias* (New York, Praeger, 1970), and Edmund G. Brown (Pat) and Bill Brown, *Reagan: The political chameleon* (New York, Praeger, 1976), barely qualify as biographies as they are quite weak in describing Reagan's life before he became involved in California politics. Essentially, both books are warnings that Reagan is, well Reagan. James D. Barber identified the role of the media in building Reagan's career in *The Pulse of Politics* (New York, Norton, 1980).

Some of Reagan's own team saw his success in turning back the tide of history as limited: David Stockman, *The Triumph of Politics: Why the Reagan Revolution failed* (New York, Harper and Row, 1986); Lawrence I. Barrett, *Gambling with History: Reagan in the White House* (New York, Doubleday, 1983).

Valuable studies of Ronald Reagan's economic policies are George Gilder, *Wealth and Poverty* (New York, Basic Books, 1981), and Jude Wanniski, *The Way The World Works* (New York, Basic Books, 1978); the former of which served almost as Bible to the "Reaganauts." Compare also Thomas D. Edsall, *The New Politics of Inequality* (New York, Norton, 1984); one-time administrator David Stockman's *The Triumph of Politics* (New York, Harper and Row, 1986); "The 400 richest people in America," *Forbes* magazine, Oct. 26, 1987; and Geoffrey Smith, *Reagan and Thatcher* (London, Bodley Head, 1990), a valuable compare-and-contrast.

At the beginning of his presidency, Reagan's foreign policy was more than hostility to Communism, wherever it appeared. Indeed, for his first term Jeane J. Kirkpatrick, his ambassador at the UN, was his main voice: see her collection of speeches and articles in *The Reagan Phenomenon* (Washington, American Enterprise Institute, 1981). See also the many references to him in Margaret Thatcher, *The Downing Street Years* (London, Harper Collins, 1993).

Finally, the US in the immediate post-Reagan situation is well portrayed by Kevin Phillips in *The Politics of Rich and Poor: Wealth and the American electorate in the Reagan aftermath* (New York, Random House, 1990). Cf. Robert Kuthner, *The End of Laissez-Faire* (New York, Knopf, 1991).

17 THE FRAGMENTATION OF THE DREAM

For general overviews of the changes in modern America, see William H. Chafe, *The Unfinished Journey: America since World War II* (New York, Oxford University Press, 1986); Allan M. Winkler, *Modern America: The US from World War II to the Present* (New York and London, Harper and Row, 1986); William Issel, *Social Change in the United States 1945–1983* (London, Macmillan, 1985); Donald L. Barlett and James B. Steele, *America: What Went Wrong?* (Kansas City, Andrews and McMeel, 1992); Kenneth Fox, *Metropolitan America: Urban Life and Urban Policy in the United States 1940–1980* (London, Macmillan, 1985). See too Arthur M. Schlesinger Jr's *The Disuniting of America, reflections on a multicultural society* (New York, Norton, 1992), and John Ehrman, *The Rise of Neo-Conservatism: Intellectuals and Foreign Affairs 1945–1994* (New Haven, Yale University Press, 1995).

Readers interested in historical works dealing with poverty in America will do well to begin with Robert H. Bremner, *From the Depths: The Discovery of Poverty in the United States* (New York, New York University Press, 1956), a balanced, readable account of poverty from the 1830s to the 1920s. Another broad study is Paul Boyer, *Urban Masses and Moral Order in America, 1820–1920* (Cambridge, Mass., Harvard University Press, 1978). Walter I. Trattner's *From Poor Law to Welfare State: A history of social welfare in America* (New York, Free Press, 1974) is a useful brief survey, while James T. Patterson's *America's Struggle Against Poverty, 1930–1980* (Cambridge, Mass., Harvard University Press, 1981) and *The Welfare State in America 1930–1980* (London, British

Association for American Studies, 1983); provide the most recent full treatment of the subject.

For federal policy in the 1930s, see Harry Hopkins, *Spending to Save: The complete story of relief* (New York, Harper and Row, 1936), and Donald Howard, *The WPA and Federal Relief Policy* (New York, Russell Sage Foundation, 1943). An intelligent monograph on the subject is Barbara Blumberg, *The New Deal and the Unemployed: The view from New York City* (Lewisburg, Pa., Bucknell University Press, 1979).

Consult also the excellent overview by Henry Aaron, *Politics and the Professors: The Great Society in perspective* (Washington, DC, Brookings Institute, 1978); H. Haveman (ed.), *A Decade of Federal Antipoverty Programs: Achievements, failures, and lessons* (Madison, Wisconsin University Press, 1977); and Robert D. Plotnick and Felicity Skidmore, *Progress Against Poverty, 1964–1974* (New York, Academic Press, 1975). For the story of President Nixon's Family Assistance Plan, see Vincent and Vee Burke, *Nixon's Good Deed: Welfare reform* (New York, Columbia University Press, 1974).

A large body of works now exists on non-white poverty in America. Among the most accessible are Kenneth B. Clark, *The Dark Ghetto: Dilemmas of social power* (New York, Harper and Row, 1965), and Lee Rainwater, *Behind Ghetto Walls: Black families in a federal slum* (Chicago, Aldine Publishing Co., 1970). Elliot Liebow's *Tally's Corner: A study of Negro streetcorner men* (Boston, Little, Brown, 1967) is an especially cogent work. For black life prior to World War II, the starting place remains the massive study headed by Gunnar Myrdal, *An American Dilemma: The Negro problem and American democracy* (New York, Harper, 1942); but see also Gilbert Osofsky, *Harlem: The making of a ghetto* (New York, Harper and Row, 1966). Manning Marable, *Race, Reform and Rebellion: The second Reconstruction in black America 1945–82* (New York, Macmillan, 1984), brings the story up to the 1980s.

For crime in the USA, see Michael Woodiwiss, *Organized Crime USA: from Prohibition to the present day* (London, British Association for American Studies, 1990). More recently published studies of the mid-Twentieth century include Terry Cooney, *Balancing Acts, American Thought and Culture in the 1930s* (New York, Twayne, 1995); William Graebner, *The Age of Doubt, American Thought and Culture in the 1940s* (New York, Twayne 1990); Neil Jamieson, *Understanding Vietnam* (University of California Press 1993); Gary Hess, *Vietnam and the United States Origins and Legacy of War* (New York, Twayne 1990); (ed) William Whyte Jr., *The Exploding Metropolis* (University of California Press 1993); Kirkpatrick Sale, *The Green Revolution: The American Environmental Movement 1962–1992* (New York, Hill & Wang 1994); John Earl Haynes and Harvey Klehr, *The Secret World of American Communism* (Yale University Press 1995), especially for its freshly-informed view of the role of Senator McCarthy; Reed Veda, *Postwar Immigrant America* (New York, St Martin's Press 1995); Peter Brimelow, *Alien Nation: Common Sense about America's Immigration Disaster* (New York, Random House, 1995); Byron M. Roth, *Prescription for Failure, Race Relations in the Age of Social Science* (New Brunswick, Rutgers University Press, 1995).

For the environmental movement see Samuel P. Hays, *Beauty, Health and Permanence: Environmental Politics in the United States, 1955–1985* (Cambridge, Cambridge University Press, 1987) and *Conservation and the Gospel of Efficiency: The Progressive Conservation Movement, 1890–1920* (Cambridge, Harvard University Press, 1959).

Index

Index compiled by Meg Davies (Society of Indexers).